The Mutual
BASEBALL
ALMANAC

Edited by

ROGER KAHN

Baseball Writer for the New York Herald Tribune

and

AL HELFER

Sports Announcer for Mutual Broadcasting's "Game of the Day"

in co-operation with

THE MUTUAL SPORTS STAFF

1954

DOUBLEDAY & COMPANY, INC.
Garden City, New York

CONTENTS

FOREWORD

Baseball books run in two patterns. Some are listings of statistics or records and appeal as much to slide rule fans as to baseball fans. Others, the monumental works, contain more—so much more—that they consign themselves to reference shelves.

The Baseball Almanac contains statistics and records. In fact, the Who's Who section encompasses all the important figures on the professional career of every major league player. In addition, tips on watching baseball written by the game's greatest stars, diagrams of the seating plans and fields of all the big league ball parks, an outline of how a typical club runs and many other features have been included. But the Almanac has not outgrown readable size.

The aim of the editors was to produce a book of real interest and real value to baseball fans, but without the cooperation of many leading baseball figures, no book would have been possible. Thanks are due to Walter F. O'Malley, President of the Brooklyn Dodgers, for his invaluable help in explaining the inner workings of a typical major league organization. Bob Cooke, sports editor of the New York *Herald Tribune,* graciously consented to the use of a portion of his poem on the climax of the greatest pennant race in baseball history.

Charles Segar, of the Commissioner's office, Earl Hilligan, director of the American League Service Bureau, Dave Grote, his National League counterpart, the publicity director of every major league team, Sid Keener, director of the Hall of Fame, lent needed aid.

We, the editors, also wish to thank the sports staff of the Mutual Broadcasting System for their indispensable and most valuable help. At the same time we should like to extend our sincere appreciation to the staff of Mutual's "Game of the Day," which, each day from a different ball park, brings a live play-by-play broadcast of a major-league baseball game to such a large section of America.

May we say in closing that to work on this book was particularly gratifying as it represents in a sense the combined efforts of the communications industry from radio broadcast to printed page. The fact of such an effort is certainly a tribute to what is truly a national sport.

To all the above people then, to the contributing sports figures and to many others go our many, many thanks.

THE EDITORS

COVERING A GAME

By RED SMITH
Syndicated Columnist New York Herald Tribune

From the Yankee Stadium press box, a man watched as the batter hit a ground ball, dashed for first base, and was retired. The man bent over his scorebook, then hesitated. "How'd that play go?" he asked John Drebinger, the distinguished gentleman from the distinguished New York *Times*.

"Six to three," Mr. Drebinger said, which meant, in the baseball writer's code, that the shortstop had thrown the batter out at first. Then he recited evilly:

> *"When the One Great Scorer comes to*
> *write against your name,*
> *"He marks—not that you won or lost—*
> *but how did that last guy go out?"*

Put the question to nine out of ten sports writers: "How do you watch a ball game?" If they are honest they will reply, "Not half attentively enough," and all ball players within earshot will roar amen. It is, of course, the considered opinion of every player whoever was charged with an error on a tough chance that them meatheaded newspaper guys don't know their ear from their appetite and if you was to put a ape in uniform and call him Ty Cobb, why, they ain't one of them meatheads could spot the difference at ten paces, the meatheads.

Everybody's attention wanders, of course. Yet when a sports writer watches a play with his eyes and not his mind, it doesn't necessarily mean he is doing a bad job. More likely it means that his work has conditioned him to be alert for the unusual, the bizarre or dramatic or comical, and not to clutter his mind with the commonplace.

The keenest baseball observer I have known in the press box was Garry Schumacher, now a member of the Giants' official family, who was a sports writer before he went square. He watched a game as a good manager does, analyzing the strategy pitch by pitch.

Late one season a lot of us were in Washington for an important series between the Senators and Tigers. Detroit won the first game of a double-header by something like 8–3, and to most of us it was a game without distinction, to be got through in the hope of livelier doings later. When it was over, Garry turned to a Washington writer.

"I think your guy was a little timid," he said, referring to the Senators' manager. "There in the fifth inning when he had the Detroit pitcher on the ropes, he might have knocked him out of there if he'd been hitting and running——"

Obviously Garry had seen more in the game than the rest of us because he was better.

However, though he had the gift of concentration, some jobs seem to call for a quality of non-concentration. Take the fellow writing a sports column on a New York paper when the Yankees and Dodgers are in a World Series.

From the same staff there's a man writing the lead story which will tell who won and how, there's another doing notes and "color," two others are assigned to the clubhouses, and there may be still another describing the crowd. What's left for the guy with the column if he is to avoid duplication?

Well, he can go expert and second-guess the manager, if he likes. I don't like, for several reasons. One is that dumb managers are smarter than I am. An alternative is to try for a piece that will capture what a man has described as the "smell of cabbage cooking in the halls"—to try, in other words, to catch the special flavor of the show.

That's where the quality of non-concentration comes in. It's a matter of keeping the mind open and receptive to impressions, like soft wax. (This is not difficult if the columnist is fairly soft in the head to begin with.) Maybe an individual player will pop up and make the story. Perhaps the picture will be drawn in one dramatic moment. Possibly the watcher sees the pitcher's shoulders sag as a home run reaches the seats, and he puts himself in the pitcher's place and sees the game through the pitcher's eyes.

Chances are every witness has his own memory of the finish of the National League race of 1951, when Bobby Thomson of the Giants won the last playoff game from Brooklyn with a home run in the ninth inning. It was the triumphant end of a crazy rush which saw the Giants cut away Brooklyn's big lead and win in the last stride. The experts still argue about that game, wrangling over the Dodger pitching strategy, but to one spectator it remains simply a tale of two third basemen—Thomson and Billy Cox.

For eight innings, Cox played marvelously well and Thomson indifferently or worse. Thomson ruined one promising inning for the Giants by trying to take second base with a teammate already there. Cox smothered several more with dazzling plays in the field. The hits that put Brooklyn ahead in the seventh inning went hopping through Thomson's territory, and although they could not have been scored as errors, they were the sort of chances that Cox had been eating up

8

all afternoon. Brooklyn's fourth run was driven in by Cox, and his hit flashed right past his third base rival.

As the Giants went out in order in the eighth, trailing by 4–1, a glance at the score card made it clear that if they should manage to mount a rally in the ninth, the situation would be loaded by the time Thomson went to bat. And even as that possibility was rejected as too ridiculously melodramatic, it came to pass.

Even Thomson's home run went out Cox's way, but this was one ball Billy couldn't handle—he who had handled so many so magnificently. He turned as it whistled overhead, stood frozen until it settled into the grandstand, and then started the long walk to the clubhouse.

Well, that's how one man may see one game. Maybe none of the others in the crowd would see it quite the same way, but most of them are watching for fun, without a column to write.

If this falls short as an answer to the question: How do you watch a ball game? then it's probably because I don't know the answer. Certainly the answer has little to do with technical details that would be important to a scout, like how the second baseman pivots on a double play.

Maybe that's because people always seem more interesting than technicalities or statistics. Away back in 1906, watching the Cubs beat Nick Altrock, pitcher for the White Sox, in a World Series game, Charley Dryden wrote that "poor Nick left the yard with his usually sunny smile hanging down like a torn pocket."

To perceive that was better than to know by heart every batting average for ten years. Similarly, when the World Series of 1931 is recalled, it isn't Mickey Cochrane who comes to mind, or Lefty Grove or Al Simmons or Burleigh Grimes or Frank Frisch or Bill Hallahan. Instead, there's a memory of Pepper Martin coming to bat for the Cardinals in a crucial moment of the fifth game with the teams tied at two victories apiece.

"Well," said a fellow in the press box, "any hack could write this script. This guy has hit singles and doubles and beaten out bunts and stolen every base in sight. There's nothing left for him to do now except belt one right up there in the sta——"

Just then, naturally, Martin hit one up there. It was minutes before the fellow upstairs could get his slack jaw to close.

That was the Series when Martin took the Athletics apart like a manly lad plucking the wings off a housefly. The story of that series was Pepper Martin . . . Up at the plate "just takin' my natural swing, and the ball hittin' the fat part of the bat" . . . Pepper tearing around the bases and diving into his headlong slide, his great hooked nose splitting the wind . . . Pepper buffeted and good-natured in the crowds that swirled about him in the hotel lobby . . . Pepper grinning at Judge Kenesaw Mountain Landis's bellowed salute, "Young man, I'd like to be in your place tonight," and responding, "Well, Judge, $75,000 a year instead of $7,500; I'll swap you."

How do you watch a ball game? In those games you watched one man.

Perhaps the point here is that every game is a new game, different from any other that's ever been played or ever will be played, and it is the reporter's job to discern that difference and write it. So he must watch every game differently.

Sometimes technical minutiae can be revealing. The Athletics had a pitcher named Russ Christopher, who mastered an underhand delivery after a sore arm made it difficult to "come over the top." An observer familiar with his work could decide almost from his first pitch how effective he would be on a given day. If he was throwing from around his shoetops, he had evil stuff that whistled past the batters' knees. When he didn't get all the way down, they hit him.

Somehow, probably by osmosis, the reporter learns to see some of these things. He misses more. Most of us wrote rhapsodically of Al Gionfriddo's catch in the 1947 World Series, when he ran approximately three miles to the left field fence and grabbed a fly by Joe DiMaggio. It was midwinter before an old pro pointed out that an outfielder who had properly analyzed the situation of the moment would have been standing with the blouse of his britches against the fence before DiMaggio swung.

After the Yankees' Billy Martin tried unwisely to score from second base on a single in the 1953 World Series—he was out at the plate and that killed the Yankees' last chance to win the game—Frank Crosetti, the coach at third base, took the blame. He said he had waved Martin home. If a single man among the hundreds in the press box noted Crosetti's signals on that play, his identity is not known here.

Maybe details like that should not escape the reporter, but somehow it didn't seem to matter. Watching the ball and watching Martin, it was possible to see that even before he reached third base Martin was resolved to keep going for the plate. The way he was running, Crosetti would have needed an elephant gun to stop him.

Martin, it seems to me, was the man to watch. Whether Crosetti actually made a mistake of judgment or was only trying to protect the young man from censure afterward—that's academic.

It is an article of the ballplayer's faith that all newspapermen are purblind and mentally incompetent, and that the one currently doubling as official scorer is a troglodyte as well. As for the scorer in any rival city, he never gives one of our guys a break and probably is in the pay of a foreign power.

During World War II an amiable young man named Irvin Hall was an infielder with the Athletics. He was popular with everyone who knew him, including the enemy pitchers. One day he made what would ordinarily be a routine single, but the center fielder played the ball dreamily, it hopped past him untouched, and Hall circled the bases. The scorer hesitated, then ruled a single and a three-base error.

The scorer rode home from the game with his neighbor, Earle Brucker, then a coach with the Athletics.

"Golly," the scorer said, "I was sorry I couldn't call that a home run for Hall. He's such a nice kid, and he's never had a homer in the majors. Hasn't had one since he played in Pocomoke City, Md."

"That wasn't a home run?" Brucker asked.

"No. What do you think?"

Brucker thought it over. "Well," he said, "if this is the big leagues, it should have been a single. But if this was in St. Louis and Hall was playing for the Browns. . . ."

Fact is, of course, that the scorer watches the game more closely than anyone else in the press box. Sometimes others nod, like the veteran who yawned loudly in the sixth inning on opening day and moaned, "Lord! Won't this season ever end?"

Nor can it be claimed that the strictest attention was invariably paid by the men assigned to watch the Phillies of about fifteen years ago accept almost daily defeat. Baker Bowl, the scene of those horrors, no longer stands. In fact, the old joint was staggering then.

The press box was narrow and deep, with about six rows of desks set one behind the other. Occupants of the rear ranks lightened the weary afternoons by throwing peanuts at the heads of authors in the front rows. One day when the Cubs were in town, the litterateurs took to throwing paper cups of water, some of which dripped into the sparsely settled stands below. This brought the club president, Gerry Nugent, up to protest.

"After all," he said indignantly, "we have patrons downstairs."

"Great God!" said Warren Brown, of Chicago. "What a story!"

TIPS ON WATCHING BASEBALL

THE BATTER

By STAN MUSIAL *of the St. Louis Cardinals*
Six-Time National League Batting Champion

For the single instant when a speeding pitch reaches home plate, virtually every eye in the ball park is focused on the batter. But if the hitter swings, a scout may learn all he wants in a split second, while less expert baseball followers see only a healthy cut.

If you're wondering how you can glance at a batter's stance, watch him swing and decide on the spot whether he's a good hitter or not, the answer is that you probably can't do it at all. On rare occasions experts may, but they always spend more time watching a hitter to confirm their first impression.

There are many batting stances. I'm reminded of that every time I see my own stance described as "unorthodox." My stance is comfortable to me. To someone else it might be uncomfortable.

There are level swings and uppercutting swings. Generally the level swing is best, but some power hitters are uppercutters and are successful.

The one unbreakable rule about hitting is this: if a batter hits well with his own particular stance and swing, think twice—or more—before suggesting a change. There is no one correct way to bat, and so of course there is no one correct stance to look for.

All the variations, however, come only after a few basic principles are followed.

Look for a batter to keep his eye on the ball, not merely when it's on the way, but also up until the time it hits his bat. A batter who looks up and swings can be badly fooled by a pitch that breaks in the last fraction of a second.

Look for a batter to hold his bat still just before the pitch is released. There's nothing wrong with pumping a bat back and forth while the pitcher is preparing to throw, but when he's about to throw, the bat should be back, still, and ready to be whipped into the ball.

Look for a batter to stride with the pitch. By that I mean a batter stepping to meet an outside pitch and stepping back from an inside pitch.

Look for a batter who does not overstride. Some hitters have been

12

successful with very long strides, but generally an overstrider has trouble with change-of-pace pitches and with breaking stuff.

Look for a batter to hold his arms away from his body. That's necessary for a free full swing.

Look for the batter who waits for a pitch in the strike zone. There have been and still are some good bad ball hitters in the majors, but, logically, most batters don't hit pitches at ankle level as well as they do strikes.

Of course, a short cut which eliminates this and a great deal of additional painstaking observation is to look at what happens after the batter swings. You want to see how often a batter hits—something probably learned most quickly from the batting averages—and you want to see what power he has.

Most power hitters pull. For a left-hander like myself, that means hitting the ball to right field; for a right-hander, it means hitting the ball to left. Pull hitters generally have two advantages. They meet the ball when their swing is at maximum power. The fences down the foul lines are closer than the fences in center field.

Occasionally you'll see a right-hander drive a long shot into right center; more rarely to dead right. But usually the home-run kings are pull hitters.

Don't look for a good hitter to pull outside pitches, however. Sometimes it can be done; more often it can't. My power is to right and right center, but many times I'll deliberately slap an outside pitch to left field. This is "hitting the ball where it's pitched." Clearly, it requires tremendous wrist action to catch a pitch near the end of the bat and pull it. A few sluggers can do it, but watch for most hitters to slap to the opposite field.

Some hitters, like the Phils' Richie Ashburn, rarely try to overpower the ball. They choke up on the bat—hold it a few inches from the end—and try to place their hits. A choke hitter bats that way by choice. If he wanted to hold a bat at the end, he could always use a lighter bat. But some batters prefer to slap the ball, going for singles instead of home runs, and men like Ashburn are particularly valuable for their ability to reach base safely and start rallies.

I stand far from the plate and deep in the batters' box. Some hitters stand close and up forward in the box. Some coaches point out that by standing deep and striding forward, the batter hits the ball as it is crossing the plate, and can tell up to the last instant whether the pitch will be a strike or a ball, and gets a trifle more distance between himself and the pitcher—helpful when the pitcher is fast. But, as always in batting, individual styles vary, and success is the thing to look for.

It's a good idea to watch hitters on the hit-and-run play. This tests their ability to hit behind a runner. When a left-handed batter wants to hit to right, he need only try to pull. The good right-handed batter generally drops his right foot back, so that as he swings he's almost facing right field. There are other more radical techniques, but this is the one that seems to work best for most big-leaguers and is the one to look for.

There are several batting traits that usually indicate weakness. Some hitters sweep at the ball, using their entire bodies but little wrist. Good wrist action is a key to batting success, and there isn't any substitute for it.

Others follow through poorly. This serves to rob the hitter of power. Still others lunge at the ball and end up swinging off balance, with the upper part of the body moving farther forward than the lower part. A good many slumps are due to unconscious lunging. It's tough enough to time the variety of pitches thrown in the majors, even with a perfectly smooth swing. Lunging means that timing suffers and base hits grow more uncommon.

Then there are late swingers and chop swingers, and batters who get so entangled with their swing that they can't break fast from the plate and lose a great many base hits.

Everyone is tempted at times to grab a bat and just swing away. Hitting is a science—and when pitchers are mixing curves, fast balls and change-ups, it is an exact science. I guess, after all, the best tip I can give you is simply to look for the hitter who hits the most line drives. And if you want to vary your study, look for the hitter who hits the most high drives that don't come down until they've reached the bleachers.

THE PITCHER

By ROBIN ROBERTS *of the Philadelphia Phils*
National League All-Star in 1952 and 1953

Often I've learned more by watching a losing pitcher than a winner. That's because the loser usually gets into more trouble, and when trouble comes there's more to be learned in a few minutes than during an entire trouble-free game.

You're watching a scoreless tie and suddenly one team gets a couple of men on base with nobody out. Here's what to do:

Up to now, the pitcher in a jam has been getting the hitters out. From your seat in the stands you've decided that he's been doing it with a fast ball or a curve. But you can't be sure what the pitcher's best pitch is until the game starts tumbling down around him. Then if he goes to his fast ball, you know the fast ball is the pitch that supports his family.

But in the majors it isn't always that simple. When Sal Maglie or Larry Jansen of the New York Giants or Warren Spahn of the Milwaukee Braves is in trouble, you can't pick out a single money pitch. Men like Maglie, Jansen, and Spahn have been successful because they have two or more pitches they can use in the clutch—pitches they can control, pitches good enough to get good batters out.

Good control of an assortment of pitches is essential to the sort of success Maglie, Jansen, and Spahn have enjoyed. It's probably tough, from most sections of the stands, to differentiate between the different types of curves one pitcher throws. Don't worry. A lot of batters have the same trouble. Pitching can be an art designed to fool rather than overpower batters. If you're fooled in your grandstand seat, blame the pitcher. He's doing his job and doing it well.

What you can spot pretty easily is the speed of a pitch. Changing speeds is the mark of many master pitchers. I'd like to tell you just how a pitcher goes about throwing full speed, three-quarter speed, half speed, and everything in between, all with the same motion. The hitch is that I don't have that technique down myself. [EDITOR'S NOTE: Roberts won twenty-eight games in 1952 and twenty-three games last season without having that technique "down."]

A pitcher who varies his speeds but doesn't vary his motion gets batters to swing at his arm instead of the ball. He throws a fast one past the hitter and then, with the same motion, lets up. The batter thinks "fast ball," and this time he swings when the ball is way out in front of him. A tremendous change in speed is not necessary. Just a little added or a little taken off is enough to upset a hitter's timing.

You have to watch carefully, but it is possible to observe even these slight variations in speed. Ignore the pitcher's motion and concentrate on the flight of the ball. You may not see the way one curve Spahn throws breaks differently from another, but you will see that one is a shade faster—or a lot faster—than the other.

An essential in observing a pitcher requires a careful look beyond the mound. Without eight good fielders supporting him, a good pitcher can look bad. And sometimes fine fielding—outfielders making tough catches appear easy—can convince you that a pitcher is more effective than he actually is.

When I study a pitcher I look first for speed. That's the way a great many scouts operate, too. Curves and change-ups can be taught, but it is a rare pitcher who can learn to throw harder. The co-ordination and strength once there, steps are possible to smooth out the delivery and add a trifle to the speed of a fast ball. But the co-ordination and

15

the strength must first be there. When you watch a young big-league pitcher, look for speed. Chances are you'll find it.

Speed alone is not enough. Control is absolutely essential. And remember, there's more to control than just throwing the ball over the plate. If a major-leaguer throws down the middle with good speed, the ball will likely head toward the grandstands with great speed. "Throwers" have speed; pitchers have speed and control and more.

One way to check a major-leaguer's control is to check the count. He may not be walking anyone, but if he is getting behind the hitters, he may get out of the game in a hurry.

Major-league control calls for pitching to spots. Some hitters blast fast balls below the belt, and the faster the pitch, the bigger the blast. Others ask only for high ones. After a hitter has been in a league for a while, teams make a book on him. They list his batting strengths and weaknesses and review them constantly, and pitchers pitch with the book in mind.

Before each game there's a clubhouse meeting; a large portion of each meeting is devoted to discussion of opposing hitters. Sometimes a pitcher, catcher, and manager may agree to feed a particular hitter high fast balls. This doesn't mean *only* high fast balls. Rather, it means that the pitcher intends to make a high fast ball the pitch that the batter hits—or tries to.

Then, on the mound, the pitcher works on the batter. Maybe he leads off with a high fast one for a strike. He gets a second strike when the batter fouls a low outside curve (a tough pitch for almost anyone) into the dirt. Next he comes back with the curve even farther outside, hoping the batter will go for it.

He doesn't, but he has seen two straight curves. Now the pitcher blazes in the high fast one. The batter, behind in the count, must swing and pops up. The pitcher has set him up and got him out according to the book.

Sure the pitch was fast. That much you can see from the stands. It was high, and if you go to enough games you may notice that certain batters get a steady dose of high pitches. And possibly you've been able to see just what the pitcher was doing as he went about getting the hitter to pop up. But it takes careful concentration.

You'll notice quickly whether a pitcher has a good move to first base. If the runners seem to be taking big leads, and the pitcher isn't doing much about it, you're safe in guessing that his move to first is weak. But watch Spahn, or young Johnny Podres of the Brooklyn Dodgers. The runners don't dare lead off too far, because that's nothing more than a short cut back to the bench after a successful pick-off. I can't write much on the mechanics of a good move to first. I don't have a good move.

Some pitchers seem to have special trouble with special teams. Last year for me the St. Louis Cardinals in general and Solly Hemus in particular gave me a lot of trouble. But frankly, I find that every year it seems a different team and a different batter bother me most.

On the whole, I don't think there's a set pattern to watch for in pitching. Like Stan Musial's stance, the pitching method that proves successful is correct for the individual, whether it's unusual or not. Look for speed and control in a pitcher, but don't forget something else. It isn't a bad idea to look for results.

THE CATCHER

By ROY CAMPANELLA *of the Brooklyn Dodgers*
The National League's Most Valuable Player in 1953

Secrecy is the idea behind the signs a catcher gives a pitcher, but a few catchers are so bad at keeping secrets that you can discover what the next pitch is going to be from a seat in the stands.

I don't mean that you can spot the number of fingers the catcher sticks out to tell the pitcher what to throw. You can't, and in the majors the signs themselves aren't that simple, anyway. It's just that some catchers hold their gloves one way for a curve and another for a fast ball, or squat a little differently depending on the pitch.

Don't expect to spot that in a hurry. First of all, it's only a few catchers who tip their hands. Second, the way they give away a pitch may come in some small thing that you see only after you spend time in studying. But the best way to watch a catcher is to study what kind of receiver he is. I don't care whether a catcher has the best arm in the world and can call pitches like a wonder, if he isn't a good receiver, he isn't a good catcher.

Perhaps the word "receiver" has you confused. A catcher does a lot of things. Receiving is one of them—it's the way he handles the pitches he has to catch.

Receiving is the first thing I look for in a catcher. I want to see a catcher who can handle those wide-breaking curves, who can go up for the high fast balls and save wild pitches by staying with the mean ones that bounce in the dirt. Two things go into receiving, agility and hands. Speed—running speed—doesn't matter.

A good catcher tries to handle every pitch cleanly. For that he needs quick hands. Maybe one curve a pitcher throws breaks more sharply than another. The catcher knows the curve is coming both times, but only quick hands can help him when that second pitch acts like it's falling off a table.

But even the best catcher can't handle everything. Sometimes, on a pitch into the dirt, a catcher realizes that he probably won't be able to glove it. That's where the agility comes in. If the catcher can get his body behind the ball he can block it, with his chest protector, usually.

I figure this: that as long as I can keep the ball in front of me, I'm okay. If I see I don't have full control of a low pitch, I'll try to swipe it in front of me or block it with my body. If the ball's in front of me, no runner is going to move up. Our team doesn't get hurt. Of course, if a runner has been going with the pitch, he steals a base, but my way he doesn't get two bases while I go looking for the ball behind me.

It isn't important for a catcher to run a hundred yards in ten seconds. All he has to do is move a few feet to one side or the other in a split second.

After receiving, I guess the next thing I look for in a catcher is his arm. He has to be able to throw, but he should be able to do more. Watch some catchers when a runner breaks for second and you'll see them come out of their squat and then throw. That costs time and maybe an out. A catcher should throw from his squatting position, or just as he starts to rise. But if a catcher doesn't throw until he's up, word will get around—and so will base runners.

I think throwing gives me one of the toughest plays I have to handle. It's that double steal, with men on first and third. The runners break when you have the ball, the man on first breaking full, the man on third taking a few steps down the line.

A lot of times, catchers just hold the ball to keep that man at third from trying to score, but then the man on first makes second without a play. I try to look the man on third back to his base then and throw to second. It feels as though I were looking one way and throwing another, and maybe I am. But you have to watch that man on third. If he gets off too far, you nail him. If not, you want to get the man going to second. It isn't easy, and it's a good play to watch catchers make.

That isn't the toughest play I have to make, though. Those pop flies right over my head are murder. Not the ones in back or behind, but the ones straight up. All you can do is run out from under them and then judge just where they're going to fall. If you keep looking straight up, you don't have a chance.

On all pop flies, it's smart to watch what the catcher does with his mask. He rips it off, but he doesn't just throw it. First he spots the ball; then he flings his mask the other way. If he didn't, he might trip over it.

Up to now I've written about things you can see. Here's something

18

you can't—the way the catcher and the pitcher r
majors, signs aren't the way they are some other p
fast ball—two fingers, curve—three fingers, chang
teams use a series of signs: one finger, two fingers, o.
ball. Things like that.

Then, too, the signs are changed pretty often. People ask n.
times how I work with pitchers. It just sort of comes to you. .
you've been around a league awhile and you get to know the hitters
and your pitchers, you just do it right. When I'm catching a veteran
like Preacher Roe, I know what he's going to want to throw. You
work with a pitcher and you get to know the way his mind runs. Of
course, with a kid pitcher it's different. You have to call the pitches for
him and guide him along.

The catcher has to guide a lot of plays along, too. He's the only
man on his team who faces away from home plate. On a bunt he can't
reach, he can see whether the fielder should make the play at first or
second. On a throw from the outfield, he can see whether the ball
should be cut off or let alone. A good catcher calls a lot of things
besides pitches.

The good catcher—the catcher you want to look for—has agility,
quick hands, and a good arm, can handle pop flies and pitchers and
can take charge. But there's more to it. I don't exactly know what it is,
and I don't know exactly how to express it, but suppose you were in
my house talking baseball with me. I could tell you how a catcher does
this and how a catcher does that. It isn't the same as when I'm out
there on the field. Then I don't think what to do. I do it. I can't say just
how I throw to second. I just throw.

As I say, I'm not positive what this thing is, but I've got a pretty
good idea. I think it's instinct. I don't know any way that you can
look for it but this: if you see a catcher who makes the big throw in
the clutch, or talks to the rookie pitcher at just the right time, you're
seeing a catcher who's really got it.

THE FIRST BASEMAN

By WHITEY LOCKMAN *of the New York Giants*
National League All-Star in 1952

When I switched from the outfield to first base a few years ago, I
didn't have much trouble with pop flies or with catching throws or
fielding grounders. But if you think that's all there is to playing first
base, think again, and the next time you're watching a ball game,
watch more closely.

19

...bothered me most was the mental adjustment to patterns of ...d play. I don't suppose even a psychiatrist can spot a mentally ...djusted player from the stands. But what bothered me, too—and every fan can look for these in every first baseman—were footwork and the science of making the double play.

When I see a first baseman working, the first things I look for are speed and agility. They both go into footwork. Unless a first baseman handles his feet properly, he might as well forget about handling his glove. No glove will help if you're tied up in a knot when the throw arrives. First basemen who tie themselves in knots are not popular with second basemen, third basemen, and shortstops.

Actually, I've learned that the key to keeping your left foot off your right foot is simple. But it took me some time to master, and many an apprentice first baseman is in constant danger of being spiked—by himself.

A right-handed first baseman must remember to take almost every throw with his right foot on the bag. A left-handed first baseman must remember to take almost every throw with his left foot on the bag. The exceptions occur on bad throws, and then the individual must shift in whichever way suits him best. A bad shift on a bad throw can put the first baseman directly in the runner's path. This is never suitable, particularly if the runner is, say Ted Kluszewski. The good shift on the bad throw takes practice.

You're probably in the habit of following the ball on all plays at first base. Try watching the first baseman's feet at times, instead of the ball. That's the best way to understand the problems of footwork.

Something else that troubled me when I switched was the first-to-second-to-first double play. I still rate it the toughest play I have to make. In this situation, of course, there's always a man on first. He has to be held close. Suddenly a grounder rips into the first baseman's territory. He has to get into position to field the ball, throw to second in a hurry, and get back to first in time to take the return throw. When you watch this one, see how quickly the first baseman gets into position and how quickly he gets rid of the ball. That's the key.

Position is a subject in itself. On the ordinary grounder, the good first baseman stands directly facing the ball, feet slightly apart, back bent as much as possible, hands almost touching the ground. Of course, at first base you get a lot of grounders that aren't ordinary; those short-hop drives and sizzlers don't give you much time to think about position.

Watch a good first baseman and you'll see he always tries to play the ball; he tries to charge everything. But on the low line drive that hits the ground a step in front of him, even the best first baseman can't

20

play the ball. He has to let the ball play him. If he lets the ball play him on softer hits, though, he is not fielding well.

One ball that invites you to play it is about as tough as any. That's the bunt on the sacrifice. Here again, the first baseman must hold a runner on. He can't leave the bag until the pitcher delivers the ball. Then he has to leave in high gear, give the ball the quick treatment, and throw just as quickly, usually while he's off balance, to second base. That's the way to beat the sacrifice. Sometimes there's no sense in trying to get the man at second, but a first baseman has to assume there is until he learns better—perhaps from the catcher, who has the whole diamond in front of him.

The catcher comes into the cut-off play, another toughie. The throw comes in, and a split-second decision determines whether it's cut off or not. The catcher has to shout on this play, "Let it go!" or "Cut it off!" An out often hinges on the catcher's shout and the first baseman's response.

When you see a pop fly go soaring over first base, maybe you mark an out on your scorecard before the ball comes down. Very few errors are made on pop flies. Most first basemen know that the important thing in grabbing them is to follow the ball carefully. Then they try to get in position directly in front of the ball and keep their ears open, because teammates are likely to be shouting directions.

Directions on playing the hitters usually come before the game—in the clubhouse meeting. But it's always a good idea for a first baseman to study the hitters himself and make a private "book" on as many batters as he can. Some right-handed hitters can hit to right; others can't. Some lefthanded hitters pull; others don't. A first baseman always plays off the bag, of course, but how far off and how deep depends on the hitter.

First basemen also must know their infielders. A hard throw from short or third tends to move, in the same way a good fast ball moves. Some infielders' throws take off; they seem to be coming in at the shoulders and end up around the eyes. It's good to know in advance how the ball is apt to act in a case like that.

Other infielders' throws will drift slightly to one side or another. When Bucky Walters was a third baseman he used to throw sinkers to his first baseman, which is how Walters became a pitcher.

There's more to the job of playing first base than meets the eye at a quick glance. As I mentioned, I look first for speed and agility in first basemen. Then I look for mental alertness, so important on plays like the sacrifice and the cut-off. After that I check for hustle. Without hustle, a first baseman can have all the speed, agility, and alertness in the world, but no one will ever know. Finally, I want to see signs that a first baseman is trying to improve. This shows up in prac-

21

tice when a first baseman works on one play over and over again.

I think the fan who sees a big-leaguer and looks for these things will usually see them all. If he doesn't, he might remember before he starts to blast the first baseman, that no one is perfect.

As a ballplayer, I'm sure of one thing: every player in the major leagues is doing his best every second. He has to, or else he couldn't stay in the majors. We're all short of perfection in one way or another, but we're all trying to be perfect all the time. I don't think you can ask any more of anyone.

THE SECOND BASEMAN

By JACKIE ROBINSON *of the Brooklyn Dodgers*
Four-Time National League All-Star Second Baseman

I used to watch second basemen myself. That was when I was a shortstop on the Kansas City Monarchs in the Negro American League. Then I got a chance to watch second basemen again last season, when I moved to third base and the outfield and Junior Gilliam took over my old spot for the Dodgers.

There was just one difference. In between, I'd learned how to play second base.

You get a completely different viewpoint of a position after you've played it. Perhaps you think the second baseman's pivot on the double play is hard. I *know* it's hard. That's why I look for the pivot first when I see a new second baseman. I want to know if he's found out what I found out.

If a second baseman doesn't pivot right, he won't pivot often. He'll be belted, bruised, spiked, and stepped on, and he won't make double plays. On the double play that starts at shortstop, the second baseman can play two roles. He can be the pivot man. He can be the sitting duck. Myself, I preferred being a pivot man.

Picture the play. The shortstop scoops the grounder and shovels it to second. The second baseman catches the ball while moving across the bag, turns and throws to first to get the second out. That's one way. The other, the second baseman catches the ball while moving across the bag, turns and gets knocked on his head by the sliding runner, who wants to make sure the batter makes first.

What's the difference between a knocked-down second baseman and an upright one? You can see it from the stands; it's the jump.

For every hitter but the extreme left-handed pull slugger, the second baseman's fielding position is close enough to second to enable him to beat the base runner to the bag by a comfortable margin. When

22

he's there with the ball ahead of the runner, he has time to feint one way and pivot another. He can fool the runner into sliding on the right-field side of second, then pivot, throw the batter out at first, and help the base runner to his feet. The last is optional.

But if the second baseman starts late, he loses his feinting edge. He only has time to pivot before the runner is upon him, and that is a literal description.

There's no secret. The second baseman need only be alert. When you watch a second baseman, watch the break he gets for second in the double play situation. The good second baseman gets the good jump and the double play. The bad one gets the bump. With the fast break toward second and the instant of grace that gave me, I found I could keep clear of the spikes of the roughest sliders in the big leagues. So remember: watch the jump.

The best way to pivot is while going across the base, but it isn't the only way. Some second basemen kick the bag, others have other tricks. You can judge only by results, and if you see a second baseman pivoting in unorthodox style and still completing double plays, you'll realize that the style he uses suits him best. There's no unbreakable rule of pivot technique.

I can give you a pretty sound rule on pop flies, though: Go back until the outfielder hollers you off the ball. A second baseman has to have range and hustle on short flies to right. Watch to see if the second baseman goes back for everything he can possibly get. He should. I'd go back and back and back and grab the ball unless I heard Carl Furillo yell, "I got it." Then I'd get out of the way in a hurry and Carl took it.

Pop flies, in a sense, are just a diversion for a second baseman. Grounders are his stock in trade, for most of his chances are grounders. He's playing second because he's supposed to be a master at turning rollers into outs, and you'd like to be able to tell the masters from the journeymen.

Hands, of course, are the key. The hands of a second baseman must be sure and quick, but that alone is not enough. A second baseman has to know how to use his hands. Whenever I went for a grounder, I'd keep my glove as close to the ground as I possibly could. Then if the ball hopped, I'd come up for it. It's a lot easier to get your glove up than to bring it down, and besides, if your glove is low and the ball hops high, there's a good chance you'll block it with your body. If your glove is high and the ball bounces low, there's a good chance the right fielder will have to block it and a fair chance that you'll be charged with an error. Look for a glove near the ground.

At second, you can often get away with playing a ball with your chest. Except in cases of grounders back of second, the throw is short and requires no windup at all. There's no sense in looking for a strong arm in a second baseman. You won't find it often, and it doesn't mean much. What is important is the speed with which the second baseman gets rid of the ball.

Sometime when you've gotten to a ball game early enough to see infield practice, you may have seen second basemen practicing getting the ball out of their gloves after fielding grounders. That's all you can do about it—practice. If you see a second baseman who takes a long time getting his throw off, you are not seeing a good second baseman.

There's one play you'll see second basemen make where they have to get the throw off just as soon as they grab the ball. That's on those slow, topped rollers. It's a common play, and it's a tough one. You're playing deep; you come charging in, grab the ball bare-handed, and throw in one motion while you're off balance. That's a lot easier to write than to do. When you see a second baseman make that play a few times, you're seeing a star fielder.

The relay from the outfield comes up, too, but not as often for the second baseman as for the shortstop. Generally, shortstops have better arms, and the second baseman acts as relay man only on some hits to right center. It is really the shortstop's play, and Phil Rizzuto explains what to look for in a relay in his article.

If you see a second baseman who can make the double play and handle slow and hard grounders, and who roams as far for pop flies as the outfielders let him, but who is nevertheless a little weak on relays, don't be disturbed. The weakness isn't fatal or even very serious.

THE THIRD BASEMAN

By AL ROSEN *of the Cleveland Indians*
American League's Most Valuable Player in 1953

I like to watch Eddie Yost of the Washington Senators play third. He shows me what I look for—quick reactions and fast hands. George Kell of the Boston Red Sox shows me the same things.

There isn't any trick to spotting speed and agility. Major league hitters have major league muscles, and when they swing away, the third baseman who doesn't have speed and agility is in danger. The ball comes down the line like a jet, and quick reflexes are a matter of self-defense. You'll see plenty of plays where the third baseman has to get his glove up to stay healthy, and plenty more where he has to get his hands down in the dirt to keep his team's chances alive. Quickness is indispensable; without it, a third baseman will find the left fielder helping him play third.

When I've discovered that a third baseman is quick, I look to see if he's mobile. There's a difference. Watch how Yost and Kell crowd the line in a situation when a double would hurt more than a single through the hole. Watch how they edge away from the line when the single is the hit that can do the damage. Watch how they edge in a few steps on some hitters—the good bunters. Watch how they edge back on the men who can't bunt, but can slug. Watch how they play position. Speed and agility don't help a third baseman who's ten feet away from a sizzler.

You're watching a star. You see he uses his head to get the most out of his reflexes. Now you see something else. Someone hits a slow grounder toward short. Without an instant's hesitation, the third baseman cuts over, spears the ball, and throws out the hitter. If he hadn't, the shortstop would have had a tough—maybe impossible—play.

Now there's a pop fly halfway up the line. The third baseman moves in, yelling, "I got it, I got it!" And he takes it. You've seen more than just reflexes and alertness. You've seen a third baseman with a take-charge attitude. He's a defensive star.

It's tough to be a defensive star, tough just to be a competent third baseman. When I joined the Indians, I couldn't make a lot of the plays I do now. I gave third base concentration and constant practice. Techniques of playing hitters and mechanical techniques were drummed into me by Oscar Melillo and Tony Cuccinello. Al Lopez, my manager, helped with my throwing. All this just made it possible for me to learn. The actual learning came through practice.

Take the swinging bunt, the toughest play I have to make. Almost every game you see will have at least one of these roughies in it—the batter swings with all his might, tops the ball, a dribbler like a bunt comes creeping up the line, and the batter starts racing toward first. If I've been playing deep and the hitter is fast, this play is specially tough. Sometimes there's just no way it can be made. But when it is made, here are some secrets I've picked up:

I rely on instinct—that's the only word that describes it—to determine exactly how deep I play. I know the pitcher and the hitter, and that's what determines the general area. When a sinker-ball pitcher is working and a right-handed batter is up, I know the swinging bunt is a strong possibility.

I know that when the swinging bunt comes I have to charge fast and fire the ball cleanly and in a hurry. If I miss one of the three, I miss my play.

Watch third basemen on swinging bunts. There isn't a better way to spot a weakness. But a way that's almost as good is to watch one of those sliced grounders that left-handers slap toward third. The ball is spinning like a top, and gloving a top isn't easy. The tag play on a base runner is no bargain, either, when the throw is coming from center or from right. The ball is usually in a direct line with the base runner, and you're trying to catch both.

Every play at third isn't rugged, of course. A lot of pop flies are comparatively easy. Look for a third baseman who seems to be watching the ball with real concentration, who waits for it relaxed, and who follows the ball into the glove. On most grounders, my rule is that the lower I get my body, the farther out front I keep my hands. That, generally, is something to look for, but I don't think I can give you anything definite on the position of the third baseman's feet when he's scooping a grounder. A third baseman spreads his feet in whatever way suits him best. He wants to be relaxed as he fields the grounder, and footwork is important in relaxation.

Footwork is just as important in the throw to first. If you see a third baseman who seems to be throwing across his body all through a game, you're seeing a third baseman who isn't throwing correctly. The idea is to shift, and a good third baseman ends up facing the bag to which he's throwing; his arm pointed directly toward the bag in proper follow-through. Another point, but one you'll have trouble noticing even with binoculars, is the third baseman's throwing grip. It must be firm, and preferably the grip should be down the long seams.

Sometimes, though, there isn't the second to spare for checking the grip. A surprise bunt is that kind of situation. The way to beat the surprise bunt is to avoid being surprised. This isn't like the swinging bunt; it's deliberate. I try to study managers and hitters. In that way I learn bunt situations. Then the play resembles the swinging bunt. I have to charge hard and throw—whether underhand, side-arm or overhand—in a hurry.

Generally, the third baseman doesn't have to cover the ground a shortstop does. He doesn't have the double play pivot that keeps second basemen jumping. But he has his own special problems, and he has to resolve them in his own special ways. Billy Cox of the Brooklyn Dodgers plays a lot of hard smashes from the side, spearing them. That violates a lot of rules, but have you ever heard any complaints about Cox's fielding? Yost and Kell get their results in a more orthodox style.

But all third basemen must have speed, agility, and mobility. Look for those three qualities, and if you find them, you won't see many bad plays around third base.

26

THE SHORTSTOP

By PHIL RIZZUTO *of the New York Yankees*
Four-Time Major-League All-Star

There isn't any mystery to playing shortstop, and you don't have to be a detective to tell a good one from a bad.

I always ask three questions:

1. Are the shortstop's hands quick?
2. Does he have a good arm?
3. How fast does he get rid of the ball?

There's more to the business of plugging the gap between the second baseman and the third baseman, of course. But the three I've listed are basic. A big-league shortstop who is weak in one of these departments is not likely to remain a big-league shortstop for long. Let me show you what I mean.

The toughest play I have to make is the one that sends me into the hole back of third—the play you see when the hitter raps a grounder between the shortstop and the third baseman, and the shortstop reaches the ball. There is a variation of this play when the shortstop does not reach the ball. It's called a single.

Anyway, when I go into the hole, I'm moving toward my barehand side. It's best to get squarely behind the grounder, but that can't always be done, and the ball has to be scooped backhand. Suppose, as I'm about to scoop, the ball takes a slightly erratic bounce and comes up a little higher than I'd figured. If I get my glove up in time, I stay with it. If not—well, we have a single again.

Sometimes it's hard to spot those little bad hops from the stands. The big ones you can always see. But next time you're watching a big-league shortstop work, follow the ball closely, and you'll likely see a grounder that fools you and the shortstop. Then watch his hands. The quicker they move, the more hops they stay with and the more runners he throws out. But let's get back to me.

I've stayed with the hop and here I am, on the edge of the outfield grass, leaning toward third. And there's the hitter bearing down on first base. I have to get rid of the ball quickly, or else I might as well keep it as a souvenir. "Eat the ball," is the way some players put it.

The only way to avoid eating it is to reach into your glove and grab it in a hurry. That's just a matter of reflexes, but you have to have the reflexes.

Now I'll let you in on a trade secret. We've come to the key moment in this particular play. As I reach for the ball, I get my balance

27

set. When I scooped it, I was leaning toward third, but I can't get off a decent throw that way. So while I'm reaching for the ball and before I make my throw, I'm getting set. If I don't, all I've done up to now has been wasted.

With my body balanced properly, I throw. Only a strong accurate throw will retire the batter and, balance or no, only a good arm can deliver the strong accurate throw.

Say my peg is swift and true and I nip the hitter by half a step. I've made the toughest play I ever have to make at shortstop, and I've nailed my man. But take away one thing—the quickness of my hands, the speed with which I got rid of the ball, or the good throw—and what do you have? You've got a man on first or maybe second. You also have a shortstop who'll find himself on a fast bus to the minors.

All three general points contribute to the play, in addition to the specific trick of getting set. Of course, some big-league shortstops have better arms than others, some have quicker hands, some are more adept at getting rid of the ball. But none of the good ones is really weak in any of the three. Remember that, and when you watch a shortstop, check him on the Rizzuto three-point plan. If he fails badly on one point, you won't be watching him for long.

Chances are you'll never find yourself watching a very slow shortstop. If a ballplayer has no speed, he plays somewhere else where he is less apt to hurt his team, himself, and the fans who've paid to see him play. But there are degrees of speed, and the best way to spot the player who's a little slow is to look for his position with respect to the ball. If he's in front of almost every grounder when he picks it up, the boy can move. If he's playing them from the side, you're probably looking at a converted catcher.

That position tells you what sort of break the shortstop gets, too. You hear a lot more about outfielders getting the jump on flies than about infielders getting the jump on grounders. But if a shortstop doesn't leave at the crack of the bat, there's no sense in his going. So remember to watch position.

Then, of course, there's the little matter of making the double play. If a shortstop can't play his part, he won't have many pitchers among his friends, and he may have to get used to a long stay in the second division.

When the shortstop starts the double play, watch his throw. Sure, it should be chest high, but, just as important, the ball should be in view of the second baseman all the time. When the shortstop throws so that the runner screens part of the ball's flight, he's taking a chance on throwing to right field.

The double plays the second baseman starts mean one thing to me:

get rid of that ball in a hurry. Those are the most important things for you to watch in one of the most important plays in baseball.

Fans watching big-leaguers decide before long that the pop fly is an easy play. It isn't tough, usually, but remember, big-leaguers are making it look easy. When you see one of those pops go heading toward the sky over short, see if the shortstop shades his eyes from the sun. If he doesn't, you'll see the ball better than he. Pops in shallow left can cause trouble unless the shortstop races back fast. And there can be trouble even after he's raced back, if he doesn't remember to try to catch the ball squarely in front of him. The over-the-shoulder stuff looks fancy, but a good shortstop will pass up a fancy play for an easy one any time. Only when he can barely reach a pop fly should a shortstop grab it going away from the infield.

And while we have the shortstop in back of his position, let's not forget the relay play—taking an outfielder's throw and whipping it in. Look for the shortstop to give the fielder a target, to stand in line with the base he wants to throw to, and to get rid of the ball in one motion.

Remember, too, that a good shortstop fields all grounders with his hands in front of him and tries to be in position to throw.

If you remember all this, you may not qualify as a scout, but you'll certainly be able to tell a good shortstop from a bad one.

THE LEFT FIELDER

By STAN MUSIAL of the St. Louis Cardinals

Before you start watching a left fielder, remember that the left fielder has been doing some watching of his own. Chances are he's made a quick check on the distance between himself and the wall. If there's a sun, he knows its position, because he doesn't want to see the sun when he's looking for a fly ball. Then he's made sure he knows exactly what the game situation is. You may not notice a left fielder checking the points he has to, but if he hasn't checked them, you'll find out before many balls are hit his way.

What you can always spot in a left fielder is his mechanical ability. He needs reasonable speed. He doesn't need the most powerful arm in the outfield, but he should have a good one, and he needs the ability to judge drives hit his way.

The left fielder doesn't have to make a throw comparable to the right fielder's peg to third. That's why—all other factors being equal —the strong-armed outfielder plays right field. But the left fielder does have some problems of his own.

Most hitters are right-handed and give left fielders a lot of business. A common play and a tough one is the solid line drive hit near the foul line.

Line drives generally bother young left fielders. That's because liners move. Almost invariably the liner hit down the line curves toward foul territory. It can land fair, of course, and that curve often carries it away from the left fielder's reach, but not quite across the foul line. When that happens, the left fielder must decide whether to attempt to cut off the ball or to play it off the wall.

Around the National League, the walls vary. In St. Louis it's about 350 feet from the plate and falls away in a straight line. In the Polo Grounds, the left-field wall is less than 300 feet out, but it falls back sharply on a curve. In addition, the upper deck at the Polo Grounds extends far out, and sometimes balls I thought I'd catch have just grazed the upper deck and become homers.

A good left fielder remembers the ball park in which he's playing before committing himself on one of those twisting liners. A well-played rebound on a sharp liner in the Polo Grounds means only a single. In St. Louis, a ball bouncing against the left-field wall is almost always good for two bases. So a left fielder remembers his park, and checks the score of the game, before deciding how to play that particular tough chance.

When the left fielder actually does play it, there are things you can look for and, in the majors, generally spot.

When he runs, he runs on the balls of his feet. If he ran on his heels, his body would be jarred at every step and the ball would seem to come at him in jumps. The final jump, very likely, would carry the ball over his head.

He runs watching the ball. He knows where the fences are, and he also knows that the only way he can be sure of staying with a drive is to follow in from the bat to his glove.

He tries to use two hands whenever possible. I remember a drive to left center in Ebbets Field last year. I took off after it and managed to catch it with a backhand stab. On one of those desperate tries, one hand may go further than two, but only on those desperate tries.

He catches balls above the waist with his glove up, balls below the waist with his glove down. I know of a case where an outfielder—not a major-leaguer—tried to catch a sinking liner with his glove up. He went for it with two hands, as he should have; the ball kept sinking and broke a finger on his bare hand. If this outfielder had held his glove down and his bare hand down, he would have saved himself a lot of pain.

As often as you watch a left fielder handling flies, you see him playing ground balls. Singles through the left side of the infield and short line drives are both on or near the ground by the time the left fielder reaches them. There's no specific technique in handling grounders that fans can look for. There are several techniques, and here again the left fielder decides only after watching the game closely.

If there's no one on base, the left fielder may drop to one knee. The knee that touches the ground should be on the same side from which the player throws. That enables the left fielder to block the ball if it gets out of his glove and still make a fast recovery throw to the infield. Of course, no outfielder ever places both knees on the ground. That would delay the throw and in addition, if the ball should bounce away, the left fielder would lose time in regaining his feet to chase it.

If there are men on base, the situation is different. There may be no time for caution, only for speed. Then look for the left fielder to charge in, scoop the ball, and get rid of it quickly.

In watching left fielders throw, look for low pegs that can be cut off. In theory it's a good idea for the left fielder to throw the way a pitcher does a fast ball, gripping across the four seams. In practice there often is no time to check the grip.

There's one more thing to look for when you watch good left fielders work. That's hustle. A ballplayer with little natural ability cannot become great simply by hustling. But a ball player with great natural ability must always hustle if he wants to realize his potentialities.

A hustling left fielder will come running in when he spots a base runner trying to steal third. Chances are the catcher's throw will be accurate, but on the slim chance that it won't be, the left fielder should move in fast enough to prevent the runner from scoring.

I've always tried to hustle. I started out as a pitcher, fast and wild, and I remember years later seeing a scouting report in which the scout called me the wildest pitcher he had ever seen. But I wanted to be a pitcher and switched only after some arm trouble. I learned about hustle in the minors while getting used to the outfield. Later, with the Cardinals, I played first base for a while. Again it was a new position, and again I tried to hustle.

Hustle isn't all that goes into making a good left fielder. But no one can be a good left fielder without it.

THE CENTER FIELDER

By LARRY DOBY *of the Cleveland Indians*
Five-Time American League All-Star

Maybe you've played a little center field yourself; maybe you've just watched a lot of center fielders. But chances are you know how important the break is—that split-second jump that turns what looks like a double into a nice running catch. You have to study the break if you want to watch center fielders. But there's more to it than that. You have to study the times the center fielder doesn't break.

You may have seen me off with the crack of the bat at times. You may have seen me spend that split-second waiting and spear the ball in mid-stride.

"Look at that," some fans will say. "He's making an easy catch look hard."

That isn't quite right. Sometimes when I delay my break, I'm making a tough catch, and I'm making it the only way it can be made. From the stands you get one angle. When you're out on the field making a living, you get another.

From my angle, the toughest ball to handle is the low line drive—those shots that can be four feet high when the batter hits them, four feet high when they zip over second, and maybe all the way down to three feet high by the time they reach center field. The hitch is, those shots don't always act the same.

I've learned that when Mickey Mantle or Yogi Berra belts a low liner, the ball tends to sink. That's because of the way their wrist action affects the ball. Minnie Minoso hits a lot of low liners that take off and drift to one side or the other. And there's more to it even than that.

On a day when Bob Lemon is at his fastest, the low liners may act just a little differently from the way they do when Lemon is getting by with more stuff and less speed. I've found there's only one thing to do —play the ball off the bat. Wait an instant before moving. You lose a half-step, but every step you take is in the right direction.

I'm not minimizing the break. As a matter of fact, it's the first thing I look for when I see a center fielder. But the break can only be used when there's no risk of breaking in the wrong direction. And on those low liners, that risk is high.

When I've spotted a center fielder's break, I look for speed. If you can't run, you have no business playing center field. And then I want to see an arm. A center fielder either has these things or he doesn't. You either know how to break or you don't. All you can learn is what I've learned: don't break too soon on certain types of hits. And speed and an arm, basically, are talents that can be improved upon. First, though, they have to be there.

"Being there," of course, pretty well describes the whole business of playing center field. You have to be there at the same time the ball is. The way to watch for this is obvious; the *time* to watch for it is not.

I think Minoso causes more center fielders more trouble than anyone else in the American League. I play Mantle, Gus Zernial, and

ROBIN ROBERTS

Pitcher for Philadelphia Phils, National League All-Star in 1952 and 1953

STAN ("The Man") MUSIAL

Left fielder for St. Louis Cardinals, Six-Time National League Batting Champion

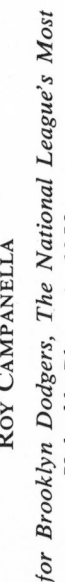

ROY CAMPANELLA

Catcher for Brooklyn Dodgers, The National League's Most
Valuable Player in 1953

WHITEY LOCKMAN

First baseman for New York Giants, National League All-Star
in 1952

AL ROSEN

Third baseman for Cleveland Indians, American League's Most Valuable Player in 1953

JACKIE ROBINSON

Second baseman for Brooklyn Dodgers, Four-Time National League All-Star Second Baseman

JIM PIERSALL

Right fielder for Boston Red Sox, fielding sensation of the
American League

LARRY DOBY

Center fielder for Cleveland Indians, Five-Time American
League All-Star

maybe some others, a little deeper than Minoso. But they don't put me to the test the way he does. Minnie bats right-handed, so the tendency is to shade him to left. The trouble is that he hits to right like a left-hander. He has really good power, so you have to play him deep. The trouble here is that he always seems to be looping one in front of you, just a step out of reach.

Then he hits a lot of those liners I mentioned. His take off and fade. For example, he'll ram one toward right center that looks like an easy play, but the ball starts to move further and further toward right, and takes off to make it harder. That's my idea of the toughest play in the book.

Normally, you'll notice the center fielder taking everything he can get. That's a sort of unwritten law of the outfield—the center fielder takes charge. But on one of those right center drives, I sometimes call the right fielder on to the ball. I might reach it, but it's moving toward him so I know he can reach it. Besides, if he's a right-handed thrower, he'll have a much better angle than I to get off that peg back to the infield.

On all other outfield plays, though, look for the center fielder, because he's the key man. What he reaches, he takes; what he can't, he supervises. The play is always in front of the center fielder. Even on a pop fly to short left. Then the left fielder moves in, the shortstop goes back and the center fielder comes over. Visualize it and you'll see that the center fielder can spot the other two players and the ball all in one quick look. If he can reach it, he yells, "I got it," and takes it. If he can't, he may yell, "George, George," if, like me, he's playing behind a shortstop named George and the shortstop seems to have the best chance at this ball.

Watch the way a center fielder moves back and comes in. In the majors you'll probably see a man who does both without much difficulty. Sometimes, though, you may spot something that can give you a private book on a particular player.

You have to be careful, though. Remember, I mentioned break, speed, and arm. Take someone like Billy Bruton of the Milwaukee Braves. I've seen him play center a lot, and he doesn't get the best break in the world. But Billy's so fast he doesn't seem to need it. He outruns the ball. His break will improve with practice, and when it does he'll be great.

If you want to appreciate a special problem in some ball parks, sit in the center field stands. All year in the Yankee Stadium and late in the season in Cleveland, the ball comes out of shadows. The center fielder stands in the sun and the batter in the shade, and if you don't think that can make it tough, sit back of the center fielder. It's only fair to warn you that you may not see the ball.

In the minors there are places where night baseball adds to the center fielder's problems, because the whole park appears to be in shadow. Not in the majors, fortunately, are there any parks like that. Perhaps big-league visibility may not be 100 per cent at night—just 99 per cent.

Watching big-league center fielders, you'll see slight variations in styles and techniques. As long as you're watching a major-leaguer, though, you can be pretty sure of this: you're watching an expert who knows what's best for him and for his team.

THE RIGHT FIELDER

By JIM PIERSALL *of the Boston Red Sox*
Fielding Sensation of the American League

The good right fielder does not ad-lib. Before the pitch is thrown, he considers every possible play. When the ball is hit to right, the good right fielder knows exactly what he's going to do because he's planned in advance. Aside from physical equipment, I think that's the most important single quality of the good right fielder.

How can you look for it? Let's take a case in point. With two out and nobody on base, a hitter bounces a single through the infield. The right fielder charges the ball so hard that he overruns it, and the hitter reaches second base on his single.

The point here is not that the right fielder failed to handle the ball cleanly. Mechanical errors are a part of baseball. Rather, it's that he charged the ball at all. There was no chance of getting the man at first. If the right fielder had come in easily, there would have been no chance of the man making second. With two out, it takes successive singles to score a man from first, but almost any hit will bring him in from second. The overcharging right fielder didn't think of that. He ad-libbed and made a bad play.

If there'd been a runner on second, the right fielder would have been wise to charge the ball, at least until he'd made sure that there could be no play at the plate. In that situation when the right fielder overruns the ball he is making an error. But he isn't making a bad play.

Of course, when you watch right fielders you notice them most when they're chasing back for long drives, not when they're coming in on grounders. The good right fielder tries to "secure" every play he makes, even the toughest.

By "secure" I mean this: he tries to catch every fly ball with both hands, and he tries to make his plays in the right position at all times.

34

Here's something that may help you in watching right fielders "secure."

More important than sheer speed is judgment—which way to move. And there can't be any waiting for this judgment. Ability to move in the right direction at the sound of ball meeting bat always gives the right fielder a great chance to rob the batter. [EDITOR'S NOTE: This is really advice from an expert. Piersall probably robbed more batters than anyone else in the majors last season.]

That's one kind of judgment, and it must be exercised in a flash. There's another kind of judgment entirely different. The good right fielder has made a study of the hitting ability of every player he faces. He learns that a Yogi Berra hits deep and pulls, that a Dale Mitchell sprays his hits. He knows where to play a Berra or a Mitchell. Sometimes he's crossed up, but more often he's right. And when the good right fielder is right, he's saved needless running and, on hits that may drop in, vital seconds.

Before each game, the good right fielder reviews his hitters. When you see him, he'll probably be relaxed, so that the ball is easier to catch, but watchful, so that he'll be where the ball is in order to catch it.

Sometimes, during a pause in the game, you may see a right fielder chatting with a center fielder. It isn't likely that they're discussing the latest movie downtown. More likely, they're discussing the situation and what each intends to do on the next play.

When there isn't time for a chat, they may shout to each other. The shouting is about where each man will play, and the reason they're shouting is that neither wants a crash when a fly is hit to right center. The center fielder is in complete charge, because he has all the plays in front of him. Look for this shouting the next time you're at the ball park. It's a sign of a good right fielder and a good outfield.

Some right fielders, you'll notice, waste no time at all in firing the ball when there's any possible play. The best right fielder is the one who throws the ball quickest—provided he knows where he's throwing it.

Usually, I'll throw to one of two cutoff men. I'll always throw low, so that the ball can be cut off. On the peg to third, the cutoff man is the shortstop. On the peg to the plate, it's usually the first baseman. The idea of the cutoff is this:

Let's say a batter singles with a man on second. Maybe there'll be a play at home, maybe not. The right fielder fires, hard and low, but there just can't be a play on the runner. But the hitter sees the throw headed home and figures he can make second base by the time the catcher gets the ball and manages to throw to second. The catcher never gets the ball. The first baseman, in line between the right fielder and the plate, cuts it off, whips it to second, and the hitter is out by yards.

Look for a right fielder to throw low. It may be possible to get more distance on a high throw, but it's impossible to cut off. The right fielder who plans ahead knows how important the cutoff is.

I look for evidence of planning by right fielders. And it's a rare game that doesn't offer plenty of evidence for examination. Besides the planning, of course, I want to see a right fielder with speed enough to cover his territory and strength enough in his arm to make the long low throws he must make.

Right field is just a part of the outfield, and chances are that every right fielder you see in the majors could move to left or center if he had to and still do fairly well. As a young outfielder, I know I talked to other outfielders, regardless of their specific position, about the hitters in the league and about outfielding in general. In big, little, or sandlot leagues there's a lot a newcomer can learn from someone who's been around awhile.

Of course, major-league right fielders have learned a great deal. They've practiced with others and by themselves for a long time. And my personal tip on the major-league right fielder, the man with the ability and experience to reach the top, is this:

He will not waste a move, because waste motion can lose the game. Every movement that you see him make counts toward winning for his whole team.

That's the sort of right fielder to look for, no matter what kind of game you're watching. That's the kind of right fielder who's best.

THE MANAGER AND THE COACH

By ED STANKY *of the St. Louis Cardinals*
Manager of the Year in 1952

There isn't any way you fans can watch a manager the way you watch his ball players. And that's the way it should be because the players make the manager. If Casey Stengel, or Leo Durocher, or Joe McCarthy, or even the great John McGraw had been managing the Pittsburgh Pirates last season, do you think any of them would have finished with a better record than Fred Haney did? I don't think so. I think a manager without good players is like a soldier going to war with a good gun but no bullets. He looks fine until the shooting starts.

Even a manager who, like myself, acts as a coach spends half the game sitting in the dugout. Maybe not sitting. Maybe walking up and down when the tension starts to mount; but, anyway, out of sight of most spectators. Once in a while the manager comes out of his dugout and marches to the mound. That always means trouble; it usually means the other team is rallying. To you fans the rally represents excitement and action, and when the manager walks to the mound the action stops. I've seen some fans grow angry every time one of those emergency meetings is held. But those meetings are a part of baseball and a part of the manager's job.

Let me pass along a little inside stuff to you. One of the biggest concerns in managing—a job not without concerns—is the handling of pitchers.

It takes at least four or five months for a manager to learn what he must learn about every pitcher—how that pitcher acts when he's tired, for example. Some hurlers go to the resin bag more frequently when they're growing weary. Others paw the rubber like a chicken looking for a worm. Still others flash a sign to an infielder. I remember when I was a second baseman I'd get signs from pitchers and trot over.

"Gee, Eddie," the pitcher would say, "stall a little. I need a breather. It's a hot day."

I'd stall, the pitcher would get his rest, and the umpire would put the blast on me. The pitcher got rest and I'd get overheated. That's fair, of course, because on the day he starts, the pitcher has the most strenuous job on the field—the catcher over a season, the pitcher for a single day.

Suppose you're watching a game and a pitcher and an infielder huddle. Then the manager comes out. You're annoyed; you want the game to continue. But think a minute and remember that there's an inside of baseball.

Perhaps they're huddling because someone suspects a Durocher or a Cavaretta has stolen a set of signs. Perhaps they're wondering about the best way for the infielder to play the hitter. That's just in the normal course of a game. When a team is in trouble, the manager is probably wondering whether the pitcher still has his stuff, trying to confirm a sign of weariness he's spotted from the bench. This may slow the game for you fans, but a player and a manager are always trying to win. And those huddles at the mound are not slow to them.

The huddles you see; the little storms in the clubhouse you don't. A manager, of course, must have patience, and managers tend to be more patient with rookies than veterans. But rookie or veteran, a loafing or an unthinking ball player tries a manager's patience to the breaking point.

I like to tell the Cardinals in the clubhouse: "The perfect ball player is in the graveyard. We don't have any." All real ball players strive for perfection, but too many things happen in too many different games for anyone to achieve perfection all the time. I never have and never will ridicule a player for a mechanical mistake like booting a grounder, dropping a fly, or striking out. But when a pitcher fails to cover first base on a ground ball to the right side or an infielder "short-legs" a grounder, that's a little different. That's what leads to those small storms.

Something else happens in the clubhouse out of your sight. A few players try to alibi after a bonehead play. When someone pulls a rock, he knows it, you fans know it, and the manager knows it. There's no sense in alibiing to save face. The only way to save face is to admit the rock and accept the consequences.

That's all part of managing—dealing with these situations. Coaching is a different job. I can think of ten reasons why a manager should coach on the lines. I can think of ten reasons why he should not. It's up to the individual manager, and the big reason for my coaching is my belief that it helps the club. When I stop helping my club, I head for my dugout and stay there.

You fans can see a coach make a snap decision. And you can second-guess his decision when a runner is out at the plate. The perfect coach, like the perfect manager and the perfect player, is extinct —if he ever lived.

You see the decision, but do you know what goes into it? Before a coach decides whether to send or hold a runner, he has to know the strengths and weaknesses of the outfielder—how well the fielder throws, whether he charges balls quickly, and whether he takes a long time to get rid of the ball once he's got it. Then the coach must consider the speed of the base runner, the number of outs, the hitters to follow, and the stage of the game. All this flashes through the coach's mind, but all you see is a man standing with palms raised in the classic stop sign, or a man with an arm waving furiously, telling the runner to go ahead.

When you don't see a coach in one of these poses, you'll likely see him flashing signs. He'll touch his cap, hitch his belt, scratch his elbow, and shout, "Get on!" Maybe one of those items means bunt. Maybe not.

Signs are specially important to a winning team, and more so to the pennant-winning team. I've seen games lost because a batter or a base runner missed a sign. And a missed hit-and-run, a missed steal, or a missed bunt can change the entire course of a game. I've also seen good alert players go through an entire season without missing a single sign.

There are a great many systems of signs and a great many systems for stealing them. Some managers have no set system of signaling players. They use complex hard-to-steal signs for the cleverest ballplayers and simpler signs for the simpler ones. Unfortunately, the importance of signs is too often overlooked by you fans and by members of the press and radio. A manager remembers always that a game lost by a missed sign in May is as important as a game lost by a bad pitch in September.

Sometimes when a pitcher loses a big game or a hitter strikes out in the clutch, people will point to the pitcher or the hitter. "He lost the big game," they'll say. "He lost his team the pennant." That's ridiculous. The home-run ball in the last week of the season may look bigger than the missed sign in May. But it is not. A manager knows it is not.

As a class, I'd say we managers refuse to believe any team has to win some and lose some. We want to win them all. So do the players, and none of us care whether the games take two or four hours, so long as we win.

When you watch me manage, you're watching a man who said when he first got the job: "I don't consider major-league managing difficult." I haven't had to eat those words. Nineteen fifty-four is my twentieth season in baseball, and baseball has been good to me. My family has always been first; baseball has always been second. Because of all my years in baseball, managing comes easily to me. Nothing would make me happier than to spend another twenty years in baseball—managing in St. Louis for my boss, Gussie Busch. Nothing, except, perhaps, if baseball should be as good to my two-year-old son Mike as it has been to me.

THE UMPIRE

By LARRY GOETZ *of the National League*
A Leading National League Umpire Since 1936

Some people see terrible things when they watch umpires. Or at least say they do. To hear them talk, you'd think it would be a good idea to station the umpires in the bleachers and let them call the plays from there. That's because these people think they can judge from their left-field seats whether a curve ball catches a corner than the umpire can from his position back of the plate.

These people aren't real baseball fans, though. The real fans know that for every pitch an umpire calls wrong, there are a hundred he calls right. The real fans know that umpires don't care who the batter is or who the pitcher is—only where the pitch is. They know that umpiring is a profession with high standards, and they understand how important good umpiring is to baseball.

I'm writing this for the real fans. There are tricks and techniques to umpiring, and a veteran umpire knows what to look for when he sees a younger man work. I supervised a clinic for young umpires at the Dodgers' base in Vero Beach, Florida, and I think if I pass along to you some of the pointers I taught then, you'll learn a lot about the way to watch an umpire work.

The first rule for umpires is the same as the first rule for ball players. In a word, "Hustle."

An umpire who does not hustle is a bad umpire. A secret of umpiring is position. You want a clear view of the play, because if the third baseman's back is in your face you aren't going to be able to tell whether the runner sliding into third is safe or out. Or, suppose the batter lifts a foul into the first row of seats and the catcher and a fan go for the ball. The only way you can tell if the catcher caught it fairly, or if he caught it off the fan's arm or grabbed it after the fan caught it, is to be right there. The catcher will be running, and the umpire has to run, too.

A hustling umpire will stay right on top of the plays. Watch for that. If he's out of position, not only can he call one wrong, but also, even if he calls it right, he's open to player protests. You never want to let a player say, "How could you call that one? You were in the next county."

If you see an umpire calling plays long-distance or calling them from behind the fielder's back, chances are you aren't watching a major-league umpire.

But hustle isn't the whole story. After I see an umpire get into perfect position, then I want to see him take his time. Hustle doesn't mean yelling "Safe!" or "Out!" because that's the first thing that comes into your head. Hustle on the play and take your time making the decision.

I've developed this deliberate style myself, and it took a long time. I simply forced myself not to make decisions on those open-and-shut plays. You know the ones: the throw has the runner out by twenty feet, or the base looks easily stolen—the sort of plays that don't seem to need an umpire to make the decision.

By not guessing how the play was going to turn out, I kept myself from raising my arm or putting my palms down too soon. And maybe changing my decision in a hurry when the throw sailed wild or the runner slid off the base.

I follow the same policy on balls and strikes. I wait until the ball has reached the catcher's glove, because then I can rule on the half-swings more accurately. And, incidentally, if the pitch is really bad, I watch the batter. Most half-swings come on bad balls that fool the batter, and when I can see that the pitch is going to hit the dirt, I watch the hitter.

When you see an umpire hustle to the scene and slow down before making the call, you're watching a mechanically good umpire. There's more to umpiring than mechanics.

Notice how the decision is made. It should be emphatic and authoritative, because it isn't enough for an umpire merely to know what he's doing. He has to *look* as though he knows what he's doing, too. That's important in winning and keeping the respect of players and fans.

And in line with that, look at the umpire's appearance. It isn't an accident that we wear dignified blue suits. Dignity is an important part of the job. An umpire should carry himself with an air of assurance. He should be neat. He should be businesslike.

Temperament is another factor. How can you sit in the stands and discover whether an umpire has the proper temperament? Watch him when players argue. Emotion has its place in baseball, and you can't expect a player to go through a tension-charged season without an occasional complaint. You can't let a player spend the whole season complaining. So you have to draw the line, and you have to know where to draw it.

Some players must be slapped down, others given a little room, kidded, or "handled." The good umpire knows how to deal with different players, and he knows, too, that no matter how wild the players may get, he must keep his head.

There are some other items, but these are the main ones. I've learned them the hard way. I spent sixteen seasons being seasoned in the minors, eleven of them in triple-A ball. Then when I did get to the majors, it took about five years for me to establish myself. And then I had to keep hustling to keep established, just like a ballplayer or anyone else at the top of his chosen profession.

But, after all these years, after work in World Series and All-Star games, after running a clinic and being in the middle of pennant race after pennant race, I've learned something else. There are still any number of things I have to learn about umpiring and watching other umpires.

I guess that's the main feature of my job. I know that's what makes it so interesting.

A CONCISE HISTORY OF BASEBALL

There is a legend about baseball and a little New York village called Cooperstown and a youth named Abner Doubleday who grew up to be a major general. According to the legend, young Doubleday labored briefly and gave birth to a game with a bat, a ball, home plate, and three bases. This was at Cooperstown in 1839.

"What is the name of this game, Abner?" the youth's parents are reported to have asked after watching a contest.

"I'm not sure," the legend says Doubleday replied, "but tentatively I'm calling it baseball."

The legend does not specify whether a flourish of trumpets from afar greeted young Abner's answer. Nor does it explain what his parents thought of the name. But no matter.

Not everything is known about the origin of baseball. Just enough to be certain that Abner Doubleday did not invent it, that it did not start in Cooperstown, and that it was played before 1839. At best, Doubleday got a good idea many years too late. At worst, as some historians suggest, he never played baseball at all. But, for better or for worse, Doubleday and the legend that surrounds him have been accepted by a great many people.

A commission especially authorized by baseball to probe old records unearthed the Doubleday story in 1907. The records the commission searched were not old enough.

Ernie Harwell, the baseball announcer, owns what is probably the most complete private library on the sport in the world. His earliest book is a reprint of *A Little Pretty Pocket Book,* an English work for children first published in 1744. It consists of poems, each with a moral attached, and was thrust upon the American public in 1787 when it was printed in Worcester, Massachusetts.

Under a woodcut of young ballplayers is the title "Baseball," and this brief rhyme appears:

> *The ball once struck off,*
> *Away flies the boy*
> *To the next destined point,*
> *And then home with joy.*

The baseball moral given by *A Little Pretty Pocket Book* will not be repeated here. The real point is that the boy striking the ball, go-

42

ing from one destined point to another, and then flying home seems to be hitting a home run. And if boys were hitting home runs before 1787, Abner Doubleday could no more have invented baseball in 1839 than you could invent the cotton gin in 1954.

In fact, by 1839 baseball was well established in New England, at least. Another of Harwell's venerable volumes proves that.

This one, called *Festivals, Games, and Amusements,* was published as part of Harper's Family Library in 1833 and was written by one Horatio Smith. In his section on festivals in New England, Smith writes:

"Young men are expert in a variety of games of ball such as cricket, base, etc."

Smith was an Englishman. That he should list baseball immediately after cricket appears to indicate that baseball had gained considerable stature by 1833. In addition, we know from this that there were expert players at that time. The game must not only have been played long before 1833, but also it must have been played often. Today young men who get into one or two games a year may be experts at watching baseball. They are never experts at playing it.

Baseball did not spring fullgrown from the brain of Abner Doubleday. It did not spring fullgrown from any single brain. Rather, it evolved, as it is still evolving, from eighteenth-century beginnings.

In the first half of the nineteenth century, the evolution speeded up, and baseball became increasingly popular with both players and fans. But in this era of our country's history—an era spanning Thomas Jefferson's retirement to his Virginia farm and Abraham Lincoln's rise from humble beginnings to a position of national importance and everlasting fame—baseball was far from the game we know today.

At one time stakes were used for bases. These were discarded in the 1830s because base runners kept running into the stakes and limping away. Flat stones were substituted, and the runners, no longer running into stakes, began stumbling over stones. Finally, about 1840 an unknown humanitarian conceived the idea of filling sacks with sand and using them for bases. But the humanitarian did not foresee the speed with which fielders would master techniques of kicking bases away from runners—a manuever which aided enormously in tagging out runners who would otherwise have been safe. Within a year, some practical man decreed that bases were to be staked down, which ended the problem of kicking.

Well into the 1840s, runners were put out by "plugging." This meant simply throwing the ball at the base runner and hitting him. Before this practice was eliminated, "putout" was a literal term.

Then, too, the teams were of indeterminate size, ranging from eleven players to twenty. Against one of those twenty-man teams, even a Wee Willie Keeler could not have "hit 'em where they ain't." They was everywhere.

But by 1845 rules and regulations had advanced far enough for the first baseball team to be organized. It was called the Knickerbocker Club of New York.

The Knickerbockers codified the rules and issued a challenge to all comers to meet under the "Knickerbocker Rules of Baseball." The first response came from a club called simply the "New York Team," which, upon learning that Knickerbocker rules limited players to nine on a side, obliged by changing its name to the "New York Nine." This was in the spring of 1846, a time when troubles that led to the Mexican War were brewing, and the cry of "Fifty-four Forty or fight!" resounded east from Oregon. Let's look in on that first formal baseball game ever played.

There is no set number of innings. In fact, there aren't any innings at all, because what we call innings, people then called "hands." The game ends when one team scores twenty-one runs, only there aren't even any runs. The word for runs is "aces."

But the diamond looks familiar, even though it's called a "square." Alexander Cartwright, a good man with a drawing board, has sketched the model for the playing area and has decided that the bases should be ninety feet apart. True, the pitcher stands only forty-five feet from home, but don't feel sorry for the hitters. The curve ball hasn't been invented.

The plate itself is a surprise. It really is a plate, this flat circular iron disc that covers an area about equal to a square foot. And look at the players. They're wearing mustaches but they aren't wearing gloves. Uniforms are a thing of the future, to say nothing of numerals. We won't be able to tell which player is which, but let's watch the game anyway.

The powerful Knickerbockers, who wrote the rules, don't seem to know about hitting. They aren't doing much of it. Their pitching doesn't seem to be too good, either. And there's room for improvement in their fielding. After four innings, the game ends in a tidy 23–1 victory for the New York Nine. We've not only seen the first formal baseball game, but we've also seen the first formal baseball upset. And we've come to the end of the age of baseball's dawn. Now, as the nineteenth century move toward its mid-point, it is morning.

It was a long morning, lasting until 1900, when baseball came into its own, and it was an exciting morning. Men began to explore the wonders of baseball. The curve ball was discovered. Scientists insisted the curve ball was an illusion. A pitcher said scientists were an illusion. Someone who was not concerned with illusions thought of charging admission. People paid. Leagues were formed and battled each other, and the hardiest survived. The game became more popular than ever.

But to return to the Knickerbockers, who wrote the rules and couldn't win. Disheartened, perhaps, they decided to practice. They practiced and practiced, taking time out in 1849 to turn fashion plate and don blue-and-white uniforms. These baseball suits bore so striking a resemblance to cricket uniforms that it has been suggested that what each Knickerbocker wore was just that—an old, used cricket suit. These were, at any rate, the first uniforms worn in baseball.

The uniform idea stuck and, resplendent in blue and white, the Knickerbockers continued to practice. That the New York Nine disbanded right after the 1846 game must have heartened them, and by 1851 the slaughter was only a memory. Besides, the Knickerbockers assumed that after five years of practice they were an improved ball club. Back they went into action again.

The Knickerbockers were indeed improved, and they beat a team called the "Washingtons of New York" twice at the Red House Grounds in New York City, 21–11 the first time, 22–20 the second —the latter being probably the first "squeaker" in the history of baseball.

Whether the Knickerbocker victory cheered the baseball world or not, the number of teams increased immediately after it. By 1858 there were so many of them that a convention was held.

The first convention differed from many of its successors. A major step was taken in that umpires were given complete authority over games. Also, control of baseball was wrested from the powerful Knickerbockers, but this was only a foreshadowing of the wars that were to shake the sport later on.

Under the old set-up, two umpires, one selected by each team, shared control with a referee. When a home-team star came in with the tie-breaking run, arriving at the same time as the ball, complete chaos resulted.

"Safe!" the umpire selected by the home team would shout.

"Out!" the umpire selected by the visiting team would bellow.

The referee would then be summoned to cast the deciding vote. First, this took time. Second, it made the umpires appear useless. Third, it did little to bolster public confidence in the impartiality of umpires. The new rule placed the home team's umpire in charge. No revolutions followed, only better umpiring.

And this was not the only step baseball took that year. The season before, a rule had gone through limiting games to nine innings and eliminating the twenty-one-run regulation. Now, with the conservative Knickerbockers losing power, conventions mushroomed. One adopted the called strike. Another formed the National Association of Baseball

Players, an amateur group that was the first league. A third conference wiped from the books the regulation allowing fielders to retire hitters by catching a ball on the first bounce.

All these were secondary. In 1858 a Brooklyn team met a New York team at a spot called Fashion Race Course, near Jamaica, Long Island. Admission of fifty cents was charged. Fifteen hundred people paid, and the practice of charging admission was a success the day it was born.

With money came trouble. The National Association, determined to be amateur, adopted a rule a year later barring players from taking money for playing. There are no concrete instances of players being paid, but if it had not happened would there have been a rule?

Amateur or professional, the idea in baseball is to win, and it was with this in mind that hitters began developing newer and better bats. There was no question of hitting the side of a barn door with these bats; the bats themselves were barn-door size. So another rule was born, one that required bats to be round and no more than two and a half inches in diameter at their thickest point.

That was a small burden for the hitters to bear. William A. (Candy) Cummings, a pitcher for the Brooklyn Stars, had the really bad news. One afternoon in 1864 Cummings, facing the Brooklyn Atlantics, began snapping his wrist as he delivered his pitches. At that instant the curve ball was born. Today, even big-league hitters have been heard to call the pitch "Public Enemy Number One."

No sooner had word of Cummings's discovery spread than scientists and semi-scientists cried hoax.

"It is against the laws of physics," one wrote, "an illusion."

The point is still being made—witness recent *Life* magazine photos —although a plea by the Yankees' Lefty Gomez some years back should have been enough to squelch it.

"Here I am trying to make a comeback," Gomez complained, "and now they tell me my best pitch is an optical illusion."

Cummings was not concerned with the laws of physics. He got the hitters out with his sharp-breaking illusion and let it go at that. On August 16, 1870, Fred Goldsmith, a young man from New Haven, Connecticut, came to New York determined to prove that his best pitch was not an illusion.

Goldsmith had a forty-five foot chalk line drawn, and had poles placed at each end. Remember, the pitching distance was forty-five feet in those days. A third pole was planted halfway down the line. Then, with a large crowd watching, Goldsmith threw a pitch that went to the left of the pole nearest him; to the right of the center pole and to the left of the far pole. He did it again. An eyewitness reported that he threw "six or eight" pitches. Each time the ball seemed to travel in an arc; each time the ball seemed to curve.

46

To some, the curve ball was established as a true curve. To others, it remained merely one of the most baffling of all illusions.

The curve ball was an eastern product, as baseball itself largely was. But it was the Midwest that contributed a pair of early records likely to stand for all time.

In 1867 a team called "Western Indianapolis" lost a game to a Washington squad, 106–21. Until a better claim comes along, this is offered as the worst catastrophe ever to befall a baseball team.

The other midwestern record is a more justifiable source of pride. It was in 1860 that baseball came to Cincinnati, and in a few years the Ohio city boasted an amateur team. The squad found the customary long pants uncomfortable, and one afternoon, summoning their courage, the players took the field in knickers. There were a great many jokes in Cincinnati during the summer of 1868 about this squad of grown men wearing knickers. The idea still strikes some people as funny, but it has ceased to be a legitimate basis for baseball humor.

The knickers revealed that the Cincinnati club was wearing stockings of bright red: the Cincinnati Red Stockings were in business. Or rather, almost in business. They did not turn professional until 1869.

This was no Knickerbocker-type organization. When the Red Stockings turned pro, they were ready. In their first ninety-four games, they won ninety-three and tied one. Par was established. It has not since been equalled.

The Red Stockings were the first salaried team, although the term "salary" is applied loosely. Some players were paid $600 for a season. The captain and shortstop, George Wright, received $1400. But George Wright earned every cent of it in a single game. This was the contest that ended the Red Stockings' unbeaten string (the Brooklyn Atlantics beat them, 8–7) but it produced baseball's first double play. Wright pulled it with a hidden ball trick in the tenth inning.

Now, with the double play, the curve, admission prices, and the Red Stockings in business, it was just a matter of time before baseball as a whole became professional. It happened in 1871, when the National Association of Professional Baseball Players was organized and the amateur National Association of Baseball Players collapsed.

Nine teams started the first professional league's first season. Fort Wayne dropped out in midsummer, the Philadelphia Athletics won the pennant and Boston finished second. In descending order, the other clubs were the Chicago White Stockings, the Troy (New York) Haymakers, the New York Mutuals, the Cleveland Forest Citys, the Washington Nationals, and the Rockford (Illinois) Forest Citys.

A major league with franchises in cities as small as Troy and Rockford would not seem to be on a very sound footing. The National

Association was not. It had succeeded in eliminating amateur baseball as a sport, but it succeeded in very little else.

There were constant switches in teams. Before the citizens of a city had a chance to work up a rooting interest in a club, the club had folded. At one time there were eleven teams; at another eight; finally there were thirteen. Schedules conflicted. Baseball was chaotic. It may also have been dishonest.

Baseball's difficulties did not lie in the franchise-shifting, for this was no more than the normal pains of growing. The danger lay in the grandstands.

Liquor was sold at ball parks. Worse, it was bought in large quantities. And along with intoxicated fans went gambling. A man untroubled by ethics knows no better way to turn a quick dollar than to bait a drunk into a bet. A man untroubled by ethics also knows how to turn others' discontent to his own personal gain. Players were discontented with their earnings; gamblers filled the stands. It was not hard for players to supplement their earnings.

By 1875 even the naive were convinced that baseball was dishonest. To go to a ball game meant to sit among drunks and gamblers and to see a contest quite possibly fixed. So people stopped going to ball games. It was then, with baseball rushing headlong toward oblivion, that the National League was born. A great ballplayer and an executive shrewd beyond measure were its midwives.

During the 1875 season, William A. Hulbert, president of the Chicago National Association club, came to realize that the bright future he was planning for himself in baseball stood in peril. There might be no more baseball before long. Hulbert chatted with someone else whose baseball future was to be even brighter—A. G. Spalding, then a star pitcher for Boston and later founder of the sporting goods concern bearing his name. The two men thought and planned. In January of 1876 Hulbert was ready.

Secretly he invited his fellow western officials, men from Louisville, St. Louis, and Cincinnati, to meet with him in Louisville. When they met, Hulbert proposed a new league and made his point so convincingly that he was authorized to speak on baseball for all the West. Hulbert went East to New York.

There he invited four eastern officials, from New York, Hartford, Boston, and Philadelphia, to the Grand Central Hotel. None knew that the others were coming. Hulbert met with each Easterner privately for half an hour. Then he brought the four men together in the hotel's meeting room.

It is not known whether William A. Hulbert ever acted on a stage. But certainly he didn't need a stage. With the four Easterners assembled, Hulbert strode to the door, locked it, and put the key in his pocket. According to the official National League history, this is what happened then:

"Do not be alarmed, gentlemen," boomed Hulbert's voice from beneath his handlebar mustache. "I have merely taken the precaution of seeing that there will be no intrusion from the outside."

There were sounds of protest.

"There is some business that has to be finished," Hulbert continued. "No one will leave the room until I have explained everything."

With that Hulbert began. For every further protest he had an answer. He even had answers when there weren't any protests. He explained that baseball could not remain as it was. He added he had the three other western votes behind him. Finally he reached into an inside coat pocket and whipped out a constitution for the new league. He did not just happen to have it with him; he and Spalding had struggled over it for many days and had called on a St. Louis judge for legal help. They'd also worked out a standard player contract.

Against this barrage of facts, explanations, and eloquence aimed at them by the Chicagoan, the Easterners were defenseless. They capitulated.

Hulbert was smart enough to realize that gambling and the sale of liquor in ball parks had to go, of course. He demanded a strong stand on that, and the Easterners agreed. He demanded that a five-man committee be established to run the league. Again the Easterners agreed.

Hulbert did not demand the league presidency for himself. He knew that the league might have a bad first year or might even flop. So he campaigned for Morgan Bulkeley of Hartford as league president. A Hulbert campaign guaranteed results: Bulkeley won unanimously, and the National League of Professional Baseball was born.

On that day in 1876 the Atlantic seaboard was lashed by a wintry gale. Next day the morning newspapers were filled with items about the storm and about a bill introduced in the New York State Legislature to abolish the Tammany Society. The papers printed not one word about William A. Hulbert, or Morgan Bulkeley, or the National League.

It was three days before the news crept into the morning papers, and even then only careful scrutiny would reveal it. Under the headline "Sporting," one paper informed its readers that the previous day's races of the Savannah Jockey Club had been canceled. Beneath that was an item about pigeon shooting. At the bottom of the column, a few lines told of the formation of a new baseball league.

The National League was formed quietly—and wisely. One rule required all franchises to represent cities over 75,000 in population. Another priced the franchises at $100, as compared to the $10.00 the

49

National Association had charged and the minimum of $2,000,000 a major-league franchise would cost today.

Seventy games were scheduled for each of the teams, and admission was set at fifty cents. It paid to come late: after the third inning, admission was a dime. The season began with eight charter clubs. When it had run its course there were six, and Chicago, under Hulbert's direction, had won the first pennant.

At the start, attendance was poor. Late in the season the New York Mutuals and the Philadelphia Athletics refused to make the last western trip for reasons of economy. It was too much for Bulkeley. He resigned, and Hulbert, now ready to take charge, accepted a draft and assumed the presidency. His first move was to expel the Mutuals and the Athletics, who were left telling each other how the league would fold without them.

In the long run, their self-evaluation might have proved correct. It is hard to envision major-league baseball today without the three teams from New York City and the two from Philadelphia. But in the short run, the Mutuals and the Athletics were guilty of a gross overestimate of their own importance. The league did not flourish, but it survived. When the 1877 season ended the six-team National League had avoided disaster and had won a position of public trust.

During the year, four Louisville players were charged with "throwing" games. Hulbert launched an investigation which proved that the four had dealt with gamblers. He banished the players for life. The public and the press took notice that baseball was giving dishonesty no sanction, and they applauded.

But applause itself was not enough, and the league was still on shaky ground. It was not until 1882 that the loop was doing well enough to prompt the formation of the American Association as a rival. This led to the first in the series of struggles that were to grip the infant league.

The game of that day was markedly different from modern baseball. In 1866 Robert Addy of Rockford, hurrying to a base, skidded along the ground. The fielder tagged where Addy would have been had he not skidded. Addy was safe. The slide had been invented. But the glove had to wait until 1875 when a Harvard man, weary of sore hands, appeared with an unpadded catcher's glove. His hands improved, but only slightly.

In those days it was becoming increasingly difficult to find anyone willing to catch. Foul tips had a way of smashing noses. So in 1875 Fred W. Thayer hit upon the nose-saver we call a mask, but which people then called a "bird cage." Professional catchers began sporting "bird cages" two years later. Now able to stop worrying about their noses, catchers began to count body bruises. The count was so high

50

that a Hartford man devised the chest protector. It was not very appealing; the general sentiment among catchers was not that they'd rather die than wear one, but simply that they'd rather be bruised. However, over the course of the next few years the bruises continued, and chest protectors became standard gear.

Pitchers had one advantage in the early days. It took nine balls to walk a batter, until the 1880s, when five rule changes were made scaling the number of balls down to four. But batters had an even bigger advantage; they could call for a high or low pitch and the pitcher had to oblige. There was no sense in studying a batter's weaknesses, because the batter wouldn't let the pitcher exploit them. This was ended in 1887, six years after the pitching distance had been increased to fifty feet.

Base runners had their moments of glory, too. Any runner who came near a ground ball did his best to kick it away from the fielder. These potential soccer players became so adroit that an 1880 edict decreed the runner out if he was hit by a batted ball.

Then, no one was quite sure where home plate belonged. In the early days, it had sometimes been well inside the diamond itself. Later it was fixed at a point just outside the diamond. Finally in 1877 the plate was moved just within the limits of the diamond, and there it had stayed ever since.

Business heads were busy, too. Club owners were allowed to deduct $30 from each player's salary for the cost of a uniform. A smarter step, however, was the introduction of the turnstile. Still smarter was the move in 1888 to end for all time the prospect of a team refusing to make a trip. Visiting teams were given fifteen cents on each paid admission, and thus no trip could be entirely fruitless. Today the cut has jumped to about twenty-five cents and the idea of giving the visiting team an interest in home attendance seems, from our perspective, one of the soundest financial policies ever established in baseball.

In line with the idea of the visitors' cut, the home team was required to pay the umpires. There are no instances of owners going broke paying umpires. The standard rate was $5.00 a game. But the cost of living at the time is indicated by the fifty cents a day that ball clubs deducted from the earnings of traveling players for meals.

Before 1880, only a secret agreement among owners kept players tied to the same club season after season. It was not sufficient, and the owners decided to hold a secret meeting about their secret agreement. Out of this came the reserve clause, the provision in a player's contract that enables an owner to reserve his services from year to year.

During its life the reserve cause has been a popular target for abuse. It prevents a player from selling his services to the highest bidder, a privilege most Americans enjoy. It binds a player to an organization for as long as the organization wants him, and it does not concern itself with the player's wants. But it is indispensable to modern baseball.

Suppose there were no reserve clause. The Cardinals' Stan Musial, after winning a batting championship, could announce that he was open to offers. Allie Reynolds, after pitching the Yankees to a world championship, could do the same. So could young Harvey Kuenn of Detroit, using his 1953 rookie-of-the-year award as ammunition.

Each year would see a realignment of stars. The Yankees, with the most money, would never lose, and under the present system—despite present appearances—they will not win forever. Washington, a poorer club, would have to content itself with players the Yankees did not want. The judgment of scouts and the teaching talents of managers would mean nothing. Why, without the reserve clause, should another club develop a player for the rich Yankees to steal? The reserve clause does not challenge the Magna Carta as a concept of human freedom; it is a practical device. Baseball is a game of practicalities.

A few minor leagues, notably the International, had been established during the first seasons of the National League's existence, but until 1882 its exclusive place in the baseball world was not challenged. In that year, however, the American Association was formed. The Association was a direct ancestor of neither the American League nor the present-day American Association, and it lived only until 1891. But it produced competition, and with competition came progress.

Baseball's future brightened when the American Association was formed. Ten years after the Association died, baseball was soundly in business. It has remained so to this day.

The American Association selected as its cities those where Sunday baseball was allowed. It permitted the sale of beer at its ball parks. It raided the National League for some of its talent, but obtained most of its players from a minor league. Once in operation, it instituted two major changes.

The Association decided to use won-and-lost percentages as the method of determining standings. Two years later, the National League purchased a few slide rules and followed suit. The Association hired a staff of permanent umpires; it took the National League only one year to realize that this was a good idea.

In the second season of the Association's life, raiding was ended by the adoption of a stronger reserve clause. The Association and the National League agreed that each club could reserve eleven players and that there was to be no tampering. By 1886 the two major leagues had signed a working agreement. (Meanwhile, a third major league, the Union Association, had appeared in 1884. It had also disappeared in 1884.)

52

The National League and the American Association worked together and kept their accounts balanced until 1889, when a number of players concluded that the balance was resting heavily on their wallets. During the winter of 1889 they organized the Players (or Brotherhood) League.

As executives, ballplayers today tend to be good ballplayers, and such was the case in 1890, also. American Association salaries were lower than those in the National League, and when Association players were through jumping to the newly formed Players League, the Association was left with little first-class talent. During the 1890 season, the American Association endured a terrible financial beating, as did the Players League and the National League. The Players League collapsed at once.

The Association itself never recovered, but it did not collapse until 1892. The National League, however, struggled through all the hard times and in 1893 found that it had the field of major-league baseball to itself. The number of its clubs varied, finally dropping from twelve to eight just before the turn of the century. The 1900 make-up of Boston, Brooklyn, Chicago, Cincinnati, Philadelphia, Pittsburgh, New York, and St. Louis remained unchanged until 1953.

It was ten years after the American Association failed before another rival arose to share the business of baseball with the National League. On the morning of November 21, 1900, B. B. (Ban) Johnson, a former sportswriter, organized the American League. Johnson had been heading the minor Western League, but at the end of the 1899 season he took stock. The first item he checked was the list of stars.

During the 1880s there had been some standout figures to draw fans to ball parks. Mike Kelly, Boston's catcher, became identified with the cry of "Slide, Kelly, slide." Charles (Old Hoss) Radbourne brought customers to the Providence park to see him pitch. In fact, nearly every time they came he did pitch. In 1884 he started seventy-four games and won sixty. Providence was sending twenty-game winners back to the minors in those days.

Moses (Fleet) Walker caught for the Toledo American Association team. He was a Negro, the first ever to play in the major leagues. It was later that Negroes were to be kept out of the game, and much, much later that Branch Rickey was to defy tradition by signing Jackie Robinson.

The final decade of the 1890s saw swarms of young men turn to baseball. One of them, a cab driver in Woonsocket, Rhode Island, was supplementing his income in 1896 by commuting to Fall River often enough to play first base for its New England league team. He was good, but not spectacular.

That particular year, the Philadelphia Phillies were doing badly, and their manager went to Fall River to see an outfielder named Paul Geier. The manager liked what he saw and paid $1500 for Geier's contract. The Fall River club, stricken with feelings of guilt, tossed in the cab-driving first baseman—Napoleon (Larry) Lajoie—as a bonus. Once Lajoie made the major leagues he stopped driving his cab.

He could afford to. In 1897 he was moved to second base, and there he remained, fielding with sure-handed grace, hitting with tremendous power and skill. When Lajoie's career ended, he had made 3,242 hits and was hailed as one of the game's greats; time has not dimmed his glory. Lajoie was baseball's biggest bonus ever.

The Phils had more than Lajoie. They had a slugger named Ed Delehanty who hit four home runs in a single game, a mark since equalled but never exceeded. In the West, Chicago was delighted with a big, florid-faced first baseman named Adrian (Cap) Anson. A team called the Cleveland Spiders featured a young pitcher named Denton (Cy) Young. When Young finished his baseball travels he had won 511 games, a figure no one else has ever come close to.

In Pittsburgh, a tall, skinny catcher named Connie Mack was a competent but by no means great ballplayer. He left Pittsburgh for Milwaukee and then left Milwaukee to visit Philadelphia. He stayed there.

But the gayest stars and the gayest team of the Gay Nineties played in Baltimore and called themselves the Orioles. It was in Baltimore that Wee Willie Keeler explained, "I hit 'em where they ain't." It was also in Baltimore that Keeler batted .432 in one season and hit safely in forty-four straight games in another.

A heavy-set man who had quit the meat business for baseball was Baltimore's catcher—Wilbert Robinson. Under the nickname of Uncle Robby, he was to dominate baseball in Brooklyn decades later. The Baltimore third baseman was the most fiery battler on a fiery team. His name was John McGraw.

Baltimore won three pennants in the 1890s. Along with Boston, a club bolstered by Hugh Duffy, who hit .438 one season, Baltimore dominated the National League until Brooklyn won the final flag of the nineteenth century. And when the American League came into being and caused baseball's last major war to be fought, the Orioles were in the midst of the fighting. There were Orioles, of course, on both sides of the fence.

During the 1900 season, the National League inaugurated its eight-team setup, leaving Cleveland, Washington and Baltimore free areas. Johnson, looking east from his Western League, saw enough stars and enough territory to prompt thoughts of a second major loop. He sprang into action.

Johnson called a meeting in Chicago's Grand Pacific Hotel in

54

November. The records are not sufficient to contrast his organizing skill with that of William A. Hulbert, but Johnson's results would have made even Hulbert proud.

"We hereby covenant and agree each with the other," the secretary of the group wrote, "that the name of this organization shall be the 'American League of Professional Base Ball Clubs' . . . that B. B. Johnson shall be elected president, secretary, and treasurer."

The president, secretary, and treasurer formed a league consisting of Buffalo, Chicago, Cleveland, Detroit, Grand Rapids, Indianapolis, Kansas City, and Milwaukee. Johnson was not seeking war, only success, and he asked the National League for peaceful recognition of his loop. "This is protection against some unfriendly group," Johnson wrote, "and the American League desires to act wholly in concert with the Nationals."

The National League had been completely successful in beating back all previous competitors, and it now ignored Johnson's request. Johnson informed the National League that he planned to move east the following year, but his second letter, too, was left to gather dust.

Johnson organized a circuit commission; dropped Buffalo, Indianapolis, Kansas City, and Minneapolis; and added Boston, St. Louis, Washington and, of course, Baltimore. Now, with enough cities, Johnson wanted enough stars. His league began raiding the Nationals, and through the lure of money it won Lajoie from the Phillies to the Athletics. This was too much for the Phils, and baseball had its first day in court.

Three different state courts offered two different rulings on the legality of the reserve clause. This was no help, and so the National League decided to take action on its own. Or rather, John McGraw, by now manager of Baltimore, decided to take action on *his* own.

McGraw obtained a major share of the Orioles' stock, raising capital by disposing of his interest in a saloon. Then he sold his stock to the new Baltimore president, a man named Mahon, and jumped to the New York Giants. Mahon, probably at McGraw's direction, sold his stock to John T. Brush, head of the Giants and president of the National League executive committee. To raise capital for Brush, the rest of the National League kicked in on a pro rata basis.

As a result of all this, the National League in 1902 owned the Baltimore American League franchise. If Hulbert had been around, the American League might have died on the spot. But he was not, and the American League lived.

The lifesaver was a National League order sending four Baltimore players to the Giants and two more to Cincinnati. Baltimore suffered a few injuries and one July day could not field a team to meet St. Louis, Milwaukee's American League successor. The Orioles forfeited the game, and more. For American League rules specifically stated that failure to field a team was an act calling for cancellation of a franchise. The Baltimore franchise was canceled; Brush's $15,000 worth of stock was worthless; the Orioles were through.

But the National League had blundered in the clutch. With an opportunity to disrupt its rival league beyond repair, it had overstepped the mark and disrupted instead only one team—and that the team it owned itself. The American League at once organized a new Baltimore franchise and finished the season.

Something in that wild season, however, frightened the National League. During the winter a series of peace talks was arranged, at which baseball's major-and-minor-league system was organized largely as it is today. Some stolen players were returned, but nearly half a million dollars' worth were not. When Ban Johnson promised in that January, 1903, session that the American League wanted only to move the Baltimore team to New York and had no intentions of moving into Pittsburgh, final truce was declared.

The American League, people insisted, had won; the National League had lost. But the National League did not lose in 1903; nobody lost—baseball won. The game's alignment was established, and all teams have been helped by it ever since.

Just one more explosion was to disturb the peace. In the first modern World Series in 1903, the Boston Americans defeated the Pittsburgh Nationals, five games to three. In 1904 the Giants won the pennant. Their manager, John McGraw, was still raging at the upstart American League, and their president, John T. Brush, was still angry about his $15,000 of worthless stock. Boston, which again finished first in the American League, looked forward to another World Series victory. But no one will ever know who baseball's world's champions were in 1904.

"Play those minor-leaguers?" stormed McGraw. "Never!"

Brush supported his manager, and thus in 1904 there was no World Series. This angered Johnson, a dangerous man when angry. He laid plans for a new war.

The National League executives talked fast and furiously, even apologized. Brush wrote a set of rules for the conduct of future World Series. Both the American and National leagues adopted them, and ever since the two leagues have worked wholly in concert.

With the last war—but not the last battle—ended, less and less baseball news was made in hotel rooms, more and more on the field. The stars of the 1890s had been the vanguard; now in the twentieth century the stars were better known and more numerous.

Brooklyn had won the National League pennant in 1900, but Pittsburgh won for the next three seasons. It's doubtful if there has ever been a shortstop to equal the Pirates' shortstop, Honus Wagner. For the rest of the first decade of the 1900s, the Chicago Cubs and the New York Giants were National League powers. In the American League it was Chicago winning for the first two years, and Boston, Philadelphia, and Detroit after that.

No single giant dominated the game of baseball in the first decade of the twentieth century as Babe Ruth was to dominate it twenty years later. But it was not because of a shortage of giants. Rather, it was that there were so many of them.

New York had its own giant in John McGraw. He had one gospel, the gospel of victory and his sermons were on scientific baseball. With McGraw doing the thinking, the Giants played scientific baseball as it had never before been played. They used the squeeze play, the sacrifice, the steal.

And there were signs. Sitting on the bench, McGraw would blow his nose; the New York batter would bunt. One day the manager had a cold and the Giants were to face a pitcher notoriously poor at fielding. Throughout the first inning, McGraw blew and Giants bunted. Finally the pitcher was taken out and was replaced by one who was more agile. McGraw had outsmarted himself. For the rest of the game he had to sit on the bench with his heavy cold, not daring to blow his nose.

On another occasion, McGraw flashed one of his other bunt signs and Sam Strang, the Giant batter, swung. He belted a homer and, all smiles, trotted around the bases. His smiles ceased when he returned to the dugout.

"You're fined $50," McGraw thundered, "for missing a sign!"

In addition to McGraw, the Giants had playing talent. Christy Mathewson, a young right-hander out of Bucknell University, came to the Giants in 1900. He developed a new breaking ball and called it a "fade-away," although a modern pitcher with the same pitch calls it a screwball. Mathewson won 373 games in his career. His control was perfect, as it is with all great pitchers. But some who saw Mathewson insist he was the greatest pitcher of all.

Mathewson's catcher, a former Baltimore star named Roger Bresnahan, in 1908 invented shin guards. The wisdom of shin guards was not challenged, as that of the chest protector had been years earlier.

But the wisdom of John McGraw and the strength of his Giants were challenged. The Pirates, under Fred Clarke, were an early power and always a threat. And in the midst of the 1905 season, the Chicago Cubs hired Frank Chance, their graceful first baseman, as manager. The next season the Cubs won 116 games. In his first full season, Chance had become the best manager in major-league history.

With Chance there were, of course, Johnny Evers and Joe Tinker.

57

Evers and Tinker were not on speaking terms for years, but every afternoon they put personal feelings aside, and "Tinkers-to-Evers-to-Chance" came to mean "double play" to every baseball fan in the country.

It was inevitable that the Giants and Cubs should crash head on, and they did, but never more violently than in September of 1908, when the two teams were battling for the pennant, with the Giants in first place. The score was tied, 1–1, in the last of the ninth inning, with Moose McCormick on third and Fred Merkle on first for the Giants and two men out. Al Birdwell laced a single to center, McCormick trotted home and Merkle trotted into the Giant clubhouse, not bothering to touch second base.

Evers, always alert, stood screaming for the ball at second, surrounded by the fans who had rushed onto the field. He finally got a ball and claimed Merkle was out, forced at second. Hank O'Day, the umpire, honored the claim, and so did Harry Pulliam, the league president. The game was ruled a tie.

It is not likely that the baseball Evers gloved was the same one Birdwell hit. Iron Man Joe McGinnity, a Giant pitcher, probably threw that ball into the grandstands. But that Evers had any baseball at all was enough, and the Giants and Cubs finished the season with exactly the same percentage.

A play-off was arranged in New York. McGraw led with Mathewson, his ace, and Chance selected Mordecai (Three-Finger) Brown, a pitcher whose duels with Mathewson were examples of pitching at its best.

"My arm had been dead," Mathewson wrote later. "I hadn't pitched for a while, and that only made it deader."

Mathewson's arm, while hardly dead, was not as lively as Brown's. The Giants lost an early lead, and the Cubs won, 4–2.

The American League underwent no such hectic race. But it had a pitcher who provided hectic personal races—with fire engines. Rube Waddell, a big, gawky left-hander who pitched for the Athletics, could throw with incredible speed. He set a strikeout record that stood until Bob Feller broke it in 1948. But Waddell loved fire engines more than baseball.

Mathewson in his book *Pitching in a Pinch* recalls days when Waddell would be blazing his fast ball past hitters until the sound of a siren reached his ears. Then Waddell would desert the game and race through the stands for the street and after the engines. Since he was a great pitcher, he had many fans, mostly small boys. A sight Mathewson insists was common in Philadelphia included fire engines speeding down the street, followed by Waddell, anxious to see a fire, followed by small boys anxious to get his autograph.

More stable and even more talented than Waddell was a youth who came from Georgia to join Detroit in 1906, Tyrus Raymond (Ty) Cobb. For twenty-two years Cobb played for Detroit, and when he finished his lifetime batting average was .368. Once he batted .420; twelve times he led the American League in hitting, and in the period from 1907 through 1915, he won the batting title every year.

But Cobb was more than a hitter. His talent as a base runner is indicated by the ten times he led the league in stolen bases. But there was still more. Cobb made sliding an art, and spiking a thought to keep infielders awake nights and a reality to trouble them afternoons. He slid hard, spikes high. To tag Cobb meant to run the risk of contusions, lacerations, and abrasions. Many stood up to Cobb and took the cuts and bruises; many did not.

A great baseball player, he wanted only to win and usually did. If someone stood in his way, Cobb cut him down. If he was tagged hard on the nose by a fielder seeking vengeance, Cobb would come back even harder with spikes even higher the next time. Once he climbed into the stands in New York to punch an abusive fan. Once, in Philadelphia's Shibe Park, a swarm of threatening fans surrounded him. Discretion would have called for stalling until the police and his own teammates arrived. Cobb ignored discretion, walked through the throng, and no one moved a hand to touch him.

Cobb may have been the greatest of all baseball players. He was not the greatest home-run hitter, but for most of his era baseball was not a game of home runs. Though the cork-center ball was introduced in 1909, the first baseball with as much life as the modern one did not appear until 1920.

Still, more than one early player had enough muscle to blast occasional wallops into the stands. The Athletics' Frank Baker even won himself the nickname of "Home Run Baker" during the 1911 Series.

By that time, baseball writing had advanced so much that a number of writers had launched side careers as "ghosts." Christy Mathewson had a ghost writer during the 1911 World Series. So did Rube Marquard, the fine left-hander who teamed with Mathewson on the Giant pitching staff. Baker beat Marquard in the second game of the 1911 Series by belting a homer. The next morning, Mathewson was surprised to find a newspaper article under his by-line blasting Marquard for pitching to Baker's strength.

By nightfall, however, Mathewson was no longer surprised—he was embarrassed. For in the third game Baker had hit a tenth-inning home run and beaten him. Marquard's enraged ghost now got even. He blasted Mathewson for pitching to Baker's weakness. The Athletics had a good laugh and called their third baseman "Home Run Baker" after that.

Laughter was not, however, an earmark of baseball in the second decade of this century. In 1914 the Boston Braves, last team in the league on July 4, stormed to a pennant and became the first team ever to sweep a World Series when they beat the Athletics four games to none. But in 1914, too, an organization known as the United States League changed its name to the Federal League and demanded major status. Its backers consisted of multi-millionaires and a few millionaires who had sneaked in when no one was looking.

The Federal League raided the National and American leagues and stole more than fifty players. It held pennant races in 1914 and 1915. Against this threat the majors put up a solid front, and after the 1915 season, the Federal League announced that it was closing. A backer explained that money had not influenced the decision; rather, it had been the belief that there was no place for a third major league in America.

One major-league owner had predicted, when the Federal League was born, that it would be "a flea on an elephant's back." It was more than this, but baseball survived. And just in time to withstand impact of World War I.

War drove countless minor leagues out of business. The majors were hurt. In 1918 the Secretary of War asked the major leagues to close their season on September 1. Realizing that a government request is equal to anyone else's order, the majors complied.

With the end of the war came an even worse blow—the worst that modern baseball has ever endured—the Black Sox scandal.

The 1919 Chicago White Sox were one of the strongest baseball teams ever assembled. They had "Shoeless Joe" Jackson, a near-illiterate who had walked out of the hills with the smoothest swing anyone had ever seen. They had a brilliant second baseman in Eddie Collins. They had brilliant pitchers in Eddie Cicotte and Claude (Lefty) Williams. The White Sox won the pennant in the American League and went into the 1919 World Series prohibitive favorites over the first Cincinnati team ever to win a National League pennant. But the Sox looked bad in the Series; Cincinnati looked good; and the Reds won, five games to three.

It was a tremendous upset, but baseball is full of upsets. The newspapers reported the 1919 World Series as a form reversal, nothing more. It was more.

Officials in Chicago were suspicious. Some of the White Sox had not been keeping good company. Law-enforcement officers shared the suspicions, and an investigation was launched. Nearly a year later, while the White Sox were battling Cleveland in a bid for another pennant, baseball's most shocking story landed on front pages from California to Maine. The Chicago White Sox had "thrown" the 1919 World

Series. The name White Sox was too good for them. They were the Black Sox. Working hand in hand with some of the most notorious gamblers in the country, they had arranged to lose baseball's biggest prize.

Eight Sox—Jackson, Cicotte, Buck Weaver, Chic Gandil, Charley Risberg, Williams, Fred McMullin, and Happy Felsh—were suspended. Though this move cost the White Sox a pennant, and Cleveland went on to win, the public confidence baseball had strived so hard to attain was shattered.

If there was ever to be a time for baseball greatness, it was now. The greatness came, too—from a shaggy-maned, incorruptible federal judge named Kenesaw Mountain Landis and from a tall, skinny kid out of a Baltimore home for boys—George Herman Ruth.

Baseball had been run by a commission. The commission was junked and Landis was installed as commissioner. At once he barred the eight Sox from baseball for life. From that moment until the day in 1944 when he died, Kenesaw Mountain Landis wielded almost limitless baseball power. He wielded it wisely.

"I remember," Warren Giles, president of the National League, recalls, "that whenever I talked to the judge and he wanted to make a point, he'd jab one of his long bony fingers against one of my ribs. And he'd keep jabbing the same rib. He made his points." The point Landis made to the American people was that baseball was honest.

Babe Ruth's point was that a game was well worth the admission price. The Babe did not use a finger, as the judge did; he used a bat.

Between 1910 and 1920, a new group of stars had entered the baseball picture. The Phils came up with Grover Cleveland Alexander, and in one year Alexander pitched sixteen shutouts. That record still stands. A young Washington fast-ball hurler named Walter Johnson had made his debut in 1907. Now people were saying he was the fastest pitcher ever. He probably was. Cleveland discovered a center-fielder, Tris Speaker, who played close back of second base and got away with it because no one ever went back for flies the way he did. St. Louis brought up a young second baseman, Rogers Hornsby, who dominated National League hitters the way Cobb ruled the American Leaguers.

But in April 1914 a young left-handed pitcher broke in with Baltimore of the International League by pitching a six-hit shutout and drilling two singles. Babe Ruth was to outshine all other stars of his time and remodel baseball in his own image.

Ed Barrow, general manager of the Yankees, pried Ruth loose from the Boston Red Sox in 1919 and stuck him in the Yankee outfield. It was no accident that the Yankees, "also-rans" until then, grew into a team which was to rule baseball as no one else had. To this day, losers wail about Yankee luck, and there was some element of it in 1920. That was the year the manufacturer of the American League baseballs decided to try Australian yarn instead of the American yarn that had been used. The Australian product was stronger, wound tighter. The lively ball was born.

In 1919, before the lively ball, Ruth hit twenty-nine homers—a record total. In 1920 the Babe hit fifty-four. Under manager Miller Huggins, the Yankees won pennants in 1921, 1922 and 1923. In '23 they won the World Series from the Giants. Heywood Broun, who was there, reported: "The Ruth is mighty and shall prevail."

Ruth did prevail, and McGraw's scientific baseball—the importance of the bunt, the stolen base, the single run—was to perish before his flailing bat. Babe went for homers. In 1927 he hit sixty. No one else has ever hit as many.

By then, still tall but no longer skinny, Ruth was a national hero. He never remembered names, and everyone thought that was funny. He always ate oversized portions of food, and that was funny, too. Once Ruth was stricken with a violent stomach-ache, a result of too many hot dogs; the ache was duly reported on front pages across the land.

But there was nothing funny about Babe Ruth on the field. Those who saw him insist his baseball instinct was such that he never threw to the wrong base. And many of those who saw him joined in a singular tribute to Ruth's crowd appeal. "It was more exciting to see the Babe strike out," runs a classic phrase, "than to see someone else hit a home run."

Pitching could not stop him. Once, after he had battered the White Sox in the opener of a two-game series in Chicago, a White Sox official called in a few of his reserves.

"Take Ruth out tonight," the official ordered. "Show him the town. Keep him up until you see the sun rise."

The subs did what they were told. Finally, as morning approached, the Chicago players left Ruth and staggered to their homes.

That afternoon the White Sox reserves summoned all their strength and dragged themselves to Comiskey Park. Through blood-shot, half-closed eyes they saw a sight they'd never forget. Ruth belted two more homers and beat the White Sox again. When the game ended he trotted over.

"It sure was nice of you guys to take me out last night," he boomed. "We gotta do it again next trip."

This was Babe Ruth, a modern Gargantua blessed with the talent to hit a baseball higher, harder, and farther than anyone else. As Ruth put on more weight, his legs remained thin, and his pigeon-toed home-run jog around the bases became a Yankee trade-mark.

Under the sure hand of Barrow, the Yankees built a dynasty in the Bronx. Lou Gehrig came from the Columbia University campus to line up with Ruth and play day after day until disease cut off his career and killed him before his time. As quiet as Ruth was garrulous, Gehrig set a record for consecutive games as remarkable as Ruth's home-run record. And the powerful first baseman stood right behind Ruth as a Yankee slugger. There were others—so many that the Yankee batting order was called "Murderer's Row."

The Yankees' stress was on hitting, but even before then, rule-makers had whipped a fast ball past the pitchers. Until 1920, the spit ball had been legal. By wetting their fingers pitchers had learned to add to the effectiveness of their breaking balls. Spit balls broke sharply and erratically. In 1920, an edict barred the spitter, exempting only a few long-time users. When they passed from the majors, so did the pitch.

The twenties were a Yankee era (as were the eras to follow). But in the thirties Branch Rickey, a wily, spellbinding ex-catcher who was running the St. Louis Cardinals, perfected the system of developing talent that is used today by every club that has enough money. Long before the thirties, major-league teams had worked with and owned minor-league clubs, but never on the scale that Rickey set up. Players joked bitterly about slavery in the Cardinal chain, and Rickey got results.

The "Gashouse Gang" was the most obvious result. It could not be ignored. A rough and boisterous band of stars—Dizzy Dean, Leo Durocher, Paul Dean, Joe Medwick—they won pennants, organized a band complete with washboard and sweet potato, and knew nothing of conventions save that they were to be broken.

Even the front offices were growing less conventional. Leland Stanford (Larry) MacPhail, who had tried to kidnap the Kaiser after World War I and failed, had better luck when he introduced major-league night baseball at Cincinnati in 1935.

The Yankees, not worried about night ball just then, were not worried because they were about to obtain Joe DiMaggio. The Giants had Mel Ott. A Detroit first baseman named Hank Greenberg hit fifty-eight home runs in 1938.

Then there were the pitchers. A rookie named Bob Feller joined Cleveland. A veteran left-hander named Bob Grove was nearing the end with the Athletics. A left-hander named Carl Hubbell won so often for the Giants that he gained the nickname of "Meal Ticket." In 1933 the All-Star game was inaugurated, and in 1934 Hubbell fanned Ruth, Gehrig, Al Simmons, Jimmy Foxx and Joe Cronin in succession. Hubbell had a screw ball. He had a lot more.

By 1941 the Yankees were still winning, and Larry McPhail, who

63

had moved to Brooklyn from Cincinnati, got the Dodgers a pennant winner for the first time since 1920. This was the year that DiMaggio broke Wee Willie Keeler's record by hitting safely in fifty-six successive games. It was also one of the years when the Dodgers lost a World Series to the Yankees.

The Cardinals, with a rookie named Stan Musial in left field, won a pennant in 1942, but World War II stopped everything. Teams trained in the North instead of going South; all but nine minor leagues quit; and major-league games sometimes looked like minor-league ones. Before the Tigers met the Cubs in the 1945 World Series, one sports writer remarked, "I don't see how either team can possibly win."

In the postwar era, Albert B. (Happy) Chandler, a United States Senator, followed Judge Landis as commissioner. Angry owners followed Chandler, barking at his heels, after he'd made a few decisions, and when his term was up he was released. There was little mourning, and Ford Frick, a former sports writer, moved up from the National League presidency to become baseball commissioner.

One highlight of postwar baseball was Commissioner Chandler's suspension of Leo Durocher, then the Dodger manager, for reasons never disclosed. Another was the formation of the Mexican League and its raids on American leagues for talent. Big money was offered in the United States, but some players reported it was not paid in Mexico. The threat, at any rate, soon passed.

It was Branch Rickey who provided the biggest postwar surprise. Now working in Brooklyn, in 1946 he hired Jackie Robinson, a former All-American halfback at UCLA, assigned him to the Dodgers' Montreal club for one season, and then brought him to the Dodgers. The shattering of baseball's color line was not easily achieved, but Robinson kept his head high and his mouth closed. He had to be above reproach until Negroes were established in the majors. And he was. Behind Robinson came others—Roy Campanella, Larry Doby, and the rest—and when they did, Robinson abandoned his role of symbol and became a battling ball player in the classic manner.

In 1951 baseball produced the greatest pennant race ever. The Giants, thirteen and a half games behind in August, came thundering up and tied the Dodgers for the pennant. A three-game play-off was arranged. New York won the first game, Brooklyn the second. The third was probably the most implausibly exciting game ever played.

The whole country was wrapped up in the events at the Polo Grounds that day. One man who was there, Bob Cooke, sports editor and columnist for the New York *Herald Tribune,* has added to sports literature with his description of the game. Drawing freely on *Horatius at the Bridge,* Cooke composed a poem which is quoted here in part but which is displayed in its entirety in Baseball's Hall of Fame at Cooperstown, New York:

> . . . Then came the ninth
>   And with it, a 4–1 Brooklyn lead,
> Surely New York was beaten now,
>   Why did it not concede?
>
> But up spake Dark, young Alvin,
>   A great clutch hitter, he,
> "I'll take two and hit to right,
>   I'll prolong the race, you'll see."
> Then up spake young Don Mueller,
>   A batsman brave was he,
> "I'll belt a single, too,
>   Just you wait and see."
>
> Then up spake Whitey Lockman,
>   A solid slugger, he:
> "And I will hit for two," said he,
>   "To mar the Flatbush glee."
> But meanwhile in the bullpen,
>   Ralph Branca's arm is warm.
> And now he's plodding to the mound,
>   Big Newk can't brave the storm.
>
> But from the Giant dugout
>   Bob Thomson then appears.
> He takes his place up at the plate,
>   'Mid Giant hopes and fears.
> Bob looked toward Staten Island,
>   Which he still calls his home,
> And Leo on the coaching line
>   Composed this pretty poem:
>
> "Oh, Thomson, Bobby Thomson,
>   To whom the Giants pray,
> A Giant's life, a Giant's dream
>   Take you in charge this day!"
> And so Lip spake and speaking,
>   With Thomson at the plate,
> And thousands cheering in the stands,
>   Awaiting Thomson's fate.
> Branca throws, it is a strike,
>   But tension sets the pace,

It could not have been otherwise,
  Was ever such a race?
Then the next pitch came winging
  Straight down the narrow lane,
Bobby Thomson took a cut,
  He swung with might and main.

No sound of joy or sorrow
Arose from either side,
As friend and foe in dumb surprise,
With parted lips and straining eyes,
Stood staring where it sank.
But when the panting patrons
Saw the baseball disappear,
New York sent forth a rapturous shout
And even ranks of Flatbush fans
Could scarce forbear to cheer.

. . . Now when Giants of the future
  Prepare for the great quest,
When Durocher starts spring training
  And asks each man his best,
With weeping and with laughter
  Still is the story told:
How well Bob Thomson kept the bridge
  In the brave days of old.

After Thomson's homer, everyone called the World Series an anti-climax—everyone except the Yankees. They won it and two more, and in 1953 they became the first team ever to win five straight world championships. Something happened that had never happened before, as something new is always happening in baseball.

To many, baseball's wonder lies in its humor and its laughter, laughter that rings through clubhouses and grandstands from Shawnee to the Yankee Stadium. But baseball is essentially a serious game.

To others, baseball's wonder lies in the stars—Ruth, Cobb, Lajoie. But before the stars could burn brightly, admirers had to be willing to watch.

To still others, baseball's wonder lies in its honesty. But honesty is not the monopoly of baseball.

And to the rest, perhaps it lies in the remembrance of bright days spent hitting and fielding and pitching.

Americans play baseball when they are young and watch it when they are old. They are caught up in its wonder. But no one can explain the wonder. One only knows it is there.

66

HOW THE BIG LEAGUES ARE RUN

Out of countless wars for survival, out of the shattering Black Sox scandal, and out of self-defense, organized baseball forged itself into the form it retains today. Basic have been the beliefs that the game itself must be above suspicion and that there must be unity enough to meet any outside threat.

All is not always harmony within the structure of organized ball, but considering the vast gap between the interests of a major league club and the interests of a Class D team, it is remarkable that there should be any harmony at all.

Players entering the minor leagues remain only until their skill and promise prompt a larger minor league or a major league to grab them. But at the same time, money is constantly funneled downward in baseball to allow the small circuits to continue. Interdependence is a fact of baseball life.

Organized baseball polices itself and in most cases has proved a stern disciplinarian. It makes its own rules, and nearly always the rules make sense. The rules cover many pages of small print, and the structure is complex and is replete with checks and balances.

To understand the administration of baseball, it is necessary to understand the "house rules." They are contained in five documents:

1. The Major-League Agreement
2. The Major-League Rules
3. The Major-Minor League Agreement
4. The Major-Minor League Rules
5. The National Association Agreement

This is not as confusing as it sounds. Each document serves its purpose and has its scope. The Major-League Agreement covers government; the Major-League Rules cover the conduct of business.

The Major-League Agreement is particularly important because it was baseball's answer to the Black Sox scandal—the "throwing" of the 1919 World Series by the Chicago White Sox. The Agreement discarded the unwieldy National Commission as baseball's top body and replaced it with a single commissioner.

Kenesaw Mountain Landis, the first commissioner, won back public confidence but also was so powerful that newspapers referred to him as "baseball's czar." A. B. (Happy) Chandler, the next commissioner, had neither Landis's practical power nor his prestige. The present commissioner, Ford C. Frick, while not as forceful as Landis, has won a great deal of respect for his sincerity and devotion to the game.

Under the Major-League Agreement, Frick draws a salary of $65,000 a year. In return for this, the Agreement calls for him to fulfill the following functions:

1. To investigate on his own, or upon someone else's complaint, any act even suspected of being detrimental to baseball, and to summon anyone in baseball or demand any document in baseball needed for the investigation.

2. To determine, if the party or club or league is guilty in his eyes, remedial, preventive, or punitive action.

3. To resolve any dispute between the major leagues which a league president asks him to resolve.

4. To settle disputes among clubs involving players, and to settle disputes in which players themselves are involved, when asked.

5. To formulate and from time to time announce the rules of procedure for the commissioner's office and for parties, clubs, or leagues taking their problems to the commissioner. These rules must always recognize the right of any interested party to come before the commissioner and be heard.

As punishment for conduct detrimental to baseball, the commissioner has a wide range of choices. He may issue a public reprimand to either league, to any club, to any player or club employee. He may fine a league or a club up to $5000 for any one offense. He may bar a player for life or suspend him, and he may do the same to any club executive or employee. He may deprive a club of its right to representation at the major league joint meetings.

However, the commissioner's judgment of what is "detrimental to baseball" is kept under check. He cannot apply the term to a rule lawfully passed by either major league or by the two leagues. All he can do in this case is to express disapproval and call a special meeting for reconsideration of the rule.

In the case of something detrimental to baseball which originates outside organized baseball, the commissioner is empowered to resort to the courts or to do whatever else he considers appropriate.

The commissioner's term is for seven years, but he can hold any number of terms. He is elected at a meeting of both major leagues, with twelve of the sixteen votes required.

The commissioner has an additional role. He is chairman of the executive council, a body including both league presidents and one representative of the club owners in each league. Players are represented on the executive council, too, but only in matters concerning them.

The council operates on a majority-rule basis. It is designed to "promote and protect interests of leagues and clubs and especially to protect the interests of players." It checks major-league rules with an eye toward revision, and handles whatever major-league problems are not in the province of the commissioner. The players' pension fund is an example of a matter handled by the executive council.

The executive council meets four times a year and at least once with the representatives of National League and American League players. The council can appropriate funds for itself or for the commissioner's office, but must report all its actions to each of the sixteen clubs.

Neither the council nor the commissioner can change a rule. This must be done at a joint meeting, usually held semiannually, at which the sixteen clubs and the two leagues are represented and the commissioner presides.

Funds for all this administration come from World Series and All-Star games, and whatever else is needed is taken on a pro rata basis from the sixteen clubs. The present Major-League Agreement, signed in 1946, is scheduled to remain in force until 1970.

The Agreement merely implements the Rules. The body of the Rules is enormous, but here is a brief summary:

Rule 1 covers the make-up of the leagues and requires that each have an aggregate population of 15,000,000 in its eight cities. It calls for a balanced 154-game schedule, ball parks of at least 25,000 capacity, and acceptance of the uniform player's contract, and it lists requirements for franchise application.

Rule 2 limits to forty the number of players (excluding returning servicemen) a club may carry on its roster. It sets at twenty-five, again excluding veterans, the number of active players a club may carry with it from the thirty-first day of the season to August 31.

Rule 3 deals with the contract, and requires that contracts be mailed to players on or before February 1. It makes binding any written agreement by a player to financial terms, even a telegram of agreement. Tampering with a player under contract to any other club is outlawed, and also the signing of—but not the talking to—high-school students. American Legion junior-team players are similarly protected, and clubs signing schoolboys or Legion athletes not only end up with an invalid contract but also are fined $500.

Rule 4 allows clubs to reserve, under the reserve clause, forty players.

Rule 5 sets up the draft of minor-league players for prices ranging from $15,000 for the top minor league to $1500 for the lowest. Big-league clubs pick players in their reverse order of finish for the pennant, with the last club getting first choice, and which alternates between the National and American leagues annually.

69

Rule 6 covers the return of drafted players to the minors. This cannot be done before the April 1 following the draft, then requires waivers, and return prices run from $7500 to $200.

Rule 7 allows a club to end its relationship with a player by trading, selling, or releasing his contract, but

Rule 8 sets restrictions on unconditional releases. Waivers are required, and any other club may purchase the contract of the player up for release for $1.00.

Rule 9 enlarges on the business of assigning contracts to another club and provides for "reasonable" moving expenses for the player.

Rule 10 outlines the complicated waiver procedure, and fixes $10,000 as the price for a player obtained on waivers. It prohibits a club from dealing from June 16 to the close of the season unless waivers first have been obtained.

Rule 11 allows fifteen options to each major-league team. Options mean simply that a player transferred to a team in a lower league may be recalled on short notice. This, of course, is basic to farm-system operation, where big-league teams often release players to the minors in the spring and call them back when the pennant race points up a squad's hidden weaknesses.

Rule 12 touches on procedure in cases of options.

Rule 13 gives a club power to suspend or fine a player for misconduct, insubordination, failure to get into playing condition, and similar offenses. However, the player retains the right to appeal to the commissioner, provided he does so within ten days.

Rule 14 merely describes retirement procedure for players, but

Rule 15 defines actions that lead to a player's being declared ineligible. Contract-jumping is specifically mentioned—a result of outside raids for players.

Rule 16 discusses player reinstatement.

And then the rules get around to salary.

The sum of $6000 is set as the minimum for a major-league season in Rule 17, but Rule 18 forbids a player from adding to his income in a season by appearing for any team but the one to which he is contracted. This prevents players from picking up a quick $100 in a semipro game on a day off.

Umpires get the right to take salary grievances to the commission in Rule 19 and in Rule 20, which covers stock ownership, umpires are forbidden to borrow money from anyone owning stock in a club in the same league in which the umpire works. Stockholders may not own stock in more than one club and, further, major-league clubs may not own or work with two minor-league teams in the same league.

Misconduct is the subject of Rule 21 and here gifts to umpires are outlawed. Anyone connected with a club who bets on a game is declared ineligible for a year if his own team is not involved in the game. If it is, the penalty is life.

Rules 22 to 24 are minor, but Rule 25 fixes the committee that writes the rules of play at nine men, three from each major league and three from the minors. Rule 26 deals with the conduct of executive council meetings, 27 with joint meetings, and Rules 28 to 32 with less important procedural matters.

Rules 33 through 48 apply to the World Series, placing the classic under the commissioner's supervision, fixing the schedule pattern, and requiring a player to be under contract to a pennant-winning team on August 31 to be eligible. The rules provide for the following division of receipts:

15 per cent of all receipts to the commissioner's office.

60 per cent of the balance in the first four games to the players' pool. Of this amount, thirty per cent goes to second-, third-, and fourth-place teams, and the remaining 70 per cent to the Series winner and loser on a 60–40 basis.

After the 15 per cent and the 60 per cent are deducted in the first four games, the remainder is divided equally between the two Series clubs and their respective leagues.

Voluminous though the complete rules are, they do not cover every facet of major-league operation nor is that their intention. Some matters are left to each league to decide for itself. The question of the number of night games to be allowed is typical, and on so important a matter as the visiting team's share of receipts the two leagues do not agree. The National League in 1953 increased the visitor's take from twenty-two and a half cents per ticket to twenty-seven and a half cents, while the American League left its arrangement at an even twenty-five cents.

Actual administration of the leagues is handled by league presidents, and umpires work under them. All battles between players and umpires are settled in the league president's office if they are violent enough to merit special attention.

The Major-League Agreement is the minors' recognition of the commissioner's powers, a recognition tempered by the reservation that the agreement may be terminated by a three-fourths vote of the National Association, the organization into which all minor leagues are banded. A major-minor league executive council, on the lines of the major-league executive council, is provided for.

The Major-Minor League Rules make for consistency throughout organized ball. Much here is duplication of major league rules, but the first provision is not. This prohibits major-league franchises from moving into minor-league territory without "just and reasonable compensation."

71

The National Association Agreement vests minor-league supervisory power in an executive committee and a president. The executive committee consists of one representative from the top minor leagues, one from middle, and one from lower classifications.

The president is elected annually, and a prime difference between the National Association Agreement and the Major League Agreement is that appeals in some cases go from the president to the executive council. There is no appeal from the commissioner.

The National Association Agreement explains conditions for membership in the National Association, delegates authority, and touches on a score of minor matters.

Plainly, the administration of baseball is not simple. The body of rules and agreements is more than twice as long as the United States Constitution, and the commissioner earns more than the governor of any state. His job, while perhaps not as taxing as that of a governor, is not easy. The administration of baseball requires experts and much legal advice, and it offers headaches more than balancing the free tickets the commissioner receives.

Some critics say that baseball is not well run. But the game is alive and healthy and has public confidence. Perhaps the administrative setup might be made simpler, but baseball is reluctant to change radically a structure so successful for so long.

HOW A BIG-LEAGUE CLUB OPERATES

Because there are sixteen different major-league clubs, there are probably sixteen different ways of operating a major-league club.

In some clubs, such as the Chicago White Sox, the president delegates the job of running the organization to a general manager. In others, such as the Philadelphia Phillies, the president is his own general manager. The Chicago Cubs have a president active in matters of policy, and two men—a director of player personnel and a business manager—who share the duties assumed by some individual general managers.

On pages 75 and 78 appear a financial statement and an organizational chart of the Brooklyn Baseball Club. These documents are typical, but they merely illustrate one way of operating a successful team.

Neither the Dodgers nor any baseball team is big business in the sense that a large industrial corporation is. In a borough of New York City with a population of more than 2,000,000, the Dodgers find their income limited by the 31,902 seating capacity of Ebbets Field. Plans are being readied for a new stadium, but until the plans become reality, a matter of years, the small ball park will remain the chief handicap to more profitable operation of the Dodgers.

Insufficient playing talent is a handicap under which many other clubs work. The Dodgers have had ample talent for years because of their fifteen-team farm system, a system which annually runs at a loss and must be subsidized from the profits of the parent club.

Walter F. O'Malley, president of the Dodgers, takes an active interest in the club, but relies heavily on the judgment of two vice-presidents. One, E. J. (Buzzie) Bavasi, oversees the Dodger team and the two top farm clubs. The other, Fresco Thompson, is in charge of the other farms and the vast Brooklyn scouting network. But the final responsibility for the success or failure of the entire Brooklyn organization rests with O'Malley.

At major press conferences it is usually the president who answers the volleys of questions fired by reporters. When big decisions are to be made, such as the one to retain the policy of one-year contracts for

73

field managers even at the cost of losing manager Charley Dressen, it is the president who makes them. But O'Malley, a highly successful attorney before entering baseball, decides only after consultation with Bavasi, Thompson, and any other officials whose experience makes their opinion valuable in the particular case.

Bavasi is a career baseball executive who worked his way up from the front office of a Class D club. In addition to the Dodgers themselves, he is in charge of the farm teams at Montreal and St. Paul, since both these clubs feed talent directly to Brooklyn. Included in his duties are the signing of Dodger players each year, determining with the field manager the make-up of the team, and generally making sure that the entire operation in Brooklyn runs smoothly.

Thompson, a onetime standout major-league second baseman, works with Bavasi in handling Montreal and St. Paul and, besides supervising the other thirteen farm teams, runs the scouting program. A man of particularly acute baseball judgment, Thompson is often asked to step out of his formal role as farm boss to offer an opinion about some problem of the parent club.

Under Thompson there work a great many former ballplayers. One, Andy High, a former third baseman, is chief scout. Brooklyn scouts cover every state in the union and parts of Canada and Latin America. They are experts, because no one but an expert can look at a seventeen-year-old boy and decide accurately whether the youth merits the investment of a contract. Some seventeen-year-olds never improve; others develop suddenly. But in the Brooklyn organization there are rarely surprises. Each day a report on every minor-league player in the Dodger system is sent to the club's central office in downtown Brooklyn. On pages 76, 77 and 79 appear a player questionnaire filled in by a young catcher and actual Dodger scouting reports.

It is rarely possible to purchase an established major-league star any more, regardless of the price offered. Major-league clubs must produce their own stars, and without thorough, accurate, nationwide scouting, production falls off.

Only a portion of the Dodgers' employees are ballplayers and ex-ballplayers. Lee Scott, the traveling secretary, is a former newspaperman. Allan Roth, the Dodger statistician, is a native of Canada who did statistics for the Montreal Canadiens hockey team before turning to baseball and inventing new means of statistical analysis of this country's national game.

But everyone in the Brooklyn organization is working toward one end—the protection of the stockholders' investment. Victories, of course, offer the best protection, and the form all labors take is an effort to bring winning teams to Brooklyn and as many minor-league cities as possible.

Most of the club's income arrives in the form of small bills, paid in by fans for tickets. Another portion comes from the sale of radio and television rights. Additional cash is derived from the concessions at the ball park.

Because of their vast minor-league chain, the Dodgers have another source of revenue. Every year some young players, usually those not as promising as others, are sold to organizations less rich in talent than Brooklyn. These annual sales are regularly included in the Brooklyn budget.

The 1952 season was a good one for the Brooklyn organization. The team won the National League pennant and went seven games before losing the World Series to the New York Yankees. World Series tickets are priced high, and because of the Series the Dodgers managed to show a sizeable profit.

Throughout the entire organization and during the entire season, including World Series and minor-league play-off games, ticket sales totaled about $4,500,000. Concessions brought in an extra sum equal to about 10 per cent of that figure. Player sales amounted to close to $200,000. The actual figures involved in radio and television cannot be revealed.

This is one side of the Brooklyn ledger. On the other are countless small items from baseballs to ushers' caps. The major Dodger expenses for 1952 are presented here, with actual figures, each carried to the nearest thousand.

Federal, state, and city taxes	$ 926,000.00
Team salaries, player pensions, and traveling expenses	1,119,000.00
Team replacement expenses, scouts, payments to free agents, deficits of owned minor-league farm clubs, and spring training	428,000.00
Stadium maintenance	589,000.00
Game expenses, ticket printing and selling, ushers, and staffing	184,000.00
Advertising and publicity, office personnel and staff salaries, and insurance	80,000.00
Administrative expenses, insurance, telephone, and office supplies	417,000.00
	$3,743,000.00

BROOKLYN ORGANIZATION PLAYER QUESTIONNAIRE

IMPORTANT

To: This questionnaire, carefully completed by you, will help our publicity department and you personally. The information supplied at this time will be made a permanent part of your Brooklyn organization file, eliminating the necessity of asking you to complete similar forms in the future. Please give this matter your immediate attention.

Full name (Please print) OMER *(first)* DEAN *(middle)* EHLERS *(last)* — Position CATCHER

Permanent home address BOX 12 — CAMPBELL HILL — ILLINOIS *(number and street)* *(city)* *(state)*

Social security number 349-22-4057 — Birth Date JUNE *(month)* 22 *(date)* 1929 *(year)*

Birth Place CAMPBELL HILL, ILLINOIS — Your nationality AMERICAN (GERMAN) *(city)* *(state)*

Father's nationality AMERICAN (GERMAN); Mother's nationality AMERICAN (GERMAN)

Draft classification 1-A — Do you throw right or left? R

Do you bat right or left? R — Height 6-1 — Weight 175

Color of your hair BROWN — Color of your eyes BLUE

Do you wear glasses when playing? No ; off the field? No

Nickname NONE — How did your nickname originate?

With what club and organization, if any, did you sign your first contract in professional baseball?

GEORGIA *(organization)* — BORDER *(league)* — 1948 *(season)* — BROOKLYN *(organization)*

What circumstances led to your being offered your first contract? Agreed by me and scout Lefty Phillips to see how play a couple of game & if good enough atta try offered me a contract.

Name of person by whom you were signed to play in Brooklyn organization Lefty "Patterson"

Name of club you were first signed to in Brooklyn organization Border *(club)* — *(league)* — 1948 *(season)*

Through what person, persons or circumstances did you first come in contact with Brooklyn organization? Answer during offical first contacted

High school(s) attended Campbell Hill Com. Campbell Hill, Illinois 43-47 *(name)* *(city)* *(what years?)*

High school graduation date Friday Hill 1947 — High school sports in which you participated Baseball until Basketball

---

Did you receive any athletic distinction in high school such as varsity letter, captainships or were you selected on any all-star teams? Varsity letters in baseball, varsity in basketball, all state basketball from my senior year.

Were you a member of any championship teams? No — If yes, give details:

College(s) attended Central College — Fayette, Missouri *(name)* *(city)* *(state)*

1947-48 1948-49 — College graduation date June 1951 *(what years?)* *(date)*

College sports in which you participated Basketball (2 yrs) Football (1 yr)

Did you receive any athletic distinction at college or were you selected on any all-star teams? 2 years letter in basketball, 2 yrs letter in football. Captain of basketball team two years. Captain of football team one year. All conference basketball selection two years.

Were you a member of any championship teams? No — If yes, give details:

Did you ever play American Legion Jr. baseball? If so, give name of team, city and years in which you played.

List sandlot and semi-pro teams you have played with and years in which you played.

Did you receive any honors or distinction in American Legion Jr., sandlot or semi-pro baseball?
If so, please give details

Were you a member of any championship teams? — If so, name the players)

Did you play in amateur, sandlot or semi-pro baseball on the same club or in the same league with players now prominent in the major leagues? (If so, name the players) *(player's name)* *(team)* *(league)*

Is there any individual, club, organization or specialized type of instruction to which you particularly owe your success in baseball?

Who is your baseball hero? STAN MUSIAL

-2-

Tell about your greatest thrill in baseball: _hitting my first home run in pro ball_
Have you ever led a professional league in any department of play over a full season? _No_ If so, give full details, including year:

If a pitcher, have you ever pitched a no-hit game in professional baseball? _____ If yes, give details:

List ALL clubs with which you have played in professional baseball:

Year	Club	Organization (if any)	League	Manager
1948	Geneva	Brooklyn	Border	Shuk Jones
1949	Ponca City	"	K.O.M.	Boyd Bartley

With what pennant or play-off winning teams have you played? Give names of clubs and years

Have you ever been named the "Most Valuable Player" in any professional league? _No_ If yes, give details:

What is your winter occupation? _Attending College_

What position(s) did you play before entering professional baseball? _Pitcher & Catcher_
What position(s) have you played since entering professional baseball? (Please list in order of sequence) _Catcher outfield 1st base_

Are you still playing the first position you played professionally? _yes_
If not, what was the reason for the change?

Who changed your position? _____ When?
What is your favorite position among those you have played? _Catcher_
If you "had it to do all over again," what position would you point for? _Pitcher Catcher Outfield_
Why? _I believe I would have better chance for advancement in pitching_

-3-

Did you serve in World War II? _No_ What branch of service? _____
Length of Service _____ Were you awarded any military decorations or honors? If so, please give details.

Did you suffer any injuries in military service? _____ If so, please give details.

While in military service, were you involved in any events of particular interest? (i.e.—major battles, campaigns, hazardous or unusual mission, etc.)

Rate or rank upon entering service? _____
Rate or rank upon discharge from service. _____ Are you a member of any active or inactive reserve group, National Guard unit, etc. _____ If so, please specify.

What is your pet superstition, if any? _None_

What are your hobbies? _None_

Do you play any musical instrument(s)? _No_ If so, please specify
Do you sing? _No_ Have you ever made any speeches before schools, clubs or at banquets? _No_
Of what clubs, fraternities (honorary or social) or societies are you a member? _Beta Sigma fraternity (social)_

Are you a bachelor, widower or married man? _bachelor_ If married, give date of marriage
Have you any children? _____ What are their names and ages?

What was your wife's maiden name? _____
Are you related to or descended from anyone of particular prominence in any field? _No_
If so, please give names and relationship.

What are your plans for the future (after your playing career is ended)? _Coaching in a high school_ Signature _Glenn Ebbens_
Date _July 7, 1950_
NOTE: Please re-read this completed questionnaire. Have you fully answered all questions? Is the information correct in all details?

-4-

77

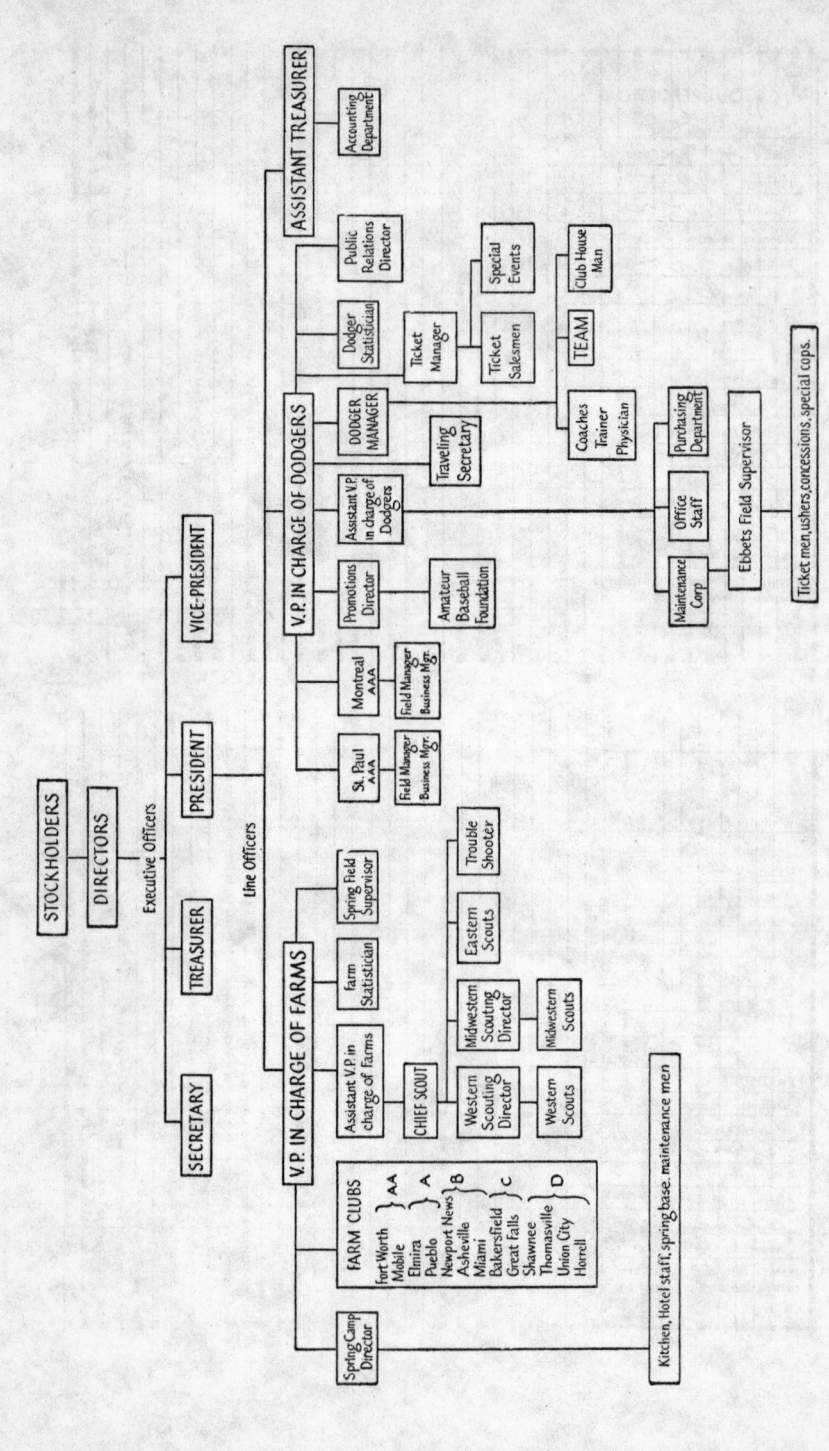

SCOUT REPORT CARD **Snider**

Name in Full Ed. Snider

Pos. OF. Age 17
Hgt. 5-11 Wgt. 165

Club Newport News League Piedmont   Bats R Throws R

Hitting	good	Power	good
Throwing	very good	Accuracy	very good
Running Speed	good	Base Running	good
Fielding	good		

PITCHER
Speed	
Curve	
Change	
Control	

Definite Prospect? ✓   Has Chance?   Habits

Physical Description (Build, Size, Agility, Etc.) Well built and moves good.

Remarks: Must improve on hitting curve ball. Has lot of ability, might go all the way.

Report By Jake Pitler   Date Sept 2, 1944

Note: This card to be used in reporting on ALL PLAYERS in Brooklyn organization and any PROSPECTS outside Brooklyn organization.

SCOUT REPORT CARD **Campanella**

Name in Full Roy Campanella

Pos. C Age 25
Hgt. 5-9½ Wgt. 208

Club Nashua League N.E.   Bats R Throws R

Hitting	+	Power	+
Throwing	++	Accuracy	+
Running Speed	ave	Base Running	ave
Fielding			

PITCHER
Speed	
Curve	
Change	
Control	

APTITUDE

Definite Prospect? ✓   Has Chance?   Habits

Physical Description (Build, Size, Agility, Etc.) Well built, moves very good.

Remarks: Very good receiver, hits ball where it is pitched with power. Uses good judgement.

Report By Jake Pitler   Date Sept 9, 1946.

Note: This card to be used in reporting on ALL PLAYERS in Brooklyn organization and any PROSPECTS outside Brooklyn organization.

79

HOW TO SCORE AND READ A SCORE CARD

The only consistent element in scoring a baseball game is its purpose. The scorer wants to have a record of what went on, and he does not want it to be the length of a novel. Though certain patterns are generally followed by major-league baseball writers, broadcasters, and telecasters, each tends to develop individual quirks and short cuts.

For example, there is a commonly accepted system of numbering players according to position. Under this setup, the pitcher is 1, the catcher 2, the first baseman 3, the second baseman 4, the third baseman 5, the shortstop 6, the left fielder 7, the center fielder 8 and the right fielder 9. But one baseball writer has developed his own numbering system which, if nothing else, prevents his colleagues from understanding his score card.

Reproduced on these pages is another baseball writer's score card. The game is the final one of the 1953 World Series, and from the score card we can follow the progress of the battle through Carl Furillo's exciting game-tying ninth-inning home run to Billy Martin's climactic

TOWN *N.Y.(Yankee Stadium)* UMPIRES *Stewart, Hurley, Gore, Grieve, Dascoli, Soar* TIME 2:55

RBI	PLAYERS	1	2	3	4	5	6	7	8	9	10	11	12	13	14	AB	R	H	PO	A	E
•	Woodling 7		L7					FC								4	1	2	1	0	0
	Collins 3/3 Mizz Seling (9th)	Ks		9			33									3/0	0/0	1/0	5/0	1/0	0/0
	Bauer 9			FO	P6											3	2	1	3	0	0
•	Berra 2		DP 842		P4			L9								5	0	2	10	0	0
	Mantle 8	DW	43	8		7										4	0	1	5	0	0
••	Martin 4	E4	7			143										5	0	2	1	0	0
	McDougald 5	543	ES	63		K										4	0	0	0	0	0
	Rizzuto 6		F3		8											4	1	2	2	2	0
	Ford 1		8	63		1										3	0	1	0	1	0
	Reynolds (8th) 1															1	0	1	0	0	0
	TOTALS																				

ER		BB			SO			DP	
Left		2-B		3-B		HR		SB	
Sacrifices		PB		WP		HB		Balks	

INNINGS	1	2	3	4	5	6	7	8	9	10	11	12	13	14	15	16	17	18	19	20	21	R	H	E
Dodgers	0	0	0	0	0	1	0	0	2													3	8	3
Yankees	2	1	0	0	0	0	0	0	1													4	13	0

winning single. Remember that the idea of a score card is to show each play in a game. It's all there, and here's how to read it:

The players are listed in batting order, with the number after each name representing the man's defensive position. Visualize the four corners of the boxes as the three bases and home plate. Gilliam's "P3" indicates a pop fly to the Yankee first baseman. "P" is often used for pop, "L" for line drive, "F" for foul, and "D" for deep fly by those who want to know more than just which fielder caught a ball hit into the air.

Reese's first-inning symbol shows a line single to left—the horizontal single line signifying a one-base hit, the vertical line angled to left, the field to which the ball was driven. Looping lines below indicate looping hits, and wavy lines indicate ground singles.

Reese's symbol in the first corner puts him on first base, and from there he moves counterclockwise. Robinson hits into a force-out (FO) with Reese retired at second, 4 unassisted (4X). Campanella grounds a single to center, and Robinson stops at second on the hit, as is shown by the 2, Campanella's defensive number, in the second corner of Robinson's box. Hodges lines to short, ending the half-

DATE *October 5 1953* TEAM *Dodgers*   *Reynolds, lights on*   ATTENDANCE *62,370*

RBI	PLAYERS		1	2	3	4	5	6	7	8	9	10	11	12	13	14	AB	R	H	PO	A	E
	Gilliam	4	P3		7		K		/	D9	/						4	0	0	4	4	1
	Reese	6	/	8			/	8		9							4	0	1	1	4	0
	Robinson	7	2 FO		/	63		⌐S		/							4	1	2	3	0	0
•	Campanella	2	/		Ks		63		Ks								4	0	1	4	0	0
	Hodges	3	L6		13		33		/	8							4	0	0	7	0	0
	Snider	8	/	Ks	/	Ks	/	Ks		/							3	1	0	4	1	0
••	Furillo	9	3X3					8		◇							4	1	3	2	0	0
	Cox	5	Ks		8		/	Kc									4	0	1	0	1	1
	Erskine / A-Williams –	1		/	Ks		L9	Kc									1 / 0	0 / 0	0 / 0	0 / 0	0 / 0	1 / 0
	Milliken (5th) / B-Morgan –	1															0 / 1	0 / 0	0 / 0	0 / 0	0 / 0	0 / 0
	Labine (7th)	1															1	0	0	0	1	0
	TOTALS		0/02	0/0	0/0	0/0	0/02	1/0	0/01	0/01	2/0											

ER		BB		SO		DP	
Left		2-B		3-B		HR		SB
Sacrifices		PB		WP		HB		Balks

WINNING PITCHER— *Reynolds*   LOSING PITCHER— *Labine*

A—Walked for Erskine in 5th
B—Lined out for Milliken in 7th.

inning, and the totals are no runs, two hits, no Yankee errors, two Dodgers left on base.

That's the general idea. Symbols used later are an arrow for an advance of more than one base, "Ks" for a swinging strikeout, "Kc" for a call-out on strikes, a boxed "W" for a full-count walk, a circled "W" for a four-pitch walk, "DW" for a deliberate walk, "S" for steal, with a connecting line indicating who was at bat when the base was stolen, "E" for error, with the defensive player's number listed, "ET" for throwing error, and "FC" for fielder's choice.

In showing hits, the scorer has used two lines for doubles and would have used three for triples had there been any. To make Furillo's home run easier to spot, however, he has used a diamond within the box to indicate a home run and the usual directional line showing that the ball went to right field.

For most double plays, such as the one Martin hit in the Yankee sixth inning, mention of the defenders involved within the hitter's box, with a line to the box of the runner put out, is sufficient. However, in the complex second-inning double play, it was necessary to write "DP" in Berra's box as a reminder.

No baseball writer can cover games without often falling back on notes to supplement his scoring. But for ordinary purposes a fan who masters a scoring technique of whatever style will have a record of all he need know about any game.

HOW TO READ A BOX SCORE

In its few inches of space, a box score reveals a great deal about a game. It is concise and exact, and requires only an understanding of its abbreviations for proper reading. Reproduced below is the box score of the sixth and final game of the 1953 World Series, which brought the New York Yankees their fifth consecutive world championship.

Brooklyn (NL)	AB	R	H	PO	A	New York (AL)	AB	R	H	PO	A
Gilliam, 2b. ...	4	0	0	4	4	Woodling, lf. ...	4	1	2	1	0
Reese, ss.	4	0	1	1	4	Collins, 1b.	3	0	1	5	1
Robinson, lf. ..	4	1	2	3	0	C-Mize	1	0	0	0	0
Campanella, c. .	4	0	1	4	0	Bollweg, 1b.	0	0	0	0	0
Hodges, 1b. ...	4	0	0	7	0	Bauer, rf.	3	2	1	3	0
Snider, cf.	3	1	0	4	1	Berra, c.	5	0	2	10	0
Furillo, rf.	4	1	3	2	0	Mantle, cf.	4	0	1	5	0
Cox, 3b.	4	0	1	0	1	Martin, 2b.	5	0	2	1	0
Erskine, p.	1	0	0	0	0	McDougald, 3b. .	4	0	0	0	0
A-Williams	0	0	0	0	0	Rizzuto, ss.	4	1	2	2	2
Milliken, p. ...	0	0	0	0	0	Ford, p.	3	0	1	0	1
B-Morgan	1	0	0	0	0	Reynolds, p.	1	0	1	0	0
Labine, p.	1	0	0	0	1						
Totals	34	3	8	y25	11	**Totals**	37	4	13	27	4

A—Walked for Erskine in 5th.
B—Lined out for Milliken in 7th.
C—Grounded out for Collins in 8th.
y—One out when winning run was scored.

Brooklyn 000 001 002—3
New York 210 000 001—4

E—Gilliam, Erskine, Cox. RBI—Berra, Martin 2, Woodling, Campanella, Furillo 2. 2B—Berra, Furillo, Martin, Robinson. HR—Furillo. SB—Robinson. DP—Cox-Gilliam-Hodges, Snider-Gilliam-Campanella, Labine-Gilliam-Hodges. Left—Brooklyn 6, New York 13. BB—Ford 1, Reynolds 1, Erskine 3, Milliken 1, Labine 1. SO—Ford 7, Reynolds 3, Erskine 1, Labine 1. HO—Erskine 6 in 4 innings, Milliken 2 in 2, Ford 6 in 7, Labine 5 in 2⅓, Reynolds 2 in 2. R-ER—Erskine 3-3, Milliken 0-0, Ford 1-1, Labine 1-1, Reynolds 2-2. Winner—Reynolds. Loser—Labine. U—Stewart, Hurley, Gore, Grieve, Dascoli, Soar. T—2:55. A—62,370 (paid).

We don't learn from the box score in what inning the hits, strike-outs, and such took place, but we learn almost everything else. The letters in parentheses after the names of the teams indicate the leagues in which each club plays, "NL" for the National and "AL" for the American League. After that, the abbreviations are "AB" for at-bats, "R" for runs, "H" for hits, "PO" for put-outs, and "A" for assists. The players are listed according to the order in which they bat, and the abbreviations after their names show their positions.

Those players with a letter preceding their names have no position indicated. The notes at the bottom of the line-up section indicate that these men were pinch hitters or pinch runners. The "y" next to Brooklyn's put-out total is necessary because in a full nine innings each team makes twenty-seven put-outs, and in this game Brooklyn only made twenty-five.

Below the line-up portion of the box is the score by innings, and then the lower portion with its own set of abbreviations. "E" stands for error, "RBI" for runs batted in, "2B" for double, "HR" for home run, "DP" for double play, "Left" for left on base, "BB" for bases on balls, "SO" for strike-outs, "R-ER" for runs and earned runs, "U" for umpires, "T" for time, and "A" for attendance.

Different newspapers follow slightly different styles in the printing of box scores, and a common practice during the season is to list the won-and-lost record of the winning and losing pitchers in parentheses after their names.

HOW TO FIGURE AVERAGES

Averages are baseball's yardsticks. Even the casual fan knows that a .300 hitter is a good hitter and that a club winning at a .667 pace is a good club. Slightly more obscure to some is the exact meaning of the slugging percentage and earned-run average, but all baseball averages, from the simplest to the most complex, are easy to calculate. None requires more than simple arithmetic. All are expressed in three figures, which means dividing to four places and rounding off to the nearest thousandth (except in the case of the earned-run average).

Here are baseball's key averages, with an explanation of the figuring of each:

Batting Average—Divide the number of hits by the number of at-bats. The quotient is the batting average. Thus a player making three hits in ten at-bats is batting .300. The numbers change, but the principle does not.

Won-and-Lost Percentage—Add the won and lost figures to find the total number of games. Divide the number of victories by this total, and again the quotient is the percentage sought. For a team winning seven games and losing three, the total number of games is ten. The division of seven by ten yields .700. Won-and-lost percentages for pitchers are calculated in the same way.

Fielding Percentage—Take the total number of chances accepted (put-outs plus assists) and divide by the total number of chances (put-outs, assists plus errors). The quotient is the fielding percentage. A player with forty-five put-outs, forty-four assists and one error has a fielding percentage of .990—the quotient of 99 divided by 100.

Slugging Percentage—Divide the number of total bases of a player's singles, doubles, triples, and home runs by his number of at-bats. A player who in 100 times at bat makes 20 singles, five doubles, two triples and one home run has a total of 40 bases and a slugging percentage of .400. This is an excellent gauge of a hitter's power, and league leaders in this department customarily slug at a clip of over .600.

Earned-run Average—This is the only figure that is a true average rather than a percentage. To find it, multiply by nine the total of earned runs a pitcher has allowed. Earned runs are those not made possible by errors. Then divide this figure by the total number of innings the pitcher has worked. This gives the number of earned runs a pitcher has allowed for each nine innings he has pitched. A pitcher who allows 50 runs in 300 innings has an earned-run average of 1.50, the quotient of 450 (nine times the 50 runs) divided by 300. It's no trick to tell that a pitcher who allows an average of 1.50 runs a game is a top hurler. Actually, that's almost unheard-of, and an earned-run average of 2.30 is often sufficient to lead the major leagues.

THE HALL OF FAME

The Hall of Fame and the National Museum comprise baseball's shrine. Cooperstown, New York, a hamlet of less than three thousand population, is the site, and was selected when organized baseball accepted the legend that Abner Doubleday invented the game there in 1839.

Discovery of a baseball dating from Doubleday's time in the nearby town of Fly Creek gave the museum a start in 1935. Soon after, Ford Frick, now baseball commissioner but then president of the National League, suggested the establishment of the Hall of Fame.

The museum now contains a vast collection of memorabilia, ranging from the sheepskin sliding pads Ty Cobb used when he set a stolen base record in 1916 to an 1891 photograph of nine young ladies, garbed in a strange variation of a baseball uniform and said to be the first women's team ever.

The Hall of Fame consists of bronze plaques of baseball's immortals, bearing brief descriptions of their achievements and busts engraved upon the bronze. The immortals have been selected in several ways. The current system calls for an annual election among members of the Baseball Writers' Association who have ten or more years' standing. Baseball figures retired for at least one year but active in the quarter-century preceding the election are eligible.

An example of the plaques is the one bearing the bust of Christy Mathewson. His years with the New York Giants and his one year with the Cincinnati Reds are listed, and the following inscription appears:

> Born Factoryville, Pa., August 12, 1880.
> Greatest of all the great pitchers
> In the 20th century's first quarter.
> Pitched 3 shutouts in 1905 World Series.
> First pitcher of the century ever to
> win 30 games in 3 successive years.
> Won 37 games in 1908.
> "Matty was master of them all."

Here is a list of the immortals in baseball's Hall of Fame:

Lifetime Records of Immortals

Year elected	Name and playing years	Games	Batting Average	Year elected	Name and playing years	Games	Batting Average
1939	Anson, Adrian C., 1876–97......	2253	.339	1953	Simmons, Al H., 1924–44.......	2215	.334
1945	Bresnahan, Roger, 1897–1915....	1410	.279	1939	Sisler, George H., 1915–30......	2055	.340
1945	Brouthers, Dan, 1879–96.......	1653	.348	1937	Speaker, T. E., 1907–28........	2789	.344
1946	Burkett, Jesse C., 1890–1905....	2063	.342	1954	Terry, William H.	1721	.341
1946	Chance, Frank L., 1898–1914....	1232	.297	1946	Tinker, Joseph B., 1902–16......	1641	.264
1945	Clarke, Fred C., 1894–1915......	2204	.315	1948	Traynor, Harold J., 1920–37.....	1941	.320
1936	Cobb, Tyrus R., 1905–28........	3033	.367	1936	Wagner, John P., 1897–1917....	2785	.329
1947	Cochrane, Gordon S., 1925–37...	1482	.320	1953	Wallace, Rhoderick J., ...	2369	.267
1939	Collins, Edward T., 1906–30.....	2826	.333	1952	Waner, Paul G., 1926–45........	2549	.333
1945	Collins, James J., 1895–1908....	1718	.294	1937	Wright, George, 1876–82........	315	.251
1939	Comiskey, C. A., 1882–94.......	1383	.269				
1945	Delahanty, E. J., 1888–1903.....	1825	.346		**PITCHERS**		
1954	Dickey, William M.	1789	.313				
1945	Duffy, Hugh, 1888–1906.........	1722	.330	Year elected	Name and playing years	Won	Lost
1946	Evers, John J., 1902–19.........	1776	.270				
1939	Ewing, Wm. B., 1880–97.......	1280	.311	1938	Alexander, Grover C., 1911–30....	373	208
1951	Foxx, James E., 1925–1945......	2317	.325	1953	Bender, Charles A., 1903–1917....	212	128
1947	Frisch, Frank F., 1919–37......	2311	.316	1949	Brown, Mordecai, 1903–16......	239	131
1939	Gehrig, H. Louis, 1923–39......	2164	.340	1946	Chesbro, John D., 1899–1909.....	199	128
1949	Gehringer, Charles L., 1924–42..	2323	.321	1953	Dean, Jerome H., 1930–41........	150	83
1952	Heilmann, Harry E., 1914–32...	2146	.342	1946	Griffith, Clark C., 1891–1908......	237	140
1942	Hornsby, Rogers, 1915–37......	2259	.358	1947	Grove, Robert M., 1925–41.......	300	141
1945	Jennings, H. A., 1891–1908......	1264	.314	1947	Hubbell, Carl O., 1928–43.......	253	154
1939	Keeler, Wm. H., 1892–1910.....	2124	.345	1936	Johnson, Walter P., 1907–27....	414	276
1945	Kelly, Michael J., 1878–93.....	1493	.315	1946	McGinnity, Joseph J., 1899–1908..	248	141
1937	Lajoie, Napoleon, 1896–1916....	2475	.338	1936	Mathewson, Christopher, 1900–16.	373	188
1954	Maranville, Walter J.	2670	.258	1949	Nichols, Charles A., 1890–1906...	360	202
1946	McCarthy, Thomas, 1884–96.....	1268	.294	1948	Pennock, Herbert J., 1912–34.....	239	161
1937	McGraw, John J., 1891–1906....	1082	.334	1946	Plank, Edward S., 1901–17.......	324	190
1937	Mack, Connie, 1886–96.........	736	.249	1939	Radbourne, Charles G., 1880–91..	308	191
1945	O'Rourke, James, 1876–94......	1750	.315	1946	Waddell, George E., 1897–1910....	203	143
1951	Ott, Melvin T., 1926–1947......	2730	.304	1946	Walsh, Edward A., 1904–17.....	195	126
1945	Robinson, Wilbert, 1886–1902...	1316	.280	1937	Young, Denton T., 1890–1911.....	511	315
1936	Ruth, G. H. (Babe), 1914–35....	2503	.342				

SELECTED FOR MERITORIOUS SERVICE

Edward G. Barrow (1953), Morgan G. Bulkeley (1937), Alexander J. Cartwright (1938), Henry Chadwick (1938), Thomas Connelly (1953), William A. Cummings (1939), B. Bancroft Johnson (1937), William Klem (1953), Judge Kenesaw M. Landis (1944), Albert G. Spalding (1939), Harry Wright (1953).

BALTIMORE ORIOLES ROSTER

Manager: Jimmy Dykes.   Coaches: Tom Oliver, Frankie Skaff, Harry Brecheen.

Name	Pos.	B	T	Hgt.	Wgt.	Age	1953 Club	Won	Lost
Bickford, Vern	P	R	R	6:00	185	32	Milwaukee	2	5
Blyzka, Mike	P	R	R	6:00	200	25	Browns	2	6
Coleman, Joe	P	R	R	6:03	200	31	Philadelphia	3	4
Duren, Rinold	P	R	R	6:01	180	25	San Antonio	12	12
Fanovich, Frank	P	L	L	5:11	180	31	Philadelphia	0	3
Fox, Howard	P	R	R	6:03	220	33	Baltimore (Int.)	15	10
Habenicht, Robert	P	R	R	6:02	185	28	Charleston	4	7
Heard, Jehosie	P	L	L	5:08	150	29	Portland	16	12
Held, Melvin	P	R	R	6:00	178	25	Wichita	8	8
Kretlow, Louis	P	R	R	6:01	190	30	Browns	1	5
Larsen, Don	P	R	R	6:04	210	24	Browns	7	12
Littlefield, Richard	P	L	L	6:00	175	28	Browns	7	12
Locke, Charles	P	R	R	6:00	185	21	Wichita	8	18
Perkins, Vachel	P	R	R	6:02	205	23	San Antonio	9	16
Pilgram, William	P	R	R	6:03	190	24	Wichita	6	11
Pillette, Duane	P	R	R	6:04	195	30	Browns	7	13
Post, Carlton	P	L	L	5:11	165	28	Toronto	10	8
Stuart, Marlin	P	L	R	6:02	190	35	Browns	8	2
Turley, Robert	P	R	R	6:04	218	23	Browns	2	6

Name	Pos.	B	T	Hgt.	Wgt.	Age	1953 Club	Batting Average
Courtney, Clint	C	L	R	5:08	173	27	Browns	.251
Johnson, Darrell	C	R	R	6:01	176	26	Memphis	.249
Moss, Lester	C	R	R	5:11	188	28	Browns	.276
Berry, Neil	Inf.	R	R	5:10	175	32	Browns	.271
Caffery, Robert	Inf.	L	R	6:00	165	24	San Antonio	.266
Dyck, James	Inf.	R	R	6:02	190	32	Browns	.213
Garcia, Viniciot	Inf.	R	R	5:09	160	25	Shreveport	.305
Hunter, Bill	Inf.	R	R	6:00	175	25	Browns	.219
Kellert, Frank	Inf.	R	R	6:03	180	29	Oklahoma City	.289
Kryhoski, Dick	Inf.	L	L	6:02	215	29	Browns	.278
Mickelson, Edward	Inf.	R	R	6:04	200	27	San Antonio	.296
Sievers, Roy	Inf.	R	R	6:01	190	27	Browns	.270
Stephens, Vernon	Inf.	R	R	5:10	190	33	Browns	.262
Young, Robert	Inf.	L	R	6:00	160	29	Browns	.255
Balcana, Robert	Of.	R	L	5:07	160	25	San Antonio	.274
Diering, Charles	Of.	R	R	5:10	165	31	Minneapolis	.322
Fridley, James	Of.	R	R	6:02	205	28	San Antonio	.293
Ippolito, Rocco	Of.	R	R	6:01	208	25	San Antonio	.234
Kokos, Richard	Of.	L	L	5:08	175	26	Browns	.241
Kwak, Karol	Of.	L	L	5:10	170	24	Anderson	.359
Lenhardt, Don	Of.	R	R	6:03	187	31	Browns	.317
Masser, Robert	Of.	L	R	5:09	175	25	Wichita	.281
Niele, Sam	Of.	R	R	6:01	178	31	Chicago	.274
Pisoni, James	Of.	R	R	5:10	172	23	Anderson	.323
Wertz, Victor	Of.	L	R	6:00	196	29	Browns	.268

BOSTON RED SOX ROSTER

Manager: Lou Boudreau. Coaches: Del Baker, Paul Schreiber, George Susce, Buster Mills.

Name	Pos.	B	T	Hgt.	Wgt.	Age	1953 Club	Won	Lost
Brown, Hector	P	R	R	6:02	180	29	Boston	11	6
Delock, Ivan	P	R	R	5:11	175	24	Boston	3	1
Dobson, Joe	P	R	R	6:02	200	37	Chicago	5	5
Flowers, Bennett	P	R	R	6:04	195	26	Boston	1	4
Freeman, Hershell	P	R	R	6:02	215	25	Boston	1	4
Henry, Bill	P	L	L	6:02	180	26	Boston	5	5
Herrin, Tom	P	R	R	6:03	175	24	Baltimore	8	4
Hudson, Sid	P	R	R	6:04	185	37	Boston	6	9
Kiely, Leo	P	L	L	6:02	185	24	In Service	--	--
Kinder, Ellis	P	R	R	6:01	195	39	Boston	10	6
Nixon, Willard	P	L	R	6:03	192	25	Boston	4	8
Parnell, Mel	P	L	L	6:00	180	31	Boston	21	8
Sullivan, Franklin	P	R	R	6:07	220	24	Albany	9	6
Werle, Bill	P	L	L	6:02	192	31	Louisville	13	8

Name	Pos.	B	T	Hgt.	Wgt.	Age	1953 Club	Batting Average
Daley, Pete	C	R	R	6:00	195	24	Louisville	.256
Morton, Guy	C	R	R	6:02	200	22	Roanoke	.302
Niarhos, Gus	C	R	R	6:00	165	32	Boston	.200
White, Sammy	C	R	R	6:03	195	25	Boston	.273
Wilber, Del	C	R	R	6:03	208	35	Boston	.241
Baker, Floyd	Inf.	L	R	5:09	165	34	Boston	.263
Bolling, Milton	Inf.	R	R	6:01	175	23	Boston	.263
Consolo, Bill	Inf.	R	R	5:11	180	19	Boston	.215
Damman, Louis	Inf.	L	R	5:09	160	26	Louisville	.265
Furfaro, Vince	Inf.	R	R	5:09	186	22	Roanoke	.205
Gernert, Dick	Inf.	R	R	6:03	205	24	Boston	.253
Goodman, Billy	Inf.	L	R	5:12	165	28	Boston	.313
Kell, George	Inf.	R	R	5:10	175	31	Boston	.307
Lepcio, Ted	Inf.	R	R	5:10	176	23	Boston	.236
Broome, Robert	Of.	L	L	6:00	190	29	Louisville	.306
Evers, Hoot	Of.	R	R	6:02	180	33	Boston	.240
Jensen, Jack	Of.	R	R	5:11	190	27	Washington	.266
Maxwell, Charles	Of.	L	L	5:11	185	27	Louisville	.305
Olson, Karl	Of.	R	R	6:04	204	23	Boston	.123
Piersall, Jim	Of.	R	R	6:00	185	24	Boston	.272
Stephens, Gene	Of.	L	R	6:03	175	21	Boston	.204
Van Alstyne, Allen	Of.	R	R	6:01	190	24	Albany	.284
Williams, Ted	Of.	L	R	6:04	198	35	Boston	.407

CHICAGO WHITE SOX ROSTER

Manager: Paul Richards.   Coaches: Roger Cramer, Ray Berres, Luman Harris.

Name	Pos.	B	T	Hgt.	Wgt.	Age	1953 Club	Won	Lost
Aloma, Luis	P	R	R	6:02	190	30	Chicago	2	0
Consuegra, Sandy	P	R	R	5:11	165	33	Chicago	7	5
Dorish, Harry	P	R	R	5:11	202	30	Chicago	10	6
Fornieles, Mike	P	R	R	5:11	160	22	Chicago	8	7
Harshman, Jack	P	L	L	6:02	185	27	Nashville	23	7
Hurd, Tom	P	R	R	5:09	155	30	Memphis	17	11
Johnson, Connie	P	R	R	6:04	182	31	Chicago	4	4
Johnson, Don	P	R	R	6:02	200	27	Toronto	15	12
Keegan, Bob	P	R	R	6:02	190	31	Chicago	7	5
Keriazakos, Gus	P	R	R	6:03	190	22	Charleston	1	6
Pierce, Bill	P	L	L	5:10	165	27	Chicago	18	12
Strahs, Dick	P	R	R	6:00	196	29	Memphis	16	8
Trucks, Virgil	P	R	R	6:00	198	35	Chicago	20	10
Valentinetti, Vito	P	R	R	6:00	195	25	Charleston	0	1
Zilian, Al	P	R	R	6:01	180	29	Oklahoma City	16	12

Name	Pos.	B	T	Hgt.	Wgt.	Age	1953 Club	Batting Average
Lollar, Sherman	C	R	R	6:00	195	29	Chicago	.287
Sawatski, Carl	C	L	R	5:11	219	27	Cubs	.27
Sheely, Bud	C	L	R	6:00	207	32	Chicago	.217
Wilson, Bob	C	R	R	6:00	187	25	Chicago	.250
Boyd, Robert	Inf.	L	L	5:10	170	27	Chicago	.297
Carrasquel, Chico	Inf.	R	R	6:00	172	26	Chicago	.279
Elliott, Bob	Inf.	R	R	6:00	185	37	Chicago	.256
Fain, Ferris	Inf.	L	L	5:11	186	32	Chicago	.256
Fox, Nelson	Inf.	L	R	5:10	160	26	Chicago	.285
Kirrene, Joseph	Inf.	R	R	6:02	190	23	In Service	--
Landenberger, Ken	Inf.	L	L	6:03	200	26	Memphis	.256
Lipon, John	Inf.	R	R	5:11	171	31	Boston	.214
Marsh, Fred	Inf.	R	R	5:11	180	30	Chicago	.200
York, Earl	Inf.	L	L	6:02	195	27	Charleston	.246
Groth, John	Of.	R	R	6:00	180	27	Brown	.253
Marshall, Willard	Of.	L	R	6:00	190	33	Cincinnati	.266
Minoso, Orestes	Of.	R	R	5:11	175	30	Chicago	.313
Nicholas, Don	Of.	L	R	5:07	150	23	Charleston	.263
Rivera, Jim	Of.	R	R	6:00	189	32	Chicago	.259
Stewart, Ed	Of.	L	R	5:11	170	38	Chicago	.271
White, Ed	Of.	R	R	6:02	195	27	Memphis	.330
Wilson, Bill	Of.	R	R	6:03	195	25	Memphis	.311
Wright, Tom	Of.	L	R	6:00	190	30	Chicago	.250

CLEVELAND INDIANS ROSTER

Manager: Al Lopez.   Coaches: Tony Cuccinello, Mel Harder, Ralph Kress,, Bill Lobe.

Name	Pos.	B	T	Hgt.	Wgt.	Age	1953 Club	Won	Lost
Chakales, Bob	P	R	R	6:01	185	26	Indianapolis	4	2
Feller, Bob	P	R	R	6:01	190	35	Cleveland	10	7
Garcia, Mike	P	R	R	6:01	210	30	Cleveland	18	9
Hooper, Bob	P	R	R	5:11	200	31	Cleveland	5	4
Hoskins, Dave	P	L	R	6:01	180	28	Cleveland	9	3
Houtteman, Art	P	R	R	6:02	188	26	Cleveland	9	13
Lemon, Bob	P	L	R	6:00	185	33	Cleveland	21	15
Murszewski, Marian	P	L	L	6:03	175	23	Reading	10	5
Mossi, Don	P	L	L	6:01	185	24	Tulsa	12	11
Narleski, Ray	P	R	R	6:00	170	25	Indianapolis	6	8
Rodemoyer, Howard	P	R	R	5:11	180	24	Tulsa	9	8
Santiago, Jose	P	R	R	5:10	160	25	Dallas	13	11
Tomanek, Dick	P	L	L	6:00	165	23	Indianapolis	13	8
Upton, Bill	P	B	R	6:00	162	24	Indianapolis	10	6
Wheat, Leroy	P	R	R	6:04	175	24	Tulsa	0	1
Wight, Bill	P	L	L	6:02	190	32	Cleveland	2	4
Wynn, Early	P	B	R	6:00	200	34	Cleveland	17	12

Name	Pos.	B	T	Hgt.	Wgt.	Age	1953 Club	Batting Average
Ginsberg, Joe	C	L	R	5:11	180	27	Cleveland	.290
Grasso, Mickey	C	R	R	6:00	190	31	Washington	.209
Hegan, Jim	C	R	R	6:02	190	33	Cleveland	.217
Avila, Bob	Inf.	R	R	5:10	175	27	Cleveland	.286
Dente, Sam	Inf.	R	R	5:11	175	32	Indianapolis	.269
Easter, Luke	Inf.	L	R	6:05	235	32	Cleveland	.303
Friend, Owen	Inf.	R	R	6:01	180	27	Cleveland	.201
Glynn, Bill	Inf.	L	L	5:12	195	28	Cleveland	.243
Majeski, Hank	Inf.	R	R	5:09	185	38	Cleveland	.300
Nelson, Glenn	Inf.	L	L	5:11	175	29	Montreal	.310
Prentice, Bob	Inf.	R	R	6:00	178	25	Tulsa	.276
Rosen, Al	Inf.	R	R	5:11	185	29	Cleveland	.336
Strickland, George	Inf.	R	R	6:01	178	28	Cleveland	.284
Doby, Larry	Of.	L	R	6:01	180	29	Cleveland	.263
Kennedy, Bob	Of.	R	R	6:02	195	33	Cleveland	.236
Lemon, Jim	Of.	R	R	6:04	200	26	Indianapolis	.218
Mitchell, Dale	Of.	L	L	6:01	200	32	Cleveland	.300
Pope, Dave	Of.	L	R	5:10	165	28	Indianapolis	.287
Simpson, Harry	Of.	L	R	6:02	175	28	Cleveland	.227
Smith, Al	Of.	R	R	6:00	189	26	Cleveland	.240
Wade, Galeard	Of.	R	L	6:01	190	24	Fort Worth	.314
Westlake, Wally	Of.	R	R	6:00	195	33	Cleveland	.330

DETROIT TIGERS ROSTER

Manager: Fred Hutchinson. **Coaches:** Lynwood Rowe, Bob Swift, Johnny Hopp.

Name	Pos.	B	T	Hgt.	Wgt.	Age	1953 Club	Won	Lost
Aber, Albert	P	L	L	6:02	206	26	Detroit	5	4
Branca, Ralph	P	R	R	6:03	220	28	Detroit	4	7
Bunning, James	P	R	R	6:03	185	22	Little Rock	5	12
Cruze, Robert	P	R	L	5:11	175	24	In Service	--	--
Donovan, Richard	P	L	R	6:03	200	25	Atlanta	11	8
Foytack, Paul	P	R	R	5:11	175	23	Buffalo	13	10
Garver, Ned	P	R	R	5:10	180	28	Detroit	11	11
Gray, Ted	P	L	L	5:11	160	29	Detroit	10	15
Gromek, Steve	P	B	R	6:02	195	33	Detroit	7	9
Harrist, Earl	P	R	R	6:00	185	33	Buffalo	9	5
Herbert, Ray	P	R	R	5:11	185	24	Detroit	4	6
Hoeft, Bill	P	L	L	6:03	180	22	Detroit	9	14
Johnson, Milo	P	R	R	6:01	165	33	Little Rock	16	12
Jordan, Milton	P	R	R	6:02	190	25	Buffalo	12	1
Lary, Frank	P	R	R	5:11	180	23	Buffalo	17	11
Marlowe, Richard	P	R	R	6:02	165	24	Detroit	6	7
Miller, Robert	P	R	L	6:01	180	18	Detroit	1	2
Weik, Richard	P	R	R	6:05	185	26	Detroit	0	1

Name	Pos.	B	T	Hgt.	Wgt.	Age	1953 Club	Batting Average
Batts, Matt	C	R	R	5:11	200	30	Detroit	.278
Bucha, John	C	R	R	5:12	195	29	Detroit	.222
Streuli, Walter	C	R	R	6:02	192	18	Montgomery	.250
Baumgartner, John	Inf.	R	R	6:01	205	22	Little Rock	.305
Bertoia, Reno	Inf.	R	R	6:00	180	19	Little Rock	.288
Bolling, Frank	Inf.	R	R	6:01	175	22	Buffalo	.318
Boone, Ray	Inf.	R	R	6:00	182	30	Detroit	.296
Bright, Harry	Inf.	R	R	6:00	185	24	Memphis	.295
Dropo, Walter	Inf.	R	R	6:05	220	30	Detroit	.248
Hatfield, Fred	Inf.	L	R	6:01	171	29	Detroit	.254
Hicks, Clarence	Inf.	B	R	5:10	165	27	Buffalo	.295
Kress, Charles	Inf.	L	L	6:00	175	32	Rochester	.319
Kuenn, Harvey	Inf.	R	R	6:02	183	23	Detroit	.308
Little, Keith	Inf.	R	R	6:02	210	24	Montgomery	.238
Pesky, John	Inf.	L	R	5:09	165	34	Detroit	.292
Crawford, Rufus	Of.	R	R	6:01	185	26	Buffalo	.242
Delsing, Jim	Of.	L	R	5:11	178	28	Detroit	.288
Flemming, Fred	Of.	L	R	6:01	180	21	Durham	.211
Kaline, Albert	Of.	R	R	6:01	170	19	Detroit	.250
Linhart, Carl	Of.	L	R	5:11	175	24	Little Rock	.274
Lund, Don	Of.	R	R	6:00	200	30	Detroit	.257
Mullin, Pat	Of.	L	R	6:02	190	36	Detroit	.268
Nieman, Robert	Of.	R	R	5:11	190	27	Detroit	.281
Souchock, Steve	Of.	R	R	6:02	200	35	Detroit	.302
Tuttle, Bill	Of.	R	R	6:00	190	24	Buffalo	.276

NEW YORK YANKEES ROSTER

Manager: Casey Stengel.   Coaches: Bill Dickey, Jim Turner, Frank Crosetti, Ralph Houk.

Name	Pos.	B	T	Hgt.	Wgt.	Age	1953 Club	Won	Lost
Burnette, Wallace	P	R	R	6:01	175	24	Binghamton	21	10
Byrd, Harry	P	R	R	6:01	188	29	Philadelphia	11	20
Cicotte, Al	P	L	L	5:10	180	24	Birmingham	4	8
Ford, Ed	P	L	L	5:10	165	25	New York	18	6
Gorman, Tom	P	R	R	6:02	195	28	New York	4	5
Kraly, Steve	P	L	L	5:08	160	24	Binghamton	19	2
Kuzava, Bob	P	B	L	6:02	194	30	New York	6	5
Lopat, Ed	P	L	L	5:10	195	35	New York	16	4
McDonald, Jim	P	R	R	5:11	192	26	New York	9	7
Miller, Bill	P	L	L	6:00	182	26	Kansas City	5	6
Reynolds, Allie	P	R	R	6:00	200	37	New York	13	7
Sain, John	P	R	R	6:02	194	37	New York	14	7
Schallock, Art	P	L	L	5:09	160	28	Kansas City	9	3
Terry, Ralph	P	R	R	6:03	195	18	Free Agent	--	--
Wiesler, Bob	P	B	L	6:03	175	23	Kansas City	8	7
Wright, Mel	P	R	R	6:03	210	25	Kansas City	13	2

Name	Pos.	B	T	Hgt.	Wgt.	Age	1953 Club	Batting Average
Berberet, Louis	C	L	R	5:11	206	24	Binghamton	.251
Berra, Larry	C	L	R	5:08	194	28	New York	.296
Silvera, Charles	C	R	R	5:10	181	29	New York	.280
Smith, Hal	C	R	R	6:00	195	23	Birmingham	.311
Triandos, Gus	C	R	R	6:03	205	23	Birmingham	.368
Brideweser, Jim	Inf.	R	R	6:00	167	27	Syracuse	.282
Carey, Andy	Inf.	R	R	6:01	190	22	New York	.321
Coleman, Jerry	Inf.	R	R	5:11	168	29	New York	.200
Collins, Joe	Inf.	L	L	6:00	189	31	New York	.269
Leja, Frank	Inf.	L	L	6:04	210	18	Free Agent	--
Martin, Billy	Inf.	R	R	5:11	161	25	New York	.257
Miranda, Willie	Inf.	B	R	5:09	150	25	New York	.219
McDougald, Gil	Inf.	R	R	6:00	178	25	New York	.285
Rizzuto, Phil	Inf.	R	R	5:07	153	35	New York	.271
Robinson, Eddie	Inf.	L	R	6:03	210	33	Philadelphia	.247
Segrist, Kal	Inf.	R	R	6:00	180	22	Kansas City	.211
Bauer, Hank	Of.	R	R	6:00	188	31	New York	.304
Cerv, Bob	Of.	R	R	6:00	200	27	Kansas City	.317
Howard, Elston	Of.	R	R	6:02	191	25	Kansas City	.286
Mantle, Mickey	Of.	B	R	5:10	191	22	New York	.295
Noren, Irv	Of.	L	L	6:00	184	29	New York	.267
Schult, Art	Of.	R	R	6:04	210	25	Syracuse	.243
Tellinger, Emil	Of.	R	R	6:03	200	25	Birmingham	.316
Virdon, Bill	Of.	L	R	6:00	170	22	Birmingham	.317
Woodling, Gene	Of.	L	R	5:09	194	31	New York	.306

PHILADELPHIA ATHLETICS ROSTER

Manager: Eddie Joost. Coaches: Rollie Hemsley, Augie Galan, Wally Moses, Les McCrabb

Name	Pos.	B	T	Hgt.	Wgt.	Age	1953 Club	Won	Lost
Bishop, Charles	P	R	R	6:02	195	30	Philadelphia	3	14
Burtschy, Ed	P	R	R	6:03	208	31	Ottawa	12	7
Cain, Robert	P	L	L	6:00	165	29	Browns	4	10
Ditmar, Arthur	P	R	R	6:02	180	25	Savannah	7	0
Fricano, Marion	P	R	R	6:00	175	30	Philadelphia	9	12
Gray, John	P	R	R	6:02	200	26	Kansas City	9	7
Kellner, Alex	P	R	L	6:00	205	29	Philadelphia	11	12
Kellner, Walter	P	R	R	6:00	205	25	Williamsport	7	14
Martin, Morris	P	R	L	6:00	175	31	Philadelphia	10	12
Monahan, Ed	P	R	R	6:01	195	25	Philadelphia	0	0
Portocarrero, Al	P	R	R	6:03	195	22	In Service	--	--
Scheib, Carl	P	R	R	6:02	202	27	Philadelphia	3	7
Shantz, Bobby	P	R	L	5:07	150	28	Philadelphia	5	9
Trice, Robert	P	R	R	6:03	190	25	Ottawa	21	10

Name	Pos.	B	T	Hgt.	Wgt.	Age	1953 Club	Batting Average	
Astroth, Joe	C	R	R	5:10	187	31	Philadelphia	.296	
Minor, Harry	C	R	R	6:02	210	26	Savannah	.258	
Murray, Ray	C	R	R	6:03	200	34	Philadelphia	.284	
Robertson, Al	C	R	R	5:10	185	26	Kansas City	.278	
Bollweg, Don	Inf.	L	L	6:01	175	32	Yankees	.297	
DeMaestri, Joe	Inf.	R	R	6:00	174	25	Philadelphia	.255	
Finigan, James	Inf.	R	R	5:11	175	25	Binghamton	.303	
Giordano, Thomas	Inf.	R	R	6:00	175	27	Savannah	.281	
Jacobs, Forest	Inf.	R	R	5:09	155	28	Fort Worth	.282	
Joost, Eddie	Inf.	R	R	6:00	175	37	Philadelphia	.249	
Limmer, Louis	Inf.	L	L	6:02	190	27	Ottawa	.274	
Littrell, Jack	Inf.	R	R	5:11	170	25	Ottawa	.243	
Shantz, Wilmer	Inf.	R	R	6:01	160	23	Ottawa	.227	
McGhee, Edward	Of.	R	R	5:11	176	27	Philadelphia	.263	
Philley, Dave	Of.	B	R	6:00	190	33	Philadelphia	.303	
Power, Victor	Of.	R	R	6:00	170	23	Kansas City	.349	
Renna, Bill	Of.	R	R	6:02	220	27	Yankees	.314	
Valo, Elmer	Of.	L	R	5:10	189	33	Philadelphia	.224	
Zernial, Gus	Of.	R	R	6:03	210	30	Philadelphia	.284	

WASHINGTON SENATORS ROSTER

Manager: Bucky Harris. Coaches: George Myatt, Joe Haynes, Joe Fitzgerald.

Name	Pos.	B	T	Hgt.	Wgt.	Age	1953 Club	Win	Lost
Clark, Larry	P	R	R	6:00	170	24	Chattanooga	4	4
Dixon, John	P	R	R	6:03	205	29	Washington	5	8
Lane, Jerry	P	R	R	6:03	195	28	Chattanooga	11	10
Marrero, Connie	P	R	R	5:06	165	38	Washington	8	7
McDermott, Mickey	P	L	L	6:04	190	25	Boston	18	10
Porterfield, Bob	P	R	R	6:00	190	29	Washington	22	10
Ross, Robert	P	R	L	6:00	170	26	In Service	--	--
Sanchez, Paul	P	R	R	6:00	150	23	Chattanooga	9	11
Schmitz, John	P	R	L	6:02	168	33	Washington	2	7
Shea, Frank	P	R	R	6:00	205	31	Washington	12	7
Stewart, Veston	P	L	L	6:00	154	23	Chattanooga	14	10
Stobbs, Charles	P	L	L	6:00	188	24	Washington	11	8
Stone, Dean	P	L	L	6:04	205	23	Chattanooga	8	10

Name	Pos.	B	T	Hgt.	Wgt.	Age	1953 Club	Batting Average
FitzGerald, Ed	C	R	R	6:00	180	29	Washington	.250
Oldis, Bob	C	R	R	6:01	186	24	Chattanooga	.266
Sacka, Frank	C	R	R	6:00	195	29	Chattanooga	.292
Tipton, Joe	C	R	R	5:11	188	32	Cleveland	.229
Becquer, Julio	Inf.	L	L	6:00	162	22	Havana	.296
Davalillo, Pompeyo	Inf.	R	R	5:04	145	22	Charlotte	.305
Hoderlein, Mel	Inf.	R	R	5:10	180	29	Washington	.191
Roig, Tony	Inf.	R	R	6:01	180	24	Chattanooga	.303
Runnels, Pete	Inf.	L	R	5:11	170	26	Washington	.257
Snyder, Jerry	Inf.	R	R	5:11	165	24	Chattanooga	.307
Terwilliger, Wayne	Inf.	R	R	5:11	170	27	Washington	.252
Vernon, Mickey	Inf.	L	L	6:02	180	35	Washington	.337
Yost, Eddie	Inf.	R	R	5:10	180	27	Washington	.272
Barmes, Bruce	Of.	L	R	5:08	165	24	Chattanooga	.320
Busby, Jim	Of.	R	R	6:01	175	27	Washington	.312
Campos, Frank	Of.	L	L	5:11	180	27	Charleston	.294
Coan, Gil	Of.	L	R	6:00	180	29	Washington	.198
Delis, Juan	Of.	R	R	5:11	170	26	Havana	.287
Paula, Carlos	Of.	R	R	6:03	195	26	Havana	.309
Porter, David	Of.	L	L	6:00	170	23	In Service	--
Scull, Angel	Of.	R	R	5:08	162	23	Charleston	.286
Thomas, Kite	Of.	R	R	6:02	195	29	Washington	.215
Umphlett, Tom	Of.	R	R	6:02	180	22	Boston	.283
Vollmer, Clyde	Of.	R	R	6:02	190	32	Washington	.260

BROOKLYN DODGERS ROSTER

Manager: Walter Alston.   Coaches: Jake Pitler, Billy Herman, Ted Lyons

Name	Pos.	B	T	Hgt.	Wgt.	Age	1953 Club	Won	Lost
Bessent, Don	P	B	T	6:00	175	23	St. Paul	11	10
Black, Joe	P	R	R	6:02	220	30	Brooklyn	6	3
Coleman, Hamp	P	R	R	6:02	175	26	Montreal	8	4
Erskine, Carl	P	R	R	5:09	165	27	Brooklyn	20	6
Hughes, Jim	P	R	R	6:01	200	30	Brooklyn	4	3
Labine, Clem	P	R	R	6:00	180	27	Brooklyn	11	6
LaSorda, Tom	P	L	L	5:10	175	26	Montreal	17	8
Lehman, Ken	P	L	L	6:00	160	25	Montreal	13	9
Loes, Billy	P	R	R	6:01	165	24	Brooklyn	14	8
Meyer, Russ	P	B	R	6:01	175	29	Brooklyn	15	5
Mickens, Glenn	P	R	R	6:00	170	23	Fort Worth	8	5
Milliken, Bob	P	R	R	6:00	190	27	Brooklyn	8	4
Moore, Ray	P	R	R	6:00	195	27	St. Paul	11	14
Negray, Ron	P	R	R	6:01	170	24	St. Paul	10	12
Newcombe, Don	P	L	R	6:04	230	28	In Service	--	--
Palica, Erv	P	R	R	6:01	190	26	Brooklyn	0	0
Podres, John	P	L	L	6:00	170	22	Brooklyn	9	4
Roe, Preacher	P	R	L	6:01	165	36	Brooklyn	11	3
Roebuck, Ed	P	R	R	6:02	185	23	Montreal	15	14
Wade, Ben	P	R	R	6:03	200	31	Brooklyn	7	5
Wojey, Pete	P	R	R	6:00	185	31	Fort Worth	14	9

Name	Pos.	B	T	Hgt.	Wgt.	Age	1953 Club	Batting Average
Campanella, Roy	C	R	R	5:08	205	33	Brooklyn	.312
Staples, Ken	C	R	R	5:08	175	27	Fort Worth	.225
Thompson, Chas.	C	L	R	5:11	180	29	Montreal	.293
Walker, Al	C	L	R	6:01	185	28	Brooklyn	.242
Baxes, Jim	Inf.	R	R	6:01	190	25	Fort Worth	.269
Belardi, Wayne	Inf.	L	L	6:01	185	23	Brooklyn	.239
Cox, Billy	Inf.	R	R	5:08	150	35	Brooklyn	.291
Gilliam, Jim	Inf.	B	R	5:11	175	25	Brooklyn	.278
Hoak, Don	Inf.	R	R	6:00	165	26	Montreal	.269
Hodges, Gil	Inf.	R	R	6:02	200	30	Brooklyn	.302
Reese, Pee Wee	Inf.	R	R	5:10	175	35	Brooklyn	.260
Robinson, Jack	Inf.	R	R	6:00	205	35	Brooklyn	.329
Zimmer, Don	Inf.	R	R	5:09	165	23	St. Paul	.300
Amoros, Ed	Of.	L	L	5:08	170	22	Montreal	.353
Antonello, Bill	Of.	R	R	5:11	185	27	Brooklyn	.163
Bartz, Ted	Of.	R	R	6:03	190	28	St. Paul	.280
Cimoli, Gino	Of.	R	R	6:01	180	25	St. Paul	.262
Furillo, Carl	Of.	R	R	6:00	190	32	Brooklyn	.344
Morasco, Vic	Of.	R	R	5:07	175	25	Fort Worth	.306
Moryn, Walt	Of.	L	R	6:02	205	28	St. Paul	.306
Shuba, George	Of.	L	R	6:00	180	29	Brooklyn	.254
Snider, Duke	Of.	L	R	6:00	190	27	Brooklyn	.336
Thompson, Don	Of.	L	L	6:00	185	30	Brooklyn	.242
Williams, Dick	Of.	R	R	6:00	190	25	Brooklyn	.242

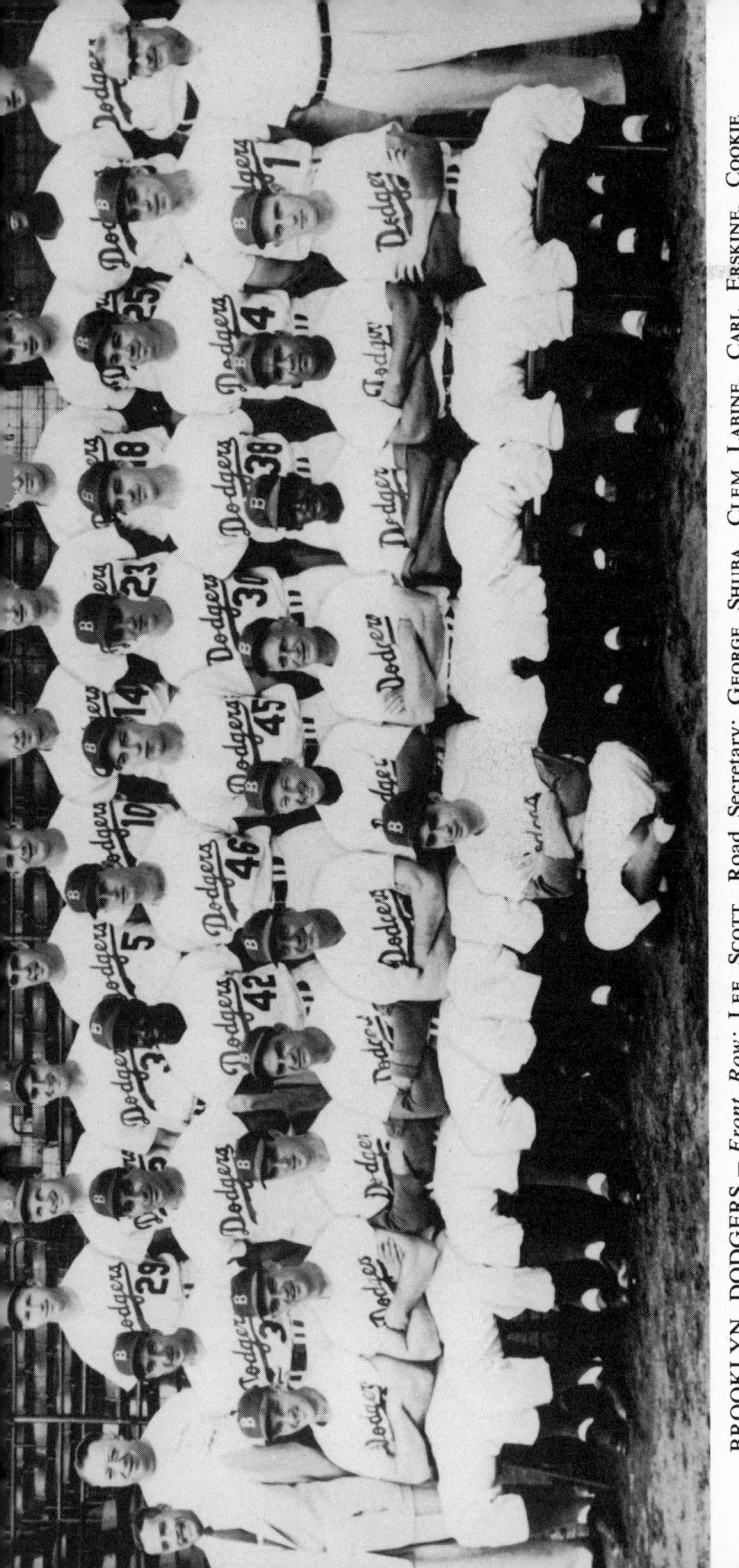

BROOKLYN DODGERS – *Front Row:* LEE SCOTT, Road Secretary; GEORGE SHUBA, CLEM LABINE, CARL ERSKINE, COOKIE LAVAGETTO, Coach; BILLY HERMAN, Coach; CHUCK DRESSEN, Manager; JAKE PITLER, Coach; JUNIOR GILLIAM, ROY CAMPANELLA, RUSS MEYER. *Center Row:* JOHN GRIFFIN, Clubhouse manager; BILLY COX, CARL FURILLO, JACKIE ROBINSON, BEN WADE, JOHN PODRES, BILLY LOES, DICK WILLIAMS, DUKE SNIDER, PEEWEE REESE, HAROLD (Doc) WENDLER, Trainer. *Back Row:* DON THOMPSON, BOBBY MORGAN, BILL ANTONELLO, WAYNE BELARDI, RUBE WALKER, GIL HODGES, ERV PALICA, JIM HUGHES, BOB MILLIKEN, JOE BLACK, PREACHER ROE. *Seated in Front:* CHARLIE DI GIOVANNI, *Bat Boy.*

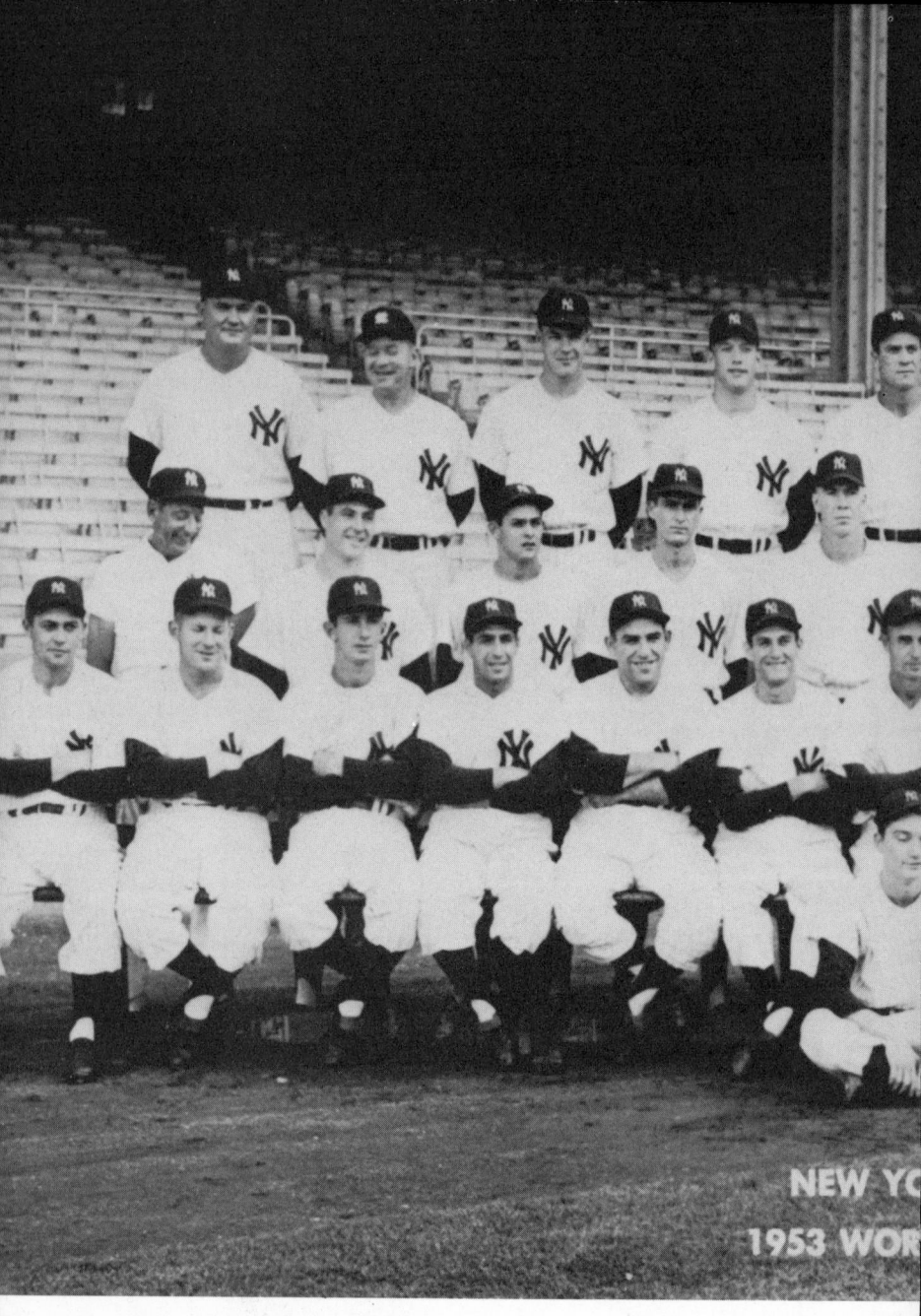

Back Row: JOHNNY MIZE, ED LOPAT, ANDY CAREY, MICKEY MANTLE, H
COLLINS. *Second Row:* GUS MAUCH, Trainer; JIM McDONALD, WI
RENNA, GUS TRIANDOS, VIC RASCHI. *Front Row:* ART SCHALLOCK, WH
CROSETTI, Coach; CASEY STENGEL, Manager; BILL DICKEY, Coach;

ER, RALPH HOUK, JOHNNY SAIN, DON BOLLWEG, ALLIE REYNOLDS, JOE
ANDA, JERRY COLEMAN, BOB KUZAVA, BILL MILLER, TOM GORMAN, BILL
D, BILLY MARTIN, PHIL RIZZUTO, LARRY BERRA, STEVE KRALY, FRANK
NER, *Coach;* GIL McDOUGALD, IRV NOREN, GENE WOODLING, CHARLES
ERA. *Bat Boys:* JOE CARRIERI *and* IGGY MANZIDELIS.

PHIL ("Scooter") RIZZUTO

Shortstop for New York Yankees, Four-Time Major League All-Star

EDDIE STANKY

Manager of the St. Louis Cardinals, Manager of the Year in 1952

CHICAGO CUBS ROSTER

Manager: Phil Cavarretta. Coaches: Ray Blades, Dutch Leonard, Bob Scheffing.

Name	Pos.	B	T	Hgt.	Wgt.	Age	1953 Club	Won	Lost
Brosnan, Jim	P	R	R	6:04	197	24	Springfield	4	17
Church, Bubba	P	R	R	6:00	180	28	Chicago	7	8
Elston, Don	P	R	R	6:00	165	25	Springfield	9	17
Hacker, Warren	P	R	R	6:01	180	29	Chicago	12	19
Hartig, Bob	P	R	R	6:02	200	23	Des Moines	4	9
Klippstein, John	P	R	R	6:01	174	26	Chicago	10	11
Kuncl, Joe	P	R	R	6:01	180	27	Macon	16	18
Lown, Omar	P	R	R	6:00	181	30	Chicago	8	7
Minner, Paul	P	L	L	6:04	204	31	Chicago	12	15
Moisan, William	P	L	R	6:01	170	29	Los Angeles	10	11
Pollet, Howie	P	L	L	6:01	175	33	Chicago	6	7
Pyecha, John	P	R	R	6:05	200	22	Springfield	7	11
Rush, Bob	P	R	R	6:05	204	28	Chicago	9	14
Watkins, Don	P	R	R	6:00	179	28	Des Moines	14	9
Willis, Jim	P	L	R	6:03	175	27	Chicago	2	1
Zick, Bob	P	L	R	6:01	168	27	Des Moines	14	12

Name	Pos.	B	T	Hgt.	Wgt.	Age	1953 Club	Batting Average
Garagiola, Joe	C	L	R	6:00	190	28	Chicago	.262
McCullough, Clyde	C	R	R	5:11	190	36	Chicago	.258
Meek, Harold	C	R	R	6:02	180	24	Springfield	.215
Murray, Bob	C	R	R	6:01	195	25	Des Moines	.231
Tappe, Elvin	C	R	R	5:11	180	25	Los Angeles	.281
Baker, Gene	Inf.	R	R	6:01	170	28	Los Angeles	.284
Banks, Ernie	Inf.	R	R	6:01	180	23	Chicago	.314
Edwards, Bruce	Inf.	R	R	5:08	194	31	Springfield	.282
Fondy, Dee	Inf.	L	L	6:03	196	30	Chicago	.310
Jackson, Ransom	Inf.	R	R	6:02	179	28	Chicago	.285
Kitsos, Chris	Inf.	B	R	5:09	165	25	Des Moines	.221
Miksis, Eddie	Inf.	R	R	6:00	186	28	Chicago	.251
Serena, Bill	Inf.	R	R	5:10	181	30	Chicago	.251
Smalley, Roy	Inf.	R	R	6:03	191	28	Chicago	.249
Baumholtz, Frank	Of.	L	L	5:10	176	35	Chicago	.306
Brinkopf, Leon	Of.	R	R	6:00	180	28	Vol. Ret. List	--
Jeffcoat, Hal	Of.	R	R	5:11	186	30	Chicago	.234
Kiner, Ralph	Of.	R	R	6:02	190	32	Chicago	.279
Marquez, Luis	Of.	R	R	5:10	190	28	Toledo	.292
McDaniel, Jim	Of.	R	R	6:01	181	21	Des Moines	.227
Robertson, Don	Of.	L	L	5:09	175	23	In Service	--
Sauer, Henry	Of.	R	R	6:03	199	35	Chicago	.263
Talbot, Bob	Of.	R	R	6:00	170	26	Los Angeles	.287
Thurlby, Burdette	Of.	L	R	6:02	190	26	Des Moines	.263

CINCINNATI REDLEGS ROSTER

Manager: Birdie Tebbetts. Coaches: Dick Bartell, Tom Ferrick.

Name	Pos.	B	T	Hgt.	Wgt.	Age	1953 Club	Won	Lost
Acker, Tom	P	R	R	6:04	210	24	In Service	--	--
Baczewski, Fred	P	L	L	6:02	192	27	Cincinnati	11	4
Collum, Jackie	P	L	L	5:07	160	26	Cincinnati	7	11
Crimian, Jack	P	R	R	5:11	170	27	Rochester	13	5
Fisher, Maurice	P	R	R	6:05	200	23	Columbia	16	7
Fowler, Arthur	P	R	R	5:11	180	30	Atlanta	18	10
Judson, Howard	P	R	R	6:01	195	28	Tulsa	11	0
Kelly, Robert	P	R	R	6:00	180	26	Cincinnati	1	3
King, Clyde	P	R	R	6:01	183	28	Cincinnati	3	6
Martin, Barney	P	R	R	5:11	170	31	Columbia	17	6
Melton, James	P	R	R	6:02	195	23	Mobile	10	10
Minarcin, Rudy	P	R	R	6:00	195	24	In Service	--	--
Nuxhall, Joe	P	L	L	6:03	220	25	Cincinnati	9	11
Perkowski, Harry	P	L	L	6:02	190	31	Cincinnati	12	11
Podbielan, Bud	P	R	R	6:02	180	30	Cincinnati	6	16
Powell, Bill	P	L	R	6:02	195	29	Charleston	14	9
Raffensberger, Ken	P	R	L	6:01	205	36	Cincinnati	7	14
Rogovin, Saul	P	R	R	6:03	205	30	White Sox	7	12
Ross, Cliff	P	L	L	6:04	195	25	Tulsa	7	8
Savransky, Moe	P	L	L	5:11	175	25	In Service	--	--
Smith, Frank	P	R	R	6:03	200	26	Cincinnati	8	1
Valentine, Hal	P	R	R	6:01	203	24	Columbia	13	6
Wehmeier, Herm	P	R	R	6:03	200	27	Cincinnati	1	6
Zuverink, George	P	R	R	6:04	195	27	Indianapolis	13	8

Name	Pos.	B	T	Hgt.	Wgt.	Age	1953 Club	Batting Average
Bailey, Ed	C	L	R	6:02	205	23	Tulsa	.243
Baldwin, Frank	C	R	R	5:11	195	25	Cincinnati	.100
Kinaman, Dick	C	R	R	6:00	190	28	Syracuse	.232
Landrith, Hobie	C	L	R	5:08	170	24	Cincinnati	.240
Seminick, Andy	C	R	R	5:10	187	33	Cincinnati	.235
Adams, Bobby	Inf.	R	R	5:10	170	32	Cincinnati	.275
Bridges, Rocky	Inf.	R	R	5:08	175	26	Cincinnati	.227
Harmon, Charley	Inf.	R	R	6:02	175	28	Tulsa	.311
Hatton, Gene	Inf.	R	R	6:01	175	24	Columbia	.260
Hatton, Gray	Inf.	L	R	5:09	175	31	Cincinnati	.233
Krsnich, Rocco	Inf.	R	R	6:01	175	26	White Sox	.202
Kluszewski, Ted	Inf.	L	L	6:02	225	29	Cincinnati	.316
McMillan, Roy	Inf.	R	R	5:11	170	23	Cincinnati	.233
Ryan, Connie	Inf.	R	R	5:11	175	34	Philadelphia	.296
Temple, John	Inf.	R	R	5:11	175	24	Cincinnati	.264
Bell, Gus	Of.	L	R	6:02	190	25	Cincinnati	.300
Bolger, Jim	Of.	R	R	6:02	180	22	Columbia	.301
Borkowski, Bob	Of.	R	R	6:00	180	27	Cincinnati	.269
Escalera, Nino	Of.	L	L	5:10	165	24	Tulsa	.305
Greengrass, Jim	Of.	R	R	6:01	200	26	Cincinnati	.285
Hazle, Bob	Of.	L	R	6:00	190	23	Tulsa	.272
Merriman, Lloyd	Of.	L	L	6:00	195	29	In Service	--
Post, Wally	Of.	R	R	6:01	190	24	Indianapolis	.289
Szekely, Joe	Of.	R	R	5:11	180	27	Shreveport	.273

MILWAUKEE BRAVES ROSTER

Manager: Charley Grimm.   Coaches: Johnny Cooney, Bucky Walters, Bob Keely.

Name	Pos.	B	T	Hgt.	Wgt.	Age	1953 Club	Won	Lost
Buhl, Bob	P	R	R	6:02	180	24	Milwaukee	13	8
Burdette, Lew	P	R	R	6:02	180	26	Milwaukee	15	5
Cole, Dave	P	R	R	6:02	175	22	Milwaukee	0	1
Conley, Gene	P	R	R	6:08	225	22	Toledo	23	9
Crone, Ray	P	R	R	6:02	165	21	Jacksonville	19	11
Denney, Bill	P	R	R	6:00	175	21	Lincoln	8	8
Jay, Joe	P	R	R	6:01	178	18	Milwaukee	1	0
Johnson, Ben	P	R	R	6:00	176	22	In Service	--	--
Johnson, Ernie	P	R	R	6:04	195	29	Milwaukee	4	3
Jolly, Dave	P	R	R	6:00	160	28	Milwaukee	0	1
Nichols, Chet	P	R	L	6:02	165	23	In Service	--	--
Paine, Phil	P	R	R	6:02	175	23	In Service	--	--
Spahn, Warren	P	L	L	6:00	175	32	Milwaukee	23	7
Thompson, Glenn	P	R	R	6:00	177	24	Toledo	8	6
Wilson, Jim	P	R	R	6:01	195	31	Milwaukee	4	9

Name	Pos.	B	T	Hgt.	Wgt.	Age	1953 Club	Batting Average
Calderone, Sam	C	R	R	5:10	185	27	New York	.222
Casey, Bill	C	R	R	5:10	180	23	Jacksonville	.253
Crandall, Del	C	R	R	6:02	185	23	Milwaukee	.272
Laguna, Ted	C	R	R	5:11	190	20	Hagerstown	.289
Linden, Walter	C	R	R	6:01	190	28	Lincoln	.220
Adcock, Joe	Inf.	R	R	6:04	210	25	Milwaukee	.285
Dittmer, Jack	Inf.	L	R	6:01	175	25	Milwaukee	.266
Logan, Johnny	Inf.	R	R	5:11	175	26	Milwaukee	.273
Mathews, Ed	Inf.	L	R	6:02	185	22	Milwaukee	.302
O'Connell, Danny	Inf.	R	R	5:11	180	24	Pittsburgh	.294
Roach, Mel	Inf.	R	R	6:00	175	20	Milwaukee	.000
Sisti, Sibby	Inf.	R	R	5:11	185	33	Milwaukee	.227
Bruton, Bill	Of.	L	R	6:01	169	23	Milwaukee	.250
Metkovich, George	Of.	L	L	6:01	185	32	Chicago	.212
Morgan, Collins	Of.	L	R	6:01	180	21	Jacksonville	.272
Pafko, Andy	Of.	R	R	6:00	190	33	Milwaukee	.297
Pendleton, Jim	Of.	R	R	6:00	185	27	Milwaukee	.299
Queen, Billy	Of.	R	R	6:00	178	24	Toledo	.281
Sinovic, Dick	Of.	R	R	6:01	190	26	Atlanta	.342
Thomson, Bob	Of.	R	R	6:02	190	30	New York	.288
Thorpe, Bob	Of.	R	R	6:01	182	28	Milwaukee	.162
Whisenant, Pete	Of.	R	R	6:02	190	23	Atlanta	.266

NEW YORK GIANTS ROSTER

Manager: Leo Durocher. **Coaches:** Fred Fitzsimmons, Herman Franks, Frank Shellenback.

Name	Pos.	B	T	Hgt.	Wgt.	Age	1953 Club	Won	Lost
Atonelli, John	P	R	L	6:01	183	23	Milwaukee	12	12
Corwin, Al	P	R	R	6:01	170	27	New York	6	4
Fowler, Charles	P	R	R	6:02	175	24	In Service	--	--
Gomez, Ruben	P	R	R	6:00	175	26	New York	13	11
Grissom, Marvin	P	R	R	6:03	195	36	New York	4	2
Hearn, Jim	P	R	R	6:03	200	31	New York	9	12
Jansen, Larry	P	R	R	6:02	190	33	New York	11	16
Koslo, Dave	P	L	L	5:11	185	34	New York	6	12
Liddle, John	P	L	L	5:10	165	27	Milwaukee	7	6
Maglie, Sal	P	R	R	6:02	190	37	New York	8	9
McCall, John	P	L	L	6:00	180	28	San Francisco	12	7
Modica, Pete	P	R	R	6:00	155	31	Nashville	9	5
Nicholas, Harry	P	R	R	6:02	180	24	Minneapolis	7	13
Picone, Mario	P	R	R	5:10	190	27	Minneapolis	14	8
Wilhelm, Hoyt	P	R	R	6:00	190	30	New York	7	8
Worthington, Allan	P	R	R	6:02	205	24	New York	4	8

Name	Pos.	B	T	Hgt.	Wgt.	Age	1953 Club	Batting Average	
Katt, Ray	C	R	R	6:02	200	26	Minneapolis	.326	
Noble, Ray	C	R	R	5:11	190	32	New York	.206	
St. Claire, Ebba	C	B	R	6:01	219	32	Milwaukee	.200	
Westrum, Wes	C	R	R	5:11	190	31	New York	.224	
Castleman, Foster	Inf.	R	R	6:00	175	23	Minneapolis	.368	
Dark, Alvin	Inf.	R	R	5:11	185	31	New York	.300	
Gardner, William	Inf.	R	R	6:00	170	26	Nashville	.308	
Gilbert, Harold	Inf.	L	R	6:03	185	25	New York	.169	
Harris, Gail	Inf.	L	L	6:00	195	22	Nashville	.281	
Hofman, Bob	Inf.	R	R	5:11	175	28	New York	.266	
Klaus, Bill	Inf.	L	R	5:09	160	24	Toledo	.275	
Lockman, Whitey	Inf.	L	R	6:02	180	27	New York	.295	
Samford, Ronald	Inf.	R	R	5:09	165	24	Minneapolis	.280	
Spencer, Daryl	Inf.	R	R	6:02	190	24	New York	.208	
Thompson, Hank	Inf.	L	L	5:10	175	28	New York	.302	
Williams, Dave	Inf.	R	R	5:10	165	25	New York	.297	
Berns, Ray	Of.	L	R	5:11	180	26	Minneapolis	.283	
Gentry, Harvey	Of.	L	R	6:00	170	27	Nashville	.294	
Irvin, Monte	Of.	R	R	6:01	195	33	New York	.329	
Mays, Willie	Of.	R	R	5:11	170	22	In Service	--	
Mueller, Don	Of.	L	R	6:00	180	27	New York	.333	
Rhodes, Jim	Of.	L	R	6:00	180	26	New York	.233	
Taylor, Bill	Of.	L	R	6:04	210	24	Nashville	.350	

PHILADELPHIA PHILLIES ROSTER

Manager: Steve O'Neill.   Coaches: Benny Bengough, Cy Perkins, Eddie Mayo.

Name	Pos.	B	T	Hgt.	Wgt.	Age	1953 Club	Won	Lost
Casagrande, Tom	P	L	L	6:03	210	23	Schenectady	16	7
Dickson, Murry	P	R	R	5:11	160	37	Pittsburgh	10	19
Drews, Karl	P	R	R	6:04	198	33	Philadelphia	9	10
Greenwood, Robert	P	R	R	6:04	190	26	Baltimore	11	12
Kipper, Thornton	P	R	R	6:03	190	25	Philadelphia	3	3
Konstanty, Jim	P	R	R	6:02	195	37	Philadelphia	14	10
Lindell, John	P	R	R	6:05	220	37	Pittsburgh	6	17
Markell, Harry	P	R	R	6:02	209	30	Syracuse	11	17
Miller, Bob	P	R	R	6:03	194	26	Philadelphia	8	9
Mrozinski, Ronald	P	R	L	5:11	160	23	Baltimore	2	5
Penson, Paul	P	R	R	6:01	185	22	Free Agent	--	--
Qualters, Tom	P	R	R	6:01	190	19	Philadelphia	0	0
Ridzik, Steve	P	R	R	5:11	170	25	Philadelphia	9	6
Roberts, Robin	P	B	R	6:02	190	27	Philadelphia	23	16
Sanford, John	P	R	R	5:11	175	23	Baltimore	14	13
Simmons, Curt	P	L	L	6:00	175	24	Philadelphia	16	13

Name	Pos.	B	T	Hgt.	Wgt.	Age	1953 Club	Batting Average
Burgess, Forrest	C	L	R	5:08	181	27	Philadelphia	.292
Lonnett, Joe	C	B	R	5:10	180	27	Baltimore	.154
Lopata, Stan	C	R	R	6:02	210	28	Philadelphia	.239
Sandlock, Mike	C	B	R	6:01	185	37	Pittsburgh	.231
Silvestri, Ken	C	B	R	6:01	200	37	Philadelphia	.000
Hamner, Granville	Inf.	R	R	5:11	160	27	Philadelphia	.276
Jones, Willie	Inf.	R	R	6:01	192	28	Philadelphia	.225
Kazanski, Ted	Inf.	R	R	6:01	175	20	Philadelphia	.217
Micelotta, Robert	Inf.	R	R	5:11	170	25	Terre Haute	.297
Torgeson, Earl	Inf.	L	L	6:03	180	30	Philadelphia	.274
Waitkus, Eddie	Inf.	L	L	6:01	175	33	Philadelphia	.291
Young, Richard	Inf.	B	R	5:11	175	25	Louisville	.236
Ashburn, Richie	Of.	L	R	5:11	170	27	Philadelphia	.330
Bowman, Robert	Of.	R	R	6:01	194	22	Schenectady	.257
Clark, Mel	Of.	R	R	6:00	180	27	Philadelphia	.298
Ennis, Del	Of.	R	R	6:00	195	28	Philadelphia	.285
Jok, Stanley	Of.	R	R	6:01	205	27	Baltimore	.279
Mayo, John	Of.	L	R	6:01	190	27	Baltimore	.286
Palys, Stanley	Of.	R	R	6:00	187	23	Spokane	.331
Schell, Danny	Of.	R	R	6:01	195	26	Schenectady	.333
Wyrostek, John	Of.	L	R	6:02	185	34	Philadelphia	.271

PITTSBURGH PIRATES ROSTER

Manager: Fred Haney. Coaches: John Fitzpatrick, Clyde Sukeforth, Sam Narron, Hans Wagner (Emeritus)

Name	Pos.	B	T	Hgt.	Wgt.	Age	1953 Club	Won	Lost
Churn, Clarence	P	R	R	6:02	205	24	Charleston, S.C.	5	5
Face, Elroy	P	R	R	5:08	155	26	Pittsburgh	6	8
Friend, Robert	P	R	R	6:00	190	23	Pittsburgh	8	11
Garber, Robert	P	R	R	6:01	190	25	Charleston, S.C.	2	1
Hall, Robert	P	R	R	6:02	195	30	Pittsburgh	3	6
Hansen, Andy	P	R	R	6:03	190	29	Philadelphia	0	2
Hetki, John	P	R	R	6:01	205	31	Pittsburgh	3	6
Hogue, Calvin	P	R	R	6:01	195	26	Oklahoma City	7	5
King, Nelson	P	R	R	6:06	185	26	Denver	15	3
LaPalme, Paul	P	L	L	5:11	184	29	Pittsburgh	8	16
Lassalle, Larry	P	R	L	5:11	188	24	Jacksonville	19	5
Law, Verne	P	R	R	6:03	200	24	In Service	--	--
O'Donnell, George	P	R	R	6:02	175	24	Hollywood	20	12
Pettit, Paul	P	L	L	6:02	205	22	Pittsburgh	1	2
Pritts, Harry	P	L	L	6:00	170	24	Denver	9	5
Purkey, Robert	P	R	R	6:02	175	24	New Orleans	11	13
Schultz, Robert	P	R	L	6:03	200	30	New Orleans	9	4
Surkont, Matthew	P	R	R	6:00	210	31	Milwaukee	11	5
Thies, Vernon	P	R	R	5:11	170	26	Denver	16	6
Waugh, James	P	R	R	6:03	185	20	Pittsburgh	4	5
Waters, Fred	P	L	L	5:11	185	26	Lincoln	10	10
Yochim, Leonard	P	L	L	6:02	195	25	New Orleans	14	14

Name	Pos.	B	T	Hgt.	Wgt.	Age	1953 Club	Batting Average
Atwell, Toby	C	L	R	5:10	185	30	Pittsburgh	.239
Cooper, Walker	C	R	R	6:03	195	38	Milwaukee	.219
Hall, William	C	L	R	5:11	165	25	New Orleans	.281
Janowicz, Victor	C	R	R	5:09	190	24	Pittsburgh	.252
Koback, Nicholas	C	R	R	6:00	187	18	Pittsburgh	.125
Naton, Pete	C	R	R	6:01	200	22	Charleston, S. C.	.205
Shepard, Jack	C	R	R	6:02	195	22	Pittsburgh	.250
Cole, Richard	Inf.	R	R	6:02	175	27	Pittsburgh	.272
Coogan, Dale	Inf.	L	L	6:01	190	24	In Service	--
Freese, George	Inf.	R	R	6:00	190	27	Springfield,Mass.	.266
Gordon, Sid	Inf.	R	R	5:10	180	35	Milwaukee	.274
Grunwald, Alfred	Inf.	L	L	6:03	180	24	New Orleans	.293
Hall, Richard	Inf.	R	R	6:06	205	23	Waco	.246
Lohrke, Jack	Inf.	R	R	5:12	175	30	Baltimore	.194
Long, Richard	Inf.	L	L	6:04	210	28	Hollywood	.272
Pellagrini, Edward	Inf.	R	R	5:09	160	35	Pittsburgh	.253
Roberts, Curtis	Inf.	R	R	5:08	165	24	Denver	.291
Smith, Paul	Inf.	L	L	5:09	165	23	Pittsburgh	.283
Smith, Richard	Inf.	R	R	5:08	160	26	New Orleans	.281
Ward, Preston	Inf.	L	L	6:04	198	26	Pittsburgh	.215
Abrams, Calvin	Of.	L	L	6:00	185	30	Pittsburgh	.286
Bernier, Carlos	Of.	R	R	5:09	180	25	Pittsburgh	.213
Davis, Robert	Of.	R	R	5:11	170	25	Pittsburgh	.205
Henley, Gail	Of.	L	R	5:10	175	24	New Orleans	.290
Hermanski, Gene	Of.	L	R	5:11	190	32	Pittsburgh	.167
Jethroe, Sam	Of.	B	R	6:01	178	32	Toledo	.309
Lynch, Gerald	Of.	L	R	6:01	180	23	Norfolk	.333
Rice, Harold	Of.	L	R	6:02	195	30	Pittsburgh	.310
Thomas, Frank	Of.	R	R	6:03	200	24	Pittsburgh	.255

Manager: Eddie Stanky. Coaches: Mike Ryba, John Riddle, Bill Posedel.

Name	Pos.	B	T	Hgt.	Wgt.	Age	1953 Club	Won	Lost
Blaylock, Gary	P	R	R	6:00	175	22	Columbus, O.	7	13
Boyer, Cloyd	P	R	R	6:01	188	26	Houston	4	1
Brazle, Alpha	P	L	L	6:03	185	39	St. Louis	6	7
Deal, Ellis	P	R	R	5:11	185	30	Rochester	17	8
Haddix, Harvey	P	L	L	5:09	155	28	St. Louis	20	9
Jordan, Niles	P	L	L	6:00	180	28	Rochester	8	1
Lint, Royce	P	L	L	6:01	150	33	Portland	22	10
Luna, Memo	P	L	L	6:00	168	23	San Diego	17	12
Miller, Stuart	P	R	R	5:11	155	26	St. Louis	7	8
Montgomery, Walter	P	R	L	5:11	181	23	Omaha	13	9
Poholsky, Tom	P	R	R	6:03	195	24	In Service	--	--
Presko, Joe	P	R	R	5:10	165	25	St. Louis	6	13
Raschi, Vic	P	R	R	6:01	210	34	New York, A.L.	13	6
Romonosky, John	P	R	R	6:03	190	24	Lynchburg	10	4
Schmidt, Willard	P	R	R	6:01	187	24	Columbus, O.	5	9
Staley, Gerald	P	R	R	6:00	195	30	St. Louis	18	9
Tiefenauer, Bobby	P	R	R	6:02	185	24	Rochester	9	3
Walsh, Jim	P	R	R	6:00	190	34	Hollywood	16	9
White, Harold	P	R	R	5:10	165	35	Cardinals	6	5
Wooldridge, Floyd	P	R	R	6:01	182	25	Houston	15	13
Yuhas, Eddie	P	R	R	6:02	165	30	St. Louis	0	0

Name	Pos.	B	T	Hgt.	Wgt.	Age	1953 Club	Batting Average
Rand, Dick	C	R	R	6:02	185	23	Houston	.283
Rice, Del	C	R	R	6:02	195	31	St. Louis	.236
Sarni, Bill	C	R	R	5:11	187	26	Columbus, O.	.277
Yvars, Sal	C	R	R	5:10	187	30	St. Louis	.260
Alston, Tom	Inf.	L	R	6:05	210	23	San Diego	.297
Bilko, Steve	Inf.	R	R	6:01	230	25	St. Louis	.252
Castiglione, Pete	Inf.	R	R	5:11	175	33	St. Louis	.199
Grammas, Alex	Inf.	R	R	6:00	175	26	Kansas City	.307
Hemus, Solly	Inf.	L	R	5:09	175	30	St. Louis	.278
Jablonski, Ray	Inf.	R	R	5:10	185	27	St. Louis	.269
Marolewski, Fred	Inf.	R	R	6:02	215	25	Houston	.252
Ortiz, Lou	Inf.	R	R	6:02	198	30	Rochester	.298
Phillips, Eddie	Inf.	R	R	6:01	170	22	Houston	.308
Schoendienst, Al	Inf.	B	R	6:00	168	31	St. Louis	.342
Schofield, Dick	Inf.	B	R	5:09	155	18	St. Louis	.179
Burgess, Tom	Of.	L	L	6:00	175	26	Rochester	.345
Elliott, Harry	Of.	R	R	5:10	180	28	Houston	.323
Frazier, Joe	Of.	L	R	6:00	200	31	Oklahoma City	.332
Lowrey, Peanuts	Of.	R	R	5:09	172	35	St. Louis	.269
Musial, Stan	Of.	L	L	6:00	175	33	St. Louis	.337
Rac, Russell	Of.	R	R	5:10	185	23	Omaha	.302
Repulski, Rip	Of.	R	R	6:00	195	25	St. Louis	.275
Slaughter, Enos	Of.	L	R	5:09	195	38	St. Louis	.291

OFFICIAL AMERICAN LEAGUE SCHEDULE, 1954

Asterisks Denote Night Games   **Bold Face Figures Denote Doubleheaders**

	AT CHICAGO	AT DETROIT	AT CLEVELAND	AT BALTIMORE	AT WASH.	AT PHILA.	AT NEW YORK	AT BOSTON
CHICAGO		Apr. 19, 20 May 21*, 22, 23 July 6, 7, 8 Aug. 20*, 21, 22	Apr. 17, 18 May 31 July 2*, 3*, 4 Sept. 20*, 21*, 22	Apr. 15 May 28*, 29*, 30 July 17, 18*, 19 Sept. 24, 25, 26	May 4*, 5*, 6 June 5*, 6, 7 July 15*, 16*, 17 Aug. 24*, 25	May 2, 3 June 8*, 9*, 10 July 18 Aug. 26*, 27*, 28	Apr. 27, 28, 29 June 11*, 12, 13 July 20*, 21, 22 Aug. 29	Apr. 30, May 1 June 2*, 3, 4 July 23*, 24, 25 Aug. 31, Sept. 1
DETROIT	May 8, 9 June 29*, 30 Aug. 13, 14, 15 Sept. 6		Apr. 15 May 28*, 29*, 30 Aug. 17*, 18, 19 Sept. 24, 25, 26	Apr. 17, 18 May 31, June 1* July 2*, 3*, 4 Sept. 20*, 21*, 22	Apr. 30*, May 1 June 2*, 3*, 4 Aug. 31*, Sept. 1*, 2	Apr. 27*, 28* June 11*, 12, 13 July 20*, 21*, 22* Aug. 29	May 2 June 8*, 9, 10 July 18, 19 Aug. 26, 27*, 28	May 4, 5, 6 June 5*, 6, 7 July 15*, 16, 17 Aug. 24, 25
CLEVELAND	Apr. 13, 14 May 25*, 26 July 9*, 10, 11 Sept. 3*, 4*, 5	Apr. 23, 24, 25 July 5 Aug. 10* 11, 12 Sept. 17*, 18, 19		Apr. 21*, 22 May 8*, 9 June 29*, 30* Aug. 20*, 21*, 22 Sept. 6	May 4*, 5*, 6* June 5, 6 July 15*, 16*, 17 Aug. 24*, 25*	May 4*, 5, 6* June 8*, 9 July 18, 19 Aug. 26*, 27*, 28	Apr. 30*, May 1 June 2*, 3, 4 Aug. 31*, Sept. 1, 2	Apr. 27, 28, 29 June 11*, 12, 13 July 20*, 21, 22 Aug. 29, 30
BALTIMORE	Apr. 23, 24, 25 July 5 Aug. 10*, 11 Sept. 17*, 18, 19	Apr. 13, 14 May 25*, 26, 27 July 9, 10, 11 Sept. 3*, 4, 5	May 21, 22, 23 July 6*, 7*, 8 Aug. 13*, 14, 15		Apr. 27*, 28*, 29* June 11*, 12*, 13 July 20*, 21*, 22* Aug. 29, 30	Apr. 30*, May 1 June 2*, 3*, 4 July 23*, 24, 25 Aug. 31*, Sept. 1*	May 4, 5, 6 June 5, 6 July 15*, 16*, 17 Aug. 24*, 25	May 2 June 8*, 9, 10 July 18, 19 Aug. 26*, 27, 28
WASHINGTON	May 16 June 22*, 23, 24 Aug. 6*, 7, 8 Sept. 8*, 9	May 11, 12 June 25*, 26, 27 Aug. 2*, 3, 4, 5 Sept. 12, 13	May 13, 14*, 15 June 15*, 16*, 17 July 30*, 31, Aug. 1 Sept. 14*	May 18*, 19* June 18, 19, 20 July 27*, 28*, 29 Sept. 11		Apr. 21* May 28*, 29*, 30 June 29*, 30* Aug. 20*, 21, 22	Apr. 17, 18 May 31 July 2*, 3*, 4 Sept. 20*, 21, 22	Apr. 15 May 7*, 8, 9 Aug. 10*, 11, 12 Sept. 24, 25, 26
PHILADELPHIA	May 13, 14*, 15 June 15*, 16, 17 July 30*, 31, Aug. 1 Sept. 14*	May 18, 19*, 20 June 18*, 19, 20 July 27*, 28, 29 Sept. 10, 11	May 16 June 22, 23, 24 Aug. 6*, 7, 8 Sept. 8*, 9	May 10*, 11* June 25*, 26, 27 Aug. 2*, 3*, 4* Sept. 12	Apr. 19*, 20* May 21*, 22*, 23 July 6* Aug. 13*, 14*, 15 Sept. 6		Apr. 15 May 7, 8, 9 Aug. 10*, 11, 12 Sept. 24, 25*, 26	Apr. 17, 18 May 31 July 2*, 3, 4 Sept. 20, 21, 22
NEW YORK	May 18*, 19 June 18*, 19, 20 July 27*, 28, 29 Sept. 10*, 11	May 13*, 14, 15 June 22, 23, 24 Aug. 6*, 7, 8 Sept. 14, 15	May 10*, 11*, 12 June 25*, 26, 27 Aug. 3*, 4*, 5 Sept. 12	May 16 June 15*, 16*, 17 July 30*, 31 Aug. 1 Sept. 8*, 9	Apr. 13, 14 May 25*, 26*, 27 Aug. 17*, 18*, 19 Sept. 17*, 18*, 19	Apr. 23*, 24, 25 July 5 Aug. 17*, 18* Sept. 17*, 18*, 19		Apr. 19 May 28*, 29, 30 June 29*, 30 Aug. 20*, 21, 22
BOSTON	May 11*, 12 June 25*, 26, 27 Aug. 3*, 4, 5 Sept. 12	May 16, 17 June 15*, 16, 17 July 30*, 31 Aug. 1 Sept. 8, 9	May 18, 19 June 18*, 19, 20 July 27*, 28*, 29 Sept. 10*, 11	May 13*, 14*, 15 June 22*, 23* Aug. 6*, 7, 8 Sept. 14, 15*	Apr. 23*, 24*, 25 July 5 Aug. 17*, 18*, 19 Sept. 17*, 18*, 19	Apr. 13 May 25*, 26* July 9*, 10, 11 Sept. 3*, 4, 5	Apr. 21 May 21*, 22, 23 July 6*, 7 Aug. 13*, 14, 15 Sept. 6	

ALL STAR GAME—CLEVELAND—TUESDAY, JULY 13

OFFICIAL NATIONAL LEAGUE SCHEDULE, 1954

Asterisks Denote Night Games — *Bold Face Figures Denote Doubleheaders*

	AT BROOKLYN	AT CHICAGO	AT CINCINNATI	AT MILWAUKEE	AT NEW YORK	AT PHILA.	AT PITTSBURGH	AT ST. LOUIS
BROOKLYN		May 4, 5, 6 / June 4, 5, 6 / July 18, 19, 20 / Sept. 1, 2	Apr. 29, 30* / May 1 / June 11*, 12, 13 / July 21*, 22 / Aug. 24*, 25*	May 2, 3 / June 1*, 2*, 3 / July 15*, 16*, 17 / Aug. 29, 30*, 31	Apr. 13, 14* / May 28*, 29, 30 / June 29*, 30 / July 1 / Sept. 3*, 4, 5	Apr. 19*, 20* / May 7*, 8, 9 / May 31 / July 2*, 3*, 4 / Aug. 10*, 11*	Apr. 23*, 24, 25 / July 5 / Aug. 17*, 18*, 19 / Sept. 17*, 19	Apr. 27*, 28 / June 7*, 8*, 9* / 10 / July 23*, 24*, 25 / Aug. 27*, 28
CHICAGO	May 18*, 19 / June 18*, 19, 20 / July 27, 28*, 29 / Sept. 12		Apr. 23*, 24, 25 / July 5 / Aug. 10*, 11*, 12 / Sept. 18, 19	Apr. 21*, May 7*, 8, 9 / June 29, 30 / Aug. 13*, 14*, 15 / Sept. 6	May 13, 14*, 15 / June 25*, 26, 27 / Aug. 3*, 4, 5 / Aug. 8, 9	May 11*, 12* / June 22*, 23*, 24* / Aug. 6*, 7, 8 / Sept. 10*, 11	May 16, 17 / June 14*, 16*, 17 / July 30*, 31 / Aug. 1 / Sept. 14	Apr. 13 / May 24*, 25*, 26*, 27 / July 9*, 10*, 11 / Sept. 3*, 4*, 5
CINCINNATI	May 16 / June 22, 23*, 24 / Aug. 6*, 7, 8 / Sept. 14*, 15, 16	Apr. 25, 28, 29, 30 / May 28, 29, 30 / Aug. 17, 18, 19 / Sept. 25, 26		May 11, 12 / May 31 / July 2*, 3*, 4 / Sept. 20, 21, 22	May 11, 12 / June 15*, 16, 17 / July 30*, 31 / Aug. 1 / Sept. 10, 11	May 13*, 14*, 15 / June 18*, 19, 20 / July 27*, 28*, 29* / Sept. 8*	May 18*, 19* / June 25*, 26, 27 / Aug. 3*, 4*, 5 / Sept. 12	Apr. 19*, 20* / May 21*, 22*, 23 / July 6*, 7*, 8* / Aug. 20*, 21*, 22
MILWAUKEE	May 11*, 12 / June 15*, 16*, 17 / July 30*, 31 / Aug. 1, 2 / Sept. 10*, 11	Apr. 21, 22, 23 / May 21, 22, 23 / July 6, 7, 8 / Aug. 20, 21, 22	Apr. 13 / May 25*, 26* / July 9*, 10, 11 / Sept. 3*, 4, 5		May 16 / June 22*, 23, 24 / Aug. 6*, 7, 8 / Sept. 14*, 15, 16	May 18*, 19* / June 18*, 19, 20 / July 27*, 28*, 29* / Sept. 8*	May 13*, 14*, 15 / June 25*, 26*, 27 / July 26*, 28*, 29 / Sept. 8	Apr. 23*, 24*, 25 / July 5 / Aug. 10*, 11*, 12* / Sept. 17*, 18*, 19
NEW YORK	Apr. 17, 18 / July 6*, 7*, 8 / Aug. 13*, 14, 15 / Sept. 20*, 21, 22	Apr. 30, May 1 / June 11, 12, 13 / July 21, 22 / Aug. 24, 25, 26	May 4*, 5*, 6 / June 4*, 5, 6 / July 18, 20 / Sept. 1*	Apr. 27*, 28 / June 7*, 8*, 9* / 10 / July 23*, 24, 25 / Aug. 27*, 28		Apr. 15 / May 20*, 21*, 22*, 23, 24* / Sept. 6*, 25*, 26	Apr. 21*, 22 / May 7*, 8*, 9 / May 31 / July 2*, 3, 4	May 2, 3* / June 2*, 3* / July 15*, 16*, 17 / Aug. 29, 30*, 31*
PHILADELPHIA	Apr. 21* / May 25, 26*, 27 / July 9, 10, 11 / Aug. 20*, 21, 22	Apr. 28 / June 8, 9, 10 / July 23, 24, 25 / Aug. 27, 28	Apr. 27*, 28 / June 8*, 9*, 10 / July 23*, 24, 25 / Aug. 27*, 28	Apr. 29*, 30* / May 1 / June 11*, 12, 13 / July 21*, 22 / Aug. 24*, 25*, 26	Apr. 23*, 24, 25 / July 5 / Aug. 17*, 18, 19 / Sept. 17, 18, 19		Apr. 13, 14 / May 28*, 29, 30 / June 29*, 30* / Sept. 3, 4, 5	May 4*, 5*, 6 / June 4*, 5*, 6 / July 18, 19*, 20* / Sept. 1*, 2
PITTSBURGH	Apr. 15 / May 21*, 22, 23, 24* / Sept. 6 / Sept. 24, 25, 26	May 2, 3 / June 2, 3 / July 15, 16, 17 / Aug. 29, 31	Apr. 27*, 28 / June 8*, 9*, 10 / July 27*, 28 / Aug. 27*, 28	Apr. 15 / May 28*, 29*, 30 / July 1 / Aug. 17*, 18*, 19 / Sept. 24, 25, 26	Apr. 19, 20 / May 9, 10, 11 / July 9, 10, 11 / Aug. 20, 21, 22	Apr. 17, 18 / July 6*, 7* / Aug. 13, 14, 15 / Aug. 21*, 22*		Apr. 29*, 30* / May 1 / June 11*, 12*, 13 / July 21*, 22 / Aug. 24*, 25*, 26*
ST. LOUIS	May 13, 14*, 15 / June 25*, 26*, 27 / Aug. 3*, 4*, 5 / Sept. 8*, 9	Apr. 17, 18 / May 31 / June 1 / July 2, 3, 4 / Sept. 22	Apr. 21* / May 7*, 8, 9 / June 29*, 30* / Aug. 13*, 14*, 15 / Sept. 6	Apr. 15 / May 28*, 29*, 30 / July 1 / Aug. 17*, 18*, 19 / Sept. 24, 25, 26	Apr. 18*, 19 / June 18*, 19, 20 / July 27*, 28, 29 / Sept. 12, 13	May 16, 17* / June 15*, 16*, 17* / July 30*, 31* / Aug. 1 / Sept. 14*, 15*	May 11*, 12 / June 22*, 23*, 24 / Aug. 6*, 7, 8 / Sept. 10, 11	

ALL STAR GAME—CLEVELAND—TUESDAY, JULY 13

105

FINAL STANDING OF CLUBS

CLUB	N.Y.	CLEV.	CHI.	BOS.	WASH.	DET.	PHIL.	ST.L.	WON	LOST	PCT.
New York	--	11	13	11	14	16	17	17	99	52	.656
Cleveland	11	--	11	9	11	14	19	17	92	62	.597
Chicago	9	11	--	16	12	14	10	17	89	65	.578
Boston	10	13	6	--	10	13	15	17	84	69	.549
Washington	8	11	10	12	--	11	14	12	76	76	.500
Detroit	6	8	8	9	11	--	11	7	60	94	.390
Philadelphia	6	3	12	7	8	11	--	18	59	95	.383
St. Louis	5	6	5	5	10	16	9	-	54	100	.351

INDIVIDUAL BATTING
(400 or More Times at Bat)

NAME AND CLUB	BATS	G	AB	R	H	2B	3B	HR	SB	RBI	PCT
Vernon, James B., Wash.	L	152	608	101	205	43	11	15	4	115	.337
Rosen, Albert L., Cleve.	R	155	599	115	201	27	5	43	8	145	.336
Minoso, Orestes A., Chi.	R	151	556	104	174	24	8	15	25	104	.313
Goodman, William D., Bos	L	128	514	73	161	33	5	2	1	41	.313
Busby, James F., Wash.	R	150	586	68	183	28	7	6	13	82	.312
Kuenn, Harvey E., Det.	R	155	679	94	209	33	7	2	6	48	.308
Kell, George C., Bos.	R	134	460	68	141	41	2	12	6	73	.307
Bauer, Henry A., N.Y.	R	133	437	77	133	20	6	10	2	57	.304
Philley, David E., Phil.	BOTH	157	620	80	188	30	9	9	13	59	.303
Mitchell, L. Dale, Clev.	L	134	500	76	150	26	4	13	3	60	.300
Berra, Lawrence P., N.Y.	L	137	503	80	149	23	5	27	0	108	.296
Boone, Raymond O., 34 Clv.-101 Det.	R	135	497	94	147	17	8	26	3	114	.296
Mantle, Mickey C., N.Y.	BOTH	127	461	105	136	24	3	21	8	92	.295
Delsing, James H., Det.	L	138	479	77	138	26	6	11	1	62	.288
Avila, Roberto, Clev.	R	141	559	85	160	22	3	8	10	55	.286
Suder, Peter, Phil.	R	115	454	44	130	11	3	4	3	35	.286
Fox, J. Nelson, Chi.	L	154	624	92	178	31	8	3	4	72	.285
McDougald, Gilbert J., N.Y.	R	141	541	82	154	27	7	10	3	83	.285
Zernial, Gus E., Phil.	R	147	556	85	158	21	3	42	4	108	.284
Strickland, George B., Clev.	R	123	419	43	119	17	4	5	0	47	.284
Umphlett, Thomas M., Bos.	R	137	495	53	140	27	5	3	4	59	.283
Nieman, Robert C., Det.	R	142	508	72	143	32	5	15	0	69	.281
Carrasquel, Alfonso, Chi.	R	149	552	72	154	30	4	2	5	47	.279
Mele, Sabath A., Chi.	R	140	481	64	132	26	8	12	3	82	.274
White, Samuel C., Bos.	R	136	476	59	130	34	2	13	3	64	.273
Piersall, James A., Bos.	R	151	585	76	159	21	9	3	11	52	.272
Yost, Edward F., Wash.	R	152	577	107	157	39	7	9	7	45	.272
Rizzuto, Philip F., N.Y.	R	134	413	54	112	21	3	2	4	54	.271
Wertz, Victor W., St.L.	L	128	440	61	118	18	6	19	1	70	.268
Jensen, Jack E., Wash.	R	147	552	87	147	32	8	10	18	84	.266
Doby, Lawrence E., Clev.	L	149	513	92	135	18	5	29	3	102	.263
Vollmer, Clyde F., 1 Bos.-118 Wash.	R	119	408	54	106	15	3	11	0	74	.260
Rivera, Manuel J., Chi.	R	156	567	79	147	26	16	11	22	78	.259
Martin, Alfred M., N.Y.	R	149	587	72	151	24	6	15	6	75	.257
Runnels, James E., Wash.	L	137	486	64	125	15	5	2	3	50	.257
Lund, Donald A., Det.	R	131	421	51	108	21	4	9	3	47	.257
Fain, Ferris R., Chi.	L	128	446	73	114	18	2	6	3	52	.256
Young, Robert G., St.L.	L	148	537	48	137	22	2	4	2	25	.255
DeMaestri, Joseph P., Phil.	R	111	420	53	107	17	3	6	0	35	.255
Groth, John T., St. L.	R	141	557	65	141	27	4	10	6	57	.253
Gernert, Richard E., Bos.	R	139	494	73	125	15	1	21	0	71	.253
Terwilliger, W. Wayne, Wash.	R	134	464	62	117	24	4	4	7	46	.252
Michaels, Casimer E., Phil.	R	117	411	53	103	10	0	12	7	42	.251
Dropo, Walter O., Det.	R	152	600	61	150	30	3	13	2	96	.248

NAME AND CLUB	BATS	G	AB	R	H	2B	3B	HR	SB	RBI	PCT
Robinson, Wm. Edward, Phil.	L	156	615	64	152	28	4	22	1	102	.247
Glynn, William V., Clev.	L	147	411	60	100	14	2	3	1	30	.243
Hunter, G. William, St. L.	R	154	567	50	124	18	1	1	3	37	.219

Players in Ten or More Games but Less Than 400 Times at Bat

NAME AND CLUB	BATS	G	AB	R	H	2B	3B	HR	SB	RBI	PCT
Weik, Richard H., 1 Clev.-12 Det.	R	13	2	2	1	1	0	0	0	1	.500
Kennedy, William A., Bos.	L	16	2	0	1	0	0	0	0	0	.500
Williams, Theodore S., Bos	L	37	91	17	37	6	0	13	0	34	.407
Kinder, Ellis R., Bos.	R	69	29	3	11	1	0	0	0	2	.379
Snyder, Jerry G., Wash.	R	29	62	10	21	4	0	0	1	4	.339
Westlake, Waldon T., Clev.	R	82	218	42	72	7	1	9	2	46	.330
Carey, Andrew A., N.Y.	R	51	81	14	26	5	0	4	2	8	.321
Keegan, Robert C., Chi.	R	22	28	4	9	0	0	0	0	5	.321
Lenhardt, Donald E., St. L.	R	97	303	37	96	15	0	10	1	35	.317
Renna, William B., N.Y.	R	61	121	19	38	6	3	2	0	13	.314
Woodling, Eugene R., N.Y.	L	125	395	64	121	26	4	10	2	58	.306
Easter, Luscious, Clev.	L	68	211	26	64	9	0	7	0	31	.303
Souchock, Stephen, Det.	R	89	278	29	84	13	3	11	5	46	.302
McDermott, Maurice, Bos	L	45	93	9	28	8	0	1	0	13	.301
Majeski, Henry, Clev.	R	50	50	6	15	1	0	2	0	12	.300
Boyd, Robert R., Chi.	L	55	165	20	49	6	2	3	1	23	.297
Bollweg, Donald R., N.Y.	L	70	155	24	46	6	4	6	1	24	.297
Astroth, Joseph H., Phil.	R	82	260	28	77	15	2	3	1	24	.296
Brown, Hector H., Bos.	R	30	58	5	17	5	0	1	0	10	.293
Davalillo, Pompeyo, Wash.	R	19	58	10	17	1	0	0	1	2	.293
Pesky, John M., Det.	L	103	308	43	90	22	1	3	2	24	.292
Ginsberg, Myron N., 18 Det.-46 Clev.	L	64	162	16	47	6	0	0	0	13	.290
Lollar, J. Sherman, Chi.	R	113	334	46	96	19	0	8	1	54	.287
Coleman, Joseph P., Phil.	R	21	28	1	8	2	0	0	0	1	.286
Murray, Raymond L., Phil.	R	84	268	25	76	14	3	6	0	41	.284
Larsen, Donald J., St. L.	R	50	81	11	23	3	1	3	0	10	.284
Silvera, Charles A., N.Y	R	42	82	11	23	3	1	0	0	12	.280
Batts, Matthew D., Det.	R	116	374	38	104	24	3	6	2	42	.278
Kryhoski, Richard D., St. L.	L	104	338	35	94	18	4	16	0	50	.278
Turley, Robert L., St. L.	R	10	18	2	5	0	0	1	0	1	.278
Moss, John Lester, St. L.	R	78	239	21	66	14	1	2	0	28	.276
Wynn, Early, Clev.	BOTH	37	91	11	25	2	0	3	0	10	.275
Berry, Cornelius J., 57 St.L.-5 Chi.	R	62	107	15	29	1	2	0	1	11	.271
Stewart, Edward P., Chi.	L	53	59	16	16	2	0	2	1	13	.271
Sievers, Roy E., St. L.	R	92	285	37	77	15	0	8	0	35	.270
Collins, Joseph E., N.Y.	L	127	387	72	104	11	2	17	2	44	.269
Mullin, Patrick J., Det.	L	79	97	11	26	1	0	4	0	17	.268
Noren, Irving A., N.Y.	L	109	345	55	92	12	6	6	3	46	.267
Ford, Edward C., N.Y.	L	33	75	10	20	2	0	0	0	10	.267
Carswell, Frank W., Det.	R	16	15	2	4	0	0	0	0	2	.267
McGhee, W. Edward, Phil.	R	104	358	36	94	11	4	1	4	29	.263
Bolling, Milton J., Bos.	R	109	323	30	85	12	1	5	1	28	.263
Baker, Floyd W., 9 Wash.-81 Bos.	L	90	179	22	47	4	2	0	0	24	.263
Stephens, Vernon D., 44 Chi.-46 St.L.	R	90	294	30	77	14	0	5	2	31	.262
Hoskins, David T., Clev.	R	38	58	10	15	2	0	1	0	9	.259
Elliott, Robert I., 48 St.L.-67 Chi.	R	115	368	43	94	19	2	9	1	61	.255
Mauro, Carmen L., 17 Wash.-64 Phil.	L	81	188	15	48	4	5	0	3	19	.255
Porterfield, Ervin C., Wash.	R	37	98	8	25	7	0	3	1	16	.255
Hatfield, Fred J., Det.	L	109	311	41	79	11	1	3	3	19	.254
Courtney, Clinton D., St. L.	L	106	355	28	89	12	2	4	0	19	.251
Fitzgerald, Edward R., Wash.	R	88	288	23	72	13	0	3	2	39	.250
Wilson, Robert J., Chi.	R	71	164	21	41	6	1	0	2	10	.250
Wright, Thomas E., Chi.	L	77	132	14	33	5	3	2	0	25	.250
Mize, John R., N.Y.	L	81	104	6	26	3	0	4	0	27	.250
Garcia, Edward M., Clev.	R	38	96	8	24	5	0	0	0	5	.250
Sullivan, Russell G., Det.	L	23	72	7	18	5	1	1	0	6	.250
Sain, John F., N.Y.	R	41	68	8	17	3	1	0	0	8	.250
Kaline, Albert W., Det.	R	30	28	9	7	0	0	1	1	2	.250
Wight, William R., 13 Det.-20 Clev.	L	33	12	0	3	0	0	0	0	1	.250
Sullivan, Franklin L., Bos.	R	14	4	0	1	0	0	0	0	0	.250
Joost, Edwin D., Phil.	R	51	177	39	44	8	0	6	8	15	.249

NAME AND CLUB	BATS	G	AB	R	H	2B	3B	HR	SB	RBI	PCT
Kokos, Richard J., St. L.	L	107	299	41	72	12	0	13	0	38	.241
Wilber, Delbert Q., Bos.	R	58	112	16	27	6	1	7	0	29	.241
Evers, Walter A., Bos.	R	99	300	39	72	10	1	11	2	31	.240
Smith, Alphonse E., Clev.	R	47	150	28	36	9	0	3	2	14	.240
Shantz, Robert C., Phil.	R	21	38	6	9	1	1	0	1	4	.237
Lepcio, Thaddeus S., Bos.	R	66	161	17	38	4	2	4	0	11	.236
Kennedy, Robert D., Clev.	R	100	161	22	38	5	0	3	0	22	.236
Priddy, Gerald E., Det.	R	65	196	14	46	6	2	1	1	24	.235
Lemon, Robert G., Clev.	L	51	112	12	26	8	1	2	2	17	.232
Babe, Loren R., 5 N.Y.-103 Phil.	L	108	361	36	83	17	2	2	0	26	.230
Gray, Theodore G., Det.	BOTH	32	61	5	14	0	1	0	0	7	.230
Tipton, Joseph J., Clev.	R	47	109	17	25	2	0	6	0	13	.229
Simpson, Harry L., Clev.	L	82	242	25	55	3	1	7	0	22	.227
Stobbs, Charles K., Wash.	L	27	44	11	10	0	0	0	1	3	.227
Valo, Elmer W., Phil.	L	50	85	15	19	3	0	0	0	9	.224
Parnell, Melvin L., Bos.	L	38	94	7	21	4	0	0	1	9	.223
Bucha, John G., Det.	R	60	158	17	35	9	0	1	1	14	.222
Byrd, Harry G., Phil.	R	40	81	8	18	0	0	0	0	6	.222
Ryan, Cornelius J., Chi.	R	17	54	6	12	1	0	0	2	6	.222
Miranda, Guillermo P., 17 St. L.-48 N.Y.	BOTH	65	64	14	14	0	0	1	2	5	.219
Marlowe, Richard B., Det.	R	42	32	0	7	0	0	0	0	2	.219
Hegan, James E., Clev.	R	112	299	37	65	10	1	8	1	37	.217
Kellner, Alexander R., Phil.	R	25	69	4	15	2	0	0	0	6	.217
Sheely, Hollis K., Chi.	L	31	46	4	10	1	0	0	0	2	.217
Trucks, Virgil O., 16 St. L.-24 Chi.	R	40	88	6	19	4	0	1	0	7	.216
Thomas, Keith M., 24 Phil.-38 Wash.	R	62	107	11	23	3	2	1	0	14	.215
Consolo, William A., Bos.	R	47	65	9	14	2	1	1	1	6	.215
Lipon, John J., 60 Bos.-7 St. L.	R	67	154	18	33	7	0	0	1	14	.214
Dyck, James R., St. L.	R	112	334	38	71	15	1	9	3	27	.213
Wood, Kenneth L., Wash.	R	12	33	0	7	1	0	0	0	3	.212
Hitchcock, William C., Det.	R	22	38	8	8	0	0	0	0	0	.211
Grasso, Newton M., Wash.	R	61	196	13	41	7	0	2	0	22	.209
Stephens, G. Eugene, Bos.	L	78	221	30	45	6	2	3	3	18	.204
Krsnich, Peter R., Chi.	R	64	129	9	26	8	0	1	0	14	.202
Friend, Owen L., 31 Det.-34 Clev.	R	65	164	17	33	6	0	5	0	23	.201
Marsh, Fred F., Chi.	R	67	95	22	19	1	0	2	0	2	.200
Niarhos, Constantine G., Bos.	R	16	35	6	7	1	1	0	0	2	.200
Cain, Robert M., St. L.	L	34	30	3	6	2	0	0	0	2	.200
Miller, William P., N.Y.	L	13	10	1	2	1	0	0	0	1	.200
Edwards, Henry A., St. L.	L	65	106	6	21	3	0	0	0	9	.198
Coan, Gilbert F., Wash.	L	68	168	28	33	1	4	2	7	17	.196
Hamilton, Thomas C., Phil.	R	58	56	8	11	2	0	0	0	5	.196
Scheib, Carl A., Phil.	R	35	41	4	8	0	0	0	0	4	.195
Zarilla, Allen L., Bos.	L	57	67	11	13	2	0	0	0	4	.194
Stuart, Marlin H., St. L.	R	60	26	3	5	1	0	0	0	1	.192
Hoderlein, Melvin A., Wash.	BOTH	23	47	5	9	0	0	0	0	5	.191
Lopat, Edmund W., N.Y.	L	26	63	5	12	3	0	0	0	1	.190
Nixon, Willard L., Bos.	L	23	42	4	8	1	0	0	0	3	.190
Littlefield, Richard B., St. L.	L	38	42	4	8	0	0	0	0	2	.190
McCosky, W. Barney, Clev.	L	22	21	3	4	3	0	0	0	3	.190
Bearden, H. Eugene, Chi.	L	31	21	2	4	0	0	0	0	3	.190
Verble, Eugene K., Wash.	R	13	21	4	4	0	0	0	0	2	.190
Henry, William R., Bos.	L	21	32	2	6	1	1	0	0	4	.188
Fanovich, Frank J., Phil.	L	26	11	1	2	0	0	0	0	0	.182
Clark, Alfred A., 20 Phil.-9 Chi.	R	29	89	6	16	4	0	3	0	13	.180
Brecheen, Harry D., St. L.	L	27	39	1	7	0	0	0	0	2	.179
Shea, Frank J., Wash.	R	23	62	2	11	1	1	0	0	6	.177
Giordano, Thomas A., Phil.	R	11	40	6	7	2	0	2	0	5	.175
Lemon, James R., Clev.	R	16	46	5	8	1	0	1	0	5	.174
Hoeft, William F., Det.	L	30	64	8	11	1	0	0	0	4	.172
Kretlow, Louis A., 9 Chi.-22 St. L.	R	31	29	2	5	0	0	0	0	1	.172
Dorish, Harry, Chi.	R	55	41	4	7	0	0	0	0	1	.171
Newsom, Louis N., Phil.	R	17	6	1	1	0	0	0	0	0	.167
Lanier, H. Max, St. L.	R	10	6	0	1	0	0	0	0	0	.167
Watlington, J. Neal, Phil.	L	21	44	4	7	1	0	0	0	3	.159
Flowers, Bennett, Bos.	R	32	19	0	3	2	0	0	0	1	.158
Herbert, Raymond E., Det.	R	43	19	0	3	0	0	0	0	0	.158

108

NAME AND CLUB	BATS	G	AB	R	H	2B	3B	HR	SB	RBI	PCT
Triandos, Gus, N.Y.	R	18	51	5	8	2	0	1	0	6	.157
Dixon, John C., Wash.	BOTH	43	26	1	4	1	0	0	0	0	.154
Garver, Ned F., Det.	R	30	72	3	11	0	0	1	0	6	.153
Houtteman, Arthur J.,16 Det.-23 Clv.	R	39	53	7	8	2	0	1	0	2	.151
Fricano, Marion J., Phil.	R	46	69	6	10	1	0	0	1	1	.145
Raschi, Victor J., N.Y.	R	28	63	4	9	1	0	0	0	11	.143
Hudson, Sidney C., Bos.	R	30	50	3	7	1	1	0	0	6	.140
Masterson, Walter E., Wash.	R	29	51	2	7	0	0	0	0	5	.137
Rogovin, Saul, Chi.	R	22	37	5	5	0	0	0	1	3	.135
Gorman, Thomas A., N.Y.	R	40	15	0	2	0	0	0	0	0	.133
Pillette, Duane X., St. L.	R	31	53	4	7	1	0	1	0	4	.132
Aber, Albert J., 6 Clev. -17 Det.	L	23	23	2	3	0	0	0	0	2	.130
Pierce, W. William, Chi.	L	42	87	4	11	0	0	0	0	4	.126
Marrero, Conrado, Wash.	R	22	48	5	6	0	0	0	0	1	.125
Miller, Robert G., Det.	R	13	8	0	1	0	0	0	0	0	.125
Olson, Karl A., Bos.	R	25	57	5	7	2	0	1	0	6	.123
Reynolds, Allie P., N. Y.	R	42	41	3	5	2	0	0	0	2	.122
Branca, Ralph T., Det.	R	17	34	3	4	0	1	0	0	4	.118
Sima, Albert, Wash.	R	31	17	1	2	0	0	0	0	0	.118
Byrne, Thomas J., 18 Chi.-14 Wash.	L	32	35	2	4	0	0	1	0	5	.114
Lane, Jerald H., Wash.	R	20	9	2	1	1	0	0	0	0	.111
Campos, Francisco J., Wash.	L	10	9	0	1	0	0	0	0	2	.111
Feller, Robert W., Clev.	R	25	56	3	6	1	0	0	0	1	.107
Holloman, Alva L., St. L.	R	22	19	0	2	0	0	0	0	3	.105
Delock, Ivan M,, Bos.	R	23	10	1	1	0	0	0	0	0	.100
Fornieles, Miguel J., Chi.	R	39	41	2	4	1	0	0	0	5	.098
McDonald, James L., N. Y.	R	29	41	2	4	0	0	0	0	4	.098
Martin, Morris W., Phil.	L	58	42	0	4	0	0	0	0	1	.095
Madison, David P., Det.	R	32	11	1	1	0	0	0	0	0	.091
Freeman, Hershell B., Bos.	R	18	11	0	1	0	0	0	0	0	.091
Bishop, Charles T., Phil.	R	40	56	2	5	2	0	0	0	6	.089
Hooper, Robert N., Clev.	R	43	12	0	1	0	0	0	0	0	.083
Scarborough, Ray W., 25 N.Y.-13 Det.	R	38	14	1	1	0	0	1	0	3	.071
Gromek, Stephen J., 5 Clev.-19 Det.	BOTH	24	43	0	3	0	0	0	0	2	.070
Dobson, Joseph G., Chi.	R	23	29	0	2	1	0	0	0	2	.069
Paige, Leroy, St. L.	R	57	29	1	2	0	0	0	0	2	.069
Schmitz, John A., 3 N.Y.-24 Wash.	R	27	34	0	2	0	0	0	0	0	.059
Consuegra, Sandalio S., 4 Wash.-29 Chi.	R	33	35	1	2	0	0	0	0	3	.057
Johnson, Clifford, Chi.	R	15	20	4	1	0	0	0	0	1	.050
Kuzava, Robert L., N. Y.	BOTH	33	21	3	1	0	0	0	0	0	.048
Blyzka, Michael, St. L.	R	33	23	1	0	0	0	0	0	1	.000
Grissom, Marvin E., Bos.	R	13	18	0	0	0	0	0	0	0	.000
Moreno, Julio, Wash.	R	12	9	0	0	0	0	0	0	0	.000
Aloma, Luis B., Chi.	R	24	6	0	0	0	0	0	0	0	.000
Erickson, Harold J., Det.	R	18	4	0	0	0	0	0	0	0	.000
Harrist, Earl, 7 Chi.-8 Det.	R	15	4	0	0	0	0	0	0	0	.000
White, Harold G., St. L.	R	10	1	0	0	0	0	0	0	0	.000
Leslie, Leland V., Clev.	L	16	0	0	0	0	0	0	0	0	.000

CLUB BATTING

Club	G	AB	R	OR	H	2B	3B	HR	SB	RBI	PCT
New York	151	5194	801	547	1420	226	52	139	34	762	.273
Cleveland	155	5285	770	627	1426	201	29	160	33	729	.270
Detroit	158	5553	695	923	1479	259	44	108	30	660	.266
Boston	153	5246	656	632	1385	255	37	101	33	613	.264
Washington	152	5149	687	614	1354	230	53	69	65	647	.263
Chicago	156	5212	716	592	1345	226	53	74	73	676	.258
Philadelphia	157	5455	632	799	1398	205	38	116	41	588	.256
St. Louis	154	5264	555	778	1310	214	25	112	17	522	.249
TOTALS		42358	5512	5512	11117	1816	331	879	326	5197	.262

PITCHERS' RECORDS

Pitchers with at least 154 Innings Rated According to Earned Run Average Per Nine Inning Game

Name and Club	Throws	G	GS	CG	W	L	PCT	IP	H	HR	R	ER	BB	SO	ERA
Lopat, Edmund W., N.Y.	L	25	24	9	16	4	.800	178	169	13	58	48	32	50	2.43
Pierce, W. William, Chi.	L	40	33	19	18	12	.600	271	216	20	94	82	102	186	2.72
Trucks, Virgil O., 16 St. L.-24 Chi.	R	40	33	17	20	10	.667	264	234	18	97	86	99	149	2.93
Ford, Edward C., N.Y.	L	32	30	11	18	6	.750	207	187	13	77	69	110	110	3.00
Sain, John F., N.Y.	R	40	19	10	14	7	.667	189	189	16	68	63	45	84	3.00
McDermott, Maurice, Bos.	L	32	30	8	18	10	.643	206	169	9	82	69	109	92	3.01
Parnell, Melvin L., Bos.	L	38	34	12	21	8	.724	241	217	15	98	82	116	136	3.06
Garcia, Edward M., Clev.	R	38	35	21	18	9	.667	272	260	18	106	98	81	134	3.24
Raschi, Victor J., N.Y.	R	28	26	7	13	6	.684	181	150	11	74	67	55	76	3.33
Porterfield, Ervin C., Wash.	R	34	32	24	22	10	.688	255	243	19	99	95	73	77	3.35
Lemon, Robert G., Clev.	R	41	36	23	21	15	.583	287	283	16	119	107	110	98	3.36
Hudson, Sidney C., Bos.	R	30	17	4	6	9	.400	156	164	13	65	61	49	60	3.52
Feller, Robert W., Clev.	R	25	25	10	10	7	.588	176	163	16	78	70	60	60	3.58
Masterson, Walter E., Wash.	R	29	20	10	10	12	.455	166	145	16	79	67	62	95	3.63
Fricano, Marion J., Phil.	R	39	23	9	9	12	.429	211	206	21	105	91	90	67	3.88
Kellner, Alexander R., Phil.	L	25	25	14	11	12	.478	202	210	8	98	88	51	81	3.92
Wynn, Early, Clev.	R	36	34	16	17	12	.586	252	234	19	121	110	107	138	3.93
Shea, Frank J., Wash.	R	23	23	11	12	7	.632	165	151	11	82	72	75	38	3.93
Larsen, Donald J., St. L.	R	38	22	7	7	12	.368	193	201	11	99	89	64	96	4.15
Martin, Morris W., Phil.	L	58	11	2	10	12	.455	156	158	12	85	77	59	64	4.44
Garver, Ned F., Det.	R	30	26	13	11	11	.500	198	228	16	107	98	66	69	4.45
Pillette, Duane X., St. L.	R	31	25	5	7	13	.350	167	181	16	90	83	62	58	4.47
Houtteman, Arthur J., 16 Det.-22 Clev.	R	38	22	9	9	13	.409	178	200	15	106	91	54	68	4.60
Gray, Theodore G., Det.	L	30	28	8	10	15	.400	176	166	25	102	90	76	115	4.60
Brown, Hector H., Bos.	R	30	25	6	11	6	.647	166	177	16	94	86	57	62	4.66
Hoeft, William F., Det.	L	29	27	9	9	14	.391	198	223	24	113	106	58	90	4.82
Byrd, Harry G., Phil.	R	40	37	11	11	20	.355	237	279	23	155	145	115	122	5.51
Bishop, Charles T., Phil.	R	39	20	1	3	14	.176	161	174	15	106	101	86	66	5.65

BALKS: Lopat, Trucks, Sain, McDermott, Feller, Masterson, Fricano, Shea, Garver, Hoeft, Byrd, 1 each.

Pitchers in Ten or More Games with Less Than 154 Innings Rated
According to Earned Run Average Per Nine Inning Game

Name and Club	Throws	G	GS	CG	W	L	PCT	IP	H	HR	R	ER	BB	SO	ERA
Kinder, Ellis R., Bos.	R	69	0	0	10	6	.625	107	84	8	30	22	38	39	1.85
White, Harold G., St. L.	R	10	0	0	0	0	.000	10	8	1	3	3	3	2	2.70
Keegan, Robert C., Chi.	R	22	11	4	7	5	.583	99	80	4	34	30	33	32	2.73
Moreno, Julio, Wash.	R	12	2	1	3	1	.750	35	41	2	11	11	13	13	2.83
Consuegra, Sandalio S., 4 Wash.-29 Chi.	R	33	13	5	7	5	.583	129	131	9	45	41	32	30	2.86
Bearden, H. Eugene, Chi.	L	25	3	0	3	3	.500	58	48	8	27	19	33	24	2.95
Marrero, Conrado E., Wash.	R	22	20	10	8	7	.533	146	130	11	56	49	48	65	3.02
Brecheen, Harry D., St. L.	L	26	16	3	5	13	.278	117	122	7	51	40	31	44	3.08
Henry, William R., Bos.	L	21	12	4	5	5	.500	86	86	4	39	31	33	56	3.24
Stobbs, Charles K., Wash.	L	27	20	8	11	8	.579	153	146	11	64	56	44	67	3.29
Turley, Robert L., St. L.	R	10	7	3	2	6	.250	60	39	4	24	22	44	61	3.30
Kuzava, Robert L., N. Y.	R	33	6	2	6	5	.545	92	92	9	35	34	34	48	3.33
Dorish, Harry, Chi.	R	55	6	2	10	6	.625	146	140	9	59	55	52	69	3.39
Gorman, Thomas A., N. Y.	R	40	1	0	4	5	.444	77	65	5	32	29	32	38	3.39
Reynolds, Allie P., N. Y.	R	41	15	5	13	7	.650	145	140	9	64	55	61	86	3.41
Sima, Albert, Wash.	L	31	5	1	2	3	.400	68	63	7	31	26	31	25	3.44
Paige, Leroy, St. L.	R	57	4	0	3	9	.250	117	114	12	51	46	39	51	3.54
Johnson, Clifford, Chi.	R	14	10	2	4	4	.500	61	55	4	27	24	38	44	3.54
Fornieles, Miguel J., Chi.	R	39	16	5	8	7	.533	153	160	8	68	61	61	72	3.59
Schmitz, John A., 3 N. Y.-24 Wash.	L	27	13	5	2	7	.222	112	120	10	53	45	40	39	3.62
Dobson, Joseph G., Chi.	R	23	15	3	5	5	.500	101	96	10	46	41	37	50	3.65
Dixon, John C., Wash.	R	43	6	0	5	8	.385	120	123	13	57	50	31	40	3.75
Kennedy, William A., Bos.	L	16	0	0	0	0	.000	24	24	2	13	10	17	14	3.75
McDonald, James L., N. Y.	R	27	18	6	9	7	.563	130	128	4	64	55	39	43	3.81
Flowers, Bennett, Bos.	R	32	6	1	1	4	.200	79	87	6	39	34	24	36	3.87
Nixon, Willard L., Bos.	R	23	15	5	5	8	.333	117	114	6	57	51	59	57	3.92
Stuart, Marlin H., St. L.	R	60	2	0	8	2	.800	114	136	6	62	50	44	46	3.95
Hoskins, David T., Clev.	R	26	7	3	9	3	.750	113	102	9	57	50	38	55	3.98
Coleman, Joseph P., Phil.	R	21	9	2	3	4	.429	90	85	8	46	40	49	18	4.00
Hooper, Robert N., Clev.	R	43	0	0	5	5	.556	69	50	4	37	37	38	16	4.04
Shantz, Robert C., Phil.	L	16	16	6	5	9	.357	106	107	10	52	48	26	58	4.08
Branca, Ralph T., Det.	R	17	14	7	4	7	.364	102	98	7	55	47	31	50	4.15
Gromek, Stephen J., 5 Clev.-19 Det.	R	24	18	6	7	9	.438	137	149	17	74	67	39	67	4.40

Name and Club	Throws	G	GS	CG	W	L	PCT	IP	H	HR	R	ER	BB	SO	ERA
Delock, Ivan M., Bos.	R	23	1	0	3	1	.750	49	60	2	27	24	20	22	4.41
Scarborough, Ray W., 25 N.Y.-13 Det.	R	38	1	0	2	4	.333	75	86	7	47	39	37	32	4.68
Aber, Albert J., 6 Clev.-17 Det.	L	23	10	2	5	4	.556	73	69	3	41	38	50	38	4.68
Grissom, Marvin E., Bos.	R	13	11	1	2	6	.250	59	61	5	34	31	30	31	4.73
Aloma, Luis B., Chi.	R	24	0	0	2	0	1.000	38	41	7	20	20	23	23	4.74
Kretlow, Louis A., 9 Chi.-22 St. L.	R	31	14	0	1	5	.167	102	105	7	67	54	82	52	4.76
Miller, William P., N.Y.	L	13	3	0	2	1	.667	34	46	3	19	18	17	17	4.76
Erickson, Harold J., Det.	R	18	0	0	0	1	.000	32	43	4	23	17	10	19	4.78
Newsom, Louis N., Phil.	R	17	2	1	2	1	.667	39	44	3	24	21	24	16	4.85
Scheib, Carl A., Phil.	R	28	8	3	3	7	.300	96	99	9	57	52	29	25	4.88
Lane, Jerald H., Wash.	R	20	2	0	1	4	.200	57	64	3	33	31	16	26	4.89
Littlefield, Richard B., St. L.	L	36	22	2	7	12	.368	152	153	17	93	86	84	104	5.09
Rogovin, Saul, Chi.	R	22	19	4	7	12	.368	131	151	17	82	76	48	62	5.22
Herbert, Raymond E., Det.	R	43	3	1	4	6	.400	88	109	5	58	51	46	37	5.22
Marlowe, Richard B., Det.	R	42	11	2	6	7	.462	120	152	13	74	70	42	52	5.25
Holloman, Alva L., St. L.	R	22	10	1	3	7	.300	65	69	2	41	38	50	25	5.26
Fanovich, Frank J., Phil.	L	26	3	0	0	3	.000	62	62	5	41	38	37	37	5.52
Freeman, Hershell B., Bos.	R	18	2	0	1	4	.200	39	50	2	31	24	17	15	5.54
Sullivan, Franklin L., Bos.	L	14	0	0	1	1	.500	26	24	3	16	16	11	17	5.54
Miller, Robert G., Det.	L	13	1	0	1	2	.333	36	43	3	25	24	21	9	6.00
Byrne, Thomas J., 6 Chi.-6 Wash.	L	12	11	2	2	5	.286	50	53	3	35	34	48	26	6.12
Cain, Robert M., St. L.	L	32	13	1	4	10	.286	100	129	8	74	69	45	36	6.21
Wight, William R., 13 Det.-20 Clev.	R	33	4	0	2	4	.333	52	64	5	45	36	30	24	6.23
Blyzka, Michael, St. L.	R	33	9	0	3	9	.250	94	110	6	78	67	56	23	6.41
Madison, David P., Det.	R	32	1	0	3	4	.429	62	76	7	55	47	44	27	6.82
Lanier, H. Max, St. L.	L	10	1	0	0	1	.000	22	28	2	18	18	19	8	7.36
Brissie, Leland V., Clev.	L	16	1	0	0	0	.000	13	21	1	11	11	13	5	7.62
Harrist, Earl, 7 Chi.-8 Det.	L	15	1	0	1	2	.333	27	34	2	26	25	20	8	8.33
Wetk, Richard H., Det.	R	12	1	0	0	1	.000	19	32	3	30	30	23	6	14.21

BALKS: Kinder, Brecheen, Dorish, Paige, Fornieles, Hoskins, Delock, Aloma, Rogovin, Holloman, 1 each.

CLUB PITCHING RECORDS

	IP	H	HR	R	ER	BB	SO	CG	E. R. Avg. Per G.
New York	1358-1/3	1286	94	547	483	500	604	50	3.20
Chicago	1403-2/3	1299	113	592	532	683	714	57	3.41
Boston	1373	1333	92	632	546	584	642	41	3.58
Cleveland	1373	1311	92	627	556	519	586	81	3.64
Washington	1344-2/3	1313	112	614	547	478	515	76	3.66
St. Louis	1383-2/3	1467	101	778	688	626	639	28	4.47
Philadelphia	1408-2/3	1475	121	799	731	594	566	51	4.67
Detroit	1415	1633	154	923	826	585	645	50	5.25
TOTALS	11060	11117	879	5512	4909	4469	4911	434	3.99

INDIVIDUAL FIELDING RECORDS
Ten or More Games
FIRST BASEMEN

Name and Club	Throws	G	PO	A	E	TC	DP	PCT.
Boyd, Chi.	L	29	275	16	0	291	25	1.000
Mize, N.Y.	R	15	113	7	0	120	19	1.000
Priddy, Det.	R	11	92	9	0	101	7	1.000
Glynn, Clev.	L	135	1036	81	8	1125	133	.993
Vernon, Wash.	L	152	1376	94	12	1482	158	.992
Kryhoski, St. L.	L	88	685	66	6	757	77	.992
Sievers, St. L.	R	76	604	31	5	640	64	.992
Triandos, N.Y.	R	12	100	6	1	107	8	.991
Dropo, Det.	R	150	1260	127	14	1401	121	.990
Fain, Chi.	L	127	1108	106	13	1227	98	.989
Collins, N.Y.	L	113	826	65	10	901	100	.989
Robinson, Phil.	R	155	1366	71	17	1454	135	.988
Gernert, Bos.	R	136	1223	84	19	1326	139	.986
Bollweg, N.Y.	L	43	323	15	6	344	37	.983
Easter, Clev.	R	56	442	30	9	481	64	.981
Goodman, Bos.	R	20	151	13	6	170	18	.965

TRIPLE PLAYS -- Vernon, Kryhoski, Bollweg, Fain, 1 each.

SECOND BASEMEN

Name and Club	G	PO	A	E	TC	DP	PCT.
Majeski, Clev.	10	8	8	0	16	2	1.000
Pesky, Det.	73	166	224	3	393	49	.992
Baker, Wash.-Bos.	16	45	36	1	82	12	.988
Avila, Clev.	140	346	445	11	802	114	.986
Martin, N.Y.	146	376	390	12	778	121	.985
Suder, Phil	88	89	105	3	197	23	.985
Giordano, Phil.	11	31	32	1	64	11	.984
Fox, Chi.	154	451	426	15	892	101	.983
Terwilliger, Wash.	133	333	395	13	741	108	.982
McDougald, N.Y.	26	23	33	1	57	9	.982
Lepcio, Bos.	34	71	85	3	159	25	.981
Consolo, Bos.	11	23	29	1	53	10	.981
Young, St. L.	148	397	363	18	778	120	.977
Priddy, Det.	45	111	106	5	222	28	.977
Goodman, Bos.	112	267	306	15	588	88	.974
Berry, St. L.-Chi.	18	31	37	2	70	9	.971
Michaels, Phil.	110	304	302	19	625	81	.970
Hatfield, Det.	28	64	87	5	156	21	.968
Friend, Det.-Clev.	45	106	111	8	225	36	.964
Hoderlein, Wash.	11	18	23	2	43	6	.953
Runnels, Wash.	11	24	27	3	54	7	.944

TRIPLE PLAY - Young

THIRD BASEMEN

Name and Club	G	PO	A	E	TC	DP	PCT.
Carey, N.Y.	40	29	55	1	85	8	.988
Hatfield, Det.	54	56	121	4	181	13	.978
Suder, Phil.	72	89	174	7	270	19	.974
Kell, Bos.	124	114	231	10	355	23	.972
Stephens, Chi.-St. L.	84	84	158	8	250	16	.968
Yost, Wash.	152	190	300	18	508	31	.965
Rosen, Clev.	154	174	338	19	531	38	.964
Elliott, St.L.-Chi.	103	105	197	13	315	21	.959
Boone, Clev.-Det.	97	111	211	14	336	32	.958
McDougald, N.Y.	136	147	299	22	468	36	.958
Baker, Wash.-Bos.	38	22	57	4	83	6	.953
Babe, N.Y.-Phil.	98	122	207	18	347	27	.952
Marsh, Chi.	32	17	30	3	50	5	.948
Lepcio, Bos.	11	10	18	2	30	2	.940
Krsnich, Chi.	57	31	100	10	141	7	.933
Hitchcock, Det.	12	9	17	2	28	1	.929
Ryan, Chi.	16	20	31	4	55	1	.929
Dyck, St. L.	51	62	101	13	176	12	.927
Minoso, Chi.	10	3	14	2	19	0	.926
Berry, St. L.-Chi.	18	15	18	7	40	1	.895
Consolo, Bos.	16	3	18	5	26	3	.825

SHORTSTOPS

Name and Club	G	PO	A	E	TC	DP	PCT.
Snyder, Wash.	17	28	54	1	83	10	.988
Lepcio, Bos.	20	15	52	1	68	10	.985
Miranda, St. L.-N.Y.	53	60	80	3	143	20	.979
Carrasquel, Chi.	149	278	462	18	758	87	.976
Strickland, Clev.	122	238	400	17	655	103	.974
Kuenn, Det.	155	308	441	21	770	78	.973
Hunter, St. L.	152	284	512	25	821	99	.970
DeMaestri, Phil.	108	191	297	18	506	53	.964
Marsh, Chi.	17	17	36	2	55	5	.964
Rizzuto, N.Y.	133	214	409	24	647	100	.963
Runnels, Wash.	121	195	324	23	542	87	.958
Joost, Phil.	51	102	147	11	260	33	.958
Bolling, Bos.	109	174	321	23	518	71	.956
Lipon, Bos.-St. L.	58	85	150	12	247	26	.951
Boone, Clev.-Det.	34	68	102	9	179	26	.950
Martin, N.Y.	18	13	19	2	34	5	.941
Davalillo, Wash.	17	39	47	6	92	10	.935

TRIPLE PLAYS - Carrasquel, Hunter, Rizzuto, Runnels, 1 each

OUTFIELDERS

Name and Club	Throws	G	PO	A	E	TC	DP	PCT.
Coan, Wash.	R	46	105	2	0	107	1	1.000
Kennedy, Clev.	R	89	91	2	0	93	0	1.000
Valo, Phil.	R	25	46	1	0	47	1	1.000
Thomas, Phil.-Wash.	R	23	42	0	0	42	0	1.000
Edwards, St. L.	L	21	36	2	0	38	0	1.000
Clark, Phil.-Chi.	R	20	34	2	0	36	0	1.000
Kaline, Det.	R	20	11	1	0	12	0	1.000
Stewart, Chi.	R	16	12	0	0	12	0	1.000
Woodling, N.Y.	R	119	240	6	1	247	2	.996
Mele, Chi.	R	138	213	14	1	228	1	.996

Name and Club	Throws	G	PO	A	E	TC	DP	PCT.
Delsing, Det.	R	133	354	7	3	364	2	.992
Bauer, N.Y.	R	126	230	13	2	245	3	.992
Groth, St. L.	R	141	425	18	4	447	5	.991
Noren, N.Y.	L	96	208	11	2	221	1	.991
Busby, Wash.	R	150	482	15	6	503	4	.988
Evers, Bos.	R	93	161	3	2	166	0	.988
Piersall, Bos.	R	151	352	15	5	372	7	.987
Doby, Clev.	R	146	354	10	6	370	3	.984
Umphlett, Bos.	R	136	382	12	7	401	1	.983
Jensen, Wash.	R	146	274	9	5	288	0	.983
Renna, N.Y.	R	40	57	0	1	58	0	.983
Mantle, N.Y.	R	121	322	10	6	338	2	.982
McGhee, Phil.	R	99	319	4	6	329	0	.982
Philley, Phil.	R	157	296	18	6	320	0	.981
Dyck, St. L.	R	55	100	5	2	107	1	.981
Lund, Det.	R	123	275	12	6	293	0	.980
Nieman, Det.	R	135	271	10	6	287	1	.979
Vollmer, Bos.-Wash.	R	106	227	8	5	240	1	.979
Wright, Chi.	R	33	44	1	1	46	0	.978
Rivera, Chi.	L	156	385	15	10	410	5	.976
Wertz, St. L.	R	121	243	15	7	265	4	.974
Zernial, Phil.	R	141	300	17	9	326	2	.972
Mauro, Wash.-Phil.	R	55	129	6	4	139	0	.971
Mitchell, Clev.	L	125	224	2	7	233	1	.970
Williams, Bos.	R	26	31	1	1	33	1	.970
Olson, Bos.	R	24	31	1	1	33	0	.970
Lenhardt, St. L.	R	77	148	8	5	161	1	.969
Simpson, Clev.	R	69	118	4	4	126	0	.968
Minoso, Chi.	R	147	279	15	10	304	3	.967
Stephens, Bos.	R	72	113	2	4	119	0	.966
Kokos, St. L.	L	83	152	5	6	163	1	.963
Westlake, Clev.	R	72	128	3	5	136	2	.963
Boyd, Chi.	L	16	26	0	1	27	0	.963
Souchock, Det.	R	80	144	7	6	157	3	.962
Sullivan, Det.	R	20	42	4	2	48	1	.958
Zarilla, Bos.	R	18	17	1	1	19	0	.947
Mullin, Det.	R	14	16	1	1	18	0	.944
Smith, Clev.	R	39	67	2	6	75	0	.920
J. Lemon, Clev.	R	11	20	1	2	23	0	.913

TRIPLE PLAY - Noren

CATCHERS

Name and Club	G	PO	A	E	TC	DP	PB	PCT.
Tipton, Clev.	46	114	18	0	132	1	3	1.000
Sheeley, Chi.	17	60	2	0	62	1	0	1.000
Lollar, Chi.	107	470	51	3	524	2	3	.994
Silvera, N. Y.	39	113	15	1	129	1	2	.992
Murray, Phil.	78	330	45	4	379	8	8	.989
FitzGerald, Wash.	85	319	33	4	356	3	8	.989
Astroth, Phil.	79	341	47	5	393	13	7	.987
White, Bos.	131	588	68	9	665	9	5	.986
Berra, N. Y.	133	566	64	9	639	9	8	.986
Batts, Det.	103	463	44	7	514	7	13	.986
Niarhos, Bos.	16	61	5	1	67	2	1	.985
Grasso, Wash.	59	219	24	4	247	4	4	.984
Bucha, Det.	56	218	22	4	244	4	5	.984
R. Wilson, Chi.	63	282	24	6	312	1	1	.981
Courtney, St. L.	103	436	47	10	493	7	4	.980
Wilber, Bos.	28	90	7	2	99	0	2	.980
Moss, St. L.	71	296	21	7	324	4	4	.978
Hegan, Clev.	106	399	42	11	452	3	5	.976
Ginsberg, Det.-Clev.	54	201	22	6	229	4	4	.974

CLUB FIELDING

CLUB	G	DP	TP	PB	PO	A	E	TC	PCT
Chicago	156	144	1	4	4211	1779	125	6115	.980
Cleveland	155	197	0	3	4119	1794	127	6040	.979
New York	151	182	1	10	4075	1747	126	5948	.979
Washington	152	173	1	12	4033	1638	120	5791	.979
Detroit	158	149	0	20	4245	1742	135	6122	.978
Philadelphia	157	161	0	15	4227	1709	137	6073	.977
Boston	153	173	0	8	4119	1732	148	5999	.975
St. Louis	154	165	1	8	4151	1644	152	5947	.974
TOTALS		1344	4	90	33180	13785	1070	48035	.978

Triple Play: Chicago, N. Y., Wash., St. Louis.

INDIVIDUAL RECORDS

Includes all players with 20 or more runs batted in, rated according to runs batted in.

NAME AND CLUB	G	BB	HB	RBI	SO	GI DP	SLUG PCT
Rosen, Clev.	155	85	4	145	48	19	.613
Vernon, Wash.	152	63	4	115	57	15	.518
Boone, Clev.-Det.	135	72	5	114	68	9	.519
Berra, N. Y.	137	50	3	108	32	7	.523
Zernial, Phil.	147	57	4	108	79	12	.559
Minoso, Chi.	151	74	17	104	43	23	.466
Doby, Clev.	149	96	6	102	121	7	.487
Robinson, Phil.	156	63	5	102	56	13	.413
Dropo, Det.	152	29	6	96	69	22	.371
Mantle, N. Y.	127	79	0	92	90	2	.497
Jensen, Wash.	147	73	5	84	51	19	.408
McDougald, N. Y.	141	60	5	83	65	9	.416
Mele, Chi.	140	58	0	82	47	14	.437
Busby, Wash.	150	38	4	82	45	8	.415
Rivera, Chi.	156	53	6	78	70	15	.420
Martin, N. Y.	149	43	6	75	56	19	.395
Vollmer, Bos.-Wash.	119	49	3	74	59	6	.392
Kell, Bos.	134	52	5	73	22	10	.483
Fox, Chi.	154	49	7	72	18	15	.375
Gernert, Bos.	139	88	5	71	82	9	.415
Wertz, St. L.	128	72	4	70	44	13	.466
Nieman, Det.	142	57	0	69	57	13	.453
White, Bos.	136	29	2	64	48	15	.435
Delsing, Det.	138	66	5	62	39	8	.436
Elliott, St. L.-Chi.	115	61	1	61	39	7	.391
Mitchell, Clev.	134	42	0	60	20	11	.446
Umphlett, Bos.	137	34	2	59	30	11	.376
Philley, Phil.	157	51	2	59	35	22	.424
Woodling, N. Y.	125	82	3	58	29	14	.468
Bauer, N. Y.	133	59	6	57	45	8	.446
Groth, St. L.	141	42	2	57	53	14	.370
Avila, Clev.	141	58	2	55	27	18	.379
Lollar, Chi.	113	47	8	54	29	7	.416
Rizzuto, N. Y.	134	71	4	54	39	6	.351
Fain, Chi.	128	108	4	52	28	11	.345
Piersall, Bos.	151	41	9	52	52	12	.354
Kryhoski, St. L.	104	26	2	50	33	10	.497
Runnels, Wash.	137	64	3	50	36	18	.321
Kuenn, Det.	155	50	1	48	31	10	.388
Strickland, Clev.	123	51	0	47	52	4	.379
Lund, Det.	131	39	2	47	65	11	.390
Carrasquel, Chi.	149	38	4	47	47	15	.359
Westlake, Clev.	82	35	2	46	29	6	.495
Souchock, Det.	89	8	2	46	35	10	.489

NAME AND CLUB	G	BB	HB	RBI		GI DP	SLUG PCT
Noren, N. Y.	109	42	2	46	39	5	.388
Terwilliger, Wash.	134	64	0	46	65	13	.347
Yost, Wash.	152	123	4	45	59	12	.395
Collins, N. Y.	127	59	0	44	36	6	.439
Batts, Det.	116	24	0	42	36	9	.406
Michaels, Phil.	117	51	1	42	56	6	.363
Murray, Phil.	84	18	1	41	25	6	.425
Goodman, Bos.	128	57	2	41	11	2	.409
FitzGerald, Wash.	88	19	1	39	34	10	.326
Kokos, St. L.	107	56	0	38	53	4	.411
Hegan, Clev.	112	25	1	37	41	8	.348
Hunter, St. L.	154	24	2	37	45	12	.259
Sievers, St. L.	92	32	0	35	47	9	.407
Lenhardt, St. L.	97	41	1	35	41	8	.465
DeMaestri, Phil.	111	24	1	35	39	15	.352
Suder, Phil.	115	17	0	35	35	10	.350
Williams, Bos.	37	19	0	34	10	1	.901
Easter, Clev.	68	15	4	31	35	13	.445
Stephens, Chi-St. L.	90	31	0	31	42	10	.361
Evers, Bos.	99	23	8	31	41	9	.390
Glynn, Clev.	147	44	5	30	65	5	.309
Wilber, Bos.	58	6	1	29	21	5	.500
McGhee, Phil.	104	32	3	29	43	12	.324
Moss, St. L.	78	18	1	28	31	10	.368
Bolling, Bos.	109	23	3	28	41	4	.353
Mize, N. Y.	81	12	2	27	17	1	.394
Dyck, St. L.	112	38	3	27	40	15	.344
Babe, N. Y.-Phil.	108	35	2	26	22	9	.305
Wright, Chi.	77	12	2	25	21	1	.379
Young, St. L.	148	41	1	25	40	12	.326
Priddy, Det.	65	17	1	24	19	6	.301
Bollweg, N. Y.	70	21	1	24	31	0	.503
Astroth, Phil.	82	27	2	24	12	11	.404
Baker, Wash.-Bos.	90	25	2	24	10	5	.307
Pesky, Det.	103	27	2	24	10	4	.390
Boyd, Chi.	55	13	1	23	11	3	.412
Friend, Det.-Clev.	65	11	1	23	25	7	.329
Grasso, Wash.	61	9	2	22	20	8	.276
Simpson, Clev.	82	18	1	22	27	6	.335
Kennedy, Clev.	100	19	1	22	11	7	.323

Includes all players in ten or more games with less than 20 runs batted in, rated according to runs batted in.

NAME AND CLUB	G	BB	HB	RBI	SO	GI DP
Mauro, Wash.-Phil.	81	20	0	19	24	6
Courtney, St. L.	106	25	1	19	20	14
Hatfield, Det.	109	40	1	19	34	7
Stephens, Bos.	78	29	2	18	56	1
R. Lemon, Clev.	51	7	0	17	20	1
Coan, Wash.	68	22	3	17	23	3
Mullin, Det.	79	14	0	17	15	3
Porterfield, Wash.	37	6	0	16	20	2
Joost, Phil.	51	45	0	15	24	1
Smith, Clev.	47	20	3	14	25	0
Bucha, Det.	60	20	0	14	14	3
Thomas, Phil.-Wash.	62	14	1	14	13	7
Krsnich, Chi.	64	12	0	14	11	2
Lipon, Bos.-St. L.	67	14	0	14	17	5
Clark, Phil.-Chi.	29	3	0	13	10	5
McDermott, Bos.	45	2	0	13	13	2
Tipton, Clev.	47	19	3	13	13	7
Stewart, Chi.	53	14	0	13	3	1
Renna, N. Y.	61	13	1	13	31	2

NAME AND CLUB	G	BB	HB	RBI	SO	GI DP
Ginsberg, Det.-Clev.	64	24	2	13	5	4
Silvera, N. Y.	42	9	0	12	5	0
Majeski, Clev.	50	3	1	12	8	1
Raschi, N. Y.	28	3	0	11	13	4
Berry, St. L.-Chi.	62	10	0	11	11	5
Lepcio, Bos.	66	17	1	11	24	5
Brown, Bos.	30	2	1	10	5	0
Ford, N. Y.	33	9	0	10	13	3
Wynn, Clev.	37	7	0	10	17	0
Larsen, St. L.	50	4	0	10	14	1
R. Wilson, Chi.	71	26	0	10	12	3
Parnell, Bos.	38	4	0	9	16	0
Hoskins, Clev.	38	3	1	9	11	1
Valo, Phil.	50	22	0	9	7	2
Edwards, St. L.	65	13	0	9	10	1
Sain, N. Y.	41	5	0	8	1	4
Carey, N. Y.	51	9	0	8	12	1
Gray, Det.	32	6	0	7	14	1
Trucks, St. L.-Chi.	40	0	1	7	13	1
Ryan, Chi.	17	9	0	6	12	4
Triandos, N. Y.	18	3	0	6	9	0
Sullivan, Det.	23	13	2	6	5	4
Shea, Wash.	23	2	0	6	9	3
Olson, Bos.	25	1	0	6	9	4
Garver, Det.	30	6	0	6	12	4
Hudson, Bos.	30	2	0	6	4	3
Bishop, Phil.	40	2	0	6	27	0
Byrd, Phil.	40	1	0	6	13	3
Consolo, Bos.	47	2	0	6	23	0
Giordano, Phil.	11	5	0	5	6	0
J. Lemon, Clev.	16	3	0	5	15	0
Keegan, Chi.	22	1	0	5	5	2
Hoderlein, Wash.	23	6	0	5	9	2
Masterson, Wash.	29	6	0	5	21	1
Byrne, Chi.-Wash.	32	5	0	5	13	0
Garcia, Clev.	38	3	0	5	15	2
Fornieles, Chi.	39	1	0	5	5	1
Hamilton, Phil.	58	7	0	5	11	2
Miranda, St. L.-N. Y.	65	6	0	5	11	4
Branca, Det.	17	2	0	4	14	2
Shantz, Phil.	21	2	0	4	3	1
Henry, Bos.	21	0	0	4	10	1
Snyder, Wash.	29	5	0	4	8	2
McDonald, N. Y	29	2	0	4	18	0
Hoeft, Det.	30	9	0	4	17	1
Pillette, St. L	31	5	0	4	16	1
Scheib, Phil.	35	2	0	4	1	1
Pierce, Chi.	42	4	1	4	16	3
Zarilla, Bos.	57	14	0	4	13	3
Wood, Wash.	12	2	0	3	3	1
Watlington, Phil.	21	3	0	3	8	1
Rogovin, Chi.	22	7	0	3	9	2
McCosky, Clev.	22	1	0	3	4	0
Holloman, St. L.	22	0	0	3	6	0
Nixon, Bos.	23	5	0	3	9	0
Stobbs, Wash.	27	4	0	3	14	1
Bearden, Chi.	31	0	0	3	4	1
Consuegra, Wash.-Chi.	33	1	0	3	7	0
Scarborough, N. Y.-Det.	38	0	0	3	2	1
Campos, Wash.	10	1	0	2	0	1
Verble, Wash.	13	2	0	2	1	1
Niarhos, Bos.	16	4	1	2	4	0
Carswell, Det.	16	3	0	2	1	0
Davalillo, Wash.	19	1	0	2	7	1
Dobson, Chi.	23	1	0	2	11	1
Aber, Clev.-Det.	23	3	0	2	6	0
Gromek, Clev.-Det	24	1	0	2	11	0
Brecheen, St. L.	27	1	0	2	10	1

NAME AND CLUB	G	BB	HB	RBI	SO	GI DP
Kaline, Det.	30	1	1	2	5	1
Sheely, Chi.	31	9	0	2	8	1
Cain, St. L.	34	1	0	2	3	1
Littlefield, St. L.	38	2	0	2	17	1
Houtteman, Det.-Clev	39	1	0	2	7	1
Reynolds, N. Y.	42	7	1	2	11	4
Marlowe, Det.	42	0	0	2	13	1
Paige, St. L.	57	0	0	2	9	0
Marsh, Chi.	67	13	1	2	26	2
Kinder, Bos.	69	0	0	2	6	0
Turley, St. L.	10	1	0	1	6	0
Weik, Clev.-Det.	13	0	0	1	1	0
Miller, N. Y.	13	0	0	1	1	0
Johnson, Chi.	15	2	0	1	7	1
Coleman, Phil.	21	1	0	1	7	0
Marrero, Wash.	22	5	0	1	8	0
Feller, Clev	25	6	0	1	23	0
Lopat, N. Y.	26	5	0	1	13	2
Kretlow, Chi.-St. L.	31	1	0	1	16	0
Flowers, Bos.	32	0	0	1	8	1
Blyzka, St. L.	33	1	0	1	9	0
Wight, Det.-Clev	33	0	0	1	3	0
Fricano, Phil.	46	4	0	1	30	0
Dorish, Chi.	55	0	0	1	5	1
Martin, Phil.	58	0	0	1	16	1
Stuart, St. L.	60	0	0	1	11	1
Dixon, Wash.	43	4	0	0	7	0
Kuzava, N. Y.	33	4	0	0	7	1
A. Kellner, Phil.	25	3	2	0	8	3
Hitchcock, Det.	22	3	0	0	3	4
Herbert, Det.	43	2	0	0	7	1
Lane, Wash.	20	2	0	0	2	0
Hooper, Clev	43	1	0	0	0	0
White, St. L.	10	1	0	0	0	0
Harrist, Chi.-Det.	15	1	0	0	0	0
Moreno, Wash.	12	1	0	0	0	0
Sima, Wash.	31	1	0	0	8	0
Gorman, N. Y.	40	1	0	0	7	0
Delock, Bos.	23	1	0	0	5	0
Schmitz, N. Y.-Wash.	27	0	0	0	13	0
Aloma, Chi.	24	0	0	0	4	0
Grissom, Bos.	13	0	0	0	4	0
Freeman, Bos.	18	0	0	0	3	1
Madison, Det.	32	0	0	0	2	1
Fanovich, Phil.	26	0	0	0	2	1
Newsom, Phil.	17	0	0	0	1	0
Kennedy, Bos.	16	0	0	0	1	0
Sullivan, Bos.	14	0	0	0	1	0
Lanier, St. L.	10	0	0	0	1	0
Miller, Det.	13	0	0	0	0	0
Brissie, Clev.	16	0	0	0	0	0
Erickson, Det.	18	0	0	0	0	1

CLUB RECORDS

CLUB	BB	HBP	SO	RBI	GI DP
New York	656	34	644	762	105
Cleveland	609	35	683	729	125
Chicago	601	54	530	676	146
Detroit	506	30	603	660	139
Washington	596	31	604	647	134
Boston	496	38	601	613	109
Philadelphia	498	24	602	588	141
St. Louis	507	17	644	522	144
TOTALS	4469	263	4911	5197	1043

OFFICIAL NATIONAL LEAGUE RECORDS, 1953

FINAL STANDING OF CLUBS

Club	Bkn.	Milw.	Phil.	St.L.	N.Y.	Cinn.	Chi.	Pitt.	Won	Lost	Pct.
Brooklyn	-	13	14	15	15	15	13	20	105	49	.682
Milwaukee	9	--	13	13	14	14	14	15	92	62	.597
Philadelphia	8	9	--	11	13	10	17	15	83	71	.539
St. Louis	7	9	11	--	13	15	11	17	83	71	.539
New York	7	8	9	9	--	13	13	11	70	84	.455
Cincinnati	7	8	12	7	9	--	10	15	68	86	.442
Chicago	9	8	5	11	9	12	--	11	65	89	.422
Pittsburgh	2	7	7	5	11	7	11	--	50	104	.325

INDIVIDUAL BATTING

(400 or more times at bat)

Player and Club	BATS	G	AB	R	H	2B	3B	HR	SB	RBI	PCT
Furillo, Carl A., Brooklyn	R	132	479	82	165	38	6	21	1	92	.344
Schoendienst, Albert F., St. L.	BOTH	146	564	107	193	35	5	15	3	79	.342
Musial, Stanley F., St. L.	L	157	593	127	200	53	9	30	3	113	.337
Snider, Edwin D., Brooklyn	L	153	590	132	198	38	4	42	16	126	.336
Mueller, Donald F., N. Y.	L	131	480	56	160	12	2	6	2	60	.333
Ashburn, Richie, Phil.	L	156	622	110	205	25	9	2	14	57	.330
Robinson, Jack R., Brooklyn	R	136	484	109	159	34	7	12	17	95	.329
Irvin, Monford, N. Y.	R	124	444	72	146	21	5	21	2	97	.329
Kluszewski, Theodore, Cinn.	L	149	570	97	180	25	0	40	2	108	.316
Campanella, Roy, Brooklyn	R	144	519	103	162	26	3	41	4	142	.312
Fondy, Dee, Chicago	L	150	595	79	184	24	11	18	10	78	.309
Baumholtz, Frank, Chicago	L	133	520	75	159	36	7	3	3	25	.306
Mathews, Edwin L., Milw.	L	157	579	110	175	31	8	47	1	135	.302
Hodges, Gilbert R., Brooklyn	R	141	520	101	157	22	7	31	1	122	.302
Dark, Alvin R., N. Y.	R	155	647	126	194	41	6	23	7	88	.300
Bell, David R., Cinn.	L	151	610	102	183	37	5	30	0	105	.300
Pafko, Andrew, Milw.	R	140	516	70	153	23	4	17	2	72	.297
Lockman, Carroll W., N. Y.	L	150	607	85	179	22	4	9	3	61	.295
O'Connell, Daniel F., Pitts.	R	149	588	88	173	26	8	7	3	55	.294
Slaughter, Enos B., St. L.	L	143	492	64	143	34	9	6	4	89	.291
Thomson, Robert B., N. Y.	R	154	608	80	175	22	6	26	4	106	.288
Abrams, Calvin, Pitts.	L	119	448	66	128	10	6	15	4	43	.286
Greengrass, James, Cinn.	R	154	606	86	173	22	7	20	6	100	.285
Adcock, Joseph W., Milw.	R	157	590	71	168	33	6	18	3	80	.285
Ennis, Delmer, Phil.	R	152	578	79	165	22	3	29	1	125	.285
Jackson, Ransom J., Chicago	R	139	498	61	142	22	8	19	8	66	.285
Hemus, Solomon J., St. L.	L	154	585	110	163	32	11	14	2	61	.279
Kiner, Ralph M., 41 Pitts.-117 Chi.	R	158	562	100	157	20	3	35	2	116	.279
Gilliam, James, Brooklyn	BOTH	151	605	125	168	31	17	6	21	63	.278
Hamner, Granville W., Phil.	R	154	609	90	168	30	8	21	2	92	.276
Adams, Robert H., Cinn.	R	150	607	99	167	14	6	8	3	49	.275
Repulski, Eldon J., St. L.	R	153	567	75	156	25	4	15	3	66	.275
Gordon, Sidney, Milw.	R	140	464	67	127	22	4	19	1	75	.274
Logan, John, Milw.	R	150	611	100	167	27	8	11	2	73	.273
Reese, Harold H., Brooklyn	R	140	524	108	142	25	7	13	22	61	.271
Wyrostek, John, Phil.	L	125	409	42	111	14	2	6	0	47	.271
Jablonski, Raymond L., St. L.	R	157	604	64	162	23	5	21	2	112	.268
Dittmer, John D., Milw.	L	138	504	54	134	22	1	9	1	63	.266
Thomas, Frank J., Pitts.	R	128	455	68	116	22	1	30	1	102	.255
Miksis, Edward T., Chicago	R	142	577	61	145	17	6	8	13	39	.251
Bilko, Stephen T., St. L.	R	154	570	72	143	23	3	21	0	84	.251
Bruton, William H., Milw.	L	151	613	82	153	18	14	1	26	41	.250
Rice, Delbert W., St. L.	R	135	419	32	99	22	1	6	0	37	.236

Player and Club	BATS	G	AB	R	H	2B	3B	HR	SB	RBI	PCT
McMillan, Roy D., Cinn.	R	155	557	51	130	15	4	5	2	43	.233
Bridges, Everett L., Cinn.	R	122	432	52	98	13	2	1	6	21	.227
Jones, Willie E., Phil.	R	149	481	61	108	16	2	19	1	70	.225
Spencer, Daryl, N. Y.	R	118	408	55	85	18	5	20	0	56	.208

Players in ten or more games but less than 400 times at bat.

Player and Club	BATS	G	AB	R	H	2B	3B	HR	SB	RBI	PCT
Hiller, Frank W., N. Y.	R	19	4	0	2	0	0	0	0	0	.500
Jolly, David, Milw.	R	24	2	1	1	0	0	0	0	0	.500
Cole, David B., Milw.	R	10	2	1	1	0	0	1	0	1	.500
Dunlap, Grant, St. L.	R	16	17	2	6	0	1	1	0	3	.353
Brazle, Alpha E., St. L.	L	60	15	2	5	1	0	0	0	0	.333
Nuxhall, Joseph H., Cinn.	L	30	49	6	16	2	0	3	0	8	.327
Banks, Ernest, Chicago	R	10	35	3	11	1	1	2	0	6	.314
Rice, Harold H., 8 St.L.-78 Pitts.	L	86	294	39	91	16	1	4	0	42	.310
Podres, John, Brooklyn	L	34	36	5	11	0	0	0	1	1	.306
Lindell, John H., 58 Pitts.-11 Phil.	R	69	109	14	33	7	1	4	0	17	.303
Thompson, Henry, N. Y.	L	114	388	80	117	15	8	24	6	74	.302
Leonard, Emil J., Chicago	R	45	10	0	3	1	0	0	0	2	.300
Pendleton, James E., Milw.	R	120	251	48	75	12	4	7	6	27	.299
Clark, Melvin J., Phil.	R	60	198	31	59	10	4	0	1	19	.298
Williams, David C., N. Y.	R	112	340	51	101	11	2	3	2	34	.297
Ryan, Cornelius J., Phil.	R	90	247	47	73	14	6	5	5	26	.296
Lerchen, George, Cinn.	L	22	17	2	5	1	0	0	0	2	.294
Burgess, Forrest H., Phil.	L	102	312	31	91	17	5	4	3	36	.292
Cox, William R., Brooklyn	R	100	327	44	95	18	1	10	2	44	.291
Waitkus, Edward S., Phil.	L	81	247	24	72	9	2	1	1	16	.291
Haddix, Harvey, St. L.	L	48	97	21	28	3	3	1	0	11	.289
Surkont, Matthew C., Milw.	R	28	56	10	16	5	1	0	0	6	.286
Crowe, George D., Milw.	L	47	42	6	12	2	0	2	0	6	.286
Anderson, Ferrell, St. L.	R	18	35	1	10	2	0	0	0	1	.286
Cavarretta, Philip J., Chicago	L	27	21	3	6	3	0	0	0	3	.286
Hughes, James R., Brooklyn	R	48	14	1	4	0	0	0	0	1	.286
Bowman, Roger C., Pitts.	R	30	7	0	2	0	0	0	0	0	.286
Hansen, Andrew V., Phil.	R	30	7	0	2	0	0	0	0	0	.286
Smith, Paul, Pitts.	L	118	389	41	110	12	7	4	3	44	.283
Corwin, Elmer N., N. Y.	R	54	32	5	9	1	1	2	0	4	.281
Torgeson, Earl C., Phil.	L	111	379	58	104	25	8	11	7	64	.274
Marquis, Robert R., Cinn.	L	40	44	9	12	1	1	2	0	3	.273
Crandall, Delmar, Milw.	R	116	382	55	104	13	1	15	2	51	.272
Cole, Richard R., Pitts.	R	97	235	29	64	13	1	0	2	23	.272
Maglie, Salvatore A., N. Y.	R	27	48	6	13	1	0	0	0	9	.271
Borkowski, Robert V., Cinn.	R	94	249	32	67	11	1	7	0	29	.269
Lowrey, Harry L., St. L.	R	104	182	26	49	9	2	5	1	27	.269
Stanky, Edward R., St. L.	R	17	30	5	8	0	0	0	1	0	.267
Marshall, Willard W., Cinn.	L	122	357	51	95	14	6	17	0	62	.266
Hofman, Robert G., N. Y.	R	74	169	21	45	7	2	12	1	34	.266
Temple, John E., Cincinnati	R	63	110	14	29	4	0	1	1	9	.264
Sauer, Henry J., Chicago	R	108	395	61	104	16	5	19	0	60	.263
Garagiola, Joseph, 27 Pitts.-74 Chi.	L	101	301	30	79	14	4	3	1	35	.262
Morgan, Robert M., Brooklyn	R	69	196	35	51	6	2	7	2	33	.260
Yvars, Salvador A., 23 N.Y.-30 St.L.	R	53	104	5	27	2	0	1	0	7	.260
McCullough, Clyde E., Chicago	R	77	229	21	59	3	2	6	0	23	.258
Sisler, Richard A., St. L.	L	32	43	3	11	1	1	0	0	4	.256
Collum, Jack D., 7 St.L.-30 Cinn.	L	37	39	3	10	2	0	0	0	3	.256
Shuba, George T., Brooklyn	L	74	169	19	43	12	1	5	1	23	.254
Elliott, Harry, St. L.	R	24	59	6	15	6	1	1	0	6	.254
Pellagrini, Edward C., Pitts.	R	78	174	16	44	3	2	4	1	19	.253
Janowicz, Victor F., Pitts.	R	42	123	10	31	3	1	2	0	8	.252
Serena, William R., Chicago	R	93	275	30	69	10	5	10	0	52	.251
Rigney, Willian J., N. Y.	R	19	20	2	5	0	0	0	0	1	.250
Simpson, Thomas L., Chicago	R	30	8	1	2	0	0	0	0	0	.250
Fusselman, Lester L., St. L.	R	11	8	1	2	1	0	0	0	0	.250
Pettit, Paul G., Pitts.	L	11	8	0	2	0	0	0	0	0	.250
Smalley, Roy F., Chicago	R	82	253	20	63	9	0	6	0	25	.249

121

Player and Club	BATS	G	AB	R	H	2B	3B	HR	SB	RBI	PCT
O'Brien, John, Pitts.	R	89	279	28	69	13	2	2	1	22	.247
Thompson, Donald N., Brooklyn	L	96	153	25	37	5	0	1	2	12	.242
Walker, Albert B., Brooklyn	L	43	95	5	23	6	0	3	0	9	.242
Post, Walter C., Cincinnati	R	11	33	3	8	1	0	1	1	4	.242
Landrith, Hobart N., Cinn.	L	52	154	15	37	3	1	3	2	16	.240
Lopata, Stanley E., Phil.	R	81	234	34	56	12	3	8	3	31	.239
Atwell, Maurice D., 24 Chi.-53 Pitts.	R	77	213	21	51	8	0	1	0	25	.239
Belardi, Wayne C., Brooklyn	L	69	163	19	39	3	2	11	0	34	.239
O'Brien, Edward, Pitts.	R	89	261	21	62	5	3	0	6	14	.238
Hanebrink, Harry A., Milw.	L	51	80	8	19	1	1	1	1	8	.238
Seminick, Andrew W., Cinn.	R	119	387	46	91	12	0	19	2	64	.235
Jeffcoat, Harold B., Chicage	R	106	183	22	43	3	1	4	5	22	.235
Black, Joseph, Brooklyn	R	34	17	1	4	0	0	0	0	1	.235
Rhodes, James L., N. Y.	L	76	163	18	38	7	0	11	0	30	.233
Hatton, Grady E., Cinn.	L	83	159	22	37	3	1	7	0	22	.233
Sandlock, Michael J., Pitts.	BOTH	64	186	10	43	5	0	0	0	12	.231
Church, Emory N., 12 Cinn.-27 Chi.	R	39	48	4	11	2	0	1	0	3	.229
Waugh, James E., Pitts.	R	29	22	2	5	0	0	0	0	1	.227
Westrum, Wesley N., N. Y.	R	107	290	40	65	5	0	12	2	30	.224
Calderone, Samuel F., N. Y.	R	35	45	4	10	2	0	0	0	8	.222
Minner, Paul E., Chicago	L	31	68	5	15	1	1	1	0	6	.221
Cawatski, Carl E., Chicago	L	43	59	5	13	3	0	1	0	5	.220
Presko, Joseph E., St. Louis	R	35	59	6	13	1	0	0	0	2	.220
Konstanty, C. James, Phil.	R	48	50	3	11	0	0	0	0	5	.220
Cooper, Walker W., Milw.	R	53	137	12	30	6	0	3	1	16	.219
Spahn, Warren E., Milw.	L	38	105	6	23	5	0	2	0	12	.219
Hacker, Warren L., Chicago	R	42	78	8	17	1	1	0	0	4	.218
Williams, Richard H., Brooklyn	R	30	55	4	12	2	0	2	0	5	.218
Kazanski, Theodore S., Phil.	R	95	360	39	78	17	5	2	1	27	.217
Sisti, Sebastian D., Milw.	R	38	23	8	5	1	0	0	0	4	.217
Ward, Preston M., 33 Chi.-88 Pitts.	L	121	381	45	82	12	1	12	4	39	.215
Erskine, Carl D., Brooklyn	R	43	93	12	20	2	0	0	0	8	.215
Bernier, Carlos R., Pitts.	B	105	310	48	66	7	8	3	15	31	.213
Metkovich, George M., 26 Pitts.-61 Chicago	L	87	165	24	35	8	1	3	2	19	.212
Nicholson, William B., Phil.	L	38	62	12	13	5	1	2	0	16	.210
Gomez, Ruben, N. Y.	R	61	72	15	15	1	0	0	0	4	.208
Hetki, John E., Pitts.	R	54	24	2	5	1	2	0	0	2	.208
Noble, Rafael M., N. Y.	R	46	97	15	20	0	1	4	1	14	.206
Davis, Brandon R., Pitts.	R	12	39	5	8	2	0	0	0	2	.205
Glaviano, Thomas G., Phil.	R	53	74	17	15	1	2	3	2	5	.203
Perkowski, Harry W., Cinn.	L	33	69	7	14	4	0	0	0	5	.203
St. Claire, Edward J., Milw.	BOTH	33	80	7	16	3	0	2	0	5	.200
Wehmeier, Herman R., Cinn.	R	29	20	1	4	0	0	0	0	0	.200
Johnson, William R., St. L.	R	11	5	0	1	1	0	0	0	1	.200
Castiglione, Peter R., 45 Pitts.-67 St. L.	R	112	211	23	42	4	1	4	1	24	.199
Brown, Thomas M., Chicago	R	65	138	19	27	7	1	2	1	13	.196
Ridzik, Stephen G., Phil.	R	42	36	3	7	3	0	1	0	4	.194
Baczewski, Frederick J., 9 Chicago-24 Cinn.	L	33	47	4	9	0	0	1	0	2	.191
Miller, Stuart L., St. L.	R	42	43	4	8	2	0	0	0	1	.186
Miller, Robert J., Phil.	R	35	55	5	10	1	0	0	0	3	.182
Roberts, Robin E., Phil.	BOTH	44	123	14	22	5	1	1	0	7	.179
Schofield, Richard, St. L.	BOTH	33	39	9	7	0	0	2	0	4	.179
Antonelli, John, Milw.	R	31	62	7	11	2	0	0	0	4	.177
Burdette, Lewis S., Milw.	R	46	53	4	9	0	0	0	0	1	.170
Gilbert, Harold J., N. Y.	L	70	160	12	27	3	0	3	1	16	.169
Hermanski, Eugene V., 18 Chicago-41 Pitts.	L	59	102	8	17	1	0	1	1	5	.167
Wilson, James A., Milw.	R	20	36	2	6	0	0	1	0	2	.167
Wade, Benjamin S., Brooklyn	R	32	24	1	4	0	0	1	0	2	.167
Antonello, William J., Brooklyn	R	40	43	9	7	1	1	1	0	4	.163
Smith, Richard H., Pitts.	R	13	43	4	7	0	1	0	0	2	.163
Thorpe, Benjamin V., Milw.	R	27	37	1	6	1	0	0	0	5	.162
Hall, Robert L., Pitts.	R	37	38	1	6	1	0	1	0	2	.158
Klippstein, John C., Chicago	R	48	58	5	9	2	0	1	0	4	.155
Ramazzotti, Robert L., Chicago	R	26	39	3	6	2	0	0	0	4	.154

122

Player and Club	BATS	G	AB	R	H	2B	3B	HR	SB	RBI	PCT
Smith, Frank T., Cinn.	R	50	13	0	2	0	0	0	0	1	.154
Lohrke, Jack W., Phil.	R	12	13	3	2	0	0	0	0	0	.154
Wilhelm, Hoyt J., N. Y.	R	68	33	5	5	2	1	0	0	1	.152
Meyer, Russell C., Brooklyn	BOTH	34	75	6	11	1	0	0	0	2	.147
Pollet, Howard J., 5 Pitts.-25 Chi.	L	30	34	3	5	0	0	0	0	2	.147
Erautt, Edward L., 4 Cinn.-20 St.L.	R	24	7	0	1	0	0	0	0	0	.143
Simmons, Curtis T., Phil.	L	32	93	6	13	1	1	0	1	3	.140
Raffensberger, Kenneth D., Cinn.	R	26	57	2	8	3	0	1	0	8	.140
Hearn, James T., New York	R	27	66	5	9	1	2	0	0	7	.136
Friend, Robert B., Pitts.	R	32	52	4	7	1	0	0	0	1	.135
Jansen, Lawrence J., N. Y.	R	36	60	5	8	0	0	0	0	2	.133
Face, Elroy L., Pitts.	R	43	30	1	4	1	0	0	0	2	.133
Addis, Robert G., 10 Chi.-4 Pitts.	L	14	15	2	2	1	0	0	0	1	.133
Podbielan, Clarence A., Cinn.	R	36	56	2	7	0	0	0	0	2	.125
Loes, William, Bklyn.	R	32	56	2	7	1	1	0	0	4	.125
Lown, Omar J., Chi.	R	49	48	3	6	1	0	0	0	2	.125
Wilson, George W., N. Y.	L	11	8	0	1	0	0	0	0	0	.125
Drews, Karl A., Phila.	R	47	59	3	7	0	0	0	0	1	.119
Milliken, Robert, Bklyn.	R	37	34	1	4	2	0	0	0	1	.118
Chambers, Clifford D., St. Louis	L	32	17	1	2	1	0	0	0	0	.118
Dickson, Murry M., Pitts.	R	45	61	0	7	0	0	0	0	2	.115
Buhl, Robert R., Milw.	R	30	53	3	6	0	0	0	0	0	.113
Rush, Robert R., Chi.	R	29	54	2	6	0	1	0	0	5	.111
Kelly, Robert E., 14 Chi.-28 Cinn.	R	42	18	0	2	0	0	0	0	0	.111
Judson, Howard K., Cinn.	R	10	9	3	1	0	0	0	0	0	.111
Montemayor, Felipe, Pitts.	L	28	55	5	6	4	0	0	0	2	.109
Staley, Gerald L., St. Louis	R	40	78	4	8	0	0	0	0	2	.103
Baldwin, Frank D., Cinn.	R	16	20	0	2	0	0	0	0	0	.100
Kipper, Thornton, Phila.	R	20	11	0	1	0	0	0	0	1	.091
Liddle, Donald E., Milw.	L	31	34	2	3	0	0	0	0	1	.088
La Palme, Paul E., Pitts.	L	35	59	6	5	0	0	0	0	1	.085
Mizell, Wilmer D., St. Louis	R	33	83	4	7	1	1	1	0	8	.084
Grissom, Marvin, N. Y.	R	21	27	2	2	1	0	0	0	1	.074
Labine, Clement W., Bklyn.	R	37	28	1	2	1	0	0	0	0	.071
Johnson, Ernest T., Milw.	R	36	14	0	1	0	0	0	0	0	.071
Bickford, Vernon E., Milw.	R	20	15	1	1	0	0	0	0	0	.067
Worthington, Allan, N. Y.	R	20	31	5	2	1	0	0	0	0	.065
Roe, Elwin C., Bklyn.	R	25	57	4	3	0	0	1	0	2	.053
Koslo, George B., N. Y.	L	37	30	0	1	0	0	0	0	0	.033
Nevel, Ernie W., Cinn.	R	10	0	0	0	0	0	0	0	0	.000
Kennedy, Montia C., N. Y.	R	19	2	0	0	0	0	0	0	0	.000
Benson, Vernon A., St. Louis	L	13	4	2	0	0	0	0	0	0	.000
Schultz, Robert D., 7 Chi.-11 Pitts.	R	18	5	1	0	0	0	0	0	0	.000
Clark, Michael J., St. Louis	R	23	6	0	0	0	0	0	0	0	.000
Jones, Sheldon L., Chi.	R	22	7	0	0	0	0	0	0	0	.000
Peterson, Kent F., Phila.	R	15	7	1	0	0	0	0	0	0	.000
Willis, James G., Chi.	L	13	9	1	0	0	0	0	0	1	.000
King, Clyde E., Cinn.	BOTH	35	10	0	0	0	0	0	0	0	.000
White, Harold G., St. Louis	R	49	16	0	0	0	0	0	0	0	.000

CLUB BATTING

Club	G.	AB.	R.	Opp. Runs	H.	2B.	3B.	HR.	SB.	RBI.	PCT.
Brooklyn	155	5373	955	689	1529	274	59	208	90	887	.285
St. Louis	157	5397	768	713	1474	281	56	140	18	722	.273
New York	155	5362	768	747	1452	195	45	176	31	739	.271
Milwaukee	157	5349	738	589	1422	227	52	156	46	691	.266
Philadelphia	156	5290	716	666	1400	228	62	115	42	657	.265
Cincinnati	155	5343	714	788	1396	190	34	166	25	669	.261
Chicago	155	5272	633	835	1372	204	57	137	49	588	.260
Pittsburgh	154	5253	622	887	1297	178	49	99	41	571	.247
Totals		42639	5914	5914	11342	1777	414	1197	342	5524	.266

123

PITCHERS' RECORDS

Pitchers With at Least 154 Innings Rated According to Earned Run Average Per Nine Inning Game

Pitcher and Club	Thrs.	G	GS	CG	W	L	PCT	IP	R	ER	H	HR	BB	SO	ERA
Spahn, Warren E., Milw.	L	35	32	24	23	7	.767	266	75	62	211	14	70	148	2.10
Roberts, Robin E., Phil.	R	44	41	33	23	16	.590	347	119	106	324	30	61	198	2.75
Buhl, Robert R., Milw.	R	30	18	8	13	8	.619	154	59	51	133	9	73	83	2.98
Haddix, Harvey, St. L.	L	36	33	19	20	9	.690	253	97	86	220	24	69	163	3.06
Antonelli, John, Milw.	L	31	26	11	12	12	.500	175	83	62	167	15	71	131	3.19
Simmons, Curtis T., Phil.	L	32	30	19	16	13	.552	238	102	85	211	17	82	138	3.21
Burdette, Lewis S., Milw.	R	46	13	6	15	5	.750	175	73	63	177	7	56	58	3.24
Gomez, Ruben, N. Y.	R	29	26	13	13	11	.542	204	89	77	166	17	101	113	3.40
Mizell, Wilmer D., St. L.	L	33	33	10	13	11	.542	224	93	87	193	12	114	173	3.50
Erskine, Carl D., Brooklyn	R	39	33	16	20	6	.769	247	106	97	213	21	95	187	3.53
Raffensberger, Kenneth D., Cinn.	L	26	26	9	7	14	.333	174	87	76	200	23	33	47	3.93
Staley, Gerald L., St. L.	R	40	32	10	18	9	.667	230	118	103	243	31	54	88	3.99
Miller, Robert J., Phil.	R	35	20	8	8	9	.471	157	76	70	169	14	42	63	4.01
Jansen, Lawrence J., N. Y.	R	36	26	6	11	16	.407	185	96	85	185	24	55	88	4.14
Surkont, Matthew C., Milw.	R	28	24	11	11	5	.688	170	82	79	168	22	64	83	4.18
Minner, Paul E., Chicago	L	31	27	9	12	15	.444	201	109	94	227	15	40	64	4.21
Roe, Elwin C., Brooklyn	L	25	24	9	11	3	.786	157	78	76	171	27	40	85	4.36
Hacker, Warren L., Chicago	R	39	32	9	12	19	.387	222	123	108	225	35	54	106	4.38
Konstanty, C. James, Phil.	R	48	19	7	14	10	.583	171	90	84	198	18	42	45	4.42
Dickson, Murry M., Pitts.	R	45	26	10	10	19	.345	201	121	101	240	27	58	88	4.52
Hearn, James T., N. Y.	R	36	32	6	9	12	.429	197	111	99	206	22	84	77	4.52
Perkowski, Harry W., Cinn.	L	33	25	7	12	11	.522	193	107	97	204	26	62	70	4.52
Drews, Karl A., Phil.	R	47	27	6	9	10	.474	185	116	93	218	26	50	72	4.52
Rush, Robert R., Chicago	R	29	28	8	8	14	.391	167	97	84	177	17	66	84	4.53
Loes, William, Brooklyn	R	32	25	9	14	8	.636	163	92	82	165	21	53	75	4.53
Meyer, Russell C., Brooklyn	R	34	32	10	15	5	.750	191	109	97	201	25	63	106	4.57
La Palme, Paul E., Pitts.	L	35	24	7	8	16	.333	176	107	90	191	20	64	86	4.60
Lindell, John H., 27 Pitts.-5 Phil.	R	32	26	15	6	17	.261	199	122	103	195	17	139	118	4.66
Podbielan, Clarence A., Cinn.	R	36	24	8	6	16	.273	186	112	98	214	21	67	74	4.74
Klippstein, John C., Chicago	R	48	20	5	10	11	.476	168	115	90	169	15	107	113	4.82
Friend, Robert B., Pitts.	R	32	24	8	8	11	.421	171	103	93	193	18	57	66	4.89
Presko, Joseph E., St. L.	R	34	25	4	6	13	.316	162	95	90	165	19	65	56	5.00

BALKS - Loes, 3; Spahn, Mizell, Surkont, 2 each. Staley, Buhl, Rush, Friend, 1 each.

Pitchers in Ten or More Games With Less Than 154 Innings Rated According to Earned Run Average Per Nine Inning Game

Pitcher and Club	Thrs.	G	GS	CG	W	L	PCT	IP	R	ER	H	HR	BB	SO	ERA
Johnson, Ernest T., Milw.	R	36	1	0	4	3	.571	81	34	24	79	4	22	36	2.67
Labine, Clement W., Brooklyn	R	37	7	0	11	6	.647	110	39	34	92	9	30	44	2.78
White, Harold G., St. L.	R	49	0	0	6	5	.545	85	32	28	84	5	39	32	2.96
Wilhelm, Hoyt J., N. Y.	R	68	0	0	7	8	.467	145	61	49	127	13	77	71	3.04
Liddle, Donald E., Milw.	L	31	15	4	7	6	.538	129	54	44	119	6	55	63	3.07
Willis, James G., Chicago	R	13	3	2	2	1	.667	43	15	15	37	1	17	15	3.14
Milliken, Robert, Brooklyn	R	37	10	3	5	4	.667	118	52	44	94	13	42	65	3.36
Worthington, Allan, N. Y.	R	20	17	5	4	8	.333	102	55	39	103	6	54	52	3.44
Hughes, James R., Brooklyn	R	48	0	0	4	3	.571	86	33	33	80	6	41	49	3.45
Jolly, David, Milw.	R	24	0	0	0	1	.000	38	16	15	34	4	27	23	3.55
Baczewski, Frederick J.. 9 Chi.-24 Cinn.	L	33	18	10	11	4	.733	148	65	60	145	14	58	61	3.65
Ridzik, Stephen G., Phil.	R	42	12	1	9	6	.600	124	61	52	119	15	48	53	3.77
Wade, Benjamin S., Brooklyn	R	32	0	0	7	5	.583	90	40	38	79	15	33	65	3.80
Grissom, Marvin, N. Y.	R	21	7	3	4	2	.667	84	40	37	83	6	31	46	3.96
Collum, Jack D., 7 St.L.-30 Cinn.	L	37	12	4	7	11	.389	136	67	60	138	9	43	56	3.97
Hetki, John E., Pitts.	R	54	2	0	3	6	.333	118	60	52	120	9	33	37	3.97
Hansen, Andrew V., Phil.	R	30	1	0	0	0	.000	51	30	23	60	6	24	17	4.06
Maglie, Salvatore A., N. Y.	R	27	24	9	8	9	.471	145	79	67	158	19	47	80	4.16
Brazle, Alpha E., St. L.	L	60	0	0	6	7	.462	92	47	43	101	8	43	57	4.21
Podres, John, Brooklyn	L	33	18	3	9	4	.692	115	62	54	126	12	64	82	4.23
Nuxhall, Joseph H., Cinn.	L	30	17	5	9	11	.450	142	77	68	136	13	69	52	4.31
Wilson, James A., Milw.	R	20	18	5	4	9	.308	114	59	55	107	16	43	71	4.34
Leonard, Emil J., Chicago	R	45	0	0	2	3	.400	63	34	32	72	9	24	27	4.57
Kipper, Thornton, Phil.	R	20	3	0	2	3	.500	46	26	24	59	8	12	15	4.70
Koslo, George B., N. Y.	L	37	12	2	6	12	.333	112	70	59	135	8	36	36	4.74
Clark, Michael J., St. L.	R	23	2	0	1	0	1.000	36	21	19	46	2	21	17	4.75
Pollet, Howard J., 5 Pitts.-25 Chi.	L	30	18	2	6	7	.462	124	77	66	147	8	50	53	4.79
Chambers, Clifford D., St. L.	L	32	8	0	3	6	.333	80	50	43	82	7	43	26	4.84
Bowman, Roger C., Pitts.	L	30	2	0	0	4	.000	65	42	35	65	9	29	36	4.85
Corwin, Elmer N., N. Y.	R	48	7	2	6	4	.600	107	65	59	122	17	68	49	4.96
Lown, Omar J., Chicago	R	49	12	2	8	7	.533	148	93	85	166	20	84	76	5.17
King, Clyde E., Cinn.	R	35	4	0	3	6	.333	76	47	44	78	15	32	21	5.21

Pitcher and Club	Thrs.	G	GS	CG	W	L	PCT	IP	R	ER	H	HR	BB	SO	ERA
Bickford, Vernon E.., Milw.	R	20	9	2	2	5	.286	58	35	34	60	8	35	25	5.28
Church, Emery N..11Cinn.-27Chi.	R	38	18	3	7	8	.467	148	99	87	170	25	68	59	5.29
Black, Joseph, Brooklyn	R	34	3	0	6	3	.667	73	46	43	74	12	27	42	5.30
Hall, Robert L., Pitts.	R	37	17	6	3	12	.200	152	99	91	172	17	72	68	5.39
Kelly, Robert E.. 14 Chi.-28 Cinn.	R	42	5	0	1	3	.250	83	55	50	98	9	35	35	5.42
Jones, Sheldon L., Chi.	R	22	2	0	0	2	.000	38	24	23	47	3	16	9	5.45
Smith, Frank T., Cinn.	R	50	1	0	8	1	.889	84	64	51	89	15	25	42	5.46
Miller, Stuart L., St. L.	R	40	18	8	7	8	.467	138	86	85	161	19	47	79	5.54
Judson, Howard K., Cinn.	R	10	6	0	0	1	.000	39	28	24	58	8	11	11	5.54
Hiller, Frank W.. N.Y.	R	19	1	0	2	1	.667	34	29	23	43	6	15	10	6.09
Erautt, Edward L.. 4Cinn.-20 St. L.	R	24	1	0	3	1	.750	40	28	28	54	7	19	16	6.30
Nevel, Ernie W., Cinn.	R	10	0	0	0	0	.000	10	7	7	16	0	1	5	6.30
Waugh, James E., Pitts.	R	29	11	1	4	5	.444	90	70	65	108	21	56	23	6.50
Face, Elroy L., Pitts.	R	41	13	2	6	8	.429	119	90	87	145	19	30	56	6.58
Peterson, Kent F., Phil.	L	15	0	0	0	1	.000	27	20	20	26	3	21	20	6.67
Kennedy, Montia C.. N.Y.	R	18	0	0	0	0	.000	23	18	18	30	2	19	11	7.04
Wehmeier, Herman R., Cinn.	R	28	10	2	1	6	.143	82	71	65	100	20	47	32	7.13
Schultz, Robert D.. 7 Chi.-11 Pitts.	L	18	4	0	0	4	.000	30	29	24	39	5	21	9	7.20
Pettit, Paul G., Pitts.	L	10	5	0	1	2	.333	28	27	24	33	1	20	14	7.71
Simpson, Thomas L., Chicago	L	30	1	0	1	2	.333	45	47	40	60	8	25	21	8.00
Cole, David B., Milw.	R	10	0	0	0	0	.000	15	14	14	17	1	14	13	8.40

BALKS - Johnson, White, Hetki, Leonard, Kipper, Koslo, Chambers, Corwin, Bickford, Black, Jones, Hiller, Erautt, Waugh, Face, Simpson, 1 each.

CLUB PITCHING RECORDS

Club	IP	R	ER	H	HR	BB	SO	CG	ERA
Milwaukee	1387	589	508	1282	107	539	738	72	3.30
Philadelphia	1369	666	578	1410	138	410	637	76	3.80
Brooklyn	1381	689	629	1337	169	509	817	51	4.10
St. Louis	1387	713	651	1406	139	533	732	51	4.22
New York	1366	747	645	1403	146	610	647	46	4.25
Cincinnati	1365	788	703	1484	179	488	506	47	4.64
Chicago	1359	835	723	1491	151	554	623	38	4.79
Pittsburgh	1358	887	788	1529	168	577	607	49	5.22
TOTALS	10972	5914	5225	11342	1197	4220	5307	430	4.29

INDIVIDUAL FIELDING (Ten or more games)

FIRST BASEMEN

Player and Club	Throws	G.	PO.	A.	E.	TC.	DP.	PCT.
Hatton, Grady E., Cinn.	R	10	72	3	0	75	14	1.000
Sisler, Richard A., St. L.	R	10	42	6	0	48	5	1.000
Kluszewski, Theodore, Cinn.	L	147	1285	58	7	1350	149	.995
Gilbert, Harold J., N. Y.	R	44	381	26	2	409	34	.995
Hodges, Gilbert R., Brooklyn	R	127	1025	99	8	1132	105	.993
Bilko, Stephen T., St. L.	R	154	1446	124	15	1585	145	.991
Adcock, Joseph W., Milw.	R	157	1389	96	13	1498	146	.991
Ward, Preston M., 7 Chi.-78 Pitts.	R	85	742	65	7	814	74	.991
Lockman, Carroll W., N. Y.	R	120	1042	100	13	1155	96	.989
Waitkus, Edward S., Phil.	L	59	480	37	6	523	65	.989
Fondy, Dee, Chicago	L	149	1274	115	18	1407	105	.987
Torgeson, C. Earl, Phil.	L	105	916	65	13	994	83	.987
Smith, Paul, Pitts.	L	74	622	52	10	684	53	.985
Belardi, Wayne C., Brooklyn	L	38	283	23	5	311	34	.984
Metkovich, George M., 5 Pitts.-7 Chi.	L	12	84	1	2	87	4	.977

Triple Play-Kluszewski

SECOND BASEMEN

Player and Club	Throws	G.	PO.	A.	E.	TC.	DP.	PCT.
Sisti, Sebastian D., Milw	R	13	10	9	0	19	1	1.000
Hatton, Grady E., Cinn.	R	35	56	49	1	106	15	.991
Dark, Alvin R., N. Y.	R	26	68	72	2	142	17	.986
Schoendienst, Albert F., St. L.	R	140	365	430	14	809	109	.983
Serena, William R., Chicago	R	49	106	120	4	230	24	.983
Williams, David C., N. Y.	R	95	191	254	8	453	54	.982
O'Brien, John, Pitts.	R	77	172	210	7	389	48	.982
Hanebrink, Harry A., Milw.	R	21	38	55	2	95	18	.979
Gilliam, James, Brooklyn	R	149	332	426	19	777	102	.976
Bridges, Everett L., Cinn.	R	115	329	320	16	665	94	.976
Hofman, Robert G., N. Y.	R	17	34	48	2	84	13	.976
Pellagrini, Edward C., Pitts.	R	31	69	72	4	145	12	.972
Hamner, Granville W., Phil.	R	93	194	290	15	499	65	.970
O'Connell, Daniel F., Pitts.	R	47	107	149	8	264	27	.970
Dittmer, John D., Milw.	R	138	290	343	23	656	95	.965
Temple, John E., Cinn.	R	44	71	90	6	167	20	.964
Spencer, Daryl, N. Y.	R	32	66	85	6	157	23	.962
Ryan, Cornelius J., Phil.	R	65	134	166	13	313	39	.958
Miksis, Edward T., Chicago	R	92	210	262	23	495	65	.954
Glaviano, Thomas G., Phil.	R	12	17	19	2	38	3	.947
Lowrey, Harry L., St. L.	R	10	22	19	3	44	6	.932
Ramazzotti, Robert L., Chicago	R	18	28	23	5	56	6	.911

Triple Play-Bridges

THIRD BASEMEN

Player and Club	Throws	G.	PO.	A.	E.	TC.	DP.	PCT.
Johnson, William R., St. L.	R	11	1	8	0	9	1	1.000
Castiglione, Peter R., 43 Pitts.-51 St. L.	R	94	51	110	4	165	10	.976
Jones, Willie E., Phil.	R	147	176	253	11	440	36	.975
Robinson, Jack R., Brooklyn	R	44	34	84	3	121	14	.975
Cox, William R., Brooklyn	R	89	86	142	6	234	20	.974
O'Connell, Daniel F., Pitts.	R	104	119	221	15	355	16	.958
Serena, William R., Chicago	R	28	29	40	3	72	7	.958
Thompson, Henry, N. Y.	R	101	90	194	13	297	18	.956
Adams, Robert H., Cinn.	R	150	159	324	25	508	39	.951
Jackson, Ransom J., Chicago	R	133	141	265	22	428	24	.949
Mathews, Edwin L., Milw.	R	157	154	311	30	495	33	.939
Pellagrini, Edward C., Pitts.	R	12	6	23	2	31	1	.935
Jablonski, Raymond L., St. L.	R	157	94	278	27	399	27	.932
Morgan, Robert M., Brooklyn	R	36	22	58	7	87	6	.920
Hofman, Robert G., N. Y.	R	23	21	35	5	61	5	.918
Spencer, Daryl, N. Y.	R	36	33	47	9	89	3	.899
Glaviano, Thomas G., Phil.	R	14	14	19	4	37	2	.892

SHORTSTOPS

Player and Club	Throws	G.	PO.	A.	E.	TC.	DP.	PCT.
Banks, Ernest, Chicago	R	10	19	33	1	53	9	.981
Logan, John, Milw.	R	150	295	481	20	796	104	.975
McMillan, Roy D., Cinn.	R	155	288	519	23	830	114	.972
Morgan, Robert M., Brooklyn	R	21	49	47	3	99	13	.970
Dark, Alvin R., N. Y.	R	110	219	343	19	581	79	.967
Reese, Harold H., Brooklyn	R	135	265	380	23	668	83	.966
Cole, Richard R., Pitts.	R	77	139	192	12	343	40	.965
Hemus, Solomon J., St. L	R	150	257	476	27	760	90	.964
Smith, Richard H., Pitts.	R	13	18	56	3	77	10	.961
Miksis, Edward T., Chicago	R	53	105	144	12	261	31	.954
Kazanski, Theodore S., Phil	R	95	185	239	23	447	53	.949
O'Brien, Edward, Pitts.	R	81	122	207	23	352	39	.935
Smalley, Roy F., Chicago	R	77	153	191	25	369	39	.932
Spencer, Daryl, N. Y.	R	53	80	137	17	234	26	.927
Hamner, Granville W., Phil.	R	71	91	169	22	282	40	.922
Schofield, Richard, St. L.	R	15	19	36	5	60	8	.917
Brown, Thomas M., Chicago	R	28	44	68	12	124	13	.903

Triple Play-McMillan

OUTFIELDERS

Player and Club	Throws	G.	PO.	A.	E.	TC.	DP.	PCT.
Metkovich, George M., 4 Pitts.-38 Chi	L	42	74	2	0	76	0	1.000
Lockman, Carroll W., N. Y.	R	30	64	2	0	66	0	1.000
Hermanski, Eugene V., 13 Chi.-13 Pitts.	R	26	44	0	0	44	0	1.000
Lowrey, Harry L., St. L.	R	38	42	1	0	43	0	1.000
Elliott, Harry, St. L.	R	17	34	1	0	35	0	1.000
Montemayor, Felipe, Pitts.	L	12	29	2	0	31	0	1.000
Dark, Alvin R., N. Y.	R	17	26	1	0	27	1	1.000
Nicholson, William B., Phil	R	12	13	0	0	13	0	1.000
Thorpe, Benjamin R., Milw.	R	18	12	0	0	12	0	1.000
Slaughter, Enos B., St. L.	R	137	235	2	1	238	0	.996
Marshall, Willard W., Cinn	R	95	187	11	1	199	1	.995
Clark, Melvin E., Phil.	R	51	104	2	1	107	0	.991
Ashburn, Richie, Phil.	R	156	496	18	5	519	4	.990
Thompson, Donald N., Brooklyn	L	81	84	5	1	90	1	.989
Furillo, Carl A., Brooklyn	R	131	232	11	3	246	3	.988
Snider, Edwin D., Brooklyn	R	151	370	7	5	382	3	.987
Repulski, Eldon J., St. L.	R	153	361	7	5	373	1	.987
Musial, Stanley F., St. L.	L	157	294	9	5	308	1	.984
Shuba, George T., Brooklyn	R	44	59	1	1	61	1	.984
Thomson, Robert B., N. Y.	R	154	391	16	7	414	0	.983
Greengrass, James, Cinn.	R	153	341	11	6	358	0	.983
Borkowski, Robert V., Cinn.	R	67	104	3	2	109	0	.982
Robinson, Jack R., Brooklyn	R	76	145	9	3	157	0	.981
Ennis, Delmer, Phil.	R	150	284	14	6	304	4	.980
Baumholtz, Frank, Chicago	L	130	290	6	6	302	0	.980
Bruton, William H., Milw.	R	150	397	15	9	421	5	.979
Bell David R., Cinn.	R	151	447	16	11	474	5	.977
Gordon, Sidney, Milw.	R	137	245	10	6	261	2	.977
Pafko, Andrew, Milw.	R	139	241	5	6	252	1	.976
Thomas, Frank J., Pitts.	R	118	306	17	8	351	1	.976
Hodges, Gilbert R., Brooklyn	R	24	37	2	1	40	1	.975
Kiner, Ralph M., 41 Pitts.-116 Chi	R	157	282	11	8	301	3	.973
Irvin, Monford, N. Y.	R	113	244	10	7	261	4	.973
Abrams, Calvin, Pitts.	L	112	205	13	6	224	3	.973
Rice, Harold H., 0 St. L.-70 Pitts.	R	70	167	14	5	186	2	.973
Jeffcoat, Harold B., Chicago	R	100	175	6	5	186	2	.973
Mueller, Donald F., N. Y.	R	122	203	7	6	216	0	.972
Smith, Paul, Pitts.	L	19	31	2	1	34	0	.971
Bernier, Carlos R., Pitts.	R	86	220	8	7	235	1	.970
Sauer, Henry J., Chicago	R	105	221	5	7	233	1	.970
Rhodes, James L., N. Y.	R	47	76	6	3	85	4	.965
Antonello, William J., Brooklyn	R	25	27	0	1	28	0	.964
Wyrostek, John, Phil.	R	110	102	11	8	211	2	.962

128

Player and Club	Throws	G.	PO.	A.	E.	TC.	DP.	PCT.
Pendleton, James E., Milw.	R	105	141	7	6	154	1	.961
Ward, Preston M., 27 Chi.- 0 Pitts.	R	27	49	0	2	51	0	.961
Post, Walter C., Cinn.	R	11	22	2	1	25	0	.960
Williams, Richard H., Brooklyn	R	24	24	0	2	26	0	.923
Marquis, Robert R., Cinn.	L	10	19	0	2	21	0	.905

CATCHERS

Player and Club	Throws	G.	PO.	A.	E.	TC.	DP.	PB.	PCT.
Anderson, Ferrell, St. L.	R	12	32	4	0	36	0	1	1.000
Fusselman, Lester L., St. L.	R	11	20	2	0	22	0	0	1.000
Yvars, Salvador A., 20 N. Y.-26 St. L.	R	46	146	20	1	167	4	2	.994
Burgess, Forrest H., Phil.	R	95	395	23	3	421	8	10	.993
St. Claire, Edward J., Milw.	R	27	106	11	1	118	3	4	.992
Sandlock, Michael J., Pitts.	R	64	290	49	3	342	4	15	.991
Campanella, Roy, Brooklyn	R	140	807	57	10	874	9	3	.989
Rice, Delbert W., St. L.	R	135	627	60	8	695	6	8	.988
Garagiola, Joseph, 22 Pitts.-68 Chi.	R	90	378	44	5	427	2	6	.988
Lopata, Stanley E., Phil	R	80	344	27	5	376	2	4	.987
McCullough, Clyde E., Chicago	R	73	273	31	4	308	7	1	.987
Crandall, Delmar, Milw.	R	108	566	62	9	637	13	6	.986
Landrith, Hobart N., Cinn.	R	47	179	13	3	195	4	2	.985
Cooper, Walker W., Milw.	R	35	165	6	3	174	1	0	.983
Westeum, Wesley N., N. Y.	R	106	441	53	9	503	9	6	.982
Seminick, Andrew W., Cinn.	R	112	436	44	9	489	2	4	.982
Noble, Rafael M., N. Y.	R	41	152	13	3	168	0	7	.982
Walker, Albert B., Brooklyn	R	28	120	12	3	135	2	1	.978
Calderone, Samuel F., N. Y.	R	31	50	6	2	58	2	0	.966
Atwell, Maurice D., 24 Chi.-45 Pitts.	R	69	295	37	15	347	2	7	.957
Sawatski, Carl E., Chicago	R	15	45	5	3	53	0	0	.943
Janowicz, Victor F., Pitts.	R	35	104	15	8	127	2	7	.937

CLUB FIELDING

Club	G.	DP.	PB.	PO.	A.	E.	TC.	PCT.
Brooklyn	155	161	4	4142	1608	118	5868	.980
Cincinnati	155	176	7	4094	1713	129	5936	.978
St. Louis	157	161	10	4160	1823	138	6121	.977
Milwaukee	157	169	10	4161	1711	143	6015	.976
New York	155	151	16	4097	1721	151	5969	.975
Philadelphia	156	161	14	4107	1578	147	5832	.975
Pittsburgh	154	139	32	4074	1759	163	5996	.973
Chicago	155	141	8	4079	1627	193	5899	.967
Totals	1259	101		32914	13540	1182	47636	.975

Triple Play-Cincinnati

INDIVIDUAL MISCELLANEOUS RECORDS

(Qualifiers for Slugging Championship)

Player and Club	G.	AB.	TB.	Slug PCT.	RBI.	BB.	SO.	HP.	Gr. Into DP.
Snider, Brooklyn	153	590	370	.6271	126	82	90	3	10
Mathews, Milw.	157	579	363	.6269	135	99	83	2	6
Campanella, Brooklyn	144	519	317	.610	142	67	58	4	13
Musial, St. L.	157	593	361	.609	113	105	32	0	10
Furillo, Brooklyn	132	479	278	.580	92	34	32	4	15
Kluszewski, Cinn.		570	325	.570	108	55	34	4	13
Hodges, Brooklyn	141	520	286	.550	122	75	84	3	4
Irvin, N. Y.	124	444	240	.541	97	55	34	3	20
Bell, Cinn.	151	610	320	.525	105	48	72	3	14
Kiner, Pitts.-Chi.	158	562	288	.512	116	100	88	3	11
Thomas, Pitts	128	455	230	.505	102	50	93	2	12
Schoendienst, St. L.	146	564	283	.502	79	60	23	0	19
Robinson, Brooklyn	136	484	243	.502	95	74	30	7	12
Dark, N. Y.	155	647	316	.488	88	28	34	6	19
Ennis, Phil.	152	578	280	.484	125	57	53	5	14
Fondy, Chicago	150	595	284	.477	78	44	106	1	6
Jackson, Chicago	139	498	237	.476	66	42	61	0	20
Thomson, N. Y.	154	608	287	.472	106	43	57	3	18
Gordon, Milw.	140	464	214	.461	75	71	40	2	14
Hamner, Phil.	154	609	277	.455	92	32	28	1	17
Pafko, Milw.	140	516	235	.455	72	37	33	3	14
Adcock, Milw.	157	590	267	.453	80	42	82	2	22
Greengrass, Cinn.	154	606	269	.444	100	47	83	3	18
Hemus, St. L.	154	585	259	.443	61	86	40	12	10
Abrams, Pitts.	119	448	195	.435	43	58	70	0	2
Slaughter, St. L.	143	492	213	.433	89	80	28	5	10
Jablonski, St. L.	157	604	258	.427	112	34	61	1	15
Spencer, N. Y.	118	408	173	.424	56	42	74	3	11
Reese, Brooklyn	140	524	220	.420	61	82	61	4	15
Baumholtz, Chicago	133	520	218	.419	25	42	36	1	5
Gilliam, Brooklyn	151	605	251	.415	63	100	38	3	7
Repulski, St. L.	153	567	234	.413	66	33	71	9	14
Bilko, St. L.	154	570	235	.412	84	70	125	1	17
Ashburn, Phil.	156	622	254	.408	57	61	35	5	3
Mueller, N. Y.	131	480	194	.404	60	19	13	1	7
O'Connell, Pitts.	149	588	236	.401	55	57	42	4	13
Logan, Milw.	150	611	243	.398	73	41	33	7	13
Lockman, N. Y.	150	607	236	.389	61	52	36	0	5
Jones, Phil.	149	481	185	.385	70	85	45	1	10
Dittmer, Milw.	138	504	185	.367	63	18	35	1	11
Wyrostek, Phil.	125	409	147	.359	47	38	43	4	9
Adams, Cinn.	150	607	217	.357	49	58	67	0	7
Miksis, Chicago	142	577	198	.343	39	33	59	1	18
Rice, St. L.	135	419	141	.337	37	48	49	6	13
Bruton, Milw.	151	613	202	.330	41	44	100	6	9
McMillan, Cinn.	155	557	168	.302	43	43	52	1	11
Bridges, Cinn.	122	432	118	.273	21	37	42	0	10

(Non-Qualifiers -- Ten or More Games)

Cole, Milw.	10	2	4	2.000	1	0	0	3	0
Dunlap, St. L.	16	17	11	.647	3	0	2	0	1
Banks, Chicago	10	35	20	.571	6	4	5	0	0
Thompson, N.Y.	114	388	220	.567	74	60	39	4	5
Corwin, N.Y.	54	32	18	.563	4	0	12	0	1
Nuxhall, Cinn.	30	49	27	.551	8	4	13	0	1
Hofman, N.Y.	74	169	92	.544	34	12	23	0	7
Hiller, N. Y.	19	4	2	.500	0	0	0	0	0
Jolly, Milw.	24	2	1	.500	0	1	1	0	0
Lindell, Pitts.-Phil.	69	109	54	.495	17	22	17	2	6
Belardi, Brooklyn	69	163	79	.485	34	16	40	1	2

Player and Club	G.	AB.	TB.	Slug P.C.	RBI.	BB.	SO.	HP.	Gr. Into DP.
Marshall, Cinn.	122	357	172	.482	62	41	28	0	10
Rhodes, N. Y.	76	163	78	.479	30	10	28	0	3
Marquis, Cinn.	40	44	21	.477	3	4	11	0	0
Crowe, Milw.	47	42	20	.476	6	2	7	1	1
Sauer, Chicago	108	395	187	.473	60	50	56	2	12
Torgeson, Phil.	111	379	178	.470	64	53	57	2	7
Pendleton, Milw.	120	251	116	.462	27	7	36	2	5
Ryan, Phil.	90	247	114	.462	26	30	35	0	4
Cox, Brooklyn	100	327	145	.443	44	37	21	0	7
Elliott, St. L.	24	59	26	.441	6	3	8	1	3
Serena, Chicago	93	275	119	.433	52	41	46	1	9
Crandall, Milw.	116	382	164	.429	51	33	47	0	13
Cavaretta, Chicago	27	21	9	.429	3	6	3	0	0
Shuba, Brooklyn	74	169	72	.426	23	17	20	1	5
Lowrey, St. L.	104	182	77	.423	27	15	21	0	8
Lopata, Phil.	81	234	98	.419	31	28	39	0	0
Nicholson, Phil.	38	62	26	.419	16	12	20	0	2
Morgan, Brooklyn	69	196	2	.418	33	33	47	1	7
Burgess, Phil.	102	312	130	.417	36	37	17	2	11
Hetki, Pitts.	54	24	10	.417	2	1	1	0	1
Seminick, Cinn.	119	387	160	.413	64	49	82	1	10
Rice, St. L.-Pitts.	86	294	121	.412	42	17	25	0	5
Haddix, St. L.	48	97	40	.412	11	5	19	2	2
Surkont, Milw.	28	56	23	.411	6	5	7	0	1
Borkowski, Cinn.	94	249	101	.406	29	21	41	1	5
Walker, Brooklyn	43	95	38	.400	9	7	11	1	1
Brazzle, St. L.	60	15	6	.400	0	0	1	0	0
Leonard, Chicago	45	10	4	.400	2	0	1	0	0
Johnson, St. L.	11	5	2	.400	1	1	1	0	0
Hatton, Cinn.	83	159	63	.396	22	29	24	0	3
Glaviano, Phil.	53	74	29	.392	5	24	20	2	4
Clark, Phil.	60	198	77	.389	19	11	17	1	10
P. Smith, Pitts.	118	389	148	.380	44	24	23	3	8
Fusselman, St. L.	11	8	3	.375	0	0	0	0	1
Williams, N. Y.	112	340	125	.368	34	44	19	3	6
McCullough, Chicago	77	229	84	.367	23	15	23	0	9
Westrum, N. Y.	107	290	106	.366	30	56	73	1	8
Garagiola, Pitts.-Chi.	101	301	110	.365	35	31	34	3	10
Williams, Brooklyn	30	55	20	.364	5	3	10	1	1
Post, Cinn.	11	33	12	.364	4	4	6	0	2
Pellagrini, Pitts.	78	174	63	.362	19	14	20	0	1
Ridzik, Phil.	42	36	13	.361	4	2	9	0	1
Smalley, Chicago	82	253	90	.356	25	28	57	2	4
Waitkus, Phil.	81	247	88	.356	16	13	23	1	3
Lerchen, Cinn.	22	17	6	.353	2	5	6	0	0
Noble, N. Y.	46	97	34	.351	14	19	14	3	2
Ward, Chi.-Pitts.	121	381	132	.346	39	62	60	1	9
Anderson, St. L.	18	35	12	.343	1	0	4	0	0
Janowicz, Pitts.	42	123	42	.341	8	5	31	1	3
Cole, Pitts.	97	235	79	.336	23	38	26	0	6
Metkovich, Pitts.-Chi.	87	165	55	.333	19	22	13	1	6
Church, Cinn.-Chi.	39	48	16	.333	3	2	10	0	1
Schofield, St. L.	33	39	13	.333	4	2	11	0	0
Landrith, Cinn.	52	154	51	.331	16	12	8	1	2
J. O'Brien, Pitts.	89	279	92	.330	22	21	36	4	9
Jeffcoat, Chicago	106	183	60	.328	22	21	26	0	5
Cooper, Milw.	53	137	45	.328	16	12	15	1	6
Temple, Cinn.	63	110	36	.327	9	7	12	1	0
Sisler, St. L.	32	43	14	.326	4	1	4	0	1
Spahn, Milw.	38	105	34	.324	12	1	22	0	1
Sawatski, Chicago	43	59	19	.322	5	7	7	0	2
Bernier, Pitts.	105	310	98	.316	31	51	53	4	11
Hanebrink, Milw.	51	80	25	.313	8	6	8	0	0
St. Claire, Milw.	33	80	25	.313	5	3	9	0	0
Minner, Chicago	31	68	21	.309	6	3	16	0	2
Kazanski, Phil.	95	360	111	.308	27	26	53	3	7

	G	AB	TB	Slug PC.	RBI	BB	SO	HP	Gr. Into DP
Yvars, N. Y.- St. L.	53	104	32	.308	7	11	7	1	7
Collum, St. L. - Cinn.	37	39	12	.308	3	4	1	0	1
Podres, Brooklyn	34	36	11	.306	1	0	1	1	1
Brown, Chicago	65	138	42	.304	13	13	17	3	9
Antonello, Brooklyn	40	43	13	.302	4	2	11	0	1
Thompson, Brooklyn	96	153	45	.294	12	14	13	1	6
Maglie, N. Y.	27	48	14	.292	9	2	13	0	3
Rigney, N. Y.	19	20	5	.250	1	0	4	0	0
Simpson, Chicago	30	8	2	.250	0	0	1	0	0
Pettit, Pitts.	11	8	2	.250	0	2	2	0	0
Raffensberger, Cinn.	26	57	14	.246	8	0	22	0	3
Gilbert, N. Y.	70	160	39	.244	16	22	21	0	2
Klippstein, Chicago	48	58	14	.241	4	1	20	0	0
Erskine, Brooklyn	43	93	22	.237	8	1	17	0	1
Presko, St. L.	35	59	14	.237	2	4	5	0	3
Black, Brooklyn	34	17	4	.235	1	0	5	0	0
Miller, St. L.	42	43	10	.233	1	3	2	0	2
Waugh, Pitts.	29	22	5	.227	1	1	5	0	1
Gomez, N. Y.	61	72	16	.222	4	1	8	0	2
Konstanty, Phil.	48	50	11	.220	5	0	7	0	0
Hearn, N. Y.	37	66	14	.212	7	8	27	0	3
Antonelli, Milw.	31	62	13	.210	4	3	14	0	0
R. Smith, Pitts.	13	43	9	.209	2	6	6	0	1
Hermanski, Chi.-Pitts.	59	102	21	.206	5	12	21	1	3
Ramazzotti, Chi.	26	39	8	.205	4	3	4	0	1
Miller, Phil.	35	55	11	.200	3	0	17	0	1
Wehmeier, Cinn.	29	20	4	.200	0	1	6	0	1
Addis, Chi.-Pitts.	14	15	3	.200	1	2	2	0	0
Thorpe, Milw.	27	37	7	.189	5	1	6	0	0
Montemayor, Pitts.	28	55	10	.182	2	4	13	3	1
Loes, Brooklyn	32	56	10	.179	4	1	13	0	2
Milliken, Brooklyn	37	34	6	.176	1	1	10	0	1
Chambers, St. L.	32	17	3	.176	0	0	4	0	0
Simmons, Phil.	32	93	16	.172	3	2	15	1	0
Burdetter, Milw.	46	53	9	.170	1	0	13	0	0
Face, Pitts.	43	30	5	.167	2	0	10	0	0
Meyer, Brooklyn	34	75	12	.160	2	3	21	0	2
Mizell, St. L.	33	83	13	.157	8	3	42	0	0
Friend, Pitts.	32	52	8	.154	1	1	16	0	1
Smith, Cinn.	50	13	2	.154	1	0	6	0	0
Lohrke, Phil.	12	13	2	.154	0	1	2	0	0
Rush, Chicago	29	54	8	.148	5	3	23	0	0
Pollet, Pitts.-Chi.	30	34	5	.147	2	3	6	0	0
Lown, Chicago	49	48	7	.146	2	2	8	0	2
Erautt, Cinn.-St.L.	24	7	1	.143	0	0	4	0	0
Jansen, N. Y.	36	60	8	.133	2	6	21	0	0
Podbielan, Cinn.	36	56	7	.125	2	2	11	0	0
Wilson, N. Y.	11	8	1	.125	0	2	2	1	0
Drews, Phil.	47	59	1	.119	1	4	20	0	0
Dickson, Pitts.	45	61	7	.115	2	2	11	0	2
Buhl, Milw.	30	53	6	.113	2	2	18	0	1
Grissom, N. Y.	21	27	3	.111	1	2	7	0	1
Kelly, Chi.-Cinn.	42	18	2	.111	0	0	7	0	0
Judson, Cinn.	10	9	1	.111	0	5	6	0	0
Labine, Brooklyn	37	28	3	.107	0	3	18	0	0
Roe, Brooklyn	25	57	6	.105	2	3	18	0	0
Staley, St. L.	40	78	8	.103	2	4	21	0	3
Baldwin, Cinn.	16	20	2	.100	0	1	9	0	1
Worthington, N. Y.	20	31	3	.097	0	2	14	0	0
Kipper, Phil.	20	11	1	.091	1	0	6	0	0
Liddle, Milw.	31	34	3	.088	1	3	9	0	0
La Palme, Pitts.	35	59	5	.085	1	1	13	0	2
Johnson, Milw.	36	14	1	.071	0	0	4	0	0
Bickford, Milw.	20	15	1	.067	0	1	7	0	0
Koslo, N. Y.	37	30	1	.033	0	1	11	0	1

	G	AB	TB	Slug PC.	RBI	BB	SO	HP	Gr. Into DP
White, St. L.	49	16	0	.000	0	1	8	0	1
King, Cinn.	35	10	0	.000	0	2	2	0	0
Clark, St. L.	23	6	0	.000	0	0	1	0	1
Jones, Chicago	22	7	0	.000	0	0	2	0	0
Kennedy, N. Y.	19	2	0	.000	0	0	2	0	0
Schultz, Chi.-Pitts.	18	5	0	.000	0	1	3	0	0
Peterson, Phil.	15	7	0	.000	0	0	2	0	2
Benson, St. L.	13	4	0	.000	0	1	2	0	0
Willis, Chicago	13	9	0	.000	1	1	3	0	0
Nevel, Cinn.	10	0	0	.000	0	0	0	0	0

CLUB MISCELLANEOUS RECORDS

Club	G	AB	TB	Slug PC.	RBI	BB	SO	HP	Gr. Into DP
Brooklyn	155	5373	2545	.474	887	655	686	35	115
St. Louis	157	5397	2287	.424	722	574	617	39	141
New York	155	5362	2265	.422	739	499	608	28	129
Milwaukee	157	5349	2221	.415	691	439	637	27	122
Cincinnati	155	5343	2152	.403	669	485	701	16	113
Chicago	155	5272	2101	.399	588	514	746	14	140
Philadelphia	156	5290	2097	.396	657	530	597	29	109
Pittsburgh	154	5253	1870	.356	571	524	715	36	117
TOTALS		42639	17538	.411	5524	4220	5307	224	986

1903: Boston A.L., 5; Pittsburgh N.L., 3.
1904: Not held.
1905: New York N.L., 4; Philadelphia A.L., 1.
1906: Chicago A.L., 4; Chicago N.L., 2.
1907: Chicago N.L., 4; Detroit A.L., 0.
1908: Chicago N.L., 4; Detroit A.L., 1.
1909: Pittsburgh N.L., 4; Detroit A.L., 3.
1910: Philadelphia A.L., 4; Chicago N.L., 1.
1911: Philadelphia A.L., 4; New York N.L., 2.
1912: Boston A.L., 4; New York N.L., 3.
1913: Philadelphia A.L., 4; New York N.L., 1.
1914: Boston N.L., 4; Philadelphia A.L., 0.
1915: Boston A.L., 4; Philadelphia N.L., 1.
1916: Boston A.L., 4; Brooklyn N.L., 1.
1917: Chicago A.L., 4; New York N.L., 2.
1918: Boston A.L., 4; Chicago N.L., 2.
1919: Cincinnati N.L., 5; Chicago A.L., 3.
1920: Cleveland A.L., 5; Brooklyn N.L., 2.
1921: New York N.L., 5; New York A.L., 3.
1922: New York N.L., 4; New York A.L., 0.
1923: New York A.L., 4; New York N.L., 2.
1924: Washington A.L., 4; New York N.L., 3.
1925: Pittsburgh N.L., 4; Washington A.L., 3.
1926: St. Louis N.L., 4; New York A.L., 3.
1927: New York A.L., 4; Pittsburgh N.L., 0.
1928: New York A.L., 4; St. Louis N.L., 0.
1929: Philadelphia A.L., 4; Chicago N.L., 1.
1930: Philadelphia A.L., 4; St. Louis N.L., 2.
1931: St. Louis N.L., 4; Philadelphia A.L., 3.
1932: New York A.L., 4; Chicago N.L., 0.
1933: New York N.L., 4; Washington A.L., 1.
1934: St. Louis N.L., 4; Detroit A.L., 3.
1935: Detroit A.L., 4; Chicago N.L., 2.
1936: New York A.L., 4; New York N.L., 2.
1937: New York A.L., 4; New York N.L., 2.
1938: New York A.L., 4; Chicago N.L., 0.
1939: New York A.L., 4; Cincinnati N.L., 0.
1940: Cincinnati N.L., 4; Detroit A.L., 3.
1941: New York A.L., 4; Brooklyn N.L., 1.
1942: St. Louis N.L., 4; New York A.L., 1.
1943: New York A.L., 4; St. Louis N.L., 1.
1944: St. Louis N.L., 4; St. Louis A.L., 2.
1945: Detroit A.L., 4; Chicago N.L., 3.
1946: St Louis N.L., 4; Boston A.L., 3.
1947: New York A.L., 4; Brooklyn N.L., 3.
1948: Cleveland A.L., 4; Boston N.L., 2.
1949: New York A.L., 4; Brooklyn N.L., 1.
1950: New York A.L., 4; Philadelphia N.L., 0.
1951: New York A.L., 4; New York N.L., 2.
1952: New York A.L., 4; Brooklyn N.L., 3.
1953: New York A.L., 4; Brooklyn N.L., 2.

CHAMPION BATTERS IN MAJOR LEAGUES

1901–1953

National League		American League	
1901—J. Burkett, St. Louis	.382	N. Lajoie, Philadelphia	.405
1902—C. H. Beaumont, Pittsburgh	.357	E. J. Delahanty, Washington	.376
1903—J. P. Wagner, Pittsburgh	.355	N. Lajoie, Cleveland	.355
1904—J. P. Wagner, Pittsburgh	.349	N. Lajoie, Cleveland	.381
1905—J. B. Seymour, Cincinnati	.377	Elmer Flick, Cleveland	.306
1906—J. P. Wagner, Pittsburgh	.339	G. Stone, St. Louis	.358
1907—J. P. Wagner, Pittsburgh	.350	T. R. Cobb, Detroit	.350
1908—J. P. Wagner, Pittsburgh	.354	T. R. Cobb, Detroit	.324
1909—J. P. Wagner, Pittsburgh	.339	T. R. Cobb, Detroit	.377
1910—S. N. Magee, Philadelphia	.331	T. R. Cobb, Detroit	.385
1911—J. P. Wagner, Pittsburgh	.334	T. R. Cobb, Detroit	.420
1912—H. Zimmerman, Chicago	.372	T. R. Cobb, Detroit	.410
1913—J. Daubert, Brooklyn	.350	T. R. Cobb, Detroit	.390
1914—J. Daubert, Brooklyn	.329	T. R. Cobb, Detroit	.368
1915—L. Doyle, New York	.320	T. R. Cobb, Detroit	.369
1916—H. Chase, Cincinnati	.339	T. Speaker, Cleveland	.386
1917—E. J. Roush, Cincinnati	.341	T. R. Cobb, Detroit	.383
1918—Z. D. Wheat, Brooklyn	.335	T. R. Cobb, Detroit	.382
1919—E. J. Roush, Cincinnati	.321	T. R. Cobb, Detroit	.384
1920—Rogers Hornsby, St. Louis	.370	G. H. Sisler, St. Louis	.407
1921—Rogers Hornsby, St. Louis	.397	H. E. Heilmann, Detroit	.394
1922—Rogers Hornsby, St. Louis	.401	G. H. Sisler, St. Louis	.420
1923—Rogers Hornsby, St. Louis	.384	H. E. Heilmann, Detroit	.403
1924—Rogers Hornsby, St. Louis	.424	G. H. Ruth, New York	.378
1925—Rogers Hornsby, St. Louis	.403	H. E. Heilmann, Detroit	.393
1926—Eugene Hargrave, Cincinnati	.353	H. E. Manush, Detroit	.378
1927—Paul G. Waner, Pittsburgh	.380	H. E. Heilmann, Detroit	.398
1928—Rogers Hornsby, Boston	.387	L. A. Goslin, Washington	.379
1929—Frank J. O'Doul, Philadelphia	.398	L. A. Fonseca, Cleveland	.369
1930—Wm. H. Terry, New York	.401	A. H. Simmons, Philadelphia	.381
1931—C. J. Hafey, St. Louis	.349	A. H. Simmons, Philadelphia	.390
1932—F. J. O'Doul, Brooklyn	.368	D. Alexander, Detroit-Boston	.367
1933—C. H. Klein, Philadelphia	.368	J. E. Foxx, Philadelphia	.356
1934—P. G. Waner, Pittsburgh	.362	H. L. Gehrig, New York	.363
1935—F. Vaughan, Pittsburgh	.385	C. S. Meyer, Washington	.349
1936—P. G. Waner, Pittsburgh	.373	L. B. Appling, Chicago	.388
1937—J. M. Medwick, St. Louis	.374	C. L. Gehringer, Detroit	.371
1938—E. N. Lombardi, Cincinnati	.342	J. E. Foxx, Boston	.349
1939—J. R. Mize, St. Louis	.349	J. P. DiMaggio, New York	.381
1940—D. Garms, Pittsburgh	.355	J. P. DiMaggio, New York	.352
1941—H. P. Reiser, Brooklyn	.343	T. S. Williams, Boston	.406
1942—E. N. Lombardi, Boston	.330	T. S. Williams, Boston	.356
1943—S. F. Musial, St. Louis	.357	L. B. Appling, Chicago	.328
1944—F. Walker, Brooklyn	.357	L. Boudreau, Cleveland	.327
1945—P. J. Cavarretta, Chicago	.355	G. H. Stirnweiss, New York	.309
1946—S. F. Musial, St. Louis	.365	Jas. B. Vernon, Washington	.353
1947—H. W. Walker, St. Louis Philadelphia	.363	T. S. Williams, Boston	.343
1948—S. F. Musial, St. Louis	.376	T. S. Williams, Boston	.369
1949—J. R. Robinson, Brooklyn	.342	G. C. Kell, Detroit	.342
1950—S. F. Musial, St. Louis	.346	W. D. Goodman, Boston	.354
1951—S. F. Musial, St. Louis	.355	F. R. Fain, Philadelphia	.344
1952—S. F. Musial, St. Louis	.336	F. R. Fain, Philadelphia	.327
1953—C. A. Furillo, Brooklyn	.344	Jas. B. Vernon, Washington	.337

LEADING PITCHERS IN MAJOR LEAGUES
Won and Lost Percentage, 1901–1953
(15 or more decisions)

	NATIONAL LEAGUE				AMERICAN LEAGUE			
	Name and Club	W.	L.	PC.	*Name and Club*	W.	L.	PC.
1901	Samuel L. Leever, Pitts. ..	14	5	.737	Clark C. Griffith, Chi.	24	7	.774
1902	John D. Chesbro, Pitts. ...	28	6	.824	William Bernhard, Cleve.	18	5	.783
1903	Samuel L. Leever, Pitts. ..	25	7	.781	Earl L. Moore, Cleve	22	7	.759
1904	Joseph J. McGinnity, N.Y.	35	8	.814	John D. Chesbro, N.Y. ...	41	12	.774
1905	Samuel L. Leever, Pitts. ..	20	5	.800	George E. Waddell, Phila.	27	10	.730
1906	Edward M. Reulbach, Chi.	19	4	.826	Edward S. Plank, Phila. ..	19	6	.760
1907	Edward M. Reulbach, Chi.	17	4	.810	Wm. E. Donovan, Detroit	25	4	.862
1908	Edward M. Reulbach, Chi.	24	7	.774	Edward A. Walsh, Chi. ...	40	15	.727
1909	{ S. Howard Camnitz, Pitts.	25	6	.806				
	{ Chris. Mathewson, N.Y. ..	25	6	.806	George J. Mullin, Detroit	29	8	.784
1910	Chas. L. Phillippe, Pitts. ..	14	2	.875	Charles A. Bender, Phila.	23	5	.821
1911	Rich. W. Marquard, N.Y. ..	24	7	.774	Charles A. Bender, Phila.	17	5	.773
1912	Claude R. Hendrix, Pitts. .	24	9	.727	Joseph Wood, Bos.	34	5	.872
1913	Albert Humphries, Chi. ...	16	4	.800	Walter P. Johnson, Wash.	36	7	.837
1914	William L. James, Bos.	26	7	.788	Charles A. Bender, Phila.	17	3	.850
1915	Grover C. Alexander, Phila.	31	10	.756	George H. Ruth, Bos.	18	6	.750
1916	Thomas Hughes, Bos.	16	3	.842	H. Coveleskie, Detroit	23	10	.697
1917	Ferd. N. Schupp, N.Y.	21	7	.750	Edward L. Klepfer, Cleve.	13	4	.765
1918	Claude R. Hendrix, Chi. ...	20	7	.741	Sam P. Jones, Bos.	16	5	.762
1919	Walter H. Reuther, Cinn. ..	19	6	.760	E. V. Cicotte, Chi.	29	7	.805
1920	Burleigh A. Grimes, Bklyn.	23	11	.676	James C. Bagby, Cleve. ..	31	12	.721
1921	{ Charles B. Adams, Pitts. .	14	5	.737				
	{ Chas. F. Glazner, Pitts. ..	14	5	.737	Carl W. Mays, N.Y.	27	9	.750
1922	Philip B. Douglas, N.Y. ...	11	4	.733	Leslie J. Bush, N.Y.	26	7	.788
1923	Adolfo Luque, Cinn.	27	8	.771	Herbert J. Pennock, N.Y. .	19	6	.760
1924	Emil Yde, Pitts.	16	3	.842	Walter P. Johnson, Wash.	23	7	.767
1925	Wm. H. Sherdel, St. L.	15	6	.714	S. Coveleskie, Wash.	20	5	.800
1926	Ray Kremer, Pitts.	20	6	.769	George E. Uhle, Cleve. ...	27	11	.711
1927	Lawrence J. Benton, N.Y. .	17	7	.708	Waite C. Hoyt, N.Y.	22	7	.759
1928	Lawrence J. Benton, N.Y. .	25	9	.735	A. F. Crowder, St. L.	21	5	.808
1929	Charles H. Root, Chi.	19	6	.760	Robert M. Grove, Phila. ..	20	6	.769
1930	Fred Fitzsimmons, N.Y. ...	19	7	.731	Robert M. Grove, Phila. ..	28	5	.848
1931	Jesse L. Haines, St. L.	12	3	.800	Robert M. Grove, Phila. ..	31	4	.886
1932	Lonnie Warneke, Chi.	22	6	.786	John T. Allen, N.Y.	17	4	.810
1933	Lyle Tinning, Chi.	13	6	.684	Robert M. Grove, Phila. ..	24	8	.750
1934	Jerome H. Dean, St. L.	30	7	.811	Vernon Gomez, N.Y.	26	5	.839
1935	William C. Lee, Chi.	20	6	.769	Eldon L. Auker, Detroit ..	18	7	.720
1936	Carl O. Hubbell, N.Y.	26	6	.813	Irving D. Hadley, N.Y. ...	14	4	.778
1937	Carl O. Hubbell, N.Y.	22	8	.733	John T. Allen, Cleve.	15	1	.938
1938	William C. Lee, Chi.	22	9	.710	Robert M. Grove, Bos. ...	14	4	.778
1939	Paul Derringer, Cinn.	25	7	.781	R. Atley Donald, N.Y.	13	3	.813
1940	Fred L. Fitzsimmons, Bklyn.	16	2	.889	Lynwood T. Rowe, Detroit	16	3	.842
1941	Elmer R. Riddle, Cinn.	19	4	.826	Vernon Gomez, N.Y.	15	5	.750
1942	Howard W. Krist, St. L. ...	13	3	.813	Ernest E. Bonham, N.Y. ..	21	5	.808
1943	{ Clyde M. Shoun, Cinn. ...	14	5	.737				
	{ J. Whitlow Wyatt, Bklyn.	14	5	.737	Spurgeon F. Chandler, N.Y.	20	4	.833
1944	Theodore Wilks, St. L.	17	4	.810	Cecil C. Hughson, Bos. ...	18	5	.783
1945	Harry D. Brecheen, St. L. .	15	4	.789	Robert C. Muncrief, St. L.	13	4	.765
1946	Lynwood T. Rowe, Phila. ..	11	4	.733	David M. Ferriss, Bos. ...	25	6	.806
1947	Lawrence Jansen, N.Y.	21	5	.808	Frank J. Shea, N.Y.	14	5	.737
1948	Truett B. Sewell, Pitts. ..	13	3	.813	John H. Kramer, Bos.	18	5	.783
1949	Ralph T. Branca, Bklyn. ...	13	5	.722	Ellis R. Kinder, Bos.	23	6	.793
1950	Salvatore A. Maglie, N.Y. .	18	4	.818	Victor J. Raschi, N.Y.	21	8	.724
1951	Elwin C. Roe, Bklyn.	22	3	.880	{ Robert W. A. Feller, Cleve.	22	8	.733
					{ Morris W. Martin, Phila. ..	11	4	.733
1952	J. Hoyt Wilhelm, N.Y.	15	3	.833	Robert C. Schantz, Phila.	24	7	.774
1953	Carl D. Erskine, Bklyn. ...	20	6	.769	Edmund W. Lopat, N.Y. ..	16	4	.800

RUNS BATTED IN LEADERS
(official tabulation adopted in 1920)

NATIONAL LEAGUE		AMERICAN LEAGUE	
1920—Kelly, George L., New York	94	Ruth, George H., New York	137
Hornsby, Rogers, St. Louis	94		
1921—Hornsby, Rogers, St. Louis	126	Ruth, George H., New York	170
1922—Hornsby, Rogers, St. Louis	152	Williams, Kenneth R., St. Louis	155
1923—Meusel, Emil F., New York	125	Speaker, Tris, Cleveland	130
		Ruth, George H., New York	130
1924—Kelly, George L., New York	136	Goslin, Leon A., Washington	129
1925—Hornsby, Rogers, St. Louis	143	Meusel, Robert W., New York	138
1926—Bottomley, James L., St. Louis	120	Ruth, George H., New York	155
1927—Waner, Paul G., Pittsburgh	131	Gehrig, Henry L., New York	175
1928—Bottomley, James L., St. Louis	136	Ruth, George H., New York	142
		Gehrig, Henry L., New York	142
1929—Wilson, Lewis R., Chicago	159	Simmons, Al H., Philadelphia	157
1930—Wilson, Lewis R., Chicago	190	Gehrig, Henry L., New York	174
1931—Klein, Charles H., Philadelphia	121	Gehrig, Henry L., New York	184
1932—Hurst, Frank O., Philadelphia	143	Foxx, James E., Philadelphia	169
1933—Klein, Charles H., Philadelphia	120	Foxx, James E., Philadelphia	163
1934—Ott, Melvin T., New York	135	Gehrig, Henry L., New York	165
1935—Berger, Walter A., Boston	130	Greenberg, Henry, Detroit	170
1936—Medwick, Joseph M., St. Louis	138	Trosky, Harold, Cleveland	162
1937—Medwick, Joseph M., St. Louis	154	Greenberg, Henry, Detroit	183
1938—Medwick, Joseph M., St. Louis	122	Foxx, James E., Boston	175
1939—McCormick, Frank A., Cincinnati	128	Williams, Theodore S., Boston	145
1940—Mize, John R., St. Louis	137	Greenberg, Henry, Detroit	150
1941—Camilli, Adolph, Brooklyn	120	DiMaggio, Jos. P., New York	125
1942—Mize, John R., New York	110	Williams, Theodore S., Boston	137
1943—Nicholson, William B., Chicago	128	York, P. Rudolph, Detroit	118
1944—Nicholson, William B., Chicago	122	Stephens, Vernon D., St. Louis	109
1945—Walker, Frederick, Brooklyn	124	Etten, Nicholas R., New York	111
1946—Slaughter, Enos B., St. Louis	130	Greenberg, Henry B., Detroit	127
1947—Mize, John R., New York	138	Williams, Theodore S., Boston	114
1948—Musial, Stanley F., St. Louis	131	DiMaggio, Joseph P., New York	155
1949—Kiner, Ralph M., Pittsburgh	127	Williams, Theodore S., Boston	159
		Stephens, Vernon D., Boston	159
1950—Ennis, Delmer, Philadelphia	126	Stephens, Vernon D., Boston	144
		Dropo, Walter O., Boston	144
1951—Irvin, Monford, New York	121	Zernial, Gus E., Chic-Phila.	129
1952—Sauer, Henry J., Chicago	121	Rosen, Albert L., Cleveland	105
1953—Campanella, Roy, Brooklyn	142	Rosen, Albert L., Cleveland	145

HOME RUN LEADERS
1901–1953

NATIONAL LEAGUE	No.	AMERICAN LEAGUE	No.
1901—Crawford, Samuel, Cincinnati	16	Lajoie, Napoleon, Philadelphia	13
1902—Leach, Thomas W., Pittsburgh	6	Seybold, Ralph O., Philadelphia	16
1903—Sheckard, James, T., Brooklyn	9	Freeman, John B., Boston	13
1904—Lumley, Harry G., Brooklyn	9	Davis, Harry H., Philadelphia	10
1905—Odwell, Fred, Cincinnati	9	Davis, Harry H., Philadelphia	8
1906—Jordan, Timothy J., Brooklyn	12	Davis, Harry H., Philadelphia	12
1907—Brain, David L., Boston	10	Davis, Harry H., Philadelphia	8
1908—Jordan, Timothy J., Brooklyn	12	Crawford, Samuel, Detroit	7
1909—Murray, John J., New York	7	Cobb, Tyrus R., Detroit	9
1910—Beck, Boston, Schulte, Chicago	10	Stahl, J. Garland, Boston	10
1911—Schulte, Frank, Chicago	21	Baker, J. Franklin, Philadelphia	9
1912—Zimmerman, Henry, Chicago	14	Baker, J. Franklin, Philadelphia	10
1913—Cravath, Clifford C., Philadelphia	19	Baker, J. Franklin, Philadelphia	12
1914—Cravath, Clifford C., Philadelphia	19	Baker, Phila.; Crawford, Detroit	8
1915—Cravath, Clifford C., Philadelphia	24	Roth, Robert F., Chic.-Cleveland	7
1916—Robertson, N. Y.; Williams, Chicago	12	Pipp, Walter C., New York	12
1917—Robertson, N. Y.; Cravath, Phila.	12	Pipp, Walter C., New York	9
1918—Cravath, Clifford C., Philadelphia	8	Walker, Phila.; Ruth, Boston	11
1919—Cravath, Clifford C., Philadelphia	12	Ruth, George H., Boston	29
1920—Williams, Fred C., Philadelphia	15	Ruth, George H., New York	54
1921—Kelly, George L., New York	23	Ruth, George H., New York	59
1922—Hornsby, Rogers, St. Louis	42	Williams, Kenneth R., St. Louis	39
1923—Williams, Fred C., Philadelphia	41	Ruth, George H., New York	41
1924—Fournier, Jacques F., Brooklyn	27	Ruth, George H., New York	46
1925—Hornsby, Rogers, St. Louis	39	Meusel, Robert W., New York	33
1926—Wilson, Lewis R., Chicago	21	Ruth, George H., New York	47
1927—Wilson, Chi.; Williams, Phila.	30	Ruth, George H., New York	60
1928—Bottomley, St. Louis; Wilson, Chi.	31	Ruth, George H., New York	54
1929—Klein, Charles H., Philadelphia	43	Ruth, George H., New York	46
1930—Wilson, Lewis R., Chicago	56	Ruth, George H., New York	49
1931—Klein, Charles H., Philadelphia	31	Ruth, N. Y.; Gehrig, N. Y.	46
1932—Klein, Phila.; Ott, New York	38	Foxx, James E., Philadelphia	58
1933—Klein, Charles H., Philadelphia	28	Foxx, James E., Philadelphia	48
1934—Collins, St. Louis; Ott, New York	35	Gehrig, Henry L., New York	49
1935—Berger, Walter A., Boston	34	Foxx, Phila.; Greenberg, Detroit	36
1936—Ott, Melvin T., New York	33	Gehrig, Henry L., New York	49
1937—Ott, New York; Medwick, St. Louis	31	DiMaggio, Joseph P., New York	46
1938—Ott, Melvin T., New York	36	Greenberg, Henry, Detroit	58
1939—Mize, John R., St. Louis	28	Foxx, James E., Boston	35
1940—Mize, John R., St. Louis	43	Greenberg, Henry, Detroit	41
1941—Camilli, Adolph, Brooklyn	34	Williams, Theodore S., Boston	37
1942—Ott, Melvin T., New York	30	Williams, Theodore S., Boston	36
1943—Nicholson, William B., Chicago	29	York, P. Rudolph, Detroit	34
1944—Nicholson, William B., Chicago	33	Etten, Nicholas R., New York	22
1945—Holmes, Thomas F., Boston	28	Stephens, Vernon D., St. Louis	24
1946—Kiner, Ralph M., Pittsburgh	23	Greenberg, Henry B., Detroit	44
1947—Kiner, Pitts.; Mize, New York	51	Williams, Theodore S., Boston	32
1948—Kiner, Pitts.; Mize, New York	40	DiMaggio, Joseph P., New York	39
1949—Kiner, Ralph M., Pittsburgh	54	Williams, Theodore S., Boston	43
1950—Kiner, Ralph M., Pittsburgh	47	Rosen, Albert L., Cleveland	37
1951—Kiner, Ralph M., Pittsburgh	42	Zernial, Gus E., Chic.-Phila.	33
1952—Kiner, Pitts., Sauer, Chicago	37	Doby, Lawrence E., Cleveland	32
1953—Mathews, Edwin L., Milwaukee	47	Rosen, Albert L., Cleveland	43

POSITION OF MAJOR LEAGUE CLUBS AT CLOSE OF SEASON
1901–1953

NATIONAL LEAGUE

	Boston	Brooklyn	Chicago	Cincinnati	New York	Philadelphia	Pittsburgh	St. Louis
1901	5	3	6	8	7	2	1	4
1902	3	2	5	4	8	7	1	6
1903	6	5	3	4	2	7	1	8
1904	7	6	2	3	1	8	4	5
1905	7	8	3	5	1	4	2	6
1906	8	5	1	6	2	4	3	7
1907	7	5	1	6	4	3	2	8
1908	6	7	1	5	2*4	4	2*	8
1909	8	6	2	4	3	5	1	7
1910	8	6	1	5	2	4	3	7
1911	8	7	2	6	1	4	3	5
1912	8	7	3	4	1	5	2	6
1913	5	6	3	7	1	2	4	8
1914	1	5	4	8	2	6	7	3
1915	2	3	4	7	8	1	5	6
1916	3	1	5	7*	4	2	6	7*
1917	6	7	5	4	1	2	8	3
1918	7	5	1	3	2	6	4	8
1919	6	5	3	1	2	8	4	7
1920	7	1	5	3	2	8	4	6
1921	4	5	7	6	1	8	2	3
1922	8	6	5	2	1	7	3*	3*
1923	7	6	4	2	1	8	3	5
1924	8	2	5	4	1	7	3	6
1925	5	6*	8	3	2	6*	1	4
1926	7	6	4	2	5	8	3	1
1927	7	6	4	5	3	8	1	2
1928	7	6	3	5	2	8	4	1
1929	8	6	1	7	3	5	2	4
1930	6	4	2	7	3	8	5	1
1931	7	4	3	8	2	6	5	1
1932	5	3	1	8	6*	4	2	6*
1933	4	6	3	8	1	7	2	5
1934	4	6	3	8	2	7	5	1
1935	8	5	1	6	3	7	4	2
1936	6	7	2*	5	1	8	4	2*
1937	5	6	2	8	1	7	3	4
1938	5	7	1	4	3	8	2	6
1939	7	3	4	1	5	8	6	2
1940	7	2	5	1	6	8	4	3
1941	7	1	6	3	5	8	4	2
1942	7	2	6	4	3	8	5	1
1943	6	3	5	2	8	7	4	1
1944	6	7	4	3	5	8	2	1
1945	6	3	1	7	5	8	4	2
1946	4	2	3	6	8	5	7	1
1947	3	1	6	5	4	7*	7*	2
1948	1	3	8	7	5	6	4	2
1949	4	1	8	7	5	3	6	2
1950	4	2	7	6	3	1	8	5
1951	4	2	8	6	1	5	7	3
1952	7	1	5	6	2	4	8	3
Milw.								
1953	2	1	7	6	5	3*	8	3*

*Indicates ties.

AMERICAN LEAGUE

	Boston	Chicago	Cleveland	Detroit	New York	Philadelphia	St. Louis	Washington
					Balto	Milw		
1901	2	1	7	3	5	4	8	6
					Balto			
1902	3	4	5	7	8	1	2	6
1903	1	7	3	5	4	2	6	8
1904	1	3	4	7	2	5	6	8
1905	4	2	5	3	6	1	8	7
1906	8	1	3	6	2	4	5	7
1907	7	3	4	1	5	2	6	8
1908	5	3	2	1	8	6	4	7
1909	3	4	6	1	5	2	7	8
1910	4	6	5	3	2	1	8	7
1911	5	4	3	2	6	1	8	7
1912	1	4	5	6	8	3	7	2
1913	4	5	3	6	7	1	8	2
1914	2	6*	8	4	6*	1	5	3
1915	1	3	7	2	5	8	6	4
1916	1	2	6	3	4	8	5	7
1917	2	1	3	4	6	8	7	5
1918	1	6	2	7	4	8	5	3
1919	6	1	2	4	3	8	5	7
1920	5	2	1	7	3	8	4	6
1921	5	7	2	6	1	8	3	4
1922	8	5	4	3	1	7	2	6
1923	8	7	3	2	1	6	5	4
1924	7	8	6	3	2	5	4	1
1925	8	5	6	4	7	2	3	1
1926	8	5	2	6	1	3	7	4
1927	8	5	6	4	1	2	7	3
1928	8	5	7	6	1	2	3	4
1929	8	7	3	6	2	1	4	5
1930	8	7	4	5	3	1	6	2
1931	6	8	4	7	2	1	5	3
1932	8	7	4	5	1	2	6	3
1933	7	6	4	5	2	3	8	1
1934	4	8	3	1	2	5	6	7
1935	4	5	3	1	2	8	7	6
1936	6	3	5	2	1	8	7	4
1937	5	3	4	2	1	7	8	6
1938	2	6	3	4	1	8	7	5
1939	2	4	3	5	1	7	8	6
1940	4*	4*	2	1	3	8	6	7
1941	2	3	4*	4*	1	8	6*	6*
1942	2	6	4	5	1	8	3	7
1943	7	4	3	5	1	8	6	2
1944	4	7	5*	2	3	5*	1	8
1945	7	6	5	1	4	8	3	2
1946	1	5	6	2	3	8	7	4
1947	3	6	4	2	1	5	8	7
1948	2	8	1	5	3	4	6	7
1949	2	6	3	4	1	5	7	8
1950	3	6	4	2	1	8	7	5
1951	3	4	2	5	1	6	8	7
1952	6	3	2	8	1	4	7	5
1953	4	3	2	6	1	7	8	5

139

AMERICAN LEAGUE PARKS

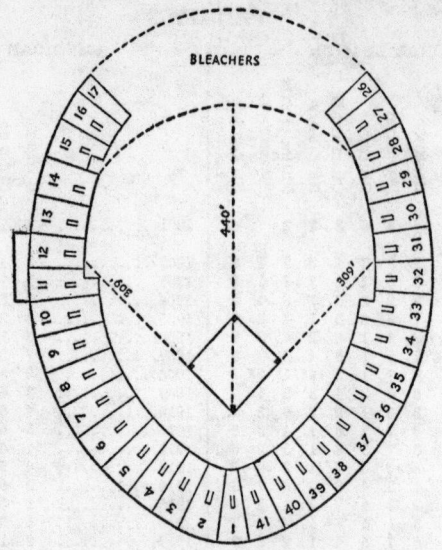

Memorial Stadium, Baltimore, Maryland
Double-decked stands. Bleachers

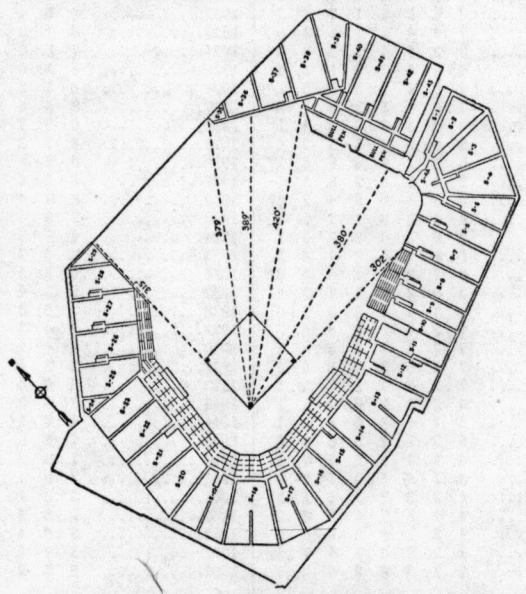

Fenway Park, Boston, Massachusetts
Double-decked stands. Bleachers
Seating capacity 34,822

140

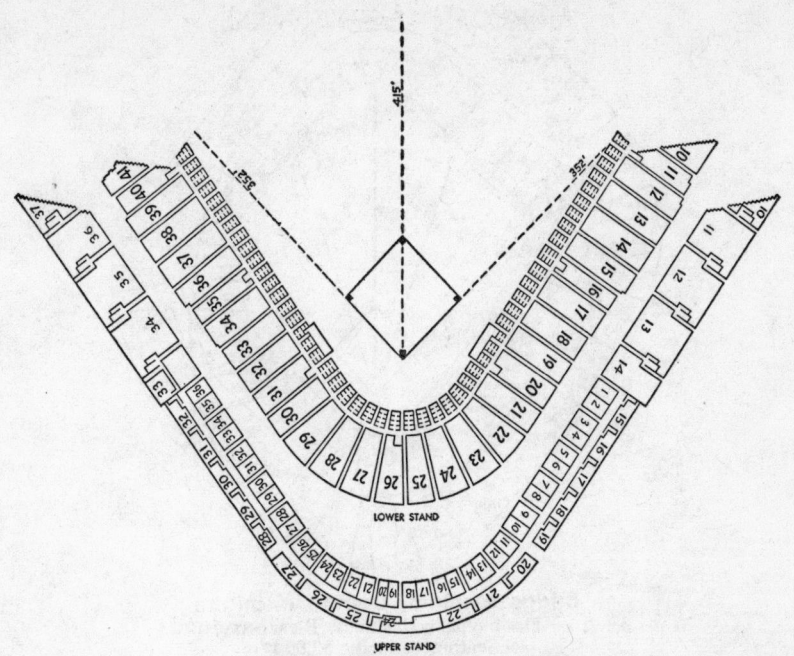

Comisky Park, Chicago, Illinois
Double-decked stands. Bleachers
Seating capacity 46,550

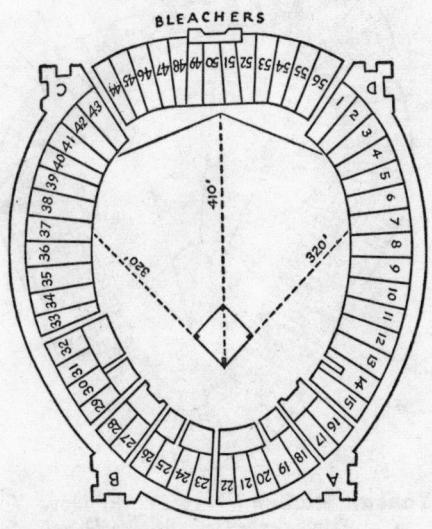

Municipal Stadium, Cleveland, Ohio
Double-decked stands. Bleachers
Seating capacity 73,500

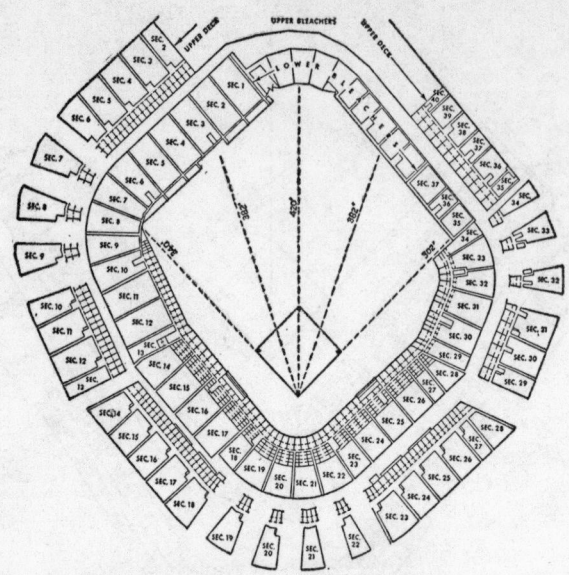

Briggs Stadium, Detroit, Michigan
Double-decked stands. Bleachers
Seating capacity 52,954

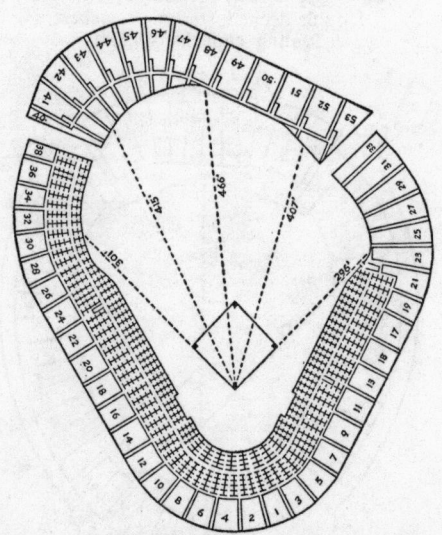

Yankee Stadium, New York, New York
Triple-decked stands. Bleachers
Seating capacity 67,000

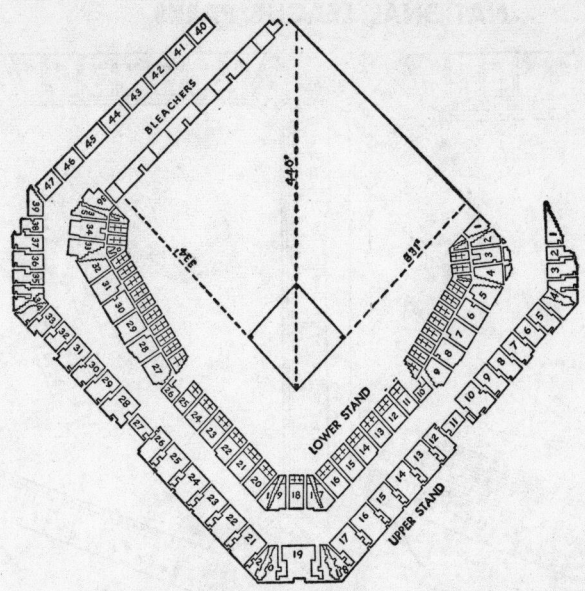

Connie Mack Stadium, Philadelphia, Pennsylvania
Double-decked stands. Bleachers covered
Seating capacity 33,223

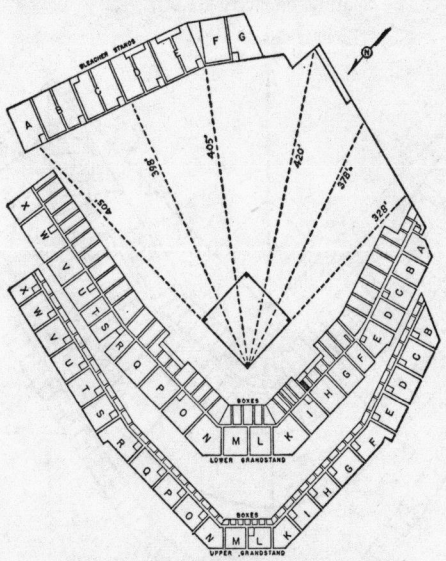

Griffith Stadium, Washington, D.C.
Double-decked stands. Bleachers
Seating capacity 27,523

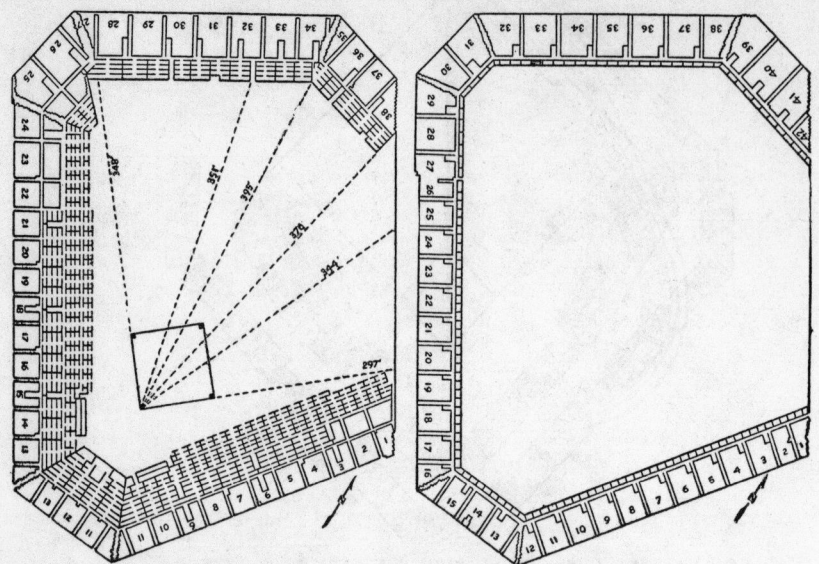

Ebbets Field, Booklyn, New York
Double-decked stands. Bleachers covered
Seating capacity 31,902

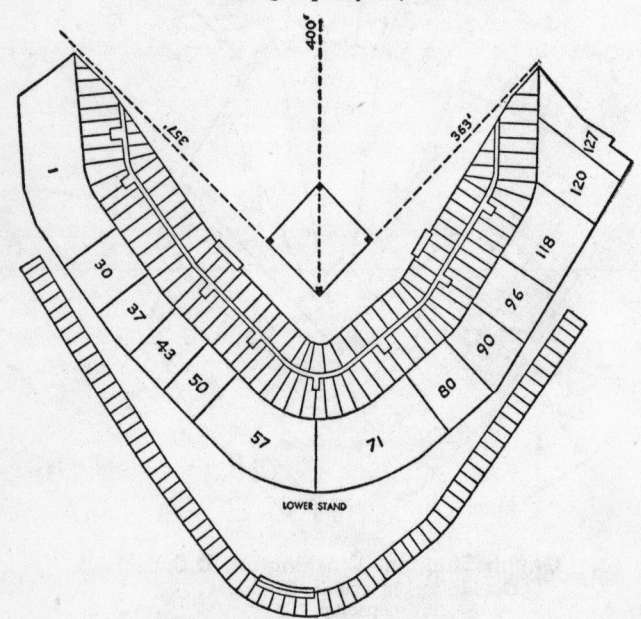

144   **Wrigley Field, Chicago, Illinois**
Double-decked stands. Bleachers
Seating capacity 36,755

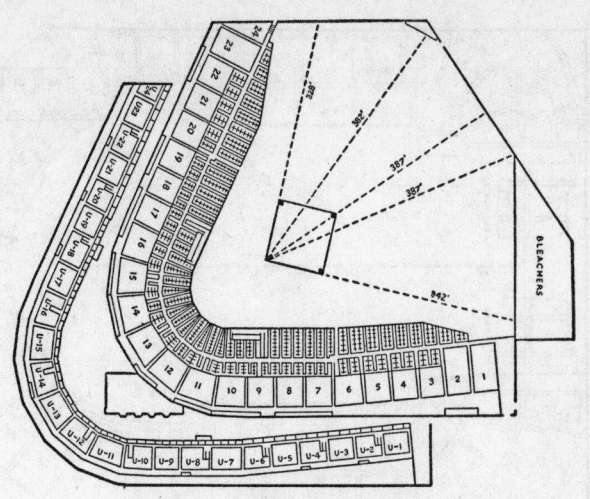

Crosley Field, Cincinnati, Ohio
Double-decked stands. Bleachers
Seating capacity 30,000

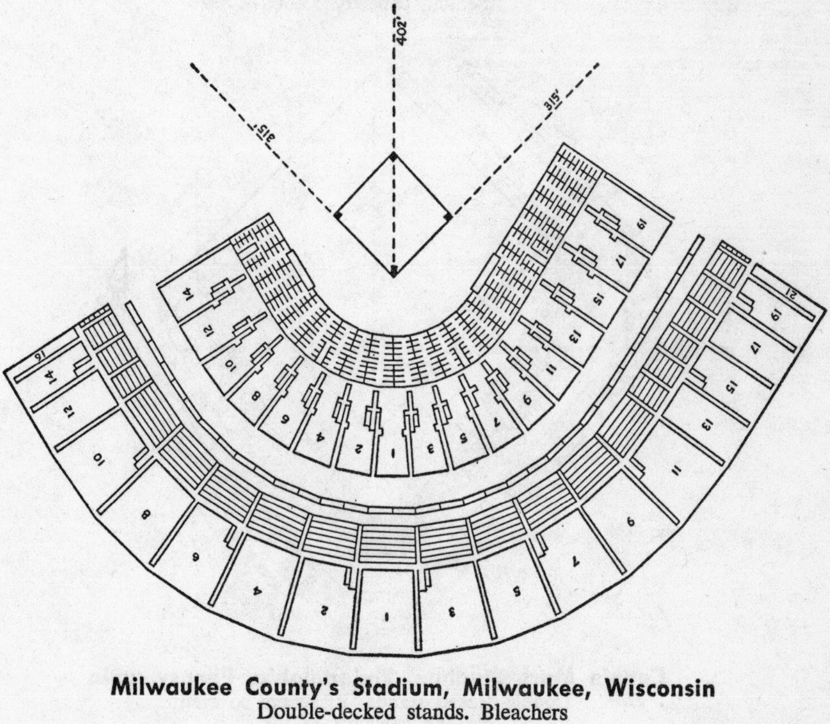

Milwaukee County's Stadium, Milwaukee, Wisconsin
Double-decked stands. Bleachers

145

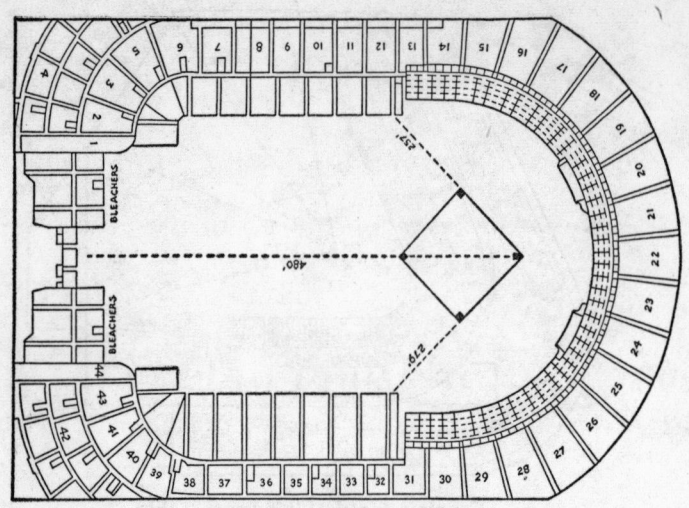

Polo Grounds, New York, New York
Double-decked stands. Bleachers
Seating capacity 55,000

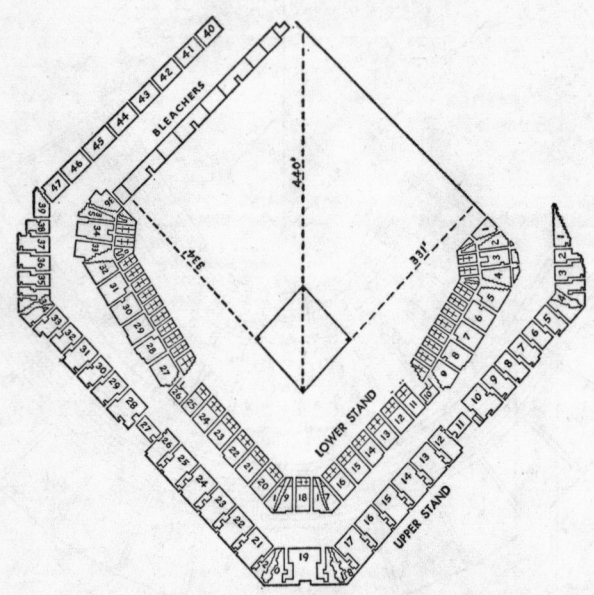

Connie Mack Stadium, Philadelphia, Pennsylvania
Double-decked stands. Bleachers covered
Seating capacity 33,223

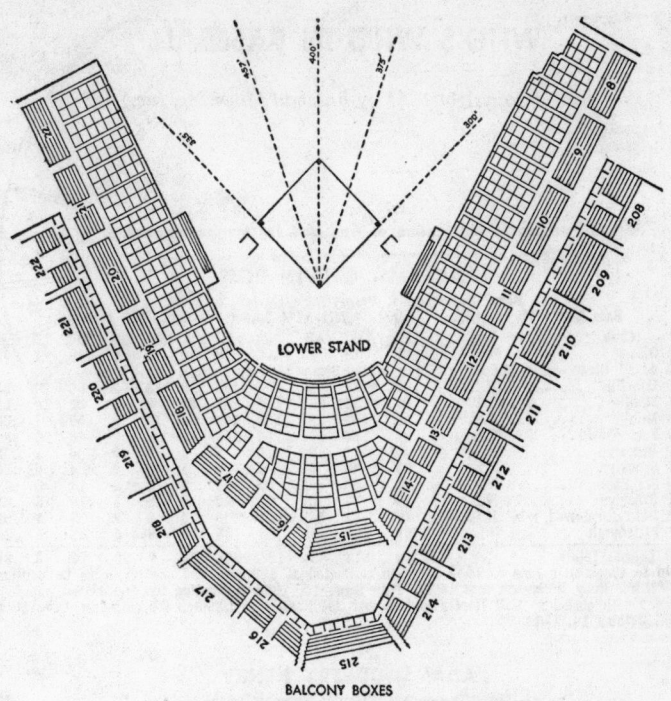

Forbes Field, Pittsburgh, Pennsylvania
Double-decked stands. Three tiers of boxes. Bleachers
Seating capacity 34,249

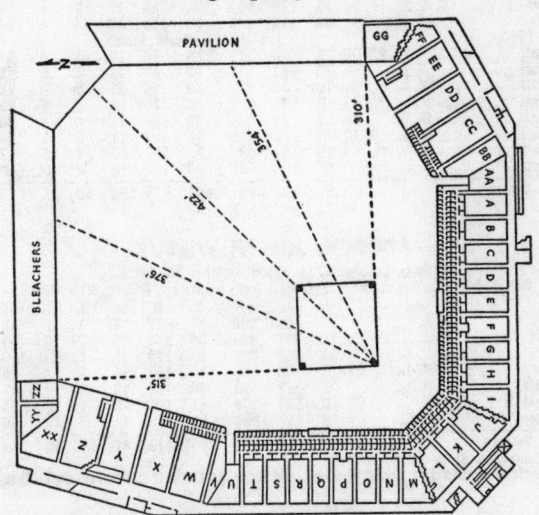

Sportsman's Park, St. Louis, Missouri
Double-decked stands. Pavilion covered. Bleachers
Seating capacity 30,808

WHO'S WHO IN BASEBALL

(Copyright 1954 by *Baseball Magazine, Inc.*)

* Indicates led league or was tied for league leadership.

ABRAMS, CALVIN ROSS

Born, Philadelphia, Pennsylvania, March 2, 1924.
Bats Left.   Throws Left.   Height, 5 feet 11½ inches.   Weight, 195 pounds.

Year	Club	Lea	Pos	G	AB	R	H	2B	3B	HR	RBI	SB	Avg
1942	Olean	Pony	OF	19	55	16	18	6	0	0	9	1	.327
1943-44-45	Olean	Pony	(In United States Military Service)										
1946	Danville	I.I.L.	OF	*123	441	100	*146	16	*13	2	56	20	.331
1947	Mobile	S.A.	OF	*154	589	*134	203	38	9	9	63	10	.345
1948	Mobile	S.A.	OF	131	487	120	164	23	10	6	59	7	.337
1949	Fort Worth	T.L.	OF	120	431	116	145	29	9	3	46	22	.336
1949	Brooklyn	N.L.	OF	8	24	6	2	1	0	0	1	.083
1950	Brooklyn	N.L.	OF	38	44	5	9	1	0	0	4	0	.205
1950	St. Paul	A.A.	OF	58	192	52	64	8	1	3	16	5	.333
1951	Brooklyn	N.L.	OF	67	150	27	42	8	0	3	19	3	.280
1952	Bkln.-Cincinnati a-b	N.L.	OF	81	168	24	46	9	2	2	13	1	.274
1953	Pittsburgh	N.L.	OF	119	448	66	128	10	6	15	43	4	.286
Major League Totals			5 Yrs	313	834	128	227	29	8	20	79	9	.272

a Sold to Cincinnati, June 8, 1952 for cash estimated at $30,000, and one player to be delivered in future. Rudy Rufer was sent to St. Paul Sept. 15, 1952 completing the transaction.
b Traded with outfielder Gail Henley and catcher Joe Rossi to Pittsburgh for outfielder Dave (Gus) Bell, October 14, 1952.

ADAMS, ROBERT HENRY

Born, Tuolumne, California, December 14, 1921.
Bats Right.   Throws Right.   Height, 5 feet, 10½ inches.   Weight, 170 pounds.

Year	Club	Lea	Pos	G	AB	R	H	2B	3B	HR	RBI	SB	Avg
1939	Ogden	Pio.	2B	64	236	33	79	7	7	1	46	2	.335
1940	Ogden	Pio.	OF-2B	105	444	81	158	16	13	1	47	17	*.356
1941	Columbia	S.A.L.	2B	137	561	100	*195	46	9	4	92	17	.348
1942	Syracuse	I.L.	2B	115	425	53	110	30	4	4	43	10	.259
1943, 1944, 1945			(In United States Army)										
1946	Cincinnati	N.L.	2B-OF-3B	94	311	35	76	13	3	4	24	16	.244
1947	Cincinnati	N.L.	2B	81	217	39	59	11	2	4	20	9	.272
1948	Cincinnati	N.L.	2B-3B	87	262	33	78	20	3	1	21	6	.298
1949	Cincinnati	N.L.	2B-3B	107	277	32	70	16	2	0	25	4	.253
1950	Cincinnati	N.L.	2B-3B	115	348	57	98	21	8	3	25	7	.282
1951	Cincinnati	N.L.	2B-3B-OF	125	403	57	107	12	5	5	24	4	.266
1952	Cincinnati	N.L.	3B	*154	*637	85	180	25	4	6	48	11	.283
1953	Cincinnati	N.L.	3B	150	607	99	167	14	6	8	49	3	.275
Major League Totals			8 Yrs	913	3062	437	835	132	33	31	236	60	.273

ADCOCK, JOSEPH WILBUR

Born, Coushatta, Louisiana, October 30, 1927.
Bats Right.   Throws Right.   Height, 6 feet, 4 inches.   Weight, 210 pounds.

Year	Club	Lea	Pos	G	AB	R	H	2B	3B	HR	RBI	SB	Avg
1947	Columbia a	S.A.L.	1B	73	280	35	74	11	5	7	43	0	.264
1948	Columbia	S.A.L.	1B	117	434	58	121	25	2	6	64	7	.279
1949	Tulsa	T.L.	1B	149	598	95	178	41	7	19	116	18	.298
1950	Cincinnati	N.L.	OF-1B	102	372	46	109	16	1	8	55	2	.293
1951	Cincinnati	N.L.	OF	113	395	40	96	16	4	10	47	1	.243
1952	Cincinnati b	N.L.	OF-1B	117	378	43	105	22	4	13	52	1	.278
1953	Milwaukee	N.L.	1B	157	590	71	168	33	6	18	80	3	.285
Major League Totals			4 Yrs	489	1735	200	478	87	15	49	234	7	.276

a Signed off Louisiana State Univ. campus.
b Traded to Boston Braves for Rocky Bridges and cash as part of four-club deal, Feb. 16, 1953.

ASHBURN, RICHIE

Born, Tilden, Nebraska, March 19, 1927.
Bats Left. Throws Right. Height, 5 feet, 10½ inches. Weight, 175 pounds.

Year	Club	Lea	Pos	G	AB	R	H	2B	3B	HR	RBI	SB	Avg
1945	Utica	E. L.	OF-C	106	356	63	111	17	6	1	42	21	.312
1946		(In United States Military Service)											
1947	Utica	E. L.	OF	137	536	*128	*194	21	12	8	52	*24	.362
1948	Philadelphia	N. L.	OF	117	463	78	154	17	4	2	40	*32	.333
1949	Philadelphia	N. L.	OF	154	*662	84	188	18	11	1	87	9	.284
1950	Philadelphia	N. L.	OF	151	594	84	180	25	*14	2	41	14	.303
1951	Philadelphia	N.L.	OF	154	643	92	*221	31	5	4	63	29	.344
1952	Philadelphia	N. L.	OF	*154	613	93	173	31	6	1	42	16	.282
1953	Philadelphia	N. L.	OF	156	622	110	*205	25	9	2	57	14	.330
Major League Totals			6 Yrs	886	8597	541	1121	147	49	12	280	114	.312
World's Series Record													
1950	Philadelphia	N. L.	OF	4	17	0	3	1	0	0	1	0	.176

ASTROTH, JOSEPH HENRY

Born East Alton, Illinois, September 1, 1922.
Bats Right. Throws Right. Height, 5 feet, 10 inches. Weight, 187 pounds.

Year	Club	Lea	Pos	G	AB	R	H	2B	3B	HR	RBI	SB	Avg
1945	Philadelphia	A.L.	C	10	17	1	1	0	0	0	1	0	.059
1946	Philadelphia	A.L.	C	4	7	0	1	0	0	0	0	0	.143
1946	Toronto	I.L.	C	1	3	0	0	0	0	0	0	0	.000
1946	Lancaster	Inter. St.	C	97	301	58	87	13	3	6	47	6	.289
1947	Savannah	S.A.L.	C	141	475	81	133	22	6	7	76	4	.280
1948	Memphis	S.A.	C	116	349	66	123	22	9	4	55	3	.352
1949	Philadelphia	A.L.	C	55	148	18	36	4	1	0	12	1	.243
1950	Philadelphia	A.L.	C	89	110	11	36	8	1	1	18	0	.327
1951	Philadelphia	A. L.	C	64	187	30	46	10	2	2	19	0	.246
1952	Philadelphia	A. L.	C	104	337	24	84	7	2	1	36	2	.249
1953	Philadelphia	A. L.	C	82	260	28	77	15	2	3	24	1	.296
Major League Totals			7 Yrs	358	1066	112	281	39	8	7	110	4	.264

ATWELL, MAURICE DAILEY, JR. (TOBY)

Born, Leesburg, Va., March 8, 1924.
Bats Left. Throws Right. Height, 5 feet 9½ inches. Weight, 185 pounds.

Year	Club	Lea	Pos	G	AB	R	H	2B	3B	HR	RBI	SB	Avg
1946	Danville	I. I. L.	C-OF	114	387	76	127	19	11	3	63	25	.328
1947	Montreal	I. L.	PH	2	1	0	0	0	0	0	0	0	.000
1947	Fort Worth	Texas	OF-C	80	238	88	64	7	5	0	23	11	.269
1948	Fort Worth	Texas	C	32	92	15	31	2	1	0	10	2	.337
1948	St. Paul	A. A.	OF-C	60	203	37	70	16	8	3	39	3	.345
1949	Montreal	I. L.	C	52	145	14	38	5	0	0	22	5	.262
1950	Montreal	I. L.	C	112	338	48	93	13	2	9	41	2	.275
1951	Montreal	I. L.	C	122	395	58	92	18	0	9	45	4	.233
1952	Chicago	N. L.	C	107	362	36	105	16	3	2	31	2	.290
1953	Chic.-Pitts. a	N. L.	C	77	213	21	51	8	0	1	25	0	.239
Major League Totals			2 Yrs	184	575	57	156	24	3	3	56	2	.271

a Traded to Pittsburgh with Bob Addis, Gene Hermanski, Bob Schultz, Preston Ward, option to purchase George Freese and cash for Joe Garagiola, Ralph Kiner, George Metkovich and Howie Pollet, June 4, 1953.

AVILA, ROBERTO FRANCISCO (GONZALEZ)

Born, Vera Cruz, Mexico, June 7, 1926.
Bats Right. Throws Right. Height, 5 feet, 10 inches. Weight, 170 pounds.

Year	Club	Lea	Pos	G	AB	R	H	2B	3B	HR	RBI	SB	Avg
1948	Baltimore	I. L.	2B-OF	56	182	18	40	9	0	0	12	6	.220
1949	Cleveland	A. L.	2B	31	14	3	3	0	0	0	3	0	.214
1950	Cleveland	A. L.	2B-SS	80	201	39	60	10	2	1	21	5	.299
1951	Cleveland	A. L.	2B	141	541	76	165	21	3	10	58	14	.305
1952	Cleveland	A. L.	2B	150	597	102	179	26	*11	7	45	12	.300
1953	Cleveland	A. L.	2B	141	559	85	160	22	3	8	55	10	.286
Major League Totals			5 Yrs	543	1912	305	567	79	19	26	182	41	.297

149

BAKER, FLOYD WILSON

Born, Luray, Virginia, October 10, 1918.
Bats Left. Throws Right. Height, 5 feet, 9 inches. Weight, 160 pounds.

Year	Club	Lea	Pos	G	AB	R	H	2B	3B	HR	RBI	SB	Avg
1938	Mayfield	Kitty	SS	125	457	111	158	25	9	2	85	24	.346
1939	Youngstown	M. A. L.	SS	103	406	67	108	14	7	1	44	4	.266
1940	Youngstown	M. A. L.	SS	124	465	83	141	23	5	0	48	18	.303
1941	Springfield	I. I. L.	SS	124	486	79	154	25	8	8	65	5	.317
1942	San Antonio	T. L.	SS	100	374	44	122	12	4	0	31	4	.326
1943	St. Louis	A. L.	3B-SS	22	46	5	8	2	0	0	4	0	.174
1943	Toledo	A. A.	SS	37	149	21	38	3	1	1	14	1	.255
1944	St. Louis a	A. L.	2B-SS	44	97	10	17	3	0	0	5	2	.175
1945	Chicago	A. L.	2B-3B	82	208	22	52	8	0	0	19	3	.250
1946	Chicago	A. L.	3B	9	24	2	6	1	0	0	3	0	.250
1946	Milwaukee	A. A.	INF	120	464	81	133	23	4	0	35	7	.287
1947	Chicago	A. L.	3B-2B-SS	105	371	61	98	12	3	0	22	9	.264
1948	Chicago	A. L.	3B-2B-SS	104	335	47	72	8	3	0	18	4	.215
1949	Chicago	A. L.	3B-SS-2B	125	388	38	101	15	4	1	40	3	.260
1950	Chicago	A. L.	3B-2B-OF	83	186	26	59	7	0	0	11	1	.317
1951	Chicago b	A. L.	3B-2B-SS	82	133	24	35	6	1	0	14	0	.263
1952	Washington	A. L.	2B-SS-3B	79	263	27	69	8	0	0	33	1	.262
1953	Wash.-Bost. c	A. L.	3B-2B	90	179	22	47	4	2	0	24	0	.263

Major League Totals 11 Yrs 825 2230 284 564 74 13 1 193 23 .253
World's Series Record

| 1944 | St. Louis .... | A. L. | 2B | 2 | 2 | 0 | 0 | 0 | 0 | 0 | 0 | 0 | .000 |

a Sold to Chicago White Sox, December 30, 1944.
b Traded to Washington for Guillermo Miranda, October 24, 1951.
c Sold to Boston Red Sox, May 12, 1953.

BATTS, MATTHEW DANIEL

Born, San Antonio, Texas, October 16, 1922.
Bats Right. Throws Right. Height, 5 feet, 11 inches. Weight, 200 pounds.

Year	Club	Lea	Pos	G	AB	R	H	2B	3B	HR	RBI	SB	Avg
1942	Canton	M. A. L.	C-1B-OF	126	483	63	142	20	4	10	82	8	.294
1943-44-45	Louisville	A. A.	(In Military Service)										
1946	Lynn	N. Eng	C-OF	98	359	56	121	17	7	12	86	3	.337
1947	Scranton	E. L.	C-1B-OF	8	30	3	7	1	0	1	4	0	.233
1947	Toronto	I. L.	C-OF	110	359	32	94	4	2	7	40	3	.262
1947	Boston	A. L.	C	7	16	3	8	1	0	1	5	0	.500
1948	Boston	A. L.	C	46	118	13	37	12	0	1	24	0	.314
1949	Boston	A. L.	C	60	157	23	38	9	1	3	31	1	.242
1950	Boston	A. L.	C	75	238	27	65	15	3	4	34	0	.273
1951	Boston-St. L. a ...	A. L.	C	90	277	27	79	18	1	5	33	2	.285
1952	Detroit b	A. L.	C	56	173	11	41	4	1	3	13	1	.237
1953	Detroit	A. L.	C	116	374	38	104	24	3	6	42	2	.278

Major League Totals 7 Yrs 450 1353 142 372 83 9 23 182 6 .275
a Traded with Jim McDonald, Jim Suckecki and $100,000 to St. Louis Browns for Les Moss, May 17, 1951.
b Traded with Dick Littlefield, Cliff Mapes, Ben Taylor to Detroit for Gene Bearden, Bob Cain and Dick Kryhoski, February 14, 1952.

BAUER, HENRY ALBERT (HANK)

Born, East St. Louis, Illinois, July 31, 1922.
Bats Right. Throws Right. Height, 6 feet, Weight, 185 pounds.

Year	Club	Lea	Pos	G	AB	R	H	2B	3B	HR	RBI	SB	Avg
1941	Oshkosh	Wisc. St.	OF-IF-P	108	405	63	106	22	6	10	64	11	.262
1942-43-44-45	Oshkosh	Wisc. St.	(In Military Service)										
1946	Quincy	I. I. L.	OF	109	430	85	139	24	8	12	90	27	.323
1947	Kansas City	A. A.	OF	131	457	90	143	32	5	16	79	13	.313
1948	Kansas City	A. A.	OF	132	541	103	165	32	11	23	100	26	.305
1948	New York	A. L.	OF	19	50	6	9	1	1	1	9	1	.180
1949	New York	A. L.	OF	103	301	56	82	6	6	10	45	2	.272
1950	New York	A. L.	OF	113	415	72	133	16	2	13	70	2	.320
1951	New York	A. L.	OF	118	348	53	103	19	3	10	54	5	.296
1952	New York	A. L.	OF	141	553	86	162	31	6	17	74	6	.293
1953	New York	A. L.	OF	133	437	77	133	20	6	10	57	2	.304

Major League Totals 6 Yrs 627 2104 350 622 93 24 61 309 18 .296
World's Series Record

1949	New York	A. L.	OF	3	6	0	1	0	0	0	0	0	.167
1950	New York	A. L.	OF	4	15	0	2	0	0	0	1	0	.133
1951	New York	A. L.	OF	6	18	0	3	0	1	0	3	0	.167
1952	New York	A. L.	OF	7	18	2	1	0	0	0	1	0	.056
1953	New York	A. L.	OF	6	23	6	6	0	1	0	1	0	.261

World's Series Totals 26 80 8 13 0 2 0 6 0 .163

BAUMHOLTZ, FRANK CONRAD

Born, Midvale, Ohio, October 7, 1919.
Bats Left. Throws Left. Height 5 feet, 10½ inches. Weight, 175 pounds.

Year	Club	Lea	Pos	G	AB	R	H	2B	3B	HR	RBI	SB	Avg
1941	Riverside	Calif.	OF	19	79	9	22	4	0	1	10	3	.278
1941	Ogden	Pio.	OF	74	279	36	79	12	5	1	42	16	.283
1941, 1942, 1943, 1944, 1945		(In U. S. Navy)											
1946	Columbia	S. A. L.	OF	119	472	85	•162	•43	18	2	81	12	.343
1947	Cincinnati	N. L.	OF	151	643	96	182	32	9	5	45	6	.283
1948	Cincinnati	N. L.	OF	123	415	57	123	19	5	4	30	8	.296
1949	Cincinnati-Chicago a	N. L.	OF	85	245	27	56	9	5	2	23	2	.229
1950	Los Angeles	P. C. L.	OF	172	670	126	254	•53	10	15	89	27	•.379
1951	Chicago	N. L.	OF	146	560	62	159	28	10	2	50	5	.284
1952	Chicago	N. L.	OF	103	409	59	133	17	4	4	35	5	.325
1953	Chicago	N. L.	OF	133	520	75	159	36	7	8	25	8	.306

Major League Totals   6 Yrs   746 2792 376 812 141 40 20 208 29 .291
a Traded with Hank Sauer by Cincinnati to Chicago for outfielders Peanuts Lowrey and Harry Walker.
June 15.

BELARDI, CARROLL WAYNE

Born, St. Helena, Calif., September 5, 1930.
Bats Left. Throws Left. Height, 6 feet, 1 inch. Weight, 185 pounds.

Year	Club	Lea	Pos	G	AB	R	H	2B	3B	HR	RBI	SB	Avg
1949	Nashua	New Eng.	1B	69	274	53	84	11	2	14	40	11	.307
1949	Greenville	S. A. L.	1B	16	58	13	18	3	2	1	13	1	.310
1949	St. Paul	A. A.	1B	28	99	14	24	4	0	4	18	1	.242
1950	Brooklyn	N. L.	1B	10	10	0	0	0	0	0	0	0	.000
1951	Mobile	S. A.	1B	155	597	80	155	23	4	22	98	1	.260
1951	Brooklyn	N. L.	PH	8	8	1	.1	0	1	0	0	0	.333
1952	Ft. Worth	T. L.	1B	149	520	85	157	33	2	20	90	8	.302
1953	Brooklyn	N. L.	1B	69	163	19	39	3	2	11	34	0	.239

Major League Totals   3 Yrs.   82 176 20 40 3 3 11 34 0 .227
World's Series Record
1953 Brooklyn .... N. L.   PH   2   2   0   0   0   0   0   0   0   .000

BELL, DAVID RUSSELL (GUS)

Born, Louisville, Kentucky, November 15, 1928.
Bats Left. Throws Right. Height, 6 feet, 1½ inches. Weight, 190 pounds.

Year	Club	Lea	Pos	G	AB	R	H	2B	3B	HR	RBI	SB	Avg
1947	Keokuk	Cen. Assn.	OF	23	95	11	24	3	3	1	17	2	.253
1947	Leesburg	Fla. St.	OF	53	194	22	46	7	2	1	23	7	.237
1948	Keokuk	Cen. Assn.	OF	123	502	86	160	27	•20	6	98	12	•.319
1949	Albany	E. L.	OF	134	535	100	•174	27	13	12	85	5	.325
1950	Indianapolis	A. A.	OF	33	165	33	66	10	6	5	21	1	.400
1950	Pittsburgh	N. L.	OF	111	422	62	119	22	11	8	53	4	.282
1951	Pittsburgh	N. L.	OF	149	600	80	167	27	•12	16	89	1	.278
1952	Hollywood a	P. C. L.	OF	17	64	12	19	3	1	2	13	1	.297
1952	Pittsburgh b	N. L.	OF	131	468	53	117	21	5	16	59	1	.250
1953	Cincinnati	N. L.	OF	151	610	102	183	37	5	30	105	0	.300

Major League Totals   4 Yrs   542 2100 297 586 107 33 70 306 6 .279
a On option from Pittsburgh to Hollywood, Apr. 22 to May 12.
b Traded by Pittsburgh to Cincinnati for outfielders Cal Abrams and Gail Henley and catcher Joe
Rossi, Oct. 14, 1952.

BERNIER, CARLOS

Born, Juana Diaz, Puerto Rico, January 28, 1929.
Bats Right. Throws Right. Height, 5 feet, 9 inches. Weight, 180 pounds.

Year	Club	Lea	Pos	G	AB	R	H	2B	3B	HR	RBI	SB	Avg
1948	Port Chester	Colon.	OF-2B	104	270	72	67	7	7	3	29	24	.248
1949	Indianapolis	A. A.	OF	2	0	0	0	0	0	0	0	0	.000
1949	Bristol	Colon.	OF	120	444	•136	149	25	5	15	56	•89	.336
1950	St. Jean	Province.	OF	64	242	69	81	9	2	15	39	41	.335
1950	Bristol	Colon.	OF	52	192	67	55	10	2	9	33	•53	.287
1951	Tampa	Fla. Int.	OF	135	501	•124	136	11	•21	5	58	•51	.271
1952	Hollywood	P. C. L.	OF-SS	171	652	•105	196	24	9	9	79	•65	.301
1953	Pittsburgh	N. L.	OF	105	310	48	66	7	8	3	31	15	.213

BERRA, LAWRENCE PETER (YOGI)

Born, St. Louis, Missouri, May 12, 1925.
Bats Left.   Throws Right.   Height, 5 feet, 8 inches.   Weight, 180 pounds.

Year	Club	Lea	Pos	G	AB	R	H	2B	3B	HR	RBI	SB	Avg
1943	Norfolk	Pied.	C	111	376	52	95	17	8	7	56	9	.253
1944-45	Kansas City	A.A.	(In Military Service)										
1946	Newark	I.L.	C-OF	77	277	41	87	14	1	15	59	5	.314
1946	New York	A.L.	C	7	22	3	8	1	0	2	4	0	.364
1947	New York	A.L.	C-OF	83	293	41	82	15	3	11	54	0	.280
1948	New York	A.L.	C-OF	125	469	70	143	24	10	14	98	3	.305
1949	New York	A.L.	C	116	415	59	115	20	2	20	91	2	.277
1950	New York	A.L.	C	151	597	116	192	30	6	28	124	4	.322
1951	New York a	A.L.	C	141	547	92	161	19	4	27	88	5	.294
1952	New York	A.L.	C	142	534	97	146	17	1	30	98	2	.273
1953	New York	A.L.	C	137	503	80	149	23	5	27	108	0	.296
Major League Totals			8 Yrs	902	3380	558	996	149	31	159	665	16	.295
World's Series Record													
1947	New York	A.L.	C-OF	6	19	2	3	0	0	1	2	0	.158
1949	New York	A.L.	C	4	16	2	1	0	0	0	1	0	.063
1950	New York	A.L.	C	4	15	2	3	0	0	1	2	0	.200
1951	New York	A.L.	C	6	23	4	6	1	0	0	0	0	.261
1952	New York	A.L.	C	7	28	2	6	1	0	2	3	0	.214
1953	New York	A.L.	C	6	21	3	9	1	0	1	4	0	.429
World's Series Totals				33	122	15	28	3	0	5	12	0	.230

a Selected Most Valuable Player in American League for 1951.

BERRY, CORNELIUS JOHN

Born, Kalamazoo, Michigan, January 11, 1922.
Bats Right.   Throws Right.   Height, 5 feet, 10 inches.   Weight, 168 pounds.

Year	Club	Lea	Pos	G	AB	R	H	2B	3B	HR	RBI	SB	Avg
1942	Winston-Salem	Pied.	SS	135	503	63	116	12	6	0	28	14	.231
1943-44-45	Win.-Salem	Pied.	(In Military Service)										
1946	Buffalo	I.L.	SS	136	556	93	159	21	8	0	86	8	.286
1947	Buffalo	I.L.	SS	123	428	64	128	20	4	1	50	8	.299
1948	Detroit	A.L.	2B-SS	87	256	46	68	8	1	0	16	1	.266
1949	Detroit	A.L.	2B-SS	109	329	38	78	9	1	0	18	4	.237
1950	Detroit	A.L.	SS-2B-3B	38	39	9	10	1	0	0	7	0	.256
1951	Detroit	A.L.	SS-2B-3B	67	157	17	36	5	2	0	9	4	.229
1952	Detroit a	A.L.	SS-3B	73	189	22	43	4	3	0	13	1	.228
1953	St. L.-Chic. b	A.L.	2B-3B-SS	62	107	15	29	1	2	0	11	1	.271
Major League Totals			6 Yrs	436	1077	147	264	28	9	0	74	11	.245

a Traded with outfielder Cliff Mapes, by Detroit to St. Louis Browns, for outfielder Rufus (Jake) Crawford (with Scranton in 1952), Sept. 1, 1952.
b Sold to Chicago White Sox, September 1, 1953.

BILKO, STEPHEN THOMAS

Born, Nanticoke, Pennsylvania, November 13, 1928.
Bats Right.   Throws Right.   Height, 6 feet, 1 inch.   Weight, 230 pounds.

Year	Club	Lea	Pos	G	AB	R	H	2B	3B	HR	RBI	SB	Avg
1945	Allentown	Int.-St.	OF	1	1	0	1	0	0	0	1	0	1.000
1946	Allentown	Int.-St.	PH	1	1	0	0	0	0	0	0	0	.000
1946	Salisbury	E. S. L.	1B	122	441	73	121	28	4	12	90	6	.274
1947	Winston-Salem	Car.	1B	116	438	109	148	26	3	29	120	12	.338
1948	Rochester	I.L.	1B	12	41	5	6	1	0	0	3	0	.146
1948	Lynchburg	Pied.	1B	128	463	89	154	*34	6	*20	92	3	*.333
1949	Rochester	I.L.	1B	139	503	101	156	32	5	34	*125	1	.310
1949	St. Louis	N.L.	1B	6	17	3	5	2	0	0	2	0	.294
1950	St. Louis	N.L.	1B	10	33	1	6	1	0	0	2	0	.182
1950	Rochester	I.L.	1B-2B	109	334	71	97	18	6	15	58	1	.290
1951	Columbus	A. A.	1B	26	74	13	21	2	0	1	6	0	.284
1951	Rochester	I.L.	1B	73	273	41	77	14	6	8	50	0	.282
1951	St. Louis	N.L.	1B	21	72	5	16	4	0	2	12	0	.222
1952	Rochester	I.L.	1B	82	286	55	92	22	5	12	55	0	.322
1952	St. Louis	N.L.	1B	20	72	7	19	6	1	1	6	0	.264
1953	St. Louis	N.L.	1B	154	570	72	143	23	3	21	84	0	.251
Major League Totals			5 Yrs	211	764	88	189	36	4	24	106	0	.247

BOLLING, MILTON JOSEPH, III

Born, Mississippi City, Mississippi, August 9, 1930.
Bats Right.   Throws Right.   Height, 6 feet, 1 inch.   Weight, 180 pounds.

Year	Club	Lea	Pos	G	AB	R	H	2B	3B	HR	RBI	SB	Avg
1948	Roanoke	Pied.	SS	85	293	22	54	13	3	1	23	0	.184*

Year	Club	Lea	Pos	G	AB	R	H	2B	3B	HR	RBI	SB	Avg
1949	Roanoke	Pied.	SS	139	521	70	120	28	2	12	67	6	.230
1950	Scranton	E. L.	SS-3B	119	459	73	132	21	3	5	37	8	.288
1950	Birmingham	S. A.	3B	10	27	1	2	0	0	0	0	0	.074
1951	Scranton	E. L.	SS	71	221	20	56	16	1	0	29	4	.253
1952	Birmingham	S. A.	SS	94	332	42	83	12	0	8	32	3	.250
1952	Boston	A. L.	SS	11	36	4	8	1	0	1	3	0	.222
1953	Boston	A. L.	SS	109	323	30	85	12	1	5	28	1	.263
Major League Totals			2 Yrs	120	359	34	93	13	1	6	31	1	.259

BOLLWEG, DONALD RAYMOND

Born, Wheaton, Illinois, February 12, 1922.
Bats Left. Throws Left. Height, 6 feet, 1 inch. Weight, 190 pounds.

Year	Club	Lea	Pos	G	AB	R	H	2B	3B	HR	RBI	SB	Avg
1942	Washington	A. L.	1B	112	427	89	126	18	8	*25	105	13	.295
1943-44-45	Columbus	S. A. L.	(In Military Service)										
1946	Columbus	S. A. L.	1B	127	437	52	97	16	10	7	63	6	.222
1947	Columbus	S. A. L.	1B	145	536	100	157	26	15	18	115	5	.293
1948	Houston	T. L.	OF-1B	142	494	69	118	24	9	13	96	2	.239
1949	Houston	T. L.	1B	142	494	85	128	26	10	10	82	6	.259
1950	Rochester	I. L.	1B	92	256	61	80	18	0	17	60	6	.313
1950	St. Louis	N. L.	1B	4	11	1	2	0	0	0	1	0	.182
1951	St. Louis a	N. L.	1B	6	9	1	1	1	0	0	2	0	.111
1951	Kansas City	A. A.	1B	122	426	109	129	26	12	20	69	1	.303
1952	Kansas City	A. A.	1B	126	464	108	151	27	14	23	81	10	.325
1953	New York b	A. L.	1B	70	155	24	46	6	4	6	24	1	.297
Major League Totals			3 Yrs	80	175	26	49	7	4	6	27	1	.280

World's Series Record

Year	Club	Lea	Pos	G	AB	R	H	2B	3B	HR	RBI	SB	Avg
1953	New York	A. L.	PH	3	2	0	0	0	0	0	0	0	.000

a Traded to New York Yankees with cash for Billy Johnson, May 14, 1951; assigned to Kansas City.
b Traded with Vic Power and Bill Renna for Harry Byrd and Eddie Robinson, Dec. 16, 1953.

BOONE, RAYMOND OTIS

Born, San Diego, California, July 27, 1923.
Bats Right. Throws Right. Height, 6 feet. Weight, 185 pounds.

Year	Club	Lea	Pos	G	AB	R	H	2B	3B	HR	RBI	SB	Avg
1942	Wausau	No. L.	C	89	304	47	93	13	8	4	41	6	.306
1943-44-45	Wilkes-Barrre	E. L.	(In Military Service)										
1946	Wilkes-Barre	E. L.	C	77	213	37	55	7	3	4	31	2	.258
1947	Okla. City	T. L.	C-SS	130	402	47	106	25	4	6	48	8	.264
1948	Hollywood	P. C. L.	SS	23	96	14	24	3	2	1	11	1	.250
1948	Okla. City	T. L.	SS	87	318	40	113	16	9	3	48	9	.355
1948	Cleveland	A. L.	SS	6	5	0	2	1	0	0	1	0	.400
1949	Cleveland	A. L.	SS	86	258	39	65	4	4	4	26	0	.252
1950	Cleveland	A. L.	SS	109	365	53	110	14	6	7	58	4	.301
1951	Cleveland	A. L.	SS	151	544	65	127	14	1	12	51	5	.233
1952	Cleveland	A. L.	SS-3B-2B	103	316	57	83	8	2	7	45	0	.263
1953	Cleve.-Detroit a	A. L.	3B-SS	135	497	94	147	17	8	26	114	3	.296
Major League Totals			6 Yrs	590	1985	308	534	58	21	56	295	12	.269

World's Series Record

Year	Club	Lea	Pos	G	AB	R	H	2B	3B	HR	RBI	SB	Avg
1948	Cleveland	A. L.	PH	1	1	0	0	0	0	0	0	0	.000

a Traded to Detroit with Al Aber, Steve Gromek and Dick Weik for Owen Friend, Joe Ginsberg, Art Houtteman and Bill Wight, June 15, 1953.

BORKOWSKI, ROBERT VILIRIAN

Born, Dayton, Ohio, January 27, 1927.
Bats Right. Throws Right. Height, 6 feet. Weight, 182 pounds.

Year	Club	Lea	Pos	G	AB	R	H	2B	3B	HR	RBI	SB	Avg
1946	Elizabethton	App. L.	OF-P	114	406	81	156	23	12	12	90	21	.384
1947	Des Moines	W. L.	OF-P	119	474	74	132	21	5	6	87	15	.278
1948	Des Moines	W. L.	OF	124	476	88	141	30	4	7	70	3	.296
1949	Nashville	S. A.	OF-C	140	471	83	177	34	5	9	78	1	*.376
1950	Springfield	I. L.	OF	6	21	2	6	3	0	0	3	0	.286
1950	Chicago	N. L.	OF-1B	85	256	27	70	7	4	4	29	1	.273
1951	Chicago a	N. L.	OF	58	89	9	14	1	0	0	10	0	.157
1952	Cincinnati	N. L.	OF-1B	126	377	42	95	11	4	4	24	1	.252
1953	Cincinnati	N. L.	OF-2B	94	249	32	67	11	1	7	29	0	.269
Major League Totals			4 Yrs	363	971	110	246	30	9	15	92	2	.253

a Traded to Cincinnati Reds with Forrest Burgess for Bob Usher and John Pramesa, Oct. 4, 1951.

BOYD, ROBERT RICHARD

Born, Potts Camp, Mississippi, October 1, 1926.
Bats Left. Throws Left. Height, 5 feet, 9 inches. Weight, 167 pounds.

Year	Club	Lea	Pos	G	AB	R	H	2B	3B	HR	RBI	SB	Avg
1950	Colorado Springs	W. L.	1B	42	158	39	59	6	5	9	39	3	.373
1951	Sacramento	P. C. L.	1B	145	555	82	190	32	11	5	64	*41	.342
1951	Chicago	A. L.	1B	12	18	3	3	0	1	0	4	0	.167
1952	Seattle	P. C. L.	1B-OF	161	641	100	205	29	*18	3	75	33	*.320
1953	Charleston	A. A.	OF-1B	49	198	33	64	8	6	2	22	12	.323
1953	Toronto	I. L.	OF-1B	31	120	16	37	4	4	3	12	1	.308
1953	Chicago	A. L.	1B-OF	55	165	20	49	6	2	3	23	1	.297
Major League Totals			2 Yrs	67	183	23	52	6	3	3	27	1	.284

BRIDGES, EVERETT LAMAR (ROCKY)

Born, Refugio, Texas, August 7, 1927.
Bats Right. Throws Right. Height, 5 feet, 8 inches. Weight, 176 pounds.

Year	Club	Lea	Pos	G	AB	R	H	2B	3B	HR	RBI	SB	Avg
1947	Santa Barbara	Cal. L.	SS-P	39	120	15	22	5	0	2	16	0	.183
1948	Greenville	S. A. L.	SS	154	626	85	157	18	3	7	50	21	.251
1949	Montreal	I. L.	2B-SS	151	504	77	139	28	3	7	73	3	.276
1950	Montreal	I. L.	SS	153	553	90	155	24	9	5	83	16	.280
1951	Brooklyn	N. L.	2B-SS-3B	63	134	13	34	7	0	1	15	0	.254
1952	Montreal	I. L.	3B	5	19	2	7	1	0	0	3	0	.368
1952	Brooklyn a	N. L.	2B-SS-3B	51	56	9	11	3	0	0	2	0	.196
1953	Cincinnati	N. L.	2B-SS-3B	122	432	52	98	13	2	1	21	6	.227
Major League Totals			3 Yrs	236	622	74	143	23	2	2	38	6	.230

a Traded to Boston Braves with Jim Pendleton for Russ Meyer, and then traded by Boston to Cincinnati, with cash for Joe Adcock, Feb. 16, 1953.

BRUTON, WILLIAM HARON

Born, Panola, Alabama, December 22, 1929.
Bats Left. Throws Right. Height, 6 feet, ½ inch. Weight, 169 pounds.

Year	Club	Lea	Pos	G	AB	R	H	2B	3B	HR	RBI	SB	Avg
1950	Eau Claire	Northern	OF	*128	*545	*126	157	25	13	5	58	*66	.288
1951	Denver	West. L.	OF	133	518	104	157	18	*27	2	38	19	.303
1952	Milwaukee	A. A.	OF	*154	*650	*130	*211	37	7	5	62	30	.325
1953	Milwaukee	N. L.	OF	151	613	82	153	18	14	1	41	*26	.250

BUCHA, JOHN GEORGE

Born, Allentown, Pennsylvania, January 22, 1925.
Bats Right. Throws Right. Height, 6 feet. Weight, 190 pounds.

Year	Club	Lea	Pos	G	AB	R	H	2B	3B	HR	RBI	SB	Avg
1943	Allentown	Inter-St.	C	26	78	6	18	3	1	1	13	1	.231
1944	Columbus	A. A.	C	2	2	0	0	0	0	0	0	0	.000
1944	Allentown	Inter-St.	C	101	331	71	112	15	6	16	83	5	.338
1945	Columbus	A. A.	C	119	396	54	130	17	5	3	47	4	.328
1946	Columbus	A. A.	C	6	10	2	2	0	0	0	0	0	.200
1946	Rochester	I. L.	C	40	90	6	19	2	1	0	11	0	.211
1947	Columbus	Sally	C	18	60	5	13	1	3	0	11	0	.217
1947	Omaha	West. L.	C	73	241	57	87	21	4	7	55	11	.361
1948	St. Louis	N. L.	C	2	1	0	0	0	0	0	0	0	.000
1948	Houston	T. L.	C	32	89	7	21	1	2	1	17	0	.236
1948	Rochester	I. L.	C	54	132	20	40	6	1	2	24	1	.303
1949	Rochester	I. L.	C	114	329	47	95	19	3	8	47	2	.289
1950	St. Louis	N. L.	C	22	36	1	5	1	0	0	1	0	.139
1951	Rochester	I. L.	C	110	349	89	91	17	4	3	45	1	.261
1952	Rochester a	I. L.	C	144	500	75	142	25	3	6	72	4	.284
1953	Detroit	A. L.	C	60	158	17	35	9	0	1	14	1	.222
Major League Totals			3 Yrs	84	195	18	40	10	0	1	15	1	.205

a Drafted by Detroit, December 1, 1952.

BURGESS, FORREST HARRILL (SMOKY)

Born, Caroleen, North Carolina, February 6, 1927.
Bats Left. Throws Right. Height, 5 feet, 8 inches. Weight, 180 pounds.

Year	Club	Lea	Pos	G	AB	R	H	2B	3B	HR	RBI	SB	Avg
1944	Lockport	Pony	C-OF	54	203	31	66	6	3	2	32	10	.325
1945	Portsmouth	Pied.	C-OF	12	45	8	18	2	4	0	3	1	.400
1945-46	Los Angeles	P. C. L.	(In Military Service)										
1946	Los Angeles	P. C. L.	C	1	2	0	1	0	0	0	0	0	.500

Year	Club	Lea	Pos	G	AB	R	H	2B	3B	HR	RBI	SB	Avg
1947	Macon	S. A. L.	C	16	38	3	11	3	2	0	7	0	.289
1947	Fayetteville	Tri-St.	C-OF	99	388	79	150	28	2	11	76	8	*.387
1948	Nashville	S. A.	C-OF	116	433	93	167	38	6	22	102	2	*.386
1949	Los Angeles	P. C. L.	OF	19	43	5	12	1	0	2	12	1	.279
1949	Chicago	N. L.	C	46	56	4	15	0	0	1	12	0	.268
1950	Springfield	I. L.	C	88	315	55	103	15	10	8	52	4	.327
1951	Chicago a-b	N. L.	C	94	219	21	55	4	2	2	20	2	.251
1952	Philadelphia	N. L.	C	110	371	49	110	27	2	6	56	3	.296
1953	Philadelphia	N. L.	C	102	312	31	91	17	5	4	36	3	.292

| Major League Totals | | | | 4 Yrs | 352 | 958 | 105 | 271 | 48 | 9 | 13 | 124 | 8 | .283 |

a Traded with Bob Borkowski to Cincinnati Reds for Bob Usher and John Pramesa, Oct. 4, 1951.
b Traded with Howie Fox and Connie Ryan to Philadelphia Phillies for Dick Sisler, Andy Seminick, Eddie Pellagrini and Niles Jordan, December 11, 1951.

BUSBY, JAMES FRANKLIN

Born, Kenedy, Texas, January 8, 1927.

Bats Right. Throws Right. Height, 6 feet, 1 inch. Weight, 175 pounds.

Year	Club	Lea	Pos	G	AB	R	H	2B	3B	HR	RBI	SB	Avg
1948	Muskegon	Cent.	PH	2	2	1	1	0	1	0	0	0	.500
1948	Waterloo	I. I. L.	OF	68	293	65	89	11	8	9	40	18	.304
1949	Muskegon	Cent.	OF	9	30	2	5	1	0	0	1	0	.167
1949	Waterloo	I. I. L.	OF	78	333	62	106	15	5	4	29	23	.318
1950	Sacramento	P. C. L.	OF	111	416	76	129	23	8	3	31	17	.310
1950	Chicago	A. L.	OF	18	48	5	10	0	0	0	4	0	.208
1951	Chicago	A. L.	OF	143	477	59	135	15	2	5	68	26	.283
1952	Chi.-Washington a	A. L.	OF	145	551	63	130	24	4	2	47	5	.236
1953	Washington	A. L.	OF	150	586	68	183	28	7	6	82	13	.312

| Major League Totals | | | | 4 Yrs | 456 | 1662 | 195 | 458 | 67 | 13 | 13 | 201 | 44 | .276 |

a Traded with infielder Mel Hoderlein, by Chicago to Washington, in exchange for outfielder Sam Mele, May 3, 1952.

CALDERONE, SAMUEL FRANCIS

Born, Beverly, New Jersey, February 6, 1926.

Bats Right. Throws Right. Height, 5 feet, 11 inches. Weight, 185 pounds.

Year	Club	Lea	Pos	G	AB	R	H	2B	3B	HR	RBI	SB	Avg
1945	Newport News	Pied.	C	130	482	64	144	28	3	2	79	2	.299
1946	Newport News	Pied.	C	8	20	1	2	1	0	0	1	0	.100
1946	Meridian	So'east.	C	82	244	20	57	9	1	2	28	3	.234
1947	Pueblo	West.	C	101	331	52	105	15	1	8	67	2	.317
1948	Mobile	S. A.	C	113	396	46	116	19	2	2	46	1	.293
1949	St. Paul a	A. A.	C	60	136	20	43	5	0	4	29	1	.316
1950	New York	N. L.	C	34	67	9	20	1	0	1	12	0	.299
1951-52	New York	N. L.		(In Military Service)									
1953	New York	N. L.	C	35	45	4	10	2	0	0	8	0	.222

| Major League Totals | | | | 2 Yrs | 69 | 112 | 13 | 30 | 3 | 0 | 1 | 20 | 0 | .268 |

a Drafted by New York Giants, November 17, 1949.

CAMPANELLA, ROY

Born, Philadelphia, Pennsylvania, November 19, 1921.

Bats Right. Throws Right. Height, 5 feet, 8 inches. Weight, 205 pounds.

Year	Club	Lea	Pos	G	AB	R	H	2B	3B	HR	RBI	SB	Avg
1946	Nashua	New Eng.	C	113	396	75	115	19	8	13	96	16	.290
1947	Montreal	I. L.	C	135	440	64	120	25	3	13	75	7	.273
1948	St. Paul	A. A.	C-OF	35	123	31	40	5	2	13	39	0	.325
1948	Brooklyn	N. L.	C	83	279	32	72	11	3	9	45	3	.258
1949	Brooklyn	N. L.	C	130	436	65	125	22	2	22	82	3	.287
1950	Brooklyn	N. L.	C	126	437	70	123	19	3	31	89	1	.281
1951	Brooklyn a	N. L.	C	143	505	90	164	33	1	33	108	1	.325
1952	Brooklyn	N. L.	C	128	468	73	126	18	1	22	97	8	.269
1953	Brooklyn b	N. L.	C	144	519	103	162	26	3	41	*142	4	.312

Major League Totals				6 Yrs	754	2644	433	772	129	13	158	563	20	.292
World's Series Record													
1949	Brooklyn	N. L.	C	5	15	2	4	1	0	1	2	0	.267
1952	Brooklyn	N. L.	C	7	28	0	6	0	0	0	1	0	.214
1953	Brooklyn	N. L.	C	6	22	6	6	0	0	1	2	0	.273

| World's Series Totals | | | | 18 | 65 | 8 | 16 | 1 | 0 | 2 | 5 | 0 | .246 |

a Selected Most Valuable Player in National League for 1951.
b Selected Most Valuable Player in National League for 1953.

CAREY, ANDREW ARTHUR

Born, Oakland, California, October 18, 1931.
Bats Right. Throws Right. Height, 6 feet 1 inch. Weight, 190 pounds.

Year	Club	Lea	Pos	G	AB	R	H	2B	3B	HR	RBI	SB	Avg
1951	Kansas City	A. A.	3B	120	424	47	122	15	6	14	72	3	.288
1952	Kansas City	A. A.	3B-SS	82	324	44	92	18	8	16	45	4	.284
1952	New York	A. L.	3B-SS	16	40	6	6	0	0	0	1	0	.150
1952	Syracuse	I. L.	3B	24	94	8	24	4	2	2	11	0	.255
1953	New York	A. L.	3B-SS-2B	51	81	14	26	5	0	4	8	2	.321
Major League Totals			2 Yrs	67	121	20	32	5	0	4	9	2	.264

CARRASQUEL, ALFONSO COLON (CHICO)

Born, Caracas, Venezuela, January 23, 1928.
Bats Right. Throws Right. Height, 6 feet. Weight, 170 pounds.

Year	Club	Lea	Pos	G	AB	R	H	2B	3B	HR	RBI	SB	Avg
1949	Fort Worth	T. L.	SS	128	445	63	140	13	9	6	69	6	.315
1950	Chicago	A. L.	SS	141	524	72	148	21	5	4	46	0	.282
1951	Chicago	A.L.	SS	147	538	41	142	22	4	2	58	14	.264
1952	Chicago	A. L.	SS	100	359	36	89	7	4	1	42	2	.248
1953	Chicago	A. L.	SS	149	552	72	154	30	4	2	47	5	.279
Major League Totals			4 Yrs	537	1973	221	533	80	17	9	193	21	.270

CASTIGLIONE, PETER PAUL

Born, Greenwich, Connecticut, February 13, 1922.
Bats Right. Throws Right. Height, 5 feet, 11 inches. Weight, 170 pounds.

Year	Club	Lea	Pos	G	AB	R	H	2B	3B	HR	RBI	SB	Avg
1940	Hutchinson	W. A.	3B	64	248	42	68	11	4	0	29	1	.274
1941	Hutchinson	W. A.	3B	23	103	14	20	2	2	0	3	0	.194
1941	Moultrie	Ga.-Fla.	3B	92	403	68	113	20	4	0	42	1	.280
1942	Harrisburg	Inter. St.	SS	123	472	67	125	21	4	0	22	8	.265
1943-44-45	Harrisburg	Inter. St.	(In Military Service)										
1946	Selma	So'east.	SS	134	476	79	163	43	6	8	81	10	.342
1947	Indianapolis	A. A.	SS	146	567	74	153	26	9	2	40	3	.270
1947	Pittsburgh	N. L.	SS	13	50	6	14	0	0	0	1	0	.280
1948	Indianapolis	A. A.	SS	148	578	87	178	33	16	5	88	3	.308
1948	Pittsburgh	N. L.	SS	4	3	0	0	0	0	0	0	1	.000
1949	Pittsburgh	N. L.	3B-SS-OF	118	448	57	120	20	2	6	43	2	.268
1950	Pittsburgh	N. L.	INF	94	263	29	67	10	3	3	22	1	.255
1951	Pittsburgh	N. L.	3B-SS	132	482	62	126	19	4	7	42	2	.261
1952	Pittsburgh a	N. L.	3B-1B-OF	67	214	27	57	9	1	4	18	3	.266
1953	Pitt.-St. L. b	N. L.	3B-2B-SS	112	211	23	42	4	1	4	24	1	.199
Major League Totals			7 Yrs	540	1670	204	426	62	11	24	150	10	.255

a Disabled with broken elbow most of season.
b Traded to St. Louis Cardinals for Hal Rice, June 14, 1953.

CLARK, MELVIN EARL

Born, Letart, W. Va., July 7, 1926.
Bats Right. Throws Right. Height, 6 feet. Weight, 180 pounds.

Year	Club	Lea	Pos	G	AB	R	H	2B	3B	HR	RBI	SB	Avg
1947	Appleton	Wis. St.	OF-3B	41	147	26	51	7	4	1	18	3	.347
1948	Baton Rouge	Evang.	OF	137	550	95	191	30	*22	8	91	13	.347
1949	Utica	Eastern	OF	71	282	46	71	9	6	2	24	4	.252
1949	Terre Haute	I. I. L.	OF	33	130	20	38	7	4	0	20	3	.292
1950	Utica	Eastern	OF	91	352	59	117	19	7	2	62	2	.332
1951	Schenectady	Eastern	OF	131	500	65	147	29	10	10	87	6	.294
1951	Philadelphia	N. L.	OF	10	31	2	10	1	0	1	8	0	.323
1952	Philadelphia	N. L.	OF-3B	47	155	20	52	6	4	1	15	2	.335
1953	Philadelphia	N. L.	OF	60	198	31	59	10	4	0	19	1	.298
Major League Totals			3 Yrs	117	384	53	121	17	8	2	37	3	.315

COAN, GILBERT FITZGERALD

Born, Monroe, North Carolina, May 18, 1924.
Bats Left. Throws Right. Height, 6 feet. Weight, 180 pounds.

Year	Club	Lea	Pos	G	AB	R	H	2B	3B	HR	RBI	SB	Avg
1944	Kingsport	App. L.	OF	72	267	76	98	16	4	*18	64	17	.367
1944	Chattanooga	S. A.	OF	48	194	47	65	5	8	0	15	9	.335
1945	Chattanooga	S. A.	OF	*140	540	126	*201	*40	*28	*16	117	*37	.372
1946	Washington	A. L.	OF	59	134	17	28	8	2	3	9	2	.209

Year	Club	Lea	Pos	G	AB	R	H	2B	3B	HR	RBI	SB	Avg
1947	Washington	A. L.	OF	11	42	5	21	3	2	0	3	2	.500
1947	Chattanooga	S. A.	OF	151	585	126	199	34	*17	22	92	*42	.340
1948	Washington	A. L.	OF	138	513	56	119	13	9	7	60	23	.232
1949	Washington	A.L.	OF	111	358	36	78	7	8	3	25	9	.218
1950	Washington	A. L.	OF	104	366	58	111	17	4	7	50	10	.303
1951	Washington	A. L.	OF	135	538	85	163-	25	7	9	62	8	.303
1952	Washington	A. L.	OF	107	332	50	68	11	6	5	20	9	.205
1953	Washington	A. L.	OF	68	168	28	33	1	4	2	17	7	.196
Major League Totals		8 Yrs		733	2451	335	621	80	42	86	246	70	.253

COLE, RICHARD ROY

Born, Long Beach, California, May 6, 1926.
Bats Right. Throws Right. Height, 6 feet 2 inches. Weight, 182 pounds.

Year	Club	Lea	Pos	G	AB	R	H	2B	3B	HR	RBI	SB	Avg
1943	Sacramento	P. C. L.	SS	26	76	8	17	0	1	0	0	0	.224
1944	Allentown	Int.-St.	SS	97	398	76	112	22	2	4	46	8	.281
1945	Columbus	A. A.		(In Military Service)									
1946	Columbus	A. A.	SS-2B	37	108	8	26	2	0	1	12	0	.241
1947	Columbus	A. A.	2B	15	50	8	11	0	1	0	4	1	.220
1947	Omaha	Western	SS	4	3	1	2	0	0	0	0	0	.667
1947	Fresno	Calif.	2B	83	345	88	133	24	2	1	51	4	*.386
1948	Rochester	I. L.	INF	91	226	33	57	11	0	4	22	7	.252
1949	Rochester	I. L.	2B-SS	141	454	64	107	16	4	7	43	8	.236
1950	Rochester	I. L.	SS-2B	135	528	93	147	17	5	4	44	8	.278
1951	St. Louis-Pitts. a	N. L.	2B-SS	57	142	13	32	5	0	1	14	0	.225
1951	Indianapolis	A. A.	SS	57	195	37	58	8	5	2	28	2	.297
1952	Hollywood	P. C. L.	SS	*178	602	75	172	22	1	8	73	2	.286
1953	Pittsburgh	N. L.	SS-2B-1B	97	235	29	64	13	1	0	23	2	.272
Major League Totals		2 Yrs		154	377	42	96	18	1	1	37	2	.255

a Traded to Pittsburgh with Joe Garagiola, Bill Howerton, Howie Pollet and Ted Wilks for Cliff
Chambers and Wally Westlake, June 15, 1951.

COLEMAN, GERALD FRANCIS (JERRY)

Born, San Jose, California, September 14, 1924.
Bats Right. Throws Right. Height, 6 feet. Weight, 165 pounds.

Year	Club	Lea	Pos	G	AB	R	H	2B	3B	HR	RBI	SB	Avg
1942	Wellsville	Pony	SS-3B	83	289	56	88	22	1	4	52	5	.304
1943-44-45	Kansas City	A. A.		(In United States Military Service)									
1946	Kansas City	A. A.	2B	5	3	0	1	0	0	0	0	0	.333
1946	Binghamton	E. L.	INF	134	487	76	134	25	3	4	53	17	.275
1947	Kansas City	A. A.	3B-SS	131	446	60	124	15	6	6	57	12	.278
1948	Newark	I. L.	INF	142	491	65	123	26	1	8	62	7	.251
1949	New York	A. L.	2B-SS	128	447	54	123	21	5	2	42	8	.275
1950	New York	A. L.	2B-SS	153	522	69	150	19	6	6	69	8	.287
1951	New York	A. L.	2B-SS	121	362	48	90	11	2	3	43	6	.249
1952	New York a	A. L.	2B	11	42	6	17	2	1	0	4	0	.405
1953	New York b	A. L.	2B-SS	8	10	1	2	0	0	0	0	0	.200
Major League Totals		5 Yrs		421	1383	178	382	53	14	11	158	17	.276

World's Series Record

Year	Club	Lea	Pos	G	AB	R	H	2B	3B	HR	RBI	SB	Avg
1949	New York	A. L.	2B	5	20	0	5	3	0	0	4	0	.250
1950	New York	A. L.	2B	4	14	3	4	1	0	0	3	0	.286
1951	New York	A. L.	2B	5	8	2	2	0	0	0	0	0	.250
World's Series Totals				14	42	4	11	4	0	0	7	0	.262

a Entered U. S. Military Service April 30, 1952.
b Reinstated from NDS list September 1, 1953.

COLLINS, JOSEPH EDWARD

Born, Scranton, Pennsylvania, December 3. 1922.
Bats Left. Throws Left. Height, 6 feet. Weight, 185 pounds.

Year	Club	Lea	Pos	G	AB	R	H	2B	3B	HR	RBI	SB	Avg
1939	Butler	Penn. St.	1B	5	17	3	3	1	0	0	1	0	.176
1939	Easton	E. Shore	1B	9	28	3	3	1	1	0	1	0	.107
1940	Butler	Penn. St.	1B	99	381	80	122	16	5	9	69	23	.320
1941	Akron	M. A. L.	1B	116	459	77	114	27	10	4	52	18	.248
1942	Norfolk	Pied.	1B	23	90	11	12	0	0	0	7	3	.133
1942	Amsterdam	Can. Am.	OF-1B	73	270	42	92	18	5	6	48	11	.341
1943	Springfield	E. L.	OF	70	254	41	66	12	6	0	80	7	.260
1943-44-45	Newark	I. L.		(In United States Military Service)									
1946	Beaumont	T. L.	1B	52	184	19	42	6	8	1	12	5	.228
1946	Newark	I. L.	OF-1B	67	243	29	66	10	8	6	81	4	.272

Year	Club	Lea	Pos	G	AB	R	H	2B	3B	HR	RBI	SB	Avg
1947	Birmingham	S. A.	1B-OF	48	189	40	68	13	7	6	31	4	.360
1947	Newark	I. L.	1B-OF	98	364	52	99	10	4	17	53	5	.272
1948	Newark	I. L.	OF-1B	139	512	84	140	25	6	23	76	5	.273
1948	New York	A. L.	PH	5	5	0	1	1	0	0	2	0	.200
1949	Kansas City	A. A.	1B	146	530	104	169	25	*18	20	83	6	.319
1949	New York	A. L.	1B	7	10	2	1	0	0	0	4	0	.100
1950	New York	A. L.	1B-OF	108	205	47	48	8	3	8	28	5	.234
1951	New York	A. L.	1B-OF	125	262	52	75	8	5	9	48	9	.286
1952	New York	A. L.	1B	122	428	69	120	16	8	18	59	4	.280
1953	New York	A. L.	1B-OF	127	387	72	104	11	2	17	44	2	.269
Major League Totals		6 Yrs		494	1297	242	849	44	18	52	185	20	.269

World's Series Record

Year	Club	Lea	Pos	G	AB	R	H	2B	3B	HR	RBI	SB	Avg
1950	New York	A. L.	1B	1	0	0	0	0	0	0	0	0	.000
1951	New York	A. L.	1B-OF	6	18	2	4	0	0	1	3	0	.222
1952	New York	A. L.	1B	6	12	1	0	0	0	0	0	0	.000
1953	New York	A. L.	1B	6	24	4	4	1	0	1	2	0	.167
World's Series Totals				19	54	7	8	1	0	2	5	0	.148

COOPER, WILLIAM WALKER

Born, Atherton, Mo., January 8, 1915.
Bats Right. Throws Right. Height, 6 feet, 3 inches. Weight, 205 pounds.

Year	Club	Lea	Pos	G	AB	R	H	2B	3B	HR	RBI	SB	Avg
1935	Rogers	Ark. St.	C-OF	91	334	64	120	26	4	14	79	11	.359
1936	Springfield	W. A.	C	129	486	60	136	28	8	6	95	13	.280
1937	Sacramento	P. C. L.	C	83	241	28	64	12	6	3	29	8	.266
1938	Mobile	S'East.	C-OF	61	233	25	67	9	2	4	42	8	.288
1938	Houston	T. L.	C	41	141	14	33	9	4	0	13	3	.234
1939	Asheville	Pied.	C	130	497	80	167	22	15	8	80	9	.336
1940	Columbus	A. A.	C	131	477	61	144	29	12	8	53	12	.302
1940	St. Louis	N. L.	C	6	19	3	6	1	0	0	2	1	.316
1941	St. Louis	N. L.	C	68	200	19	49	9	1	1	20	1	.245
1942	St. Louis	N. L.	C	125	438	58	123	32	7	7	65	4	.281
1943	St. Louis	N. L.	C	122	449	52	143	30	4	9	81	1	.318
1944	St. Louis	N. L.	C	112	397	56	126	25	5	13	72	4	.317
1945	St. Louis a	N. L.	C	4	18	3	7	0	0	0	1	0	.389
1946	New York b	N. L.	C	87	280	29	75	10	1	8	46	0	.268
1947	New York	N. L.	C	140	515	79	157	24	8	35	122	2	.305
1948	New York	N. L.	C	91	290	40	77	12	0	16	54	1	.266
1949	N.Y.-Cincinnati c	N. L.	C	124	454	48	117	13	4	20	83	0	.258
1950	Cincinnati-Bost. d	N. L.	C	117	384	55	120	22	8	14	64	1	.313
1951	Boston	N. L.	C	109	342	42	107	14	1	18	59	1	.313
1952	Boston	N. L.	C	102	349	33	82	12	1	10	55	1	.235
1953	Milwaukee	N. L.	C	53	137	12	30	6	0	8	16	1	.219
Major League Totals		14 Yrs		1260	4272	529	1219	210	35	154	740	18	.285

World's Series Record

Year	Club	Lea	Pos	G	AB	R	H	2B	3B	HR	RBI	SB	Avg
1942	St. Louis	N. L.	C	5	21	3	6	1	0	0	4	0	.286
1943	St. Louis	N. L.	C	5	17	1	5	0	0	0	0	0	.294
1944	St. Louis	N. L.	C	6	22	1	7	2	1	0	2	0	.318
World's Series Totals				16	60	5	18	3	1	0	6	0	.300

a Spent most of season in U. S. Navy.
b Sold to New York Giants for $175,000, January 5, 1946 while in Navy.
c Traded to Cincinnati for Ray Mueller, June 13, 1949.
d Traded to Boston Braves for Connie Ryan, May 10, 1950.

COURTNEY, CLINTON DAWSON

Born, Hall Summit, La., March 16, 1927.
Bats Left. Throws Right. Height, 5 feet, 8 inches. Weight, 180 pounds.

Year	Club	Lea	Pos	G	AB	R	H	2B	3B	HR	RBI	SB	Avg
1947	Beaumont	T. L.	C	4	8	1	4	1	0	0	1	0	.500
1947	Bisbee	Ari.-Tex	C	114	427	71	136	23	13	5	80	6	.318
1948	Augusta	So. Atl.	C	64	188	21	47	20	1	0	25	0	.250
1948	Norfolk	Piedmont	C	29	96	5	22	4	0	1	8	1	.229
1949	Manchester	New Eng.	C	58	209	33	73	13	0	5	32	1	.349
1949	Norfolk	Piedmont	C	48	169	24	41	4	0	5	24	1	.243
1950	Beaumont	Texas	C	146	521	62	137	17	2	4	79	4	.263
1951	Kansas City	A. A.	C	103	343	34	101	14	2	3	35	1	.294
1951	New York a	A. L.	C	1	2	0	0	0	0	0	0	0	.000
1952	St. Louis	A. L.	C	119	413	38	118	24	3	5	50	0	.286
1953	St. Louis	A. L.	C	106	355	28	89	12	2	4	19	0	.251
Major League Totals		8 Yrs		226	770	66	207	36	5	9	69	0	.269

a Traded to St. Louis Browns for pitcher Jim McDonald, Nov. 23, 1951.

COX, WILLIAM RICHARD

Born, Newport, Pennsylvania, August 29, 1919.
Bats Right. Throws Right. Height, 5 feet, 8½ inches. Weight, 150 pounds.

Year	Club	Lea	Pos	G	AB	R	H	2B	3B	HR	RBI	SB	Avg
1940	Harrisburg	Inter-St.	SS	120	462	55	133	24	5	8	53	8	.288
1941	Harrisburg	Inter-St.	SS	128	496	104	*180	*42	15	6	99	14	*.363
1941	Pittsburgh	N. L.	SS	10	37	4	10	3	1	0	2	1	.270
1942, 1943, 1944, 1945				(In United States Army)									
1946	Pittsburgh	N. L.	SS	121	411	82	119	22	6	2	36	4	.290
1947	Pittsburgh a	N. L.	SS	132	529	75	145	30	7	15	54	5	.274
1948	Brooklyn	N. L.	3B-SS-2B	88	237	36	59	13	2	8	15	8	.249
1949	Brooklyn	N. L.	3B	100	390	48	91	18	2	8	40	5	.233
1950	Brooklyn	N. L.	3B-2B-SS	119	451	62	116	17	2	8	44	6	.257
1951	Brooklyn	N. L.	3B-SS	142	455	62	127	25	4	9	51	5	.279
1952	Brooklyn	N. L.	3B-2B-SS	116	455	56	118	12	3	6	84	10	.259
1953	Brooklyn	N. L.	3B-2B-SS	100	327	44	95	18	1	10	44	2	.291
Major League Totals			9 Yrs	928	8292	419	880	158	28	61	320	41	.267
World's Series Record													
1949	Brooklyn	N. L.	3B	2	3	0	1	0	0	0	0	0	.333
1952	Brooklyn	N. L.	3B	7	27	4	8	2	0	0	0	0	.296
1953	Brooklyn	N. L.	3B	6	23	3	7	3	0	1	6	0	.304
World's Series Totals				15	53	7	16	5	0	1	6	0	.302

a Traded with Elwin Roe and Gene Mauch to Brooklyn for Fred Walker, Vic Lombardi and Hal Gregg. December 8.

CRANDALL, DEMAR WESLEY

Born, Ontario, California, March 5, 1930.
Bats Right. Throws Right. Height, 6 feet, 1½ inches. Weight, 180 pounds.

Year	Club	Lea	Pos	G	AB	R	H	2B	3B	HR	RBI	SB	Avg
1948	Leavenworth	W. A.	C	123	425	81	129	27	4	15	84	31	.304
1948	Milwaukee	A. A.	C	5	12	1	1	0	0	0	0	0	.083
1949	Evansville	I. L. L.	C	38	154	28	54	13	3	8	36	5	.351
1949	Boston	N. L.	C	67	228	21	60	10	1	4	34	2	.263
1950	Boston	N. L.	C-1B	79	255	21	56	11	0	4	37	0	.220
1951-52	Boston	N. L.		(In United States Military Service)									
1953	Milwaukee	N. L.	C	116	382	55	104	13	1	15	51	2	.272
Major League Totals			3 Yrs	262	865	97	220	34	2	23	122	4	.254

DARK, ALVIN RALPH

Born, Comanche, Oklahoma, January 7, 1923.
Bats Right. Throws Right. Height, 5 feet 11½ inches. Weight, 184 pounds.

Year	Club	Lea	Pos	G	AB	R	H	2B	3B	HR	RBI	SB	Avg
1946	Boston	N. L.	SS-OF	15	13	0	3	3	0	0	1	0	.231
1947	Milwaukee	A. A.	SS	149	*614	*121	186	*49	7	10	66	14	.303
1948	Boston	N. L.	SS	137	543	85	175	39	6	3	48	4	.322
1949	Boston a	N. L.	3B-SS	130	529	74	146	23	5	3	53	5	.276
1950	New York	N. L.	SS	154	587	79	164	36	5	16	67	9	.279
1951	New York	N. L.	SS	156	646	114	196	*41	7	14	69	12	.303
1952	New York	N. L.	SS	151	589	92	177	29	8	14	73	6	.301
1953	New York	N. L.	S-2-3-0-P	155	*647	126	194	41	6	23	88	7	.300
Major League Totals			7 Yrs	898	3554	570	1055	212	32	73	399	43	.297
World's Series Record													
1948	Boston	N. L.	SS	6	24	2	4	1	0	0	0	0	.167
1951	New York	N. L.	SS	6	24	5	10	3	0	1	4	0	.417
World's Series Totals				12	48	7	14	4	0	1	4	0	.292

a Traded with Eddie Stanky to New York Giants for Sid Gordon, Willard Marshall, Buddy Kerr and Sam Webb. December 14, 1949

DELSING, JAMES HENRY

Born, Rudolph, Wisconsin, November 13, 1925
Bats Left. Throws Right. Height, 5 feet, 11 inches. Weight, 180 pounds.

Year	Club	Lea	Pos	G	AB	R	H	2B	3B	HR	RBI	SB	Avg
1942	Green Bay ..	Wisc. St.	SS	49	173	38	43	12	4	3	30	0	.249
1943	Lockport	Pony	OF-3B	86	317	55	99	15	5	8	69	2	.312
1944-45	Milwaukee	A. A.		(In United States Military Service)									
1946	Eau C'aire	No. L.	OF	65	252	59	95	11	11	7	61	8	.377
1946	Milwaukee	A. A.	OF	40	157	21	50	5	2	0	20	2	.318
1947	Hollywood ...	P. C. L.	OF	153	572	92	181	24	12	5	53	3	.316

159

Year	Club	Lea	Pos	G	AB	R	H	2B	3B	HR	RBI	SB	Avg
1948	Chicago	A.L.	OF	20	63	5	12	0	0	0	5	0	.190
1948	Hollywood a	P.C.L.	OF	122	463	82	154	80	5	6	56	4	.333
1949	Kansas City ...	A.A.	OF	151	545	89	173	24	5	7	77	11	.317
1949	New York	A.L.	OF	9	20	5	7	1	0	1	8	0	.350
1950	N.Y.-St. Louis b ...	A.L.	OF	81	219	27	59	5	3	0	17	1	.269
1951	St. Louis	A.L.	OF	131	449	59	112	20	2	8	45	2	.249
1952	St. L.-Detroit c ...	A.L.	OF	126	411	48	107	15	7	4	49	4	.260
1953	Detroit	A.L.	OF	138	479	77	138	26	6	11	62	1	.288
Major League Totals		6 Yrs		505	1641	221	435	67	17	24	181	8	.265

a Traded by Chicago White Sox to New York Yankees for Steve Souchok, December 14, 1948.
b Traded to St. Louis Browns with Don Johnson, Duane Pillette, George Stirnweiss and $50,000 for Tom Ferrick, Joe Ostrowski and Leo Thomas, June 15, 1950.
c Traded to Detroit with Ned Garver, Dave Madison and Bud Black for Don Lenhardt, Dick Littlefield, Marlin Stuart and Vic Wertz, August 14, 1952.

DeMAESTRI, JOSEPH PAUL

Born, San Francisco, California, December 9, 1928.
Bats Right. Throws Right. Height, 6 feet. Weight, 170 pounds.

Year	Club	Lea	Pos	G	AB	R	H	2B	3B	HR	RBI	SB	Avg
1947	El Paso	Ariz.-Tex.	SS	76	299	37	79	11	4	0	37	8	.264
1948	San Jose	Cal. L.	2B-SS	131	535	71	153	12	1	2	71	15	.286
1949	Oneonta	Can. Am.	SS	125	506	83	140	22	14	4	74	4	.277
1950	Birmingham a	S.A.	SS	143	569	72	161	18	6	8	58	8	.283
1951	Chicago b	A.L.	SS-3B-2B	56	74	8	15	0	2	1	8	0	.203
1952	St. Louis c-d ...	A.L.	SS-3B-2B	81	186	13	42	9	1	1	18	0	.226
1953	Philadelphia	A.L.	SS	111	420	53	107	17	8	6	85	0	.255
Major League Totals		3 Yrs		248	680	74	164	26	6	8	56	0	.241

a Drafted by Chicago White Sox from Louisville, November 16, 1950.
b Traded with outfielder Manny Rivera, infielder Gordon Goldsberry, catcher Gus Niarhos and pitcher Dick Littlefield, by Chicago to St. Louis Browns, for catcher Sherman Lollar, infielder Tom Upton and pitcher Al Widmar, Nov. 26, 1951.
c Traded with pitcher Tommy Byrne, by St. Louis to Chicago, for shortstop Willie Miranda and outfielder Hank Edwards, Oct. 17, 1952.
d Traded to Philadelphia Athletics with Ed McGhee and Eddie Robinson for Ferris Fain and Bob Wilson, January 27, 1953.

DIERING, CHARLES EDWARD (CHUCK)

Born, St. Louis, Missouri, February 5, 1923.
Bats Right. Throws Right. Height, 5 feet, 10 inches. Weight, 165 pounds.

Year	Club	Lea	Pos	G	AB	R	H	2B	3B	HR	RBI	SB	Avg
1941	Daytona Beach ..	Fla. St.	OF	59	197	20	42	7	2	0	15	1	.213
1942	Albany	Ga.-Fla.	OF	*126	472	*102	144	25	6	8	64	8	.305
1943-44-45	Rochester ...	I.L.	(In U. S. Military Service)										
1946	Rochester	I.L.	OF	141	533	84	142	22	13	10	60	19	.266
1947	St. Louis	N.L.	OF	105	74	22	16	3	1	2	11	3	.216
1948	St. Louis	N.L.	OF	7	7	2	0	0	0	0	0	1	.000
1948	Rochester	I.L.	OF	149	546	91	146	31	11	5	61	11	.267
1949	St. Louis	N.L.	OF	131	369	60	97	21	8	8	88	1	.263
1950	St. Louis	N.L.	OF	89	204	34	51	12	0	8	18	1	.250
1951	St. Louis a	N.L.	OF	64	85	9	22	5	1	0	8	0	.259
1952	New York	N.L.	OF	41	23	2	4	1	1	0	2	0	.174
1952	Minneapolis	A.A.	OF	55	177	34	46	10	2	4	16	4	.260
1953	Minneapolis b	A.A.	OF	152	584	116	188	39	10	12	74	4	.322
Major League Totals		6 Yrs		437	762	129	190	42	11	8	77	6	.249

a Traded to New York Giants with Max Lanier for Eddie Stanky, Dec. 11, 1951.
b Drafted by Baltimore Orioles, Nov. 30, 1953.

DITTMER, JOHN DOUGLAS

Born, Elkader, Iowa, Jan. 10, 1928.
Bats Left. Throws Right. Height, 6 feet, 1 inch. Weight, 175 pounds.

Year	Club	Lea	Pos	G	AB	R	H	2B	3B	HR	RBI	SB	Avg
1950	Denver	West. L.	2B	72	255	43	95	18	5	2	59	1	.373
1951	Atlanta	S.A.	2B-3B	153	581	91	194	*42	11	9	105	6	.334
1952	Milwaukee	A.A.	2B	57	222	40	79	14	2	8	55	1	.356
1952	Boston	N.L.	2B	93	326	26	63	7	2	7	41	1	.193
1953	Milwaukee	N.L.	2B	138	504	54	134	22	1	9	63	1	.266
Major League Totals		2 Yrs		231	830	80	197	29	3	16	104	2	.237

DOBY, LAWRENCE EUGENE

Born, Camden, South Carolina, December 13, 1924.
Bats Left. Throws Right. Height, 6 feet, 1 inch. Weight, 185 pounds.

Year	Club	Lea	Pos	G	AB	R	H	2B	3B	HR	RBI	SB	Avg
1947	Cleveland	A. L.	1B-2B-SS	29	32	3	5	1	0	0	2	0	.156
1948	Cleveland	A. L.	OF	121	439	83	132	23	9	14	66	9	.301
1949	Cleveland	A. L.	OF	147	547	106	153	25	3	24	85	10	.280
1950	Cleveland	A. L.	OF	142	503	110	164	25	5	25	102	8	.326
1951	Cleveland	A. L.	OF	134	447	84	132	27	5	20	69	4	.295
1952	Cleveland	A. L.	OF	140	519	*104	143	26	8	*32	104	5	.276
1953	Cleveland	A. L.	OF	149	513	92	135	18	5	29	102	3	.263
Major League Totals		7 Yrs		862	3000	582	864	145	35	144	530	39	.288
World's Series Record													
1948	Cleveland	A. L.	OF	6	22	1	7	1	0	1	2	0	.318

DROPO, WALTER

Born, Moosup, Connecticut, January 30, 1923.
Bats Right. Throws Right. Height, 6 feet, 5 inches. Weight, 220 pounds.

Year	Club	Lea	Pos	G	AB	R	H	2B	3B	HR	RBI	SB	Avg
1947	Scranton	E. L.	1B	87	337	54	100	18	1	12	59	0	.297
1948	Louisville	A. A.	1B	28	109	9	22	1	2	3	12	2	.202
1948	Birmingham	S. A.	1B	118	454	74	163	34	7	14	102	3	.359
1949	Boston	A. L.	1B	11	41	3	6	2	0	0	1	0	.146
1949	Sacramento	P. C. L.	1B	132	481	60	138	30	3	17	85	6	.287
1950	Louisville	A. A.	1B	11	47	5	12	1	1	2	11	0	.255
1950	Boston	A. L.	1B	136	559	101	180	28	8	34	*144	0	.322
1951	San Diego	P. C. L.	1B	33	126	17	36	4	0	5	13	0	.286
1951	Boston	A. L.	1B	99	360	37	86	14	0	11	57	0	.239
1952	Bos.-Detroit a	A. L.	1B	152	591	69	163	24	4	29	97	2	.276
1953	Detroit	A. L.	1B	152	606	61	150	30	3	13	96	2	.248
Major League Totals		5 Yrs		550	2157	271	585	98	15	87	395	4	.271

a Traded with Fred Hatfield, Don Lenhardt, Johnny Pesky and Bill Wight to Detroit for Hoot Evers, George Kell, Johnny Lipon and Dizzy Trout, June 3, 1952.

DYCK, JAMES ROBERT

Born, Omaha, Neb., Feb. 3, 1922.
Bats Right. Throws Right. Height, 6 feet 2½ inches. Weight, 205 pounds.

Year	Club	Lea	Pos	G	AB	R	H	2B	3B	HR	RBI	SB	Avg
1941	Norfolk	West.	P-OF	48	125	13	28	1	2	1	12	2	.224
1942	Fond Du Lac	Wis. St.	P-IN-OF	80	264	41	72	10	1	2	87	10	.273
1943-44-45	Norfolk	I. I. I.	(In U. S. Military Service)										
1946	Quincy	I. I. I.	3B	14	43	4	9	0	0	0	4	1	.209
1946	Joplin	Wes. Asn.	3B-P	106	412	89	150	31	13	13	*104	12	*.364
1947	Binghamton	Eastern	3B	73	265	40	80	14	3	8	37	7	.302
1947	Newark	I. L.	3B	46	166	17	48	4	0	4	15	1	.289
1947	Kansas City	A. A.	3B	11	26	5	5	1	0	0	8	1	.192
1948	Kansas City	A. A.	OF-3B	106	407	71	115	25	4	2	61	8	.283
1949	Kansas City	A. A.	OF-3B	53	174	24	50	8	2	8	26	8	.287
1949	Binghamton	Eastern	3B	20	67	8	19	1	0	8	12	0	.284
1949	Newark	I. L.	OF-3B	45	168	22	41	6	0	5	22	1	.244
1950	Baltimore	I. L.	OF	12	11	2	3	0	0	1	1	0	.273
1950	San Antonio	T. L.	OF-3B-1B	102	355	64	114	19	4	10	63	2	.321
1951	San Antonio	T. L.	INF-OF	161	587	102	167	30	3	27	*127	11	.284
1951	St. Louis	A. L.	3B	4	15	1	1	0	0	0	0	0	.067
1952	St. Louis	A. L.	3B-OF	122	402	60	108	22	3	15	64	0	.269
1953	St. Louis	A. L.	OF-3B	112	334	38	71	15	1	9	27	3	.213
Major League Totals		8 Yrs		238	751	99	180	37	4	24	91	3	.240

EASTER, LUSCIOUS (LUKE)

Born, St. Louis. Missouri, August 4. 1921.
Bats Left. Throws Right. Height, 6 feet, 4½ inches. Weight, 235 pounds.

Year	Club	Lea	Pos	G	AB	R	H	2B	3B	HR	RBI	SB	Avg
1949	San Diego	P. C. L.	1B	80	273	56	99	23	0	25	92	1	.363
1949	Cleveland	A. L.	OF	21	45	6	10	3	0	0	2	0	.222
1950	Cleveland	A. L.	1B-OF	141	540	96	151	20	4	28	107	0	.280
1951	Cleveland	A. L.	1B	128	486	65	131	12	5	27	103	0	.270
1952	Indianapolis a	A. A.	1B	14	50	13	17	2	0	6	12	1	.340
1952	Cleveland	A. L.	1B	127	437	63	115	10	3	31	97	1	.263
1953	Cleveland b	A. L.	1B	68	211	26	64	9	0	7	31	0	.303
Major League Totals		5 Yrs		485	1719	256	471	54	12	93	340	1	.274

a On option from Cleveland to Indianapolis, June 30-July 15.
b On Disabled List April 25 to June 20.

EDWARDS, CHARLES BRUCE

Born, Quincy, Illinois, July 15, 1923.
Bats Right. Throws Right. Height, 5 feet, 8 inches. Weight, 180 pounds.

Year	Club	Lea	Pos	G	AB	R	H	2B	3B	HR	RBI	SB	Avg
1941	Santa Barbara	Calif.	OF-C	53	185	29	48	10	1	1	27	6	.259
1942	Santa Barbara	Calif.	C	6	18	0	5	0	0	0	8	0	.278
1942	Durham ·	Pied.	C	32	90	7	21	1	0	0	5	1	.233
1943-44-45	Montreal	I. L.	(In Military Service)										
1946	Mobile	S. A.	C	62	208	43	69	13	1	2	24	9	.332
1946	Brooklyn	N. L.	C	92	292	24	78	13	5	1	25	1	.267
1947	Brooklyn	N. L.	C	130	471	53	139	15	8	9	80	2	.295
1948	Brooklyn	N. L.	C-OF-INF	96	286	36	79	17	2	8	54	4	.276
1949	Brooklyn	N. L.	C-OF-3B	64	148	24	31	3	0	8	25	0	.209
1950	Brooklyn	N. L.	C-1B	50	142	16	26	4	1	8	16	1	.183
1951	Bklyn.-Chic. a	N. L.	C-1B	68	177	25	42	11	2	4	25	1	.237
1952	Chicago	N. L.	C	50	94	7	23	2	2	1	12	0	.245
1953	Springfield b	I. L.	1B	38	112	17	32	4	1	1	13	0	.286
1953	Des Moines b	West.	3B	50	166	19	53	10	1	7	42	0	.319
Major League Totals		7 Yrs		550	1610	185	418	65	20	39	237	9	.260
Year	Club	Lea	Pos	G	AB	R	H	2B	3B	HR	RBI	SB	Avg
World's Series Record													
1947	Brooklyn	N. L.	C	7	27	3	6	1	0	0	2	0	.222
1949	Brooklyn	N. L.	PH	2	2	0	1	0	0	0	0	0	.500
World's Series Totals				9	29	3	7	1	0	0	2	0	.241

a Traded to Chicago Cubs with Joe Hatten, Gene Hermanski, and Eddie Miksis for Andy Pafko, Johnny Schmitz, Wayne Terwilliger and Al Walker, June 15, 1951.
b Playing manager.

EDWARDS HENRY ALBERT (HANK)

Born, Elmwood Place, Ohio, January 29, 1919.
Bats Left. Throws Left. Height, 6 feet. Weight, 190 pounds.

Year	Club	Lea	Pos	G	AB	R	H	2B	3B	HR	RBI	SB	Avg
1939	Mansfield	Ohio St.	OF	130	529	135	209	41	14	18	129	0	*.395
1940	Charleston	M. A. L.	OF	69	254	43	72	12	3	·2	33	3	.283
1941	Wilkes-Barre	E. L.	PH	4	4	1	0	0	0	0	1	0	.000
1941	Cedar Rapids	I. I. I.	OF	121	473	*101	*172	31	10	*23	*113	5	*.364
1941	Cleveland	A. L.	OF	16	68	10	15	1	1	1	6	0	.221
1942	Baltimore	I. L.	OF	137	496	82	132	18	5	18	69	6	.266
1942	Cleveland	A. L.	OF	13	48	6	12	2	1	0	7	2	.250
1943	Cleveland	A. L.	OF	92	297	33	82	18	6	3	28	4	.276
1944-45	Cleveland.......	A. L.	(In United States Military Service)										
1946	Cleveland	A. L.	OF	124	458	62	138	33	*16	10	54	1	.301
1947	Cleveland	A. L.	OF	108	393	54	102	12	3	15	59	1	.260
1948	Cleveland	A. L.	OF	55	160	27	43	9	2	3	18	1	.269
1949	Cleveland a	A. L.	OF	5	15	3	4	0	0	1	1	0	.267
1949	Chicago	N. L.	OF	58	176	25	51	8	4	7	21	0	.290
1950	Chicago	N. L.	OF	41	110	13	40	11	1	2	21	0	.364
1950	Springfield	I. L.	OF	17	41	6	11	3	0	1	9	0	.268
1951	Brooklyn-Cin b ...	N. L.	OF	76	158	15	47	12	1	8	23	0	.297
1952	Cincinnati c	N. L.	OF	74	184	24	52	7	6	6	28	0	.283
1952	Chicago d	A. L.	OF	8	18	2	6	0	0	0	1	0	.333
1953	St. Louis	A. L.	OF	65	106	6	21	3	0	0	9	0	.198
Major League Totals		11 Yrs		735	2191	285	613	116	41	51	276	9	.280

a Sold to Chicago Cubs, May 7, 1949.
b Claimed by Cincinnati on waivers, July 18, 1951.
c Traded by Cincinnati to Chicago White Sox for cash and pitcher Howie Judson, Sept. 1, 1952.
d Traded to St. Louis Browns with Willie Miranda for Tommy Byrne and Joe DeMaestri, October 17, 1952.

ENNIS, DELMER

Born, Philadelphia, Pennsylvania, June 8, 1925.
Bats Right. Throws Right. Height, 6 feet. Weight, 195 pounds.

Year	Club	Lea	Pos	G	AB	R	H	2B	3B	HR	RBI	SB	Avg
1943	Trenton	Inter St.	OF	*140	570	104	197	37	16	18	93	7	.346
1944-45	Philadelphia.....	N. L.	(In United States Navy)										
1946	Philadelphia	N. L.	OF	141	540	70	169	30	6	17	73	5	.313
1947	Philadelphia	N. L.	OF	139	541	71	149	25	6	12	81	9	.275
1948	Philadelphia	N. L.	OF	152	589	86	171	40	4	30	95	2	.290
1949	Philadelphia	N. L.	OF	154	610	92	184	39	11	25	110	2	.302
1950	Philadelphia	N. L.	OF	153	595	92	185	34	8	31	*126	2	.311

Year	Club	Lea	Pos	G	AB	R	H	2B	3B	HR	RBI	SB	Avg
1951	Philadelphia	N. L.	OF	144	532	76	142	20	5	15	73	4	.267
1952	Philadelphia	N. L.	OF	151	592	90	171	30	10	20	107	6	.289
1953	Philadelphia	N. L.	OF	152	578	79	165	22	3	29	125	1	.285
Major League Totals			8 Yrs	1186	4577	656	1336	240	53	179	790	31	.292
World's Series Record													
1950	Philadelphia	N. L.	OF	4	14	1	2	1	0	0	0	0	.143

EVERS, WALTER ARTHUR (HOOT)

Born, St. Louis, Missouri, February 8, 1921.
Bats Right. Throws Right. Height, 6 feet, 2 inches. Weight, 180 pounds.

Year	Club	Lea	Pos	G	AB	R	H	2B	3B	HR	RBI	SB	Avg
1941	Beaumont	T. L.	OF	7	23	2	4	0	0	0	2	0	.174
1941	Winston-Salem	Pied.	OF	117	415	41	96	14	1	4	86	8	.231
1941	Detroit	A. L.	OF	1	4	0	0	0	0	0	0	0	.000
1942	Beaumont	T. L.	OF	152	556	92	179	28	8	10	92	15	.322
1943-44-45	Detroit	A. L.		(In United States Army)									
1946	Detroit	A. L.	OF	81	304	42	81	8	4	4	33	7	.266
1947	Detroit	A. L.	OF	126	460	67	136	24	5	10	67	8	.296
1948	Detroit	A. L.	OF	139	538	81	169	33	6	10	103	3	.314
1949	Detroit	A. L.	OF	132	432	68	131	21	6	7	72	6	.303
1950	Detroit	A. L.	OF	143	526	100	170	35	*11	21	103	5	.323
1951	Detroit	A. L.	OF	116	393	47	88	15	2	11	46	5	.224
1952	Det.-Boston a ...	A. L.	OF	107	402	53	106	17	4	14	59	5	.264
1953	Boston ...: ...	A. L.	OF	99	300	39	72	10	1	11	31	2	.240
Major League Totals			9 Yrs	944	3359	497	953	163	39	88	514	41	.284

a Traded to Boston Red Sox with George Kell, Johnny Lipon and Dizzy Trout for Walt Dropo, Fred Hatfield, Don Lenhardt, Johnny Pesky and Bill Wight, June 8, 1952.

FAIN, FERRIS ROY

Born, San Antonio, Texas, March 29, 1922.
Bats Left. Throws Left. Height, 5 feet, 11 inches. Weight, 183 pounds.

Year	Club	Lea	Pos	G	AB	R	H	2B	3B	HR	RBI	SB	Avg
1939	San Francisco	P. C. L.	1B	12	33	4	7	2	0	1	8	0	.212
1940	San Francisco ...	P. C. L.	1B	146	446	64	106	21	7	7	50	3	.238
1941	San Francisco ...	P. C. L.	1B	174	649	*122	201	27	8	5	66	8	.310
1942	San Francisco	P. C. L.	1B	162	519	57	112	17	4	4	53	3	.216
1943, 1944, 1945			(In United States Military Service)										
1946	San Francisco a	P. C. L.	1B	180	615	*117	185	35	6	11	*112	24	.301
1947	Philadelphia	A. L.	1B	136	461	70	134	28	6	7	71	4	.291
1948	Philadelphia . ..	A. L.	1B	145	520	81	146	27	6	7	88	10	.281
1949	Philadelphia	A. L.	1B	150	525	81	138	21	5	3	78	8	.263
1950	Philadelphia	A. L.	1B	151	522	83	147	25	4	10	83	8	.282
1951	Philadelphia	A. L.	1B-OF	117	425	63	146	30	3	6	57	0	* .344
1952	Philadelphia b ...	A. L.	1B	145	538	82	176	*43	3	2	59	3	*.327
1953	Chicago	A. L.	1B	128	446	73	114	18	2	6	52	3	.256
Major League Totals			7 Yrs	972	3437	533	1001	192	29	41	488	36	.291

a Drafted by Philadelphia Athletics, November 11, 1946.
b Traded to Chicago White Sox with Bob Wilson for Joe DeMaestri, Ed McGhee and Eddie Robinson, Jan. 27, 1953.

FITZGERALD, EDWARD RAYMOND

Born, Santa Ynez, California, May 21, 1924.
Bats Right. Throws Right. Height, 6 feet. Weight, 180 pounds.

Year	Club	Lea	Pos	G	AB	R	H	2B	3B	HR	RBI	SB	Avg
1946	Wenatchee	W. I. L.	C	91	287	58	97	16	8	13	48	8	.338
1946	Sacramento	P. C. L.	C	11	38	7	10	2	1	0	0	0	.263
1947	Sacramento	P. C. L.	C	144	411	62	149	22	9	5	49	26	.363
1948	Pittsburgh	N. L.	C	102	262	31	70	9	8	1	35	3	.267
1949	Pittsburgh	N. L.	C	75	160	16	42	7	0	2	18	1	.263
1950	Pittsburgh	N. L.	C	6	15	1	1	1	0	0	0	0	.067
1950	Indianapolis .,....	A. A.	C	103	310	43	97	14	6	0	42	3	.313
1951	Pittsburgh	N. L.	C	55	97	8	22	6	0	0	13	1	.227
1952	Pittsburgh	N. L.	C-3B	51	73	4	17	1	0	1	7	0	.233
1953	Pittsburgh a	N. L.	C	6	17	2	2	1	0	0	1	0	.118
1953	Washington	A. L.	C	88	288	23	72	13	0	3	39	2	.250
Major League Totals			6 Yrs	883	912	85	226	38	8	7	113	7	.248

a Sold to Washington, May 13, 1953.

FONDY, DEE VIRGIL, JR.

Born, Slaton, Texas, October 31, 1924.
Bats Left. Throws Left. Height, 6 feet, 3 inches. Weight, 195 pounds.

Year	Club	Lea	Pos	G	AB	R	H	2B	3B	HR	RBI	SB	Avg
1946	Santa Barbara ...	Cal. L.	1B	59	221	34	74	14	2	3	36	9	.335
1947	Newport News	Pied.	1B	136	511	109	172	39	*13	14	99	*37	.337
1948	Fort Worth	T. L.	1B	153	588	92	*193	24	11	5	86	34	.328
1949	Fort Worth	T. L.	OF	6	15	3	4	0	0	1	5	1	.267
1949	Mobile	S. A.	1B	128	496	62	146	14	10	4	62	20	.294
1949	Montreal	I. L.	1B	16	56	5	14	1	1	1	4	5	.250
1950	Fort Worth a	T. L.	1B	141	528	69	157	22	9	5	54	*39	.297
1951	Los Angeles	P. C. L.	1B	70	274	46	103	16	6	11	45	7	.376
1951	Chicago	N. L.	1B	49	170	23	46	7	2	3	20	5	.271
1952	Chicago	N. L.	1B	145	554	69	166	21	9	10	67	13	.300
1953	Chicago	N. L.	1B	150	595	79	184	24	11	18	78	10	.309

Major League Totals   3 Yrs 344 1319 171 396 52 22 31 165 28 .300

a Sold to Chicago Cubs with Kevin Connors by Brooklyn, October 10, 1950, for Hank Edwards and cash.

FOX, JACOB NELSON (NELLIE)

Born, St. Thomas, Pennsylvania, December 25, 1927.
Bats Left. Throws Right. Height, 5 feet, 10 inches. Weight, 160 pounds.

Year	Club	Lea	Pos	G	AB	R	H	2B	3B	HR	RBI	SB	Avg
1944	Jamestown	Pony	OF	56	230	40	70	11	0	0	18	3	.304
1944	Lancaster	Inter-St.	1B	24	77	11	25	6	0	0	12	0	.325
1945	Lancaster	Inter-St.	2B	*140	*573	*128	*180	19	*19	1	68	14	.314
1946	Philadelphia........	A. L.		(In United States Military Service)									
1947	Lancaster	Inter-St.	2B	55	228	42	64	8	4	1	22	0	.281
1947	Philadelphia	A. L.	2B	7	3	2	0	0	0	0	0	0	.000
1948	Philadelphia	A. L.	2B	3	13	0	2	0	0	0	1	0	.154
1948	Lincoln	W. L.	2B	136	*576	97	*179	28	14	5	67	19	.311
1949	Philadelphia a	A. L.	2B	88	247	42	63	6	2	0	21	2	.255
1950	Chicago	A. L.	2B	130	457	45	113	12	7	0	30	4	.247
1951	Chicago	A. L.	2B	147	604	93	189	32	12	4	55	9	.313
1952	Chicago	A. L.	2B	152	*648	76	*192	25	10	0	39	5	.296
1953	Chicago	A. L.	2B	154	624	92	178	31	8	3	72	4	.285

Major League Totals   7 Yrs 681 2596 350 737 106 39 7 217 25 .284

a Traded to Chicago, A. L. for Joe Tipton, October 18, 1949.

FRIEND, OWEN LACEY, JR.

Born, Granite City, Illinois, March 21, 1927.
Bats Right. Throws Right. Height, 6 feet, 1 inch. Weight, 175 pounds.

Year	Club	Lea	Pos	G	AB	R	H	2B	3B	HR	RBI	SB	Avg
1944	Newark	Ohio St.	2B	129	488	80	137	25	7	2	52	15	.281
1945	Memphis	S. A.	2B	8	29	1	10	3	0	0	2	0	.345
1945	Raleigh	Carol.	2B	106	424	76	119	26	5	5	68	16	.281
1946	Elmira	E. L.	2B	114	388	42	89	18	8	2	37	0	.229
1947	San Antonio	T. L.	2B	46	162	12	36	1	2	2	13	5	.222
1947	Springfield	I. I. I.	2B	88	346	53	83	16	3	10	41	5	.240
1948	Muskegon	Cent.	2B	141	500	77	139	25	13	21	104	5	.278
1949	Elmira	E. L.	2B	139	523	75	138	23	7	20	88	12	.264
1949	St. Louis	A. L.	2B	2	8	1	3	0	0	0	1	0	.375
1950	St. Louis	A. L.	2B	119	372	48	88	15	3	8	50	2	.237
1951-52	St. Louis a.....	A. L.		(In United States Military Service)									
1953	Det.-Cleve. b	A. L.	2B-SS-3B	65	164	17	33	6	0	5	23	0	.201

Major League Totals   3 Yrs 186 544 66 124 21 2 13 74 2 .228

a Traded to Detroit with Bob Nieman and J. W. Porter for Johnny Groth, Virgil Trucks and Hal White, December 4, 1952.

b Traded to Cleveland with Joe Ginsberg, Art Houtteman and Bill Wight for Al Aber, Ray Boone, Steve Gromek and Dick Weik, June 15, 1953.

FURILLO, CARL ANTHONY

Born, Stony Creek Mills, Pennsylvania, March 8, 1922.
Bats Right.   Throws Right.   Height, 5 feet, 11 inches.   Weight, 190 pounds.

Year	Club	Lea	Pos	G	AB	R	H	2B	3B	HR	RBI	SB	Avg
1940	Pocomoke City	E. S. L.	OF-P	71	235	36	75	15	3	9	39	4	.319
1940	Reading	Inter-St.	OF	8	30	3	11	0	1	0	2	0	.367
1941	Reading	Inter-St.	OF-P	125	482	87	151	23	16	10	76	8	.313
1942	Montreal	I. L.	OF	129	445	55	125	21	6	3	51	13	.281
1943-44-45 Montreal	I. L.		(In United States Army)										
1946	Brooklyn	N. L.	OF	117	335	29	95	18	6	3	35	6	.284
1947	Brooklyn	N. L.	OF	124	437	61	129	24	7	8	88	7	.295
1948	Brooklyn	N. L.	OF	108	364	55	108	20	4	4	44	6	.297
1949	Brooklyn	N. L.	OF	142	549	95	177	27	10	18	106	4	.324
1950	Brooklyn	N. L.	OF	153	620	99	189	30	6	18	106	8	.305
1951	Brooklyn	N. L.	OF	*158	*667	93	197	32	4	16	91	8	.295
1952	Brooklyn	N. L.	OF	134	425	52	105	18	1	8	59	1	.247
1953	Brooklyn	N. L.	OF	132	479	82	165	38	6	21	92	1	*.344
Major League Totals		8 Yrs		1068	3876	566	1165	207	44	96	621	41	.301

World's Series Record

Year	Club	Lea	Pos	G	AB	R	H	2B	3B	HR	RBI	SB	Avg
1947	Brooklyn	N. L.	OF	6	17	2	6	2	0	0	3	0	.353
1949	Brooklyn	N. L.	OF	3	8	0	1	0	0	0	0	0	.125
1952	Brooklyn	N. L.	OF	7	23	1	4	2	0	0	0	0	.174
1953	Brooklyn	N. L.	OF	6	24	4	8	2	0	1	4	0	.333
World's Series Totals				22	72	7	19	6	0	1	7	0	.264

GARAGIOLA, JOSEPH HENRY

Born, St. Louis, Missouri, February 12, 1926.
Bats Left.   Throws Right.   Height, 6 feet.   Weight, 195 pounds.

Year	Club	Lea	Pos	G	AB	R	H	2B	3B	HR	RBI	SB	Avg
1942	Springfield	W. A.	C-OF	67	181	20	46	4	1	5	26	1	.254
1943	Columbus	A. A.	C	81	205	27	60	7	3	4	27	2	.293
1944	Columbus	A. A.	C	1	3	1	0	0	0	0	0	0	.000
1944-45-46 St. Louis	N. L.		(In United States Military Service)										
1946	St. Louis	N. L.	C	74	211	21	50	4	1	3	22	0	.237
1947	St. Louis	N. L.	C	77	183	20	47	10	2	5	25	0	.257
1948	St. Louis	N. L.	C	24	56	9	6	1	0	2	7	0	.107
1948	Columbus	A. A.	C	65	202	38	72	11	3	7	45	0	.356
1949	St. Louis	N. L.	C	81	241	55	63	14	0	3	26	0	.261
1950	St. Louis	N. L.	C	34	88	8	28	6	1	2	20	0	.318
1951	St. L.-Pittsb. a	N. L.	C	99	284	33	68	11	4	11	44	4	.239
1952	Pittsburgh	N. L.	C	118	344	35	94	15	4	8	54	0	.273
1953	Pitts.-Chic. b	N. L.	C	101	301	30	79	14	4	3	35	1	.262
Major League Totals		8 Yrs		608	1708	211	435	75	16	37	233	5	.255

World's Series Record

Year	Club	Lea	Pos	G	AB	R	H	2B	3B	HR	RBI	SB	Avg
1946	St. Louis	N. L.	C	5	19	2	6	2	0	0	4	0	.316

a Traded with Pitchers Howie Pollet and Ted Wilks, Outfielder Bill Howerton and Infielder Dick Cole to Pittsburgh for Pitcher Cliff Chambers and Outfielder Wally Westlake, June 15, 1951.

b Traded to Chicago Cubs with Ralph Kiner, George Metkovich and Howie Pollet for Bob Addis, Toby Atwell, Gene Hermanski, Bob Schultz, Preston Ward, option to purchase George Freese, and cash, June 4, 1953.

GARCIA, VINICIO

Born, Vera Cruz, Mexico, December 13, 1930.
Bats Right.   Throws Right.   Height, 5 feet, 8 inches.   Weight, 165 pounds.

Year	Club	Lea	Pos	G	AB	R	H	2B	3B	HR	RBI	SB	Avg
1949	Juarez	Ariz.-Tex.	2B	148	602	*170	*227	42	*20	4	88	41	*.377
1950	Shreveport	T. L.	2B	142	485	53	104	17	1	1	35	9	.214
1951	Corpus Christi	Gulf Ct.	2B	34	145	35	52	6	4	1	21	6	.359
1951	Shreveport	T. L.	2B-3B-SS	77	235	28	57	10	1	0	20	4	.243
1952	Shreveport	T. L.	2B	158	585	88	162	20	7	2	62	6	.277
1953	Shreveport a	T. L.	2B	155	601	82	183	34	4	2	51	8	.305

a Drafted by Baltimore, Nov. 30, 1953.

GERNERT, RICHARD EDWARD

Born, Reading, Pa., Sept. 12, 1929.
Bats Right. Throws Right. Height, 6 feet, 3 inches. Weight, 205 pounds.

Year	Club	Lea	Pos	G	AB	R	H	2B	3B	HR	RBI	SB	Avg
1950	San Jose	Calif.	1B	21	94	26	36	9	4	2	24	0	.383
1950	Scranton	Eastern	1B	69	234	40	62	11	3	6	40	0	.265
1950	Louisville	A. A.	1B	26	73	6	16	1	0	0	3	0	.219
1951	Scranton	Eastern	1B	124	431	72	132	28	3	9	78	4	.306
1952	Louisville	A. A.	1B	19	73	17	23	7	0	4	16	0	.315
1952	Boston	A. L.	1B	102	367	53	89	20	2	19	67	4	.243
1953	Boston	A. L.	1B	139	494	73	125	15	1	21	71	0	.253
Major League Totals			2 Yrs	241	861	131	214	35	3	40	138	4	.249

GILLIAM, JAMES (JUNIOR)

Born, Nashville, Tennessee, October 17, 1928.
Bats Both. Throws Right. Height, 5 feet, 11 inches. Weight, 175 pounds.

Year	Club	Lea	Pos	G	AB	R	H	2B	3B	HR	RBI	SB	Avg
1951	Montreal	I. L.	2B-OF-3B	152	565	*117	162	22	9	7	73	15	.287
1952	Montreal	I. L.	2B-OF-3B	151	561	*111	169	39	9	9	112	18	.301
1953	Brooklyn	N. L.	2B	151	605	125	168	31	*17	6	63	21	.278
World's Series Record													
1953	Brooklyn	N. L.	2B	6	27	4	8	3	0	2	4	0	.296

GINSBERG, MYRON NATHAN (JOE)

Born, New York City, New York, October 11, 1926.
Bats Left. Throws Right. Height, 5 feet, 11 inches. Weight, 175 pounds.

Year	Club	Lea	Pos	G	AB	R	H	2B	3B	HR	RBI	SB	Avg
1944	Jamestown	Pony	C	88	273	41	74	12	6	4	43	7	.271
1945, 1946		(In United States Military Service)											
1947	Williamsport	E. L.	C	92	250	35	55	9	5	3	34	2	.220
1948	Williamsport	E. L.	C	107	340	55	111	21	8	1	53	8	.326
1948	Detroit	A. L.	C	11	36	7	13	0	0	0	1	0	.361
1949	Toledo	A. A.	C	102	336	43	95	17	1	5	43	2	.283
1950	Detroit	A. L.	C	36	95	12	22	6	0	0	12	1	.232
1950	Toledo	A. A.	C	63	214	32	72	13	2	7	39	0	.336
1951	Detroit	A. L.	C	102	304	44	79	10	2	8	37	0	.260
1952	Detroit	A. L.	C	113	307	29	68	13	2	6	36	1	.221
1953	Det.-Cleve. a	A. L.	C	64	162	16	47	6	0	0	13	0	.290
Major League Totals			5 Yrs	326	904	108	229	35	4	14	99	2	.253

a Traded to Cleveland with Owen Friend, Art Houtteman and Bill Wight for Al Aber, Ray Boone, Steve Gromek and Dick Weik, June 15, 1953.

GOODMAN, WILLIAM DALE

Born, Concord, North Carolina, March 22, 1926.
Bats Left. Throws Right. Height, 5 feet, 11½ inches. Weight, 160 pounds.

Year	Club	Lea	Pos	G	AB	R	H	2B	3B	HR	RBI	SB	Avg
1944	Atlanta	S. A.	OF	137	*554	*122	186	22	*13	2	64	19	.336
1945	Atlanta	S. A.	(In United States Military Service)										
1946	Atlanta	S. A.	1B-OF	86	332	65	129	14	3	1	46	6	.389
1947	Boston	A. L.	OF	12	11	1	2	0	0	0	1	0	.182
1947	Louisville	A. A.	SS-OF	94	329	55	112	18	3	2	49	3	.340
1948	Boston	A. L.	INF	127	445	65	138	27	2	1	66	5	.310
1949	Boston	A. L.	1B	122	443	54	132	23	3	0	56	2	.298
1950	Boston	A. L.	INF-OF	110	424	91	150	25	3	4	68	2	*.354
1951	Boston	A. L.	INF-OF	141	546	92	162	34	4	0	50	7	.297
1952	Boston	A. L.	INF-OF	138	513	79	157	27	8	4	56	8	.306
1953	Boston	A. L.	2B-1B	128	514	73	161	33	5	2	41	1	.313
Major League Totals			7 Yrs	778	2896	455	902	169	20	11	338	25	.311

GORDON, SIDNEY

Born, Brooklyn, New York, August 13, 1918.
Bats Right. Throws Right. Height, 5 feet, 10½ inches. Weight, 180 pounds.

Year	Club	Lea	Pos	G	AB	R	H	2B	3B	HR	RBI	SB	Avg
1938	Milford	E. S. L.	3B	112	412	104	*145	18	*9	25	83	16	*.352
1939	Clinton	I. I.	2B-3B	121	459	89	150	14	*24	8	83	9	.327
1939	Jersey City	I. L.	3B	8	9	1	2	0	0	0	0	1	.222
1940	Jersey City	I. L.	3B	136	501	76	131	21	7	5	89	7	.261
1941	Jersey City	I. L.	INF-OF	150	523	69	159	15	6	7	76	15	.304
1941	New York	N. L.	OF	9	31	4	8	1	1	0	4	0	.258
1942	New York	N. L.	3B	6	19	4	6	0	1	0	2	0	.316
1942	Jersey City	I. L.	OF-INF-P	145	517	68	155	17	5	10	85	15	.300
1943	New York	N. L.	1F-OF	131	474	50	119	9	11	9	63	2	.251
1944-45	New York	N. L.	(In United States Coast Guard)										
1946	New York	N. L.	3B-OF	135	450	64	132	15	4	5	45	1	.293
1947	New York	N. L.	3B-OF	130	437	57	119	19	8	13	57	2	.272
1948	New York	N. L.	3B-OF	142	521	100	156	26	4	30	107	8	.299
1949	New York a	N. L.	1B-3B-OF	141	489	87	139	26	2	26	90	1	.284
1950	Boston	N. L.	3B-OF	134	481	78	146	33	4	27	103	2	.304
1951	Boston	N. L.	3B-OF	150	550	96	158	28	1	29	109	2	.287
1952	Boston	N. L.	OF-3B	144	522	69	151	22	2	25	75	0	.289
1953	Milwaukee b	N. L.	OF	140	464	67	127	22	4	19	75	1	.274

Major League Totals 11 Yrs 1262 4438 676 1261 201 42 183 730 19 .284

a Traded with Buddy Kerr, Willard Marshall and Sam Webb to Boston Braves for Eddie Stanky and Alvin Dark, December 14, 1949.
b Traded to Pittsburgh with Max Surkont, Sam Jethroe, Larry Lassalle, Fred Waters, Curt Raydon and cash for Danny O'Connell, Dec. 26, 1953.

GRAMMAS, ALEXANDER PETER

Born, Birmingham, Alabama, April 3, 1927.
Bats Right. Throws Right. Height, 6 feet. Weight, 175 pounds.

Year	Club	Lea	Pos	G	AB	R	H	2B	3B	HR	RBI	SB	Avg
1949	Muskegon	Central	3B	87	294	42	96	12	3	0	30	2	.327
1950	Memphis	S. A.	SS-3B	135	457	49	102	16	6	1	41	3	.223
1951	Memphis	S. A.	3B-SS	52	185	35	47	6	1	2	16	2	.254
1951	Tulsa	T. L.	SS-3B	88	302	29	83	10	3	2	32	9	.275
1952	Tulsa	T. L.	SS-2B-3B	158	602	80	146	28	9	2	51	3	.243
1953	Kansas City a	A. A.	SS	140	584	93	179	29	3	2	62	5	.307

a Traded by Cincinnati to St. Louis Cardinals for Jack Crimian and cash, Dec. 2, 1953.

GRASSO, NEWTON MICHAEL (MICKEY)

Born, Newark, New Jersey, May 10, 1922.
Bats Right. Throws Right. Height, 6 feet. Weight, 195 pounds.

Year	Club	Lea	Pos	G	AB	R	H	2B	3B	HR	RBI	SB	Avg
1941	Trenton	Inter.-St.	C	52	124	16	29	8	0	1	14	2	.234
1942-43-44-45	Trenton	Int. St.	(In United States Military Service)										
1946	Jersey City	I. L.	C	106	303	31	69	8	0	13	46	1	.228
1946	New York	N. L.	C	7	22	1	3	0	0	0	1	0	.136
1947	Jersey City	I. L.	C	117	388	55	104	17	1	16	52	7	.268
1948	Seattle	P. C. L.	C	140	380	35	99	13	1	5	27	1	.261
1949	Seattle a	P. C. L.	C	109	299	29	75	11	0	7	31	1	.251
1950	Washington	A. L.	C	75	195	25	56	4	1	1	22	1	.287
1951	Washington	A. L.	C	52	175	16	36	3	0	1	15	0	.206
1952	Washington	A. L.	C	115	361	22	78	9	0	0	27	1	.216
1953	Washington	A. L.	C	61	196	13	41	7	0	2	22	0	.209

Major League Totals 5 Yrs 310 949 77 214 23 1 4 87 2 .226

a Drafted by Washington, November 17, 1949.

GREENGRASS, JAMES RAYMOND

Born, Addison, N. Y., Oct. 24, 1927.
Bats Right. Throws Right. Height, 6 feet, 1 inch. Weight, 200 pounds.

Year	Club	Lea	Pos	G	AB	R	H	2B	3B	HR	RBI	SB	Avg
1944	Wellsville	Pony	3B-SS	66	261	42	69	15	2	0	33	5	.264
1945	Wellsville	Pony	3B-P	75	284	57	99	15	12	8	59	11	.349

Year	Club	Lea	Pos	G	AB	R	H	2B	3B	HR	RBI	SB	Avg
1945	Binghamton	Eastern	3B	6	25	1	3	0	1	0	1	0	.120
1946-1947	Binghamton .	Eastern	(In U. S. Military Service)										
1948	Binghamton	Eastern	3B	131	481	61	125	21	8	7	60	15	.260
1949	Newark	I. L.	3B	29	75	8	18	2	0	4	6	1	.240
1949	Binghamton	Eastern	3B	103	364	50	96	19	4	7	60	0	.264
1950	Muskegon	Central	OF-P	62	137	23	46	13	0	3	22	0	.336
1951	Muskegon	Central	3B-OF	99	377	84	143	22	9	18	90	8	*.379
1952	Beaumont a	T. L.	3B-OF	151	540	88	149	31	15	22	101	3	.276
1952	Cincinnati	N. L.	OF	18	68	10	21	2	1	5	24	0	.309
1953	Cincinnati	N. L.	OF	154	606	86	173	22	7	20	100	6	.285
Major League Totals			2 Yrs	172	674	96	194	24	8	25	124	6	.288

a New York Yankee property; was sent to Cincinnati Reds with cash estimated at $40,000, plus Johnny Schmitz, Ernie Nevel and Bob Marquis in exchange for pitcher Ewell Blackwell, Aug. 28. 1952.

GROTH, JOHN THOMAS
Born, Chicago, Illinois, July 23, 1926.
Bats Right. Throws Right. Height, 6 feet. Weight, 182 pounds.

Year	Club	Lea	Pos	G	AB	R	H	2B	3B	HR	RBI	SB	Avg
1946	Detroit	A. L.	OF	4	9	1	0	0	0	0	0	0	.000
1947	Williamsport	E. L.	OF	121	426	88	136	26	*14	10	78	9	.319
1947	Detroit	A. L	OF	2	4	1	1	0	0	0	0	0	.250
1948	Buffalo	I. L.	OF	150	*586	*124	*199	*37	*16	30	97	7	.340
1948	Detroit	A. L.	OF	6	17	3	8	3	0	1	5	0	.471
1949	Detroit	A. L.	OF	103	348	60	102	19	5	11	73	3	.293
1950	Detroit	A. L.	OF	*157	566	95	173	30	8	12	85	1	.306
1951	Detroit	A. L.	OF	118	428	41	128	29	1	3	49	1	.299
1952	Detroit a	A. L.	OF	141	524	56	149	22	2	4	51	2	.284
1953	St. Louis	A. L.	OF	141	557	65	141	27	4	10	57	5	.253
Major League Totals			8 Yrs	672	2453	322	702	130	20	41	320	12	.286

a Traded to St. Louis Browns with Virgil Trucks and Hal White for Owen Friend, Bob Nieman and J. W. Porter, December 4, 1952.

HAMNER, GRANVILLE WILBUR (GRANNY)
Born, Richmond, Virginia, April 26, 1927.
Bats Right. Throws Right. Height, 5 feet, 11 inches. Weight, 160 pounds.

Year	Club	Lea	Pos	G	AB	R	H	2B	3B	HR	RBI	SB	Avg
1944	Philadelphia	N. L.	SS	21	77	6	19	1	0	0	5	0	.247
1945	Utica	E. L.	SS	104	364	39	94	11	7	1	58	7	.258
1945	Philadelphia	N. L.	SS	14	41	3	7	2	0	0	6	0	.171
1946			(In United States Military Service)										
1946	Philadelphia	N. L.	SS	2	7	0	1	0	0	0	0	0	.143
1947	Utica	E. L.	2B-SS	138	*609	90	177	26	6	4	79	10	.291
1947	Philadelphia	N. L.	SS	2	7	1	2	0	0	0	0	0	.286
1948	Philadelphia	N. L.	2B-SS-3B	129	446	42	116	21	5	3	48	2	.260
1949	Philadelphia	N. L.	SS	154	*662	83	174	32	5	6	53	6	.263
1950	Philadelphia	N. L.	SS	*157	637	78	172	27	5	11	82	2	.270
1951	Philadelphia	N. L.	SS	150	589	61	150	23	7	9	72	10	.255
1952	Philadelphia	N. L.	SS	151	596	74	164	30	5	17	87	7	.275
1953	Philadelphia	N. L.	2B-SS	154	609	90	168	30	8	21	92	2	.276
Major League Totals			10 Yrs	934	3671	438	973	166	35	67	445	29	.265
World's Series Record													
1950	Philadelphia	N. L.	SS	4	14	1	6	2	1	0	0	1	.429

HATFIELD, FRED JAMES
Born, Lanett, Alabama, March 18, 1925.
Bats Left. Throws Right. Height, 6 feet, ½ inch. Weight, 171 pounds.

Year	Club	Lea	Pos	G	AB	R	H	2B	3B	HR	RBI	SB	Avg
1942	Canton	M. A. L.	3B	12	36	3	6	0	0	0	1	0	.167
1942	Danville-Schoolfield .	Bi-St.	3B	81	335	31	87	13	3	1	37	2	.260
1943-44-45	Louisville ...	A. A.	(In United States Military Service)										
1946	Roanoke	Pied.	3B-P	114	440	66	118	7	9	3	42	11	.268
1947	Scranton	E L	8B-SS	137	525	72	143	22	8	7	74	6	.272
1948	Louisville	A. A.	3B	39	155	12	39	8	2	0	12	2	.252
1948	Lynn	N. E. L.	3B	108	402	104	114	20	6	14	74	10	.284
1949	Birmingham	S. A.	3B	154	597	98	156	21	13	25	101	6	.261
1950	Birmingham	S A.	3B	141	544	113	163	22	9	27	101	3	.300
1950	Boston	A. L.	3B	10	12	3	3	0	0	0	2	0	.250
1951	Boston	A. L.	3B	80	163	23	28	4	2	2	14	1	.172

Year	Club	Lea	Pos	G	AB	R	H	2B	3B	HR	RBI	SB	Avg
1952	Bos.-Detroit a	A. L.	3B-SS	131	466	48	112	13	3	3	28	2	.240
1953	Detroit	A. L.	3B-2B-SS	109	311	41	79	11	1	3	19	3	.254

| Major League Totals | | | 4 Yrs | 330 | 952 | 115 | 222 | 28 | 6 | 8 | 63 | 6 | .233 |

a Traded to Detroit with Walt Dropo, Don Lenhardt, Johnny Pesky and Bill Wight for Hoot Evers, George Kell, Johnny Lipon and Dizzy Trout, June 3, 1952.

HATTON, GRADY EDGEBERT, JR.

Born, Beaumont, Texas, October 7, 1922.
Bats Left. Throws R.ght. Height, 5 feet, 9 inches. Weight, 175 pounds.

Year	Club	Lea	Pos	G	AB	R	H	2B	3B	HR	RBI	SB	Avg
1946	Cincinnati	N. L.	3B-OF	116	436	56	118	18	3	14	69	6	.271
1947	Cincinnati	N. L.	3B	146	524	91	147	24	8	16	77	7	.281
1948	Cincinnati	N. L.	INF-OF	133	458	58	110	17	2	9	44	7	.240
1949	Cincinnati	N. L.	3B	137	537	71	141	38	5	11	69	4	.263
1950	Cincinnati	N. L.	3B-2B-SS	130	438	67	114	17	1	11	54	6	.260
1951	Cincinnati	N. L.	3B-0F	96	331	41	84	9	3	4	37	4	.254
1952	Cincinnati	N. L.	2B	128	433	48	92	14	1	9	57	5	.212
1953	Cincinnati	N. L.	2B-1B-3B	83	159	22	37	3	1	7	22	0	.233

| Major League Totals | | | 8 Yrs | 969 | 3316 | 454 | 843 | 140 | 24 | 81 | 429 | 39 | .254 |

HEGAN, JAMES EDWARD

Born, Lynn, Massachusetts, August 3, 1920.
Bats Right. Throws Right. Height, 6 feet, 2 inches. Weight, 195 pounds.

Year	Club	Lea	Pos	G	AB	R	H	2B	3B	HR	RBI	SB	Avg
1938	Springfield	M. A. L.	OF-C	62	185	33	54	10	3	5	19	1	.292
1939	Springfield	M. A. L.	OF-C	103	342	46	83	13	1	13	53	0	.243
1940	Wilkes Barre	E. L.	C	32	78	7	19	3	3	0	7	0	.244
1940	Oklahoma City	T. L.	C	44	138	16	39	7	3	2	18	3	.283
1941	Oklahoma City	T. L.	C	77	256	30	62	9	7	1	26	3	.242
1941	Wilkes Barre	E. L.	C	34	98	9	23	2	4	2	12	0	.235
1941	Cleveland	A. L.	C	16	47	4	15	2	0	1	5	0	.319
1942	Baltimore	I. L.	C	4	8	1	2	1	0	0	0	0	.250
1942	Cleveland	A. L.	C	68	170	10	33	5	0	0	11	1	.194
1943-44-45	Cleveland ...	A. L.	(In U. S. Coast Guard)										
1946	Cleveland .. .	A. L.	C	88	271	29	64	11	5	0	17	1	.236
1947	Cleveland	A. L.	C	135	378	38	94	14	5	4	42	3	.249
1948	Cleveland	A. L.	C	144	472	60	117	21	6	14	61	6	.248
1949	Cleveland	A. L.	C	152	468	54	105	19	5	8	55	1	.224
1950	Cleveland	A. L.	C	131	415	53	91	16	5	14	58	1	.219
1951	Cleveland	A. L.	C	133	416	60	99	17	5	6	43	3	.238
1952	Cleveland	A. L.	C	112	333	39	75	17	2	4	41	0	.225
1953	Cleveland	A. L.	C	112	299	37	65	10	1	9	37	1	.217

Major League Totals			10 Yrs	1091	3269	384	758	132	34	60	370	17	.232
World's Series Record													
1948	Cleveland	A. L.	C	6	19	2	4	0	0	1	5	1	.211

HEMUS, SOLLY JOSEPH

Born, Phoenix, Arizona, April 17, 1924.
Bats Left. Throws Right. Height, 5 feet, 9 inches. Weight, 175 pounds.

Year	Club	Lea	Pos	G	AB	R	H	2B	3B	HR	RBI	SB	Avg
1946	Pocatello	Pio.	2B	120	449	112	163	24	4	3	58	20	.363
1947	Houston	T. L	2B	141	546	89	151	20	11	0	43	12	.277
1948	Houston	T. L.	2B	•156	570	101	164	27	11	1	70	7	.288
1949	Houston	T. L.	2B-SS	109	384	79	126	26	9	6	55	13	.328
1949	St. Louis	N. L.	2B	20	33	8	11	1	0	0	2	0	.333
1950	St. Louis	N. L.	3B	11	15	1	2	1	0	0	0	0	.133
1950	Columbus	A. A.	2B	84	296	51	88	23	4	6	49	11	.297
1951	St. Louis	N. L.	SS-2B	120	420	68	118	18	9	2	32	7	.281
1952	St. Louis	N. L.	SS-3B	151	570	•105	153	28	8	15	52	1	.268
1953	St. Louis	N. L.	SS-2B	154	585	110	163	32	11	14	61	2	.279

| Major League Totals | | | 5 Yrs | 456 | 1623 | 292 | 447 | 80 | 28 | 31 | 147 | 10 | .275 |

HERMANSKI, EUGENE VICTOR (GENE)

Born, Pittsfield, Massachusetts, May 11, 1921.
Bats Left. Throws Right. Height, 5 feet, 11 inches. Weight, 185 pounds.

Year	Club	Lea	Pos	G	AB	R	H	2B	3B	HR	RBI	SB	Avg
1939	Federalsburg	E. Shore	OF	10	46	18	9	0	0	3	7	8	.196
1939	Kinston	Coast-PL	OF	66	179	27	46	5	4	2	21	5	.257
1940	Kinston	Coast-PL	OF	9	27	2	4	0	0	0	1	0	.148
1940	Feder-Poc. C.	E. Shore	OF	121	431	79	133	20	4	11	54	24	.309
1941	Olean	Pony	OF	105	422	84	144	22	7	8	63	12	.341
1942	Durham	Pied.	(In United States Military Service)										
1943	Durham	Pied.	OF	10	39	7	16	1	8	1	8	0	.410
1943	Brooklyn	N. L.	OF	18	60	6	18	2	1	0	12	1	.300
1943-44-45	Brooklyn	N. L.	(In United States Military Service)										
1946	Brooklyn	N. L.	OF	64	110	15	22	2	2	0	8	2	.200
1947	Brooklyn	N. L.	OF	79	189	36	52	7	1	7	39	5	.275
1948	Brooklyn	N. L.	OF	133	400	63	116	22	7	15	60	15	.290
1949	Brooklyn	N. L.	OF	87	224	48	67	12	8	8	42	12	.299
1950	Brooklyn	N. L.	OF	94	289	36	86	17	8	7	34	2	.298
1951	Bklyn.-Chi. a	N. L.	OF	106	311	36	85	16	1	4	25	3	.273
1952	Chicago	N. L.	OF	99	275	28	70	6	0	4	34	2	.255
1953	Chic.-Pitts. b	N. L.	OF	59	102	8	17	1	0	1	5	1	.167
Major League Totals			9 Yrs	739	1960	276	533	85	18	46	259	43	.272
World's Series Record													
1947	Brooklyn	N. L.	OF	7	19	4	3	0	1	0	1	0	.153
1949	Brooklyn	N. L.	OF	4	13	1	4	0	1	0	2	0	.308
World's Series Totals				11	32	5	7	0	2	0	3	0	.219

a Traded to Chicago Cubs with Ed Miksis, Joe Hatten and Bruce Edwards for Andy Pafko, John Schmitz, Al Walker and Wayne Terwilliger, June 15, 1951.
b Traded to Pittsburgh with Bob Addis, Toby Atwell, Bob Schultz, Preston Ward, option to purchase George Freese, and cash for Joe Garagiola, Ralph Kiner, George Metkovich and Howie Pollet, June 4, 1953.

HODERLEIN, MELVIN ANTHONY

Born, Newtown, Ohio, June 24, 1923.
Bats Both. Throws Right. Height, 5 feet, 10 inches. Weight, 180 pounds.

Year	Club	Lea	Pos	G	AB	R	H	2B	3B	HR	RBI	SB	Avg
1942	Cordele	Ga-Fla.	SS	87	354	56	88	15	5	0	28	8	.249
1942	Columbia	S. A. L.	SS-OF	9	36	5	14	3	0	1	7	0	.389
1943-44-45	Macon	S. A. L.	(In United States Military Service)										
1946	Macon	S. A. L.	3B	28	97	13	27	4	1	1	11	8	.273
1946	Anniston	S. E. L.	SS	34	117	17	38	5	1	1	7	3	.325
1947	Birmingham	S. A.	OF-SS-2B	95	314	50	84	12	4	2	37	4	.268
1948	Birmingham	S. A.	INF-OF	130	518	79	145	17	8	2	56	7	.280
1949	Louisville	A. A.	SS-2B-3B	127	444	71	119	22	1	2	44	7	.268
1950	Louisville	A. A.	INF-OF	107	377	66	110	21	2	5	50	1	.292
1951	Louisville	A. A.	INF	111	407	59	127	15	2	5	40	8	.312
1951	Boston a	A. L.	2B-3B	9	14	1	5	1	1	0	1	0	.357
1952	Washington b	A. L.	2B	72	208	16	56	3	2	0	17	2	.269
1953	Washington	A. L.	2B-SS	23	47	5	9	0	0	0	5	0	.191
Major League Totals			3 Yrs	104	269	22	70	9	3	0	23	2	.260

a Traded with pitcher Chuck Stobbs, by Boston to Chicago White Sox, for pitcher Randy Gumpert and outfielder Don Lenhardt, Nov. 13.
b Traded with outfielder Jim Busby, by Chicago to Washington, for outfielder Sam Mele, May 3, 1952. (No games with Chicago.)

HODGES, GILBERT RAY (GIL)

Born, Princeton, Indiana, April 4, 1924.
Bats Right. Throws Right. Height, 6 feet, 1½ inches. Weight, 200 pounds.

Year	Club	Lea	Pos	G	AB	R	H	2B	3B	HR	RBI	SB	Avg
1943	Brooklyn	N. L.	3B	1	2	0	0	0	0	0	0	1	.000
1944-45	Brooklyn	N. L.	(In U. S. Marine Corps)										
1946	Newport News	Pied.	C	129	406	65	118	27	7	8	64	12	.278
1947	Brooklyn	N. L.	C	28	77	9	12	3	1	1	7	0	.156
1948	Brooklyn	N. L.	1B-C	134	481	48	120	18	5	11	70	7	.249
1949	Brooklyn	N. L.	1B	156	596	94	170	23	4	23	115	10	.285
1950	Brooklyn	N. L.	1B	153	561	98	159	26	2	32	113	6	.283
1951	Brooklyn	N. L.	1B	*158	582	118	156	25	3	40	103	9	.268
1952	Brooklyn	N. L.	1B	153	508	87	129	27	1	32	102	2	.254

Year	Club	Lea	Pos	G	AB	R	H	2B	3B	HR	RBI	SB	Avg
1953	Brooklyn	N. L.	1B-OF	141	520	101	157	22	7	81	122	1	.302
	Major League Totals		8 Yrs	924	8327	555	903	144	23	170	632	36	.271

World's Series Record

Year	Club	Lea	Pos	G	AB	R	H	2B	3B	HR	RBI	SB	Avg
1947	Brooklyn	N. L.	PH	1	1	0	0	0	0	0	0	0	.000
1949	Brooklyn	N. L.	1B	5	17	2	4	0	0	1	4	0	.235
1952	Brooklyn	N. L.	1B	7	21	1	0	0	0	0	1	0	.000
1953	Brooklyn	N. L.	1B	6	24	3	8	0	0	1	1	1	.364
	World's Series Totals			19	63	6	12	0	0	2	6	1	.190

HOFMAN, ROBERT GEORGE

Born, St. Louis, Missouri, October 5, 1925.
Bats Right.   Throws Right.   Height, 5 feet, 10 inches.   Weight, 170 pounds.

Year	Club	Lea	Pos	G	AB	R	H	2B	3B	HR	RBI	SB	Avg
1944	Springfield	Ohio St.	2B	18	65	10	20	4	0	0	10	2	.308
1945		(In Military Service)											
1946	Trenton	Inter-St.	2B	59	209	20	54	11	2	0	27	0	.258
1947	Trenton	Inter-St.	2B	130	512	92	141	30	13	5	59	4	.275
1948	Sioux City	Western	2B	120	501	104	160	33	5	10	72	7	.319
1949	New York	N. L.	2B	19	48	4	10	0	0	0	3	0	.208
1949	Minneapolis	A. A.	2B	92	395	66	111	15	4	9	83	2	.281
1950	Oakland	P. C. L.	2B-OF	166	558	79	165	30	9	15	83	2	.296
1951	Ottawa	I. L.	2B	72	263	36	72	13	1	2	29	0	.274
1951	Minneapolis	A. A.	2B	67	241	40	70	11	2	10	45	3	.290
1952	New York	N. L.	2B-3B-1B	32	63	11	18	2	2	2	4	0	.286
1953	New York ..	N. L.	3B-2B	74	169	21	45	7	2	12	34	1	.266
	Major League Totals		3 Yrs	125	280	36	73	9	4	14	41	1	.261

HUNTER, GORDON WILLIAM

Born, Punxsutawney, Pennsylvania, June 4, 1928.
Bats Right.   Throws Right.   Height, 6 feet.   Weight, 180 pounds.

Year	Club	Lea	Pos	G	AB	R	H	2B	3B	HR	RBI	SB	Avg
1948	Three Rivers ..	Can.-Am.	SS	138	541	71	132	17	8	4	64	17	.244
1949	Nashua	New Eng.	SS	95	362	39	85	15	3	1	44	11	.235
1949	Newport News	Pied.	SS	6	26	3	7	0	0	0	1	0	.269
1950	Pueblo	West.	SS-2B	137	497	80	125	23	5	5	50	17	.252
1951	Fort Worth	T. L.	SS	141	480	43	121	17	6	1	49	15	.252
1952	Fort Worth a	T. L.	SS	161	610	81	174	25	5	8	75	*24	.234
1953	St. Louis	A. L.	SS	154	567	50	124	18	1	1	37	8	.219

a Sold to St. Louis Browns for $95,000 and Pitcher Bob Mahoney, Shortstop Stan Rojek and Outfielder Ray Coleman, October 14, 1952.

IRVIN, MONFORD MERRILL (MONTY)

Born, Columbia, Alabama, February 25, 1919.
Bats Right.   Throws Right.   Height, 6 feet, 1 inch.   Weight, 195 pounds.

Year	Club	Lea	Pos	G	AB	R	H	2B	3B	HR	RBI	SB	Avg
1949	Jersey City	I. L.	OF	63	204	55	76	18	5	9	52	14	.373
1949	New York	N. L.	OF-1B-3B	36	76	7	17	8	2	0	7	0	.224
1950	Jersey City	I. L.	OF	18	51	28	26	4	1	10	33	2	.510
1950	New York	N. L.	3B-1B-OF	110	374	61	112	19	5	15	66	3	.299
1951	New York	N. L.	OF-1B	151	558	94	174	19	11	24	*121	12	.312
1952	New York a	N. L.	OF	46	126	10	39	2	1	4	21	0	.310
1953	New York	N. L.	OF	124	444	72	146	21	5	21	97	2	.329
	Major League Totals		5 Yrs	467	1578	244	488	64	24	64	312	17	.309

World's Series Record

Year	Club	Lea	Pos	G	AB	R	H	2B	3B	HR	RBI	SB	Avg
1951	New York ....N. L.		OF	6	24	3	11	0	3	0	2	2	.458

a Out with broken ankle, April 4 to July 27.

JABLONSKI, RAYMOND LEO

Born, Chicago, Illinois, December 17, 1926.
Bats Right.   Throws Right.   Height, 5 feet, 10 inches.   Weight, 185 pounds.

Year	Club	Lea	Pos	G	AB	R	H	2B	3B	HR	RBI	SB	Avg
1947	Milford	E. S. L.	SS	67	261	45	85	15	1	10	49	3	.326
1948	Milford	E. S. L.	SS-OF	123	*486	108	*172	24	2	26	131	5	.354
1949	Columbus	S. A. L.	2B-OF	140	524	65	144	17	5	7	55	1	.275
1950	Columbus	S. A. L.	3B	29	87	15	19	6	1	2	8	2	.218
1950	Lynchburg	Pied.	3B-OF	121	461	70	133	*33	3	17	83	0	.289
1951	Winston-Salem ..	Carol.	3B-OF	139	551	100	*200	*45	3	*28	*127	4	*.363

171

Year	Club	Lea	Pos	G	AB	R	H	2B	3B	HR	RBI	SB	Avg
1952	Rochester	I. L.	INF	152	592	82	177	27	10	18	103	0	.299
1953	St. Louis	N. L.	3B	157	604	64	162	23	5	21	112	2	.268

JACKSON, RANSOM JOSEPH, JR. (RANDY)

Born, Little Rock, Arkansas, February 10, 1926.
Bats Right.   Throws Right.   Height, 6 feet, 1½ inches.   Weight, 181 pounds.

Year	Club	Lea	Pos	G	AB	R	H	2B	3B	HR	RBI	SB	Avg
1948	Des Moines	W. L.	3B	132	485	100	156	31	9	6	76	7	.322
1949	Los A. geles	P. C. L.	3B	14	44	6	14	3	0	2	6	0	.318
1949	Okla. City	T. L.	3B	138	524	89	156	22	*13	19	109	11	.298
1950	Springfield	I. L.	3B	117	425	78	134	22	5	20	68	4	.315
1950	Chicago	N. L.	3B	34	111	13	25	4	3	3	6	4	.225
1951	Chicago	N. L.	3B	145	557	78	153	24	6	16	76	14	.275
1952	Chicago	N. L.	3B-OF	116	379	44	88	3	5	9	34	6	.232
1953	Chicago	N. L.	3B	139	498	61	237	22	8	19	66	8	.285
Major League Totals			4 Yrs	434	1545	196	408	58	22	47	182	32	.264

JACOBS, FORREST VANDERGRIFT

Born, Cheswold, Delaware, November 4, 1925.
Bats Right.   Throws Right.   Height, 5 feet, 9 inches.   Weight, 155 pounds.

Year	Club	Lea	Pos	G	AB	R	H	2B	3B	HR	RBI	SB	Avg
1946	Thomasville ..	N. Car. St.	2B	68	266	35	68	10	0	1	15	3	.256
1947	Johnstown	M. A. L.	2B	125	534	114	170	28	7	2	50	*33	.318
1948	Asheville	Tri.-St.	2B	137	549	111	180	21	13	2	92	*47	.328
1949	Mobile	S. A.	2B	99	332	60	88	6	1	2	22	10	.265
1950	Mobile	S. A.	2B	150	589	101	179	36	4	0	38	*22	.304
1951	Mobile	S. A.	2B	142	514	108	153	24	7	1	41	24	.298
1952	St. Paul ., ...	A. A.	2B	17	56	13	13	4	1	0	5	2	.232
1952	Mobile	S. A.	2B	120	478	95	151	22	3	1	32	18	.316
1953	Fort Worth a	T. L.	2B-SS	154	645	102	182	23	5	0	40	28	.282

a Drafted by Philadelphia Athletics from Montreal, Nov. 30, 1953.

JANOWICZ, VICTOR FELIX

Born, Elyria, Ohio, February 26, 1930.
Bats Right.   Throws Right.   Height, 5 feet, 9 inches.   Weight, 190 pounds.

Year	Club	Lea	Pos	G	AB	R	H	2B	3B	HR	RBI	SB	Avg
1953	Pittsburgh a	N. L.	C	42	123	10	31	3	1	2	8	0	.252

a Bonus Player.

JEFFCOAT, HAROLD BENTLEY

Born, West Columbia, South Carolina, September 6, 1924.
Bats Right.   Throws Right.   Height, 5 feet, 11 inches.   Weight, 185 pounds.

Year	Club	Lea	Pos	G	AB	R	H	2B	3B	HR	RBI	SB	Avg
1946	Nashville	S. A.	OF	13	30	3	7	1	0	0	1	0	.233
1946	Shelby	Tri.-St.	OF-P	123	496	81	146	19	6	15	74	14	.294
1947	Nashville	S. A.	OF	153	*630	120	*218	36	13	4	118	22	.346
1948	Chicago	N. L.	OF	134	473	53	132	16	4	4	42	8	.279
1949	Chicago	N. L.	OF	108	363	43	89	18	6	2	26	12	.245
1950	Chicago	N. L.	OF	66	179	21	42	13	1	2	18	7	.235
1951	Chicago	N. L.	OF	113	278	44	76	20	2	4	27	8	.273
1952	Chicago	N. L.	OF	102	297	29	65	17	2	4	30	7	.219
1953	Chicago	N. L.	OF	106	183	22	43	3	1	4	22	5	.235
Major League Totals			6 Yrs	629	1778	212	447	87	16	20	165	47	.252

JENSEN, JACK EUGENE

Born, San Francisco, California, March 9, 1927.
Bats Right.   Throws Right.   Height, 5 feet, 11 inches.   Weight, 190 pounds.

Year	Club	Lea	Pos	G	AB	R	H	2B	3B	HR	RBI	SB	Avg
1949	Oakland	P. C. L.	OF	125	467	63	122	21	7	9	77	5	.261
1950	New York	A. L.	OF	45	70	13	12	2	2	1	5	4	.171
1951	Kansas City	A. A.	OF	42	160	23	42	4	1	9	26	2	.263
1951	New York	A. L.	OF	56	168	30	50	8	1	8	25	8	.298
1952	N. Y.-Washington a .	A. L.	OF	151	589	83	165	30	6	10	82	18	.280

Year	Club	Lea	Pos	G	AB	R	H	2B	3B	HR	RBI	SB	Avg
1953	Washington b	A. L.	OF	147	552	87	147	32	8	10	84	18	.266
Major League Totals			4 Yrs	899	1379	213	374	72	17	29	196	48	.271

World's Series Record

Year	Club	Lea	Pos	G	AB	R	H	2B	3B	HR	RBI	SB	Avg
1950	New York	A. L.	PR	1	0	0	0	0	0	0	0	0	.000

a Traded with pitcher Frank Shea, outfielder Archie Wilson and infielder Jerry Snyder, by New York to Washington, for outfielder Irv Noren and infielder Tom Upton, May 3, 1952.
b Traded to Boston Red Sox for Maurice McDermott and Tom Umphlett, Dec. 8, 1953.

JETHROE, SAMUEL

Born, East St. Louis, Illinois, January 20, 1922.
Bats Both. Throws Right. Height, 6 feet, 1 inch. Weight, 178 pounds.

Year	Club	Lea	Pos	G	AB	R	H	2B	3B	HR	RBI	SB	Avg
1948	Montreal	I. L.	OF	76	292	64	94	19	11	1	25	18	.322
1949	Montreal	I. L.	OF-C-3B	153	•635	•154	•207	34	•19	17	83	•89	.326
1950	Boston	N. L.	OF	141	582	100	159	28	8	18	58	•35	.273
1951	Boston	N. L.	OF	148	572	101	160	29	10	18	65	•35	.280
1952	Boston	N. L.	OF	151	608	79	141	23	7	13	58	28	.232
1953	Toledo a	A. A.	OF	145	543	•137	168	32	10	28	74	27	.309
Major League Totals			3 Yrs	440	1762	280	460	80	25	49	181	98	.261

a Traded by Milwaukee to Pittsburgh with Sid Gordon, Max Surkont, Larry Lassalle, Fred Waters, Curt Raydon and cash for Danny O'Connell, Dec. 26, 1953.

JONES, WILLIE EDWARD (PUDDIN' HEAD)

Born, Dillon, South Carolina, August 16, 1925.
Bats Right. Throws Right. Height, 6 feet, 1 inch. Weight, 192 pounds.

Year	Club	Lea	Pos	G	AB	R	H	2B	3B	HR	RBI	SB	Avg
1947	Terre Haute	I. I. L.	SS-P	123	489	99	150	•37	9	10	107	11	.307
1947	Philadelphia	N. L.	3B	18	62	5	14	0	1	0	10	2	.226
1948	Utica	E. L.	3B	26	94	12	27	6	0	4	19	1	.287
1948	Toronto	I. L.	3B	118	443	69	122	22	9	6	58	5	.275
1948	Philadelphia	N. L.	3B	17	60	9	20	2	0	2	9	0	.333
1949	Philadelphia	N. L.	3B	149	532	71	130	35	1	19	77	8	.244
1950	Philadelphia	N. L.	3B	•157	610	100	163	28	6	25	88	5	.267
1951	Philadelphia	N. L.	3B	148	564	79	161	23	5	22	81	6	.285
1952	Philadelphia	N. L.	3B	147	541	60	135	12	8	18	72	5	.250
1953	Philadelphia	N. L.	3B	149	481	61	108	16	2	19	70	1	.225
Major League Totals			7 Yrs	785	2850	385	731	121	18	105	407	22	.256

World's Series Record

Year	Club	Lea	Pos	G	AB	R	H	2B	3B	HR	RBI	SB	Avg
1950	Philadelphia	N. L.	3B	4	14	1	4	1	0	0	0	0	.286

JOOST, EDWIN DAVID

Born, San Francisco, California, June 5, 1916.
Bats Right. Throws Right. Height, 6 feet. Weight, 175 pounds.

Year	Club	Lea	Pos	G	AB	R	H	2B	3B	HR	RBI	SB	Avg
1933	Mission	P. C. L.	SS	25	64	8	16	0	1	0	1	0	.250
1934	Omaha	W. L.	SS	9	40	5	11	1	2	0	0	0	.275
1934	Mission	P. C. L.	3B	7	14	0	2	0	0	0	0	0	.143
1935	Mission	P. C. L.	3B	147	533	72	153	32	6	1	83	8	.287
1936	Mission	P. C. L.	3B-SS	167	668	120	191	40	7	6	72	36	.286
1936	Cincinnati	N. L.	2B-SS	13	26	1	4	1	0	0	1	0	.154
1937	Syracuse	I. L.	INF	151	553	78	149	21	12	8	52	9	.269
1937	Cincinnati	N. L.	2B	6	12	0	1	0	0	0	0	0	.083
1938	Kansas City	A. A.	INF	145	578	96	167	33	6	5	70	23	.289
1939	Cincinnati	N. L.	2B	42	143	23	36	6	3	0	14	1	.252
1940	Cincinnati	N. L.	INF	38	278	24	60	7	2	1	24	4	.216
1941	Cincinnati	N. L.	INF	152	537	67	136	25	4	4	40	9	.253
1942	Cincinnati a	N. L.	2B-SS	142	562	65	126	30	3	6	41	9	.224
1943	Boston	N. L.	3B-2B-SS	124	421	34	78	16	3	2	20	5	.185
1944	Boston	N. L.	(Voluntarily Retired)										
1945	Boston	N. L.	2B-3B	35	141	16	35	7	1	0	9	0	.248
1946	Rochester	I. L.	SS	143	493	85	136	•35	5	19	101	5	.276
1947	Philadelphia	A. L.	SS	151	540	76	111	22	3	13	64	6	.206
1948	Philadelphia	A. L.	SS	135	509	99	127	22	2	16	55	2	.250
1949	Philadelphia	A. L.	SS	144	525	128	138	25	3	23	81	2	.263
1950	Philadelphia	A. L.	SS	131	476	79	111	12	3	18	58	5	.233
1951	Philadelphia ..,...	A. L.	SS	140	553	107	160	28	5	19	78	10	.289
1952	Philadelphia	A. L.	SS	146	540	94	132	26	8	20	75	5	.244

Year	Club	Lea	Pos	G	AB	R	H	2B	3B	HR	RBI	SB	Avg
1953	Philadelphia b	A. L.	SS	51	177	39	44	6	0	6	15	3	.249
Major League Totals			15 Yrs	1500	5440	852	1299	233	35	128	575	61	.239

World's Series Record

Year	Club	Lea	Pos	G	AB	R	H	2B	3B	HR	RBI	SB	Avg
1940	Cincinnati	N. L.	2B	7	25	0	5	0	0	0	2	0	.200

a Traded to Boston Braves with Nate Andrews and $25,000 for Eddie Miller, December 4, 1942.
b Appointed Manager of Philadelphia, Nov. 4, 1953.

KATT, RAYMOND

Born, New Braunfels, Texas, May 9, 1927.
Bats Right. Throws Right. Height, 6 feet, 2 inches. Weight, 190 pounds.

Year	Club	Lea	Pos	G	AB	R	H	2B	3B	HR	RBI	SB	Avg
1948	St. Cloud	Northern	C-OF	97	335	52	107	23	6	6	57	3	.319
1949	Trenton	Int.-St.	C	33	116	22	43	6	2	1	23	1	.371
1949	Sioux City	West.	C-OF	82	241	38	59	9	0	·9	42	0	.245
1950	Sioux City	West.	C	134	465	81	130	25	1	10	80	4	.280
1951	Minneapolis	A. A.	C	117	354	56	109	27	0	11	57	0	.308
1952	Minneapolis	A. A.	C	123	448	57	136	24	1	15	68	0	.304
1952	New York	N. L.	C	9	27	4	6	0	0	·0	1	0	.222
1953	Buffalo	I. L.	C	17	53	7	13	3	0	2	3	0	.245
1953	Minneapolis	A. A.	C	114	448	76	146	31	3	28	98	0	.326
1953	New York ...	N. L.	C	8	29	2	5	1	0	0	1	0	.172
Major League Totals			2 Yrs	17	56	6	11	1	0	0	2	0	.196

KAZANSKI, THEODORE

Born, Detroit, Michigan, January 25, 1934.
Bats Right. Throws Right. Height, 6 feet, 2 inches. Weight, 175 pounds.

Year	Club	Lea	Pos	G	AB	R	H	2B	3B	HR	RBI	SB	Avg
1951	Terre Haute	I. I. L.	SS	88	306	43	66	3	2	0	24	2	.216
1952	Schenectady	E. L.	SS	125	449	52	114	14	1	10	50	8	.254
1952	Baltimore	I. L.	SS	12	35	5	9	1	1	0	4	1	.257
1953	Baltimore	I. L.	SS	60	217	36	63	12	2	3	12	0	.290
1953	Philadelphia	N. L.	SS	95	360	39	78	17	5	2	27	1	.217

KELL, GEORGE CLYDE

Born, Swifton, Arkansas, August 23, 1922.
Bats Right. Throws Right. Height, 5 feet, 9 inches. Weight, 170 pounds.

Year	Club	Lea	Pos	G	AB	R	H	2B	3B	HR	RBI	SB	Avg
1940	Newport	N. E. Ark.	3B	48	169	14	27	2	3	0	14	1	.160
1941	Newport	N. E. Ark.	3B-SS	118	462	71	*143	26	5	1	75	18	.310
1942	Lancaster	Inter-St.	INF	127	465	56	139	18	2	0	30	2	.299
1943	Lancaster	Inter-St.	3B	138	555	*120	*220	33	*23	5	79	14	*.396
1943	Philadelphia	A. L.	3B	1	5	1	1	0	1	0	1	0	.200
1944	Philadelphia ..·...	A. L.	3B	139	514	51	138	15	3	0	44	5	.268
1945	Philadelphia	A. L.	3B	147	567	50	154	30	8	4	56	2	.272
1946	Phila.-Detroit a ..	A. L.	3B-1B	131	521	70	168	25	10	4	52	3	.322
1947	Detroit	A. L.	3B	152	588	75	188	29	5	5	93	9	.320
1948	Detroit	A. L.	3B	92	368	47	112	24	3	2	44	2	.304
1949	Detroit	A. L.	3B	134	522	97	·179	38	9	3	59	7	*.343
1950	Detroit	A. L.	3B	*157	*641	114	*218	*56	6	8	101	3	.340
1951	Detroit	A. L.	3B	147	598	92	*191	*36	3	2	59	10	.319
1952	Det.-Boston b	A. L.	3B	114	428	52	133	23	2	7	57	0	.311
1953	Boston	A. L.	3B-OF	134	460	68	141	41	2	12	73	5	.307
Major League Totals			11 Yrs	1348	5212	717	1623	317	47	47	639	46	.311

a Traded to Detroit for Barney McCosky, May 18, 1946.
b Traded with Hoot Evers, Johnny Lipon and Dizzy Trout to Boston Red Sox for Walt Dropo, Fred Hatfield, Don Lenhardt, Johnny Pesky and Bill Wight, June 3, 1952.

KENNEDY, ROBERT DANIEL

Born, Chicago, Ill., August 18, 1920.
Bats Right. Throws Right. Height, 6 feet, 2 inches. Weight, 195 pounds.

Year	Club	Lea	Pos	G	AB	R	H	2B	3B	HR	RBI	SB	Avg
1937	Dallas	T. L.	3B	21	60	7	18	1	0	0	2	0	.300
1937	Vicksburg	C. S. L.	3B	41	156	6	30	9	1	0	8	2	.192
1938	Longview	E. T. L.	3B	136	537	73	140	26	*14	3	65	11	.261
1939	Shreveport	T. L.	3B	130	493	63	140	26	7	8	74	4	.284
1939	Chicago	A. L.	3B	3	8	0	2	0	0	0	1	0	.250
1940	Chicago	A. L.	3B	154	606	74	153	23	3	3	52	3	.252
1941	Chicago	A. L.	3B	76	257	16	53	9	3	1	29	5	.206

174

Year	Club	Lea	Pos	G	AB	R	H	2B	3B	HR	RBI	SB	Avg
1942	Chicago	A. L.	3B-OF	113	412	37	95	18	5	0	88	11	.231
1943-44-45	Chicago	A. L.	(In United States Marine Corps)										
1946	Chicago	A. L.	3B-OF	113	411	43	106	13	5	5	84	6	.258
1947	Chicago	A. L.	3B-OF	115	428	47	112	19	3	6	48	8	.262
1948	Chicago-Cleve a	A. L.	1B-2B-OF	96	186	14	50	11	3	0	19	0	.269
1949	Cleveland	A. L.	OF-3B	121	424	49	117	23	5	9	57	5	.276
1950	Cleveland	A. L.	OF	146	540	79	157	27	5	9	54	8	.291
1951	Cleveland	A. L.	OF	108	321	30	79	15	4	7	29	4	.246
1952	Cleveland b	A. L.	OF-3B	22	40	6	12	3	1	0	12	1	.300
1953	Cleveland	A. L.	OF	100	161	22	38	5	0	3	22	0	.236
Major League Totals			12 Yrs	1167	3794	417	974	166	37	43	395	41	.257
World's Series Record													
1948	Cleveland	A. L.	OF	3	2	0	1	0	0	0	1	0	.500

a Traded to Cleveland for Pat Seerey and Allen Gettel, June 3.
b In Military Service for most of season.

KINER, RALPH McPHERRAN

Born, Santa Rita, New Mexico, October 27, 1922.
Bats Right. Throws Right. Height, 6 feet, 2 inches. Weight, 190 pounds.

Year	Club	Lea	Pos	G	AB	R	H	2B	3B	HR	RBI	SB	Avg
1941	Albany	E. L.	OF	*141	509	94	142	23	7	11	66	16	.279
1942	Albany	E. L.	OF	*141	483	84	124	27	7	*14	75	4	.257
1943	Toronto	I. L.	OF	43	144	22	34	6	2	2	13	4	.236
1943-44-45	Pittsburgh	N. L.	(In United States Navy Air Corps)										
1946	Pittsburgh	N. L.	OF	144	502	63	124	17	3	*23	81	3	.247
1947	Pittsburgh	N. L.	OF	152	565	118	177	23	4	*51	127	1	.313
1948	Pittsburgh	N. L.	OF	*156	555	104	147	19	5	*40	123	1	.265
1949	Pittsburgh	N. L.	OF	152	549	116	170	19	5	*54	*127	6	.310
1950	Pittsburgh	N. L.	OF	150	547	112	149	21	6	*47	118	2	.272
1951	Pittsburgh	N. L.	1B-OF	151	531	*124	164	31	6	*42	109	2	.309
1952	Pittsburgh	N. L.	OF	149	516	90	126	17	2	*37	87	3	.244
1953	Pitts.-Chic. a	N. L.	OF	*158	562	100	157	20	3	35	116	2	.279
Major League Totals			8 Yrs	1212	4327	827	1214	167	34	329	888	20	.281

a Traded to Chicago Cubs with Joe Garagiola, George Metkovich and Howie Pollet for Bob Addis, Toby Atwell, Gene Hermanski, Bob Schultz, Preston Ward, option to purchase George Freese, and cash, June 4, 1953.

KLUSZEWSKI, THEODORE BERNARD

Born, Argo, Illinois, September 10, 1924.
Bats Left. Throws Left. Height, 6 feet, 2 inches. Weight, 220 pounds.

Year	Club	Lea	Pos	G	AB	R	H	2B	3B	HR	RBI	SB	Avg
1946	Columbia	S. A. L.	1B-OF	90	335	59	118	24	5	11	87	4	*.352
1947	Cincinnati	N. L.	1B	9	10	1	1	0	0	0	2	0	.100
1947	Memphis	S. A.	1B	115	427	80	161	32	9	7	68	2	*.377
1948	Cincinnati	N. L.	1B	113	379	49	104	23	4	12	57	1	.274
1949	Cincinnati	N. L.	1B	136	531	63	164	26	2	8	68	3	.309
1950	Cincinnati	N. L.	1B	134	538	76	165	37	0	25	111	3	.307
1951	Cincinnati	N. L.	1B	154	607	74	157	35	2	13	77	6	.259
1952	Cincinnati	N. L.	1B	135	497	62	159	24	11	16	86	3	.320
1953	Cincinnati	N. L.	1B	149	570	97	180	25	0	40	108	2	.316
Major League Totals			7 Yrs	830	3132	422	930	170	19	114	509	18	.297

KOKOS, RICHARD JEROME

Born, Chicago, Illinois, February 28, 1928.
Bats Left. Throws Left. Height, 5 feet, 8 inches. Weight, 170 pounds.

Year	Club	Lea	Pos	G	AB	R	H	2B	3B	HR	RBI	SB	Avg
1945	Batavia	Pony	OF	50	190	42	61	16	4	4	55	4	.321
1946	Batavia	Pony	OF	125	482	*118	*166	*37	12	*21	*114	12	.344
1947	Wilkes-Barre	E. L.	OF	139	506	115	164	28	12	12	72	9	.324
1948	Toledo	A. A.	OF	84	314	70	99	14	8	13	44	9	.315
1948	St. Louis	A. L.	OF	71	258	40	77	15	3	4	40	4	.298
1949	St. Louis	A. L.	OF	143	501	80	131	28	1	23	77	8	.261
1950	St. Louis	A. L.	OF	143	490	77	128	27	5	18	67	8	.261
1951-52	St. Louis	A. L.	(In Military Service)										
1953	St. Louis	A. L.	OF	107	299	41	72	12	0	13	38	0	.241
Major League Totals			4 Yrs	464	1548	238	408	82	9	58	222	15	.264

175

KRYHOSKI, RICHARD DAVID

Born, Leonia, New Jersey, March 24, 1925.
Bats Left. Throws Left. Height, 6 feet, 2 inches. Weight, 200 pounds.

Year	Club	Lea	Pos	G	AB	R	H	2B	3B	HR	RBI	SB	Avg
1946	Amsterdam	Can. Am.	1B	30	116	17	26	7	1	1	16	0	.224
1946	Wellsville	Pony	1B	66	265	66	105	28	3	19	85	5	.396
1946	Binghamton	E. L.	1B	4	14	2	4	1	0	0	2	0	.286
1947	Kansas City	A. A.	PH	2	2	0	0	0	0	0	0	0	.000
1947	Binghamton	E. L.	1B	101	381	60	107	17	7	11	63	2	.281
1948	Kansas City	A. A.	1B	145	545	78	160	30	7	13	87	7	.294
1949	New York	A. L.	1B	54	177	18	52	10	3	1	27	2	.294
1949	Oakland a	P. C. L.	1B	66	253	46	83	23	5	5	50	4	.328
1950	Detroit	A. L.	1B	53	169	20	37	10	0	4	19	0	.219
1950	Toledo	A. A.	1B	29	120	18	40	11	1	6	22	1	.333
1951	Detroit b	A. L.	1B	119	421	58	121	19	4	12	57	1	.287
1952	St. Louis	A. L.	1B	111	342	38	83	13	1	11	42	2	.243
1953	St. Louis	A. L.	1B	104	338	35	94	18	4	16	50	0	.278

Major League Totals		5 Yrs	441	1447	169	387	70	12	44	195	5	.267

a Traded by New York Yankees to Detroit for Outfielder Dick Wakefield, December 17, 1949.
b Traded to St. Louis Browns with Gene Bearden and Bob Cain for Matt Batts, Dick Littlefield, Cliff Mapes and Ben Taylor, February 14, 1952.

KUENN, HARVEY EDWARD

Born, Milwaukee, Wisconsin, December 4, 1930.
Bats Right. Throws Right. Height, 6 feet, 2 inches. Weight, 185 pounds.

Year	Club	Lea	Pos	G	AB	R	H	2B	3B	HR	RBI	SB	Avg
1952	Davenport	I. I. L.	SS	63	256	46	87	17	3	1	40	3	.340
1952	Detroit	A. L.	SS	19	80	2	26	2	2	0	8	2	.325
1953	Detroit	A. L.	SS	155	*679	94	*209	33	7	2	48	6	.308

Major League Totals		2 Yrs	174	759	96	235	35	9	2	56	8	.310

LANDRITH, HOBERT NEAL

Born, Decatur, Illinois, March 16, 1930.
Bats Left. Throws Right. Height, 5 feet, 8 inches. Weight, 175 pounds.

Year	Club	Lea	Pos	G	AB	R	H	2B	3B	HR	RBI	SB	Avg
1949	Charleston	Cent.	C	110	304	38	76	16	2	5	31	4	.250
1950	Tulsa	T. L.	C	1	2	0	1	1	0	0	1	0	.500
1950	Cincinnati	N. L.	C	4	14	1	3	0	0	0	1	0	.214
1951	Buffalo	I. L.	C	98	288	20	55	13	3	3	28	1	.191
1951	Cincinnati	N. L.	C	4	13	3	5	1	0	0	0	0	.385
1952	Tulsa	T. L.	C	118	380	34	114	13	3	1	48	3	.300
1952	Cincinnati	N. L.	C	15	50	1	13	4	0	0	4	0	.260
1953	Cincinnati	N. L.	C	52	154	15	37	3	1	3	16	2	.240

Major League Totals		4 Yrs	75	231	20	58	8	1	3	21	2	.251

LENHARDT, DONALD EUGENE

Born, Alton, Illinois, October 4, 1922.
Bats Right. Throws Right. Height, 6 feet, 3 inches. Weight, 190 pounds.

Year	Club	Lea	Pos	G	AB	R	H	2B	3B	HR	RBI	SB	Avg
1946	Pittsburg	K-O-M	OF	63	250	45	92	18	9	7	58	7	.368
1946	Aberdeen	No. L.	OF	39	136	28	36	5	2	1	22	7	.265
1947	Aberdeen	No. L.	OF	62	244	45	74	16	7	5	62	1	.303
1948	Springfield	I. I. L.	3B-OF	107	390	64	119	22	5	*22	73	0	.305
1948	San Antonio	T. L.	3B-OF	4	11	1	5	1	0	0	1	0	.455
1949	San Antonio	T. L.	1B-3B-OF	131	434	65	112	23	2	26	78	3	.258
1950	St. Louis	A. L.	1B-3B-OF	139	480	75	131	22	6	22	81	3	.273
1951	St. Louis-Chic. a-b	A. L.	OF-1B	95	302	32	80	12	1	15	63	2	.265
1952	Bos.-Det.-St. L. c-d	A. L.	OF-1B	93	297	41	71	10	2	11	42	0	.239
1953	St. Louis	A. L.	OF-3B	97	303	37	96	15	0	10	35	1	.317

Major League Totals		4 Yrs	424	1382	185	378	59	9	58	221	6	.274

a Traded to Chicago White Sox for Paul Lehner, Kermit Wahl and cash, June 4, 1951.
b Traded to Boston Red Sox with Randy Gumpert for Mel Hoderlein and Chuck Stobbs, Nov. 13, 1951.
c Traded to Detroit with Walt Dropo, Fred Hatfield, Johnny Pesky and Bill Wight for George Kell, Hoot Evers, Johnny Lipon and Dizzy Trout, June 3, 1952.
d Traded to St. Louis with Dick Littlefield, Marlin Stuart and Vic Wertz for Jim Delsing, Ned Garver, Dave Madison and Bud Black, Aug. 14, 1952.

176

LEPCIO, THADDEUS STANLEY (TED)

Born, Utica, N. Y., July 28, 1930.
Bats Right.   Throws Right.   Height, 5 feet, 10 inches.   Weight, 176 pounds.

Year	Club	Lea	Pos	G	AB	R	H	2B	3B	HR	RBI	SB	Avg
1951	Roanoke	Piedmont	3B	54	190	21	51	4	0	7	27	2	.268
1951	Louisville	A. A.	2B-3B	35	137	24	36	5	3	5	11	0	.263
1952	Louisville	A. A.	PH	1	1	0	0	0	0	0	0	0	.000
1952	Boston	A. L.	2B-3B-SS	84	274	34	72	17	2	5	26	3	.263
1953	Boston	A. L.	2B-SS-3B	66	161	17	38	4	2	4	11	0	.236
Major League Totals			2 Yrs	150	435	51	110	21	4	9	37	3	.253

LIPON, JOHN JOSEPH

Born, Martin's Ferry, Ohio, November 10, 1922.
Bats Right.   Throws Right.   Height, 6 feet.   Weight, 170 pounds.

Year	Club	Lea	Pos	G	AB	R	H	2B	3B	HR	RBI	SB	Avg
1941	Muskegon	Mich. St.	SS	*119	490	*126	*176	31	2	*35	*115	8	.359
1942	Beaumont	T. L.	SS	114	385	36	116	12	1	3	52	9	.301
1942	Detroit	A. L.	SS	34	131	5	25	2	0	0	9	1	.191
1943-44-45	Detroit	A. L.	(In United States Navy)										
1946	Detroit	A. L.	SS-3B	14	20	4	6	0	0	0	1	0	.300
1947	Dallas	T. L.	SS	150	560	86	165	31	5	11	78	29	.295
1948	Detroit	A. L.	SS-2B-3B	121	458	65	133	18	8	5	52	4	.290
1949	Detroit	A. L.	SS	127	439	57	110	14	6	3	59	2	.251
1950	Detroit	A. L.	SS	147	601	104	176	27	6	2	63	9	.293
1951	Detroit	A. L.	SS	129	487	56	129	15	1	0	33	7	.265
1952	Det.-Boston a	A. L.	SS-3B	118	370	42	78	12	3	0	30	4	.211
1953	Bost.-St. Louis b	A. L.	SS-3B-2B	67	154	18	33	7	0	0	14	1	.214
Major League Totals			8 Yrs	757	2660	351	690	95	24	10	261	28	.259

a Traded to Boston Red Sox with Hoot Evers, George Kell and Dizzy Trout for Walt Dropo, Fred Hatfield, Don Lenhardt, Johnny Pesky and Bill Wight, July 3, 1952.
b Released to St. Louis Browns on waivers, September 8, 1953.

LOCKMAN, CARROLL WALTER (WHITEY)

Born, Lowell, North Carolina, July 25, 1926.
Bats Left.   Throws Right.   Height, 6 feet, 1½ inches.   Weight, 175 pounds.

Year	Club	Lea	Pos	G	AB	R	H	2B	3B	HR	RBI	SB	Avg
1943	Springfield	E. L.	OF	40	151	17	49	4	3	0	33	2	.325
1943	Jersey City	I. L.	OF	78	271	35	72	9	4	0	18	6	.266
1944	Jersey City	I. L.	OF	141	476	81	125	18	6	4	56	15	.263
1945	Jersey City	I. L.	OF	48	126	31	40	9	5	4	28	8	.317
1945	New York	N. L.	OF	32	129	16	44	9	0	3	18	1	.341
1945-46	New York	N. L.	(In United States Military Service)										
1947	New York	N. L.	PH	2	2	0	1	0	0	0	1	0	.500
1948	New York	N. L.	OF	146	584	117	167	24	10	18	59	8	.286
1949	New York	N. L.	OF	151	617	97	186	32	7	11	65	12	.301
1950	New York	N. L.	OF	129	532	72	157	28	5	6	52	1	.295
1951	New York	N. L.	1B-OF	153	614	85	173	27	7	12	73	4	.282
1952	New York	N. L.	1B	*154	606	99	176	17	4	13	58	2	.290
1953	New York	N. L.	1B-OF	150	607	85	179	22	4	9	61	3	.295
Major League Totals			8 Yrs	917	3691	571	1083	159	37	72	387	31	.293
World's Series Record													
1951	New York	N. L.	1B	6	25	1	6	2	0	1	4	0	.240

LOGAN, JOHN, JR.

Born, Endicott, N. Y., March 23, 1927.
Bats Right.   Throws Right.   Height, 5 feet, 11 inches.   Weight, 175 pounds.

Year	Club	Lea	Pos	G	AB	R	H	2B	3B	HR	RBI	SB	Avg
1947	Evansville	I. I. L.	SS	127	486	95	161	32	13	6	82	0	.331
1948	Pawtucket	N. Eng.	SS	45	188	28	61	14	3	2	25	3	.324
1948	Dallas	T. L.	SS	32	106	6	30	4	0	1	10	0	.283
1948	Milwaukee	A. A.	SS	40	151	27	38	8	3	1	20	1	.252
1949	Milwaukee	A. A.	SS	*154	548	84	157	21	5	7	69	7	.286
1950	Milwaukee	A. A.	SS	154	558	73	165	28	2	6	57	10	.296
1951	Milwaukee	A. A.	SS	57	189	25	47	8	1	4	25	2	.249
1951	Boston	N. L.	SS	62	169	14	37	7	1	0	16	0	.219
1952	Milwaukee	A. A.	SS	42	146	20	44	8	2	6	27	0	.301
1952	Boston	N. L.	SS	117	456	56	129	21	3	4	42	1	.283
1953	Milwaukee	N. L.	SS	150	611	100	167	27	8	11	73	2	.273
Major League Totals			3 Yrs	329	1236	170	333	55	12	15	131	3	.269

LOLLAR, JOHN SHERMAN

Born, Durham, Arkansas, August 23, 1924.
Bats Right.   Throws Right.   Height, 6 feet.   Weight, 180 pounds.

Year	Club	Lea	Pos	G	AB	R	H	2B	3B	HR	RBI	SB	Avg
1943	Baltimore	I. L.	C	12	34	3	4	0	0	0	1	0	.118
1944	Baltimore	I. L.	C	126	380	58	95	14	2	15	72	2	.250
1945	Baltimore	I. L.	C	139	464	104	169	27	4	34	111	5	*.364
1946	Cleveland	A. L.	C	28	62	7	15	6	0	1	9	0	.242
1946	Baltimore a	I. L.	C	67	222	37	52	6	0	20	56	3	.234
1947	Newark	I. L	C	111	357	56	100	9	5	16	64	1	.280
1947	New York	A. L.	C	11	32	4	7	0	1	1	6	0	.219
1948	New York b	A. L.	C	22	38	0	8	0	0	0	4	0	.211
1949	St. Louis	A. L.	C	109	284	28	74	9	1	8	49	0	.261
1950	St. Louis	A. L.	C	126	396	55	111	22	3	13	65	2	.280
1951	St. Louis c	A. L.	C-3B	98	310	44	78	21	0	8	44	1	.252
1952	Chicago	A. L.	C	132	375	35	90	15	0	13	50	1	.240
1953	Chicago	A. L.	C-1B	113	334	46	96	19	0	8	54	1	.287
Major League Totals			8 Yrs	639	1831	219	479	92	5	52	281	5	.262
World's Series Record													
1947	New York	A. L.	C	2	4	3	3	2	0	0	1	0	.750

a Traded by Cleveland with Ray Mack to New York Yankees for Gene Bearden, Al Gettel and Hal Peck, Dec. 6, 1946.

b Traded with Red Embree, Dick Starr and $100,000 cash to the Browns for Fred Sanford and Roy Partee, December 13, 1948.

c Traded with Al Widmar and Tom Upton to Chicago White Sox for Joe De Maestri, Gordon Goldsberry, Jim Rivera, Dick Littlefield and Gus Niarhos, November 26, 1951.

LOPATA, STANLEY EDWARD

Born, Detroit, Michigan, September 12, 1925.
Bats Right.   Throws Right.   Height, 6 feet, 2 inches.   Weight, 210 pounds.

Year	Club	Lea	Pos	G	AB	R	H	2B	3B	HR	RBI	SB	Avg
1946	Terre Haute	I. I. L.	C	67	226	40	66	7	11	9	45	2	.292
1947	Utica	E. L.	C	115	378	68	123	20	13	9	88	2	.325
1948	Toronto	I. L.	C	110	337	59	94	20	8	15	67	4	.279
1948	Philadelphia	N. L.	C	6	15	2	2	1	0	0	2	0	.133
1949	Philadelphia	N. L.	C	83	240	31	65	9	2	8	27	1	.271
1950	Philadelphia	N. L.	C	58	129	10	27	2	2	1	11	1	.209
1951	Baltimore	I. L.	C	38	102	12	20	6	1	1	6	0	.196
1951	Philadelphia	N. L.	C	3	5	0	0	0	0	0	0	0	.000
1952	Philadelphia	N. L.	C	57	179	25	49	9	1	4	27	1	.274
1953	Philadelphia	N. L.	C	81	234	34	56	12	3	8	31	3	.239
Major League Totals			6 Yrs	288	802	102	199	33	8	21	98	6	.248
World's Series Record													
1950	Philadelphia	N. L.	C	2	1	0	0	0	0	0	0	0	.000

LOWREY, HARRY LEE (PEANUTS)

Born, Los Angeles, California, August 27, 1918.
Bats Right.   Throws Right.   Height, 5 feet, 8½ inches.   Weight, 170 pounds.

Year	Club	Lea	Pos	G	AB	R	H	2B	3B	HR	RBI	SB	Avg
1937	Moline	I. I. L.	2B-SS	45	181	34	55	6	2	3	...	2	.304
1938	Ponca City	W. A.	SS	123	479	105	128	35	5	5	63	27	.267
1939	St. Joseph	W. A.	SS	137	517	122	178	39	7	15	108	30	.344
1940	Los Angeles	P. C. L.	SS-3B	70	216	36	54	7	1	1	12	12	.250
1940	Tulsa	T. L.	3B	32	110	24	33	10	0	2	14	3	.300
1941	Los Angeles	P. C. L.	3B-OF	164	653	110	203	39	4	6	69	26	.311
1942	Chicago	N. L	OF	27	58	4	11	0	0	1	4	0	.190
1942	Milwaukee	A. A.	OF	9	32	5	9	0	0	0	0	1	.281
1942	Los Angeles	P. C. L.	OF	96	393	64	101	17	0	5	39	10	.257
1943	Chicago	N. L	2B-SS-OF	130	480	59	140	25	12	1	63	13	.292
1944	Chicago	N. L	(In United States Military Service)										
1945	Chicago	N. L	SS-OF	143	523	72	148	22	7	7	89	11	.283
1946	Chicago	N. L.	3B-OF	144	540	75	139	24	5	4	54	10	.257
1947	Chicago	N. L	2B-3B-OF	115	448	56	126	17	5	5	87	2	.281
1948	Chicago	N. L.	INF-OF	129	435	47	128	12	3	2	54	2	.294
1949	Chicago-Cincinnati a	N. L.	3B-OF	127	420	66	115	21	2	4	35	4	.274
1950	Cincinnati-St. L. b	N. L.	2B 3B-OF	108	320	44	75	14	0	2	15	0	.234
1951	St. Louis	N. L.	2B-3B-OF	114	370	52	112	19	5	5	40	0	.303
1952	St. Louis	N. L.	OF-3B	132	374	48	107	18	2	1	48	3	.286

Year	Club	Lea	Pos	G	AB	R	H	2B	3B	HR	RBI	SB	Avg
1953	St. Louis	N. L.	OF-2B-3B	104	182	26	49	9	2	5	27	1	.269

Major League Totals				11 Yrs	1273	4150	549	1150	181	43	37	466	46	.277
World's Series Record														
1945 Chicago		N. L.	OF	7	29	4	9	1	0	0	0	0	.310

a Traded with Harry Walker to Cincinnati for Hank Sauer and Frank Baumholtz, June 15.
b Sold to Cardinals on waiver claim, September 7.

LUND, DONALD ANDREW

Born, Detroit, Michigan, May 18, 1923.

Bats Right. Throws Right. Height, 6 feet. Weight, 200 pounds.

Year	Club	Lea	Pos	G	AB	R	H	2B	3B	HR	RBI	SB	Avg
1945	Brooklyn	N. L.	PH	4	3	0	0	0	0	0	0	0	.000
1945	St. Paul	A. A.	OF	72	247	25	65	12	7	0	30	6	.263
1946	St. Paul	A. A.	OF	14	15	3	3	0	0	0	0	0	.200
1946	San Diego	P. C. L.	OF	12	33	4	5	1	0	0	1	0	.152
1946	Mobile	S. A.	OF	74	258	34	62	10	4	3	29	5	.240
1947	St. Paul	A. A.	OF	90	325	68	91	18	4	16	49	8	.280
1947	Brooklyn	N. L.	OF	11	20	5	6	2	0	2	5	0	.300
1948	Brooklyn a	N. L.	OF	27	69	9	13	4	0	1	5	1	.188
1948	St. Louis b	A. L.	OF	63	161	21	40	7	4	3	25	0	.248
1949	Detroit	A. L.	PH	2	2	0	0	0	0	0	0	0	.000
1949	Toledo	A. A.	OF	117	416	74	124	24	4	17	81	4	.298
1950	Toledo	A. A.	OF	150	555	88	136	22	2	23	66	1	.245
1951	Toledo	A. A.	OF	128	428	74	111	26	0	18	65	4	.259
1952	Buffalo	I. L.	OF-3B-1B	138	441	83	133	32	3	16	80	6	.302
1952	Detroit	A. L.	OF	8	23	1	7	0	0	1	0	0	.304
1953	Detroit	A. L.	OF	131	421	51	108	21	4	9	47	3	.257

Major League Totals				6 Yrs	246	699	87	174	34	8	15	83	4	.249

a Sold to St. Louis Browns for waiver price, June 28, 1948.
b Sold to Detroit Tigers for $15,000, January 20, 1949.

MAJESKI, HENRY

Born, Staten Island, New York, December 13, 1916.

Bats Right. Throws Right. Height, 5 feet, 9 inches. Weight, 180 pounds.

Year	Club	Lea	Pos	G	AB	R	H	2B	3B	HR	RBI	SB	Avg
1935	Eau Claire . ..	No. L.	2B	91	329		101	17	5	5	52	2	.307
1936	Eau Claire	No. L.	2B	122	482	88	176	*42	11	26	125	5	.365
1937	Moline	I. I. L.	3B-2B	105	403	89	139	20	15	9		7	*.345
1938	Birmingham	S. L.	2B	151	560	81	182	38	11	4	77	2	.325
1939	Boston	N. L.	3B	106	367	35	100	16	1	7	54	2	.272
1940	Boston	N. L.	PH	3	3	0	0	0	0	0	0	0	.000
1940	Newark ... ,.....	I. L.	3B	105	375	66	121	15	4	17	76	2	.323
1941	Boston	N. L.	3B	19	55	5	8	5	0	0	3	0	.145
1941	Newark ..	I. L.	3B	113	446	74	135	16	2	14	82	2	.303
1942	Newark a	I. L.	3B	151	574	112	*198	31	6	15	*121	10	*.345
1943-44-45	New York ...	A. L.		(In U. S. Coast Guard)									
1946	New York-Phila. b ..	A. L.	3B	86	276	26	67	14	4	1	25	3	.243
1947	Philadelphia	A. L.	SS-3B-2B	141	479	54	134	26	5	8	72	1	.280
1948	Philadelphia	A. L.	SS-3B	148	590	88	183	41	4	12	120	2	.310
1949	Philadelphia c	A. L.	3B	114	448	62	124	26	5	9	67	0	.277
1950	Chicago	A. L.	3B	122	414	47	128	18	2	6	46	1	.309
1951	Chicago-Phila. d ..	A. L.	3B	101	358	45	101	23	4	5	48	1	.282
1952	Phila.-Cleveland e ..	A. L.	3B-2B	70	171	21	46	4	2	2	29	0	.269
1953	Cleveland	A. L.	2B-3B-OF	50	50	6	15	1	0	2	12	0	.300

Major League Totals				11 Yrs	960	3211	389	906	174	27	52	476	10	.282

a Sold to New York Yankees by Boston Braves, Sept. 25, 1942.
b Sold to Philadelphia Athletics, June 14, 1946.
c Traded to Chicago White Sox for Ed Klieman, December 14, 1949.
d Traded to Philadelphia Athletics for Kermit Wahl, June 4, 1951.
e Sold to Cleveland, June 10, 1952.

MANTLE, MICKEY CHARLES

Born, Spavinaw, Oklahoma, October 20, 1931.

Bats Both. Throws Right. Height, 5 feet, 10 inches. Weight, 180 pounds.

Year	Club	Lea	Pos	G	AB	R	H	2B	3B	HR	RBI	SB	Avg
1949	Independence ...	K. O. M.	SS	89	323	54	101	15	7	7	63	20	.313
1950	Joplin	W. A.	SS	137	519	*141	*199	30	12	26	136	22	*.383

Year	Club	Lea	Pos	G	AB	R	H	2B	3B	HR	RBI	SB	Avg
1951	Kansas City a	...A. A.	OF	40	166	32	60	9	3	11	50	5	.361
1951	New York	A. L.	OF	96	341	61	91	11	5	13	65	8	.267
1952	New York	A. L.	OF-3B	142	549	94	171	37	7	23	87	4	.311
1953	New York	A. L.	OF-SS	127	461	105	136	24	8	21	92	8	.295
Major League Totals			8 Yrs	365	1351	260	398	72	15	57	244	20	.295
World's Series Record													
1951	New York	. A. L.	OF	2	5	1	1	0	0	0	0	0	.200
1952	New York	A. L.	OF	7	29	5	10	1	1	2	3	0	.345
1953	New York	A. L.	OF	6	24	3	5	0	0	2	7	0	.208
World's Series Totals				15	58	9	16	1	1	4	10	0	.276

a Optioned to Kansas City, July 5, 1951, and recalled by New York Yankees, August 20, 1951.

MARQUEZ, LUIS ANGEL

Born, Aguadilla, Puerto Rico, October 28, 1925.
Bats Right. Throws Right. Height, 5 feet, 10½ inches. Weight, 185 pounds.

Year	Club	Lea	Pos	G	AB	R	H	2B	3B	HR	RBI	SB	Avg
1949	Newark	I. L.	OF	18	69	13	17	3	0	1	6	3	.246
1949	Portland	P. C. L.	OF	132	511	87	150	26	7	4	46	32	.294
1950	Portland a	P. C. L.	OF	194	775	136	241	41	•19	9	86	•38	.311
1951	Boston	N. L.	OF	68	122	19	24	5	1	0	11	4	.197
1952	Milwaukee	A. A.	OF	136	521	100	180	38	10	14	99	24	.345
1953	Toledo b	A. A.	OF	130	510	77	149	28	3	13	81	37	.292

a Drafted by Boston Braves, Nov. 16, 1950.
b Drafted by Chicago Cubs, Nov. 30, 1953.

MARSH, FRED FRANCIS

Born, Valley Falls, Kans., Jan. 5, 1924.
Bats Right. Throws Right. Height, 5 feet, 10 inches. Weight, 180 pounds.

Year	Club	Lea	Pos	G	AB	R	H	2B	3B	HR	RBI	SB	Avg
1942	Zanesville	Mid-Atl.	SB-SS	124	440	47	85	14	4	1	31	10	.193
1943-44-45	Portsmouth	Pied.	(In U. S. Military Service)										
1946	Tacoma	W. Intl.	2B	131	491	88	127	22	7	4	60	26	.259
1947	Burlington	Cen. Asn.	SS-3B	89	320	62	84	15	5	1	39	22	.263
1948	Oklahoma City	T. L.	INF	115	430	77	131	20	4	11	60	7	.305
1949	Sacramento	P. C. L.	INF	101	280	36	59	11	1	3	22	8	.211
1949	Cleveland	A. L.	PR	1	0	0	0	0	0	0	0	0	.000
1950	Oklahoma City a	T. L.	SB-SS	141	564	87	169	34	3	10	96	14	.300
1951	St. Louis	A. L.	SB-SS-2B	130	445	44	108	21	4	4	43	4	.243
1952	St.L.-Wsh.-St.L. b-c-d	A.L.	INF-OF	96	271	29	70	9	1	2	28	3	.258
1953	Chicago	A. L.	INF	67	95	22	19	1	0	2	2	0	.200
Major League Totals			4 Yrs	294	811	95	197	31	5	8	73	7	.243

a Traded by Cleveland with $35,000 to St. Louis Browns for Merrill Combs and George Stirnweiss, April 1, 1951.
b Traded to Washington with Lou Sleater for Cass Michaels, May 12, 1952.
c Traded to St. Louis for Earl Rapp, June 10, 1952.
d Traded to Chicago White Sox for Dixie Upright and estimated $25,000, January 20, 1953.

MARSHALL, WILLARD WARREN

Born, Richmond, Virginia, February 8, 1921.
Bats Left. Throws Right. Height, 6 feet, 1 inch. Weight, 195 pounds.

Year	Club	Lea	Pos	G	AB	R	H	2B	3B	HR	RBI	SB	Avg
1940	Atlanta	S. A.	OF	136	500	72	157	28	9	14	•118	5	.314
1941	Atlanta	S. A.	OF	133	507	78	140	28	4	21	106	3	.276
1942	New York	N. L.	OF	116	401	41	103	9	2	11	59	1	.257
1943-44-45	New York	N. L.	(In United States Marines)										
1946	New York	N. L.	OF	131	510	63	144	18	3	13	48	3	.282
1947	New York	N. L.	OF	155	587	102	171	19	6	36	107	3	.291
1948	New York	N. L	OF	143	537	72	146	21	3	14	86	2	.272
1949	New York a	N. L.	OF	141	499	81	153	19	3	12	70	4	.307
1950	Boston	N. L.	OF	105	298	38	70	10	2	5	40	1	.235
1951	Boston	N. L.	OF	136	469	65	132	24	7	11	62	0	.281
1952	Bos.-Cincinnati b	N. L.	OF	128	463	57	121	27	2	10	57	0	.261
1953	Cincinnati c	N. L.	OF	122	357	51	95	14	6	17	62	0	.266
Major League Totals			9 Yrs	1177	4121	570	1135	161	39	129	591	14	.275

a Traded with Sid Gordon, Buddy Kerr and Sam Webb to Boston Braves for Eddie Stanky and Alvin Dark, December 14, 1949.
b Sold by Boston to Cincinnati for undisclosed sum, June 4, 1952.
c Traded to Chicago White Sox for Rocky Krsnich, Saul Rogovin and Connie Ryan, Dec. 10, 1953.

MARTIN, ALFRED MANUEL (BILLY)
Born, Berkeley, California, May 16, 1928.
Bats Right   Throws Right.   Height, 5 feet, 11 inches.   Weight, 165 pounds.

Year	Club	Lea	Pos	G	AB	R	H	2B	3B	HR	RBI	SB	Avg
1946	Idaho Falls	Pion.	3B-2B	32	114	13	29	7	0	0	12	1	.254
1947	Phoenix	Ariz.-Tex.	3B	130	*586	141	*230	*48	12	9	*174	31	*.392
1947	Oakland	P. C. L.	3B-2B	15	53	3	12	3	0	0	5	0	.226
1948	Oakland	P. C. L.	2B-3B-SS	132	401	60	111	28	2	3	42	7	.277
1949	Oakland	P. C. L.	2B-SS	172	623	90	178	27	3	12	92	11	.286
1950	New York	A. L.	2B-3B	34	36	10	9	1	0	1	8	0	.250
1950	Kansas City	A. A.	2B	29	118	15	33	6	2	4	10	2	.280
1951	New York	A. L.	INF-OF	51	58	10	15	1	2	0	2	0	.259
1952	New York	A. L.	2B	109	363	32	97	13	3	8	33	3	.267
1953	New York	A. L.	2B-SS	149	587	72	151	24	6	15	75	6	.257
Major League Totals			4 Yrs	343	1044	124	272	39	11	19	118	9	.261
World's Series Record													
1951	New York	A. L.	PR	1	0	1	0	0	0	0	0	0	.000
1952	New York	A. L.	2B	7	23	2	5	0	0	1	4	0	.217
1953	New York	A. L.	2B	6	24	5	12	1	2	2	8	1	.500
World's Series Totals				14	47	8	17	1	2	3	12	1	.362

MATHEWS, EDWIN LEE, JR.
Born, Texarkana, Tex., Oct. 13, 1931.
Bats Left.   Throws Right.   Height, 6 feet, 1 inch.   Weight, 185 pounds.

Year	Club	Lea	Pos	G	AB	R	H	2B	3B	HR	RBI	SB	Avg
1949	Hi. Pt.-Thmsvlle.	N. C. St.	3B	63	240	62	87	20	3	17	56	5	.363
1950	Atlanta	S. A.	3B	146	552	103	158	24	9	32	106	4	.286
1951	Milwaukee	A. A.	3B	12	9	2	3	0	0	1	5	0	.333
1951	Atlanta	S. A.	3B	37	128	23	37	5	4	6	29	0	.289
1952	Boston	N. L.	3B	145	528	80	128	23	5	25	58	6	.242
1953	Milwaukee	N. L.	3B	157	579	110	175	31	8	*47	135	1	.302
Major League Totals			2 Yrs	302	1107	190	303	54	13	72	193	7	.274

MAYS, WILLIE HOWARD, JR.
Born, Westfield Alabama, May 6, 1931.
Bats Right.   Throws Right.   Height, 5 feet, 10½ inches.   Weight, 170 pounds.

Year	Club	Lea	Pos	G	AB	R	H	2B	3B	HR	RBI	SB	Avg
1950	Trenton	Inter-St.	OF	81	306	50	108	20	8	4	55	7	.353
1951	Minneapolis	A. A.	OF	35	140	38	71	18	3	8	30	5	.477
1951	New York	N. L.	OF	121	464	59	127	22	5	20	68	7	.274
1952	New York a	N. L.	OF	34	127	17	30	2	4	4	23	4	.236
1952-53	New York	N. L.	(In U. S. Army)										
Major League Totals			2 Yrs	155	591	76	157	24	9	24	91	11	.266
World's Series Record													
1951	New York	N. L.	OF	6	22	1	4	0	0	0	1	0	.182

a Entered U. S. Army, May 29, 1952.

McCULLOUGH, CLYDE EDWARD
Born, Nashville, Tenn. March 14, 1918.
Bats Right.   Throws Right.   Height, 5 feet, 11 inches.   Weight, 190 pounds.

Year	Club	Lea	Pos	G	AB	R	H	2B	3B	HR	RBI	SB	Avg
1935	Lafayette	Evang. L.	C	130	453	69	119	30	7	5	70	11	.263
1936	Akron	M. A. L.	C-1B	70	225	40	70	20	3	9	50	13	.311
1936	Newark	I. L.	PH	1	1	0	0	0	0	0	0	0	.000
1937	Binghamton	N. Y.-P. L.	C	72	210	42	69	14	4	8	36	14	.329
1938	Binghamton	E. L.	C	16	40	6	9	2	0	1	3	0	.225
1938	Newark	I. L.	C	28	93	13	20	2	3	2	13	1	.215
1938	Kansas City	A. A.	C	46	132	20	33	2	2	3	12	5	.250
1939	Kansas City	A. A.	C	108	282	55	78	18	9	11	42	9	.277
1940	Buffalo	I. L.	C	145	485	69	157	21	5	27	89	4	.324
1940	Chicago	N. L.	C	9	26	4	4	1	0	0	1	0	.154
1941	Chicago	N. L.	C	125	418	41	95	9	2	9	53	5	.227
1942	Chicago	N. L.	C	109	337	39	95	22	1	5	31	7	.282
1943	Chicago	N. L.	C	87	266	20	63	5	2	2	23	6	.237
1944, 1945			(In United States Navy)										
1946	Chicago	N. L.	C	95	307	38	88	18	5	4	34	2	.287
1947	Chicago	N. L.	C	86	234	25	59	12	4	3	30	1	.252
1948	Chicago a	N. L.	C	69	172	10	36	4	2	1	7	0	.209
1949	Pittsburgh	N. L.	C	91	241	30	57	9	3	4	21	1	.237
1950	Pittsburgh	N. L.	C	103	279	28	71	16	4	6	34	3	.254

Year	Club	Lea	Pos	G	AB	R	H	2B	3B	HR	RBI	SB	Avg
1951	Pittsburgh	N. L.	C	92	259	26	77	9	2	8	39	2	.297
1952	Pittsburgh b	N. L.	C-1B	66	172	10	40	5	1	1	15	0	.233
1953	Chicago	N. L.	C	77	229	21	59	8	2	6	23	0	.258
Major League Totals				12 Yrs	1009	2940	292	744	113	28	49	311	27	.253
World's Series Record													
1945	Chicago	N. L.	PH	1	1	0	0	0	0	0	0	0	.000

a Traded to Pittsburgh with Cliff Chambers for Frank Gustine and Cal McLish, December 8, 1948.
b Sold by Pittsburgh to Chicago Cubs for cash estimated at $40,000 and pitcher Dick Manville, Dec. 1, 1952.

McDOUGALD, GILBERT JAMES

Born, San Francisco, California, May 19, 1929.
Bats Right. Throws Right. Height, 6 feet, 1 inch. Weight, 180 pounds.

Year	Club	Lea	Pos	G	AB	R	H	2B	3B	HR	RBI	SB	Avg
1948	Twin Falls	Pio.	2B	101	415	108	141	18	5	16	66	8	.340
1949	Victoria	W. I. L.	2B	140	547	128	188	*44	7	13	116	12	.344
1950	Beaumont	T. L.	2B	*152	557	106	*187	21	13	13	115	8	.336
1951	New York	A. L.	3B-2B	131	402	72	123	23	4	14	63	14	.306
1952	New York	A. L.	3B-2B	152	555	65	146	16	5	11	78	6	.263
1953	New York	A. L.	3B-2B	141	541	82	154	27	7	10	83	8	.285
Major League Totals				3 Yrs	424	1498	219	423	66	16	35	224	23	.282
World's Series Record													
1951	New York	A. L.	2B-3B	6	23	2	6	1	0	1	7	0	.261
1952	New York	A. L.	3B	7	25	5	5	0	0	1	3	1	.200
1953	New York	A. L.	3B	6	24	2	4	0	1	2	4	0	.167
World's Series Totals				19	72	9	15	1	1	4	14	1	.208

McGHEE, WARREN EDWARD

Born, Perry, Arkansas, September 29, 1926.
Bats Right. Throws Right. Height, 5 feet, 10½ inches. Weight, 175 pounds.

Year	Club	Lea	Pos	G	AB	R	H	2B	3B	HR	RBI	SB	Avg
1948	Hot Springs ...	Cott.-St.	OF	122	461	84	126	26	11	9	81	7	.273
1949	Waterloo	I. I. I.	OF	122	428	71	127	23	6	12	*88	17	.297
1950	Memphis	S. A.	OF	144	509	97	169	31	11	17	91	8	.332
1950	Chicago	A. L.	OF	3	6	0	1	0	1	0	0	0	.167
1951	Memphis	S. A.	OF	38	142	26	45	12	3	3	20	7	.317
1951	Seattle	P. C. L.	OF	38	114	13	27	4	3	1	13	0	.237
1951	Indianapolis	A. A.	OF	32	144	29	51	5	7	2	17	1	.354
1952	Memphis a	S. A.	OF	150	539	102	156	27	9	13	86	27	.289
1953	Philadelphia	A. L.	OF	104	358	36	94	11	4	1	29	4	.263
Major League Totals				2 Yrs	107	364	36	95	11	5	1	29	4	.261

a Traded by Chicago White Sox to Philadelphia Athletics with Joe DeMaestri and Eddie Robinson for Ferris Fain and Bob Wilson, January 27, 1953.

McMILLAN, ROY DAVID

Born, Bonham, Texas, July 17, 1930.
Bats Right. Throws Right. Height, 5 feet, 11 inches. Weight, 170 pounds.

Year	Club	Lea	Pos	G	AB	R	H	2B	3B	HR	RBI	SB	Avg
1947	Ballinger	Longhorn	SS	107	459	90	126	23	2	3	49	7	.275
1947	Tyler	Lone Star	SS	17	54	6	7	0	0	0	6	1	.130
1948	Tyler	Lone Star	SS	*140	*599	127	184	35	10	3	57	24	.307
1949	Columbia	So. Atl.	SS	115	431	63	100	20	1	2	46	11	.232
1949	Tulsa	T. L.	SS	4	5	0	0	0	0	0	0	0	.000
1950	Tulsa	T. L.	SS	142	562	73	154	31	2	3	51	6	.274
1951	Cincinnati	N. L.	SS-2B-3B	85	199	21	42	4	0	1	8	0	.211
1952	Cincinnati	N. L.	SS	*154	540	60	132	32	2	7	57	4	.244
1953	Cincinnati	N. L.	SS	155	557	51	130	15	4	5	43	2	.233
Major League Totals				3 Yrs	394	1296	132	304	51	6	13	108	6	.235

MELE, SABATH ANTHONY (SAM)

Born, Astoria, Long Island, New York, January 21, 1923.
Bats Right. Throws Right. Height, 6 feet, 1 inch. Weight, 183 pounds.

Year	Club	Lea	Pos	G	AB	R	H	2B	3B	HR	RBI	SB	Avg
1946	Louisville	A. A.	OF	15	53	8	12	2	2	0	8	0	.226
1946	Scranton	E. L.	OF	119	450	88	154	18	*18	6	77	17	*.342
1947	Boston	A. L.	OF-1B	123	453	71	137	14	8	12	73	0	.302
1948	Boston	A. L.	OF	66	180	25	42	12	1	2	25	1	.233

Year	Club	Lea	Pos	G	AB	R	H	2B	3B	HR	RBI	SB	Avg
1949	Boston-Washington a	A. L.	OF-1B	96	310	22	73	13	3	3	32	4	.235
1950	Washington	A. L.	OF-1B	126	435	57	119	21	6	12	86	2	.274
1951	Washington	A. L.	OF-1B	143	558	58	153	*36	7	5	94	2	.274
1952	Wash.-Chicago b ...	A. L.	OF-1B	132	451	48	117	21	2	16	69	1	.259
1953	Chicago	A. L.	OF-1B	140	481	64	132	26	8	12	82	8	.274
Major League Totals			7 Yrs	826	2868	345	773	143	35	62	461	18	.270

a Traded with Mickey Harris and cash to Washington for Walter Masterson, June 13.
b Traded to Chicago White Sox for Jim Busby and Mel Hoderlein, May 3, 1952.

MERRIMAN, LLOYD ARCHER

Born, Clovis, California, August 2, 1925.
Bats Left. Throws Left. Height, 6 feet. Weight, 190 pounds.

Year	Club	Lea	Pos	G	AB	R	H	2B	3B	HR	RBI	SB	Avg
1948	Columbia	S. A. L.	OF	152	560	*120	167	39	*18	9	75	*44	.298
1949	Cincinnati	N. L.	OF	103	287	35	66	12	5	4	26	2	.230
1950	Cincinnati	N. L.	OF	92	298	44	77	15	3	2	31	6	.258
1951	Cincinnati	N. L.	OF	114	359	34	87	23	2	5	36	8	.242
1952-53	Cincinnati	N. L.	(In Military Service)										
Major League Totals			3 Yrs	309	944	113	230	50	10	11	93	16	.244

METKOVICH, GEORGE MICHAEL

Born, Angels Camp, California, October 8, 1921.
Bats Left. Throws Left. Height, 6 feet, 1 inch. Weight, 185 pounds.

Year	Club	Lea	Pos	G	AB	R	H	2B	3B	HR	RBI	SB	Avg
1939	Henderson	E. Tex.	OF-1B	3	6	0	0	0	0	0	0	0	.000
1939	Fulton	Kitty	1B	*126	530	99	166	40	10	12	56	7	.313
1940	Evansville a	I. I. L.	1B	60	207	22	47	5	2	2	28	1	.227
1941	Evansville	I. I. L.	OF	124	449	75	129	30	10	6	65	6	.287
1942	Hartford	E. L.	1B-OF	90	320	31	76	7	3	4	15	2	.238
1942	Evansville	I. I. L.	OF	35	120	18	37	8	3	3	22	3	.308
1943	San Francisco ..	P. C. L.	OF	71	268	43	87	12	8	3	38	4	.325
1943	Boston	A. L.	OF-1B	78	321	34	79	14	4	5	27	1	.246
1944	Boston	A. L.	OF-1B	134	549	94	152	28	8	9	59	13	.277
1915	Boston	A. L.	OF-1B	138	539	65	140	26	3	5	62	19	.260
1946	Boston b	A. L.	OF	86	281	42	69	15	2	4	25	8	.246
1947	Cleveand	A. L.	OF-1B	126	473	68	120	22	7	5	40	5	.254
1948	Oakland	P. C. L.	OF	134	500	116	168	23	7	23	88	9	.336
1949	Oakland	P. C. L.	OF	77	285	50	96	13	5	14	50	9	.337
1949	Chicago	A. L.	OF	93	338	50	80	9	4	5	45	5	.237
1950	Oakland c	P. C. L.	OF	184	739	152	233	34	8	24	141	23	.315
1951	Pittsburgh	N L.	OF-1B	120	423	51	124	21	3	3	40	3	.293
1952	Pittsburgh	N. L.	1B-OF	125	373	41	101	18	3	7	41	5	.271
1953	Pitts.-Chic. d-e ..	N. L.	OF-1B	87	165	24	35	9	1	3	19	2	.212
Major League Totals			9 Yrs	987	3462	469	900	162	35	46	358	61	.260

World's Series Record

Year	Club	Lea	Pos	G	AB	R	H	2B	3B	HR	RBI	SB	Avg
1946	Boston	A. L.	PH	2	2	1	1	1	0	0	0	0	.500

a Declared Free Agent from Detroit farm system January 14, 1940 and signed with Boston Braves, March 1940.
b Sold to Cleveland, April 2, 1947.
c Drafted by Pittsburgh, November 16, 1950.
d Traded to Chicago Cubs with Joe Garagiola, Ralph Kiner and Howie Pollet for Bob Addis, Toby Atwell, Gene Hermanski, Bob Schultz, Preston Ward, option to purchase George Freese, and cash, June 4, 1953.
e Sold to Milwaukee, December 7, 1953.

MICHAELS, CASIMER EUGENE (CASS)

Born, Detroit, Michigan, March 4, 1926.
Bats Right. Throws Right. Height, 5 feet, 10 inches. Weight, 175 pounds.

Year	Club	Lea	Pos	G	AB	R	H	2B	3B	HR	RBI	SB	Avg
1943	Chicago a	A. L.	3B	2	7	0	0	0	0	0	0	0	.000
1944	Little Rock ...	S. A.	SS	54	222	40	79	15	4	0	39	1	.356
1944	Chicago	A. L.	3B-SS	27	68	4	12	4	1	0	5	0	.176
1945	Chicago ..— ...	A. L.	2B-SS	129	445	47	109	8	5	2	54	8	.245
1946	Chicago	A. L.	2B-3B-SS	91	291	37	75	8	0	1	22	9	.258
1947	Chicago	A. L.	2B-3B-SS	110	355	31	97	15	4	3	34	10	.273
1948	Chicago	A. L.	SS-2B-OF	145	484	47	120	12	6	5	56	8	.248

Year	Club	Lea	Pos	G	AB	R	H	2B	3B	HR	RBI	SB	Avg
1949	Chicago ....—	A. L.	2B	154	561	73	173	27	9	6	83	5	.308
1950	Chicago-Washington b	A. L.	2B	142	526	69	140	14	7	8	66	2	.266
1951	Washington	A. L.	2B	138	485	59	125	20	4	4	45	1	.258
1952	Wash.-St. L.-Phila. c-d	A. L.	2B-3B	132	452	53	114	16	8	5	50	4	.252
1953	Philadelphia e	A. L.	2B	117	411	58	103	10	0	12	42	7	.251
Major League Totals			11 Yrs	1187	4085	473	1068	184	44	46	457	54	.261

a Played under the name of Kwietniewski.
b Traded with John Ostrowski and Bob Kuzava to Washington, May 30, for Ray Scarborough, Al Kozar and Ed Robinson.
c Traded by Washington to St. Louis for infielder Fred Marsh and pitcher Lou Sleater, May 12, 1952.
d Sold by St. Louis Browns to Philadelphia Athletics for $10,000 waiver price, Aug. 5, 1952.
e Sold to Chicago White Sox, December 8, 1953.

MIKSIS, EDWARD THOMAS

Born Burlington, New Jersey, September 11, 1926.
Bats Right. Throws Right. Height, 6 feet, 1 inch. Weight, 180 pounds.

Year	Club	Lea	Pos	G	AB	R	H	2B	3B	HR	RBI	SB	Avg
1944	Trenton	Inter St.	LB	72	255	36	68	15	5	4	47	6	.267
1944	Brooklyn	N. L.	3B-SS	26	91	12	20	2	0	0	11	4	.220
1945-46	Brooklyn	N. L.	(In U. S. Navy)										
1946	Brooklyn	N. L.	2B-3B	23	48	8	7	0	0	0	5	0	.146
1947	Brooklyn	N. L.	INF-OF	45	86	18	23	1	0	4	10	0	.267
1948	Brooklyn	N. L.	2B-3B-SS	86	221	28	47	7	1	2	16	5	.213
1949	Brooklyn	N. L.	3B-SS-2B	50	113	17	25	5	0	1	6	8	.221
1950	Brooklyn	N. L.	2B-SS-3B	51	76	13	19	2	1	2	10	8	.250
1951	Bklyn.-Chicago a	N. L.	2B-3B	121	431	54	114	14	3	4	85	11	.265
1952	Chicago	N. L.	2B-SS	93	383	44	89	20	1	2	19	4	.232
1953	Chicago	N. L.	2B-SS	142	577	61	145	17	6	3	89	13	.251
Major League Totals			9 Yrs	637	2026	250	489	68	12	23	151	48	.241
World's Series Record													
1947	Brooklyn	N. L.	2B-OF	5	4	1	1	0	0	0	0	0	.250
1949	Brooklyn	N. L.	3B	6	7	0	2	1	0	0	0	0	.286
World's Series Totals			8	11	1	3	1	0	0	0	0	.273

a Traded to Chicago Cubs with Gene Hermanski, Joe Hatten and Bruce Edwards for Andy Pafko, John Schmitz, Al Walker and Wayne Terwilliger, June 15, 1951.

MINOSO, ORESTES (MINNY)

Born, Matanza, Cuba, November 29, 1922.
Bats Right. Throws Right. Height, 5 feet, 11 inches. Weight 180 pounds.

Year	Club	Lea	Pos	G	AB	R	H	2B	3B	HR	RBI	SB	Avg
1948	Dayton	C. L.	3B-2B	11	40	14	21	7	1	1	8	6	.525
1949	Cleveland	A. L.	OF	9	16	2	3	0	0	1	1	0	.188
1949	San Diego	P. C. L.	OF	137	532	99	158	19	7	22	75	13	.297
1950	San Diego	P. C. L.	3B-SS-OF	169	599	130	203	40	10	20	115	30	.339
1951	Cleve.-Chicago a	A. L.	1B-3B-SS-OF	146	530	112	173	34	•14	10	76	•31	.326
1952	Chicago	A. L.	OF-3B-SS	147	569	96	160	24	9	13	61	•22	.281
1953	Chicago	A. L.	OF-3B	151	556	104	174	24	8	15	104	•25	.313
Major League Totals			4 Yrs	453	1671	314	510	82	31	39	242	78	.305

a Traded to Chicago in three club deal, April 29, 1951. See footnote to Ray Murray.

MIRANDA, GUILLERMO (WILLIE)

Born, Velasco Oriente, Cuba, May 24, 1927.
Bats Both. Throws Right. Height, 5 feet, 9½ inches. Weight, 150 pounds.

Year	Club	Lea	Pos	G	AB	R	H	2B	3B	HR	RBI	SB	Avg
1948	Sherm-Den.	Big St.	SS	144	512	91	134	18	6	0	55	10	.262
1949	Chattanooga	S. A.	SS-3B	151	527	55	125	13	4	0	85	4	.237
1950	Chattanooga	S. A.	SS	141	487	55	121	17	5	1	50	9	.248
1951	Chattanooga	S. A.	SS	80	338	38	83	8	3	0	20	1	.246
1951	Washington a	A. L.	SS-1B	7	9	2	4	0	0	0	0	0.	.444
1952	Chi.-St. L.-Chi. b-c-d	A. L.	SS-3B-2B	77	161	16	34	4	2	0	8	1	.211
1953	St. L.-N.Y. e	A. L.	SS-3B	65	64	14	14	0	0	1	5	2	.219
Major League Totals			3 Yrs	149	234	32	52	4	2	1	13	3	.222

a Traded by Washington to Chicago for Floyd Baker, October 24, 1951.
b Traded to St. Louis Browns with Al Zarilla for Leo Thomas and Tom Wright, June 15, 1952.
c Released to Chicago White Sox on waivers, June 23, 1952.
d Traded to St. Louis Browns with Hank Edwards for Tommy Byrne and Joe De Maestri, Oct. 16, 1952.
e Sold to New York Yankees, June 12, 1953.

184

MITCHELL, LOREN DALE
Born, Colony, Oklahoma, August 23, 1921.
Bats Left. Throws Left. Height, 6 feet, 1 inch. Weight, 200 pounds.

Year	Club	Lea	Pos	G	AB	R	H	2B	3B	HR	RBI	SB	Avg
1946	Oklahoma City	T. L.	OF	108	415	63	140	25	8	2	63	10	*.337
1946	Cleveland	A. L.	OF	11	44	7	19	3	0	0	5	1	.432
1947	Cleveland	A. L.	OF	123	493	69	156	16	10	1	84	2	.316
1948	Cleveland	A. L.	OF	141	608	82	204	30	8	4	56	13	.336
1949	Cleveland	A. L.	OF	149	*640	81	*203	16	*28	3	56	10	.317
1950	Cleveland	A. L.	OF	130	506	81	156	27	5	8	49	8	.308
1951	Cleveland	A. L.	OF	134	510	83	148	21	7	11	62	7	.290
1952	Cleveland	A. L.	OF	134	511	61	165	26	3	5	58	6	.323
1953	Cleveland	A. L.	OF	134	500	76	150	26	4	13	60	8	.300
Major League Totals		8 Yrs		956	3812	540	1201	165	60	40	880	45	.315
World's Series Record													
1948	Cleveland	A L	OF	6	23	4	4	1	0	1	1	0	.174

MORGAN, ROBERT MORRIS
Born, Oklahoma City, Okla., June 29, 1926.
Bats Right. Throws Right. Height, 5 feet, 9½ inches. Weight, 175 pounds.

Year	Club	Lea	Pos	G	AB	R	H	2B	3B	HR	RBI	SB	Avg
1944	Newport News	Piedmont	3B	16	55	13	21	1	1	3	15	0	.382
1944	Olean	Pony	3B-SS	105	386	63	98	20	4	6	68	8	.254
1945-46	Olean	Pony	(In U. S. Military Service)										
1947	Spokane	W. Intl.	3B	149	529	116	155	32	*18	6	102	16	.293
1948	Montreal	I. L.	SS	151	516	92	137	28	9	10	75	5	.266
1949	Montreal a	I. L.	SS-3B	*154	567	109	191	*38	1	19	112	10	*.337
1950	Brooklyn	N. L.	3B-SS	67	199	38	45	10	8	7	21	0	.226
1951	Montreal	I. L.	SS	*155	575	84	156	33	3	9	75	6	.271
1952	Brooklyn	N. L.	3B-2B-SS	67	191	36	45	8	0	7	16	2	.236
1953	Brooklyn	N. L.	3B-SS	69	196	35	51	6	2	7	33	2	.260
Major League Totals		8 Yrs		203	586	109	141	24	5	21	70	4	.241
World's Series Record													
1952	Brooklyn	N. L.	3B-PH	2	1	0	0	0	0	0	0	0	.000
1953	Brooklyn	N. L.	PH	1	1	0	0	0	0	0	0	0	.000
World's Series Totals				3	2	0	0	0	0	0	0	0	.000

a Most Valuable Player, International League, 1949.

MOSS, JOHN LESTER (LES)
Born, Tulsa, Oklahoma, May 14, 1925.
Bats Right. Throws Right. Height, 5 feet, 11 inches. Weight, 200 pounds.

Year	Club	Lea	Pos	G	AB	R	H	2B	3B	HR	RBI	SB	Avg
1942	Americus	Ga.-Fla.	C	109	391	46	117	23	2	3	58	1	.299
1943	Elmira	E. L.	C	96	279	50	86	18	3	3	45	4	.308
1944-45	Toledo	A. A.	(In United States Military Service)										
1946	Toledo	A. A.	C	121	390	44	116	21	1	13	54	2	.297
1946	St. Louis	A. L.	C	12	35	4	13	3	0	0	5	1	.371
1947	St. Louis	A. L.	C	96	274	17	43	5	2	6	27	0	.157
1948	St. Louis	A L	C	107	335	35	86	12	1	14	46	0	.257
1949	St. Louis	A. L.	C	97	278	28	81	11	0	10	39	0	.291
1950	St. Louis	A. L.	C	84	222	24	59	6	0	8	34	0	.266
1951	St. L.-Boston a	A. L.	C	87	249	29	48	8	0	4	88	0	.193
1952	St. Louis	A. L.	C	52	118	11	29	8	0	8	12	0	.246
1953	St. Louis	A. L.	C	78	239	21	66	14	1	2	28	0	.276
Major League Totals		8 Yrs		613	1750	163	425	62	4	47	224	1	.248

a Traded to Boston Red Sox for Matt Batts, Jim McDonald, Jim Suchecki, and cash, May 17, 1951.
Traded back to St. Louis with Tom Wright for Gus Niarhos and Ken Wood, November 27, 1951.

MUELLER, DONALD FRED
Born, St. Louis, Missouri, April 14, 1927.
Bats Left. Throws Right. Height, 6 feet. Weight, 175 pounds.

Year	Club	Lea	Pos	G	AB	R	H	2B	3B	HR	RBI	SB	Avg
1944	Jersey City	I. L.	OF	2	6	1	1	0	0	0	8	0	.167
1945	Jersey City	I. L.	OF	8	8	2	2	0	0	0	1	0	.250
1946	Jersey City	I. L.	OF	28	78	12	28	7	0	1	9	0	.359
1947	Jacksonville	S. A. L.	OF	122	469	81	163	34	9	4	82	10	.348
1947	Jersey City	I. L.	PH	8	7	2	2	1	0	0	0	0	.286

185

Year	Club	Lea	Pos	G	AB	R	H	2B	3B	HR	RBI	SB	Avg
1948	Jersey City	I.L.	OF	99	400	67	131	17	4	10	52	3	.328
1948	New York	N.L.	OF	36	81	12	29	4	1	1	9	0	.358
1949	New York	N.L.	OF	51	56	5	13	4	0	0	1	0	.232
1949	Minneapolis	A.A.	OF	28	119	21	37	7	2	2	12	1	.311
1950	New York	N.L.	OF	132	525	60	153	15	6	7	84	1	.291
1951	New York	N.L.	OF	122	469	58	130	10	7	16	69	1	.277
1952	New York	N.L.	OF	126	456	61	128	14	7	12	49	2	.281
1953	New York	N.L.	OF	131	480	56	160	12	2	6	60	2	.333
Major League Totals			6 Yrs	598	2067	252	613	59	23	42	272	6	.297

MULLIN, PATRICK JOSEPH

Born, Trotter, Pennsylvania, November 1, 1917.
Bats Left.   Throws Right.   Height, 6 feet, 2 inches.   Weight, 190 pounds.

Year	Club	Lea	Pos	G	AB	R	H	2B	3B	HR	RBI	SB	Avg
1937	Beaumont	T.L.	OF	9	22	4	7	1	2	0	1	..	.318
1937	Lake Charles ...	Evang.L.	OF	105	407	109	156	29	17	16	89	28	.383
1938	Beaumont	T.L.	OF	154	612	94	168	30	11	5	67	40	.275
1939	Beaumont	T.L.	OF	140	547	68	152	33	7	8	61	18	.278
1940	Buffalo	I.L.	OF	157	594	85	162	25	11	15	61	18	.273
1940	Detroit	A.L.	OF	4	4	0	0	0	0	0	0	0	.000
1941	Buffalo	I.L.	OF	16	56	7	20	5	1	2	6	1	.357
1941	Detroit	A.L.	OF	54	220	42	76	11	5	5	23	5	.345
1942-43-44-45 Detroit		A.L.		(In United States Army)									
1946	Detroit	A.L.	OF	93	276	34	68	13	4	3	35	3	.246
1947	Detroit	A.L.	OF	116	398	62	102	28	6	15	62	3	.256
1948	Detroit	A.L.	OF	138	496	91	143	16	11	23	80	1	.288
1949	Detroit	A.L.	OF	104	310	55	83	8	6	12	59	1	.268
1950	Detroit	A.L.	OF	69	142	16	31	5	0	6	23	1	.218
1951	Detroit	A.L.	OF	110	295	41	83	11	8	12	51	2	.281
1952	Detroit	A.L.	OF	97	255	29	64	13	5	7	35	4	.251
1953	Detroit	A.L.	OF	79	97	11	26	1	0	4	17	0	.268
Major League Totals			10 Yrs	864	2493	381	676	106	43	87	335	20	.271

MURRAY, RAYMOND LEE

Born, Spring Hope, North Carolina, October 12, 1919.
Bats Right.   Throws Right.   Height, 6 feet, 3 inches.   Weight, 200 pounds.

Year	Club	Lea	Pos	G	AB	R	H	2B	3B	HR	RBI	SB	Avg
1940	Poco. City	E.S.L.	OF-1B-C	90	308	88	81	11	1	2	39	8	.263
1941	Tarboro	Coast. Pl.	C-OF	75	283	37	91	14	1	0	34	6	.322
1942-43-44-45 Baltimore		I.L.		(In United States Military Service)									
1946	Baltimore	I.L.	C	33	88	7	20	0	0	2	10	0	.227
1946	Okla. City	T.L.	C	42	130	11	33	2	3	2	15	1	.254
1947	Okla. City	T.L.	C	122	388	41	102	20	4	9	57	2	.263
1948	Cleveland	A.L.	PH	4	4	0	0	0	0	0	0	3	.000
1948	Okla. City	T.L.	C	64	202	19	60	8	2	5	34	0	.297
1949	Okla. City	T.L.	C	123	430	65	137	44	4	16	94	1	.319
1950	Cleveland	A.L.	C	55	139	16	38	8	2	1	13	1	.273
1951	Cleveland-Phila. a	A.L.	C	41	123	10	27	6	0	0	14	0	.220
1952	Philadelphia	A.L.	C	44	136	14	28	5	0	1	10	0	.206
1953	Philadelphia	A.L.	C	84	268	25	76	14	3	6	41	0	.284
Major League Totals			5 Yrs	228	670	65	169	33	5	8	78	4	.252

a Traded to Philadelphia Athletics as part of a three-club deal, April 29, 1951. The Athletics also received Sam Zoldak from Cleveland, Dave Philley and Gus Zernial from Chicago White Sox. Chicago received Orestes Minoso from Cleveland, Paul Lehner from the Athletics. Cleveland received Lou Brissie from the Athletics.

MUSIAL, STANLEY FRANK (THE MAN)

Born, Donora, Pennsylvania, November 21, 1920.
Bats Left.   Throws Left.   Height, 6 feet.   Weight, 175 pounds.

Year	Club	Lea	Pos	G	AB	R	H	2B	3B	HR	RBI	SB	Avg
1938	Williamson	Mt. St.	P	26	62	5	16	3	0	1	6	0	.258
1939	Williamson	Mt. St.	P	23	71	10	25	3	3	1	9	0	.352
1940	Daytona Beach ...	Fla. St.	P-OF	113	405	55	126	17	10	1	70	6	.311
1941	Springfield	W.A.	OF	87	348	100	132	27	10	*26	94	16	.379
1941	Rochester	I.L.	OF	54	221	43	72	10	4	3	21	2	.326
1941	St. Louis	N.L.	OF	12	47	8	20	4	0	1	7	1	.426
1942	St. Louis	N.L.	OF	140	467	87	147	32	10	10	72	6	.315
1943	St. Louis a	N.L.	OF	*157	617	108	*220	*48	*20	13	81	9	*.357

Year	Club	Lea	Pos	G	AB	R	H	2B	3B	HR	RBI	SB	Avg
1944	St. Louis	N. L.	OF	146	568	112	*197	*51	14	12	94	7	.347
1945	St. Louis			(In United States Navy)									
1946	St. Louis b	N. L.	1B-OF	*156	*624	*124	*228	*50	*20	16	108	7	*.365
1947	St. Louis	N. L.	1B	149	587	113	183	30	13	19	95	4	.312
1948	St. Louis c	N. L.	OF-1B	155	611	*135	*230	*46	*18	39	*131	7	*.376
1949	St. Louis	N. L.	OF-1B	*157	612	128	*207	*41	*18	36	123	8	.338
1950	St. Louis	N. L.	OF-1B	146	555	105	192	41	7	28	109	5	*.346
1951	St. Louis	N. L.	OF-1B	152	578	*124	205	30	*12	32	108	4	*.355
1952	St. Louis	N. L.	OF-1B-P	*154	578	*105	*194	*42	6	21	91	7	*.336
1953	St. Louis	N. L.	OF	157	593	127	200	*53	9	30	113	8	.337
Major League Totals				12 Yrs	1681	6437	1276	2228	468	142	257	1127	68	.345
World's Series Record													
1942	St. Louis	N. L.	OF	5	18	2	4	1	0	0	2	0	.222
1943	St. Louis	N. L.	OF	5	18	2	5	0	0	0	0	0	.278
1944	St. Louis	N. L.	OF	6	23	2	7	2	0	1	2	0	.304
1946	St. Louis	N. L.	1B	7	27	3	6	4	1	0	4	1	.222
World's Series Totals				23	86	9	22	7	1	1	8	1	.256

a Voted Most Valuable Player in National League for 1943.
b Voted Most Valuable Player in National League for 1946.
c Voted Most Valuable Player in National League for 1948.

NELSON, GLENN RICHARD

Born, Portsmouth, Ohio, November 18, 1924.
Bats Left. Throws Left. Height, 5 feet, 10½ inches. Weight, 175 pounds.

Year	Club	Lea	Pos	G	AB	R	H	2B	3B	HR	RBI	SB	Avg
1942	Johnson City	Appal.	1B-P	53	186	15	47	10	8	0	23	0	.253
1943-44-45	Columbus	A. A.		(In Military Service)									
1946	St. Joseph	W. A.	1B	135	518	92	165	31	*23	5	93	26	.319
1947	Rochester	I. L.	1B	11	18	2	1	0	0	0	2	0	.056
1947	Lynchburg	Pied.	1B	117	461	98	171	38	11	11	105	20	*.371
1948	Rochester	I. L.	1B	142	485	68	147	29	12	7	68	11	.303
1949	St. Louis	N. L.	1B	82	244	28	54	8	4	4	32	1	.221
1950	Columbus	A. A.	OF-1B	48	184	25	77	16	2	7	40	2	.418
1950	St. Louis	N. L.	1B	76	235	27	58	10	4	1	20	4	.247
1951	St. L.-Pitts.	N. L.	1B-OF	80	213	32	56	8	4	1	15	1	.263
1951	Chicago	A. L.	PH	6	5	0	0	0	0	0	0	0	.000
1952	Montreal	I. L.	1B	2	3	0	1	1	0	0	1	0	.333
1952	Brooklyn	N. L.	1B	37	39	6	10	1	0	0	3	0	.256
1953	Montreal a	I. L.	1B	154	542	117	167	33	9	34	*136	2	.308
Major League Totals				4 Yrs	281	736	93	178	27	12	6	70	6	.242
World's Series Record													
1952	Brooklyn	N. L.	PH	4	8	0	0	0	0	0	0	0	.000

a Sold to Cleveland, October 8, 1953.

NIARHOS, CONSTANTINE GREGORY (GUS)

Born, Birmingham, Alabama, December 6, 1921.
Bats Right. Throws Right. Height, 6 feet. Weight, 165 pounds.

Year	Club	Lea	Pos	G	AB	R	H	2B	3B	HR	RBI	SB	Avg
1941	Akron	M. A. L.	C-INF-OF	112	332	61	117	24	10	8	57	12	.308
1942	Binghamton	E. L.	C	127	407	78	113	14	4	0	32	12	.278
1943-44-45	Kansas City	A. A.		(In United States Military Service)									
1946	Kansas City	A. A.	C	17	51	3	12	2	0	0	3	2	.235
1946	New York	A. L.	C	37	40	11	9	1	1	0	2	1	.225
1947	Kansas City	A. A.	C	93	237	44	76	11	0	1	26	2	.321
1948	New York	A. L.	C	83	228	41	61	12	2	0	19	1	.268
1949	New York	A. L.	C	32	43	7	12	2	1	0	6	0	.279
1950	New York-Chicago a	A. L.	C	42	105	17	34	4	0	0	16	0	.324
1951	Chicago b	A. L.	C	66	168	27	43	6	0	1	10	4	.256
1952	Boston	A. L.	C	29	58	4	6	0	0	0	4	0	.103
1953	Boston	A. L.	C	16	35	6	7	1	1	0	2	0	.200
Major League Totals				7 Yrs	805	677	113	172	26	5	1	59	6	.254
World's Series Record													
1949	New York	A. L.	C	1	0	0	0	0	0	0	0	0	.000

a Sold to Chicago White Sox, June 27.

b Traded with Jim Rivera, Joe DeMaestri, Dick Littlefield and Gordon Goldsberry to St. Louis for Sherman Lollar, Al Widmar and Tom Upton, November 26, 1951. Next day traded to Boston Red Sox with Ken Wood for Les Moss and Tom Wright.

NIEMAN, ROBERT CHARLES

Born, Cincinnati, Ohio, Jan. 26, 1927.
Bats Right. Throws Right. Height, 5 feet, 11 inches. Weight, 195 pounds.

Year	Club	Lea	Pos	G	AB	R	H	2B	3B	HR	RBI	SB	Avg
1948	Muncie	Ohio-Ind.	C-OF	138	507	117	*186	*45	9	*23	*131	23	*.367
1949	Tulsa	T. L.	C	3	8	3	0	0	0	0	0	0	.000
1949	Charleston	Central	OF	92	310	53	95	16	10	9	56	1	.306
1949	Sunbury	Int. Sta.	OF-C	28	96	22	28	4	2	5	20	1	.292
1950	Columbia	So. Atl.	OF-C	87	291	42	85	10	9	6	49	2	.292
1950	Tulsa	Texas	OF	82	108	23	33	10	1	2	21	1	.306
1951	Tul.-Okla. City	Texas	OF-1B-C	144	497	79	161	88	7	14	86	7	*.324
1951	St. Louis	A. L.	OF	12	43	6	16	3	1	2	8	0	.372
1952	St. Louis a	A. L.	OF	131	478	66	138	22	2	18	74	0	.289
1953	Detroit	A. L.	OF	142	508	72	143	32	5	15	69	0	.281
Major League Totals		3 Yrs		285	1029	144	297	57	8	35	151	0	.289

a Traded with infielder Owen Friend and catcher J. W. Porter, by St. Louis to Detroit, for outfielder Johnny Groth and pitchers Virgil Trucks and Hal White, Dec. 4, 1952.

NOBLE, RAFAEL MIGUEL

Born, Central Hatillo, Cuba, March 15, 1922.
Bats Right. Throws Right. Height, 5 feet, 11½ inches. Weight, 190 pounds.

Year	Club	Lea	Pos	G	AB	R	H	2B	3B	HR	RBI	SB	Avg
1949	Jersey City	I. L.	C	67	189	33	49	6	1	7	29	1	.259
1950	Oakland	P. C. L.	C	110	345	58	109	23	8	15	76	4	.316
1951	New York	N. L.	C	55	141	16	33	6	0	5	26	1	.234
1952	Oakland	P. C. L.	C	104	366	54	109	13	8	12	60	2	.298
1953	Minneapolis	A. A.	C	29	111	21	34	5	0	4	21	2	.306
1953	New York	N. L.	C	46	97	15	20	0	1	4	14	1	.206
Major League Totals		2 Yrs		101	238	31	53	6	1	9	40	2	.223
World's Series Record													
1951	New York	N. L.	C	3	2	0	0	0	0	0	0	0	.000

NOREN, IRVING ARNOLD

Born, Jamestown, New York, November 29, 1924.
Bats Left. Throws Left. Height, 6 feet. Weight, 190 pounds.

Year	Club	Lea	Pos	G	AB	R	H	2B	3B	HR	RBI	SB	Avg
1946	Santa Barbara	Cal. L.	OF	*130	*518	138	*188	*33	*14	11	*129	28	.363
1947	Fort Worth	T. L.	OF-1B	149	598	73	162	33	10	2	72	6	.271
1948	Fort Worth	T. L.	OF-1B	135	498	85	161	34	4	10	71	8	.323
1949	Hollywood a	P. C. L.	OF	180	678	134	224	40	6	29	130	10	.330
1950	Washington	A. L.	OF-1B	138	542	80	160	27	10	14	98	5	.295
1951	Washington	A. L.	OF	129	509	82	142	33	5	8	86	10	.279
1952	Wash.-New York b	A. L.	OF-1B	105	321	40	76	16	3	5	23	5	.237
1953	New York	A. L.	OF	109	345	55	92	12	6	6	46	8	.267
Major League Totals		4 Yrs		481	1717	257	470	88	24	33	253	23	.274
World's Series Record													
1952	New York	A. L.	OF	4	10	0	3	0	0	0	1	0	.300
1953	New York	A. L.	PH	2	1	0	0	0	0	0	0	0	.000
World's Series Totals				6	11	0	3	0	0	0	1	0	.273

a Sold to Washington for estimated $80,000 by Brooklyn.
b Traded with infielder Tom Upton, by Washington to New York Yankees, for outfielder Jackie Jensen and Archie Wilson, pitcher Frank Shea and infielder Jerry Snyder, May 3, 1952.

O'CONNELL, DANIEL FRANCIS

Born, Paterson, New Jersey, January 21, 1929.
Bats Right. Throws Right. Height, 6 feet. Weight, 180 pounds.

Year	Club	Lea	Pos	G	AB	R	H	2B	3B	HR	RBI	SB	Avg
1946	Bloomingdale	No. Atl.	3B-P	121	446	91	146	27	12	4	78	11	.327
1947	Three Rivers	Can.-Am.	3B	133	485	67	151	30	7	0	49	9	.311
1948	Greenville	S. A. L.	3B-OF	146	579	91	169	34	9	10	62	10	.292
1949	St. Paul	A. A.	3B	138	493	89	155	29	1	17	102	7	.314
1950	Indianapolis	A. A.	SS	84	322	65	113	20	4	8	50	5	.351
1950	Pittsburgh	N. L.	SS-3B	79	315	39	92	16	1	8	82	7	.292
1951-52	Pittsburgh	N. L.	(In Military Service)										
1953	Pittsburgh a	N. L.	3B-2B	149	588	88	173	26	8	7	55	8	.294
Major League Totals		2 Yrs		228	903	127	265	42	9	15	87	10	.293

a Traded to Milwaukee for Sid Gordon, Max Surkont, Sam Jethroe, Larry Lassalle, Fred Waters, Curt Raydon and cash, Dec. 26, 1953.

PAFKO, ANDREW
Born, Boyceville, Wisconsin, February 25, 1921.
Bats Right. Throws Right. Height, 6 feet. Weight, 190 pounds.

Year	Club	Lea	Pos	G	AB	R	H	2B	3B	HR	RBI	SB	Avg
1940	Eau Claire	No. L.	OF	20	67	5	14	3	1	0	8	1	.209
1941	Green Bay	Wisc. St.	OF	87	318	74	111	19	8	12	66	8	.349
1942	Macon	S. A. L.	OF	126	484	88	145	20	*18	7	85	7	.300
1943	Los Angeles	P. C. L.	OF	157	604	109	*215	31	18	18	*118	18	*.356
1943	Chicago	N. L.	OF	13	58	7	22	8	0	0	10	1	.379
1944	Chicago	N. L.	OF	128	409	47	126	16	2	6	62	2	.269
1945	Chicago	N. L.	OF	144	534	64	159	24	12	12	110	5	.298
1946	Chicago	N. L.	OF	65	234	18	66	6	4	8	30	4	.282
1947	Chicago	N. L.	OF	129	513	68	155	25	7	13	66	4	.302
1948	Chicago	N. L.	2B	142	548	82	171	30	2	26	101	3	.312
1949	Chicago	N. L.	3B-OF	144	519	79	146	29	2	18	89	4	.281
1950	Chicago	N. L.	OF	146	514	95	156	24	8	36	92	4	.304
1951	Chi.-Bklyn. a	N. L.	OF	133	455	68	116	16	8	30	93	2	.255
1952	Brooklyn b	N. L.	OF-3B	150	551	76	158	17	5	19	85	4	.287
1953	Milwaukee	N. L.	OF	140	516	70	153	23	4	17	72	2	.297
Major League Totals			11 Yrs	1334	4911	674	1428	213	49	180	790	65	.291

World's Series Record

Year	Club	Lea	Pos	G	AB	R	H	2B	3B	HR	RBI	SB	Avg
1945	Chicago	N. L.	OF	7	28	5	6	2	1	0	2	1	.214
1952	Brooklyn	N. L.	OF	7	21	0	4	0	0	0	2	0	.190
World's Series Totals				14	49	5	10	2	1	0	4	1	.204

a Traded to Brooklyn with John Schmitz, Al Walker and Wayne Terwilliger for Gene Hermanski, Joe Hatten, Ed Miksis and Bruce Edwards, June 15, 1951.

b Sold by Brooklyn to Boston Braves for estimated $60,000 and infielder Roy Hartsfield, Jan. 17, 1953.

PELLAGRINI, EDWARD CHARLES
Born, Boston, Massachusetts, March 13, 1919.
Bats Right. Throws Right. Height, 5 feet, 9 inches. Weight, 160 pounds.

Year	Club	Lea	Pos	G	AB	R	H	2B	3B	HR	RBI	SB	Avg
1938	Danville	Bi-State	SS	*118	500	101	148	24	5	21	72	3	.296
1939	Rocky Mount	Pied.	SS	14	35	7	8	1	1	2	8	0	.229
1939	Canton	M. A. L.	SS	99	367	65	111	21	2	6	60	10	.302
1940	Scranton	E. L.	SS	125	421	55	109	14	6	6	48	13	.259
1941	San Diego	P. C. L.	SS	173	659	107	180	39	10	8	70	18	.273
1942	Louisville	A. A.	SS	19	68	8	14	4	0	0	1	0	.206
1942-43-44-45 Boston	A. L.	(In U. S. Navy)											
1946	Boston	A. L.	3B-SS	22	71	7	15	3	1	2	4	1	.211
1947	Boston a	A. L.	3B-SS	74	231	29	47	8	1	4	19	2	.203
1948	St. Louis	A. L.	SS	105	290	31	69	8	8	2	27	1	.238
1949	St. Louis	A. L.	SS	79	235	26	56	8	1	2	15	2	.238
1950	Baltimore	I. L.	SS	130	387	69	109	21	1	19	64	6	.282
1951	Philadelphia b	N. L.	2B-SS-3B	86	197	31	46	4	5	5	30	5	.234
1952	Cincinnati	N. L.	INF	46	100	15	17	2	0	1	8	1	.170
1953	Pittsburgh c	N. L.	2B-3B-SS	78	174	16	44	8	2	4	19	1	.253
Major League Totals			7 Yrs	490	1298	155	294	36	13	20	117	13	.227

a Traded to St. Louis Browns with Joe Ostrowski, Don Palmer, Roy Partee, Al Widmar, Jim Wilson and Pete Layden and estimated $300,000 for Vern Stephens and Jack Kramer, November 17, 1947.

b Traded to Cincinnati with Niles Jordan, Andy Seminick and Dick Sisler for Forrest Burgess, Howie Fox and Connie Ryan, December 10, 1951.

c Sold to Pittsburgh, April 17, 1953.

PENDLETON, JAMES EDWARD
Born, St. Charles, Missouri, January 7, 1926.
Bats Right. Throws Right. Height, 6 feet. Weight, 180 pounds.

Year	Club	Lea	Pos	G	AB	R	H	2B	3B	HR	RBI	SB	Avg
1949	St. Paul	A. A.	OF	105	347	88	95	9	5	6	39	27	.274
1950	St. Paul	A. A.	SS	145	571	105	171	25	*19	10	98	25	.299
1951	St. Paul	A. A.	SS	148	564	*116	170	18	18	21	79	14	.301
1952	Montreal a	I. L.	SS	151	595	87	173	24	14	11	92	14	.291
1953	Milwaukee	N. L.	OF-SS	120	251	48	75	12	4	7	27	6	.299

a Traded to Boston Braves by Brooklyn, with Rocky Bridges for Russ Meyer, as part of four club deal, February 16, 1953.

PESKY, JOHN MICHAEL
Born, Portland, Oregon, September 27, 1919.
Bats Left. Throws Right. Height, 5 feet, 9 inches. Weight, 165 pounds.

Year	Club	Lea	Pos	G	AB	R	H	2B	3B	HR	RBI	SB	Avg
1940	Rocky Mount	Pied.	SS	136	*576	114	*187	28	*16	4	55	7	.325

Year	Club	Lea	Pos	G	AB	R	H	2B	3B	HR	RBI	SB	Avg
1941	Louisville	A. A.	SS	146	600	93	*195	25	5	1	48	16	.325
1942	Boston	A. L.	SS	147	620	105	*205	29	9	2	51	12	.331
1943-44-45	Boston	A. L		(In United States Navy)									
1946	Boston	A. L.	SS	153	*621	115	*208	43	4	2	55	9	.335
1947	Boston	A. L.	3B-SS	155	*638	106	*207	27	8	0	39	12	.324
1948	Boston ....•.	A. L.	2B	143	565	124	159	26	6	8	55	3	.281
1949	Boston	A. L.	3B	148	604	111	185	27	7	2	69	8	.306
1950	Boston	A. L.	3B-SS	127	490	112	153	22	6	1	49	2	.312
1951	Boston	A. L.	3B-2B-SS	131	480	93	150	20	6	8	41	2	.313
1952	Bos.-Detroit a	A. L.	SS-3B-2B	94	244	36	55	6	0	1	11	1	.225
1953	Detroit ...	A. L.	2B	103	308	43	90	22	1	2	24	3	.292
Major League Totals			9 Yrs	1201	4570	845	1412	222	47	16	394	52	.309
World's Series Record													
1946	Boston .	A. L.	SS	7	30	2	7	0	0	0	0	1	.233

a Traded with first baseman Walt Dropo, third baseman Fred Hatfield, pitcher Bill Wight and outfielder Don Lenhardt, by Boston to Detroit, for third baseman George Kell, outfielder Hoot Evers, pitcher Dizzy Trout and infielder Johnny Lipon, June 3, 1952.

PHILLEY, DAVID EARL
Born, Garretts Bluff, Texas, May 16, 1920.
Bats Both. Throws Right. Height, 6 feet. Weight, 190 pounds.

Year	Club	Lea	Pos	G	AB	R	H	2B	3B	HR	RBI	SB	Avg
1940	Marshall	E. T. L.	OF	125	496	74	131	24	8	4	45	9	.264
1941	Monroe	C. S. L.	OF	124	503	109	174	27	5	16	110	24	.346
1941	Shreveport	T. L.	OF	6	10	1	1	0	0	0	1	0	.100
1941	Chicago	A. L.	OF	7	9	4	2	1	0	0	0	0	.222
1942	St. Paul	A. A.	OF	56	173	28	41	12	2	0	13	6	.237
1942-43-44-45	Chicago .	A. L.		(In U. S. Army)									
1946	Milwaukee	A. A.	OF	130	507	85	167	33	10	13	93	19	.329
1946	Chicago	A. L.	OF	17	68	10	24	2	3	0	17	5	.353
1947	Chicago	A. L.	OF-3B	143	551	55	142	25	11	2	45	21	.258
1948	Chicago	A. L.	OF	137	488	51	140	28	3	5	42	8	.287
1949	Chicago	A. L.	OF	146	598	84	171	20	8	0	44	13	.286
1950	Chicago	A. L.	OF	156	619	69	150	21	5	14	80	6	.242
1951	Chicago-Phila. a ...	A. L.	OF-3B	132	493	71	129	20	7	7	61	9	.262
1952	Philadelphia	A. L.	OF-3B	151	586	80	154	25	4	7	71	11	.263
1953	Philadelphia	A. L.	OF-3B	*157	620	80	188	30	9	9	59	13	.303
Major League Totals			9 Yrs	1046	4032	504	1100	172	50	44	419	86	.273

a Traded to Philadelphia Athletics as part of a three club deal, April 29, 1951. See footnote to Ray Murray.

PIERSALL, JAMES ANTHONY
Born, Waterbury, Connecticut. November 4, 1929.
Bats Right. Throws Right. Height, 6 feet. Weight, 180 pounds.

Year	Club	Lea	Pos	G	AB	R	H	2B	3B	HR	RBI	SB	Avg
1948	Scranton	E. L.	OF	141	527	74	148	*27	8	12	*92	14	.281
1949	Louisville	A. A.	OF	125	446	58	121	21	4	3	58	6	.271
1950	Louisville	A. A.	OF	131	487	97	124	25	11	8	60	14	.255
1950	Boston	A. L.	OF	6	7	4	2	0	0	0	0	0	.286
1951	Louisville	A. A.	OF	17	42	8	13	0	2	0	2	0	.310
1951	Birmingham	S. A.	OF	121	437	100	151	30	12	15	83	12	.346
1952	Boston	A. L.	OF-SS-3B	56	161	28	43	8	0	1	16	3	.267
1952	Birmingham	S. A.	OF	18	56	10	19	4	1	1	10	2	.339
1953	Boston	A. L.	OF	151	585	76	159	21	9	3	52	11	.272
Major League Totals			3 Yrs	213	753	108	204	29	9	4	68	14	.271

POST, WALTER CHARLES
Born, St. Wendelin, Ohio, July 9, 1929.
Bats Right. Throws Right. Height, 6 feet, 1 inch. Weight, 190 pounds.

Year	Club	Lea	Pos	G	AB	R	H	2B	3B	HR	RBI	SB	Avg
1946	Middletown	Ohio St.	P	2	0	0	0	0	0	0	0	0	.000
1947	Muncie	Ohio St.	P	42	77	11	26	8	0	0	14	1	.338
1948	Columbia	Sally	P-OF	47	90	10	16	2	1	1	4	1	.178
1949	Charleston	Cent.	P	6	10	2	4	0	1	0	3	0	.400
1949	Columbia	Sally	OF	123	458	60	116	19	5	14	76	18	.253
1949	Cincinnati	N. L.	OF	6	8	1	2	0	0	0	1	0	.250
1950	Tulsa	T. L.	OF	136	514	74	151	36	4	12	86	16	.294
1951	Buffalo	I. L.	OF	111	422	78	129	17	5	21	65	11	.306

Year	Club	Lea	Pos	G	AB	R	H	2B	3B	HR	RBI	SB	Avg
1951	Cincinnati	N. L.	OF	15	41	6	9	3	0	1	7	0	.220
1952	Cincinnati	N. L.	OF	19	58	5	9	1	0	2	7	0	.155
1952	Milwaukee	A. A.	OF	51	149	25	36	10	2	5	24	1	.242
1953	Cincinnati	N. L.	OF	11	83	3	8	1	0	1	4	1	.242
1953	Indianapolis	A. A.	OF	133	509	99	147	24	11	33	*120	5	.289
Major League Totals			4 Yrs	51	140	15	28	5	0	4	19	1	.200

POWER, VICTOR (PELLOT)

Born, San Juan, Puerto Rico, November 8, 1930.
Bats Right. Throws Right. Height, 6 feet. Weight, 190 pounds.

Year	Club	Lea	Pos	G	AB	R	H	2B	3B	HR	RBI	SB	Avg
1950	Drummondville	Prov.	OF-INF	105	413	63	138	20	*10	14	105	8	.334
1951	Syracuse	I. L.	OF-1B	129	489	62	129	22	5	6	56	12	.264
1952	Kansas City	A. A.	3B-OF-1B	140	550	95	182	*40	*17	16	109	10	.331
1953	Kansas City a	A. A.	OF-1B	149	*622	115	*217	39	10	16	93	8	*.349

a Traded by New York Yankees with Don Bollweg and Bill Renna for Harry Byrd and Eddie Robinson, December 16, 1953.

RAND, RICHARD HILTON

Born, South Gate, California, March 7, 1931.
Bats Right. Throws Right. Height, 6 feet, 1 inch. Weight, 175 pounds.

Year	Club	Lea	Pos	G	AB	R	H	2B	3B	HR	RBI	SB	Avg
1949	Fresno	Calif.	C	118	411	72	97	12	1	3	65	1	.236
1950	Pocatello	Pion.	C	120	396	67	127	31	5	11	87	2	.321
1951	Winst.-Salem	Carol.	C	103	357	59	100	23	4	8	53	2	.280
1952	Columbus	A. A.	C	109	309	89	79	18	3	2	51	4	.256
1953	Houston	T. L.	C	114	373	87	106	23	1	4	46	2	.284
1953	St. Louis	N. L.	C	9	31	3	9	1	0	0	1	0	.290

REESE, HAROLD HENRY (PEE WEE)

Born, Ekron, Kentucky, July 23, 1919.
Bats Right. Throws Right. Height, 5 feet, 9½ inches. Weight, 175 pounds.

Year	Club	Lea	Pos	G	AB	R	H	2B	3B	HR	RBI	SB	Avg
1938	Louisville	A. A.	SS	138	483	68	134	21	8	3	54	23	.277
1939	Louisville	A. A.	SS	149	506	78	141	22	*18	4	57	*35	.279
1940	Brooklyn	N. L.	SS	84	312	58	85	8	4	5	28	15	.272
1941	Brooklyn	N. L.	SS	152	595	76	136	23	5	2	46	10	.229
1942	Brooklyn	N. L.	SS	151	564	87	144	24	5	3	53	15	.255
1943-44-45	Brooklyn ...	N. L.		(In U. S. Navy)									
1946	Brooklyn	N. L.	SS	152	542	79	154	16	10	5	60	10	.284
1947	Brooklyn	N. L.	SS	142	476	81	135	24	4	12	73	7	.284
1948	Brooklyn .	N. L.	SS	151	566	96	155	31	4	9	75	25	.274
1949	Brooklyn	N. L.	SS	155	617	*132	172	27	3	16	73	26	.279
1950	Brooklyn	N. L.	SS-3B	141	531	97	138	21	5	11	52	17	.260
1951	Brooklyn	N. L.	SS	154	616	94	176	20	8	10	84	20	.286
1952	Brooklyn	N. L.	SS	149	559	94	152	18	6	6	58	*30	.272
1953	Brooklyn ..	N. L.	SS	140	524	108	142	25	7	13	61	22	.271
Major League Totals			11 Yrs	1571	5902	1002	1589	237	63	92	663	197	.269

World's Series Record

Year	Club	Lea	Pos	G	AB	R	H	2B	3B	HR	RBI	SB	Avg
1941	Brooklyn	N. L.	SS	5	20	1	4	0	0	0	2	0	.200
1947	Brooklyn	N. L.	SS	7	23	5	7	1	0	0	4	3	.304
1949	Brooklyn	N. L.	SS	5	19	2	6	1	0	1	2	1	.316
1952	Brooklyn	N. L.	SS	7	29	4	10	0	0	1	4	1	.345
1953	Brooklyn ..	N. L.	SS	6	24	0	5	0	1	0	0	0	.208
World's Series Totals				30	115	12	32	2	1	2	12	5	.278

RENNA, WILLIAM BENEDITTO

Born, Hanford, California, October 4, 1926.
Bats Right. Throws Right. Height, 6 feet, 3 inches. Weight, 218 pounds.

Year	Club	Lea	Pos	G	AB	R	H	2B	3B	HR	RBI	SB	Avg
1949	Twin Falls	Pion.	OF	76	330	99	127	18	6	*21	96	6	.385
1950	Kansas City	A. A.	OF	27	79	6	16	4	1	1	7	0	.203
1950	Norfolk ...	Pied.	OF	86	304	35	69	13	4	9	42	9	.227
1951	San Francisco	P. C. L.	OF	2	5	0	0	0	0	0	0	0	.000
1951	Binghamton .	E. L.	OF	6	6	2	1	0	0	0	0	0	.167
1951	Quincy	I. I. L.	OF	117	412	90	122	23	5	*26	93	13	.296
1952	Kansas City	A. A.	OF	110	414	67	122	20	8	28	90	5	.295
1953	New York a	A. L.	OF	61	121	19	38	6	3	2	18	0	.314

a Traded to Philadelphia Athletics with Don Bollweg and Vic Power for Harry Byrd and Eddie Robinson, December 16, 1953.

REPULSKI, ELDON JOHN (RIP)
Born, Sauk Rapids, Michigan, October 4, 1928.
Bats Right. Throws Right. Height, 6 feet. Weight, 195 pounds.

Year	Club	Lea	Pos	G	AB	R	H	2B	3B	HR	RBI	SB	Avg
1947	West Frankfort ..	Ill. St.	OF	111	435	73	122	9	8	*10	74	45	.280
1948	Fresno	Calif.	OF	125	510	113	164	*33	11	23	*125	15	.322
1949	Omaha	West.	OF	13	29	3	5	0	1	0	2	0	.172
1949	Winston-Salem ...	Carol.	OF	131	504	94	151	30	5	20	88	21	.300
1950	Houston	T. L.	OF	37	125	16	32	4	5	2	15	0	.256
1950	Columbus	S. A. L.	OF	105	381	76	123	12	4	17	95	13	.323
1951	Houston	T. L.	OF	21	60	5	13	3	1	0	5	2	.217
1951	Columbus	A. A.	OF	115	400	49	110	24	4	9	56	4	.275
1952	Rochester	I. L.	OF	142	521	82	154	24	7	13	65	10	.296
1953	St. Louis	N. L.	OF	153	567	75	156	25	4	15	66	3	.275

RHODES, JAMES LAMAR (DUSTY)
Born, Mathews, Ala., May 13, 1927.
Bats Left. Throws Right. Height, 6 feet. Weight, 178 pounds.

Year	Club	Lea	Pos	G	AB	R	H	2B	3B	HR	RBI	SB	Avg
1947	Hopkinsville	Kitty	OF	*125	494	112	161	19	9	12	92	18	.326
1948	Springfield	Wes. Asn.	OF-3B	131	500	84	152	21	10	13	107	17	.304
1949	Springfield	New Eng.	OF	119	451	81	131	20	9	10	82	13	.290
1950	Des Moines	West. L.	OF	45	161	24	42	11	8	2	29	0	.261
1950	Grand Rapids	Cent.	OF	2	8	4	4	1	0	1	2	0	.500
1950	Rock Hill	Tri-St.	OF	78	297	56	90	13	9	14	54	2	.303
1951	Rock Hill	Tri-St.	OF	135	529	115	*182	38	10	31	140	7	.344
1952	Nashville	S. A.	OF	90	349	71	121	29	4	18	69	0	.347
1952	New York	N. L.	OF	67	176	34	44	8	1	10	36	1	.250
1953	New York	N. L.	OF	76	163	18	38	7	0	11	30	0	.233
Major League Totals			2 Yrs.	143	339	52	82	15	1	21	66	1	.242

RICE, DELBERT, JR.
Born, Portsmouth, Ohio, October 27, 1922.
Bats Right. Throws Right. Height, 6 feet, 2 inches. Weight, 190 pounds.

Year	Club	Lea	Pos	G	AB	R	H	2B	3B	HR	RBI	SB	Avg
1941	Williamson	Mt. St.	C	88	339	39	84	9	3	3	50	2	.248
1942	Williamson	Mt. St.	C	121	468	65	135	29	3	7	77	5	.288
1943	Rochester	I. L.	C	66	182	14	36	5	3	0	18	3	.198
1944	Rochester	I. L.	C	92	296	26	78	10	8	6	50	2	.264
1945	St. Louis	N. L.	C	83	253	27	66	17	3	1	28	0	.261
1946	St. Louis	N. L.	C	55	139	10	38	8	1	1	12	0	.273
1947	St. Louis	N. L.	C	97	261	28	57	7	8	12	44	1	.218
1948	St. Louis	N. L.	C	100	290	24	57	10	1	4	34	1	.197
1949	St. Louis	N. L.	C	92	284	25	67	16	1	4	29	0	.236
1950	St. Louis	N. L.	C	130	414	39	101	20	3	9	54	0	.244
1951	St. Louis	N. L.	C	122	374	34	94	13	1	9	47	0	.251
1952	St. Louis	N. L.	C	147	495	43	128	27	2	11	65	0	.259
1953	St. Louis	N. L.	C	135	419	32	99	22	1	6	37	0	.236
Major League Totals			9 Yrs.	961	2929	262	707	140	16	57	350	2	.241
World's Series Record													
1946	St. Louis	N. L.	C	8	6	2	3	1	0	0	0	0	.500

RICE, HAROLD HOUSTEN
Born, Morganette, West Virginia, February 11, 1924.
Bats Left. Throws Right. Height, 6 feet, 1 inch. Weight, 195 pounds.

Year	Club	Lea	Pos	G	AB	R	H	2B	3B	HR	RBI	SB	Avg
1941	Williamson	Mt. St.	OF	58	225	30	58	8	6	6	38	3	.258
1942	Williamson	Mt. St.	OF	65	232	50	81	16	2	2	40	0	.349
1942	Asheville	Pied.	OF	37	108	10	22	5	1	0	16	2	.204
1943-44-45	Lynchburg ..	Pied.	(In Military Service)										
1946	Winston-Salem	Car.	OF	106	415	75	139	21	10	7	70	18	.335
1947	Rochester	I. L.	OF	120	347	42	86	15	1	5	50	4	.248
1948	Rochester	I. L.	OF-3B	146	536	80	172	36	13	7	73	9	.321
1948	St. Louis	N. L.	OF	8	31	8	10	1	2	0	8	0	.323
1949	St. Louis	N. L.	OF	40	46	3	9	2	1	1	9	0	.196
1950	Rochester ...	I. L.	OF	114	413	87	128	21	8	17	79	10	.310
1950	St. Louis	N. L.	OF	44	128	12	27	3	1	2	11	0	.211
1951	St. Louis	N. L.	OF	69	236	20	60	12	1	4	38	0	.254
1951	Rochester	I. L.	OF	54	209	30	69	10	8	12	86	0	.330
1952	St. Louis	N. L.	OF	98	295	37	85	14	5	7	45	1	.288

Year	Club	Lea	Pos	G	AB	R	H	2B	3B	HR	RBI	SB	Avg
1953	St.Louis-Pitts. a	N. L.	OF	86	294	39	91	16	1	4	42	0	.310
Major League Totals			6 Yrs	845	1030	114	282	48	11	18	148	1	.274

a Traded to Pittsburgh for Pete Castiglione, June 14, 1953.

RIVERA, MANUEL JOSEPH (JIM)
Born, Brooklyn, N. Y., July 22, 1922.
Bats Left. Throws Left. Height, 6 feet. Weight, 196 pounds.

Year	Club	Lea	Pos	G	AB	R	H	2B	3B	HR	RBI	SB	Avg
1949	Gainesville	Fla. St.	OF	*137	529	*142	177	36	*16	13	102	*55	.335
1950	Atlanta	S. A.	OF	11	34	7	9	1	0	0	3	3	.265
1950	Pensacola	S. East.	OF	124	527	*189	178	29	*12	20	135	28	.338
1951	Seattle a-b	P. C. L.	OF	166	657	*135	*231	*40	18	20	112	33	*.352
1952	St. L.-Chicago c	A. L.	OF	150	537	72	136	20	9	7	48	21	.253
1953	Chicago	A. L.	OF	156	567	79	147	26	*16	11	78	22	.259
Major League Totals			2 Yrs	306	1104	151	283	46	25	18	126	43	.256

a Bought from Seattle by Chicago White Sox for $65,000 after 1951 season.
b Traded with Dick Littlefield, Gus Niarhos, Joe DiMaestri and Gordon Goldsberry, by Chicago to St. Louis Browns for Sherman Lollar, Al Widmar and Tom Upton, Nov. 26, 1951.
c Traded with catcher Darrell Johnson, by St. Louis to Chicago White Sox. for outfielder Ray Coleman and catcher J. W. Porter, July 28, 1952.

RIZZUTO, PHILIP FRANCIS (SCOOTER)
Born, New York City, N. Y., September 25, 1918.
Bats Right. Throws Right. Height, 5 feet, 6 inches. Weight, 160 pounds.

Year	Club	Lea	Pos	G	AB	R	H	2B	3B	HR	RBI	SB	Avg
1937	Bassett	Bi-St.	SS	67	284	53	88	17	5	5		6	.310
1938	Norfolk	P. L.	3B-SS	112	446	97	150	24	10	9	58	26	.336
1939	Kansas City	A. A.	SS	135	503	99	159	21	6	5	64	33	.316
1940	Kansas City	A. A.	SS	148	579	124	201	28	10	10	73	35	.347
1941	New York	A. L.	SS	133	515	65	158	20	9	3	46	14	.307
1942	New York	A. L.	SS	144	553	79	157	24	7	4	68	22	.284
1943-44-45	New York	A. L.		(In U. S. Navy)									
1946	New York	A. L.	SS	126	471	53	121	17	1	2	38	14	.257
1947	New York	A. L.	SS	153	549	78	150	26	9	2	60	11	.273
1948	New York	A I.	SS	128	464	65	117	13	2	6	50	6	.252
1949	New York a	A. L.	SS	153	614	110	169	22	7	5	65	18	.275
1950	New York a	A. L.	SS	155	617	125	200	36	7	7	66	12	.324
1951	New York	A. L.	SS	144	540	87	148	21	6	2	43	18	.274
1952	New York	A. L.	SS	152	578	89	147	24	10	2	43	17	.254
1953	New York	A. L.	SS	134	413	54	112	21	3	2	54	4	.271
Major League Totals			10 Yrs	1422	5314	805	1479	224	61	35	533	136	.278

World's Series Record

Year	Club	Lea	Pos	G	AB	R	H	2B	3B	HR	RBI	SB	Avg
1941	New York	A. L.	SS	5	18	0	2	0	0	0	0	1	.111
1942	New York	A. L.	SS	5	21	2	8	0	0	1	1	2	.381
1947	New York	A. L.	SS	7	26	3	8	1	0	0	2	2	.308
1949	New York	A. L.	SS	5	18	2	3	0	0	0	1	1	.167
1950	New York	A L.	SS	4	14	1	2	0	0	0	0	1	.143
1951	New York	A. L.	SS	6	25	5	8	0	0	1	3	0	.320
1952	New York	A. L.	SS	7	27	2	4	1	0	0	0	0	.148
1953	New York	A. L.	SS	6	19	4	6	1	0	0	0	1	.316
World's Series Totals				45	168	19	41	8	0	2	7	8	.244

a Voted Most Valuable Player in American League for 1950.

ROBINSON, JACK ROOSEVELT
Born, Cairo, Georgia. January 81, 1919.
Bats Right. Throws Right. Height, 5 feet, 11¾ inches. Weight, 205 pounds.

Year	Club	Lea	Pos	G	AB	R	H	2B	3B	HR	RBI	SB	Avg
1946	Montreal	I. L.	2B	124	444	*113	155	25	8	3	66	40	*.349
1947	Brooklyn	N. L.	1B	151	590	125	175	31	5	12	48	*29	.297
1948	Brooklyn	N. L.	2B-1B-3B	147	574	108	170	38	8	12	85	22	.296
1949	Brooklyn a	N. L.	2B	156	593	122	203	38	12	16	124	*37	*.342
1950	Brooklyn	N. L.	2B	144	518	99	170	89	4	14	81	12	.328
1951	Brooklyn	N. L.	2B	153	548	106	185	83	7	19	88	25	.338
1952	Brooklyn	N. L.	2B	149	510	104	157	17	8	19	75	24	.308

Year	Club	Lea	Pos	G	AB	R	H	2B	3B	HR	RBI	SB	Avg
1953	Brooklyn	N. L.	INF-OF	136	484	109	159	34	7	12	95	17	.329

Major League Totals				7 Yrs	3817	773	1219	230	46	104	596	166	.319

World's Series Record

Year	Club	Lea	Pos	G	AB	R	H	2B	3B	HR	RBI	SB	Avg
1947	Brooklyn	N. L.	1B	7	27	3	7	2	0	0	3	2	.259
1949	Brooklyn	N. L.	2B	5	16	2	3	1	0	0	2	0	.188
1952	Brooklyn .\.......	N. L.	2B	7	23	4	4	0	0	1	2	2	.174
1953	Brooklyn	N. L.	OF	6	25	3	8	2	0	0	2	1	.320

World's Series Totals					25	91	12	22	5	0	1	9	5	.242

a Voted Most Valuable Player in National League for 1949.

ROBINSON, WILLIAM EDWARD (EDDIE)

Born, Paris, Texas, December 15, 1920.
Bats Left. Throws Right. Height, 6 feet, 2½ inches. Weight, 205 pounds.

Year	Club	Lea	Pos	G	AB	R	H	2B	3B	HR	RBI	SB	Avg
1939	Valdosta	Ga.-Fla.	1B	136	518	58	129	22	7	7	88	10	.249
1940	Valdosta	Ga.-Fla.	1B	137	569	90	184	20	21	8	105	11	.323
1941	Elmira	E. L.	1B	139	491	77	145	18	14	4	78	1	.295
1942	Baltimore	I. L.	1B	143	526	83	161	21	7	27	104	8	.306
1942	Cleveland	A. L.	1B	8	8	1	1	0	0	0	2	0	.125
1943-44-45	Cleveland ...		(In Military Service)										
1946	Baltimore	I. L.	1B	140	528	99	163	25	5	34	*123	8	.318
1946	Cleveland	A. L.	1B	7	27	5	11	0	0	3	4	0	.407
1947	Cleveland	A. L.	1B	95	318	52	78	10	1	14	52	1	.245
1948	Cleveland a	A. L.	1B	134	493	53	125	18	5	16	83	1	.254
1949	Washington	A. L.	1B	143	527	66	155	27	3	18	78	8	.294
1950	Washington-Chicago b	A. L.	1B	155	553	83	163	15	4	21	86	0	.295
1951	Chicago	A. L.	1B	151	564	85	159	23	5	29	117	2	.282
1952	Chicago c	A. L.	1B	155	594	79	176	33	1	22	104	2	.296
1953	Philadelphia d ...	A. L.	1B	156	615	64	152	28	4	22	102	1	.247

Major League Totals				9 Yrs	1004	3699	488	1020	154	23	145	628	10	.276

World's Series Record

Year	Club	Lea	Pos	G	AB	R	H	2B	3B	HR	RBI	SB	Avg
1948	Cleveland	A. L.	1B	6	20	0	6	0	0	0	1	0	.300

a Traded with Ed Klieman and Joe Haynes to Washington for Mickey Vernon and Early Wynn, Dec. 14, 1948.
b Traded with Ray Scarborough and Al Kozar to Chicago White Sox, May 30, for Cass Michaels, Bob Kuzava and John Ostrowski.
c Traded to Philadelphia Athletics with Joe De Maestri and Ed McGhee for Ferris Fain and Bob Wilson, Jan. 27, 1953.
d Traded to New York Yankees with Harry Byrd for Don Bollweg, Vic Power and Bill Renna, Dec. 16, 1953.

ROSEN, ALBERT LEONARD (FLIP)

Born, Spartanburg, South Carolina, March 1, 1925.
Bats Right. Throws Right. Height, 5 feet 10 inches. Weight, 175 pounds.

Year	Club	Lea	Pos	G	AB	R	H	2B	3B	HR	RBI	SB	Avg
1942	Thomasville ..	No. Car. St.	3B	86	323	55	99	12	3	7	49	24	.306
1943-44-45	Wilkes-Barre	E. L.	(In U. S. Army)										
1946	Pittsfield	Can. Am.	INF	107	375	94	121	21	*19	*15	*86	30	.323
1947	Oklahoma City	T. L.	3B-SS	146	533	115	*186	*47	11	25	*141	17	*.349
1947	Cleveland	A. L.	3B-OF	7	9	1	1	0	0	0	0	0	.111
1948	Kansas City	A. A.	SS-3B	127	462	102	151	29	8	25	110	10	.327
1948	Cleveland	A. L.	3B	5	5	0	1	0	0	0	0	0	.200
1949	San Diego	P. C. L.	1B-3B	83	273	49	87	12	1	14	51	5	.319
1950	Cleveland	A. L.	3B	23	44	3	7	2	0	0	5	0	.159
1950	Cleveland	A. L.	3B	155	554	100	159	23	4	*37	116	5	.287
1951	Cleveland	A. L.	3B	*154	573	82	152	30	1	24	102	7	.265
1952	Cleveland	A. L.	3B-1B-SS	148	567	101	171	32	5	28	*105	8	.302
1953	Cleveland a	A. L.	3B-1B-SS	155	599	*115	201	27	5	*43	*145	8	.336

Major League Totals				7 Yrs.	647	2351	402	692	114	15	132	473	28	.294

World's Series Record

Year	Club	Lea	Pos	G	AB	R	H	2B	3B	HR	RBI	SB	Avg
1948	Cleveland	A. L.	PH	1	1	0	0	0	0	0	0	0	.000

a Selected Most Valuable Player in American League for 1953.

RUNNELS, JAMES EDWARD (PETE)

Born, Lufkin, Texas, January 28, 1928.
Bats Left. Throws Right. Height, 6 feet. Weight, 170 pounds.

Year	Club	Lea	Pos	G	AB	R	H	2B	3B	HR	RBI	SB	Avg
1949	Chickasha	Sooner	3B-P	130	505	111	*188	*44	8	6	92	15	*.372

Year	Club	Lea	Pos	G	AB	R	H	2B	3B	HR	RBI	SB	Avg
1950	Texarkana	Big State	SS	144	578	131	191	38	7	10	83	4	.330
1951	Chattanooga	S. A.	SS	74	281	56	100	18	8	3	54	4	.356
1951	Washington	A. L.	SS	78	273	31	76	12	2	0	25	0	.278
1952	Washington	A. L.	SS-2B	152	555	70	158	18	3	1	64	0	.285
1953	Washington	A. L.	SS-2B	137	486	64	125	15	5	2	50	3	.257
Major League Totals			3 Yrs	367	1314	165	359	45	10	3	139	3	.273

RYAN, CORNELIUS JOSEPH (CONNIE)

Born, New Orleans, Louisiana, February 27, 1920.
Bats Right. Throws Right. Height, 5 feet, 11 inches. Weight, 175 pounds

Year	Club	Lea	Pos	G	AB	R	H	2B	3B	HR	RBI	SB	Avg
1940	Atlanta	S. A.	2B	14	42	1	7	1	0	0	2	0	.167
1940	Savannah	S. A. L.	2B	113	421	83	133	22	4	13	73	9	.316
1941	Atlanta	S. A.	2B	151	600	106	180	33	4	5	83	8	.300
1942	New York	N. L.	2B	11	27	4	5	0	0	0	2	1	.185
1942	Jersey City a	I. L.	2B	112	374	40	91	11	5	1	51	4	.243
1943	Boston	N. L.	3B-2B	132	457	52	97	10	2	1	24	7	.212
1944	Boston	N. L.	3B-2B	88	332	56	98	18	5	4	25	13	.295
1944-45	Boston	N. L.	(In U. S. Navy)										
1946	Boston	N. L.	3B-2B	143	502	55	121	28	8	1	48	7	.241
1947	Boston	N. L.	2B-SS	150	544	60	144	33	5	5	69	5	.265
1948	Boston	N. L.	2B-3B	51	122	14	26	3	0	0	10	0	.213
1949	Boston	N. L.	INF	85	208	28	52	13	1	6	20	1	.250
1950	Boston-Cincinnati b .	N. L.	2B	126	439	57	109	20	5	6	49	4	.248
1951	Cincinnati c	N. L.	INF-OF	136	473	75	112	17	4	16	53	11	.237
1952	Philadelphia	N. L.	2B	*154	577	81	139	24	6	12	49	13	.241
1953	Philadelphia d	N. L.	2B-1B	90	247	47	73	14	6	5	26	5	.296
1953	Chicago e	A. L.	3B	17	54	6	12	1	0	0	6	2	.222
Major League Totals			11 Yrs	1183	3982	535	988	181	42	56	381	69	.248
World's Series Record													
1948	Boston	N. L.	PH-PR	2	1	0	0	0	0	0	0	0	.000

a Traded by the Giants with Hugh Poland to Boston, April 27, 1943 for Ernie Lombardi.
b Traded to Cincinnati for Walker Cooper, May 10.
c Traded with Howie Fox and Forrest Burgess to Philadelphia Phillies for Dick Sisler, Andy Seminick, Eddie Pellegrini and Niles Jordan, December 11, 1951.
d Sold to Chicago White Sox on waiver claim, August 25, 1953.
e Traded to Cincinnati with Rocky Krsnich and Saul Rogovin for Willard Marshall, Dec. 10, 1953.

ST. CLAIRE, EDWARD JOSEPH JR. (EBBA)

Born, Whitehall, New York, August 5, 1921.
Bats Both. Throws Right. Height, 6 feet, 1 inch. Weight, 219 pounds.

Year	Club	Lea	Pos	G	AB	R	H	2B	3B	HR	RBI	SB	Avg
1942	Albany	E. L.	OF-P	10	20	1	3	0	1	0	3	0	.150
1943-44	Albany	E. L.	(In United States Military Service)										
1945	Albany	E. L.	C	8	22	3	7	2	0	0	7	..	.318
1945	Hornell	Pony	C-1B-P	78	297	54	103	25	6	4	57	21	.347
1946	Albany	E. L.	C	102	311	47	98	24	4	1	33	7	.315
1947	Indianapolis	A. A.	(Voluntarily Retired)										
1948	New Orleans	S. A.	C-P-3B	114	360	40	99	23	2	7	61	1	.275
1949	Atlanta	S. A.	(Voluntarily Retired)										
1950	Atlanta	S. A.	C	145	536	77	150	27	9	19	107	5	.280
1951	Boston	N. L.	C	72	220	22	62	17	2	1	25	2	.282
1952	Boston	N. L.	C	39	108	5	23	2	0	2	4	0	.213
1953	Milwaukee	N. L.	C	33	80	7	16	3	0	2	5	0	.200
Major League Totals			3 Yrs	144	408	34	101	22	2	5	34	2	.248

SAUER, HENRY JOHN (HANK)

Born, Pittsburgh, Pennsylvania, March 17, 1919.
Bats Right. Throws Right. Height, 6 feet, 3½ inches. Weight, 199 pounds.

Year	Club	Lea	Pos	G	AB	R	H	2B	3B	HR	RBI	SB	Avg
1937	Butler	P. S. A.	1B	64	235	40	63	7	3	3	38	7	.268
1938	Butler	P. S. A.	1B	*100	385	89	*135	*29	8	12	74	25	*.351
1939	Akron	M. A. L.	1B	127	472	87	142	31	8	13	92	2	.301
1940	Birmingham	S. A.	OF-1B	118	384	47	112	17	10	9	79	1	.292
1941	Birmingham	S. A.	1B	154	585	96	193	20	14	19	114	9	.330
1941	Cincinnati	N. L.	OB	9	33	4	10	4	0	0	5	0	.303
1942	Cincinnati	N. L.	1B	7	20	4	5	0	0	2	4	0	.250

Year	Club	Lea	Pos	G	AB	R	H	2B	3B	HR	RBI	SB	Avg
1942	Syracuse	I. L.	OF	82	291	35	62	9	2	11	44	1	.213
1943	Syracuse	I. L.	OF-1B	*154	571	73	157	32	9	12	75	8	.275
1944-45	Cincinnati	N. L.	(In U. S. Coast Guard)										
1945	Cincinnati	N. L.	OF-1B	31	116	18	34	1	0	5	20	2	.293
1946	Syracuse	I. L.	OF	140	517	99	146	29	2	21	90	13	.282
1947	Syracuse	I. L.	OF	146	542	*130	*182	28	1	50	*141	4	.336
1948	Cincinnati	N. L.	OF-1B	145	530	78	138	22	1	35	97	2	.260
1949	Cincinnati-Chicago a ..	N. L.	OF-1B	138	509	81	140	23	1	31	99	0	.275
1950	Chicago	N. L.	OF-1B	145	540	85	148	32	2	32	103	1	.274
1951	Chicago	N. L.	OF	141	525	77	138	19	4	30	89	2	.263
1952	Chicago b	N. L.	OF	151	567	89	153	31	3	*37	*121	1	.270
1953	Chicago	N. L.	OF	108	395	61	104	16	5	19	60	0	.263
Major League Totals		9 Yrs		875	3235	497	870	148	16	191	593	8	.269

a Traded with Frank Baumholtz to Chicago for Peanuts Lowrey and Harry Walker, June 15.
b Named National League's Most Valuable Player for 1952.

SAWATSKI, CARL ERNEST
Born, Shickshinny, Pennsylvania, November 4, 1927.
Bats Left. Throws Right. Height, 5 feet, 11 inches. Weight, 220 pounds.

Year	Club	Lea	Pos	G	AB	R	H	2B	3B	HR	RBI	SB	Avg
1945	Bradford	Pony	OF	121	461	88	136	27	10	*18	*111	5	.295
1946	Schenectady ...	Can.-Am.	OF	40	136	17	32	8	0	1	18	4	.235
1946	Bloomingdale ...	No. Atl.	C	48	154	26	43	8	1	7	35	0	.279
1947	Bloomingdale ...	No. Atl.	C-OF-P	127	457	105	161	31	6	*34	139	4	.352
1948	Des Moines	West.	C-OF	109	333	67	94	10	5	*29	111	0	.278
1948	Chicago	N. L.	PH	2	2	0	0	0	0	0	0	0	.000
1949	Nashville	S. A.	C	128	431	86	155	33	1	*45	*153	3	.360
1950	Nashville	S. A.	C	80	273	54	84	10	2	24	73	2	.308
1950	Chicago	N. L.	C	38	108	4	18	1	0	1	7	0	.175
1951-52	Chicago	N. L.	(In Military Service)										
1953	Chicago a	N. L.	C	43	59	5	13	3	0	1	5	0	.220
Major League Totals		3 Yrs		83	164	9	31	4	0	2	12	0	.189

a Sold to Chicago White Sox on waivers, December 1, 1953.

SCHOENDIENST, ALBERT FRED (RED)
Born, Germantown, Illinois, February 2, 1923.
Bats Both. Throws Right. Height, 6 feet. Weight, 165 pounds.

Year	Club	Lea	Pos	G	AB	R	H	2B	3B	HR	RBI	SB	Avg
1942	Union City	Kitty	2B	6	27	4	11	3	0	0	4	2	.407
1942	Albany	Ga.-Fla.	SS-2B	68	264	41	71	7	5	1	23	0	.269
1943	Lynchburg	Pied.	SS	9	36	3	17	2	0	0	5	3	.472
1943	Rochester	I. L.	SS	136	555	81	*187	21	5	6	37	20	*.337
1944	Rochester	I. L.	SS	25	102	26	38	3	2	2	14	16	.373
1944			(In United States Army)										
1945	St. Louis	N. L.	OF-SS-2B	137	565	89	157	22	6	1	47	*26	.278
1946	St. Louis	N. L.	2B-3B-SS	142	606	94	170	28	5	0	34	12	.281
1947	St. Louis	N. L.	2B-3B-OF	151	*659	91	167	25	9	3	48	6	.253
1948	St. Louis	N. L.	2B	119	408	64	111	21	4	4	36	1	.272
1949	St. Louis	N. L.	INF-OF	151	640	102	190	25	2	3	54	8	.297
1950	St. Louis	N. L.	2B-SS-3B	153	*642	81	177	*43	9	7	63	3	.276
1951	St. Louis	N. L.	2B-SS	135	553	88	160	32	7	6	54	0	.289
1952	St. Louis	N. L.	2B-3B-SS	152	620	91	188	40	7	7	67	9	.303
1953	St. Louis	N. L.	2B	146	564	107	193	35	5	15	79	3	.342
Major League Totals		9 Yrs		1286	5257	807	1513	271	54	46	482	63	.288
World's Series Record													
1946	St. Louis ...	N. L.	2B	7	30	3	7	1	0	0	1	1	.233

SEMINICK, ANDREW WASAL
Born, Pierce, West Virginia, September 12, 1920.
Bats Right. Throws Right. Height, 5 feet, 11 inches. Weight, 185 pounds

Year	Club	Lea	Pos	G	AB	R	H	2B	3B	HR	RBI	SB	Avg
1940	London ...	Pony	C	19	45	4	7	1	0	1	4	0	.156
1941	Elizabethtor.	App. L.	2B-OF-C	112	399	81	105	20	10	16	86	8	.263
1942	Elizabethton	App. L.	C	99	375	76	122	23	6	*15	70	13	.325
1943	Knoxville	S. A.	C-OF-1B	133	429	80	130	15	7	16	83	3	.303
1943	Philadelphia	N. L.	C-OF	22	72	9	13	2	0	2	5	0	.181
1944	Philadelphia	N. L.	OF-C	22	63	9	14	2	1	0	4	2	.222
1944	Buffalo	I. L.	OF-C	87	297	57	81	8	4	14	50	3	.273
1945	Philadelphia	N. L.	3B-OF-C	80	188	18	45	7	2	6	26	3	.239

Year	Club	Lea	Pos	G	AB	R	H	2B	3B	HR	RBI	SB	Avg
1946	Philadelphia	N. L.	C	124	406	55	107	15	5	12	52	2	.264
1947	Philadelphia	N. L.	C	111	337	48	85	16	2	13	50	4	.252
1948	Philadelphia	N. L.	C	125	391	49	88	11	8	13	44	4	.225
1949	Philadelphia	N. L.	C	109	334	52	81	11	2	24	68	0	.243
1950	Philadelphia	N. L.	C	130	393	55	113	15	8	24	68	0	.288
1951	Philadelphia a	N. L.	C	101	291	42	66	8	1	11	37	1	.227
1952	Cincinnati	N. L.	C	108	336	38	86	16	1	14	50	1	.256
1953	Cincinnati	N. L.	C	119	887	46	91	12	0	19	64	2	.235
Major League Totals			11 Yrs	1051	8198	421	789	115	20	138	468	19	.247
World's Series Record													
1950	Philadelphia	N. L.	C	4	11	0	2	0	0	0	0	0	.182

a Traded with Dick Sisler, Eddie Pellagrini and Niles Jordan to Cincinnati for Howie Fox, Connie Ryan and Forrest Burgess, December 11, 1951.

SERENA, WILLIAM ROBERT
Born, Alameda, Calif., Oct. 2, 1924.
Bats Right. Throws Right. Height, 5 feet, 9½ inches. Weight, 184 pounds.

Year	Club	Lea	Pos	G	AB	R	H	2B	3B	HR	RBI	SB	Avg
1946	Montgomery	S. East	SS	135	464	90	129	25	8	22	85	8	.278
1947	Dallas	T. L.	OF	5	12	1	3	0	0	0	0	0	.250
1947	Lubbock	W. Tex-NM.	SS	137	506	*183	189	43	9	*57	*190	26	.874
1948	Dallas	T. L.	SS-3B-OF	78	237	27	54	14	3	9	37	3	.228
1948	Buffalo	I. L.	INF-OF	63	182	43	47	8	2	13	32	3	.258
1949	Dallas	Texas	3B	151	491	102	138	28	4	28	110	8	.281
1949	Chicago	N. L.	3B	12	37	3	8	3	0	1	7	0	.216
1950	Chicago	N. L.	3B	127	435	56	104	20	*4	17	61	1	.239
1951	Chicago a	N. L.	3B	18	39	8	13	3	1	1	4	0	.333
1952	Chicago	N. L.	3B-2B	122	390	49	107	21	5	15	61	1	.274
1953	Chicago	N. L.	2B-3B	93	275	30	69	10	5	10	52	0	.251
Major League Totals			5 Yrs	867	1176	146	301	57	15	44	185	2	.256

a Broke wrist on May 6, did not play for rest of the season.

SHUBA, GEORGE THOMAS (SHOTGUN)
Born, Youngstown, Ohio, Dec. 13, 1924.
Bats Left. Throws Right. Height, 5 feet, 11½ inches. Weight, 180 pounds.

Year	Club	Lea	Pos	G	AB	R	H	2B	3B	HR	RBI	SB	Avg
1944	New Orleans	S. A.	2B	19	56	12	11	2	1	0	6	2	.196
1944	Olean	Pony	2B	105	880	79	112	17	4	*14	68	13	.295
1945	Mobile	S. A.	OF	137	528	114	169	30	15	8	103	9	.320
1946	Montreal	I. L.	OF	20	55	18	11	0	0	7	12	1	.200
1946	Mobile	S. A.	OF	112	890	74	113	18	5	11	56	8	.290
1947	Mobile	S. A.	OF	152	584	103	168	88	7	21	108	10	.288
1948	Mobile	S. A.	OF	74	280	68	109	23	7	7	60	9	.389
1948	Brooklyn	N. L.	OF	63	161	21	43	6	0	4	32	1	.267
1949	Brooklyn	N. L.	PH	1	1	0	0	0	0	0	0	0	.000
1949	Mobile	S. A.	OF	113	369	96	121	16	1	28	77	7	.328
1950	Brooklyn	N. L.	OF	34	111	15	23	8	2	3	12	2	.207
1950	St. Paul	A. A.	OF	36	117	17	30	3	1	4	19	1	.256
1950	Montreal	I. L.	OF	39	142	25	36	7	1	8	25	0	.254
1951	Montreal	I. L.	OF	92	281	54	87	25	2	20	83	8	.310
1952	Brooklyn	N. L.	OF	94	256	40	78	12	1	9	40	1	.305
1953	Brooklyn	N. L.	OF	74	169	19	43	12	1	5	23	1	.254
Major League Totals			5 Yrs	266	698	95	187	38	4	21	107	5	.268
World's Series Record													
1952	Brooklyn	N. L.	OF	4	10	0	3	1	0	0	0	0	.300
1953	Brooklyn	N. L.	PH	2	1	1	1	0	0	1	2	0	1.000
World's Series Totals				6	11	1	4	1	0	1	2	0	.364

SIEVERS, ROY EDWARD
Born, St. Louis, Missouri, November 18, 1926.
Bats Right. Throws Right. Height, 6 feet, 1 inch. Weight, 195 pounds.

Year	Club	Lea	Pos	G	AB	R	H	2B	3B	HR	RBI	SB	Avg
1947	Hannibal	Cen. Assn	OF-3B-P	*125	501	*121	*159	21	5	*34	*141	8	.817
1948	Elmira	E. L.	OF	16	56	5	10	3	0	2	8	0	.179
1948	Springfield	I. I. I.	OF	96	343	64	106	15	5	19	75	4	.309
1949	St. Louis	A. L.	OF-3B	140	471	84	144	28	1	16	91	1	.306
1950	St. Louis	A. L.	OF-3B	113	870	46	88	20	4	10	57	1	.238
1951	San Antonio	Texas	OF	39	138	16	41	8	1	2	17	6	.297
1951	St. Louis	A. L.	OF	31	89	10	20	2	1	1	11	0	.225
1952	St. Louis	A. L.	1B	11	80	3	6	3	0	0	5	0	.200
1953	St. Louis	A. L.	1B	92	285	87	77	15	0	8	35	0	.270
Major League Totals			5 Yrs	887	1245	180	835	68	6	35	199	2	.269

197

SILVERA, CHARLES RYAN

Born, San Francisco, California, October 13, 1924.
Bats Right.   Throws Right.   Height, 5 feet, 10 inches.   Weight, 175 pounds.

Year	Club	Lea	Pos	G	AB	R	H	2B	3B	HR	RBI	SB	Avg
1942	Wellsville	Pony	OF-3B-C	75	256	32	65	16	2	1	40	8	.254
1943-44-45	Kan. City	A. A.	(In Military Service)										
1946	Kansas City	A. A.	C	91	284	22	71	13	2	3	45	5	.250
1947	Portland	P. C. L.	C	120	356	40	88	12	3	1	39	0	.247
1948	Portland	P. C. L.	C	144	501	58	151	36	6	5	85	5	.301
1948	New York	A. L.	C	4	14	1	8	0	1	0	0	0	.571
1949	New York	A. L.	C	58	130	8	41	2	0	0	18	2	.315
1950	New York	A. L.	C	18	25	2	4	0	0	0	1	0	.160
1951	New York	A. L.	C	18	51	5	14	3	0	1	7	0	.275
1952	New York	A. L.	C	20	55	4	18	3	0	0	11	0	.327
1953	New York	A. L.	C-3B	42	82	11	23	3	1	0	12	0	.280
Major League Totals			6 Yrs	160	357	31	108	11	2	1	44	2	.303
World's Series Record													
1949	New York	A. L.	C	1	2	0	0	0	0	0	0	0	.000

SIMPSON, HARRY LEON (GOODY - SUITCASE)

Born, Atlanta, Georgia, December 3, 1925.
Bats Left.   Throws Right.   Height, 6 feet, 1½ inches.   Weight, 175 pounds.

Year	Club	Lea	Pos	G	AB	R	H	2B	3B	HR	RBI	SB	Avg
1949	Wilkes-Barre	E. L.	OF	139	522	*125	159	27	16	*31	*120	5	.305
1950	San Diego	P. C. L.	OF	178	697	121	225	41	*19	33	*156	2	.323
1951	Cleveland	A. L.	OF-1B	122	332	51	76	7	0	7	24	6	.229
1952	Cleveland	A. L.	OF-1B	146	545	66	145	21	10	10	65	5	.266
1953	Cleveland	A. L.	OF-1B	82	242	25	55	3	1	7	22	0	.227
Major League Totals			3 Yrs	350	1119	142	276	31	11	24	111	11	.247

SISTI, SEBASTIAN DANIEL (SIBBY)

Born, Buffalo, New York, July 26, 1920.
Bats Right.   Throws Right.   Height, 5 feet, 11 inches.   Weight, 185 pounds.

Year	Club	Lea	Pos	G	AB	R	H	2B	3B	HR	RBI	SB	Avg
1938	Hartford	E. L.	3B-SS	82	287	56	84	14	4	3	47	14	.293
1939	Hartford	E. L.	2B	54	199	35	62	7	6	3	29	7	.312
1939	Boston	N. L.	SS-3B-2B	63	215	19	49	7	1	1	11	4	.228
1940	Boston	N. L.	3B-2B	123	459	73	115	19	5	6	34	4	.251
1941	Boston	N. L.	3B-2B-SS	140	541	72	140	24	3	1	45	7	.259
1942	Boston	N. L.	2B-OF	129	407	50	86	11	4	4	35	5	.211
1943-44-45	Boston	N. L.	(In U. S. Coast Guard)										
1946	Boston	N. L.	3B	1	0	0	0	0	0	0	0	0	.000
1946	Indianapolis	A. A.	SS	149	*592	99	*203	33	*14	6	86	14	*.343
1947	Boston	N. L.	2B-SS	56	153	22	43	8	0	2	15	2	.281
1948	Boston	N. L.	2B-SS	83	221	30	54	6	2	0	21	0	.244
1949	Boston	N. L.	INF-OF	101	268	39	69	12	0	5	22	1	.257
1950	Boston	N. L.	INF-OF	69	105	21	18	3	1	2	11	1	.171
1951	Boston	N. L.	INF-OF	114	362	46	101	20	2	2	33	4	.279
1952	Boston	N. L.	INF-OF	90	245	19	52	10	1	4	24	2	.212
1953	Milwaukee	N. L.	2B-SS-3B	38	23	3	5	1	0	0	4	0	.217
Major League Totals			12 Yrs	1007	2999	399	732	†121	19	27	260	30	.244
World's Series Record													
1948	Boston	N. L.	2B	2	1	0	0	0	0	0	0	0	.000

SLAUGHTER, ENOS BRADSHER (COUNTRY)

Born, Roxboro, N. C., April 27, 1916.
Bats Left.   Throws Right.   Height, 5 feet, 9 inches.   Weight, 190 pounds.

Year	Club	Lea	Pos	G	AB	R	H	2B	3B	HR	RBI	SB	Avg
1935	Martinsville	Bi-St.	OF	109	422	68	115	25	11	18	...	11	.273
1936	Columbus	S. A. L.	OF	151	569	106	185	31	*20	9	118	9	.325
1937	Columbus	A. A.	OF	154	642	*147	*245	42	13	26	122	18	*.382
1938	St. Louis	N. L.	OF	112	395	59	109	20	10	8	58	1	.276
1939	St. Louis	N. L.	OF	149	604	95	193	*52	5	12	86	2	.320
1940	St. Louis	N. L.	OF	140	516	96	158	25	13	17	73	8	.306
1941	St. Louis	N. L.	OF	113	425	71	132	22	9	13	76	4	.311
1942	St. Louis	N. L.	OF	152	591	100	*188	31	*17	13	98	9	.318
1943-44-45	St. Louis	N. L.	(In U. S. Army Air Force)										
1946	St. Louis	N. L.	OF	*156	609	100	183	30	8	18	*130	9	.300
1947	St. Louis	N. L.	OF	147	551	100	162	31	13	10	86	4	.294
1948	St. Louis	N. L.	OF	146	549	91	176	27	11	11	90	4	.321

Year	Club	Lea	Pos	G	AB	R	H	2B	3B	HR	RBI	SB	Avg
1949	St. Louis	N. L.	OF	151	568	92	191	34	*13	13	96	3	.336
1950	St. Louis	N. L.	OF	148	556	82	161	26	7	10	101	3	.290
1951	St. Louis	N. L.	OF	123	409	48	115	17	8	4	64	7	.281
1952	St. Louis	N. L.	OF	140	510	73	153	17	12	11	101	6	.300
1953	St. Louis	N. L.	OF	143	492	64	143	34	9	6	89	4	.291
Major League Totals			13 Yrs	1820	6775	1071	2064	366	135	146	1148	64	.305
World's Series Record													
1942	St. Louis	N. L.	OF	5	19	3	5	1	0	1	2	0	.263
1946	St. Louis	N. L.	OF	7	25	5	8	1	1	1	2	1	.320
World Series Totals				12	44	8	13	2	1	2	4	1	.295

SMALLEY, ROY FREDERICK

Born, Springfield, Missouri, June 9, 1926.
Bats Right. Throws Right. Height, 6 feet, 3 inches. Weight, 185 pounds.

Year	Club	Lea	Pos	G	AB	R	H	2B	3B	HR	RBI	SB	Avg
1944	Los Angeles	P. C. L.	SS	61	160	13	30	3	0	1	11	1	.188
1945	Los Angeles	P. C. L.	(In Military Service)										
1946	Los Angeles	P. C. L.	SS	9	28	1	6	0	1	0	1	..	.214
1946	Shelby	Tri-St.	SS	30	105	16	23	3	1	4	14	1	.219
1946	Davenport	I. I. L.	3B	2	5	0	0	0	0	0	1	0	.000
1947	Des Moines	W. L.	SS	114	410	45	100	13	8	7	55	6	.244
1948	Chicago	N. L.	SS	124	361	25	78	11	4	4	36	0	.216
1949	Chicago	N. L.	SS	135	477	57	117	21	10	8	35	2	.245
1950	Chicago	N. L.	SS	154	557	58	128	21	9	21	85	2	.230
1951	Chicago a	N. L.	SS	79	238	24	55	7	4	8	31	0	.231
1952	Chicago	N. L.	SS	87	261	36	58	14	1	5	30	0	.222
1953	Chicago	N. L.	SS	82	253	20	63	9	0	6	25	0	.249
Major League Totals			6 Yrs	661	2147	220	499	83	28	52	242	4	.232

a Suffered broken left leg, April 28, and did not play until July 1.

SMITH, PAUL LESLIE

Born, New Castle, Pennsylvania, March 19, 1931.
Bats Left. Throws Left. Height, 5 feet, 8½ inches. Weight, 165 pounds.

Year	Club	Lea	Pos	G	AB	R	H	2B	3B	HR	RBI	SB	Avg
1950	Tallahassee	Ga.-Fla.	OF	139	*615	127	*196	24	8	7	76	43	.319
1951	Waco	Big St.	OF	143	552	118	178	28	8	10	62	15	.322
1952	New Orleans	S. A.	OF	153	604	95	195	27	7	5	55	23	.323
1953	Pittsburgh	N. L.	1B-OF	118	389	41	110	12	7	4	44	8	.283

SNIDER, EDWIN DONALD (DUKE)

Born, Los Angeles, California, September 19, 1926.
Bats Left. Throws Right. Height, 6 feet. Weight, 185 pounds.

Year	Club	Lea	Pos	G	AB	R	H	2B	3B	HR	RBI	SB	Avg
1944	Montreal	I. L.	PH	2	2	0	0	0	0	0	0	0	.000
1944	Newport News	Pied.	OF	131	507	87	149	34	6	9	50	10	.294
1945-46	Newport News	Pied.	(In Military Service)										
1946	Fort Worth	T. L.	OF	68	232	36	58	13	1	5	30	5	.250
1947	St. Paul	A. A.	OF	66	269	59	85	22	7	12	46	4	.316
1947	Brooklyn	N. L.	OF	40	83	6	20	3	1	0	5	2	.241
1948	Montreal	I. L.	OF	77	275	67	90	28	4	17	77	8	.327
1948	Brooklyn	N. L.	OF	53	160	22	39	6	6	5	21	4	.244
1949	Brooklyn	N. L.	OF	146	552	100	161	28	7	23	92	12	.292
1950	Brooklyn	N. L.	OF	152	620	109	*199	31	10	31	107	16	.321
1951	Brooklyn	N. L.	OF	150	606	96	168	26	6	29	101	14	.277
1952	Brooklyn	N. L.	OF	144	534	80	162	25	7	21	92	7	.303
1953	Brooklyn	N. L.	OF	153	590	*132	198	38	4	42	126	16	.336
Major League Totals			7 Yrs	838	3145	545	947	157	41	151	544	71	.301
World's Series Record													
1949	Brooklyn	N. L.	OF	5	21	2	3	1	0	0	0	0	.143
1952	Brooklyn	N. L.	OF	7	29	5	10	2	0	4	8	1	.345
1953	Brooklyn	N. L.	OF	6	25	3	8	3	0	1	5	0	.320
World's Series Totals				18	75	10	21	6	0	5	13	1	.280

SOUCHOCK, STEPHEN

Born, Yatesboro, Pennsylvania, March 8, 1919.
Bats Right. Throws Right. Height, 6 feet, 2 inches. Weight, 200 pounds.

Year	Club	Lea	Pos	G	AB	R	H	2B	3B	HR	RBI	SB	Avg
1939	Greensburg	Pa. St.	1B	39	136	31	39	5	0	4	26	10	.287
1939	Easton	E. S. L.	1B	65	241	85	62	14	9	8	36	5	.257
1940	Akron	M. A. L.	1B	•128	496	97	154	23	8	24	105	14	.310
1941	Binghamton	E. L.	1B	4	16	7	6	0	1	0	8	..	.375
1941	Norfolk	Pied.	1B-3B	125	474	82	129	18	15	8	69	10	.272
1942	Kansas City	A. A.	1B	8	28	4	6	1	0	2	5	..	.214
1942	Binghamton	E. L.	1B	129	476	•94	150	•29	•15	13	•91	25	•.315
1943-44-45	New York	A. L.	(In U. S. Army)										
1946	New York	A. L.	1B	47	86	15	26	8	8	2	10	0	.302
1947	Kansas City	A. A.	1B	136	528	86	155	25	11	17	99	19	.294
1948	New York a	A. L.	1B	44	118	11	24	8	1	3	11	3	.203
1949	Chicago	A. L.	1B-OF	84	252	29	59	13	5	7	37	5	.234
1950	Sacramento b	P. C. L.	INF	174	625	104	182	27	6	30	99	12	.291
1951	Detroit	A. L.	OF-1B-2B-3B	91	188	33	46	10	8	11	28	0	.245
1952	Detroit	A. L.	OF-3B-1B	92	265	40	66	16	4	13	45	1	.249
1953	Detroit	A. L.	OF-1B	89	278	29	84	13	3	11	46	5	.302
Major League Totals			6 Yrs	447	1187	157	305	58	19	47	177	14	.257

a Traded to Chicago White Sox for Jim Delsing, December 14, 1948.
b Drafted by Detroit, November 16, 1950.

SPENCER, DARYL DEAN

Born, Wichita, Kansas, July 13, 1929.
Bats Right. Throws Right. Height, 6 feet, 2½ inches. Weight, 185 pounds.

Year	Club	Lea	Pos	G	AB	R	H	2B	3B	HR	RBI	SB	Avg
1949	Pauls Valley	Soon. St.	SS	140	528	113	151	29	4	•23	112	20	.286
1950	Sioux City	Western	SS	•156	576	108	162	36	8	23	99	5	.281
1951	Nashville	S. A.	SS	120	398	67	100	28	8	8	61	2	.251
1952	Minneapolis	A. A.	SS	142	523	85	154	35	2	27	80	5	.294
1952	New York	N. L.	SS-3B	7	17	0	5	0	1	0	3	0	.294
1953	New York	N. L.	SS-3B-2B	118	408	55	85	18	5	20	56	0	.208
Major League Totals			2 Yrs	125	425	55	90	18	6	20	59	0	.212

STANKY, EDWARD RAYMOND

Born, Philadelphia, Pennsylvania, September 3, 1917.
Bats Right. Throws Right. Height, 5 feet, 8 inches. Weight, 165 pounds.

Year	Club	Lea	Pos	G	AB	R	H	2B	3B	HR	RBI	SB	Avg
1935	Greenville	E. Dix. L.	SS	104	396	80	119	25	4	2	46	4	.301
1936	Portsmouth	M. A. L.	3B-SS-P	111	436	96	147	23	8	8	55	9	.337
1936	Williamsport	N.Y.-P. L.	2B	11	37	5	12	1	0	0	5	1	.324
1937	Williamsport	N.Y.-P. L.	OF-2B	14	40	3	9	3	0	0	3	3	.225
1937	Portsmouth	Pied.	2B	90	314	71	86	21	1	9	36	°	.274
1938	Portsmouth	Pied.	2B-SS	137	473	110	134	18	4	9	55	15	.283
1939	Portsmouth	Pied.	3B	11	37	9	8	2	0	1	8	1	.216
1939	Macon	S. A. L.	2B-SS	123	449	109	137	28	7	4	33	17	.305
1940	Macon	S. A. L.	SS	138	529	116	160	36	3	8	55	18	.302
1941	Macon	S. A. L.	SS	139	505	112	159	26	5	1	84	11	.315
1942	Milwaukee	A. A.	SS	145	527	•124	180	•56	6	8	57	6	•.342
1943	Chicago	N. L.	2B-SS-3B	142	510	92	125	15	1	0	47	4	.245
1944	Chicago-Brooklyn a	N. L.	2B-SS-3B	102	286	36	78	9	3	0	16	4	.273
1945	Brooklyn	N. L.	2B-SS	153	555	•128	143	29	5	1	39	6	.258
1946	Brooklyn	N. L.	2B	144	483	98	132	24	7	0	36	8	.273
1947	Brooklyn	N. L.	2B	146	559	97	141	24	5	3	53	8	.252
1948	Boston b	N. L.	2B	67	247	49	79	14	2	2	29	3	.320
1949	Boston c	N. L.	2B	138	506	90	144	24	5	1	42	8	.285
1950	New York	N. L.	2B	152	527	115	158	25	5	8	51	9	.300
1951	New York d	N. L.	2B	145	515	88	127	17	2	14	43	8	.247
1952	St. Louis	N. L.	2B	53	83	13	19	4	0	0	7	0	.229
1953	St. Louis	N. L.	2B	17	30	5	8	0	0	1	0	0	.267
Major League Totals			11 Yrs	1259	4301	811	1154	185	35	29	364	48	.268
World's Series Record													
1947	Brooklyn	N. L.	2B	7	25	4	6	1	0	0	2	0	.240
1948	Boston	N. L.	2B	6	14	0	4	1	0	0	1	0	.286
1951	New York	N. L.	2B	6	22	3	3	0	0	0	1	0	.136
World's Series Totals				19	61	7	13	2	0	0	4	0	.213

c Traded to Brooklyn, June 7th for pitcher Bob Chipman.
b Traded to Boston for Carvel Rowell and an estimated $100,000, March 6, 1948.
c Traded with Alvin Dark to New York Giants for Sid Gordon, Willard Marshall, Buddy Kerr and Sam Webb, December 14, 1949.
d Traded to St. Louis for Max Lanier and Charles E Diering, December 10, 1951. Stanky succeeded Marty Marion as manager of St. Louis.

STEPHENS, VERNON DECATUR, JR. (JUNIOR)

Born. McAllister, New Mexico, October 23, 1920.
Bats Right. Throws Right. Height, 5 feet, 10½ inches. Weight, 185 pounds.

Year	Club	Lea	Pos	G	AB	R	H	2B	3B	HR	RBI	SB	Avg
1938	Springfield	I. I. I.	2B-3B	2	5	0	0	0	0	0	0	0	.000
1938	Johnstown	M. A. L.	SS	40	136	23	35	15	0	2	18	0	.257
1939	Mayfield	Kitty	SS	122	485	105	175	*44	7	30	*128	6	*.361
1940	San Antonio	T. L.	SS	159	598	60	159	27	6	22	*97	3	.266
1941	Toledo	A. A.	SS	153	*616	95	173	33	11	14	74	10	.281
1941	St. Louis	A. L.	SS	3	2	0	1	0	0	0	0	0	.500
1942	St. Louis	A. L.	SS	145	575	84	169	26	6	14	92	1	.294
1943	St. Louis	A. L.	OF-SS	137	512	75	148	27	3	22	91	8	.289
1944	St. Louis	A. L.	SS	145	559	91	164	32	1	20	*109	2	.293
1945	St. Louis	A. L.	3B-SS	149	571	90	165	27	3	*24	89	2	.289
1946	St. Louis	A. L.	SS	115	450	67	138	19	4	14	64	0	.307
1947	St. Louis a	A. L.	SS	150	562	74	157	18	4	15	83	8	.279
1948	Boston	A. L.	SS	*155	635	114	171	25	8	29	137	1	.269
1949	Boston	A. L.	SS	*155	610	113	177	31	2	39	*159	2	.290
1950	Boston	A. L.	SS	149	628	125	185	34	6	30	*144	1	.295
1951	Boston	A. L.	3B-SS	109	377	62	113	21	2	17	78	1	.300
1952	Boston b	A. L.	SS-3B	92	295	35	75	13	2	7	44	2	.254
1953	Chic.-St. L. c	A. L.	3B-SS	90	294	30	77	14	0	5	31	2	.262

Major League Totals				13 Yrs	1594	6070	960	1740	287	41	236	1121	25	.287

World's Series Record

1944	St. Louis	A. L.	SS	6	22	2	5	1	0	0	0	0	.227

a Traded to Boston Red Sox with Jack Kramer for Pete Layden, Joe Ostrowski, Don Palmer, Ed Pellagrini, Roy Partee, Al Widmar and Jim Wilson and estimated $300,000 in cash. November 17, 1947.

b Traded to Chicago White Sox for Hector Brown, Marvin Grissom and Bill Kennedy, February 14, 1953.

c Sold to St. Louis Browns, July 31, 1953.

STEWART, EDWARD PERRY

Born, Sacramento, California, June 15, 1916.
Bats Left. Throws Right. Height, 5 feet, 11 inches. Weight, 160 pounds.

Year	Club	Lea	Pos	G	AB	R	H	2B	3B	HR	RBI	SB	Avg
1937	San Diego	P. C. L.	OF	9	8	2	0	0	0	0	0	0	.000
1938	San Diego	P. C. L.	OF	94	230	33	62	8	2	0	15	0	.270
1939	San Diego	P. C. L.	OF-3B	61	186	33	57	10	8	4	17	1	.306
1939	Bellingham	W. I. L.	3B-OF	74	294	67	94	19	3	2	31	12	.320
1940	San Diego	P. C. L.	OF	*179	*723	107	231	32	12	6	71	10	.320
1941	Pittsburgh	N. L.	OF	73	172	27	46	7	0	0	10	3	.267
1942	Pittsburgh	N. L.	OF-3B-2B	82	183	21	40	8	4	0	20	2	.219
1943-44	Pittsburgh	N. L.	(Voluntarily Retired)										
1945	Hollywood a	P. C. L.	OF	63	251	38	81	6	3	0	34	9	.323
1946	Hollywood	P. C. L.	OF	33	246	43	70	12	5	2	32	8	.285
1947	Kansas City	A. A.	3B-OF	145	528	107	189	33	*17	7	102	16	.358
1948	New York-Wash. b	A. L.	OF	124	406	57	113	18	13	7	69	8	.278
1949	Washington	A. L.	OF	118	388	53	110	23	4	8	43	6	.284
1950	Washington c	A. L.	OF	118	373	46	101	15	6	4	35	5	.267
1951	Chicago	A. L.	OF	95	217	40	60	13	5	6	40	1	.276
1952	Chicago	A. L.	OF	92	225	23	60	10	0	5	30	3	.267
1953	Chicago d	A. L.	OF	53	59	16	16	2	0	2	13	1	.271

Major League Totals				8 Yrs	755	2028	288	546	96	32	32	260	29	.269

a In Military Service, June 1945 to May 1946.

b Traded to Washington for Leon Culberson and $15,000, May 13, 1948.

c Traded to Chicago White Sox for Mike McCormick, December 11, 1950.

d On disabled list, April 18 to June 8.

STRICKLAND, GEORGE BEVAN

Born, New Orleans, Louisiana, January 10, 1926.
Bats Right. Throws Right. Height, 6 feet, 1 inch. Weight, 175 pounds.

Year	Club	Lea	Pos	G	AB	R	H	2B	3B	HR	RBI	SB	Avg
1943	New Orleans	S. A.	SB	8	8	0	2	0	0	0	0	0	.250
1944-45	New Orleans	S. A.	(In Military Service)										
1946	New Orleans	S. A.	3B	73	231	25	56	11	1	2	23	5	.242
1947	Scranton	E. L.	3B-SS	134	452	70	106	20	7	4	78	11	.235
1948	Louisville	A. A.	SS-3B-1B	105	367	53	87	8	9	1	39	5	.237
1948	Scranton	E. L.	3B	35	114	5	21	1	1	0	10	0	.184
1949	Birmingham a	S. A.	SS	128	417	56	109	18	5	5	66	5	.261
1950	Pittsburgh	N. L.	SS-3B	23	27	0	3	0	0	0	2	0	.111
1951	Pittsburgh	N. L.	SS-2B	138	454	59	98	12	7	9	47	4	.216

Year	Club	Lea	Pos	G	AB	R	H	2B	3B	HR	RBI	SB	Avg
1952	Pittsburgh b	N. L.	INF	76	232	17	41	6	2	5	22	4	.177
1952	Cleveland	A. L.	SS-2B	31	88	8	19	4	0	1	8	0	.216
1953	Cleveland	A. L.	SS-1B	123	419	43	119	17	4	5	47	0	.284

Major League Totals 4 Yrs 891 1220 127 280 39 13 20 126 8 .230

a Drafted by Pittsburgh, November 17, 1949.
b Traded with Ted Wilks to Cleveland for John Berardino, Charles Sipple and cash, August 18, 1952.

SUDER, PETER

Born, Aliquippa, Pa., April 16, 1917.
Bats Right. Throws Right. Height, 6 feet. Weight, 175 pounds.

Year	Club	Lea	Pos	G	AB	R	H	2B	3B	HR	RBI	SB	Avg
1935	Washington	P. S. A.	3B	100	384	49	113	17	*18	2	46	2	.294
1936	Akron	M. A. L.	SS-3B	125	511	88	158	33	8	13	84	6	.309
1937	Norfolk	P. L.	SS-3B	137	547	100	164	34	4	22	108	15	.300
1938	Binghamton	E. L.	3B	135	539	78	150	23	5	10	97	9	.278
1939	Newark	I. L.	3B	42	143	14	85	5	8	2	17	1	.236
1939	Binghamton	E. L.	3B	67	258	83	64	11	2	4	25	4	.248
1940	Binghamton a	E. L.	3B	140	*571	78	*172	25	6	16	78	9	.301
1941	Philadelphia	A. L.	SS-3B	139	531	45	130	20	9	4	52	1	.245
1942	Philadelphia	A. L.	SS-3B-2B	123	476	46	122	20	4	4	54	4	.256
1943	Philadelphia	A. L.	2B-3B-SS	131	475	30	105	14	5	8	41	1	.221
1944-45	Philadelphia	A. L.	(In U. S. Army)										
1946	Philadelphia	A. L.	INF-OF	123	455	38	128	20	8	2	50	1	.281
1947	Philadelphia	A. L.	2B-SS-3B	145	528	45	127	28	4	5	60	0	.241
1948	Philadelphia	A. L.	2B	148	519	64	125	28	5	7	60	1	.241
1949	Philadelphia	A. L.	2B-3B-SS	118	445	44	119	24	6	10	75	0	.267
1950	Philadelphia	A. L.	INF	77	248	34	61	10	0	8	35	2	.246
1951	Philadelphia	A. L.	2B-SS-3B	123	440	46	108	18	1	1	43	5	.245
1952	Philadelphia	A. L.	2B-SS-3B	74	228	22	55	7	2	1	20	1	.241
1953	Philadelphia	A. L.	3B-2B-SS	115	454	44	130	11	8	4	85	8	.286

Major League Totals 11 Yrs 1326 4799 458 1210 195 42 49 524 19 .252

a Drafted by Philadelphia from Kansas City, October 1940.

TEMPLE, JOHN ELLIS

Born, Lexington, N. C., Aug. 8, 1929.
Bats Right. Throws Right. Height, 5 feet, 11 inches. Weight, 175 pounds.

Year	Club	Lea	Pos	G	AB	R	H	2B	3B	HR	RBI	SB	Avg
1948	Morganton	W. Car.	SS	59	263	54	83	15	6	7	89	9	.816
1949	Ogden	Pioneer	SS	116	500	122	*200	17	6	8	78	25	*.400
1950	Columbia	So. Atl.	SS-3B	130	519	75	167	17	8	1	66	7	.822
1951	Tulsa	Texas	2B	154	612	80	*180	24	5	0	52	*30	.294
1952	Tulsa	Texas	2B	103	435	64	133	32	2	2	81	19	.306
1952	Cincinnati	N. L.	2B	30	97	8	19	3	0	1	5	2	.196
1953	Cincinnati	N. L.	2B	63	110	14	29	4	0	1	9	1	.264

Major League Totals 2 Yrs 93 207 22 48 7 0 2 14 8 .232

TERWILLIGER, WILLARD WAYNE

Born, Clare, Michigan, June 27, 1925.
Bats Right. Throws Right. Height, 5 feet, 11 inches. Weight, 165 pounds.

Year	Club	Lea	Pos	G	AB	R	H	2B	3B	HR	RBI	SB	Avg
1948	Des Moines	West.	2B	18	46	10	9	2	0	0	4	2	.196
1949	Los Angeles	P. C. L.	2B	115	432	80	119	28	2	8	46	18	.275
1949	Chicago	N. L.	2B	36	112	11	25	2	1	2	10	0	.223
1950	Chicago	N. L.	INF-OF	133	480	63	116	22	8	10	32	13	.242
1951	Chic.-Brooklyn a	N. L.	2B-3B	87	242	37	55	7	0	0	14	4	.227
1952	St. Paul b	A. A.	INF-OF	77	125	32	39	6	0	4	17	1	.312
1953	Washington	A. L.	2B	134	464	62	117	24	4	4	46	7	.252

Major League Totals 4 Yrs 890 1298 173 313 55 8 16 102 24 .241

a Traded to Brooklyn with Andy Pafko, Johnny Schmitz and Al Walker for Bruce Edwards, Joe Hatten, Gene Hermanski and Eddie Miksis, June 15, 1951.
b Recalled by Brooklyn and released to Washington on waivers, September 23, 1952.

THOMAS, FRANK JOSEPH

Born, Pittsburgh, Pennsylvania, June 11, 1929.
Bats Right. Throws Right. Height, 6 feet, 8 inches. Weight, 205 pounds.

Year	Club	Lea	Pos	G	AB	R	H	2B	3B	HR	RBI	SB	Avg
1948	Tallahassee	Ga.-Fla.	3B	138	*596	106	176	89	8	14	*182	6	.295
1949	Davenport	I. I. L.	OF-3B	18	43	7	10	2	1	0	7	1	.233
1949	Tallahassee	Ga.-Fla.	OF	74	285	46	93	19	2	10	63	2	.326

Year	Club	Lea	Pos	G	AB	R	H	2B	3B	HR	RBI	SB	Avg
1949	Waco	Big St.	OF	20	73	17	25	3	0	4	17	1	.342
1950	Charleston	S.A.L.	OF	82	318	50	98	20	4	11	55	6	.308
1950	New Orleans	S.A.	OF	47	148	21	39	6	1	8	18	2	.264
1951	New Orleans	S.A.	OF	125	471	64	136	25	6	23	85	3	.289
1951	Pittsburgh	N.L.	OF	39	148	21	39	9	2	2	16	0	.264
1952	New Orleans	S.A.	OF	154	597	*112	181	40	6	*35	*131	1	.308
1952	Pittsburgh	N.L.	OF	6	21	1	2	0	0	0	0	0	.095
1953	Pittsburgh	N.L.	OF	128	455	63	116	22	1	30	102	1	.255
Major League Totals				3 Yrs	173	624	90	157	31	3	32	118	1	.252

THOMAS, KEITH MARSHALL

Born, Kansas City, Kansas, April 27, 1924.
Bats Right. Throws Right. Height, 6 feet, 1½ inches. Weight, 195 pounds.

Year	Club	Lea	Pos	G	AB	R	H	2B	3B	HR	RBI	SB	Avg
1947	Joplin	W.A.	OF	60	229	41	73	18	6	4	45	6	.319
1948	Quincy	I.I.I.	OF	125	479	87	150	24	7	17	*99	2	.313
1949	Kansas City	A.A.	1B	6	25	8	7	0	0	1	6	0	.280
1949	Beaumont	T.L.	OF-1B	134	469	66	128	23	4	23	80	2	.273
1950	Beaumont	T.L.	OF	149	552	109	156	42	8	16	111	5	.283
1951	Kansas City a	A.A.	OF-1B	138	471	59	133	24	6	14	81	0	.282
1952	Philadelphia	A.L.	OF	75	116	24	29	6	1	6	18	0	.250
1953	Phila.-Wash. b	A.L.	OF-C	62	107	11	23	3	2	1	14	0	.215
Major League Totals				2 Yrs	137	223	35	52	9	3	7	32	0	.233

a Drafted by Philadelphia Athletics, November 19, 1951.
b Traded to Washington for Carmen Mauro in waiver deal, June 30, 1953.

THOMPSON, DONALD NEWLIN

Born, Swepsonville, North Carolina, December 23, 1923.
Bats Left. Throws Left. Height, 6 feet. Weight, 185 pounds.

Year	Club	Lea	Pos	G	AB	R	H	2B	3B	HR	RBI	SB	Avg
1943	Roanoke	Pied.	P-OF	12	26	4	4	2	0	0	2	0	.154
1944	Scranton	E.L.	P	54	94	16	23	2	1	0	9	0	.245
1945	Louisville	A.A.	P-OF	34	46	9	12	2	3	0	6	0	.261
1945	Scranton	E.L.	P-OF	14	26	4	8	1	1	0	4	0	.308
1946	Louisville	A.A.	P	1	1	0	0	0	0	0	0	0	.000
1946	Scranton	E.L.	P-OF-1B	15	15	0	3	0	0	0	0	0	.200
1947	Louisville	A.A.	P	1	0	0	0	0	0	0	0	0	.000
1947	Roanoke	Pied.	P	2	2	0	1	1	0	0	0	1	.500
1947	Milford	E.S.L.	OF	107	415	93	136	23	11	6	70	33	.328
1948	Columbus a	A.A.	OF	121	446	79	127	24	3	4	51	9	.285
1949	Boston	N.L.	OF	7	11	0	2	0	0	0	0	0	.182
1949	Rochester	I.L.	OF	94	355	45	86	18	3	3	42	6	.242
1950	Montreal	I.L.	OF	142	515	91	160	24	8	11	87	16	.311
1951	Brooklyn	N.L.	OF	80	118	25	27	3	0	0	6	2	.229
1952	Montreal	I.L.	OF	71	249	42	86	9	5	4	58	11	.346
1953	Brooklyn	N.L.	OF	96	153	25	37	5	0	1	12	2	.242
Major League Totals				3 Yrs	183	282	50	66	8	0	1	18	4	.234
World's Series Record													
1953	Brooklyn	N.L.	OF	2	0	0	0	0	0	0	0	0	.000

a Drafted by Boston Braves, November 10, 1948.

THOMPSON, HENRY (HANK)

Born, Oklahoma City, Oklahoma, December 8, 1925.
Bats Left. Throws Right. Height, 5 feet, 9½ inches. Weight, 175 pounds.

Year	Club	Lea	Pos	G	AB	R	H	2B	3B	HR	RBI	SB	Avg
1947	St. Louis	A.L.	2B	27	78	10	20	1	1	0	5	2	.256
1948	(Played in Negro National League)												
1949	Jersey City	I.L.	SS-OF-2B	68	230	53	68	14	3	14	37	11	.296
1949	New York	N.L.	2B-3B	75	275	51	77	10	4	9	34	5	.280
1950	New York	N.L.	3B-OF	148	512	82	148	17	6	20	91	8	.289
1951	Minneapolis	A.A.	3B-OF-SS	14	53	18	18	2	0	7	13	5	.340
1951	New York	N.L.	3B	87	264	37	62	8	4	8	33	1	.235
1952	New York	N.L.	OF-3B-2B	128	423	67	110	13	9	17	67	4	.260
1953	New York	N.L.	3B-OF-2B	114	388	80	117	15	3	24	74	6	.302
Major League Totals				6 Yrs	579	1940	327	534	64	32	73	304	26	.275
World's Series Record													
1951	New York	N.L.	OF	5	14	3	2	0	0	0	0	0	.143

THOMSON, ROBERT BROWN

Born, Glasgow, Scotland, October 25, 1923.
Bats Right.   Throws Right.   Height, 6 feet, 2 inches.   Weight, 185 pounds.

Year	Club	Lea	Pos	G	AB	R	H	2B	3B	HR	RBI	SB	Avg
1942	Bristol	Appal.	3B	6	12	1	3	0	1	0	0	0	.250
1942	Rocky Mount	Bi-St.	3B	29	87	15	21	4	0	3	18	0	.241
1943, 1944, 1945			(In United States Military Service)										
1946	Jersey City	I. L.	3B-OF	151	533	93	149	12	7	26	92	15	.280
1946	New York	N. L.	3B	18	54	8	17	4	1	2	9	0	.315
1947	New York	N. L.	2B-OF	138	545	105	154	26	5	29	85	1	.283
1948	New York	N. L.	OF	138	471	75	117	20	2	16	63	2	.248
1949	New York	N. L.	OF	156	641	99	198	35	9	27	109	10	.309
1950	New York	N. L.	OF	149	563	79	142	22	7	25	85	3	.252
1951	New York	N. L.	OF-3B	148	518	89	152	27	8	32	101	5	.293
1952	New York	N. L.	3B-OF	153	608	89	164	29	*14	24	108	5	.270
1953	New York	N. L.	OF	154	608	80	175	22	6	26	106	4	.288

Major League Totals			8 Yrs	1054	4008	624	1119	185	52	181	666	30	.279
World's Series Record													
1951	New York	N. L.	3B	6	21	1	5	1	0	0	2	0	.238

TIPTON, JOSEPH JOHN

Born, Copperhill, Tennessee, February 18, 1922.
Bats Right.   Throws Right.   Height, 5 feet, 11½ inches.   Weight, 185 pounds.

Year	Club	Lea	Pos	G	AB	R	H	2B	3B	HR	RBI	SB	Avg
1941	Appleton	Wis.-St.	OF-C-3B-P	59	215	54	64	18	0	11	46	7	.298
1941	Flint	M. S. L.	OF-3B	10	33	5	12	3	0	2	7	0	.364
1942	Charleston	M. A. L.	C-OF	81	262	38	82	17	3	0	32	4	.313
1943-44-45	W.-Barre	E. L.	(In Military Service)										
1946	Harrisburg	Inter-St.	C-OF	104	324	59	106	28	2	7	68	3	.327
1947	Wilkes-Barre	E. L.	C	108	371	61	139	23	3	2	66	4	*.375
1948	Cleveland a	A. L.	C	47	90	11	26	3	0	1	13	0	.289
1949	Chicago b	A. L.	C	67	191	20	39	5	3	8	19	1	.204
1950	Philadelphia	A. L.	C	64	184	15	49	5	1	6	20	0	.266
1951	Philadelphia	A. L.	C	72	213	23	51	9	0	3	20	1	.239
1952	Phila.-Cleveland c	A. L.	C	66	173	21	39	6	0	9	30	1	.225
1953	Cleveland	A. L.	C	47	109	17	25	2	0	6	13	0	.229

Major League Totals			6 Yrs	363	960	107	229	30	4	28	115	3	.239
World's Series Record													
1948	Cleveland	A. L.	PH	1	1	0	0	0	0	0	0	0	.000

a Traded to Chicago, A.L., for Joe Haynes, November 24, 1948.
b Traded to Athletics for Nelson Fox, October 18, 1949.
c Sold by Philadelphia to Cleveland for $10,000 waiver price, June 23, 1952.

TORGESON, CLIFFORD EARL

Born, Snohomish, Washington, January 1, 1924.
Bats Left.   Throws Left.   Height, 6 feet, 3 inches.   Weight, 180 pounds.

Year	Club	Lea	Pos	G	AB	R	H	2B	3B	HR	RBI	SB	Avg
1941	Wenatchee	W. I. L.	1B	92	340	59	113	13	9	1	44	8	.332
1941	Seattle	P. C. L.	1B-OF	4	10	1	5	1	0	0	0	..	.500
1942	Spokane	W. I. L.	OF	7	28	12	12	2	4	0	8	7	.429
1942	Seattle	P. C. L.	1B	147	523	63	163	20	9	4	52	32	.312
1943-44-45	Seattle	P. C. L.	(In Military Service)										
1946	Seattle	P. C. L.	1B	103	354	46	101	18	5	5	53	20	.285
1947	Boston	N. L.	1B	128	399	73	112	20	6	16	78	11	.281
1948	Boston	N. L.	1B	134	438	70	111	23	5	10	67	19	.253
1949	Boston a	N. L.	1B	25	100	17	26	5	1	4	19	4	.260
1950	Boston	N. L.	1B	156	576	*120	167	30	3	23	87	15	.290
1951	Boston	N. L.	1B	155	581	99	153	21	4	24	92	20	.263
1952	Boston b	N. L.	1B-OF	122	382	49	88	17	0	5	34	11	.230
1953	Philadelphia	N. L.	1B	111	379	58	104	25	8	11	64	7	.274

Major League Totals			7 Yrs	831	2855	486	761	141	27	93	441	87	.267
World's Series Record													
1948	Boston	N. L.	1B	5	18	2	7	3	0	0	1	1	.389

a Injured left shoulder, May 14, and out for rest of season.
b Traded to Philadelphia Phillies for Russ Meyer, February 16, 1953 as part of four-club deal.

UMPHLETT, THOMAS MULLEN

Born, Scotland Neck, North Carolina, May 12, 1931.
Bats Right. Throws Right. Height, 6 feet, 1 inch. Weight, 180 pounds.

Year	Club	Lea	Pos	G	AB	R	H	2B	3B	HR	RBI	SB	Avg
1950	Marion	Ohio-Ind.	OF	94	367	80	117	16	10	8	66	9	.319
1951	H. Pt.-Th'ville	N. C. St.	OF	112	435	82	135	24	5	14	79	20	.310
1952	Louisville	A. A.	OF	124	518	75	144	24	9	8	80	6	.278
1953	Boston a	A. L.	OF	137	495	53	140	27	5	3	59	4	.283

a Traded to Washington with Maurice McDermott for Jack Jensen, Dec. 8, 1953.

VALO, ELMER WILLIAM

Born, Ribnik, Czechoslovakia, March 5, 1921.
Bats Left. Throws Right. Height, 5 feet, 10½ inches. Weight, 190 pounds.

Year	Club	Lea	Pos	G	AB	R	H	2B	3B	HR	RBI	SB	Avg
1939	Federalsburg	E. S. L.	OF	34	115	28	43	9	2	3	19	7	.374
1940	Wilmington	Inter-St.	OF	120	437	89	*159	*31	*16	6	80	31	*.364
1940	Philadelphia	A. L.	OF	6	23	6	8	0	0	0	2		.348
1941	Wilmington	Inter-St.	OF	125	447	80	145	14	7	11	67	14	.324
1941	Philadelphia	A. L.	OF	15	50	13	21	0	1	2	6	0	.420
1942	Philadelphia	A. L.	OF	133	459	64	115	13	10	2	40	13	.251
1943	Philadelphia	A. L.	OF	77	249	31	55	6	2	3	18	2	.221
1944-45	Philadelphia	A. L.		(In U. S. Army)									
1946	Philadelphia	A. L.	OF	108	348	59	107	21	6	1	31	9	.307
1947	Philadelphia	A. L.	OF	112	370	60	111	12	6	5	36	11	.300
1948	Philadelphia	A. L.	OF	113	383	72	117	17	4	3	46	10	.305
1949	Philadelphia	A. L.	OF	150	547	86	155	27	12	5	85	14	.283
1950	Philadelphia	A. L.	OF	129	446	62	125	16	5	10	46	12	.280
1951	Philadelphia	A. L.	OF	123	444	75	134	27	8	7	55	11	.302
1952	Philadelphia	A. L.	OF	129	388	69	109	26	4	5	47	12	.281
1953	Philadelphia	A. L.	OF	50	85	15	19	8	0	0	9	0	.224

Major League Totals — 12 Yrs 1145 3792 612 1076 168 58 43 419 96 .284

VERNON, JAMES BARTON (MICKEY)

Born, Marcus Hook, Pa., April 22, 1918.
Bats Left. Throws Left. Height, 6 feet, 2 inches. Weight, 170 pounds.

Year	Club	Lea	Pos	G	AB	R	H	2B	3B	HR	RBI	SB	Avg
1937	Easton	E. S. L.	1B	83	300	51	86	24	6	10	64	11	.287
1938	Greenville	S. A. L.	1B	132	524	84	172	31	12	1	72	20	.328
1939	Springfield	E. L.	1B	69	268	52	92	13	7	3	41	4	.343
1939	Washington	A. L.	1B	76	276	23	71	15	4	1	30	1	.257
1940	Jersey City	I. L.	1B	154	569	76	161	22	9	9	65	13	.283
1940	Washington	A. L.	1B	5	19	0	3	0	0	0	0	0	.158
1941	Washington	A. L.	1B	138	531	73	159	27	11	9	93	9	.299
1942	Washington	A. L.	1B	151	621	76	168	34	6	9	86	25	.271
1943	Washington	A. L.	1B	145	553	89	148	29	8	7	70	24	.268
1944-45	Washington	A. L.		(In U. S. Navy)									
1946	Wash'ngton	A. L.	1B	148	587	88	207	*51	8	8	85	14	*.353
1947	Washington	A. L.	1B	154	600	77	159	29	12	7	85	12	.265
1948	Washington a	A. L.	1B	150	558	78	135	27	7	3	48	15	.242
1949	Cleveland	A. L.	1B	153	584	72	170	27	4	18	83	9	.291
1950	Cleveland-Wash. b	A. L.	1B	118	417	55	117	17	3	9	75	8	.281
1951	Washington	A. L.	1B	141	546	69	160	30	7	9	87	7	.293
1952	Washington	A. L.	1B	154	569	71	143	33	9	10	80	7	.251
1953	Washington	A. L.	1B	152	608	101	205	*43	11	15	115	4	*.337

Major League Totals — 18 Yrs 1685 6469 872 1845 362 90 105 937 135 .285
a Traded with Early Wynn to Cleveland, December 14, for Ed Robinson, Ed Klieman and Joe Haynes.
b Traded to Washington for Dick Weik, June 14.

VOLLMER, CLYDE FRED

Born, Cincinnati, Ohio, September 24, 1921.
Bats Right. Throws Right. Height, 6 feet, 1 inch. Weight, 190 pounds.

Year	Club	Lea	Pos	G	AB	R	H	2B	3B	HR	RBI	SB	Avg
1939	Bassetts	Bi.-St.	OF	77	284	43	88	17	4	6	58	4	.310
1940	Bassetts	Bi.-St.	OF	*119	473	104	173	*45	3	21	*117	2	.366
1941	Columbia	Sally	OF	112	448	62	111	22	4	17	84	2	.248
1942	Syracuse	I. L.	OF	32	117	11	25	6	2	1	9	2	.214
1942	Cincinnati	N. L.	OF	12	43	2	4	0	0	1	4	0	.093
1942	Birmingham	S. A.	OF-3B	83	314	50	97	19	7	5	52	5	.309
1943-44-45	Cincinnati	N. L.		(In U. S. Army)									
1946	Rochester	I. L.	OF	103	338	38	93	20	8	9	53	7	.275

205

Year	Club	Lea	Pos	G	AB	R	H	2B	3B	HR	RBI	SB	Avg
1946	Cincinnati	N. L.	OF	9	22	1	4	0	0	0	1	2	.182
1947	Cincinnati	N. L.	OF	78	155	19	34	10	0	1	13	0	.219
1948	Cincinnati	N. L.	OF	7	9	0	1	0	0	0	0	0	.111
1948	Syracuse	I. L.	OF	122	440	86	127	24	4	82	104	1	.289
1948	Washington	A. L.	OF	1	5	1	2	0	0	0	0	0	.400
1949	Washington	A. L.	OF	129	443	58	112	17	1	14	59	1	.253
1950	Wash.-Bost. a	A. L.	OF	63	183	39	52	10	0	7	38	1	.284
1951	Boston ....,	A. L.	OF	115	386	66	97	9	2	22	85	0	.251
1952	Boston	A. L.	OF	90	250	35	66	12	4	11	50	2	.264
1953	Bost.-Wash. b	A. L.	OF	119	408	54	106	15	6	11	74	0	.260
	Major League Totals		9 Yrs	623	1904	275	478	73	10	67	324	6	.251

a Traded to Red Sox for Shortstop Merrill Combs and Outfielder Tom O'Brien, May 8, 1950.
b Sold to Washington, April 22, 1953.

WAITKUS, EDWARD STEPHEN

Born, Cambridge, Massachusetts, September 4, 1920.
Bats Left. Throws Left. Height, 6 feet, ½ inch. Weight, 178 pounds.

Year	Club	Lea	Pos	G	AB	R	H	2B	3B	HR	RBI	SB	Avg
1939	Moline	I. I. L.	1B	122	472	71	154	19	12	3	70	4	.326
1940	Tulsa	T. L.	1B	162	*634	89	*192	*39	*16	1	91	18	.303
1941	Tulsa	T. L.	1B	125	474	79	139	18	14	1	50	5	.293
1941	Chicago	N. L.	1B	12	28	1	5	0	0	0	0	0	.179
1942	Los Angeles	P. C. L.	1B	175	*699	108	*235	40	8	9	81	7	.336
1943-44-45	Chicago	N. L.	(In U. S. Army)										
1946	Chicago	N. L.	1B	113	441	50	134	24	5	4	55	3	.304
1947	Chicago	N. L.	1B	130	514	60	150	28	6	2	35	3	.292
1948	Chicago a	N. L.	1B-OF	139	562	87	166	27	10	7	44	11	.295
1949	Philadelphia b	N. L.	1B	54	209	41	64	16	3	1	28	3	.306
1950	Philadelphia ...	N. L.	1B	154	641	102	182	32	5	2	44	3	.284
1951	Philadelphia	N. L.	1B	145	610	65	157	27	4	1	46	0	.257
1952	Philadelphia	N. L.	1B	146	499	51	144	29	4	2	49	2	.289
1953	Philadelphia	N. L.	1B	81	247	24	72	9	2	1	16	1	.291
	Major League Totals		9 Yrs	974	3751	481	1074	192	39	20	317	26	.286

World's Series Record

| 1950 | Philadelphia ...... | N. L. | 1B | 4 | 15 | 0 | 4 | 1 | 0 | 0 | 0 | 0 | .267 |

a Traded with Hank Borowy to Philadelphia, N.L., December 14, for Emil Leonard and Walter Dubiel.
b Shot and seriously wounded by female fan he didn't know, June 15, 1949, and out for balance of season.

WALKER, ALBERT BLUFORD (RUBE)

Born, Lenoir, North Carolina, May 16, 1926.
Bats Left. Throws Right. Height, 6 feet, 1 inch. Weight, 185 pounds.

Year	Club	Lea	Pos	G	AB	R	H	2B	3B	HR	RBI	SB	Avg
1944	Erwin	App. L.	C	55	182	26	48	4	4	1	28	1	.264
1945	Nashville	S. A.	C	20	51	3	11	1	2	0	6	0	.216
1945	Portsmouth	Pied.	C	71	225	31	58	14	1	7	27	1	.258
1946	Davenport	I. I. L.	C	96	356	53	126	18	6	13	85	2	*.354
1947	Nashville	S. A.	C	128	435	67	144	20	1	22	105	0	.331
1948	Chicago	N. L.	C	79	171	17	47	8	0	5	26	0	.275
1949	Chicago	N. L.	C	56	172	11	42	4	1	3	22	0	.244
1950	Chicago	N. L.	C	74	213	19	49	7	1	6	16	0	.230
1951	Chi.-Bklyn. a	N. L.	C	73	181	15	43	8	0	4	14	0	.238
1952	Brooklyn	N. L.	C	46	139	9	36	8	0	1	19	0	.259
1953	Brooklyn	N. L.	C	43	95	5	23	6	0	3	9	0	.242
	Major League Totals		6 Yrs	371	971	76	240	41	2	22	106	0	.247

a Traded to Brooklyn with Andy Pafko, John Schmitz and Wayne Terwilliger for Gene Hermanski, Ed Miksis, Joe Hatten and Bruce Edwards, June 15, 1951.

WARD, PRESTON MEYER

Born, Columbia, Missouri, July 24, 1927.
Bats Left. Throws Right. Height, 6 feet, 4 inches. Weight, 198 pounds.

Year	Club	Lea	Pos	G	AB	R	H	2B	3B	HR	RBI	SB	Avg
1944	Newport News ...	Pied.	1B	3	2	0	0	0	0	0	1		.000
1944	Zanesville	Ohio St.	1B	74	274	51	69	12	9	4	46	5	.252
1945	Newport News ...	Pied.	1B	90	305	46	99	18	2	2	54	4	.325
1946	Danville	I. I. L.	1B	107	398	59	85	17	2	7	63	3	.214
1946	Fort Worth	T. L.	PH	1	1	0	1	0	0	0	0	0	1.000

Year	Club	Lea	Pos	G	AB	R	H	2B	3B	HR	RBI	SB	Avg
1947	Pueblo	West.	1B	125	465	*120	151	80	*21	17	*121	5	.825
1948	Brooklyn	N. L.	1B	42	146	9	88	9	2	1	21	0	.260
1948	Mobile	S. A.	1B	85	801	57	86	21	4	11	50	8	.286
1949	Fort Worth a	T. L.	1B-SS	*155	581	103	176	89	8	13	112	*29	.803
1950	Chicago	N. L.	1B	80	285	81	72	11	2	6	33	8	.253
1951-52	Chicago	N. L.	(In Military Service)										
1953	Chicago-Pitts. b	N. L.	1B-OF	121	881	45	82	12	1	12	89	4	.215
Major League Totals		8 Yrs	248	812	85	192	82	5	19	93	7	.236	

a Sold to Chicago by Brooklyn, with Paul Minner, October 14, 1949.
b Traded to Pittsburgh with Bob Addis, Toby Atwell, Gene Hermanski, Bob Schultz, option to purchase George Freese and cash for Joe Garagiola, Ralph Kiner, George Metkovich and Howie Pollet, June 4, 1953.

WERTZ, VICTOR WOODROW
Born. York, Pennsylvania, February 9, 1925.
Bats Left. Throws Right. Height, 6 feet. Weight, 190 pounds.

Year	Club	Lea	Pos	G	AB	R	H	2B	3B	HR	RBI	SB	Avg
1942	Winston-Salem	P. L.	OF	68	222	18	53	7	4	0	20	2	.239
1948	Buffalo	I. L.	OF-P	10	18	8	4	1	0	0	1	0	.222
1943-44-45	Detroit	A. L.	(In Military Service)										
1946	Buffalo	I. L.	OF	139	478	75	144	27	9	19	91	2	.301
1947	Detroit	A. L.	OF	102	833	60	96	22	4	6	44	2	.288
1948	Detroit	A. L.	OF	119	891	49	97	19	9	7	67	0	.248
1949	Detroit	A. L.	OF	*155	608	96	185	26	6	20	133	2	.304
1950	Detroit	A. L.	OF	149	559	99	172	87	4	27	123	0	.808
1951	Detroit	A. L.	OF	188	501	86	143	24	4	27	94	0	.285
1952	Det.-St. Louis a	A. L.	OF	122	415	68	115	30	8	23	70	1	.277
1958	St. Louis	A. L.	OF	128	440	61	118	18	6	19	70	1	.268
Major League Totals		7 Yrs	918	8247	519	926	166	86	129	601	6	.285	

a Traded with pitchers Marlin Stuart and Dick Littlefield. and outfielder Don Lenhardt, by Detroit to St. Louis, for pitchers Ned Garver, Bud Black and Dave Madison and outfielder Jim Delsing, Aug. 14, 1952.

WESTLAKE, WALDON THOMAS (WALLY)
Born, Gridley, California, November 8, 1920.
Bats Right. Throws Right. Height, 6 feet. Weight, 195 pounds.

Year	Club	Lea	Pos	G	AB	R	H	2B	3B	HR	RBI	SB	Avg
1940	Elmira	E. L.	OF	1	0	0	0	0	0	0	0	0	.000
1940	Dayton	M. A. L.	OF	80	131	15	23	6	0	2	9	1	.176
1941	Merced	Cal.	OF-8B-P	186	536	90	142	22	8	18	85	17	.265
1942	Oakland	P. C. L.	OF	169	598	57	159	26	6	7	74	10	.268
1943-44-45	Oakland	P. C. L	(In Military Service)										
1946	Oakland	P. C. L.	OF	136	429	60	185	19	5	7	57	5	.315
1947	Pittsburgh	N. L.	OF	112	407	59	111	17	4	17	69	5	.273
1948	Pittsburgh	N. L.	OF	132	428	78	122	10	6	17	65	2	.285
1949	Pittsburgh	N. L.	OF	147	525	77	148	24	8	23	104	6	.282
1950	Pittsburgh	N. L.	OF	139	477	69	136	15	6	24	95	1	.285
1951	Pittsb.-St. L. a	N. L.	8B-OF	123	448	64	119	12	5	22	84	1	.266
1952	St. L.-Cincinnati b	N. L.	OF	80	257	36	53	7	0	8	24	1	.206
1952	Cleveland	A. L.	OF	29	69	11	16	4	1	1	9	1	.232
1953	Cleveland	A. L.	OF	82	218	42	72	7	1	9	46	2	.830
Major League Totals		7 Yrs	844	2829	486	777	96	81	116	496	19	.275	

a Traded with Pitcher Cliff Chambers to St. Louis Cardinals for Pitchers Howie Pollet and Ted Wilks, Catcher Joe Garagiola, Outfielder Bill Howerton and Infielder Dick Cole, June 15, 1951.
b Traded with infielder Eddie Kazak, by St. Louis to Cincinnati, for first baseman Dick Sisler and shortstop Virgil Stallcup, May .13, 1952.
c Sold to Cleveland for undisclosed amount of cash on August 7, 1952, and transfer of Dick Kinaman, Oct. 7, 1952.

WESTRUM, WESLEY NOREEN
Born. Clearbrook, Minnesota, November 28, 1922.
Bats Right. Throws Right. Height, 5 feet, 11 inches. Weight, 185 pounds.

Year	Club	Lea	Pos	G	AB	R	H	2B	3B	HR	RBI	SB	Avg
1940	Crookston	No. L.	C	56	171	20	47	4	0	8	23	2	.275
1941	Minneapolis	A. A.	PH	1	1	0	0	0	0	0	0	0	.000
1941	Eau Claire	No. L.	C	98	849	69	115	82	4	7	70	18	.880
1942	Minneapolis	A. A.	C	8	1	0	0	0	0	0	0	0	.000
1942	Little Rock	S. A.	C	45	104	14	21	4	1	0	6	1	.202
1943-44-45	Minneapolis	A. A.	(In Military Service)										
1946	Jacksonville	S. A. L.	C-3B	103	327	57	90	14	8	8	56	6	.275
1947	Minneapolis	A. A	C	134	893	85	117	24	8	22	87	10	.294
1947	New York	N. L.	C	6	12	1	5	1	0	0	2	0	.417

Year	Club	Lea	Pos	G	AB	R	H	2B	3B	HR	RBI	SB	Avg
1948	New York	N. L.	C	66	125	14	20	3	1	4	16	3	.160
1949	Jersey City	I. L.	C	51	169	38	52	10	2	15	59	7	.308
1949	New York	N. L.	C	64	169	23	41	4	1	7	28	1	.243
1950	New York	N. L.	C	140	437	68	103	13	3	23	71	2	.236
1951	New York	N. L.	C	124	361	59	79	12	0	20	70	1	.219
1952	New York	N. L.	C	114	322	47	71	11	0	14	43	1	.220
1953	New York	N. L.	C-3B	107	290	40	65	5	0	12	30	2	.224
Major League Totals			7 Yrs	621	1716	252	384	49	5	80	260	10	.224
World's Series Record													
1951	New York	N. L.	C	6	17	1	4	1	0	0	0	0	.235

WHITE, SAMUEL CHARLES
Born, Wenatchee, Wash., July 7, 1928.
Bats Right. Throws Right. Height, 6 feet, 3 inches. Weight, 195 pounds.

Year	Club	Lea	Pos	G	AB	R	H	2B	3B	HR	RBI	SB	Avg
1949	Seattle	P. C. L.	C	60	173	23	52	2	2	2	20	2	.301
1949	Louisville	A. A.	C	8	21	8	3	0	1	0	3	0	.143
1949	Oneonta	Can.-Am.	C-OF	30	121	15	31	5	2	2	21	0	.256
1950	Roanoke	Piedmont	C	111	422	60	109	18	5	6	43	4	.258
1951	Scranton	Eastern	C	120	434	57	116	12	6	12	63	2	.267
1951	Boston	A. L.	C	4	11	0	2	0	0	0	0	0	.182
1952	Boston	A. L.	C	115	381	85	107	20	2	10	49	2	.281
1953	Boston	A. L.	C	136	476	59	130	34	2	13	64	3	.273
Major League Totals			3 Yrs	255	868	94	239	54	4	23	113	5	.275

WILBER, DELBERT QUENTIN
Born, Lincoln Park, Michigan, February 24, 1919.
Bats Right. Throws Right. Height, 6 feet, 2½ inches. Weight, 200 pounds.

Year	Club	Lea	Pos	G	AB	R	H	2B	3B	HR	RBI	SB	Avg
1938	Findlay	Ohio St.	C	97	398	67	121	24	4	14	62	..	.304
1939	Findlay	Ohio St.	C	121	515	112	171	33	14	16	..	..	.332
1940	Springfield	W. A.	C-OF	113	435	73	134	34	8	7	93	3	.308
1941	Columbus	S. A. L.	3B-C-OF	103	294	43	77	13	2	10	40	4	.262
1942-43-44-45	Columbus	A.A.	(In Military Service)										
1946	St. Louis	N. L.	C	4	4	0	0	0	0	0	0	0	.000
1946	Columbus	A. A.	C-1B	101	297	35	78	9	9	7	33	0	.263
1947	St. Louis	N. L.	C	51	99	7	23	8	1	0	12	0	.232
1948	St. Louis	N. L.	C	27	58	5	11	2	0	0	10	0	.190
1949	Houston a	T. L.	C-IF-OF-P	89	207	20	64	16	2	5	32	1	.309
1949	St. Louis	N. L.	C	2	4	0	1	0	0	0	0	0	.250
1950	Rochester b	I. L.	C-3B	123	440	64	130	23	7	11	80	2	.295
1951	Philadelphia	N. L.	C	84	245	30	68	7	3	8	34	0	.278
1952	Philadelphia	N. L.	PH	2	2	0	0	0	0	0	0	0	.000
1952	Boston c	A. L.	C	47	135	7	36	10	1	3	23	1	.267
1953	Boston	A. L.	C-1B	58	112	16	27	6	1	7	29	0	.241
Major League Totals			7 Yrs	275	659	65	166	33	6	18	108	1	.252

a Manager of Houston.
b Drafted by Philadelphia Phillies from Rochester, Nov. 17, 1950.
c Sold to Boston Red Sox by Philadelphia, May 12, 1952.

WILLIAMS, DAVID CARLOUS, JR.
Born, Dallas, Texas, November 2, 1928.
Bats Right. Throws Right. Height, 5 feet, 10 inches. Weight, 165 pounds.

Year	Club	Lea	Pos	G	AB	R	H	2B	3B	HR	RBI	SB	Avg
1947	Waycross	Ga.-Fla.	2B	132	464	*147	131	*34	10	8	75	28	.282
1948	Pensacola	S. E.	2B	132	535	*119	165	30	10	12	62	*35	.308
1949	Atlanta	S. A.	2B	138	513	92	149	21	7	2	62	27	.290
1949	New York	N. L.	2B	13	50	7	12	1	1	1	5	0	.240
1950	Minneapolis	A. A.	2B	138	536	*113	150	28	6	17	65	6	.280
1951	Minneapolis	A. A.	2B	80	293	61	84	9	5	12	49	2	.287
1951	New York	N. L.	2B	30	64	17	17	1	0	2	8	1	.266
1952	New York	N. L.	2B	138	540	70	137	26	3	13	55	2	.254
1953	New York	N. L.	2B	112	340	51	101	11	2	3	34	2	.297
Major League Totals			4 Yrs	293	994	145	267	39	6	19	102	5	.269
World's Series Record													
1951	New York	N. L.	PH-PR	2	1	0	0	0	0	0	0	0	.000

WILLIAMS, RICHARD HIRSCHFELD
Born, St. Louis, Mo., May 7, 1929.
Bats Right. Throws Right. Height, 6 feet. Weight, 190 pounds.

Year	Club	Lea	Pos	G	AB	R	H	2B	3B	HR	RBI	SB	Avg
1947	Santa Barbara	Calif.	OF-3B	79	313	47	77	20	2	4	50	8	.246
1948	Santa Barbara	Calif.	OF	97	385	82	129	29	2	16	90	16	.335

Year	Club	Lea	Pos	G	AB	R	H	2B	3B	HR	RBI	SB	Avg
1948	Fort Worth	T. L.	OF-3B	41	140	16	29	1	0	4	16	0	.207
1949	Fort Worth	T. L.	OF-2B-3B	154	562	109	174	30	6	23	114	13	.310
1950	Fort Worth	T. L.	OF	144	510	69	153	30	1	11	72	20	.300
1951	Brooklyn a	N. L.	OF	23	60	5	12	3	1	1	5	0	.200
1952	Brooklyn	N. L.	OF-3B-1B	36	68	13	21	4	1	0	11	0	.309
1953	Montreal	I. L.	OF	66	230	28	64	12	1	2	33	1	.278
1953	Brooklyn	N. L.	OF	30	55	4	12	2	0	2	5	0	.218
Major League Totals			3 Yrs	89	183	22	45	9	2	3	21	0	.246
World's Series Record													
1953	Brooklyn	N. L.	PH	3	2	0	1	0	0	0	0	0	.500

a In Military Service, Feb. 8, 1951 to May 25, 1951.

WILLIAMS, THEODORE SAMUEL (TED)

Born, San Diego, California, October 30, 1918.
Bats Left. Throws Right. Height, 6 feet, 3 inches. Weight, 195 pounds.

Year	Club	Lea	Pos	G	AB	R	H	2B	3B	HR	RBI	SB	Avg
1936	San Diego	P. C L.	OF	42	107	18	29	8	2	0	11	2	.271
1937	San Diego	P. C L	OF	138	454	66	132	24	2	23	98	1	.291
1938	Minneapolis	A. A.	OF	148	528	*130	193	30	9	*43	*142	6	*.366
1939	Boston	A. L.	OF	149	565	131	185	44	11	31	*145	2	.327
1940	Boston	A. L.	OF-P	144	561	*134	193	43	14	23	113	4	.344
1941	Boston	A. L.	OF	143	456	*135	185	33	3	*37	120	2	*.406
1942	Boston	A. L.	OF	150	522	*141	186	34	5	*36	*137	3	*.356
1943-44-45	Boston	A. L.	(In U. S. Naval Aviation)										
1946	Boston a	A. L.	OF	150	514	*142	176	37	8	38	123	0	.342
1947	Boston	A. L.	OF	156	528	*125	181	40	9	*32	*114	0	*.343
1948	Boston	A. L.	OF	137	509	124	188	44	3	25	127	4	*.369
1949	Boston b	A. L.	OF	*155	566	*150	194	*39	3	*43	*159	1	.343
1950	Boston	A. L.	OF	89	334	82	106	24	1	28	97	3	.318
1951	Boston	A. L.	OF	148	531	109	169	28	4	30	126	1	.318
1952	Boston c	A. L.	OF	6	10	2	4	0	1	1	3	0	.400
1953	Boston	A. L.	OF	37	91	17	37	6	0	13	34	0	.407
Major League Totals			12 Yrs	1464	5187	1292	1804	372	62	337	1298	20	.348
World's Series Record													
1946	Boston	A. L.	OF	7	25	2	5	0	0	0	1	0	.200

a Voted the Most Valuable Player in American League for 1946.
b Voted the Most Valuable Player in American League for 1949
c In Military Service from May 2, 1952 until July 28, 1953.

WILSON, ROBERT JAMES

Born, Milwaukee, Wisconsin, March 7, 1929.
Bats Right. Throws Right. Height, 6feet. Weight, 200 pounds.

Year	Club	Lea	Pos	G	AB	R	H	2B	3B	HR	RBI	SB	Avg
1950	Waterloo	I. I. I.	C	67	235	56	75	15	2	11	42	7	.319
1951	Memphis	S. A.	C	82	220	43	72	11	3	4	30	1	.327
1952	Seattle	P. C. L.	C	155	562	76	167	32	9	7	75	3	.297
1953	Chicago	A. L.	C	71	164	21	41	6	1	0	10	2	.250

WOODLING, EUGENE RICHARD

Born, Akron, Ohio, August 16, 1922.
Bats Left. Throws Right. Height, 5 feet, 9½ inches. Weight, 175 pounds.

Year	Club	Lea	Pos	G	AB	R	H	2B	3B	HR	RBI	SB	Avg
1940	Mansfield	Ohio St.	OF	85	332	78	132	29	6	4	68	7	*.398
1941	Charleston	M. A. L.	OF	13	46	8	10	2	1	0	5	5	.217
1941	Flint	Mich. St.	OF-3B-P	92	386	95	152	30	5	7	52	11	*.394
1942	Wilkes-Barre	E. L.	OF	39	120	8	23	4	2	1	11	3	.192
1943	Wilkes-Barre	E. L.	OF	128	453	91	156	30	8	5	61	6	*.344
1943	Cleveland	A. L.	OF	8	25	5	8	2	1	1	5	0	.320
1944-45	Cleveland	A. L.	(In U. S. Navy)										
1946	Cleveland a	A. L.	OF	61	133	8	25	1	4	0	9	1	.188
1947	Pittsburgh	N. L.	OF	22	79	7	21	2	2	0	10	0	.266
1947	Newark	I. L.	OF	128	477	81	138	19	8	8	54	5	.289
1948	San Francisco	P. C. L.	OF	146	524	121	202	22	*13	22	107	6	*.385
1949	New York	A. L.	OF	112	296	60	80	13	7	5	44	2	.270
1950	New York	A. L.	OF	122	449	81	127	20	10	6	60	5	.283
1951	New York	A. L.	OF	120	420	65	118	15	8	15	71	0	.281
1952	New York	A. L.	OF	122	408	58	126	19	6	12	63	1	.309
1953	New York	A. L.	OF	125	395	64	121	26	4	10	58	2	.306
Major League Totals			8 Yrs	692	2205	348	626	98	42	49	320	11	.284
World's Series Record													
1949	New York	A. L.	OF	3	10	4	4	3	0	0	0	0	.400
1950	New York	A. L.	OF	4	14	2	6	0	0	0	1	0	.429
1951	New York	A. L.	OF	6	18	6	3	1	1	1	1	0	.167

Year	Club	Lea	Pos	G	AB	R	H	2B	3B	HR	RBI	SB	Avg
1952	New York	A. L.	OF	7	23	4	8	1	1	1	1	0	.348
1953	New York	A. L.	OF	6	20	5	6	0	0	1	3	0	.300
	World's Series Totals			26	85	21	27	5	2	8	6	0	.318

a Traded to Pittsburgh for Al Lopez, December 7, 1946.

WRIGHT, THOMAS EVERETTE

Born, Rutherforton, North Carolina, September 22, 1923.
Bats Left. Throws Right. Height, 6 feet. Weight, 185 pounds.

Year	Club	Lea	Pos	G	AB	R	H	2B	3B	HR	RBI	SB	Avg
1942	Danville-S'field	Bi-St.	OF-P	107	394	52	95	21	2	5	60	7	.241
1943, 1944, 1945	(In United States Military Service)												
1946	Durham	Car. L.	OF	135	526	122	*200	36	11	14	116	11	*.380
1947	New Orleans	S. A.	OF	134	496	97	161	41	14	14	89	8	.325
1948	Louisville	A. A.	OF	151	563	89	173	31	10	13	85	12	.307
1948	Boston	A. L.	PH	8	2	1	1	0	1	0	0	0	.500
1949	Louisville	A. A.	OF	151	549	91	202	38	8	9	89	7	.368
1949	Boston	A. L.	PH	5	4	1	1	1	0	0	1	0	.250
1950	Boston	A. L.	OF	54	107	17	34	7	0	0	20	0	.318
1951	Boston	A. L.	OF	28	63	8	14	1	1	1	9	0	.222
1951	Louisville a	A. A.	OF	72	262	38	74	12	5	2	45	0	.282
1952	St. L.-Chicago b	A. L.	OF	89	198	21	50	10	2	2	27	2	.253
1953	Chicago	A. L.	OF	77	132	14	33	5	3	2	25	0	.250

Major League Totals 6 Yrs 256 506 62 133 24 7 5 82 2 .263
a Traded by Boston with Les Moss to St. Louis Browns for Gus Niarhos and Ken Wood, November 27, 1951.
b Traded to Chicago White Sox with Leo Thomas for Willie Miranda and Al Zarilla, June 15, 1952.

WYROSTEK, JOHN BARNEY

Born, Fairmont City, Illinois, July 12, 1919.
Bats Left. Throws Right. Height, 6 feet, 2 inches. Weight, 180 pounds.

Year	Club	Lea	Pos	G	AB	R	H	2B	3B	HR	RBI	SB	Avg
1937	Kinston	Coast. Pl.	OF	50	208	36	69	8	2	5	28	5	.332
1938	Kinston	Coast. Pl.	OF	112	449	89	*149	29	6	11	83	10	.332
1939	Springfield	W. A.	OF	31	114	25	44	10	1	6	30	4	.386
1939	Rochester	I. L.	OF	24	75	17	20	8	2	0	9	0	.267
1939	Houston	T. L.	OF	37	123	13	35	8	0		14	4	.285
1940	Houston	T. L.	OF	156	564	86	172	30	8	4	83	7	.305
1941	Rochester	I. L.	OF	86	298	34	75	11	3	8	39	4	.252
1941	New Orleans	S. A.	OF	48	171	29	54	16	0	1	26	2	.316
1942	Pittsburgh	N. L.	OF	9	85	0	4	0	1	0	8	0	.114
1942	Toronto	I. L.	OF	155	562	85	152	14	8	18	79	17	.270
1943	Pittsburgh a	N. L.	OF-INF	51	79	7	12	3	0	0	1	0	.152
1944	Columbus	A. A.	OF	110	416	87	149	*50	5	10	69	11	*.353
1944-45	St. Louis b	N. L.	(In U. S. Army)										
1946	Philadelphia	N. L.	OF	145	545	73	153	30	4	6	45	7	.281
1947	Philadelphia	N. L.	OF	123	454	68	124	24	7	5	51	7	.273
1948	Cincinnati c	N. L.	OF	136	512	74	140	24	9	17	76	7	.273
1949	Cincinnati	N. L.	OF	134	474	54	118	20	4	9	46	7	.249
1950	Cincinnati	N. L.	OF-1B	131	509	70	145	84	5	8	76	1	.285
1951	Cincinnati	N. L.	OF	142	537	52	167	81	8	2	61	2	.311
1952	Cinc.-Phila. d	N. L.	OF-1B	128	427	57	118	17	6	2	47	2	.265
1953	Philadelphia	N. L.	OF	125	409	42	111	14	2	6	47	0	.271

Major League Totals 10 Yrs 1129 3981 497 1087 197 41 55 453 33 .273
a Traded to Columbus (A.A.) with cash for Preacher Roe, Sept. 29, 1943.
b Sold to Philadelphia Phillies, February 5, 1946.
c Traded to Cincinnati, with cash for Eddie Miller, February 10, 1948.
d Traded with Kent Peterson to Philadelphia Phillies for Emory Church, May 23, 1952.

YOST, EDWARD FREDERICK

Born, Brooklyn, New York, October 13, 1926.
Bats Right. Throws Right. Height, 5 feet, 10 inches. Weight, 175 pounds.

Year	Club	Lea	Pos	G	AB	R	H	2B	3B	HR	RBI	SB	Avg
1944	Washington	A. L.	3B-SS	7	14	3	2	0	0	0	0	0	.143
1944-45-46	Washington	A. L.	(In U. S. Army)										
1946	Washington	A. L.	3B	8	25	2	2	1	0	0	1	2	.080
1947	Washington	A. L.	3B	115	428	52	102	17	8	0	14	3	.238
1948	Washington	A. L.	3B	145	555	74	138	32	11	2	50	4	.249
1949	Washington	A. L.	3B	124	435	57	110	19	7	9	45	3	.253
1950	Washington	A. L.	3B	155	573	114	169	26	2	11	58	6	.295

Year	Club	Lea	Pos	G	AB	R	H	2B	3B	HR	RBI	SB	Avg
1951	Washington	A. L.	3B-OF	*154	568	109	161	*36	4	12	65	6	.233
1952	Washington	A. L.	3B	*157	587	92	137	32	8	12	49	4	.233
1953	Washington	A. L.	3B	152	577	107	157	30	7	9	45	7	.272
Major League Totals			9 Yrs	1017	8762	610	978	193	87	55	827	85	.260

YOUNG, ROBERT GEORGE

Born, Granite, Maryland, January 22, 1925.
Bats Left. Throws Right. Height, 6 feet. Weight, 165 pounds.

Year	Club	Lea	Pos	G	AB	R	H	2B	3B	HR	RBI	SB	Avg
1946	Allentown	Int.-St.	2B	128	516	115	179	32	*16	5	53	13	.347
1947	Rochester	I. L.	2B-3B	118	410	63	129	19	11	0	33	8	.315
1948	Rochester	I. L.	2B	126	488	87	131	12	12	4	38	4	.268
1948	St. Louis	N. L.	3B	3	1	0	0	0	0	0	0	0	.000
1949	Rochester-Baltimore	I. L.	2B-3B	128	463	61	124	14	7	6	46	1	.268
1950	Baltimore	I. L.	2B	140	539	78	147	22	8	8	41	4	.273
1951	St. Louis	A. L.	2B	147	611	75	159	13	9	1	32	8	.260
1952	St. Louis	A. L.	2B	149	575	59	142	15	9	4	39	3	.247
1953	St. Louis	A. L.	2B	148	537	48	137	22	2	4	25	2	.255
Major League Totals			4 Yrs	447	1724	182	438	50	20	9	96	13	.254

YVARS, SALVATORE ANTHONY

Born, New York City, New York, February 20, 1924.
Bats Right. Throws Right. Height, 5 feet, 10 inches. Weight, 187 pounds.

Year	Club	Lea	Pos	G	AB	R	H	2B	3B	HR	RBI	SB	Avg
1946	Manchester	N. Eng.	C-OF	73	220	41	70	12	6	8	54	2	.318
1947	Jersey City	I. L.	C	80	208	34	61	12	0	8	43	6	.293
1947	New York	N. L.	C	1	5	0	1	0	0	0	0	0	.200
1948	Jersey City	I. L.	C	132	409	67	123	17	4	16	88	1	.301
1948	New York	N. L.	C	15	38	4	8	1	0	1	6	0	.211
1949	Minneapolis	A. A.	C	84	290	49	89	15	4	8	57	1	.307
1949	New York	N. L.	C	3	8	0	0	0	0	0	0	0	.000
1950	Jersey City	I. L.	C-3B	91	291	48	82	12	1	8	53	3	.282
1950	New York	N. L.	C	9	14	0	2	0	0	0	0	0	.143
1951	New York	N. L.	C	25	41	9	13	2	0	2	3	0	.317
1952	New York	N. L.	C	66	151	15	37	8	0	4	18	0	.245
1953	N.Y.-St. L. a	N. L.	C	53	104	5	27	2	0	1	7	0	.260
Major League Totals			7 Yrs	172	361	33	88	8	0	8	34	0	.244

World's Series Record

Year	Club	Lea	Pos	G	AB	R	H	2B	3B	HR	RBI	SB	Avg
1951	New York	N. L.	PH	1	1	0	0	0	0	0	0	0	.000

a Sold to St. Louis Cardinals, June 15, 1953.

ZERNIAL, GUS EDWARD

Born, Beaumont, Texas, June 27, 1923.
Bats Right. Throws Right. Height, 6 feet, 3 inches. Weight, 210 pounds.

Year	Club	Lea	Pos	G	AB	R	H	2B	3B	HR	RBI	SB	Avg
1942	Waycross	Ga.-Fla.	OF	95	367	54	105	25	4	3	49	0	.286
1943-44-45	Atlanta	S. A.	(In Military Service)										
1946	Burlington a	Car. L.	OF	137	501	114	167	29	3	*41	111	10	.333
1947	Baltimore	I. L.	OF	3	4	0	0	0	0	0	0	0	.000
1947	Hollywood	P. C. L.	OF	120	372	61	128	17	6	12	77	4	.344
1948	Hollywood	P. C. L.	OF	186	737	130	*237	47	7	40	*156	3	.322
1949	Chicago	A. L.	OF	73	198	29	63	17	2	*5	33	0	.318
1950	Chicago	A. L.	OF	143	543	75	152	16	4	29	93	0	.280
1951	Chicago-Phila. b	A. L.	OF	143	571	92	153	30	5	*33	*129	2	.268
1952	Philadelphia	A. L.	OF	145	549	76	144	15	1	29	100	5	.262
1953	Philadelphia	A. L.	OF	147	556	85	158	21	3	42	108	4	.284
Major League Totals			5 Yrs	651	2417	357	670	99	15	138	468	11	.277

a Purchased by Atlanta at end of season, and drafted by Cleveland, Nov. 11, 1946.
b Traded with Dave Philley to Philadelphia Athletics as part of three club deal, April 29, 1951.
See footnote to Ray Murray.

PITCHERS

ABER, ALBERT JULIUS
Born, Cleveland, Ohio, July 81, 1927.
Bats Left.   Throws Left.   Height, 6 feet, 1 inch.   Weight, 200 pounds.

Year	Club	Lea	G	IP	W	L	Pct	SO	BB	H	ERA
1946	Batavia	Pony	26	145	13	6	.684	87	85	172	4.59
1947	Burlington ..	Cent. Assn.	22	129	7	6	.538	94	79	131	3.98
1948	Spartanburg	Tri-St.	82	149	6	12	.833	93	79	183	5.86
1949	Spartanburg	Tri-St.	86	236	24	8	*.750	142	89	214	2.71
1950	Oklahoma City ...	T. L.	24	144	10	7	.588	58	65	125	8.82
1950	Cleveland·	A. L.	1	9	1	0	1.000	4	4	5	2.00
1951-52	Cleveland	A. L.	(In U. S. Army)								
1953	Clev.-Detroit a ..	A. L.	23	73	5	4	.556	88	50	69	4.68
Major League Totals		2 Yrs	24	82	6	4	.600	42	54	74	4.39

a Traded to Detroit with Ray Boone, Steve Gromek and Dick Welk for Owen Friend, Joe Ginsberg, Art Houtteman and Bill Wight, June 15, 1953.

ALOMA, LUIS (BARBA)
Born, Havana, Cuba, June 19, 1923.
Bats Right.   Throws Right.   Height, 6 feet.   Weight, 175 pounds.

Year	Club	Lea	G	IP	W	L	Pct	SO	BB	H	ERA
1944	Chattanooga	S. A.	19	71	2	6	.250	28	45	94	5.96
1944	Kingsport	App. L.	7	56	6	1	.857	53	23	49	3.05
1945	Chattanooga	S. A.	31	213	14	9	.609	89	67	214	3.17
1946	Chattanooga	S. A.	86	210	16	11	.593	104	74	203	3.56
1947	Chattanooga	S. A.	15	61	2	4	.833	20	35	86	6.93
1947	Charlotte	Tri-St.	18	117	8	7	.533	64	39	128	3.62
1948	Havana	Fla.-Int.	28	208	19	6	*.760	119	59	143	1.77
1949	Buffalo	I. L.	88	180	10	9	.526	115	94	177	4.60
1950	Chicago	A. L.	42	88	7	2	.778	49	53	77	3.78
1951	Chicago	A. L.	25	69	6	0	1.000	25	24	52	1.83
1952	Chicago	A. L.	25	40	8	1	.750	18	11	42	4.28
1953	Chicago	A. L.	24	88	2	0	1.000	23	23	41	4.74
Major League Totals		4 Yrs	116	235	18	3	.857	115	111	212	3.45

ANTONELLI, JOHN AUGUST
Born, Rochester, New York, April 12, 1930.
Bats Left.   Throws Left.   Height, 6 feet, 1 inch.   Weight, 190 pounds.

Year	Club	Lea	G	IP	W	L	Pct	SO	BB	H	ERA
1948	Boston	N. L.	4	4	0	0	.000	0	3	2	2.25
1949	Boston	N. L.	22	96	3	7	.300	48	42	99	3.56
1950	Boston	N. L.	20	59	2	8	.400	33	22	81	5.80
1951-52	Boston	N. L.	(In Military Service)								
1953	Milwaukee	N. L.	31	175	12	12	.500	131	71	167	3.19
Major League Totals		4 Yrs	77	334	17	22	.436	212	138	349	3.75

BACZEWSKI, FREDERICK
Born, St. Paul, Minnesota, May 15, 1926.
Bats Left.   Throws Left.   Height, 6 feet, 2½ inches.   Weight, 185 pounds.

Year	Club	Lea	G	IP	W	L	Pct	SO	BB	H	ERA
1947	Alexandria	Evang.	82	240	16	10	.615	242	139	159	2.10
1948	Anniston	So'east.	18	115	11	2	.846	86	72	83	3.52
1948	Shreveport	T. L.	7	18	0	1	.000	14	17	24	7.50
1948	Kilgore	Lone Star	8	60	5	0	1.000	57	35	44	3.13
1949	Shreveport	T. L.	88	141	7	5	.583	68	88	147	4.34
1950	Des Moines	West.	27	105	2	4	.333	74	46	86	2.74
1951	Los Angeles	P. C. L.	87	232	12	10	.545	129	121	206	4.03
1952	Los Angeles	P. C. L.	16	43	1	4	.200	27	31	50	5.86
1952	Shreveport	T. L.	14	97	6	4	.600	50	51	82	2.41
1953	Chi.-Cincinnati a	N. L.	33	148	11	4	.733	61	58	145	3.65

a Traded to Cincinnati with Bob Kelly for Emory (Bubba) Church, June 12, 1953.

BICKFORD, VERNON DEGELL

Born, Hellier, Kentucky, August 17, 1920.
Bats Right. Throws Right. Height, 6 feet. Weight, 185 pounds.

Year	Club	Lea	G	IP	W	L	Pct	SO	BB	H	ERA
1939	Welch	M. S. L.	10	62	5	2	.714	47	80	64	5.37
1940	Welch	M. S. L.	*37	211	15	11	.577	*163	80	219	3.50
1941	Welch	M. S. L.	31	221	13	14	.481	153	110	244	3.46
1942	Welch	M. S. L.	38	196	16	12	.571	157	107	224	...
1943-44-45	Hartford	E. L.		(In Military Service)							
1946	Hartford	E. L.	1	4	0	0	.000	0	3	2	0.00
1946	Jackson	So'east.	28	181	10	12	.455	153	91	166	3.33
1947	Milwaukee	A. A.	29	143	9	5	.643	69	72	131	3.78
1948	Boston	N. L.	33	146	11	5	.688	60	63	125	3.27
1949	Boston	N. L.	37	231	16	11	.593	101	106	246	4.25
1950	Boston a	N. L.	40	*312	19	14	.576	126	122	293	3.46
1951	Boston	N. L.	25	165	11	9	.550	76	76	146	3.11
1952	Boston	N. L.	26	161	7	12	.368	62	64	165	3.74
1953	Milwaukee	N. L.	20	58	2	5	.286	25	35	60	5.28
Major League Totals		6 Yrs	181	1073	66	56	.541	450	466	1035	3.69
World's Series Record											
1948	Boston	N. L.	1	3⅓	0	1	.000	1	5	4	2.70

a Pitched no-hit game against Brooklyn, August 11, winning 7-0.

BISHOP, CHARLES TULLER, JR.

Born, Atlanta, Georgia, January 1, 1924.
Bats Right. Throws Right. Height, 6 feet, 2 inches. Weight, 195 pounds.

Year	Club	Lea	G	IP	W	L	Pct	SO	BB	H	ERA
1942	Johnson City	Appal.	7	48	0	6	.000	37	31	53	7.13
1943	Jamestown	Pony	25	133	10	8	.556	106	102	101	3.72
1944-45	Rochester	I. L.		(In Military Service)							
1946	Columbus	S. A. L.	4	12	0	1	.000	8	16	15	...
1946	Albany	Ga.-Fla.	15	123	8	4	.667	98	74	94	2.93
1946	Winston-Salem	Carol.	5	30	2	1	.667	18	11	25	...
1947	Omaha	West.	28	153	6	8	.429	*133	107	159	4.12
1948	Lynchburg	Pied.	29	191	13	9	.591	136	137	133	2.64
1949	Columbus	S. A. L.	6	38	1	5	.167	22	37	45	6.87
1949	Lynchburg	Pied.	20	123	10	5	.667	89	115	97	4.17
1950	Sioux City	West.	32	222	16	9	.640	156	142	186	4.09
1951	Ottawa	I. L.	4	21	0	3	.000	14	16	16	4.71
1951	Oakland	P. C. L.	15	52	2	8	.200	35	35	64	5.88
1951	Jacksonville	S. A. L.	7	32	2	3	.400	27	23	33	6.19
1952	Ottawa	I. L.	27	193	12	10	.545	116	84	170	3.64
1952	Philadelphia	A. L.	6	31	2	2	.500	17	24	29	6.39
1953	Philadelphia	A. L.	39	161	3	14	.176	66	86	174	5.65
Major League Totals		2 Yrs	45	192	5	16	.238	83	110	203	5.71

BLACK, JOSEPH

Born, Plainfield, N. J., Feb. 8, 1924.
Bats Right. Throws Right. Height, 6 feet, 2 inches. Weight, 220 pounds.

Year	Club	Lea	G	IP	W	L	Pct	SO	BB	H	ERA
1951	Montreal	I. L.	26	110	7	9	.438	49	87	106	3.85
1951	St. Paul	A. A.	9	60	4	3	.571	35	24	44	2.25
1952	Brooklyn	N. L.	56	142	15	4	.789	85	41	102	2.15
1953	Brooklyn	N. L.	34	73	6	3	.667	42	27	74	5.30
Major League Totals		2 Yrs	90	215	21	7	.750	127	68	176	3.22
World's Series Record											
1952	Brooklyn	N. L.	3	21⅓	1	2	.333	9	5	15	2.53
1953	Brooklyn	N. L.	1	1	0	0	.000	2	0	1	9.00
World's Series Totals			4	22⅓	1	2	.333	11	5	16	2.82

BLYZKA, MICHAEL

Born, Hamtramck, Michigan, December 25, 1928.
Bats Right. Throws Right. Height, 6 feet. Weight, 200 pounds.

Year	Club	Lea	G	IP	W	L	Pct	SO	BB	H	ERA
1947	Madisonville	Kitty	10	45	2	6	.250	33	32	49	4.57
1947	Lima	Ohio St.	16	78	0	9	.000	58	46	109	5.65
1948	Belleville	Ill. St.	29	195	12	9	.571	*192	132	164	3.37

Year	Club	Lea	G	IP	W	L	Pct	SO	BB	H	ERA
1949	Marshall	East. Tex.	33	262	15	14	.517	173	*147	261	3.61
1950	Wichita	West.	36	152	13	6	.684	67	70	151	3.43
1951-52			(In Military Service)								
1953	St. Louis	A. L.	33	94	2	6	.250	23	56	110	6.41

BOYER, CLOYD VICTOR

Born, Liberty, Missouri, September 1, 1927.

Bats Right.　Throws Right.　Height, 6 feet, 1 inch.　Weight, 188 pounds.

Year	Club	Lea	G	IP	W	L	Pct	SO	BB	H	ERA
1945	Lynchburg	Pied.	2	2	0	0	.000	2	7	6	31.50
1945	Johnson City	App. L.	13	72	4	7	.364	55	49	70	5.00
1945, 1946			(In United States Military Service)								
1946	Carthage	K-O-M	5	26	3	1	.750	35	24	25	4.15
1947	Duluth	No. L.	32	*228	16	9	.640	*239	106	199	2.45
1948	Houston	Texas	30	228	16	10	.615	*188	126	191	3.15
1949	Rochester	I. L.	31	190	15	10	.600	143	110	147	3.18
1949	St. Louis	N. L.	4	3	0	0	.000	0	7	5	12.00
1950	St. Louis	N. L.	36	120	7	7	.500	82	49	105	3.53
1951	Columbus	A. A.	5	40	2	3	.400	44	22	29	2.03
1951	St. Louis	N. L.	19	63	2	5	.286	40	46	63	5.29
1952	St. Louis	N. L.	23	110	6	6	.500	44	47	108	4.25
1953	Houston	T. L.	28	65	4	2	.667	31	28	64	2.78
Major League Totals		4 Yrs	82	296	15	18	.455	166	149	286	4.26

BRANCA, RALPH THEODORE

Born Mt. Vernon, New York, January 6, 1926.

Bats Right.　Throws Right.　Height, 6 feet, 3 inches.　Weight, 220 pounds.

Year	Club	Lea	G	IP	W	L	Pct	SO	BB	H	ERA
1943	Olean	PONY	14	101	5	5	.500	62	48	106	4.63
1944	Montreal	I. L.	12	71	4	5	.444	37	39	69	4.44
1944	Brooklyn	N. L.	21	45	0	2	.000	16	32	46	7.00
1945	Brooklyn	N. L.	16	110	5	6	.455	69	79	73	3.03
1945	St. Paul	A. A.	15	100	6	5	.545	94	64	87	3.33
1946	Brooklyn	N. L.	24	67	3	1	.750	42	41	62	3.90
1947	Brooklyn	N. L.	43	280	21	12	.636	148	98	251	2.67
1948	Brooklyn	N. L.	36	216	14	9	.609	122	80	189	3.50
1949	Brooklyn	N. L.	34	187	13	5	.722	109	91	181	4.33
1950	Brooklyn	N. L.	43	142	7	9	.438	100	55	152	4.69
1951	Brooklyn	N. L.	42	204	13	12	.520	118	85	180	3.26
1952	Brooklyn	N. L.	16	61	4	2	.667	26	21	52	3.34
1953	Brooklyn a	N. L.	7	11	0	0	.000	5	5	15	9.82
1953	Detroit	A. L.	17	102	4	7	.364	50	31	98	4.15
Major League Totals		10 Yrs	299	1425	84	65	.564	805	618	1299	3.74
World's Series Record											
1947	Brooklyn	N. L.	8	8½	1	1	.500	8	5	12	3.64
1949	Brooklyn	N. L.	1	3⅔	0	1	.000	6	4	4	4.15
World's Series Totals			4	17	1	2	.333	14	9	16	6.85

a Sold to Detroit on waiver claim, July 10, 1953.

BRAZLE, ALPHA EUGENE

Born, Loyal, Oklahoma, October 19, 1914.

Bats Left.　Throws Left.　Height, 6 feet, 2 inches.　Weight, 182 pounds.

Year	Club	Lea	G	IP	W	L	Pct	SO	BB	H	ERA
1936	Little Rock	S. A.	37	128	7	8	.467	79	52	162	5.91
1937	Hazleton	N. Y.-P. L.	35	177	10	14	.417	91	71	185	4.02
1938	Little Rock	S. A.	33	134	7	8	.467	65	54	144	4.50
1939	Little Rock	S. A.	37	217	14	16	.467	*122	87	218	3.40
1940	Little Rock	S. A.	31	134	6	10	.375	71	55	143	4.70
1941	New Orleans	S. A.	2	3	1	0	1.000	1	0	4	12.00
1941	Houston	T. L.	21	121	11	5	.688	41	41	121	3.35
1942	Houston	T. L.	33	175	8	13	.381	74	53	176	3.45
1943	Sacramento	P. C. L.	22	160	11	8	.579	69	60	131	*1.69
1943	St. Louis	N. L.	13	88	8	2	.800	26	29	74	1.53
1944, 1945			(In United States Army)								
1946	St. Louis	N. L.	37	153	11	10	.524	58	55	152	3.29
1947	St. Louis	N. L.	44	163	14	8	.636	85	48	186	2.84
1948	St. Louis	N. L.	42	156	10	6	.625	55	50	171	3.81
1949	St. Louis	N. L.	39	206	14	8	.636	75	61	208	3.19
1950	St. Louis	N. L.	46	165	11	9	.550	47	80	188	4.09

214

Year	Club	Lea	G	IP	W	L	Pct	SO	BB	H	ERA
1951	St. Louis	N. L.	56	154	6	5	.545	66	61	139	3.10
1952	St. Louis	N. L.	46	109	12	5	.706	55	42	75	2.72
1953	St. Louis	N. L.	60	92	6	7	.462	57	43	101	4.21
Major League Totals		9 Yrs	383	1291	92	60	.605	524	469	1294	3.26
World's Series Record											
1943	St. Louis	N. L.	1	7⅓	0	1	.000	4	2	5	3.68
1946	St. Louis	N. L.	1	6⅔	0	1	.000	4	6	7	5.40
World's Series Totals			2	14	0	2	.000	8	8	12	4.50

BRECHEEN, HARRY DAVID (THE CAT)

Born, Broken Bow, Oklahoma, October 14, 1914.
Bats Left.   Throws Left.   Height, 5 feet, 10 inches.   Weight, 160 pounds.

Year	Club	Lea	G	IP	W	L	Pct	SO	BB	H	ERA
1935	Greenville	E. Dix.	12	63	5	4	.556	39	24	61	4.86
1935	Galveston	T. L.	10	24	0	8	.000	8	17	29	5.63
1936	Galveston	T. L.	7	27	0	4	.000	13	14	37	8.00
1936	Bartlesville	W. A.	38	239	6	18	.250	196	118	257	5.05
1937	Portsmouth	Pied.	39	249	21	6	.778	185	69	280	...
1938	Houston	T. L.	43	212	13	10	.565	121	87	196	3.06
1939	Houston	T. L.	42	251	18	7	*.720	146	87	216	2.51
1940	Columbus	A. A.	34	216	16	9	.640	124	52	207	2.75
1940	St. Louis	N. L.	3	3	0	0	.000	4	2	2	0.00
1941	Columbus	A. A.	35	188	16	6	.727	112	66	175	3.64
1942	Columbus	A. A.	33	246	19	10	.655	*156	53	211	*2.09
1943	St. Louis	N. L.	29	135	9	6	.600	68	39	98	2.27
1944	St. Louis ....:....	N. L.	30	189	16	5	.762	88	46	174	2.86
1945	St. Louis	N. L.	24	157	15	4	.789	63	44	136	2.52
1946	St. Louis	N. L.	36	231	15	15	.500	117	67	212	2.49
1947	St. Louis	N. L.	29	223	16	11	.593	89	66	220	3.31
1948	St. Louis	N. L.	33	233	20	7	*.741	*149	49	193	*2.24
1949	St. Louis	N. L.	32	215	14	11	.560	88	65	207	3.35
1950	St. Louis	N. L.	27	163	8	11	.421	80	45	151	3.81
1951	St. Louis	N. L.	24	139	8	4	.667	57	54	134	3.24
1952	St. Louis a	N. L.	25	100	7	5	.583	54	28	82	3.33
1953	St. Louis	A. L.	26	117	5	13	.278	44	31	122	3.08
Major League Totals		12 Yrs	318	1905	133	92	.596	901	536	1731	2.92
World's Series Record											
1943	St. Louis	N. L.	3	3⅔	0	1	.000	8	3	5	2.45
1944	St. Louis	N. L.	1	9	1	0	1.000	4	4	9	1.00
1946	St. Louis	N. L.	3	20	3	0	1.000	11	5	14	0.45
World's Series Totals			7	32⅔	4	1	.800	18	12	28	0.83

a Released by St. Louis Cardinals and signed with St. Louis Browns, Oct. 30, 1952 as Pitcher-Coach.

BRISSIE, LELAND VICTOR, JR. (LOU)

Born, Anderson, South Carolina, June 5, 1924.
Bats Left.   Throws Left.   Height, 6 feet, 4½ inches.   Weight, 208 pounds.

Year	Club	Lea	G	IP	W	L	Pct	SO	BB	H	ERA
1947	Savannah	S. A. L.	35	254	*23	5	.821	*278	100	167	*1.91
1947	Philadelphia	A. L.	1	7	0	1	.000	4	5	9	6.43
1948	Philadelphia	A. L.	39	194	14	10	.583	127	95	202	4.13
1949	Philadelphia	A. L.	34	229	16	11	.593	118	118	220	4.28
1950	Philadelphia	A. L.	46	246	7	19	.269	101	117	237	4.02
1951	Phila.-Cleveland a	A. L.	56	126	4	5	.444	53	69	110	3.57
1952	Cleveland	A. L.	42	83	8	2	.600	28	34	68	3.47
1953	Cleveland	A. L.	16	13	0	0	.000	5	13	21	7.62
Major League Totals		7 Yrs	234	898	44	48	.478	436	451	867	4.07

a Traded to Cleveland as part of three-club deal, April 29, 1951. See footnote (a) to Ray Murray.

BROWN, HECTOR HAROLD (SKINNY)

Born, Greensboro, N. C., Dec. 11, 1924.
Bats Right.   Throws Right.   Height, 6 feet, 2 inches.   Weight, 182 pounds.

Year	Club	Lea	G	IP	W	L	Pct	SO	BB	H	ERA
1946	Roanoke	Pied.	10	41	1	4	.200	30	18	37	..
1946	Durham	Carolina	21	167	15	5	.750	122	54	155	..
1947	Roanoke	Pied.	31	228	*19	8	.704	94	61	244	4.14

Year	Club	Lea	G	IP	W	L	Pct	SO	BB	H	ERA
1948	Scranton	Eastern	23	185	12	6	.667	67	44	160	2.63
1949	Louisville	A. A.	33	193	8	16	.331	70	51	217	3.31
1950	Seattle a	P. C. L.	46	222	13	13	.500	87	78	242	4.66
1951	Chicago	A. L.	3	3	0	0	.000	4	4	15	9.00
1951	Seattle	P. C. L.	27	168	16	6	*.727	70	86	151	3.05
1952	Chicago b	A. L.	24	72	2	3	.400	31	21	82	4.25
1953	Boston	A. L.	30	166	11	6	.647	62	57	177	4.66

Major League Totals .... 3 Yrs 57 247 13 9 .591 97 82 274 4.70
a Drafted by Chicago White Sox, November 16, 1950.
b Traded to Boston Red Sox with Marvin Grissom and Bill Kennedy for Vernon Stephens, Feb. 9, 1953.

BUHL, ROBERT RAY
Born, Saginaw, Michigan, August 12, 1928.
Bats Right. Throws Right. Height, 6 feet, 2 inches. Weight, 180 pounds.

Year	Club	Lea	G	IP	W	L	Pct	SO	BB	H	ERA
1947	Madisonville	Kitty	*40	216	19	10	.655	185	126	175	3.00
1948	Saginaw	Central	34	224	11	12	.478	152	*145	241	5.22
1949	Hartford	E. L.	30	120	8	8	.500	101	111	85	4.43
1950	Dallas	T. L.	35	161	8	14	.364	107	120	132	3.47
1951-52	Boston	N. L.		(In Military Service)							
1953	Milwaukee	N. L.	30	154	13	8	.619	83	73	133	2.98

BURDETTE, SELVA LEWIS, JR. (LEW)
Bórn, Nitro, W. Va., Nov. 22, 1926.
Bats Right. Throws Right. Height, 6 feet, 2 inches. Weight, 180 pounds.

Year	Club	Lea	G	IP	W	L	Pct	SO	BB	H	ERA
1947	Norfolk	Pied.	6	27	1	1	.500	10	20	23	4.33
1947	Amsterdam	Can.-Am.	24	150	9	10	.474	79	80	125	2.82
1948	Quincy	I. I. L.	31	214	*16	11	.593	185	72	164	2.02
1949	Kansas City	A. A.	36	118	6	7	.462	51	47	147	5.26
1950	Kansas City	A. A.	27	139	7	7	.500	77	52	150	4.79
1950	New York	A. L.	2	1	0	0	.000	0	0	3	9.00
1951	San Francisco a ..	P. C. L.	30	210	14	12	.538	118	78	202	3.21
1951	Boston	N. L.	3	4	0	0	.000	1	5	6	6.75
1952	Boston	N. L.	45	137	6	11	.353	47	47	138	3.61
1953	Milwaukee	N. L.	46	175	15	5	.750	58	56	177	3.24

Major League Totals .... 4 Yrs 96 317 21 16 .568 106 108 324 3.46
a New York Yankees traded Burdette, plus $50,000, to Boston Braves for pitcher Johnny Sain, Aug. 29, 1951.

BYRD, HARRY GLADWIN
Born, Darlington, S. C., Feb. 3, 1925.
Bats Right. Throws Right. Height 6 feet, 1 inch. Weight, 200 pounds.

Year	Club	Lea	G	IP	W	L	Pct	SO	BB	H	ERA
1946	Martinsville	Carolina	38	236	15	12	.556	172	108	224	...
1947	Savannah	So. Atl.	38	199	16	13	.552	115	108	221	5.56
1948	Savannah	So. Atl.	42	233	15	15	.500	118	101	223	4.09
1949	Savannah	So. Atl.	10	54	2	8	.200	42	34	51	4.67
1949	Martinsville	Carolina	5	41	3	1	.750	35	10	41	...
1950	Philadelphia	A. L.	6	11	0	0	.000	2	9	25	16.36
1950	Buffalo	I. L.	21	108	4	9	.308	66	65	184	6.75
1951	Savannah	So. Atl.	33	248	18	14	.563	*180	107	*289	3.59
1952	Philadelphia	A. L.	37	228	15	15	.500	116	98	244	3.32
1953	Philadelphia a ..	A. L.	40	237	11	*20	.355	122	115	279	5.51

Major League Totals .... 3 Yrs 83 476 26 35 .426 240 222 548 4.71
a Traded to New York Yankees with Eddie Robinson for Don Bollweg, Vic Power and Bill Renna, Dec. 16, 1953.

CAIN, ROBERT MAX
Born, Longford, Kansas, October 16, 1924.
Bats Left. Throws Left. Height, 5 feet, 11 inches. Weight, 155 pounds.

Year	Club	Lea	G	IP	W	L	Pct	SO	BB	H	ERA
1943	Bristol ...	App. L.	18	139	12	5	.706	*101	46	130	
1944-45	Jersey City	I. L.		(In United States Military Service)							
1946	Manchester ...	N. Eng.	23	151	13	4	.765	107	62	114	2.38
1947	Jersey City ...	I. L.	30	106	6	6	.500	47	53	110	4.92
1948	Jersey City ...	I. L.	17	58	1	5	.167	28	53	53	6.21
1948	Minneapolis ...	A. A.	22	78	5	5	.500	48	51	88	6.58

Year	Club	Lea	G	IP	W	L	Pct	SO	BB	H	ERA
1949	Minneapolis	A. A.	12	21	0	1	.000	8	27	16	6.00
1949	Memphis	S. A.	28	131	8	7	.533	85	60	116	3.16
1949	Chicago	A. L.	6	11	0	0	.000	5	5	7	2.45
1950	Chicago	A. L	34	172	9	12	.429	77	109	153	3.92
1951	Chi.-Detroit a	A. L.	39	176	12	12	.500	61	95	160	4.55
1952	St. Louis b	A. L.	29	170	12	10	.545	70	62	169	4.13
1953	St. Louis c	A. L.	32	100	4	10	.286	36	45	129	6.21
Major League Totals		**5 Yrs**	**140**	**629**	**37**	**44**	**.457**	**249**	**316**	**618**	**4.49**

a Traded by Chicago to Detroit for Saul Rogovin, May 16, 1951.
b Traded to St. Louis Browns with Gene Bearden and Dick Kryhoski for Matt Batts, Dick Littlefield, Cliff Mapes and Ben Taylor, Feb. 14, 1952.
c Traded to Philadelphia Athletics for Joe Coleman and Frank Fanovich. Dec. 17, 1953.

CHURCH, EMORY NICHOLAS (BUBBA)

Born, Birmingham, Alabama, September 12, 1925.
Bats Right. Throws Right. Height, 5 feet, 11 inches. Weight, 180 pounds.

Year	Club	Lea	G	IP	W	L	Pct	SO	BB	H	ERA
1947	Salina a	W. A.	30	249	21	9	.700	219	79	237	2.93
1948	Toronto	I. L.	33	119	5	9	.357	89	78	119	5.52
1949	Toronto	I. L.	34	211	15	8	.652	132	118	152	*2.35
1950	Philadelphia	N. L.	31	142	8	6	.571	50	56	113	2.73
1951	Philadelphia	N. L.	38	247	15	11	.577	104	90	246	3.53
1952	Phila.-Cincinnati b	N. L.	31	158	5	9	.357	50	49	184	4.56
1953	Cincin.-Chicago c	N. L.	33	148	7	8	.467	59	63	170	5.29
Major League Totals		**4 Yrs**	**133**	**695**	**35**	**34**	**.507**	**263**	**263**	**713**	**3.98**

a Also played outfield for Salina.
b Traded by Philadelphia to Cincinnati for outfielder John Wyrostek and pitcher Kent Peterson, May 23, 1952.
c Traded to Chicago Cubs for Fred Baczewski and Bob Kelly, June 12, 1953.

COLE, DAVID BRUCE

Born, Williamsport, Maryland, August 29, 1930.
Bats Right. Throws Right. Height, 6 feet, 2 inches. Weight, 175 pounds.

Year	Club	Lea	G	IP	W	L	Pct	SO	BB	H	ERA
1948	Pawtucket	N. Eng.	9	62	5	2	.714	42	37	48	3.34
1949	Jackson	So'east.	30	203	12	12	.500	161	*151	175	4.21
1950	Milwaukee	A. A.	30	112	6	5	.545	107	60	101	4.18
1950	Boston	N. L.	4	8	0	1	.000	3	3	7	1.18
1951	Boston	N. L.	23	68	2	4	.333	33	64	64	4.24
1952	Boston	N. L.	22	45	1	1	.500	22	42	38	4.00
1953	Milwaukee	N. L.	10	15	0	1	.000	13	14	17	8.40
Major League Totals		**4 Yrs**	**59**	**136**	**3**	**7**	**.300**	**76**	**123**	**126**	**4.43**

COLEMAN, JOSEPH PATRICK

Born, Medford, Massachusetts, July 30, 1922.
Bats Right. Throws Right. Height, 6 feet, 2½ inches. Weight, 200 pounds.

Year	Club	Lea	G	IP	W	L	Pct	SO	BB	H	ERA
1941	Newport News	Virginia	32	223	15	12	.556	177	86	251	4.86
1942	Wilmington	Int.-St.	37	213	18	9	.667	139	78	169	2.82
1942	Philadelphia	A. L.	1	6	0	1	.000	0	1	8	3.00
1943-44-45		(In Military Service)									
1946	Toronto	I. L.	26	193	14	10	.583	108	64	187	2.95
1946	Philadelphia	A. L.	4	13	0	2	.000	8	8	19	5.54
1947	Philadelphia	A. L.	32	160	6	12	.333	65	62	171	4.33
1948	Philadelphia	A. L.	33	216	14	13	.519	86	90	224	4.08
1949	Philadelphia	A. L.	36	240	13	14	.481	109	127	249	3.86
1950	Philadelphia	A. L.	15	54	0	5	.000	12	50	74	3.50
1951	Philadelphia	A. L.	28	96	1	6	.143	34	59	117	6.00
1952	Ottawa	I. L.	16	76	2	7	.222	32	64	56	3.32
1952	Savannah	S. A. L.	16	84	1	12	.077	51	63	77	5.46
1953	Philadelphia a	A. L.	21	90	3	4	.429	18	49	85	4.00
Major League Totals		**8 Yrs**	**167**	**875**	**37**	**57**	**.394**	**332**	**446**	**947**	**4.50**

a Traded to Baltimore Orioles with Frank Fanovich for Bob Cain, Dec. 17, 1953.

COLLUM, JACK DEAN

Born, Victor, Iowa, June 21, 1927.
Bats Left. Throws Left. Height, 5 feet, 7½ inches. Weight, 160 pounds.

Year	Club	Lea	G	IP	W	L	Pct	SO	BB	H	ERA
1947	St. Joseph	W. A.	32	194	15	11	.577	107	81	204	3.29
1948	St. Joseph	W. A.	32	*237	*24	2	*.923	135	104	198	*2.47
1949	Omaha	West.	23	128	3	9	.250	46	66	101	2.60
1949	Rochester	I. L.	10	42	3	2	.600	23	23	36	3.86
1950	Rochester	I. L.	40	104	3	6	.571	52	52	92	3.03
1951	Rochester	I. L.	33	222	15	8	.652	108	87	211	2.80
1951	St. Louis	N. L.	3	17	2	1	.667	5	10	11	1.59
1952	St. Louis	N. L.	2	3	0	0	.000	0	1	2	0.00
1952	Rochester	I. L.	27	167	9	10	.474	83	75	160	3.77
1953	St. L.-Cincin. a	N. L.	37	136	7	11	.389	56	43	138	3.97
Major League Totals		3 Yrs	42	156	9	12	.429	61	54	151	3.63

a Traded to Cincinnati for pitcher Ed Erautt, May 23, 1953.

CONLEY, DONALD EUGENE

Born, Muskogee, Oklahoma, November 10, 1930.
Bats Right. Throws Right. Height, 6 feet, 8 inches. Weight, 225 pounds.

Year	Club	Lea	G	IP	W	L	Pct	SO	BB	H	ERA
1951	Hartford	E. L.	33	*263	20	9	.690	173	53	207	2.16
1952	Boston	N. L.	4	13	0	3	.000	6	9	23	7.61
1952	Milwaukee	A. A.	20	160	11	4	.733	143	46	143	3.15
1953	Toledo	A. A.	36	*261	*23	9	*.719	*211	57	198	*2.90

CONSUEGRA, SANDALIO SIMEON (SANDY)

Born, Potrerillo, Las Villas, Cuba, September 3, 1920.
Bats Right. Throws Right. Height, 5 feet, 11 inches. Weight, 163 pounds.

Year	Club	Lea	G	IP	W	L	Pct	SO	BB	H	ERA
1949	Havana	Fla.-Int.	11	77	6	5	.545	23	18	81	3.04
1950	Havana	Fla.-Int.	11	83	8	2	.800	58	25	73	2.15
1950	Washington	A. L.	21	125	7	8	.467	38	57	132	4.39
1951	Washington	A. L.	40	146	7	8	.467	31	63	140	4.01
1952	Washington	A. L.	30	74	6	0	1.000	19	27	80	3.04
1953	Wash.-Chicago a	A. L.	33	129	7	5	.583	30	32	131	2.86
Major League Totals		4 Yrs	124	474	27	21	.563	118	179	483	3.65

a Sold to Chicago White Sox, May 12, 1953.

CORWIN, ELMER NATHAN, JR. (AL)

Born, Newburgh, New York, December 3, 1926.
Bats Right. Throws Right. Height, 6 feet, ½ inch. Weight, 170 pounds.

Year	Club	Lea	G	IP	W	L	Pct	SO	BB	H	ERA
1948	Reno	Sunset	40	*280	*26	9	.743	251	156	260	3.54
1949	Trenton	Inter-St.	31	220	15	11	.577	166	97	207	3.03
1950	Jacksonville	So.-Atl.	37	195	9	18	.333	149	112	216	4.57
1950	Jersey City	I. L.	1	6	0	0	.000	2	1	5	3.00
1951	Ottawa	I. L.	21	91	2	4	.333	51	51	64	2.47
1951	New York	N. L.	15	59	5	1	.833	30	21	49	3.66
1952	Minneapolis a	A. A.	26	159	8	11	.421	133	111	166	5.04
1952	New York	N. L.	21	68	6	1	.857	36	36	58	2.65
1953	New York	N. L.	48	107	6	4	.600	49	68	122	4.96
Major League Totals		3 Yrs	84	234	17	6	.739	115	125	229	3.96
World's Series Record											
1951	New York	N. L.	1	1⅔	0	0	.000	0	0	1	0.00

a On option from New York to Minneapolis, April 15 to Aug. 2.

CRIMIAN, JOHN MELVIN

Born, Philadelphia, Pennsylvania, February 17, 1927.
Bats Right. Throws Right. Height, 5 feet, 10½ inches. Weight, 175 pounds.

Year	Club	Lea	G	IP	W	L	Pct	SO	BB	H	ERA
1944	Bradford	Pony	35	206	14	14	.500	149	69	193	3.19
1944	Wilmington	Int.-St.	6	38	4	2	.667	11	17	43	...
1945		(In Military Service)									
1946	Wilmington	Int-St.	29	152	13	4	.765	132	56	138	3.26
1947	Omaha	Western	33	173	14	9	.609	105	61	169	2.86
1948	Columbus	A. A.	40	149	9	4	.692	65	64	181	4.65
1949	Columbus	A. A.	51	187	11	9	.550	52	74	209	3.47

Year	Club	Lea	G	IP	W	L	Pct	SO	BB	H	ERA
1950	Columbus	A. A.	43	122	6	8	.429	52	47	127	4.65
1951	Columbus	A. A.	36	58	5	3	.625	40	30	64	3.41
1951	St. Louis	N. L.	11	17	1	0	1.000	5	8	24	9.00
1951	Houston	T. L.	12	30	1	2	.333	12	14	15	0.90
1952	Rochester	I. L.	56	90	8	8	.727	48	37	72	2.10
1952	St. Louis	N. L.	5	8	0	0	.000	4	4	15	10.13
1953	Rochester a	I. L.	62	104	13	5	.722	52	43	91	2.85
Major League Totals		2 Yrs	16	25	1	0	1.000	9	12	39	9.36

a Traded by St. Louis Cardinals with cash to Cincinnati for Alex Grammas, December 2, 1953.

DELOCK, IVAN MARTIN

Born, Highland Park, Mich., Nov. 11, 1929.
Bats Rights. Throws Right. Height, 5 feet, 11 inches. Weight, 175 pounds.

Year	Club	Lea	G	IP	W	L	Pct	SO	BB	H	ERA
1948	Auburn	Border	24	103	5	5	.500	56	87	99	5.16
1949	Oneonta	Can.-Am.	33	199	12	13	.480	103	107	206	4.21
1950	Roanoke	Piedmont	39	213	15	8	.652	147	105	161	2.87
1951	Birmingham	S. A.	5	13	0	1	.000	5	5	17	5.54
1951	Scranton	Eastern	30	211	20	4	*.833	136	74	166	1.92
1952	Louisville	A. A.	2	16	2	0	1.000	16	5	10	2.25
1952	Boston	A. L.	39	95	4	9	.308	46	50	88	4.26
1953	Louisville	A. A.	12	85	3	6	.333	43	18	75	2.96
1953	Boston	A. L.	23	49	3	1	.750	22	20	60	4.41
Major League Totals		2 Yrs	62	144	7	10	.412	68	70	148	4.31

DICKSON, MURRY MONROE

Born, Tracy, Missouri, August 21, 1916.
Bats Right. Throws Right. Height, 5 feet, 10½ inches. Weight, 160 pounds.

Year	Club	Lea	G	IP	W	L	Pct	SO	BB	H	ERA
1937	Grand Island	Neb. St.	35	233	14	15	.483	*209	88	249	4.87
1938	Decatur	I. L. L.	*42	248	16	14	.533	151	97	239	4.07
1939	Houston	T. L.	51	263	*22	15	.595	159	85	252	3.25
1939	St. Louis	N. L.	1	4	0	0	.000	2	1	1	0.00
1940	Columbus	A. A.	36	219	17	8	.680	105	86	212	3.33
1940	St. Louis	N. L.	1	2	0	0	.000	0	1	5	18.50
1941	Columbus	A. A.	44	259	*21	11	.656	*153	*124	244	3.30
1942	St. Louis	N. L.	36	121	6	3	.667	66	61	91	2.90
1943	St. Louis	N. L.	31	116	8	2	.800	44	49	114	3.57
1944, 1945					(In United States Army)						
1946	St. Louis	N. L.	47	184	15	6	*.714	82	56	160	2.89
1947	St. Louis	N. L.	47	232	13	16	.448	111	88	211	3.06
1948	St. Louis	N. L.	42	252	12	16	.429	113	85	257	4.14
1949	Pittsburgh a	N. L.	44	224	12	14	.462	89	80	216	3.29
1950	Pittsburgh	N. L.	51	225	10	15	.400	76	83	227	3.80
1951	Pittsburgh	N. L.	45	289	20	16	.556	112	101	*294	4.02
1952	Pittsburgh	N. L.	43	278	14	*21	.400	112	76	278	3.56
1953	Pittsburgh	N. L.	45	201	10	*19	.345	88	58	240	4.52
Major League Totals		12 Yrs	433	2128	120	128	.484	895	739	2094	3.63
World's Series Record											
1943	St. Louis	N. L.	1	⅔	0	0	.000	0	1	0	0.00
1946	St. Louis	N. L.	2	14	0	1	.000	7	4	11	3.86
World's Series Totals		3	14⅔	0	1	.000	7	5	11	3.68

a Sold to Pittsburgh for undisclosed sum, January 29, 1949.

DIXON, JOHN CRAIG, JR.

Born, Charlotte, North Carolina, November 5, 1924.
Bats Both. Throws Right. Height, 6 feet, 3 inches. Weight, 205 pounds.

Year	Club	Lea	G	IP	W	L	Pct	SO	BB	H	ERA
1946	Charlotte	Tri-St.	32	*244	*19	11	.633	90	53	*246	2.62
1947	Charlotte	Tri-St.	27	165	9	9	.500	58	45	188	4.36
1948	Augusta	S. A. L.	37	190	11	7	.611	71	59	217	4.81
1949	Augusta	S. A. L.	38	217	14	14	.500	99	70	230	3.24
1950	Augusta	S. A. L.	45	230	14	13	.519	120	87	255	4.16
1951	Chattanooga	S. A.	42	255	14	13	.519	84	63	*253	5.36
1952	Chattanooga	S. A.	47	253	19	14	.576	136	71	260	3.19
1953	Washington	A. L.	43	120	5	8	.385	40	31	123	3.75

DORISH, HARRY

Born, Swoyerville, Pennsylvania, July 13, 1922.
Bats Right. Throws Right. Height, 5 feet, 11 inches. Weight, 200 pounds.

Year	Club	Lea	G	IP	W	L	Pct	SO	BB	H	ERA
1941	Canton	M. A. L.	21	120	7	6	.538	88	50	119	3.23

Year	Club	Lea	G	IP	W	L	Pct	SO	BB	H	ERA
1942	Scranton	E. L.	24	148	12	8	.600	76	49	113	2.07
1943, 1944, 1945			(In United States Military Service)								
1946	Louisville	A. A.	28	146	11	4	.733	76	47	128	3.14
1947	Boston	A. L.	41	136	7	8	.467	50	54	149	4.70
1948	Boston	A. L.	9	14	0	1	.000	5	6	18	5.79
1948	Birmingham	S. A.	16	99	9	4	.692	51	25	102	3.45
1949	Boston	A. L.	5	8	0	0	.000	5	1	7	2.25
1949	Louisville a	A. A.	15	90	8	8	.500	45	85	103	5.10
1950	St. Louis	A. L.	29	109	4	9	.308	86	86	162	6.44
1951	Chicago b	A. L.	32	97	5	6	.455	29	81	101	3.53
1952	Chicago	A. L.	89	91	8	4	.667	47	42	66	2.47
1953	Chicago	A. L.	55	146	10	8	.625	69	52	140	3.39

Major League Totals   7 Yrs   210   601   34   84   .500   241   222   643   4.16

a Sold by Boston Red Sox to St. Louis Browns, May 9, 1950.

b Drafted from Toronto, I. L., November 16, 1950, having been released by St. Louis Browns, November 14, 1950.

DREWS, KARL AUGUST

Born, Staten Island, New York, February 22, 1920.
Bats Right.   Throws Right.   Height, 6 feet, 4 inches.   Weight, 193 pounds.

Year	Club	Lea	G	IP	W	L	Pct	SO	BB	H	ERA
1939	Butler	Penn. St.	31	192	*16	5	*.762	126	123	160	3.66
1940	Norfolk	Piedmont	6	33	1	4	.200	20	23	34	4.64
1940	Akron	Mid. Atl.	30	171	11	8	.579	87	125	208	6.05
1941	Norfolk	Piedmont	2	13	1	1	.500	7	16	7	2.08
1941	Augusta	S. A. L.	1	0⅓	0	1	.000	0	2	8	81.00
1941	Amsterdam	Can.-Am.	25	128	8	6	.571	86	92	153	6.54
1942	Norfolk	Piedmont	2	9	0	1	.000	7	8	9	5.00
1942	Evansville	Three-I.	26	181	7	9	.438	78	81	125	4.81
1943	Norfolk	Piedmont	(Voluntarily Retired)								
1944	Newark	I. L.	5	28	1	8	.250	11	27	82	6.43
1944	Binghamton	Eastern	26	186	14	8	.636	158	106	151	3.19
1945	Newark	I. L.	33	240	19	9	.679	115	113	193	2.70
1946	Kansas City	A. A.	24	182	14	9	.609	89	75	174	3.86
1946	New York	A. L.	3	6	0	1	.000	4	6	6	9.00
1947	New York	A. L.	30	92	6	6	.500	45	55	92	4.89
1948	N. Y.-St. Louis a	A. L.	39	76	5	5	.500	22	69	78	5 92
1949	St. Louis	A. L.	31	140	4	12	.250	35	66	180	6.62
1950	Baltimore	I. L.	22	92	6	2	.750	42	47	84	4.11
1951	Baltimore	I. L.	33	*253	17	13	.567	127	89	211	2.85
1951	Philadelphia	N. L.	5	23	1	0	1.000	13	7	29	6 26
1952	Philadelphia	N. L.	33	229	14	15	.483	96	52	213	2.71
1953	Philadelphia	N. L.	47	185	9	10	.474	72	50	218	4.52

Major League Totals   7 Yrs   188   751   39   49   .443   287   305   816   4.64

World's Series Record

Year	Club	Lea	G	IP	W	L	Pct	SO	BB	H	ERA
1947	New York	A. L.	2	8	0	0	.000	0	6	2	3.00

a Released to St. Louis on waivers, Aug. 9, 1948.

ERAUTT, EDWARD LORENZ

Born, Portland, Oregon, September 26, 1924.
Bats Right.   Throws Right.   Height, 6 feet.   Weight, 186 pounds.

Year	Club	Lea	G	IP	W	L	Pct	SO	BB	H	ERA
1942	Salem	W. I. L.	14	89	4	7	.364	45	43	104	4.15
1942	Hollywood	P. C. L.	7	17	0	4	.000	8	11	23	7.39
1943	Hollywood	P. C. L.	20	115	5	9	.357	83	40	110	3.29
1944, 1945			(In United States Army)								
1946	Hollywood	P. C. L.	44	290	20	14	.588	*234	77	258	2.76
1947	Cincinnati	N. L.	36	119	4	9	.308	43	53	146	5.07
1948	Cincinnati	N. L.	2	3	0	0	.000	0	1	8	6.00
1948	Syracuse	I. L.	29	215	15	7	.682	141	61	202	2.97
1949	Cincinnati	N. L.	39	113	4	11	.267	43	61	99	8.35
1950	Cincinnati	N. L.	33	65	4	2	.667	35	22	82	5.68
1951	Cincinnati	N. L.	80	89	0	0	.000	20	23	50	5.77
1952	Kansas City	A. A.	30	210	*21	5	.808	104	57	189	3.00
1953	Cin.-St. Louis a	N. L.	24	40	3	1	.750	16	19	54	6.30

Major League Totals   6 Yrs   164   879   15   23   .395   157   179   434   4.87

a Traded to St. Louis Cardinals for pitcher Jack Collum, May 23, 1953.

ERSKINE, CARL DANIEL

Born, Anderson, Indiana, December 13, 1926.
Bats Right. Throws Right. Height, 5 feet, 9½ inches. Weight, 165 pounds.

Year	Club	Lea	G	IP	W	L	Pct	SO	BB	H	ERA
1946	Danville	L. I. L.	9	50	3	3	.500	52	24	41	2.16
1947	Danville	L. I. L.	37	*233	19	9	.679	191	89	200	2.94
1948	Fort Worth	T. L.	23	167	15	7	.682	112	80	136	2.59
1948	Brooklyn	N. L.	17	64	6	3	.667	29	35	51	3.23
1949	Fort Worth	T. L.	15	122	10	4	*.714	113	62	86	*2.07
1949	Brooklyn	N. L.	22	80	8	1	.889	49	51	68	4.61
1950	Montreal	I. L.	18	118	10	6	.625	89	61	103	3.74
1950	Brooklyn	N. L.	22	103	7	6	.538	50	35	109	4.72
1951	Brooklyn	N. L.	46	190	16	12	.571	95	78	206	4.45
1952	Brooklyn a	N. L.	33	207	14	6	.700	131	71	167	2.70
1953	Brooklyn	N. L.	39	247	20	6	*.769	187	95	213	3.53
Major League Totals		6 Yrs	179	891	71	34	.676	541	365	814	3.75
World's Series Record											
1949	Brooklyn	N. L.	2	1⅔	0	0	.000	0	1	3	16.20
1952	Brooklyn	N. L.	3	18	1	1	.500	10	10	12	4.50
1953	Brooklyn	N. L.	3	14	1	0	1.000	16	9	14	5.79
World's Series Totals			8	33⅔	2	1	.667	26	20	29	5.61

a Pitched no-hit, no-run game against Chicago, June 19.

FACE, ELROY LEON

Born, Stephentown, New York, February 20, 1928.
Bats Right. Throws Right. Height, 5 feet, 8 inches. Weight, 155 pounds.

Year	Club	Lea	G	IP	W	L	Pct	SO	BB	H	ERA
1949	Bradford	Pony	25	141	14	2	*.875	124	65	147	3.32
1950	Bradford	Pony	31	209	18	5	.783	150	68	193	*2.58
1951	Pueblo	Western	35	265	*23	9	.719	171	91	224	2.78
1952	Fort Worth a	T. L.	33	226	14	11	.560	130	53	216	2.88
1953	Pittsburgh	N. L.	41	119	6	8	.429	56	30	145	6.58

a Drafted by Pittsburgh from Montreal, December 1, 1952.

FELLER, ROBERT WILLIAM ANDREW

Born, Van Meter, Iowa, November 3, 1918.
Bats Right. Throws Right. Height, 6 feet. Weight, 185 pounds.

Year	Club	Lea	G	IP	W	L	Pct	SO	BB	H	ERA
1936	Cleveland	A. L.	14	62	5	3	.625	76	47	52	3.34
1937	Cleveland	A. L.	26	149	9	7	.563	150	106	116	3.38
1938	Cleveland	A. L.	39	278	17	11	.607	*240	*208	225	4.08
1939	Cleveland	A. L.	39	*297	*24	9	.727	*246	*142	227	2.85
1940	Cleveland a	A. L.	*43	*320	*27	11	.711	*261	118	245	*2.62
1941	Cleveland	A. L.	*44	*343	*25	13	.658	*260	*194	*284	3.15
1942-43-44-45	Cleveland	A. L.	(In U. S. Navy)								
1945	Cleveland	A. L.	9	72	5	3	.625	59	35	50	2.50
1946	Cleveland b	A. L.	*48	*371	*26	15	.634	*348	*153	*277	2.18
1947	Cleveland	A. L.	42	*299	*20	11	.645	*196	127	230	2.68
1948	Cleveland	A. L.	44	280	19	15	.559	*164	116	*255	3.57
1949	Cleveland	A. L.	36	211	15	14	.517	108	84	198	3.75
1950	Cleveland	A. L.	35	247	16	11	.593	119	103	230	3.43
1951	Cleveland c	A. L.	33	250	*22	8	.733	111	95	239	3.49
1952	Cleveland	A. L.	30	192	9	13	.409	81	83	219	4.73
1953	Cleveland	A. L.	25	176	10	7	.588	60	60	163	3.58
Major League Totals		15 Yrs	507	3547	249	151	.623	2479	1671	3010	3.23
World's Series Record											
1948	Cleveland	A. L.	2	14⅓	0	2	.000	7	5	10	5.02

a Pitched no-hit game against Chicago, April 16th, winning 1-0.
b Pitched no-hit game against New York, April 30, winning 1-0.
c Pitched no-hit game against Detroit, July 1, winning 2-1.

FORD, EDWARD CHARLES (WHITEY)

Born, New York, N. Y., October 21, 1928.
Bats Left. Throws Left. Height, 5 feet, 10 inches. Weight, 165 pounds.

Year	Club	Lea	G	IP	W	L	Pct	SO	BB	H	ERA
1947	Butler	M. A. L.	24	157	13	4	.765	114	53	151	3.84
1948	Norfolk	Pied.	30	216	16	8	.667	*171	112	182	2.58

221

Year	Club	Lea	G	IP	W	L	Pct	SO	BB	H	ERA
1949	Binghamton	E. L.	26	168	16	5	.762	*151	54	118	*1.61
1950	Kansas City	A. A.	12	95	6	3	.667	80	48	81	3.22
1950	New York	A. L.	20	112	9	1	.900	59	52	87	2.81
1951-52	New York	A. L.	(In Military Service)								
1953	New York	A. L.	82	207	18	6	.750	110	110	187	3.00
Major League Totals		2 Yrs	52	319	27	7	.794	169	162	274	2.93
World's Series Record											
1950	New York	A. L.	1	8⅔	1	0	1.000	7	1	7	0.00
1953	New York	A. L.	2	8	0	1	.000	7	2	9	4.50
World's Series Totals			8	16⅔	1	1	.500	14	8	16	2.18

FORNIELES, MIGUEL (TORRES)

Born, Havana, Cuba, January 18, 1932.
Bats Right. Throws Right. Height, 5 feet, 11 inches. Weight, 158 pounds.

Year	Club	Lea	G	IP	W	L	Pct	SO	BB	H	ERA
1951	Big Spring	Long.	29	208	17	6	.739	142	100	185	*2.86
1952	Havana	Fla. Int.	40	213	14	12	.538	135	102	159	2.66
1952	Washington a	A. L.	4	26	2	2	.500	12	11	13	1.38
1953	Chicago	A. L.	89	153	8	7	.533	72	61	160	3.59
Major League Totals		2 Yrs	43	179	10	9	.526	84	72	173	3.27

a Traded to Chicago White Sox for pitcher Charles Stobbs, December 10, 1952.

FRICANO, MARION JOHN JOSEPH

Born, Brant, New York, July 15, 1923.
Bats Right. Throws Right. Height, 5 feet, 11½ inches. Weight, 170 pounds.

Year	Club	Lea	G	IP	W	L	Pct	SO	BB	H	ERA
1947	Johnston	M. A. L.	14	69	5	2	.714	86	24	78	4.96
1948	Valdosta	Ga.-Fla.	82	178	13	7	.650	94	48	200	3.13
1949	Nashua	New Eng.	17	134	11	3	.786	59	49	112	*1.48
1949	Pueblo	West.	15	87	10	2	.833	52	44	88	3.52
1950	Mobile	S. A.	33	176	15	10	.600	83	60	183	4.09
1951	Mobile	S. A.	33	159	10	9	.526	64	55	137	2.77
1951	St. Paul	A. A.	9	35	2	0	1.000	14	17	29	4.88
1952	St. Paul	A. A.	2	6	0	0	.000	2	2	12	6.00
1952	Ottawa	I. L.	30	191	17	8	.680	78	64	163	*2.26
1952	Philadelphia	A. L.	2	5	1	0	1.000	0	1	5	1.80
1953	Philadelphia	A. L.	39	211	9	12	.429	67	90	206	3.88
Major League Totals		2 Yrs	41	216	10	12	.455	67	91	211	3.83

FRIEND, ROBERT BARTMESS

Born, Lafayette, Indiana, November 24, 1930.
Bats Right. Throws Right. Height, 6 feet. Weight, 190 pounds.

Year	Club	Lea	G	IP	W	L	Pct	SO	BB	H	ERA
1950	Waco	Big State	29	190	12	9	.571	107	91	173	3.08
1950	Indianapolis	A. A.	11	56	2	4	.333	34	16	75	5.46
1951	Pittsburgh	N. L.	34	150	6	10	.375	41	63	173	4.26
1952	Pittsburgh	N. L.	35	185	7	17	.292	75	84	186	4.18
1953	Pittsburgh	N. L.	82	171	8	11	.421	66	57	193	4.89
Major League Totals		3 Yrs	101	506	21	38	.356	182	209	552	4.45

GARCIA, EDWARD MIKE

Born, San Gabriel, California, November 17, 1923.
Bats Right. Throws Right. Height, 6 feet, 1½ inches. Weight, 200 pounds.

Year	Club	Lea	G	IP	W	L	Pct	SO	BB	H	ERA
1942	Appleton	Wisc. St.	20	137	10	10	.500	105	46	153	3.94
1943, 1944, 1945			(In United States Military Service)								
1946	Bakersfield	Cal. L.	*42	236	22	9	.710	*186	110	218	*2.56
1947	Wilkes-Barre	E. L.	84	*225	*17	10	.630	108	91	*219	3.24
1948	Oklahoma City	T. L.	44	259	19	16	.543	163	127	218	3.09

Year	Club	Lea	G	IP	W	L	Pct	SO	BB	H	ERA
1948	Cleveland	A. L.	1	2	0	0	.000	1	0	3	0.00
1949	Cleveland	A. L.	41	176	14	5	.737	94	60	154	2.85
1950	Cleveland	A. L.	63	184	11	11	.500	76	74	191	3.86
1951	Cleveland	A. L.	47	254	20	13	.606	118	82	239	3.15
1952	Cleveland	A. L.	46	292	22	11	.667	143	87	•284	2.37
1953	Cleveland	A. L.	38	272	18	9	.667	134	81	260	3.24
Major League Totals		6 Yrs	206	1180	85	49	.634	566	384	1131	2.97

GARVER, NED FRANKLIN

Born, Ney, Ohio, December 25, 1925.
Bats Right.   Throws Right.   Height, 5 feet, 10½ inches.   Weight, 180 pounds.

Year	Club	Lea	G	IP	W	L	Pct	SO	BB	H	ERA
1944	Newark	Ohio St.	32	•245	•21	8	.724	•221	48	169	•1.21
1945	Elmira	El. L.	4	33	3	1	.750	25	15	22	2.18
1945	Toledo	A. A.	31	132	5	8	.385	68	76	150	4.64
1946	San Antonio	T. I.	25	148	8	8	.500	76	54	140	2.86
1947	San Antonio	T. L	53	257	17	14	.548	109	92	244	3.22
1948	St. Louis	A. L.	33	198	7	11	.389	75	95	200	3.41
1949	St. Louis	A. L.	41	224	12	•17	.414	70	102	245	3.98
1950	St. Louis	A. L.	37	260	13	18	.419	85	108	264	3.39
1951	St. Louis	A. L.	33	246	20	12	.625	84	96	237	3.73
1952	St. L.-Detroit a	A. L.	23	158	8	10	.444	63	53	189	3.59
1953	Detroit	A. L.	30	198	11	11	.500	69	66	223	4.45
Major League Totals		6 Yrs	201	1284	71	79	.473	446	525	1313	3.75

a Traded with outfielder Jim Delsing and pitchers Dave Madison and Bud Black by St. Louis to Detroit for outfielders Vic Wertz and Don Lenhardt and pitchers Marlin Stuart and Dick Littlefield, Aug. 14, 1952.

GOMEZ, RUBEN

Born, Arroyo, Puerto Rico, July 13, 1927.
Bats Right.   Throws Right.   Height, 6 feet.   Weight, 175 pounds.

Year	Club	Lea	G	IP	W	L	Pct	SO	BB	H	ERA
1949	Bristol	Colonial	11	48	5	1	.833	86	68	44	2.81
1950	Bristol	Colonial	3	15	1	0	1.000	7	16	13	...
1950	St. Jean	Provincial	26	180	14	4	.778	•140	86	174	3.89
1951	Havana	Fla. Int.	4	31	1	2	.333	19	19	30	4.35
1951	St. Jean	Provincial	28	153	12	6	.667	135	81	155	4.41
1952	Kansas City	A. A.	5	10	1	0	1.000	4	6	16	1.17
1953	New York a	N. L.	29	204	13	11	.542	113	101	166	3.40

a Signed with New York Giants as a free-agent, January 30, 1953.

GORMAN, THOMAS ALOYSIUS

Born, New York City, Jan. 4, 1926.
Bats Right.   Throws Right.   Height, 6 feet, 1 inch.   Weight, 190 pounds.

Year	Club	Lea	G	IP	W	L	Pct	SO	BB	H	ERA
1946	Norfolk	Piedmont	19	93	2	9	.182	85	86	103	3.87
1946	Radford	Bl. Rdge.	10	82	8	5	.375	82	23	65	2.30
1947	Norfolk	Piedmont	35	169	8	12	.400	84	60	198	4.85
1948	Binghamton	Eastern	54	116	6	11	.353	60	41	116	4.11
1949	Binghamton	Eastern	25	159	12	8	.600	97	58	145	2.60
1949	Newark	I. L.	8	20	0	1	.000	6	18	26	6.30
1950	Kansas City	A. A.	45	97	8	5	.375	66	55	101	5.01
1951	Beaumont	Texas	26	172	12	8	.600	89	40	185	•1.94
1951	Kansas City	A. A.	8	6	0	1	.000	4	6	5	1.50
1952	Kansas City	A. A.	18	86	7	4	.636	43	22	93	3.66
1952	New York a	A. L.	12	61	6	2	.750	31	22	68	4.57
1953	New York	A. L.	40	77	4	5	.444	38	32	65	3.39
Major League Totals		2 Yrs	52	138	10	7	.588	69	54	123	3.91

World's Series Record

Year	Club	Lea	G	IP	W	L	Pct	SO	BB	H	ERA
1952	New York	A. L.	1	0⅔	0	0	.000	0	0	1	0.00
1953	New York	A. L.	1	8	0	0	.000	1	0	4	3.00
World's Series Totals		2	8⅔	0	0	.000	1	0	5	2.45

a With Kansas City on option, April 14 to July 14, 1952.

GRAY, TED GLENN

Born, Detroit, Michigan, December 31, 1924.
Bats Both.   Throws Left.   Height, 5 feet, 10 inches.   Weight, 160 pounds.

Year	Club	Lea	G	IP	W	L	Pct	SO	BB	H	ERA
1942	Winston-Salem	P. L.	30	213	13	14	.481	143	97	157	2.07
1943-44-45	Detroit	A. L.	(In U. S. Navy)								
1946	Buffalo	I. L.	25	123	7	11	.389	80	82	140	6.22
1946	Detroit	A. L.	3	12	0	2	.000	5	5	17	8.25
1947	Buffalo	I. L.	33	150	11	7	.611	138	86	128	3.42
1948	Detroit	A. L.	26	85	6	2	.750	60	72	73	4.24
1949	Detroit	A. L.	34	195	10	10	.500	96	103	163	3.51
1950	Detroit	A. L.	27	149	10	7	.588	102	72	139	4.41
1951	Detroit	A. L.	34	197	7	*14	.333	131	95	194	4.07
1952	Detroit	A. L.	35	224	12	17	.414	188	101	212	4.14
1953	Detroit	A. L.	30	176	10	15	.400	115	76	166	4.60
Major League Totals		7 Yrs	189	1038	55	67	.451	647	524	964	4.13

GRISSOM, MARVIN EDWARD

Born, Los Molinos, Calif., March 31, 1918
Bats Right.   Throws Right.   Height, 6 feet, 3 inches.   Weight, 195 pounds.

Year	Club	Lea	G	IP	W	L	Pct	SO	BB	H	ERA
1941	San Bernardino	Calif.	10	52	2	4	.333	25	27	72	4.67
1942, 1943, 1944, 1945		(In United States Military Service)									
1946	Jersey City	I. L.	34	119	4	10	.286	75	81	105	4.16
1946	New York	N. L.	4	19	0	2	.000	9	13	17	4.26
1947	Minneapolis	A. A.	37	151	9	16	.360	92	89	162	6.26
1948	Sacramento a	P. C. L.	38	190	11	7	.611	95	83	192	4.03
1949	Detroit	A. L.	27	39	2	4	.333	17	34	56	6.46
1950	Toledo	A. A.	28	156	9	10	.474	99	54	157	3.46
1951	Seattle	P. C. L.	34	252	*20	11	.645	146	100	193	3.04
1952	Chicago b	A. L.	28	166	12	10	.545	97	79	156	3.74
1953	Boston c	A. L.	13	59	2	6	.250	31	30	61	4.73
1953	New York	N. L.	21	84	4	2	.667	46	31	83	3.96
Major League Totals		4 Yrs	93	367	20	24	.455	200	187	373	4.27

a Drafted by Detroit, November 10, 1948.

b Traded to Boston Red Sox with Hector Brown and Bill Kennedy for Vernon Stephens, February 9, 1953.

c Sold to New York Giants, July 1, 1953 on waiver claim.

GROMEK, STEPHEN JOSEPH

Born, Hamtramck, Michigan, January 15, 1920.
Bats Both.   Throws Right.   Height, 6 feet, 2 inches.   Weight, 195 pounds.

Year	Club	Lea	G	IP	W	L	Pct	SO	BB	H	ERA
1940	Flint a	Mich. St.	4	28	4	0	1.000	17	7	18	1.61
1941	Flint	Mich. St.	19	143	14	2	*.875	126	44	111	*2.90
1941	Cleveland	A. L.	9	23	1	1	.500	19	11	25	4.30
1942	Baltimore	I. L.	20	63	4	6	.400	54	24	74	5.14
1942	Cleveland	A. L.	14	44	2	0	1.000	14	23	46	3.68
1943	Baltimore	I. L.	46	261	18	13	.552	*188	69	240	3.34
1943	Cleveland	A. L.	3	4	0	0	.000	4	0	6	9.00
1944	Cleveland	A. L.	35	204	10	9	.526	115	70	180	2.56
1945	Cleveland	A. L.	33	251	19	9	.679	101	66	229	2.55
1946	Cleveland	A. L.	29	164	5	15	.250	75	47	159	4.06
1947	Cleveland	A. L.	29	84	3	5	.375	39	36	77	3.75
1948	Cleveland	A. L.	38	130	9	3	.750	50	51	109	2.84
1949	Cleveland	A. L.	27	92	4	6	.400	22	40	86	3.33
1950	Cleveland	A. L.	31	118	10	7	.588	48	36	94	3.66
1951	Cleveland	A. L.	27	107	7	4	.636	40	29	93	2.73
1952	Cleveland	A. L.	29	123	7	7	.500	65	28	109	3.66
1953	Clev.-Detroit b	A. L.	24	137	7	9	.438	67	39	149	4.40
Major League Totals		13 Yrs	328	1476	84	75	.528	654	476	1347	3.30
	World's Series Record										
1948	Cleveland	A. L.	1	9	1	0	1.000	2	1	7	1.00

a Played as infielder 1939 Logan (Mt. State), 1939 Mansfield (Ohio State), 1940 Fargo-Moorhead (Northern), 1940 Flint.

b Traded to Detroit with Al Aber, Ray Boone and Dick Weik for Owen Friend, Joe Ginsberg, Art Houtteman and Bill Wight, June 15, 1953.

224

HACKER, WARREN LOUIS

Born, Marissa, Ill., Nov. 21, 1924.
Bats Right. Throws Right. Height, 6 feet, 1 inch. Weight, 185 pounds.

Year	Club	Lea	G	IP	W	L	Pct	SO	BB	H	ERA
1946	Pampa	W. Tex.-N. M.	32	213	20	4	.833	133	83	232	3.68
1947	Shreveport	Texas	7	20	2	0	1.000	5	11	22	7.65
1947	Texarkana	Big Sta.	32	146	9	5	.643	46	49	159	4.99
1948	Shreveport	Texas	*45	249	17	14	.548	32	34	226	3.18
1948	Chicago	N. L.	3	3	0	1	.000	0	8	7	21.00
1949	Shreveport	Texas	18	66	5	3	.625	29	28	75	5.18
1949	Chicago	N. L.	30	126	5	8	.385	40	53	141	4.21
1950	Springfield	I. L.	20	137	11	4	.733	61	86	137	3.35
1950	Chicago	N. L.	5	15	0	1	.000	5	8	20	5.40
1951	Chicago	N. L.	2	1	0	0	.000	2	0	3	18.00
1951	Los Angeles	P. C. L.	28	193	8	15	.348	100	54	161	3.87
1952	Chicago	N. L.	33	185	15	9	.625	84	31	144	2.58
1953	Chicago	N. L.	39	222	12	*19	.387	106	54	225	4.38
Major League Totals		6 Yrs	112	552	32	33	.457	237	149	540	3.83

HADDIX, HARVEY, JR.

Born, Medway, Ohio, September 18, 1925.
Bats Left. Throws Left. Height, 5 feet, 9½ inches. Weight, 170 pounds.

Year	Club	Lea	G	IP	W	L	Pct	SO	BB	H	ERA
1947	Winston-Salem	Carolina	27	204	19	5	*.792	268	70	144	*1.90
1948	Columbus	A. A.	32	186	11	9	.550	144	67	199	4.79
1949	Columbus	A. A.	35	219	18	18	.500	177	94	206	3.49
1950	Columbus	A. A.	30	217	*18	6	.750	*160	59	192	*2.70
1951-52	St. Louis	N. L.		(In Military Service)							
1952	St. Louis	N. L.	7	42	2	2	.500	31	10	31	2.79
1953	St. Louis	N. L.	36	253	20	9	.690	163	69	220	3.06
Major League Totals		2 Yrs	43	295	22	11	.667	194	79	251	3.02

HALL, ROBERT LOUIS

Born, Swissvale, Pennsylvania, December 22, 1923.
Bats Right. Throws Right. Height, 6 feet, 1½ inches. Weight, 195 pounds.

Year	Club	Lea	G	IP	W	L	Pct	SO	BB	H	ERA
1942	Winston-Salem	Pied.	9	48	0	8	.000	23	37	49	
1943-44-45	Winst.-Salem a	Pied.		(In Military Service)							
1946	Buffalo	I. L.	1	1	0	0	.000	0	0	2	0.00
1946	Williamsport	E. L.	6	29	1	4	.200	7	19	44	7.45
1947	Vancouver	W. I. L.	34	235	15	7	.682	216	173	235	5.21
1947	Seattle	P. C. L.	4	25	1	1	.500	12	12	30	3.60
1948	Seattle	P. C. L.	36	134	7	11	.389	96	56	119	3.96
1949	Boston	N. L.	31	74	6	4	.600	43	41	77	4.38
1950	Boston	N. L.	21	50	0	2	.000	22	33	58	7.02
1951	Milwaukee	A. A.	9	63	2	4	.333	37	36	83	4.29
1951	Seattle	P. C. L.	21	133	7	8	.467	80	51	137	3.72
1952	Sac.-Seattle b	P. C. L.	40	203	14	11	.560	119	88	180	3.28
1953	Pittsburgh	N. L.	37	152	3	12	.200	68	72	172	5.89
Major League Totals		3 Yrs	89	276	9	18	.333	133	146	307	5.41

a Declared free agent when reinstated from service, and signed with Buffalo.
b Drafted by Pittsburgh, December 1, 1952.

HANSEN, ANDREW VIGGO, JR.

Born, Lake Worth, Florida, November 12, 1924.
Bats Right. Throws Right. Height, 6 feet, 3 inches. Weight, 180 pounds.

Year	Club	Lea	G	IP	W	L	Pct	SO	BB	H	ERA
1943	Bristol	App. L.	16	115	12	3	.800	79	15	91	3.24
1944	Jersey City	I. L.	15	100	8	4	.667	31	28	90	1.89
1944	New York	N. L.	23	53	3	3	.500	15	32	63	6.45
1945	New York	N. L.	23	93	4	8	.571	37	28	98	4.65
1945	Jersey City	I. L.	5	16	1	3	.250	6	11	25	7.31
1946	New York	N. L.		(In Military Service)							
1947	New York	N. L.	27	82	1	5	.167	18	33	78	4.39
1948	New York	N. L.	36	100	5	3	.625	27	36	96	2.97
1949	New York	N. L.	33	66	2	6	.250	26	28	53	4.64
1950	New York a	N. L.	31	57	0	1	.000	19	26	64	5.53
1951	Baltimore	I. L.	19	33	1	1	.500	14	26	40	5.45
1951	Philadelphia	N. L.	24	39	3	1	.750	11	7	34	2.54

Year	Club	Lea	G	IP	W	L	Pct	SO	BB	H	ERA
1952	Philadelphia	N. L.	43	77	5	6	.455	18	27	76	3.27
1953	Philadelphia	N. L.	30	51	0	2	.000	17	24	60	4.06
	Major League Totals		9 Yrs	270	618	23	30	.434	188	246	627	4.22

a Released to Minneapolis by New York Giants, and drafted by Philadelphia Phillies, Nov. 16, 1950.

HEARN, JAMES TOLBERT
Born, Atlanta, Georgia, April 11, 1922.
Bats Right. Throws Right. Height, 6 feet, 3 inches. Weight, 200 pounds.

Year	Club	Lea	G	IP	W	L	Pct	SO	BB	H	ERA
1942	Columbus	S. A. L.	27	203	11	12	.478	119	77	188	3.24
1943, 1944, 1945		(In United States Military Service)									
1946	Columbus	A. A.	24	98	4	5	.444	48	46	103	4.13
1947	St. Louis	N. L.	37	162	12	7	.632	57	63	151	3.22
1948	St. Louis	N. L.	34	90	8	6	.571	27	35	92	4.20
1949	St. Louis	N. L.	17	42	1	3	.250	18	23	48	5.14
1949	Rochester	I. L.	13	89	8	3	.727	44	36	92	4.25
1950	St. Louis-New York a	N. L.	22	134	11	4	.733	58	44	84	*2.49
1951	New York	N. L.	34	211	17	9	.654	66	82	204	3.63
1952	New York	N. L.	37	224	14	7	.667	89	97	208	3.78
1953	New York	N. L.	36	197	9	12	.429	77	84	206	4.52
	Major League Totals		7 Yrs	217	1060	72	48	.600	392	428	993	3.73

World's Series Record

Year	Club	Lea	G	IP	W	L	Pct	SO	BB	H	ERA
1951	New York	N. L.	2	8⅔	1	0	1.000	1	8	5	1.04

a Sold to New York Giants on waivers, July 10.

HENRY, WILLIAM RODMAN
Born, Alice, Texas, October 15, 1927.
Bats Left. Throws Left. Height, 6 feet, 2 inches. Weight, 180 pounds.

Year	Club	Lea	G	IP	W	L	Pct	SO	BB	H	ERA
1948	Clarksdale	Cotton St.	27	118	6	9	.400	83	77	126	4.58
1949	Clarksdale	Cotton St.	34	195	14	14	.500	192	117	181	3.23
1950	Greenville	Big St.	26	164	11	7	.611	137	70	135	3.29
1951	Shreveport	T. L.	42	229	12	15	.444	139	125	210	4.45
1952	San Diego	P. C. L.	17	123	7	9	.438	85	55	117	3.59
1952	Boston	A. L.	13	77	5	4	.556	23	36	75	3.86
1953	Louisville	A. A.	14	96	7	3	.700	46	29	90	3.56
1953	Boston	A. L.	21	86	5	5	.500	56	33	86	3.24
	Major League Totals		2 Yrs	34	163	10	9	.526	79	69	161	3.53

HERBERT, RAYMOND ERNEST
Born, Detroit, Michigan, December 15, 1929.
Bats Right. Throws Right. Height, 5 feet, 11 inches. Weight, 185 pounds.

Year	Club	Lea	G	IP	W	L	Pct	SO	BB	H	ERA
1949	Toledo	A. A.	35	163	6	*17	.261	76	120	184	5.80
1950	Toledo	A. A.	30	188	11	12	.478	90	106	174	3.69
1950	Detroit	A. L.	8	22	1	2	.333	5	12	20	3.68
1951	Detroit	A. L.	5	13	4	0	1.000	9	9	8	1.38
1951-52	Detroit	A. L.		(In Military Service)							
1953	Detroit	A. L.	43	88	4	6	.400	37	46	109	5.22
	Major League Totals		3 Yrs	56	123	9	8	.529	51	67	137	4.54

HETKI, JOHN EDWARD
Born, Leavenworth, Kansas, May 12, 1922.
Bats Right, Throws Right. Height, 6 feet, 1 inch. Weight, 205 pounds.

Year	Club	Lea	G	IP	W	L	Pct	SO	BB	H	ERA
1941	Albuquerque ..	Ariz.-Tex.	43	243	16	10	.615	179	75	287	4.41
1942	Ogden	Pion.	22	185	13	8	.619	118	60	143	2.24
1942	Birmingham	S. A.	7	50	4	1	.800	17	22	37	2.16
1943-44	Birmingham	S. A.		(In Military Service)							
1945	Birmingham	S. A.	30	218	16	10	.615	129	93	204	2.97
1945	Cincinnati	N. L.	5	33	1	2	.333	9	11	28	3.55
1946	Cincinnati	N. L.	32	126	6	6	.500	41	31	121	3.00
1947	Cincinnati	N. L.	37	96	3	4	.429	33	48	110	5.81
1948	Cincinnati	N. L.	3	7	0	1	.000	3	3	8	9.00
1948	Syracuse	I. L.	25	143	8	12	.400	69	49	139	3.78
1949	Syracuse	I. L.	33	250	16	14	.533	108	86	*250	4.03
1950	Cincinnati	N. L.	22	53	1	2	.333	21	27	53	5.09
1951	Toronto	I. L.	37	*256	*19	10	.655	97	75	215	2.85
1952	St. Louis	A. L.	3	9	0	1	.000	4	2	15	4.00
1952	Toronto a	I. L.	30	195	13	7	.650	97	54	164	2.91
1953	Pittsburgh	N. L.	54	118	3	6	.333	37	33	120	3.97
	Major League Totals		7 Yrs	156	442	14	22	.389	148	155	455	4.28

a Drafted by Pittsburgh, December 1, 1952.

HOEFT, WILLIAM FREDERICK

Born, Oshkosh, Wisconsin, May 17, 1932.
Bats Left. Throws Left. Height, 6 feet, 2½ inches. Weight, 177 pounds.

Year	Club	Lea	G	IP	W	L	Pct	SO	BB	H	ERA
1950	Richmond	Ohio-Ind.	12	95	10	1	.909	122	34	58	1.71
1951	Toledo	A. A.	27	164	9	14	.391	124	85	171	5.43
1952	Detroit	A. L.	34	125	2	7	.222	67	63	123	4.32
1953	Detroit	A. L.	29	198	9	14	.391	90	58	223	4.82
Major League Totals		2 Yrs	63	323	11	21	.344	157	121	346	4.63

HOOPER, ROBERT NELSON

Born, Leamington, Ontario, Canada, May 30, 1922.
Bats Right. Throws Right. Height, 5 feet, 11 inches. Weight, 200 pounds.

Year	Club	Lea	G	IP	W	L	Pct	SO	BB	H	ERA
1941	Tarboro	C. P. L.	16	76	3	4	.429	39	55	78	3.79
1942	Fort Smith	W. A.	9	13	1	0	1.000	4	11	23	...
1942	Salisbury-Lex.	N. C. St.	10	72	5	3	.625	42	28	57	2.25
1942	Jacksonville	S. A. L.	6	14	0	2	.000	7	12	19	...
1942	Oklahoma City	T. L.	1	9	1	0	1.000	4	1	7	1.00
1943, 1944, 1945	(In United States Military Service)										
1946	Jacksonville	S. A. L.	29	164	9	11	.450	90	79	156	3.51
1947	Jersey City	I. L.	2	8	0	0	.000	4	2	8	10.13
1947	Jacksonville	S. A. L.	26	150	8	12	.400	73	70	151	3.48
1948	Jacksonville	S. A. L.	35	206	*20	9	.690	99	71	187	2.45
1949	Buffalo	I. L.	36	175	19	3	*.864	75	35	176	3.96
1950	Philadelphia	A. L.	45	170	15	10	.600	53	91	181	5.03
1951	Philadelphia	A. L.	38	189	12	10	.545	64	61	192	4.38
1952	Philadelphia a	A. L.	43	144	3	15	.348	40	68	158	5.19
1953	Cleveland	A. L.	43	69	5	4	.556	16	38	50	4.04
Major League Totals		4 Yrs	169	572	40	39	.506	178	253	581	4.74

a Traded to Cleveland for Dick Rozek and Bob Wilson, December 19, 1952.

HOSKINS, DAVID TAYLOR

Born, Greenwood, Mississippi, August 4, 1925.
Bats Left. Throws Right. Height, 6 feet, 1 inch. Weight, 180 pounds.

Year	Club	Lea	G	IP	W	L	Pct	SO	BB	H	ERA
1950	Dayton	Central	(Outfielder)								
1951	Wilkes-Barre	E. L.	11	60	5	1	.833	35	31	56	3.60
1952	Dallas	T. L.	35	*280	*22	10	.688	128	70	237	2.12
1953	Cleveland	A. L.	26	113	9	3	.750	55	38	102	3.98

HOUTTEMAN, ARTHUR JOSEPH

Born, Detroit, Michigan, August 7, 1927.
Bats Right. Throws Right. Height, 6 feet, 2 inches. Weight, 190 pounds.

Year	Club	Lea	G	IP	W	L	Pct	SO	BB	H	ERA
1945	Buffalo	I. L.	6	40	3	3	.500	16	15	42	4.05
1945	Detroit	A. L.	13	25	0	2	.000	9	11	27	5.40
1946	Buffalo	I. L.	32	*226	16	13	.552	147	75	217	4.22
1946	Detroit	A. L.	1	8	0	1	.000	2	0	15	9.00
1947	Buffalo	I. L.	5	29	3	1	.750	8	9	24	1.36
1947	Detroit	A. L.	23	111	7	2	.778	53	36	106	3.41
1948	Detroit	A. L.	43	164	2	16	.111	74	52	186	4.66
1949	Detroit	A. L.	34	204	15	10	.600	85	59	227	3.71
1950	Detroit	A. L.	41	275	19	12	.613	88	99	257	3.53
1951	Detroit	A. L.	(In Military Service)								
1952	Detroit	A. L.	35	221	8	*20	.286	109	65	218	4.36
1953-Det.-Cleveland a		A. L.	38	178	9	13	.409	68	54	200	4.60
Major League Totals		8 Yrs	228	1186	60	76	.441	493	376	1236	4.10

a Traded to Cleveland with Owen Friend, Joe Ginsberg and Bill Wight for Al Aber, Ray Boone, Steve Gromek and Dick Weik, June 15, 1953.

HUDSON, SIDNEY CHARLES

Born, Oliver Springs, Tenn., January 3, 1918.
Bats Right. Throws Right. Height, 6 feet, 4 inches. Weight, 175 pounds.

Year	Club	Lea	G	IP	W	L	Pct	SO	BB	H	ERA
1938	Sanford	Fla. State	27	173	11	7	.611	136	68	135	2.02
1939	Sanford	Fla. State	29	250	*24	4	*.857	*192	63	207	1.80

Year	Club	Lea	G	IP	W	L	Pct	SO	BB	H	ERA
1940	Washington	A. L.	38	252	17	16	.515	96	81	272	4.57
1941	Washington	A. L.	33	250	13	14	.481	108	97	242	3.46
1942	Washington	A. L.	35	239	10	17	.370	72	70	266	4.37
1943-44-45 Washington ..		A. L.	(In Military Service)								
1946	Washington	A. L.	31	142	8	11	.421	35	37	160	3.61
1947	Washington	A. L.	20	106	6	9	.400	37	58	113	5.60
1948	Washington ...,...	A. L.	29	182	4	16	.200	53	107	217	5.88
1949	Washington	A. L.	40	209	8	*17	.320	54	91	234	4.22
1950	Washington	A. L.	30	238	14	14	.500	75	98	261	4.08
1951	Washington	A. L.	23	139	5	12	.294	43	52	168	5.12
1952	Wash.-Boston a ...	A. L.	28	197	10	13	.435	74	65	204	3.34
1953	Boston	A. L.	30	156	6	9	.400	60	49	164	3.52

| Major League Totals | | 11 Yrs | 347 | 2110 | 101 | 148 | .406 | 707 | 805 | 2301 | 4.27 |

a Traded by Washington to Boston Red Sox for pitchers Walt Masterson and Randy Gumpert, June 10. 1952.

HUGHES, JAMES

Born, Chicago, Illinois, March 21, 1924.
Bats Right.   Throws Right.   Height, 6 feet, 1 inch.   Weight, 200 pounds.

Year	Club	Lea	G	IP	W	L	Pct	SO	BB	H	ERA
1946	Madisonville	Kitty	31	193	10	13	.435	203	63	184	3.46
1947	Waterloo	I. I. I.	34	179	12	6	.667	149	100	164	3.57
1948	Hollywood	P. C. L.	1	1	0	0	.000	1	1	2	54.00
1948	Denver	West.	2	16	1	0	1.000	18	15	14	2.81
1948	Muskegon	Cent.	36	219	16	13	.552	159	102	237	4.27
1949	Hollywood	P. C. L.	15	67	3	4	.429	39	32	73	4.29
1949	Santa Barbara	Cal.	14	121	9	4	.692	107	56	104	3.12
1950	Hollywood	P. C. L.	3	13	1	0	1.000	6	8	9	4.15
1950	St. Paul	A. A.	6	7	1	0	1.000	7	9	19	24.28
1950	Montreal	I. L.	16	86	7	2	.778	38	38	73	2.72
1951	Montreal	I. L.	27	105	10	4	.714	51	52	92	3.69
1952	Montreal	I. L.	45	95	9	7	.563	67	52	59	2.84
1952	Brooklyn	N. L.	6	19	2	1	.667	8	11	16	1.42
1953	Brooklyn	N. L.	48	86	4	3	.571	49	41	80	3.45

| Major League Totals | | 2 Yrs | 54 | 105 | 6 | 4 | .600 | 57 | 52 | 96 | 3.09 |

World's Series Record

| 1953 | Brooklyn .... | N. L. | 1 | 4 | 0 | 0 | .000 | 3 | 1 | 3 | 2.25 |

JANSEN, LAWRENCE JOSEPH

Born, Forest Grove, Oregon, July 16. 1920.
Bats Right.   Throws Right.   Height, 6 feet, 2 inches.   Weight, 190 pounds.

Year	Club	Lea	G	IP	W	L	Pct	SO	BB	H	ERA
1940	Salt Lake City	Pion.	31	214	20	7	*.741	148	69	194	*2.19
1941	San Francisco	P. C. L.	32	238	16	10	.615	70	75	220	2.80
1942	San Francisco	P. C. L.	32	173	11	14	.440	46	39	222	4.32
1943	San Francisco	P. C. L.	(Suspended)								
1944	San Francisco	P. C. L.	(Voluntarily Retired)								
1945	San Francisco	P. C. L.	7	55	4	1	.800	34	12	63	4.09
1946	San Francisco	P. C. L.	38	*321	*30	6	*.833	171	69	254	1.57
1947	New York	N. L.	42	248	21	5	*.808	104	57	241	3.16
1948	New York	N. L.	42	277	18	12	.600	126	54	283	3.61
1949	New York	N. L.	37	260	15	16	.484	113	62	271	3.84
1950	New York	N. L.	40	275	19	13	.594	161	55	238	3.01
1951	New York	N. L.	39	279	*23	11	.676	145	56	254	3.03
1952	New York	N. L.	34	167	11	11	.500	74	47	183	4.10
1953	New York	N. L.	36	185	11	16	.407	88	55	185	4.14

| Major League Totals | | 7 Yrs | 270 | 1691 | 118 | 84 | .584 | 811 | 386 | 1655 | 3.49 |

World's Series Record

| 1951 | New York .... | N. L. | 3 | 10 | 0 | 2 | .000 | 6 | 4 | 3 | 6.30 |

JOHNSON, CLIFFORD CONNIE

Born, Stone Mt., Georgia, December 27, 1922.
Bats Right.   Throws Right.   Height, 6 feet, 4 inches.   Weight, 195 pounds.

Year	Club	Lea	G	IP	W	L	Pct	SO	BB	H	ERA
1951	St. Hyacinthe	Prov.	33	250	15	14	.517	*172	112	225	3.24
1952	Colorado Springs ..	West.	30	248	18	9	.667	*233	103	215	3.38
1953	Charleston	A. A.	15	102	6	6	.500	86	50	92	3.62
1953	Chicago ...	A. L.	14	61	4	4	.500	44	38	55	3.54

228

JOHNSON, ERNEST THORWALD

Born, Brattleboro, Vermont, June 16, 1924.
Bats Right. Throws Right. Height, 6 feet, 4 inches. Weight, 195 pounds.

Year	Club	Lea	G	IP	W	L	Pct	SO	BB	H	ERA
1946	Hartford	E. L.	1	1	0	0	.000	1	1	0	0.00
1946	Pawtucket	New Eng.	15	73	4	7	.364	40	25	75	3.95
1947	Hartford	E. L.	30	142	9	8	.529	70	47	156	4.37
1948	Hartford	E. L.	25	166	12	6	.667	110	71	176	3.74
1949	Milwaukee	A. A.	7	11	0	0	.000	5	5	11	4.09
1949	Denver	Western	20	167	15	5	*.750	134	51	138	2.37
1950	Boston	N. L.	16	21	2	0	1.000	15	13	87	6.86
1950	Hartford	E. L.	7	57	5	1	.833	42	17	53	2.53
1951	Milwaugee	A. A.	32	196	15	4	*.789	133	63	168	*2.62
1952	Boston	N. L.	29	92	6	3	.667	45	31	100	4.11
1953	Milwaukee	N. L.	36	81	4	3	.571	36	22	79	2.67
Major League Totals	3 Yrs		81	194	12	6	.667	96	66	216	3.80

JOLLY, DAVID

Born, Stony Point, North Carolina, October 14, 1924.
Bats Right. Throws Right. Height, 6 feet. Weight, 160 pounds.

Year	Club	Lea	G	IP	W	L	Pct	SO	BB	H	ERA
1946	Mooresville	N. C. St.	12	75	5	3	.625	36	36	56	2.76
1947	Mooresville	N. C. St.	24	185	14	7	.667	143	58	182	3.31
1948	Tulsa	T. L.	16	59	3	5	.375	39	40	61	8.97
1949	Tulsa	T. L.	37	202	12	7	.632	124	*222	181	4.41
1950	Syracuse	I. L.	32	146	5	11	.313	73	76	162	4.32
1951	Tulsa	T. L.	37	220	9	13	.409	97	107	224	4.18
1952	Kansas City a	A. A.	40	82	6	1	.857	52	61	64	3.51
1953	Milwaukee	N. L.	24	38	0	1	.000	23	27	34	3.55

a Drafted by Boston Braves, December 1, 1952.

JUDSON, HOWARD KOLLS

Born, Hebron, Illinois, February 16, 1926.
Bats Right. Throws Right. Height, 6 feet, 1 inch. Weight, 195 pounds.

Year	Club	Lea	G	IP	W	L	Pct	SO	BB	H	ERA
1946	Waterloo	I. I. I.	7	43	2	2	.500	32	25	40	3.98
1947	Waterloo	I. L I.	29	202	16	8	.667	178	85	171	2.58
1948	Chicago	A. L.	40	107	4	5	.444	38	56	102	4.79
1949	Chicago	A. L.	26	108	1	14	.067	36	70	114	4.58
1950	Chicago	A. L.	46	112	2	3	.400	34	63	105	3.94
1951	Chicago	A. L.	27	122	5	6	.455	43	55	124	3.76
1952	Chicago a	A. L.	21	34	0	1	.000	15	22	30	4.24
1953	Cincinnati	N. L.	10	39	0	1	.000	11	11	58	5.54
1953	Indianapolis	A. A.	10	42	1	4	.200	16	18	43	4.07
1953	Tulsa	T. L.	14	90	11	0	1.000	86	40	67	1.80
Major League Totals	6 Yrs		170	522	12	30	.286	177	277	533	4.34

a Released to Cincinnati, Dec. 9, 1952 as payment for Hank Edwards, transferred to Chicago, Sept. 1, 1952.

KEEGAN, ROBERT CHARLES

Born, Rochester, New York, August 4, 1921.
Bats Right. Throws Right. Height, 6 feet, 2 inches. Weight, 195 pounds.

Year	Club	Lea	G	IP	W	L	Pct	SO	BB	H	ERA
1946	Binghamton	E. L.	13	93	5	6	.455	45	40	82	3.87
1947	Binghamton	E. L.	15	119	10	5	.667	68	52	124	3.10
1947	Newark	I. L.	11	53	1	6	.143	35	22	57	6.11
1948	Newark	I. L.	16	85	4	5	.444	40	34	98	5.51
1948	Kansas City	A. A.	9	57	4	1	.800	48	19	45	2.21
1949	Kansas City	A. A.	32	172	9	15	.375	92	88	180	4.81
1950	Kansas City	A. A.	30	127	4	12	.250	62	61	152	5.81
1951	Kansas City	A. A.	2	9	1	0	1.000	6	6	19	8.00
1951	Syracuse	I. L.	29	177	13	9	.591	86	69	162	3.51
1952	Syracuse	I. L.	35	273	*20	11	.645	111	85	*245	2.64
1953	Chicago	A. L.	22	99	7	5	.583	32	33	80	2.73

KELLNER, ALEXANDER RAYMOND

Born, Tucson, Arizona, August 26, 1924.
Bats Right. Throws Left. Height, 6 feet. Weight, 205 pounds.

Year	Club	Lea	G	IP	W	L	Pct	SO	BB	H	ERA
1941	Tucson	Ariz-Tex	22	174	18	6	.634	134	50	166	3.26
1942	Muskogee	W. A.	21	159	11	7	.611	131	39	127	..
1943-44-45	Birmingham	S. A.	(In Military Service)								
1946	Birmingham	S. A.	(Voluntarily Retired)								
1947	Birmingham	S. A.	33	176	11	9	.550	107	95	182	4.96
1948	Philadelphia	A. L.	13	23	0	0	.000	14	16	21	7.83
1948	Savannah	S. A. L.	15	112	9	3	.750	93	42	79	2.73
1949	Philadelphia	A. L.	33	245	20	12	.625	94	129	243	3.75
1950	Philadelphia	A. L.	36	225	8	*20	.286	85	112	253	5.48
1951	Philadelphia	A. L.	33	210	11	*14	.440	94	98	218	4.46
1952	Philadelphia	A. L.	34	231	12	14	.462	105	86	223	4.36
1953	Philadelphia	A. L.	25	202	11	12	.478	81	51	210	3.92
Major League Totals		6 Yrs	179	1136	62	72	.463	473	487	1168	4.46

KELLY, ROBERT EDWARD

Born, Cleveland, Ohio, October 4, 1927.
Bats Right. Throws Right. Height, 6 feet. Weight, 175 pounds.

Year	Club	Lea	G	IP	W	L	Pct	SO	BB	H	ERA
1948	Des Moines	W. L.	23	200	14	7	.667	133	94	179	2.93
1949	Los Angeles	P. C. L.	36	205	9	16	.360	77	*127	210	4.57
1950	Springfield	I. L.	19	83	3	6	.333	29	55	91	5.75
1950	Des Moines	W. L.	13	65	5	6	.455	32	30	56	3.05
1951	Chicago	N. L.	35	124	7	4	.636	48	55	130	4.65
1952	Chicago	N. L.	31	125	4	9	.308	50	46	114	3.60
1953	Chic.-Cincin. a	N. L.	42	83	1	8	.250	35	35	98	5.42
Major League Totals		3 Yrs	108	332	12	16	.429	133	136	342	4.45

a Traded to Cincinnati with Fred Baczewski for Emory (Bubba) Church, June 12, 1953.

KIELY, LEO PATRICK

Born, Hoboken, New Jersey, November 30, 1929.
Bats Left. Throws Left. Height, 6 feet, 3 inches. Weight, 180 pounds.

Year	Club	Lea	G	IP	W	L	Pct	SO	BB	H	ERA
1948	Wellsville	Pony	30	180	12	9	.571	157	80	172	3.40
1949	Scranton	E. L.	15	70	3	5	.375	43	33	58	4.24
1950	Birmingham	S. A.	34	239	18	9	.667	156	71	236	3.43
1951	Louisville	A. A.	15	108	8	4	.667	60	24	106	4.25
1951	Boston	A. L.	17	118	7	7	.500	46	39	106	3.35
1952-53	Boston	A. L.	(In Military Service)								

KINDER, ELLIS RAYMOND

Born, Atkins, Arkansas, July 26, 1914.
Bats Right. Throws Right. Height, 6 feet. Weight, 195 pounds.

Year	Club	Lea	G	IP	W	L	Pct	SO	BB	H	ERA
1938	Jackson	Kitty	1	3	0	0	.000	0	0	4	6.00
1939	Jackson	Kitty	30	223	17	12	.586	200	82	217	3.59
1940	Jackson	Kitty	32	*276	21	9	.700	*307	81	239	*2.33
1941	Binghamton	E. L.	10	43	3	3	.500	26	6	43	2.93
1941	Jackson	Kitty	18	153	11	6	.647	179	47	113	2.88
1942	Memphis	S. A.	18	62	2	3	.400	31	32	76	5.52
1942	Jackson	So'east.	9	72	6	2	.750	50	20	52	2.88
1943	Memphis	S. A	(On Suspended List)								
1944	Memphis	S. A.	30	209	*19	6	.760	132	49	197	2.80
1945	St. Louis	A. L.	(In Military Service)								
1946	St. Louis	A. L.	33	87	3	3	.500	59	36	78	3.31
1947	St. Louis a	A. L.	34	194	8	15	.348	110	32	201	4.50
1948	Boston	A. L.	28	178	10	7	.588	53	63	183	3.74
1949	Boston	A. L.	43	252	23	6	*.793	138	99	251	3.36
1950	Boston	A. L.	48	207	14	12	.538	95	78	212	4.26
1951	Boston	A. L.	*63	127	11	2	.846	84	46	108	2.55
1952	Boston b	A. L.	23	98	5	6	.455	50	28	85	2.57
1953	Boston	A. L.	*69	107	10	6	.625	39	33	84	1.85
Major League Totals		8 Yrs	341	1250	84	57	.596	628	470	1202	3.46

a Traded to Boston Red Sox with Bill Hitchcock for Clem Dreisewerd, Sam Dente, Bill Sommers and cash, November 18, 1947.
b On inactive list with back injury, June 7 to Aug. 8.

KING, CLYDE EDWARD

Born, Goldsboro, North Carolina, May 23, 1925.
Bats Right. Throws Right. Height, 6 feet, 1 inch. Weight, 183 pounds.

Year	Club	Lea	G	IP	W	L	Pct	SO	BB	H	ERA
1944	Brooklyn	N. L.	14	44	2	1	.667	14	12	42	8.07
1944	Richmond	Pied.	10	74	6	8	.667	45	20	53	1.58
1945	Brooklyn	N. L.	42	112	5	5	.500	29	48	131	4.10
1946	Mobile	S. A.	35	184	13	9	.591	72	53	200	3.57
1947	Brooklyn	N. L.	29	88	6	5	.545	31	29	85	2.79
1948	Brooklyn a	N. L.	9	12	0	1	.000	5	6	14	8.25
1948	Montreal	I. L.	13	53	2	5	.286	15	21	79	7.47
1949	Montreal	I. L.	43	197	17	7	.708	67	67	201	4.25
1950	Montreal	I. L.	32	182	13	8	.619	58	56	202	3.12
1951	Brooklyn	N. L.	48	121	14	7	.667	33	50	118	4.17
1952	Brooklyn b	N. L.	23	43	2	0	1.000	17	12	56	5.02
1953	Cincinnati	N. L.	35	76	3	6	.333	21	32	78	5.21

Major League Totals   7 Yrs   200   496   32   25   .561   150   189   524   4.14
a Sold to Philadelphia Phillies on waivers, June 9, 1948, and returned to Brooklyn on waivers, June 14.
b Sold to Cincinnati, October 10, 1952.

KIPPER, THORNTON JOHN

Born, Bagley, Wisconsin, September 27, 1928.
Bats Right. Throws Right. Height, 6 feet, 3 inches. Weight, 195 pounds.

Year	Club	Lea	G	IP	W	L	Pct	SO	BB	H	ERA
1950	Utica	E. L.	17	78	4	5	.444	30	29	97	6.23
1951	Baltimore	I. L.	(Did not play due to injured back)								
1952	Schenectady	E. L.	21	102	6	7	.462	62	30	95	3.62
1953	Schenectady	E. L.	10	76	9	1	.900	33	14	66	2.48
1953	Philadelphia	N. L.	20	46	3	3	.500	15	12	59	4.70

KLIPPSTEIN, JOHN CALVIN

Born, Washington, D. C., October 17, 1927.
Bats Right. Throws Right. Height, 6 feet, 1 inch. Weight, 170 pounds.

Year	Club	Lea	G	IP	W	L	Pct	SO	BB	H	ERA
1944	Lima	Ohio St.	7	36	3	2	.600	43	27	36	4.75
1944	Allentown	Inter-St.	6	18	1	0	1.000	14	10	25	10.50
1945	Winston-Salem	Car. L.	23	149	8	7	.533	106	75	111	2.48
1945	Allentown	Inter-St.	3	4	0	0	.000	5	3	6	15.75
1946	Columbus	A. A.	(In Military Service)								
1947	Omaha	W. L.	15	67	5	4	.556	41	51	66	5.87
1947	Lynchburg	Pied.	11	57	3	2	.600	39	33	49	4.42
1947	Columbus	A. A.	2	3	0	0	.000	1	6	8	9.00
1948	Columbus	A. A.	1	1	0	0	.000	1	3	8	9.00
1948	Lynchburg	Pied.	33	155	6	5	.545	127	119	181	4.06
1949	Mobile a	S. A.	33	195	15	8	.652	127	121	167	2.95
1950	Chicago	N. L.	33	105	2	9	.182	51	64	112	5.23
1951	Chicago	N. L.	35	124	6	6	.500	56	53	125	4.23
1952	Chicago	N. L.	41	203	9	14	.391	110	89	208	4.43
1953	Chicago	N. L.	48	163	10	11	.476	113	107	169	4.32

Major League Totals   4 Yrs   157   600   27   40   .403   330   313   614   4.65
a Drafted by Chicago Cubs from Montreal, November 17, 1949.

KONSTANTY, CASIMIR JAMES

Born, Strykersville, New York, March 2, 1917.
Bats Right. Throws Right. Height, 6 feet, 1½ inches. Weight, 195 pounds.

Year	Club	Lea	G	IP	W	L	Pct	SO	BB	H	ERA
1941	Springfield	E. L.	39	170	4	*19	.174	60	82	197	4.55
1942	Syracuse	I. L.	5	20	1	0	1.000	9	14	19	5.85
1943	Syracuse	I. L.	29	166	8	12	.400	45	72	144	3.42
1944	Syracuse	I. L.	14	115	8	6	.571	33	44	104	3.21
1944	Cincinnati	N. L.	20	113	6	4	.600	19	33	113	2.79
1945			(In United States Military Service)								
1946	Boston a	N. L.	10	15	0	1	.000	9	7	17	5.40
1946	Toronto	I. L.	20	123	4	9	.308	47	46	135	3.88
1947	Toronto	I. L.	33	197	13	13	.500	78	62	179	3.47
1948	Toronto	I. L.	*46	162	10	10	.500	78	59	163	4.06

231

			G		W	L	Pct	SO	BB	H	ERA
1948	Philadelphia	N. L.	6	10	1	0	1.000	7	2	7	0.90
1949	Philadelphia	N. L.	53	97	9	5	.643	43	29	98	3.25
1950	Philadelphia b	N. L.	*74	152	16	7	.696	56	50	108	2.66
1951	Philadelphia	N. L.	58	116	4	11	.267	27	31	127	4.03
1952	Philadelphia	N. L.	42	80	5	3	.625	16	21	87	8.94
1953	Philadelphia	N. L.	48	171	14	10	.583	45	42	198	4.42
Major League Totals		8 Yrs	811	754	55	41	.573	222	215	755	8.53
World's Series Record											
1950	Philadelphia	N. L.	8	15	0	1	.000	8	4	9	2.40

a Traded to Boston Braves with cash for Max West, April 19, 1946.
b Voted Most Valuable Player, National League, 1950.

KOSLO, GEORGE BERNARD (DAVE)

Born, Menasha, Wisconsin, March 31, 1920.
Bats Left. Throws Left. Height, 5 feet, 11 inches. Weight, 180 pounds.

Year	Club	Lea	G	IP	W	L	Pct	SO	BB	H	ERA
1939	Hopkinsville	Kitty	31	205	11	14	.440	194	*110	218	3.99
1940	Madison	I. I. I.	2	8	0	1	.000	2	8	5	12.00
1940	Paducah	Kitty	30	229	17	9	.654	246	75	202	8.03
1941	Milwaukee	A. A.	35	203	13	13	.500	96	83	211	4.43
1941	New York	N. L.	4	24	1	2	.333	12	10	17	1.88
1942	New York	N. L.	19	78	3	6	.333	42	82	79	5.08
1942	Jersey City	I. L.	12	60	8	2	.600	48	38	53	3.00
1943-44-45 New York ...	N. L.		(In U. S. Army)								
1946	New York	N. L.	40	265	14	*19	.424	121	101	*251	3.63
1947	New York	N. L.	39	217	15	10	.600	86	82	223	4.40
1948	New York	N. L.	35	149	8	10	.444	58	62	168	3.87
1949	New York	N. L.	33	212	11	14	.440	64	43	193	*2.50
1950	New York	N. L.	40	187	13	15	.464	56	68	190	3.90
1951	New York	N. L.	39	150	10	9	.526	54	45	153	8.30
1952	New York	N. L.	41	166	10	7	.588	67	47	154	3.20
1953	New York	N. L.	37	112	6	12	.333	36	86	135	4.74
Major League Totals		10 Yrs	332	1560	91	104	.467	596	526	1563	3.69
World's Series Record											
1951	New York	N. L.	2	15	1	1	.500	8	7	12	8.00

KRETLOW, LOUIS HENRY

Born, Apache, Oklahoma, June 27, 1923.
Bats Right. Throws Right. Height, 6 feet, 2 inches. Weight, 185 pounds.

Year	Club	Lea	G	IP	W	L	Pct	SO	BB	H	ERA
1946	Williamsport	E. L.	18	139	10	7	.588	123	78	118	3.56
1946	Buffalo	I. L.	11	36	0	8	.000	34	83	51	7.25
1946	Detroit	A. L.	1	7	1	0	1.000	0	4	3	0.00
1947	Buffalo	I. L.	18	77	2	7	.222	56	62	81	7.01
1948	Williamsport	E. L.	40	*268	*21	12	.636	*219	141	*238	3.32
1948	Detroit	A. L.	5	23	2	1	.667	9	11	21	4.70
1949	Detroit a	A. L.	25	76	3	2	.600	40	69	85	6.16
1950	St. Louis-Chi. b	A. L.	20	36	0	2	.000	24	45	42	7.00
1951	Chicago	A. L.	26	137	6	9	.400	89	74	129	4.20
1952	Chicago	A. L.	19	79	4	4	.500	63	56	52	2.96
1953	Chic.-St. Louis c ..	A. L.	31	102	1	5	.167	52	82	105	4.76
Major League Totals		7 Yrs	127	460	17	23	.425	277	341	437	4.62

a Traded to St. Louis Browns with $100,000 for Gerald Priddy, December 14, 1949.
b Sold to Chicago White Sox on waiver claim, July 5, 1950.
c Traded to St. Louis with Darrell Johnson and cash for Bob Elliott and Virgil Trucks, June 18, 1953.

KUZAVA, ROBERT LEROY

Born, Wyandotte, Michigan, May 28, 1923.
Bats Both. Throws Left. Height, 6 feet, 2 inches. Weight, 206 pounds.

Year	Club	Lea	G	IP	W	L	Pct	SO	BB	H	ERA
1941	Mansfield	Ohio St.	15	100	5	7	.417	104	36	103	...
1942	Charleston	M. A. L.	34	235	*21	6	*.778	129	81	188	1.73
1943, 1944, 1945		(In United States Military Service)									
1946	Wilkes-Barre	E. L.	26	*217	14	6	.700	*207	73	176	2.36
1946	Cleveland	A. L.	2	12	1	0	1.000	4	11	9	3.00
1947	Baltimore	I. L.	30	224	14	13	.519	112	76	197	3.17
1947	Cleveland	A. L.	4	22	1	1	.500	9	9	22	4.09
1948	Baltimore a	I. L.	30	192	9	*16	.360	154	*118	179	4.83
1949	Chicago	A. L.	29	157	10	6	.625	83	91	139	4.01

232

Year	Club	Lea	G	IP	W	L	Pct	SO	BB	H	ERA
1950	Chicago-Wash. b ...	A. L.	32	199	9	10	.474	105	102	199	4.34
1951	Wash.-N. Y. c ...	A. L.	31	135	11	7	.611	72	55	133	3.60
1952	New York	A. L.	28	133	8	8	.500	67	63	115	3.45
1953	New York ....,	A. L.	33	92	6	5	.545	48	34	92	3.33
	Major League Totals	7 Yrs	159	750	46	37	.554	338	365	709	3.83
	World's Series Record										
1951	New York	A. L.	1	1	0	0	.000	0	0	0	0.00
1952	New York	A. L.	1	2⅔	0	0	.000	2	0	0	0.00
1953	New York	A. L.	1	⅔	0	0	.000	1	0	2	13.50
	World's Series Totals	3	4⅓	0	0	.000	3	0	2	2.08

a Traded by Cleveland with Ernest Groth to Chicago White Sox for Frank Papish, Dec. 2, 1948
b Traded with Cass Michaels and John Ostrowski to Washington, May 30, for Ray Scarborough, Al Kozar and Ed Robinson.
c Traded to New York Yankees with Bob Ross, who went to Kansas City, Yank farm, for Tom Ferrick, Fred Sanford and Bob Porterfield, June 15, 1951.

LABINE, CLEMENT WALTER

Born, Lincoln, Rhode Island, August 6, 1926.
Bats Right. Throws Right. Height, 6 feet. Weight, 180 pounds.

Year	Club	Lea	G	IP	W	L	Pct	SO	BB	H	ERA
1944	Newport News ...	Pied.	12	56	2	4	.333	29	28	62	4.18
1945-46	Newport News ...	Pied.	(In Military Service)								
1946	Newport News ...	Pied.	3	14	1	0	1.000	11	3	16	2.52
1947	Greenville	S. A. L.	3	5	0	1	.000	3	3	14	19.80
1947	Newport News	Pied.	13	32	1	3	.250	14	21	54	9.00
1947	Asheville	Tri.-St.	3	61	6	0	1.000	33	14	53	2.07
1948	Pueblo	W. L.	40	196	13	10	.565	113	86	215	4.32
1949	St. Paul	A. A.	*64	139	12	6	.667	70	88	124	3.50
1950	Brooklyn	N. L.	1	2	0	0	.000	0	1	2	4.50
1950	St. Paul	A. A.	37	128	11	7	.611	64	64	139	4.99
1951	St. Paul	A. A.	20	117	9	6	.600	63	42	104	2.62
1951	Brooklyn	N. L.	14	65	5	1	.833	39	20	52	2.22
1952	St. Paul a	A. A.	2	14	0	1	.000	5	11	11	5.14
1952	Brooklyn	N. L.	25	77	8	4	.667	43	47	76	5.14
1953	Brooklyn	N. L.	37	110	11	6	.647	44	30	92	2.78
	Major League Totals	4 Yrs	77	254	24	11	.686	126	98	222	3.37
	World's Series Record										
1953	Brooklyn	N. L.	3	5	0	2	.000	8	1	10	3.60

a On option from Brooklyn to St. Paul, Aug. 1 to Aug. 15, 1952.

LA PALME, PAUL EDMORE

Born, Springfield, Massachusetts, December 14, 1924.
Bats Left. Throws Left. Height, 5 feet, 10½ inches. Weight, 180 pounds.

Year	Club	Lea	G	IP	W	L	Pct	SO	BB	H	ERA
1941	Bristol	Appal.	21	116	10	4	.714	65	35	129	4.50
1942	Erie	M. A. L.	30	190	12	11	.522	86	88	220	3.27
1943-44-45			(In Military Service)								
1946	Bristol	Appal.	27	191	20	2	*.909	181	55	192	3.16
1947	Jacksonville	Sally	15	53	4	2	.667	34	22	66	5.77
1947	Trenton	Int.-St.	18	114	9	4	.692	65	33	101	2.76
1948	Trenton	Int.-St.	23	159	18	3	.619	101	62	141	3.00
1949	Hartford	E. L.	31	211	14	13	.519	*162	79	175	2.90
1950	New Orleans	S. A.	9	62	4	2	.667	42	12	54	2.47
1950	Indianapolis	A. A.	31	49	6	5	.545	27	23	42	3.67
1951	Indianapolis	A. A.	5	22	1	1	.500	18	8	19	3.68
1951	Pittsburgh	N. L.	22	54	1	5	.167	24	31	79	6.33
1951	New Orleans	S. A.	5	29	2	2	.500	20	10	28	3.72
1952	Hollywood	P. C. L.	9	56	6	1	.857	33	14	36	1.29
1952	Pittsburgh	N. L.	31	60	1	2	.333	25	37	56	3.90
1953	Pittsburgh	N. L.	35	176	8	16	.333	86	64	191	4.60
	Major League Totals	3 Yrs	88	290	10	23	.303	135	132	326	4.78

LARSEN, DONALD JAMES

Born, Michigan City, Indiana, August 7, 1929.
Bats Right. Throws Right. Height, 6 feet, 4 inches. Weight, 220 pounds.

Year	Club	Lea	G	IP	W	L	Pct	SO	BB	H	ERA
1947	Aberdeen	North.	16	71	4	3	.571	38	31	65	3.42

Year	Club	Lea	G	IP	W	L	Pct	SO	BB	H	ERA
1948	Aberdeen	North.	84	211	17	11	.607	151	77	241	3.75
1949	Springfield	I. I. I.	18	74	4	4	.500	50	25	92	4.33
1949	Globe-Miami ..	Ariz.-Tex.	7	29	2	4	.333	22	24	33	...
1950	Wichita	West.	21	106	6	4	.600	47	88	103	3.14
1950	Wichita Falls	Big St.	9	44	8	8	.500	23	16	52	5.91
1951-52	San Antonio	T. L.	(In Military Service)								
1953	St. Louis	A. L.	63	193	7	12	.368	96	64	201	4.15

LEMON, ROBERT GRANVILLE

Born, San Bernardino, California, September 22, 1920.
Bats Left. Throws Right. Height, 6 feet. Weight, 180 pounds.

Year	Club	Lea	G	IP	W	L	Pct	SO	BB	H	ERA
1938	Springfield	M. A. L.	Infield and outfield								
1938	Oswego a	Can.-Am.	1	1	0	0	.000	1	0	1	0.00
1939	Springfield	M. A. L.	SS and outfield								
1939	New Orleans	S. A	3B and outfield								
1940	Wilkes-Barre	E. L.	8B and outfield								
1941	Wilkes-Barre b	E. L.	1	1	0	1	.000	0	8	0	9.00
1941	Cleveland	A. L.	3B and pinch-hitter								
1942	Baltimore	I. L.	8B and SS								
1942	Cleveland	A. L.	8B and pinch-hitter								
1943-44-45	Cleveland ...	A. L.	(In Military Service)								
1946	Cleveland c	A. L.	32	94	4	5	.444	39	68	77	2.49
1947	Cleveland c	A. L.	87	167	11	5	.688	65	97	150	3.45
1948	Cleveland d	A. L.	43	•294	20	14	.588	147	129	231	2.82
1949	Cleveland	A. L.	37	280	22	10	.688	138	137	211	2.99
1950	Cleveland	A. L.	44	•288	•23	11	.676	•170	146	•281	3.84
1951	Cleveland	A. L.	42	263	17	•14	.548	132	124	•244	3.52
1952	Cleveland	A. L.	42	•810	22	11	.667	131	105	236	2.50
1953	Cleveland	A. L.	41	•287	21	15	.583	98	110	•283	3.36
Major League Totals	10 Yrs		818	1988	140	85	.622	920	916	1713	3.15
World's Series Record											
1948	Cleveland	A. L.	2	16½	2	0	1.000	6	7	16	1.65

a Played OF and SS
b Played 3B and SS
c Also played OF
d Pitched no-hit, no-run game, June 30, defeating Detroit, 2-0.

LIDDLE, DONALD EUGENE

Born, Mt. Carmel, Illinois, May 25, 1926.
Bats Left. Throws Left. Height, 5 feet, 10 inches. Weight, 165 pounds.

Year	Club	Lea	G	IP	W	L	Pct	SO	BB	H	ERA
1946	Auburn	Border	10	49	6	3	.667	52	62	48	6.61
1947	Mt. Vernon	Ill. St.	19	181	9	7	.563	190	57	76	1.92
1948	Pawtucket	New Eng.	36	110	5	6	.455	84	85	111	3.68
1949	Pawtucket	New Eng.	16	105	11	2	.846	102	49	84	1.80
1949	Hartford	E. L.	19	117	8	5	.615	76	69	109	3.46
1950	Atlanta	S. A.	27	135	8	8	.500	84	78	141	4.84
1951	Milwaukee	A. A.	4	6	0	1	.000	4	4	10	9.00
1951	Atlanta	S. A.	86	191	14	6	.700	132	89	164	2.92
1952	Milwaukee	A. A.	34	197	17	4	.810	159	68	179	2.70
1953	Milwaukee	N. L.	81	129	7	6	.538	63	55	119	3.07

LINDELL, JOHN HARLAN

Born, Greeley, Colorado, August 30, 1916.
Bats Right. Throws Right. Height, 6 feet, 4½ inches. Weight, 210 pounds.

Year	Club	Lea	G	IP	W	L	Pct	SO	BB	H	ERA
1936	Joplin	W. A.	29	212	17	8	.680	159	97	212	4.08
1937	Binghamton ...	N. Y. P.	20	102	5	8	.385	59	32	116	2.74
1938	Newark	I. L.	4	17	1	1	.500	8	7	18	5.29
1938	Oakland	P. C. L.	33	166	9	8	.529	68	77	177	3.42
1939	Kansas City	A. A.	23	181	8	5	.615	53	45	143	4.40
1940	Kansas City	A. A.	31	203	•13	7	.720	82	69	179	2.70
1941	Newark	I. L.	81	228	23	4	•.852	100	59	205	•2.05
1941	New York	A. L.	One game as pinch-hitter								
1942	New York	A. L.	23	53	2	1	.667	23	22	52	3.74
1943-1950	New York a ...	A. L.	Outfield and First Base								
1950	St. Louis	N. L.	Outfield								
1950	Columbus .:	A. A.	Outfield								
1950	Hollywood	P. C. L.	2	7	0	1	.000	2	4	4	0.00
1951	Hollywood	P. C. L.	26	190	12	9	.571	89	112	163	3.03
1952	Hollywood	P. C. L.	37	282	•24	9	•.727	•190	•108	223	2.52

Year	Club	Lea	G	IP	W	L	Pct.	SO	BB	H	ERA
1953 Pitts.-Phila. b	N. L.		32	199	6	17	.261	118	*139	195	4.66
Major League Totals		2 Yrs	55	252	8	18	.308	146	161	247	4.46

a Sold to St. Louis Cardinals, May 15, 1950.
b Sold to Philadelphia Phillies, August 31, 1953.

LITTLEFIELD, RICHARD BERNARD
Born, Detroit, Mich., March 18, 1926.
Bats Left. Throws Left. Height, 6 feet. Weight, 180 pounds.

Year	Club	Lea	G	IP	W	L	Pct	SO	BB	H	ERA
1946 Oneonta	Can.-Am.		15	66	8	7	.800	42	67	53	5.45
1947 Oneonta	Can.-Am.		3	1	1	1	.500	..	..	..	..
1947 Wellsville	Pony		21	155	13	4	.765	141	53	122	*1.97
1948 Roanoke	Piedmont		31	227	15	11	.577	164	97	180	3.29
1949 Scranton	Eastern		31	180	12	8	.600	133	90	151	3.40
1950 Birmingham	S. A.		17	121	10	3	.769	103	46	93	2.90
1950 Boston a	A. L.		15	23	2	2	.500	13	24	27	9.39
1951 Memphis	S. A.		28	196	13	11	.542	*195	85	179	3.72
1951 Chicago b	A. L.		4	10	1	1	.500	7	17	9	8.10
1952 Buffalo	I. L.		3	20	1	1	.500	9	6	26	5.40
1952 Det.-St. Louis c-d .	A. L.		35	94	3	6	.250	66	42	81	3.54
1953 St. Louis	A. L.		36	152	7	12	.368	104	84	153	5.09
Major League Totals		4 Yrs	90	279	12	21	.364	190	167	270	5.03

a Traded to Chicago White Sox with Joe Dobson and Al Zarilla for Ray Scarborough and Bill Wight, Dec. 10, 1950.
b Traded to St. Louis Browns with Joe DeMaestri, Gordon Goldsberry, Gus Niarhos and Jim Rivera for Sherm Lollar, Tommy Upton and Al Widmar, Nov. 26, 1951.
c Traded to Detroit with Matt Batts, Cliff Mapes and Ben Taylor for Gene Bearden, Bob Cain and Dick Kryhoski, Feb. 14, 1952.
d Traded to St. Louis Browns with Don Lenhardt, Marlin Stuart, and Vic Wertz for Bud Black, Jim Delsing, Ned Garver and Dave Madison, Aug. 14, 1952.

LOES, WILLIAM
Born, Long Island City, N. Y., Dec. 13, 1929.
Bats Right. Throws Right. Height, 6 feet, 1 inch. Weight, 165 pounds.

Year	Club	Lea	G	IP	W	L	Pct	SO	BB	H	ERA
1949 Nashua	N. Eng.		17	122	11	3	.786	95	59	85	2.80
1949 Ft. Worth	Texas		15	72	5	2	.714	44	35	60	3.12
1950 Brooklyn	N. L.		10	13	0	0	.000	2	5	16	7.62
1951		(In U. S. Military Service)									
1952 Brooklyn	N. L.		39	187	13	8	.619	115	71	154	2.70
1953 Brooklyn	N. L.		32	163	14	8	.636	75	53	165	4.53
Major League Totals		3 Yrs	81	363	27	16	.628	192	129	335	3.69
World's Series Record											
1952 Brooklyn	N. L.		2	10⅓	0	1	.000	5	5	11	4.35
1953 Brooklyn	N. L.		1	3	1	0	1.000	8	2	8	3.38
World's Series Totals			3	13⅓	1	1	.500	13	7	19	3.93

LOPAT, EDMUND WALTER
Born, New York City, New York, June 21, 1918.
Bats Left. Throws Left. Height, 5 feet, 10 inches. Weight, 185 pounds.

Year	Club	Lea	G	IP	W	L	Pct	SO	BB	H	ERA
1937 Jeanerette a	Evang. L.		6	26	0	2	.000	18	18	26	4.50
1938 Jeanerette	Evang. L.		23	173	12	7	.632	103	73	159	2.73
1938 Kilgore	E. T. L.		11	79	5	4	.556	39	65	65	3.42
1938 Shreveport	T. L.		3	19	1	2	.333	7	13	23	5.21
1939 Longview	E. T. L.		29	226	16	9	.640	169	92	193	*2.11
1940 Shreveport	T. L.		15	47	0	8	.000	25	24	51	5.94
1940 Marshall	E. T. L.		24	154	7	9	.438	94	51	161	3.45
1941 Oklahoma City ...	T. L.		7	51	3	4	.429	22	13	43	1.76
1941 Salina	W. A.		31	176	11	15	.423	104	71	206	3.83
1942 Oklahoma City ..	T. L.		32	122	6	7	.462	55	52	117	3.32
1942 Little Rock	S. A.		12	71	6	4	.600	41	24	59	2.66
1943 Little Rock	S. A.		32	*245	19	10	.655	96	62	258	*3.05
1944 Chicago	A. L.		27	210	11	10	.524	75	59	217	3.26
1945 Chicago	A. L.		26	199	10	13	.435	74	56	226	4.12
1946 Chicago	A. L.		29	231	13	13	.500	89	48	216	2.73
1947 Chicago	A. L.		31	253	16	13	.552	109	73	241	2.81
1948 New York b	A. L.		33	227	17	11	.607	83	66	246	3.65
1949 New York	A. L.		31	215	15	10	.600	70	69	222	3.27
1950 New York	A. L.		35	236	18	8	.692	72	65	244	3.47
1951 New York	A. L.		31	235	21	9	.700	93	71	209	2.91
1952 New York	A. L.		20	149	10	5	.667	56	53	127	2.54
1953 New York	A. L.		25	178	16	4	*.800	50	32	169	*2.43

Year	Club	Lea	G	IP	W	L	Pct	SO	BB	H	ERA
Major League Totals		10 Yrs	288	2133	147	96	.605	771	592	2117	3.14
World's Series Record											
1949 New York	A. L.		1	5⅔	1	0	1.000	4	1	9	6.35
1950 New York	A. L.		1	8	0	0	.000	5	0	9	2.25
1951 New York	A. L.		2	18	2	0	1.000	4	3	10	0.50
1952 New York	A. L.		2	11⅓	0	1	.000	3	4	14	4.76
1953 New York	A. L.		1	9	1	0	1.000	3	4	9	2.00
World's Series Totals			7	52	4	1	.800	19	12	51	2.60

a Played 1st Base for Greensburg (Pa. State League) in 1937.
b Traded to New York Yankees for Aaron Robinson, Fred Bradley and Bill Wight, Feb. 24, 1948.

LOWN, OMAR JOSEPH (TURK)
Born, Brooklyn, N. Y., May 30, 1924.
Bats Right.   Throws Right.   Height, 6 feet.   Weight, 180 pounds.

Year	Club	Lea	G	IP	W	L	Pct	SO	BB	H	ERA
1942 Valdosta	Ga.-Fla.	30	232	18	8	.692	204	113	170	1.94
1943, 1944, 1945	(In U. S. Military Service)									
1946 Newport News ..	Piedmont	9	50	2	5	.286	19	31	49	3.60
1947 Pueblo	West. L.	33	190	13	7	.650	129	*133	172	4.50
1948 Pueblo	West. L.	27	192	17	6	*.739	161	112	191	4.03
1948 Montreal	I. L.	3	3	0	0	.000	4	5	5	12.00
1949 Montreal	I. L.	19	68	1	7	.125	48	54	57	3.97
1949 Fort Worth	Texas	12	76	8	1	.889	55	54	54	3.04
1950 Montreal a	I. L.	29	209	13	9	.591	104	122	181	3.49
1951 Chicago	N. L.	31	127	4	9	.308	39	90	125	5.46
1952 Chicago	N. L.	33	157	4	11	.267	73	93	154	4.36
1953 Chicago	N. L.	49	148	8	7	.533	76	84	166	5.17
Major League Totals		3 Yrs	113	432	16	27	.372	188	267	445	4.98

a Drafted by Chicago Cubs, November 16, 1950.

MAGLIE, SALVATORE ANTHONY
Born, Niagara Falls, New York, April 26, 1917.
Bats Right.   Throws Right.   Height, 6 feet, 2 inches.   Weight, 180 pounds.

Year	Club	Lea	G	IP	W	L	Pct	SO	BB	H	ERA
1938 Buffalo	I. L.	5	12	0	1	.000	4	8	12	3.75
1939 Buffalo	I. L.	39	101	8	7	.800	62	42	102	4.99
1940 Buffalo	I. L.	23	54	0	7	.000	22	24	80	7.17
1940 Jamestown	Pony	7	58	3	4	.429	41	15	54	2.73
1941 Elmira a	E. L.	*43	*270	20	15	.571	148	107	231	2.67
1942 Jersey City	I. L.	50	165	9	6	.600	92	74	142	2.78
1943-44 New York	N. L.	(Voluntarily Retired)								
1945 Jersey City	I. L.	21	118	6	7	.462	41	52	135	4.12
1945 New York	N. L.	13	84	5	4	.556	32	22	72	2.36
1946-47-48-49 New York	N. L.	(Ineligible due to play in Mexican League)								
1950 New York	N. L.	47	206	18	4	*.818	96	86	169	2.71
1951 New York	N. L.	42	298	*23	6	.793	146	86	254	2.93
1952 New York	N. L.	35	216	18	8	.692	112	75	199	2.92
1953 New York	N. L.	27	145	8	9	.471	80	47	158	4.16
Major League Totals		5 Yrs	164	949	72	31	.699	466	316	852	3.02
World's Series Record											
1951 New York ....N. L.		1	5	0	1	.000	3	2	8	7.20

a Drafted by New York Giants from Buffalo, November, 1941.

MARLOWE, RICHARD BURTON
Born, Hickory, North Carolina, June 27, 1929.
Bats Right.   Throws Right.   Height, 6 feet, 2 inches.   Weight, 170 pounds.

Year	Club	Lea	G	IP	W	L	Pct	SO	BB	H	ERA
1948 Flint	Cent.	21	131	12	5	.706	60	57	121	3.16
1949 Williamsport	E. L.	36	214	15	11	.577	98	95	137	4.21
1950 Toledo	A. A.	33	181	7	10	.412	81	83	181	4.57
1951 Toledo	A. A.	39	197	10	10	.500	83	78	203	4.34
1951 Detroit	A. L.	2	2	0	1	.000	1	2	5	27.00
1952 Buffalo	I. L.	35	148	10	10	.500	56	55	140	4.01
1952 Detroit	A. L.	4	11	0	2	.000	3	3	21	7.36
1953 Detroit	A. L.	42	120	6	7	.462	52	42	152	5.25
Major League Totals		3 Yrs	48	133	6	10	.375	56	47	178	5.75

MARRERO, CONRADO EUGENIO (RAMOS)

Born, Sagua LaGrande, Cuba, May 1, 1915.
Bats Right. Throws Right. Height, 5 feet, 7 inches. Weight, 165 pounds.

Year	Club	Lea	G	IP	W	L	Pct	SO	BB	H	ERA
1947	Havana	Fla.-Int.	40	271	•25	6	.806	•251	46	180	•1.66
1948	Havana	Fla.-Int.	35	264	20	11	.645	168	24	206	•1.67
1949	Havana	Fla.-Int.	35	258	•25	8	.758	•167	47	175	1.53
1950	Washington	A. L.	27	152	6	10	.375	63	55	159	4.50
1951	Washington	A. L.	25	187	11	9	.550	68	71	198	3.90
1952	Washington	A. L.	22	184	11	8	.579	77	53	175	2.89
1953	Washington	A. L.	22	146	8	7	.533	65	48	130	3.02
Major League Totals	4 Yrs		96	669	36	34	.514	271	227	662	3.57

MARTIN, MORRIS WEBSTER

Born, Dixon, Missouri, September 3, 1922.
Bats Left. Throws Left. Height, 6 feet. Weight, 180 pounds.

Year	Club	Lea	G	IP	W	L	Pct	SO	BB	H	ERA
1941	Grand Forks	North.	27	198	16	7	.696	103	58	170	•2.05
1942	St. Paul	A. A.	25	71	1	4	.200	19	87	80	4.69
1943-44-45	St. Paul	A. A.		(In Military Service)							
1946	Asheville	Tri-St.	25	173	14	6	.700	141	69	144	2.71
1947	St. Paul	A. A.	19	59	2	3	.400	30	34	47	4.12
1947	Danville	I. I. I.	7	41	3	1	.750	42	9	31	2.20
1948	St. Paul	A. A.	35	186	13	11	.542	129	71	171	4.16
1949	Brooklyn	N. L.	10	31	1	3	.250	15	15	39	6.97
1949	St. Paul	A. A.	16	79	3	6	.333	51	31	83	3.87
1950	St. Paul a	A. A.	31	197	14	9	.609	114	62	216	3.65
1951	Philadelphia	A. L.	35	138	11	4	•.733	85	63	139	3.78
1952	Philadelphia	A. L.	5	25	0	2	.000	13	15	32	6.48
1953	Philadelphia	A. L.	58	156	10	12	.455	64	59	153	4.44
Major League Totals	4 Yrs		108	350	22	21	.512	127	152	368	4.55

a Drafted by Philadelphia Athletics, November 16, 1950.

MASTERSON, WALTER EDWARD

Born, Philadelphia, Pennsylvania, June 22, 1920.
Bats Right. Throws Right. Height, 6 feet, 2 inches. Weight, 186 pounds.

Year	Club	Lea	G	IP	W	L	Pct	SO	BB	H	ERA
1939	Charlotte	Pied.	2	8	0	0	.000	3	5	11	10.13
1939	Washington	A. L.	24	58	2	2	.500	12	43	66	5.59
1940	Washington	A. L.	31	130	3	13	.188	63	88	128	4.92
1941	Washington	A. L.	34	73	4	3	.571	40	53	101	6.00
1942	Washington	A. L.	25	143	5	9	.357	63	54	138	3.34
1943-44-45	Washington	A. L.		(In Military Service)							
1945	Washington	A. L.	4	25	1	2	.333	14	10	21	1.08
1946	Washington	A. L.	29	91	5	6	.455	61	67	105	6.03
1947	Washington	A. L.	35	253	12	16	.429	135	97	215	3.13
1948	Washington	A. L.	33	188	8	15	.348	72	122	171	3.83
1949	Washington-Boston a	A. L.	28	108	6	6	.500	36	56	100	3.75
1950	Boston	A. L.	33	129	8	6	.571	60	82	145	5.65
1951	Boston	A. L.	30	59	8	0	1.000	39	32	53	3.86
1952	Bos.-Washington b	A. L.	29	170	10	9	.526	92	83	171	4.13
1953	Washington	A. L.	29	166	10	12	.455	95	62	145	3.63
Major League Totals	18 Yrs		864	1593	77	99	.438	737	854	1559	4.15

a Traded to Boston for Mickey Harris, Sam Mele and cash, June 13.
b Traded with pitcher Randy Gumpert by Boston to Washington for pitcher Sid Hudson, June 10, 1952.

McDERMOTT, MAURICE JOSEPH

Born, Poughkeepsie, New York, August 29, 1928.
Bats Left. Throws Left. Height, 6 feet, 2 inches. Weight, 170 pounds.

Year	Club	Lea	G	IP	W	L	Pct	SO	BB	H	ERA
1945	Scranton	E. L.	13	69	2	5	.286	42	81	71	3.39
1946	Scranton	E. L.	30	175	16	6	.727	144	105	136	3.29
1947	Louisville	A. A.	5	27	1	0	1.000	25	32	17	5.33
1947	Scranton	E. L.	18	132	12	4	.750	•136	71	102	2.86
1948	Boston	A. L.	7	23	0	0	.000	17	35	16	6.26
1948	Scranton	E. L.	11	87	3	6	.333	115	43	56	2.07
1949	Louisville	A. A.	11	77	6	4	.600	116	54	53	3.27
1949	Boston	A. L.	12	80	5	4	.556	50	52	63	4.05
1950	Boston	A. L.	38	130	7	3	.700	96	124	119	5.19

Year	Club	Lea	G	IP	W	L	Pct	SO	BB	H	ERA
1951	Boston	A. L.	34	172	8	8	.500	127	92	141	3.35
1952	Boston	A. L.	30	162	10	9	.526	117	92	139	3.72
1953	Boston a	A. L.	32	206	18	10	.643	92	109	169	3.01
Major League Totals		6 Yrs	153	773	48	34	.585	499	504	647	3.81

a Traded to Washington with Tom Umphlett for Jackie Jensen, December 8, 1953.

McDONALD, JAMES LEROY

Born, Grants Pass, Oregon, May 17, 1927.
Bats Right. Throws Right. Height, 5 feet, 10½ inches. Weight, 180 pounds.

Year	Club	Lea	G	IP	W	L	Pct	SO	BB	H	ERA
1945	Scranton	E. L.	11	88	7	3	.700	23	32	93	2.45
1946	Lynn	N. Eng.	15	79	6	3	.667	23	25	93	4.67
1947	Scranton	E. L.	32	152	10	8	.556	61	62	152	3.55
1948	Scranton	E. L.	25	182	13	4	.765	78	44	164	2.47
1949	Birmingham	S. A.	31	223	16	9	.640	76	98	211	3.15
1950	Louisville	A. A.	18	137	11	4	.733	47	50	117	3.35
1950	Boston	A. L.	9	19	1	0	1.000	5	10	23	3.79
1951	Louisville a	A. A.	19	144	10	7	.588	51	50	139	3.50
1951	St. Louis b	A. L.	16	84	4	7	.364	28	46	84	4.07
1952	New York	A. L.	26	69	3	4	.429	20	40	71	3.52
1953	New York	A. L.	27	130	9	7	.563	43	39	128	3.81
Major League Totals		4 Yrs	78	302	17	18	.486	96	135	306	3.81
World's Series Record											
1953	New York	A. L.	1	7⅔	1	0	1.000	3	0	12	5.87

a Traded by Boston Red Sox to St. Louis Browns with Matt Batts, Jim Suchecki and $100,000 for
Les Moss, May 17, 1951.
b Traded to New York Yankees for Clint Courtney, November 23, 1951.

MEYER, RUSSELL CHARLES

Born, Peru, Illinois, October 25, 1923.
Bats Both. Throws Right. Height, 6 feet, 1 inch. Weight, 164 pounds.

Year	Club	Lea	G	IP	W	L	Pct	SO	BB	H	ERA
1942	Superior	No. L.	32	184	7	8	.467	75	67	193	4.21
1943		(In United States Military Service)									
1944	Nashville	S. A	38	146	9	12	.429	66	70	187	5.30
1945	Nashville	S. A	34	183	11	13	.458	114	62	203	4.43
1946	Nashville	S. A.	*48	191	13	8	.619	139	91	190	3.53
1946	Chicago	N. L.	4	17	0	0	.000	10	10	21	3.18
1947	Chicago	N L	23	45	3	2	.600	22	14	43	3.40
1948	Chicago a	N. L.	29	165	10	10	.500	89	77	157	3.65
1949	Philadelphia	N. L.	37	213	17	8	.680	78	70	199	3.08
1950	Philadelphia	N. L.	32	160	9	11	.450	74	67	193	5.29
1951	Philadelphia	N. L.	28	168	8	9	.471	65	55	172	3.48
1952	Philadelphia b	N. L.	37	232	13	14	.481	92	65	235	3.14
1953	Brooklyn	N. L.	34	191	15	5	.750	106	63	201	4.57
Major League Totals		8 Yrs	224	1191	75	59	.560	536	421	1221	3.78
World's Series Record											
1950	Philadelphia	N. L.	2	1⅔	0	1	.000	1	0	4	5.40
1953	Brooklyn	N. L.	1	4⅓	0	0	.000	5	4	8	6.23
World's Series Totals		3	6	0	1	.000	6	4	12	6.00

a Sold to Philadelphia, N.L., for undisclosed sum, October 11, 1948.
b Traded to Boston for Earl Torgeson, and then to Brooklyn for Rocky Bridges and Jim Pendleton
as part of four-club deal, Feb. 16, 1953.

MILLER, ROBERT JOHN

Born, Detroit, Michigan, June 16, 1926.
Bats Right. Throws Right. Height, 6 feet, 3 inches. Weight, 190 pounds.

Year	Club	Lea	G	IP	W	L	Pct	SO	BB	H	ERA
1948	Terre Haute	I. I. I.	22	118	6	5	.545	86	41	124	3.51
1949	Terre Haute	I. I. I.	34	*255	*19	9	.679	207	59	*255	2.72
1949	Philadelphia	N. L.	3	3	0	0	.000	0	2	2	0.00
1950	Philadelphia	N. L.	35	174	11	6	.647	44	57	190	3.57
1951	Philadelphia	N. L.	17	34	2	1	.667	10	18	47	6.88
1951	Wilmington	Int.-St.	5	42	3	1	.750	21	5	30	0.86
1952	Baltimore	I. L.	32	184	12	9	.571	68	44	172	2.35
1952	Philadelphia	N. L.	3	9	0	1	.000	2	1	13	6.00
1953	Philadelphia	N. L.	35	157	8	9	.471	63	42	169	4.01
Major League Totals		5 Yrs	93	377	21	17	.553	119	120	421	4.08
World's Series Record											
1950	Philadelphia	N. L.	1	0⅓	0	1	.000	0	0	2	27.00

MILLER, STUART LEONARD

Born, Northampton, Mass., Dec. 26, 1927.
Bats Right. Throws Right. Height, 5 feet, 11 inches. Weight, 155 pounds.

Year	Club	Lea	G	IP	W	L	Pct	SO	BB	H	ERA
1949	Salisbury	E. S. L.	29	151	8	*13	.381	97	90	142	4.29
1950	Hamilton	Pony	37	244	16	*13	.552	154	93	*235	3.21
1951	Omaha	West. L.	11	32	0	0	.000	18	15	25	4.50
1951	Winston-Salem	Carolina	30	173	13	10	.565	111	59	150	2.88
1952	Columbus	A. A.	28	119	11	5	.688	82	38	113	2.34
1952	St. Louis	N. L.	12	88	6	3	.667	64	26	63	2.05
1953	St. Louis	N. L.	40	138	7	8	.467	79	47	161	5.54
Major League Totals		2 Yrs	52	226	13	11	.542	143	73	224	4.13

MILLER, WILLIAM PAUL

Born, Minersville, Pa., July 26, 1927.
Bats Left. Throws Left. Height, 6 feet. Weight, 175 pounds.

Year	Club	Lea	G	IP	W	L	Pct	SO	BB	H	ERA
1945	Lexington	N. C. Sta.	26	172	14	5	.737	191	*113	121	2.93
1946	Lexington a	N. C. Sta.	2	1	0	1	.000	3	2	1	...
1947	Lexington	N. C. Sta.	7	41	1	4	.200	44	24	47	5.71
1948	Savannah	So. Atl.	2	2	0	0	.000	...	...	...	...
1948	Statesville	N. C. Sta.	30	181	13	5	.722	*249	139	135	2.88
1949	Knoxville	Tri-St.	36	206	17	11	.607	158	*212	179	4.24
1950	Jersey City	I. L.	2	10	0	1	.000	8	13	5	4.50
1950	Sioux City	West. L.	12	64	5	3	.625	46	48	67	4.08
1950	Jacksonville	So. Atl.	7	35	2	2	.500	34	38	26	4.37
1951	Syracuse	I. L.	35	225	16	10	.615	*131	*118	204	2.96
1952	New York	A. L.	21	88	4	6	.400	45	49	78	3.48
1953	Kansas City	A. A.	12	78	5	5	.500	53	38	73	3.23
1953	New York	A. L.	13	34	2	1	.667	17	19	46	4.76
Major League Totals		2 Yrs	34	122	6	7	.462	62	68	124	3.84

a In Military Service for most of season.

MILLIKEN, ROBERT FOGLE

Born, Majorsville, West Virginia, August 25, 1926.
Bats Right. Throws Right. Height, 6 feet. Weight, 200 pounds.

Year	Club	Lea	G	IP	W	L	Pct	SO	BB	H	ERA
1947	Nashua	New Eng.	37	140	11	6	.647	113	58	115	2.70
1948	Danville	I. I. I.	24	148	9	8	.529	117	58	154	3.59
1948	Fort Worth	T. L.	9	13	1	1	.500	10	14	15	4.16
1949	Fort Worth	T. L.	34	170	12	5	.706	72	63	144	2.65
1950	Montreal	I. L.	(On Disabled List)								
1951-52	Montreal	I. L.	(In Military Service)								
1953	Brooklyn	N. L.	37	118	8	4	.667	65	42	94	3.36
World's Series Record											
1953	Brooklyn	N. L.	1	2	0	0	.000	0	1	2	0.00

MINNER, PAUL EDISON

Born, New Wilmington, Pennsylvania, July 30, 1923.
Bats Left. Throws Left. Height, 6 feet, 4½ inches. Weight, 200 pounds.

Year	Club	Lea	G	IP	W	L	Pct	SO	BB	H	ERA
1941	Knoxville	S. A.	6	15	0	2	.000	2	9	18	4.20
1941	Thomasville	Ga.-Fla.	3	14	0	2	.000	6	8	21	6.43
1942	Knoxville	S. A.	11	22	1	0	1.000	11	13	37	9.82
1942	Elizabethton	App. L.	21	179	*18	2	*.900	142	55	125	*1.41
1943, 1944, 1945			(In United States Military Service)								
1946	Mobile	S. A.	42	235	16	11	.593	147	59	245	2.72
1946	Brooklyn	N. L.	3	4	0	1	.000	3	3	6	6.75
1947	Mobile	S. A.	25	145	11	11	.500	67	34	163	3.66
1948	Montreal	I. L.	6	31	3	2	.600	17	8	31	2.90
1948	Brooklyn	N. L.	28	63	4	3	.571	23	26	61	2.43
1949	Brooklyn a	N. L.	27	47	3	1	.750	17	18	49	3.83
1950	Chicago	N. L.	39	190	8	13	.381	99	72	217	4.12
1951	Chicago	N. L.	33	202	6	*17	.261	68	64	219	3.79
1952	Chicago	N. L.	28	181	14	9	.609	61	54	180	3.73
1953	Chicago	N. L.	31	201	12	15	.444	64	40	227	4.21
Major League Totals		7 Yrs	189	888	47	59	.443	335	277	959	3.86
World's Series Record											
1949	Brooklyn	N. L.	1	1	0	0	.000	0	0	1	0.00

a Sold to Chicago along with Preston Ward, October 14.

NEWCOMBE, DONALD

Born, Madison, New Jersey, June 14, 1926.
Bats Left. Throws Right. Height, 6 feet, 4 inches. Weight, 220 pounds.

Year	Club	Lea	G	IP	W	L	Pct	SO	BB	H	ERA
1946	Nashua	N. Eng.	26	155	14	4	.778	104	79	109	2.21
1947	Nashua	N. Eng.	29	223	•19	6	.760	•186	116	180	2.91
1948	Montreal	I. L.	37	189	17	6	•.739	144	106	151	3.14
1949	Montreal	I. L.	5	34	2	2	.500	27	16	21	2.65
1949	Brooklyn	N. L.	38	244	17	8	.680	149	73	223	3.17
1950	Brooklyn	N. L.	40	267	19	11	.633	130	75	258	3.71
1951	Brooklyn	N. L.	40	272	20	9	.690	•164	91	235	3.28
1952-53	Brooklyn	N. L.		(In Military Service)							

Major League Totals		3 Yrs	118	783	56	28	.667	443	239	716	3.39
World's Series Record											
1949	Brooklyn	N. L.	2	11⅔	0	2	.000	11	3	10	3.09

NICHOLS, CHESTER RAYMOND, JR. (CHET)

Born, Providence, Rhode Island, February 22, 1931.
Bats Right. Throws Left. Height, 6 feet, 2 inches. Weight, 170 pounds.

Year	Club	Lea	G	IP	W	L	Pct	SO	BB	H	ERA
1949	Evansville	I. L. I.	27	198	14	7	.667	183	106	136	2.32
1950	Milwaukee	A. A.	29	128	7	14	.333	76	74	121	3.73
1951	Boston	N. L.	33	156	11	8	.579	71	69	142	•2.88
1952-53	Bost.-Milwaukee	N. L.		(In Military Service)							

NIXON, WILLARD LEE

Born, Taylorsville, Georgia, June 17, 1928.
Bats Left. Throws Right. Height, 6 feet, 2 inches. Weight, 190 pounds.

Year	Club	Lea	G	IP	W	L	Pct	SO	BB	H	ERA
1948	Scranton	E. L.	18	132	11	5	.688	81	58	108	2.52
1949	Birmingham	S. A.	22	177	14	7	.667	104	99	141	3.41
1949	Louisville	A. A.	4	23	0	3	.000	15	18	19	3.91
1950	Louisville	A. A.	13	117	11	2	.846	97	59	95	2.69
1950	Boston	A. L.	22	101	8	6	.571	57	58	126	6.08
1951	Boston	A. L.	33	125	7	4	.636	70	56	136	4.90
1952	Boston	A. L.	23	104	5	4	.556	50	61	115	4.85
1953	Boston	A. L.	23	117	4	8	.333	57	59	114	3.92

| Major League Totals | | 4 Yrs | 101 | 447 | 24 | 22 | .522 | 234 | 234 | 491 | 4.89 |

NUXHALL, JOSEPH HENRY

Born, Hamilton, Ohio, July 30, 1928.
Bats Left. Throws Left. Height, 6 feet, 3 inches. Weight, 220 pounds.

Year	Club	Lea	G	IP	W	L	Pct	SO	BB	H	ERA
1944	Cincinnati	N. L.	1	1	0	0	.000	0	5	2	45.00
1944	Birmingham	S. A.	1	1	0	1	.000	1	5	1	54.00
1945	Syracuse	I. L.	7	17	0	2	.000	12	21	21	7.94
1945	Lima	Ohio St.	16	126	10	5	.667	135	90	88	2.57
1946				(Voluntarily Retired)							
1947	Muncie	Ohio St.	18	100	7	7	.500	119	145	55	3.78
1948	Tulsa	T. L.	6	12	0	0	.000	9	12	10	2.25
1948	Columbia	So. Atl.	23	86	2	9	.182	52	101	79	4.81
1949	Charleston	Central	28	186	8	10	.444	139	•151	148	3.34
1950	Charleston	Central	25	138	10	9	.526	100	98	136	4.83
1951	Tulsa	T. L.	43	257	13	•22	.371	105	102	241	3.43
1952	Cincinnati	N. L.	37	92	1	4	.200	52	42	83	3.23
1953	Cincinnati	N. L.	30	142	9	11	.450	52	69	136	4.31

| Major League Totals | | 3 Yrs | 68 | 235 | 10 | 15 | .400 | 104 | 116 | 221 | 4.06 |

PAIGE, LEROY ROBERT (SATCHELL)

Born, Mobile, Alabama, September 22, 1908.
Bats Right. Throws Right. Height, 6 feet, 3½ inches. Weight, 180 pounds.

Year	Club	Lea	G	IP	W	L	Pct	SO	BB	H	ERA
1948	Cleveland	A. L.	21	73	6	1	.857	45	25	61	2.47
1949	Cleveland	A. L.	31	83	4	7	.364	54	33	70	3.04
1950				(Played in Negro League)							
1951	St. Louis	A. L.	23	62	3	4	.429	48	29	67	4.79
1952	St. Louis	A. L.	46	138	12	10	.545	91	57	116	3.07
1953	St. Louis	A. L.	57	117	3	9	.250	51	39	114	3.54

Major League Totals		5 Yrs	178	473	28	31	.475	289	183	428	3.31
World's Series Record											
1948	Cleveland	A. L.	1	⅔	0	0	.000	0	0	0	0.00

PAINE, PHILLIP STEERE

Born, Chepachet, Rhode Island, June 8, 1930.
Bats Right.   Throws Right.   Height, 6 feet, 2 inches.   Weight, 180 pounds.

Year	Club	Lea	G	IP	W	L	Pct	SO	BB	H	ERA
1948	Bradford	Pony	12	97	5	4	.556	35	32	66	2.41
1949	Vandergrift	M. A. L.	35	202	12	13	.480	108	136	239	5.48
1949	Toronto	I. L.	2	2	0	0	.000	0	1	4	4.50
1950	Hartford	E. L.	30	104	8	3	.727	56	45	105	3.12
1951	Hartford	E. L.	17	72	6	6	.500	29	40	71	3.50
1951	Boston	N. L.	21	35	2	0	1.000	17	20	36	3.09
1952-53	Bost.-Milwaukee	N. L.	(In Military Service)								

PALICA, ERVIN MARTIN

Born, Lomita, California, February 9, 1928.
Bats Right.   Throws Right.   Height, 6 feet, 1½ inches.   Weight, 180 pounds.

Year	Club	Lea	G	IP	W	L	Pct	SO	BB	H	ERA
1945	Mobile a	S. A.	6	25	1	2	.333	13	18	34	2.52
1945	Newport News	P. L.	23	146	11	8	.579	90	98	132	2.90
1946	Asheville	Tri. St.	28	215	15	6	.714	161	86	187	2.51
1947	Montreal	I. L.	29	181	12	10	.545	84	87	164	4.18
1947	Brooklyn	N. L.	8	8	0	1	.000	1	2	2	3.00
1948	Brooklyn	N. L.	41	125	6	6	.500	74	58	111	4.46
1949	Brooklyn	N. L.	49	97	8	9	.471	44	49	93	3.62
1950	Brooklyn	N. L.	43	201	13	8	.619	131	98	176	3.58
1951	Brooklyn	N. L.	19	53	2	6	.250	15	20	55	4.75
1952-53	Brooklyn	N. L.	(In Military Service)								
1953	Brooklyn	N. L.	4	6	0	0	.000	3	8	10	12.00
Major League Totals		6 Yrs	159	485	29	30	.492	268	235	447	4.05
World's Series Record											
1949	Brooklyn	N. L.	1	2	0	0	.000	1	1	1	0.00

a Also played infield and outfield for Mobile, Newport News, Asheville in 1945, 1946. Appeared in two games for Brooklyn as pinch-runner in 1945.

PARNELL, MELVIN LLOYD

Born, New Orleans, Louisiana, June 13, 1922.
Bats Left.   Throws Left.   Height, 6 feet.   Weight, 180 pounds.

Year	Club	Lea	G	IP	W	L	Pct	SO	BB	H	ERA
1941	Centreville	E. S. L.	9	48	4	4	.500	29	16	48	4.13
1942	Canton	M. A. L.	29	204	16	9	.640	125	49	157	1.59
1943, 1944, 1945		(In United States Military Service)									
1946	Scranton	E. L.	21	138	13	4	.765	111	49	97	*1.30
1947	Boston	A. L.	15	51	2	3	.400	23	27	60	6.35
1947	Louisville	A. A.	4	18	0	2	.000	11	11	24	7.50
1948	Boston	A. L.	35	212	15	8	.652	77	90	205	3.14
1949	Boston	A. L.	39	*295	*25	7	.781	122	134	258	*2.78
1950	Boston	A. L.	40	249	18	10	.643	93	106	244	3.61
1951	Boston	A. L.	36	221	18	11	.621	77	77	229	3.26
1952	Boston	A. L.	33	214	12	12	.500	107	89	207	3.62
1953	Boston	A. L.	38	241	21	8	.724	136	*116	217	3.06
Major League Totals		7 Yrs	236	1483	111	59	.653	635	639	1420	3.33

PERKOWSKI, HARRY WALTER

Born, Dante, Virginia, September 6, 1922.
Bats Left.   Throws Left.   Height, 6 feet, 2½ inches.   Weight, 196 pounds.

Year	Club	Lea	G	IP	W	L	Pct	SO	BB	H	ERA
1942	Natchez	Evang.	3	12	1	1	.500	11	2	20	6.75
1943, 1944, 1945		(In United States Navy)									
1946	Columbia	S. A. L.	3	7	0	0	.000	7	12	11	10.29
1946	Ogden	Pion.	31	224	*23	6	*.793	209	81	183	2.09
1947	Cincinnati	N. L.	3	7	0	0	.000	2	3	12	3.86
1947	Columbia	S. A. L.	32	247	17	12	.586	133	85	234	3.57
1948	Tulsa	T. L.	40	*263	*22	10	.688	163	105	231	2.98
1949	Syracuse	I. L.	32	209	14	12	.538	138	88	205	3.70
1949	Cincinnati	N. L.	5	24	1	1	.500	8	14	21	4.50
1950	Cincinnati	N. L.	22	34	0	0	.000	19	23	36	5.29
1951	Cincinnati	N. L.	35	102	3	6	.333	56	46	96	2.82
1952	Cincinnati	N. L.	33	194	12	10	.545	86	89	197	3.80
1953	Cincinnati	N. L.	33	193	12	11	.522	70	62	204	4.52
Major League Totals		6 Yrs	131	554	28	28	.500	236	237	566	4.00

PIERCE, WALTER WILLIAM

Born, Detroit, Michigan, April 2, 1927.
Bats Left. Throws Left. Height, 5 feet, 10 inches. Weight, 160 pounds.

Year	Club	Lea	G	IP	W	L	Pct	SO	BB	H	ERA
1945	Buffalo	I. L.	15	83	5	7	.417	57	71	75	5.42
1945	Detroit	A. L.	5	10	0	0	.000	10	10	6	1.80
1946	Buffalo	I. L.	10	56	3	4	.429	45	44	52	4.50
1947	Buffalo	I. L.	28	151	14	8	.636	125	125	127	3.87
1948	Detroit a	A. L.	22	55	3	0	1.000	36	51	47	6.38
1949	Chicago	A. L.	32	172	7	15	.318	95	112	145	3.87
1950	Chicago	A. L.	33	219	12	16	.429	118	137	189	3.99
1951	Chicago	A. L.	37	240	15	*14	.517	113	73	237	3.04
1952	Chicago	A. L.	33	255	15	12	.556	144	79	214	2.58
1953	Chicago	A. L.	40	271	18	12	.600	*186	102	216	2.72

Major League Totals 7 Yrs 202 1222 70 69 .504 702 564 1054 3.30
a Traded to Chicago for Aaron Robinson, November 10, 1948.

PILLETTE, DUANE XAVIER

Born, Detroit, Michigan, July 24, 1923.
Bats Right. Throws Right. Height, 6 feet, 3 inches. Weight, 195 pounds.

Year	Club	Lea	G	IP	W	L	Pct	SO	BB	H	ERA
1946	Newark	I. L.	31	194	11	10	.524	142	96	168	3.66
1947	Newark	I. L.	18	63	4	3	.571	25	48	69	5.29
1947	Portland	P. C. L.	9	57	4	2	.667	34	22	51	3.32
1948	Portland	P. C. L.	33	189	14	11	.560	83	115	184	4.00
1949	Newark	I. L.	17	109	6	7	.462	43	60	115	4.05
1949	New York	A. L.	12	37	2	4	.333	9	19	43	4.38
1950	Kansas City	A. A.	4	28	0	4	.000	8	9	37	7.07
1950	New York-St. Louis a	A. L.	28	81	3	5	.375	22	47	113	6.56
1951	St. Louis	A. L.	35	191	6	*14	.300	65	115	205	4.99
1952	St. Louis	A. L.	30	205	10	13	.435	62	55	222	3.60
1953	St. Louis	A. L.	31	167	7	13	.350	58	62	181	4.47

Major League Totals 5 Yrs 136 681 28 49 .364 216 298 764 4.60
a Traded to St. Louis Browns with Jim Delsing, Don Johnson, George Stirnweiss and $50,000 for Tom Ferrick, Joe Ostrowski and Leo Thomas, June 15, 1950.

PODBIELAN, CLARENCE ANTHONY (BUD)

Born, Curlew, Washington, March 6, 1924.
Bats Right. Throws Right. Height, 6 feet, 2 inches. Weight, 180 pounds.

Year	Club	Lea	G	IP	W	L	Pct	SO	BB	H	ERA
1946	Santa Barbara	Cal. L.	27	209	14	9	.609	112	92	208	3.83
1947	Ft. Worth	T. L.	34	212	14	8	.636	82	68	179	2.38
1948	Montreal	I. L.	35	168	13	8	.619	59	60	168	2.79
1949	Brooklyn	N. L.	7	12	0	1	.000	5	9	9	3.75
1949	Montreal	I. L.	33	174	9	13	.409	73	61	179	3.93
1950	Brooklyn	N. L.	20	73	5	4	.556	28	29	93	5.30
1950	Ft. Worth	T. L.	13	95	5	7	.417	39	52	76	3.41
1951	Montreal	I. L.	9	71	6	3	.667	22	17	57	2.92
1951	Brooklyn	N. L.	27	80	2	2	.500	26	36	67	3.49
1952	Bkln.-Cincinnati a ..	N. L.	27	89	4	5	.444	23	29	82	3.13
1953	Cincinnati	N. L.	36	186	6	16	.273	74	67	214	4.74

Major League Totals 5 Yrs 117 440 17 28 .378 156 170 465 4.25
a Traded to Cincinnati for Bud Byerly (who was sent to St. Paul), and cash, June 15, 1952.

PODRES, JOHN

Born, Witherbee, New York, September 30, 1932.
Bats Left. Throws Left. Height, 5 feet, 11 inches. Weight, 170 pounds.

Year	Club	Lea	G	IP	W	L	Pct	SO	BB	H	ERA
1951	Newport News	Pied.	7	17	0	2	.000	16	13	18	5.82
1951	Hazard	Mt. St.	26	200	21	3	*.875	*228	85	139	*1.67
1952	Montreal	I. L.	24	83	5	5	.500	47	39	76	3.27
1953	Brooklyn	N. L.	33	115	9	4	.692	82	64	126	4.23
	World's Series Record										
1953	Brooklyn	N. L.	1	2⅔	0	1	.000	0	2	1	3.38

POHOLSKY, THOMAS GEORGE
Born, Detroit, Michigan, August 26, 1929.
Bats Right. Throws Right. Height, 6 feet, 2 inches. Weight, 200 pounds.

Year	Club	Lea	G	IP	W	L	Pct	SO	BB	H	ERA
1945	Durham	Carol.	17	87	5	3	.625	29	15	104	3.31
1946	Durham	Carol.	8	35	1	3	.250	16	15	45	3.09
1946	Milford	E. S. L.	23	141	9	4	.692	75	34	145	3.64
1947	Columbus	Sally	28	174	16	3	*.842	88	42	162	2.53
1948	Houston	T. L.	4	6	1	1	.500	1	4	14	15.00
1948	Columbus	Sally	26	181	11	8	.579	95	48	161	3.13
1949	Rochester	I. L.	34	222	14	10	.583	116	69	213	3.69
1950	Rochester	I. L.	28	212	*18	6	.750	90	59	193	*2.17
1950	St. Louis	N. L.	5	15	0	0	.000	2	3	16	3.60
1951	St. Louis	N. L.	88	195	7	13	.350	70	68	204	4.43
1952-53	St. Louis	N. L.		(In Military Service)							
Major League Totals		2 Yrs	43	210	7	13	.350	72	71	220	4.37

POLLET, HOWARD JOSEPH
Born, New Orleans, La., June 26, 1921.
Bats Left. Throws Left. Height, 6 feet, ½ inch. Weight, 175 pounds.

Year	Club	Lea	G	IP	W	L	Pct	SO	BB	H	ERA
1939	Houston	T. L.	11	27	1	1	.500	14	20	26	4.67
1939	New Iberia	Evang. L.	25	163	14	5	.737	212	54	102	2.37
1940	Houston	T. L.	32	228	20	7	.741	169	82	200	2.88
1941	Houston	T. L.	25	194	20	3	*.870	*151	62	142	*1.16
1941	St. Louis	N. L.	9	70	5	2	.714	37	27	55	1.93
1942	St. Louis	N. L.	27	109	7	5	.583	42	39	102	2.89
1943	St. Louis	N. L.	16	118	8	4	.667	61	32	83	*1.75
1943, 1944, 1945			(In United States Army Air Force)								
1946	St. Louis	N. L.	40	*266	*21	10	.677	107	86	228	*2.10
1947	St. Louis	N. L.	37	176	9	11	.450	73	87	195	4.35
1948	St. Louis	N. L.	36	186	13	8	.619	80	67	216	4.55
1949	St. Louis	N. L.	39	231	20	9	.690	108	59	228	2.77
1950	St. Louis	N. L.	37	232	14	13	.519	117	68	228	3.30
1951	St. L.-Pitts. a	N. L.	27	141	6	13	.316	57	59	159	4.98
1952	Pittsburgh	N. L.	31	214	7	16	.304	90	71	217	4.12
1953	Pitts.-Chicago b	N. L.	30	124	6	7	.462	53	50	147	4.79
Major League Totals		11 Yrs	329	1867	116	98	.542	825	645	1858	3.43
World's Series Record											
1942	St. Louis	N. L.	1	⅔	0	0	.000	0	0	0	0.00
1946	St. Louis	N. L.	2	10⅓	0	1	.000	3	4	12	3.48
World's Series Totals		3	10⅔	0	1	.000	3	4	12	3.38	

a Traded with Pitcher Ted Wilks, Catcher Joe Garagiola, Outfielder Bill Howerton and Infielder Dick
Cole to Pittsburgh for Pitcher Cliff Chambers and Outfielder Wally Westlake, June 15, 1951.
b Traded To Chicago Cubs with Joe Garagiola, Ralph Kiner and George Metkovich for Bob Addis,
Toby Atwell, Gene Hermanski, Bob Schultz, Preston Ward, option to purchase George Freese, and
cash, June 4, 1953.

PORTERFIELD, ERWIN COOLIDGE (BOB)
Born, Newport, Virginia, August 10, 1924.
Bats Right. Throws Right. Height, 6 feet, 1 inch. Weight, 190 pounds.

Year	Club	Lea	G	IP	W	L	Pct	SO	BB	H	ERA
1946	Radford	Blue R.	14	105	7	5	.583	143	39	87	3.17
1946	Norfolk	P. L.	7	47	1	3	.250	36	18	52	4.60
1947	Norfolk	P. L.	32	239	17	9	.654	*208	82	191	2.37
1948	Newark	I. L.	23	178	15	6	.714	133	51	144	*2.17
1948	New York	A. L.	16	78	5	3	.625	30	34	85	4.50
1949	Newark	I. L.	5	16	1	0	1.000	16	7	16	5.63
1949	New York	A. L.	12	58	2	5	.286	25	29	53	4.03
1950	Kansas City	A. A.	3	8	0	2	.000	3	2	9	5.62
1950	New York	A. L.	10	20	1	1	.500	9	8	28	8.55
1951	Kansas City	A. A.	8	29	2	2	.500	19	14	37	4.66
1951	N. Y.-Wash. a	A. L.	21	136	9	8	.529	55	57	114	3.51
1952	Washington	A. L.	31	231	13	14	.481	80	85	222	2.73
1953	Washington	A. L.	34	255	*22	10	.688	77	73	243	3.35
Major League Totals		6 Yrs	124	778	52	41	.559	276	286	745	3.49

a Traded to Washington with Tom Ferrick and Fred Sanford for Bob Ross, who went to Kansas City,
Yankee farm, and Bob Kuzava, June 15, 1951.

PRESKO, JOSEPH EDWARD
Born, Kansas City, Missouri, October 7, 1928.
Bats Right. Throws Right. Height, 5 feet, 10 inches. Weight, 165 pounds.

Year	Club	Lea	G	IP	W	L	Pct	SO	BB	H	ERA
1948	St. Joseph	W. A.	39	197	16	8	.667	151	67	184	2.70

Year	Club	Lea	G	IP	W	L	Pct	SO	BB	H	ERA
1949	Omaha	W. L.	82	232	14	9	.609	142	85	208	3.18
1950	Houston	T. L.	86	258	16	16	.500	*165	100	239	3.14
1951	St. Louis	N. L.	15	89	7	4	.636	38	20	86	3.44
1952	St. Louis	N. L.	28	147	7	10	.412	63	57	140	4.04
1953	St. Louis	N. L.	34	162	6	13	.316	56	65	165	5.00
Major League Totals		3 Yrs	77	398	20	27	.426	157	142	391	4.30

RAFFENSBERGER, KENNETH DAVID
Born, York, Pennsylvania, August 8, 1917.
Bats Right.   Throws Left.   Height, 6 feet, 1 inch.   Weight, 205 pounds.

Year	Club	Lea	G	IP	W	L	Pct	SO	BB	H	ERA
1937	Cambridge	E. S. L.	27	*298	18	6	.750	183	47	231	...
1938	Rochester	I. L.	*53	201	15	10	.600	131	72	176	2.91
1939	Rochester	I. L.	43	242	15	15	.500	116	68	257	3.20
1939	St. Louis a	N. L.	1	1	0	0	.000	1	0	2	0.00
1940	Chicago	N. L.	43	115	7	9	.438	55	29	120	3.37
1941	Chicago	N. L.	10	18	0	1	.000	5	7	17	4.50
1941	St. Paul	A. A.	32	166	10	9	.526	89	49	183	4.85
1942	Los Angeles	P. C. L.	51	242	17	18	.486	138	51	258	3.46
1943	Los Angeles	P. C. L.	85	244	19	11	.633	134	53	228	2.14
1943	Philadelphia	N. L.	1	8	0	1	.000	8	2	7	1.13
1944	Philadelphia	N. L.	37	259	13	*20	.394	136	45	257	3.06
1945			(In United States Navy)								
1945	Philadelphia b ...	N. L.	5	24	0	8	.000	6	14	28	4.50
1946	Philadelphia	N. L.	39	196	8	15	.348	73	39	203	3.63
1947	Phila.-Cincinnati c	N. L.	29	148	8	11	.421	54	87	182	4.50
1948	Cincinnati	N. L.	40	180	11	12	.478	57	87	187	3.85
1949	Cincinnati	N. L.	41	284	18	17	.514	103	80	*289	3.39
1950	Cincinnati	N. L.	38	239	14	19	.424	87	40	271	4.26
1951	Cincinnati	N. L.	42	249	16	*17	.485	81	88	232	3.43
1952	Cincinnati	N. L.	38	247	17	13	.567	93	45	247	2.81
1953	Cincinnati	N. L.	26	174	7	14	.333	47	83	200	3.93
Major League Totals		14 Yrs	390	2142	119	152	.439	801	446	2242	3.58

a Traded to Chicago Cubs for Gene Lillard, Steve Mesner and cash, December 27, 1939.
b In U. S. Navy from May 7, 1945 to October 18, 1945.
c Traded to Cincinnati with Hugh Poland for Al Lakeman, June 14, 1947.

RASCHI, VICTOR JOHN
Born, West Springfield, Massachusetts, March 28, 1919.
Bats Right. Throws Right.   Height, 6 feet, 1 inch.   Weight, 210 pounds.

Year	Club	Lea	G	IP	W	L	Pct	SO	BB	H	ERA
1941	Amsterdam	Can. Am.	17	142	10	6	.625	117	53	167	3.67
1942	Norfolk	Pied.	17	113	4	10	.286	79	41	86	2.71
1943, 1944, 1945		(In United States Military Service)									
1946	Binghamton	E. L.	23	168	10	10	.500	160	70	153	3.16
1946	Newark	I. L.	5	33	1	2	.333	16	8	32	3.27
1946	New York	A. L.	2	16	2	0	1.000	11	5	14	3.94
1947	Portland	P. C. L.	12	85	8	2	.800	68	42	74	2.75
1947	New York	A. L.	15	105	7	2	.778	51	38	89	3.86
1948	New York	A. L.	36	223	19	8	.704	124	74	208	3.83
1949	New York	A. L.	38	275	21	10	.677	124	138	247	3.34
1950	New York	A. L.	33	257	21	8	*.724	155	116	232	3.99
1951	New York	A. L.	35	258	21	10	.677	*164	103	233	3.28
1952	New York	A. L.	81	223	16	6	.727	127	91	174	2.78
1953	New York	A. L.	28	181	13	6	.684	76	55	150	3.33
Major League Totals		8 Yrs	218	1538	120	50	.706	832	620	1347	3.47
World's Series Record											
1947	New York	A. L.	2	1⅓	0	0	.000	1	0	2	6.75
1949	New York	A. L.	2	14⅔	1	1	.500	11	5	15	4.30
1950	New York	A. L.	1	9	1	0	1.000	5	1	2	0.00
1951	New York	A. L.	2	10⅓	1	1	.500	4	8	12	0.87
1952	New York	A. L.	3	17	2	0	1.000	18	8	12	1.59
1953	New York	A. L.	1	8	0	1	.000	4	3	9	3.38
World's Series Totals			11	60⅓	5	3	.625	43	25	52	2.24

REYNOLDS, ALLIE PIERCE (THE CHIEF)
Born, Bethany, Oklahoma, February 10, 1918.
Bats Right.   Throws Right.   Height, 6 feet.   Weight, 195 pounds.

Year	Club	Lea	G	IP	W	L	Pct	SO	BB	H	ERA
1939	Springfield	M. A. L.	24	155	11	8	.579	146	107	121	3.60
1940	Cedar Rapids	I. I. L.	30	178	12	7	.632	131	88	170	3.59
1941	Wilkes-Barre	E. L.	3	7	0	0	.000	0	4	13	6.43
1941	Cedar Rapids	I. I. L.	27	167	10	10	.500	153	97	173	4.69
1942	Cleveland	A. L.	2	5	0	0	.000	2	4	5	0.00
1942	Wilkes-Barre	E. L.	32	231	18	7	.720	*193	102	143	*1.56

244

Year	Club	Lea	G	IP	W	L	Pct	SO	BB	H	ERA
1943	Cleveland	A. L.	84	199	11	12	.478	•151	109	140	2.98
1944	Cleveland	A. L.	28	158	11	8	.579	84	91	141	8.30
1945	Cleveland	A. L.	44	247	18	12	.600	112	•180	227	8.21
1946	Cleveland a	A. L.	81	188	11	15	.428	107	108	180	8.34
1947	New York	A. L.	84	242	19	8	.704	129	128	207	8.20
1948	New York	A. L.	89	236	16	7	.696	101	111	240	8.73
1949	New York	A. L.	85	214	17	6	.739	105	123	200	4.00
1950	New York	A. L.	85	241	16	12	.571	160	138	215	8.73
1951	New York b	A. L.	40	221	17	8	.680	126	100	171	8.05
1952	New York	A. L.	85	244	20	8	.714	•160	97	194	•2.07
1953	New York	A. L.	41	145	18	7	.650	86	61	140	8.41
Major League Totals		12 Yrs	898	2885	169	103	.621	1328	1195	2060	8.80
World's Series Record											
1947	New York	A. L.	2	11⅓	1	0	1.000	6	8	15	4.76
1949	New York	A. L.	2	12⅔	1	0	1.000	14	4	2	0.00
1950	New York	A. L.	2	10⅓	1	0	1.000	7	4	7	0.87
1951	New York	A. L.	2	15	1	1	.500	8	11	16	4.20
1952	New York	A. L.	4	20⅓	2	1	.667	18	6	12	1.77
1953	New York	A. L.	3	8	1	0	1.000	9	4	9	6.75
World's Series Totals		15	77⅓	7	2	.778	62	32	61	2.79	

a Traded to Yankees for Joe Gordon and Eddie Bockman, October 19, 1946.
b Pitched no-hit games against Cleveland, July 12, winning 1-0, and against Boston, September 28, winning 8-0.

RIDZIK, STEVEN GEORGE

Born, Yonkers, N. Y., April 29, 1929.
Bats Right. Throws Right. Height, 5 feet, 11 inches. Weight, 170 pounds.

Year	Club	Lea	G	IP	W	L	Pct	SO	BB	H	ERA
1945	Greensboro	Carolina	7	86	0	8	.000	18	8	86	4.75
1946	Schenectady	Can-Am.	10	57	8	4	.429	29	27	58	8.79
1947	Schenectady	Can-Am.	16	104	9	8	.750	68	45	84	2.68
1948	Toronto	I. L.	8	84	1	0	1.000	15	27	40	7.41
1948	Wilmington	Int-Sta.	20	182	10	7	.588	87	52	129	8.75
1949	Utica	Eastern	88	288	15	12	.556	188	109	216	2.99
1950	Toronto	I. L.	18	108	8	7	.588	49	57	96	4.02
1950	Philadelphia	N. L.	1	8	0	0	.000	2	1	8	6.00
1951	Baltimore	I. L.	81	188	5	11	.818	86	76	188	4.20
1952	Philadelphia	N. L.	24	98	4	2	.667	48	87	74	8.00
1953	Philadelphia	N. L.	42	124	9	6	.600	58	48	119	8.77
Major League Totals		8 Yrs	67	220	18	8	.619	98	86	196	8.48	

ROBERTS, ROBIN EVAN

Born, Springfield, Illinois, September 80, 1926.
Bats Left. Throws Right. Height, 6 feet, 1½ inches. Weight, 190 pounds.

Year	Club	Lea	G	IP	W	L	Pct	SO	BB	H	ERA
1948	Wilmington	Inter. St.	11	96	9	1	•.900	121	27	55	•2.06
1948	Philadelphia	N. L.	20	147	7	9	.438	84	61	148	8.18
1949	Philadelphia	N. L.	48	227	15	15	.500	95	75	229	8.69
1950	Philadelphia	N. L.	40	804	20	11	.645	146	77	282	8.02
1951	Philadelphia	N. L.	44	•315	21	15	.588	127	64	284	8.08
1952	Philadelphia	N. L.	89	•330	•28	7	.800	148	45	•292	2.59
1953	Philadelphia	N. L.	44	•347	•23	16	.590	•198	61	•824	2.75
Major League Totals		6 Yrs	280	1670	114	78	.610	798	883	1559	2.99	
World's Series Record											
1950	Philadelphia	N. L.	2	11	0	1	.000	5	8	11	1.64

ROE, ELWIN CHARLES (PREACHER)

Born, Ash Flat, Arkansas, February 26, 1918.
Bats Right. Throws Left. Height, 6 feet, 1 inch. Weight, 163 pounds.

Year	Club	Lea	G	IP	W	L	Pct	SO	BB	H	ERA
1988	St. Louis ...	N. L.	1	8	0	0	.000	1	2	6	12.00
1989	Rochester ...	I. L.	82	118	7	4	•.636	64	62	109	4.85
1940	Rochester ...	I. L.	81	128	5	8	.885	80	58	112	8.94
1941	Columbus ...	A. A.	80	159	11	9	.550	82	41	158	8.57
1942	Columbus ...	A. A.	88	158	6	11	.858	92	61	146	8.02
1943	Columbus ...	A. A.	24	167	15	7	.682	•186	60	128	2.87
1944	Pittsburgh ...	N. L.	89	185	18	11	.542	88	59	182	8.11
1945	Pittsburgh ...	N. L.	88	235	14	18	.519	•148	46	228	2.87
1946	Pittsburgh ...	N. L.	21	70	8	8	.278	28	25	83	5.14
1947	Pittsburgh a	N. L.	88	144	4	15	.211	59	68	156	5.25
1948	Brooklyn	N. L.	84	178	12	8	.600	86	88	156	2.68
1949	Brooklyn	N. L.	80	218	15	6	•.714	109	44	201	2.79
1950	Brooklyn	N. L.	86	251	19	11	.688	125	66	245	8.80
1951	Brooklyn	N. L.	84	258	22	8	•.880	113	64	247	8.03

Year	Club	Lea	G	IP	W	L	Pct	SO	BB	H	ERA
1952	Brooklyn	N. L.	27	159	11	2	.846	83	39	163	3.11
1953	Brooklyn	N. L.	25	157	11	3	.786	85	40	171	4.36
Major League Totals		11 Yrs	318	1853	124	80	.608	925	481	1838	3.38
World's Series Record											
1949	Brooklyn	N. L.	1	9	1	0	1.000	3	0	6	0.00
1952	Brooklyn	N. L.	3	11⅓	1	0	1.000	7	6	9	3.18
1953	Brooklyn	N. L.	1	8	0	1	.000	4	4	5	4.50
World's Series Totals			5	28⅓	2	1	.667	14	10	20	2.54

a Traded with William Cox and Gene Mauch to Brooklyn for Fred Walker, Vic Lombardi and Hal Gregg, December 8.

ROGOVIN, SAUL

Born, Brooklyn, New York, October 10, 1923.
Bats Right. Throws Right. Height, 6 feet, 3 inches. Weight, 205 pounds.

Year	Club	Lea	G	IP	W	L	Pct	SO	BB	H	ERA
1941	B. Falls-Warren	Pa. St.	Infielder and Outfielder								
1941	Youngstown	M. A. L.	Played Third Base								
1942-43			Not in organized ball								
1944	Jersey City	I. L.	Played Outfield								
1944	Williamsport	E. L.	Played Third Base and Outfield								
1944	Chattanooga a	S. A.	1	2	0	0	.000	1	0	1	0.00
1945	Chattanooga a	S. A.	1	7	1	0	1.000	3	2	4	0.00
1946	Chattanooga	S. A.	6	17	1	1	.500	3	18	13	3.71
1946	Pensacola	S'east.	22	96	8	5	.615	72	50	96	4.50
1947	Buffalo	I. L.	21	89	3	4	.429	45	53	90	4.85
1948	Buffalo	I. L.	31	172	13	7	.650	109	66	170	3.92
1949	Detroit	A. L.	5	6	0	1	.000	2	7	13	13.50
1949	Buffalo	I. L.	29	197	16	6	.727	163	101	188	3.65
1950	Detroit	A. L.	11	40	2	1	.667	11	26	39	4.50
1950	Toledo	A. A.	Played in one game as pinch-hitter								
1951	Det.-Chicago b	A. L.	27	217	12	8	.600	82	74	189	*2.78
1952	Chicago	A. L.	33	232	14	9	.609	121	79	224	3.84
1953	Chicago c-d	A. L.	22	131	7	12	.368	62	48	151	5.22
Major League Totals		5 Yrs	98	626	35	31	.530	278	234	616	3.90

a Played third-base.

b Traded to Chicago White Sox for Bob Cain, May 16, 1951.

c On disabled list, July 27 to Sept. 1, 1953.

d Traded with Rocky Krsnich and Connie Ryan to Cincinnati for Willard Marshall, Dec. 10, 1953.

RUSH, ROBERT RANSOM

Born, Battle Creek, Michigan, December 21, 1925.
Bats Right. Throws Right. Height, 6 feet, 4½ inches. Weight, 205 pounds.

Year	Club	Lea	G	IP	W	L	Pct	SO	BB	H	ERA
1947	Des Moines	W. L.	8	56	6	1	.857	44	16	39	1.61
1947	Nashville	S. A.	23	127	9	7	.563	49	37	140	3.40
1948	Chicago	N. L.	36	133	5	11	.313	72	87	153	3.92
1949	Chicago	N. L.	35	201	10	18	.357	80	79	197	4.07
1950	Chicago	N. L.	39	255	13	*20	.394	93	93	261	3.71
1951	Chicago	N. L.	37	211	11	12	.478	129	68	212	3.84
1952	Chicago	N. L.	34	250	17	13	.567	157	81	205	2.70
1953	Chicago	N. L.	29	167	9	14	.391	167	66	84	4.53
Major League Totals		6 Yrs	210	1217	65	88	.425	698	424	1112	3.72

SAIN, JOHN FRANKLIN

Born, Pine Bluff, Arkansas, September 25, 1918.
Bats Right. Throws Right. Height, 6 feet, 2 inches. Weight, 200 pounds.

Year	Club	Lea	G	IP	W	L	Pct	SO	BB	H	ERA
1936	Osceola	N. E. Ark.	11	76	5	3	.625	44	32	71	2.72
1937	Osceola	N. E. Ark.	24	135	5	8	.385	72	64	128	4.13
1938	Newport	N. E. Ark.	21	172	16	4	.800	111	48	162	2.71
1939	Newport	N. E. Ark.	29	220	18	10	.643	175	76	214	3.27
1940	Nashville	S. A.	30	97	8	4	.667	49	52	98	4.45
1941	Nashville	S. A.	41	139	6	12	.333	93	71	160	4.60
1942	Boston	N L.	40	97	4	7	.364	68	63	79	3.90
1943, 1944, 1945			(In United States Navy)								
1946	Boston	N. L.	37	265	20	14	.588	129	87	225	2.21
1947	Boston	N. L.	38	266	21	12	.636	132	79	*265	3.52
1948	Boston	N. L.	42	*315	*24	15	.615	137	83	*297	2.60
1949	Boston	N. L.	37	243	10	17	.370	73	75	285	4.81
1950	Boston	N. L.	37	278	20	13	.606	96	70	*294	3.95
1951	Boston a	N. L.	26	160	5	13	.278	63	45	195	4.22
1951	New York	A. L.	7	37	2	1	.667	21	8	41	4.14

246

Year	Club		Lea	G	IP	W	L	Pct	SO	BB	H	ERA
1952	New York	....	A. L.	35	148	11	6	.647	57	38	149	3.47
1953	New York	....	A. L.	40	189	14	7	.667	84	45	189	3.00
Major League Totals		9 Yrs	339	1998	131	105	.555	860	593	2019	3.45
World's Series Record												
1948	Boston	....	N. L.	2	17	1	1	.500	9	0	9	1.06
1951	New York	....	A. L.	1	2	0	0	.000	2	2	4	9.00
1952	New York	....	A. L.	1	6	0	1	.000	8	8	6	3.00
1953	New York	....	A. L.	2	5⅔	1	0	1.000	1	1	8	4.76
World's Series Totals		6	30⅔	2	2	.500	15	6	27	2.64

a Traded to New York Yankees for Lew Burdette and $50,000, August 29, 1951.

SCARBOROUGH, RAY WILSON
Born, Mt. Gilead, North Carolina, July 23, 1917.
Bats Right. Throws Right. Height, 6 feet. Weight, 187 pounds.

Year	Club		Lea	G	IP	W	L	Pct	SO	BB	H	ERA
1940	Chattanooga		S. A.	12	52	1	3	.250	23	37	59	5.54
1941	Selma	....	S'east.	34	244	*21	10	.677	*220	104	218	3.17
1942	Chattanooga	....	S. A.	15	99	8	5	.615	55	48	105	4.55
1942	Washington		A. L.	17	63	2	1	.667	16	32	68	4.14
1943	Washington	......	A. L.	24	86	4	4	.500	43	46	93	2.83
1943, 1944, 1945		(In United States Military Service)										
1946	Washington	....	A. L.	32	156	7	11	.389	46	74	176	4.04
1947	Washington	....	A. L.	33	161	6	13	.316	63	67	165	3.41
1948	Washington	....	A. L.	31	185	15	8	.652	76	72	166	2.82
1949	Washington	....	A. L.	34	200	13	11	.542	81	88	204	4.59
1950	Washington-Chic. a-b	A. L.	35	208	13	18	.419	94	84	222	4.93
1951	Boston	....	A. L.	37	184	12	9	.571	71	61	201	5.09
1952	Bos.-New York c	....	A. L.	37	111	6	6	.500	42	50	106	4.22
1953	N.Y.-Detroit d		A. L.	38	75	2	4	.333	32	37	86	4.68
Major League Totals		10 Yrs	318	1429	80	85	.485	564	611	1487	4.13
World's Series Record												
1952	New York	....	A. L.	1	1	0	0	.000	1	0	1	9.00

a Traded with Ed Robinson and Al Kozar to Chicago White Sox, May 30, for Cass Michaels, Bob Kuzava and John Ostrowski.
b Traded with Bill Wight to Boston Red Sox for Joe Dobson, Al Zarilla and Dick Littlefield, December 10, 1950.
c Sold to N. Y. Yankees for $10,000 waiver price, Aug. 22, 1952.
d Signed with Detroit, August 14, 1953 after being released by New York Yankees.

SCHEIB, CARL ALVIN
Born, Gratz, Pennsylvania, January 1, 1927.
Bats Right. Throws Right. Height, 6 feet, 1 inch. Weight, 192 pounds.

Year	Club		Lea	G	IP	W	L	Pct	SO	BB	H	ERA
1943	Philadelphia		A. L.	6	19	0	1	.000	3	3	24	4.26
1944	Philadelphia	......	A. L.	15	36	0	0	.000	13	11	36	4.25
1945	Philadelphia	......	A. L.	4	9	0	0	.000	2	4	6	3.00
1945, 1946		(In United States Military Service)										
1947	Philadelphia	......	A. L.	21	116	4	6	.400	28	55	121	5.04
1948	Philadelphia	......	A. L.	32	199	14	8	.636	44	76	219	3.93
1949	Philadelphia	......	A. L.	38	183	9	12	.429	43	118	191	5.11
1950	Philadelphia	......	A. L.	43	106	3	10	.231	37	70	138	7.22
1951	Philadelphia	......	A. L.	46	143	1	12	.077	49	71	132	4.47
1952	Philadelphia	......	A. L.	30	158	11	7	.611	42	50	153	4.39
1953	Philadelphia a		A. L.	28	96	3	7	.300	25	29	99	4.88
Major League Totals		10 Yrs	263	1065	45	63	.417	284	487	1119	4.82

a On disabled list, August 1 to September 2, 1953.

SCHMITZ, JOHN ALBERT
Born, Wausau, Wisconsin, November 27, 1920.
Bats Right. Throws Left. Height, 6 feet, 2 inches. Weight, 168 pounds.

Year	Club		Lea	G	IP	W	L	Pct	SO	BB	H	ERA
1938	Hopkinsville		Kitty	21	110	11	2	*.846	89	41	123	3.44
1939	Bloomington		L L L	27	208	14	12	.538	86	94	216	4.02
1939	Milwaukee	....	A. A.	2	13	0	2	.000	8	9	15	7.61
1940	Milwaukee	....	A. A.	1	3	0	0	.000	3	1	6	12.00
1940	Madison	....	L L L	31	222	15	14	.517	168	110	183	3.28
1941	Milwaukee	....	A. A.	33	157	7	14	.333	87	91	169	4.87
1941	Chicago	....	N. L.	5	21	2	0	1.000	11	9	12	1.29
1942	Chicago	....	N. L.	23	87	3	7	.300	51	45	70	3.41
1942, 1943, 1944, 1945		(In United States Navy)										
1946	Chicago	....	N. L.	41	224	11	11	.500	*135	94	184	2.61
1947	Chicago	....	N. L.	38	207	13	*18	.419	97	80	209	3.22
1948	Chicago	....	N. L.	34	242	18	13	.581	100	97	186	2.64
1949	Chicago	....	N. L.	36	207	11	13	.458	75	92	227	4.35

Year	Club	Lea	G	IP	W	L	Pct	SO	BB	H	ERA
1950	Chicago	N. L.	39	193	10	16	.385	75	91	217	4.99
1951	Chicago-Bklyn a	N. L.	24	74	2	6	.250	26	43	77	5.96
1952	Brooklyn b	N. L.	10	33	1	1	.500	11	18	29	4.36
1952	New York c	A. L.	5	15	1	1	.500	3	9	15	3.60
1952	Cincinnati d	N. L.	3	5	1	0	1.000	3	3	3	0.00
1953	N.Y.-Wash. e	A. L.	27	112	2	7	.222	39	40	120	3.62

| Major League Totals | | 10 Yrs | 285 | 1420 | 75 | 93 | .446 | 626 | 621 | 1349 | 3.61 |

a Traded to Brooklyn with Andy Pafko, Al Walker and Wayne Terwilliger for Gene Hermanski, Joe Hatten, Ed Miksis and Bruce Edwards, June 15, 1951.
b Sold to New York Yankees for estimated $20,000 and transfer of Wally Hood from Kansas City to St. Paul, August 1, 1952.
c Traded to Cincinnati with Jim Greengrass, Bob Marquis, Ernie Nevel and estimated $40,000 for Ewell Blackwell, August 28, 1952.
d Sold to New York Yankees, February 17, 1953.
e Sold to Washington on waivers, May 13, 1953.

SHANTZ, ROBERT CLAYTON

Born, Pottstown, Pennsylvania, September 26, 1925.
Bats Right. Throws Left. Height, 5 feet, 6¼ inches. Weight, 138 pounds.

Year	Club	Lea	G	IP	W	L	Pct	SO	BB	H	ERA
1948	Lincoln	W. L.	28	214	•18	7	.720	•212	55	179	2.82
1949	Philadelphia	A. L.	33	127	6	8	.429	58	74	100	3.40
1950	Philadelphia	A. L.	36	215	8	14	.364	93	85	251	4.60
1951	Philadelphia	A. L.	32	205	18	10	.643	77	70	213	3.95
1952	Philadelphia a	A. L.	33	280	•24	7	•.774	152	63	230	2.48
1953	Philadelphia	A. L.	16	106	5	9	.357	58	26	107	4.03

| Major League Totals | | 5 Yrs | 150 | 933 | 61 | 48 | .560 | 438 | 318 | 901 | 3.60 |

a Voted American League's Most Valuable Player.

SHEA, FRANK JOSEPH (SPEC)

Born, Naugatuck, Connecticut, October 2, 1922.
Bats Right. Throws Right. Height, 6 feet. Weight, 200 pounds.

Year	Club	Lea	G	IP	W	L	Pct	SO	BB	H	ERA
1940	Amsterdam	Can. Am.	20	137	11	4	.733	111	82	122	3.94
1941	Norfolk	Pied.	28	199	16	10	.615	154	92	155	3.17
1942	Kansas City	A. A.	27	100	5	8	.385	.89	75	76	3.15
1943, 1944, 1945			(In United States Military Service)								
1946	Oakland	P. C. L.	24	174	15	5	.750	124	60	125	1.66
1947	New York	A. L.	27	179	14	5	•.737	89	89	127	3.07
1948	New York	A. L.	28	156	9	10	.474	71	87	117	3.40
1949	New York	A. L.	20	52	1	1	.500	22	43	48	5.37
1949	Newark	I. L.	5	17	0	3	.000	5	18	16	8.47
1950	Kansas City	A. A.	27	116	6	11	.353	58	65	132	6.23
1951	New York	A. L.	25	96	5	5	.500	38	50	112	4.31
1952	Washington a	A. L.	22	169	11	7	.611	65	92	144	2.93
1953	Washington	A. L.	23	165	12	7	.632	38	75	151	3.93

Major League Totals		6 Yrs	145	817	52	35	.598	323	436	699	3.57
World's Series Record											
1947 New York		A. L.	3	15⅓	2	0	1.000	10	8	10	2.35

a Traded with outfielder Jackie Jensen, infielder Jerry Snyder and outfielder Archie Wilson by New York to Washington for outfielder Irv Noren and infielder Tom Upton, May 3, 1952.

SIMA, ALBERT

Born, Mahwah, New Jersey, October 7, 1922.
Bats Right. Throws Left. Height, 6 feet. Weight, 190 pounds.

Year	Club	Lea	G	IP	W	L	Pct	SO	BB	H	ERA
1942	Salisbury	N. C. St.	4	24	0	3	.000	10	3	29	4.50
1942	Bristol	Appal.	12	95	0	6	.500	37	20	87	2.65
1943	Richmond	Pied.	15	115	10	5	.667	71	39	99	2.66
1943	Jersey City	I. L.	11	46	1	4	.200	11	22	50	4.70
1944-45	Jersey City	I. L.			(In Military Service)							
1946	Jersey City	I. L.	3	31	1	3	.250	11	20	32	5.23
1946	Jacksonville	S. A. L.	18	68	3	6	.333	30	33	83	4.90
1947	Jacksonville	S. A. L.	29	184	9	9	.500	58	72	218	3.72
1948	Jacksonville	S. A. L.	30	209	14	11	.560	93	87	199	2.63
1949	Jersey City	I. L.	12	38	1	3	.250	17	26	50	6.16
1949	Minneapolis	A. A.	20	40	2	2	.500	27	21	37	4.50
1950	Chattanooga	S. A.	19	126	8	5	.615	57	48	136	3.00
1950	Washington	A. L.	17	77	4	5	.444	23	26	89	4.79
1951	Washington	A. L.	18	77	3	7	.300	26	41	79	4.79
1951	Chattanooga	S. A.	19	134	5	12	.294	88	110	144	3.24
1952	Chattanooga	S. A.	40	•279	•24	9	.727	123	73	•310	3.06
1953	Washington a	A. L.	31	68	2	3	.400	25	31	63	3.44

| Major League Totals | | 3 Yrs | 66 | 222 | 9 | 15 | .375 | 74 | 98 | 231 | 4.38 |

a Drafted by Chicago White Sox, December 1, 1953, from Chattanooga.

SIMMONS, CURTIS THOMAS

Born, Egypt, Pa., May 19, 1929.
Bats Left. Throws Left. Height, 5 feet, 11½ inches. Weight, 185 pounds.

Year	Club	Lea	G	IP	W	L	Pct	SO	BB	H	ERA
1947	Wilmington	Inter-St.	18	147	13	5	.722	197	76	107	2.69
1947	Philadelphia	N. L.	1	9	1	0	1.000	9	6	5	1.00
1948	Philadelphia	N. L.	31	170	7	13	.350	86	108	169	4.87
1949	Philadelphia	N. L.	38	131	4	10	.286	83	55	133	4.60
1950	Philadelphia	N. L.	31	215	17	8	.680	146	88	178	3.39
1951			(In U. S. Military Service)								
1952	Philadelphia	N. L.	28	201	14	8	.636	141	70	170	2.82
1953	Philadelphia	N. L.	32	238	16	13	.552	138	82	211	3.21
Major League Totals		6 Yrs	161	964	59	52	.532	603	409	866	3.63

SMITH, FRANK THOMAS

Born, Pier Point Manor, New York, April 4, 1928.
Bats Right. Throws Right. Height, 6 feet, 3 inches. Weight, 195 pounds.

Year	Club	Lea	G	IP	W	L	Pct	SO	BB	H	ERA
1946	Statesville	No. Car. St.	3	3	0	0	.000	7	11	4	2.25
1947	Marion	Ohio St.	27	147	11	7	.611	116	79	141	4.29
1948	Columbia	S. A. L.	34	226	*21	6	.778	104	76	185	2.39
1949	Tulsa	T. L.	*57	239	17	11	.607	143	100	203	2.93
1950	Cincinnati	N. L.	38	91	2	7	.222	55	39	73	3.86
1951	Cincinnati	N. L.	50	76	5	5	.500	34	22	65	3.20
1952	Cincinnati	N. L.	53	122	12	11	.522	77	41	109	3.76
1953	Cincinnati	N. L.	50	84	8	1	.889	42	25	89	5.46
Major League Totals		4 Yrs	191	373	27	24	.529	208	127	336	4.05

SPAHN, WARREN EDWARD

Born, Buffalo, New York, April 23, 1922.
Bats Left. Throws Left. Height, 6 feet. Weight, 165 pounds.

Year	Club	Lea	G	IP	W	L	Pct	SO	BB	H	ERA
1940	Bradford	Pony	12	66	5	4	.556	62	24	53	2.73
1941	Evansville	I. I. I.	28	212	*19	6	*.760	193	90	154	*1.83
1942	Hartford	E. L.	33	248	17	12	.586	141	130	148	1.96
1942	Boston	N. L.	4	16	0	0	.000	7	11	25	5.63
1943, 1944, 1945			(In United States Army)								
1946	Boston	N. L.	24	126	8	5	.615	67	36	107	2.93
1947	Boston	N. L.	40	*290	21	10	.677	123	84	245	*2.33
1948	Boston	N. L.	36	257	15	12	.556	114	77	237	3.71
1949	Boston	N. L.	38	*302	*21	14	.600	*151	86	283	3.07
1950	Boston	N. L.	41	293	*21	17	.553	*191	111	248	3.16
1951	Boston	N. L.	39	311	22	14	.611	*164	*109	278	2.98
1952	Boston	N. L.	40	290	14	19	.424	*183	73	263	2.98
1953	Milwaukee	N. L.	35	266	*23	7	.767	148	70	211	*2.10
Major League Totals		9 Yrs	297	2151	145	98	.597	1148	657	1897	2.92
World's Series Record											
1948	Boston	N. L.	3	12	1	1	.500	12	3	10	3.00

STALEY, GERALD LEE

Born, Brush Prairie, Washington, August 21, 1923.
Bats Right. Throws Right. Height, 6 feet. Weight, 190 pounds

Year	Club	Lea	G	IP	W	L	Pct	SO	BB	H	ERA
1941	Boise	Pio.	*39	*261	*22	8	.733	110	69	253	2.79
1942	Boise	Pio.	37	264	20	10	.667	143	61	250	2.72
1943, 1944, 1945			(In United States Military Service)								
1946	Sacramento	P. C. L.	31	236	13	12	.520	89	79	222	2.94
1947	St. Louis	N. L.	18	29	1	0	1.000	14	8	33	2.79
1947	Columbus	A. A.	12	66	6	1	.857	17	21	74	3.95
1948	St. Louis	N. L.	31	52	4	4	.500	23	21	61	6.92
1949	St. Louis	N. L.	45	171	10	10	.500	55	41	154	2.74
1950	St. Louis	N. L.	42	170	13	13	.500	62	61	201	4.98
1951	St. Louis	N. L.	42	227	19	13	.594	67	74	244	3.81
1952	St. Louis	N. L.	35	240	17	14	.548	93	52	238	3.26
1953	St. Louis	N. L.	40	230	18	9	.667	88	54	243	3.99
Major League Totals		7 Yrs	253	1119	82	63	.566	402	311	1174	3.86

STOBBS, CHARLES KLEIN (CHUCK)

Born, Wheeling, West Virginia, July 2, 1929.
Bats Left. Throws Left. Height, 6 feet. Weight, 195 pounds.

Year	Club	Lea	G	IP	W	L	Pct	SO	BB	H	ERA
1947	Lynn	N. Eng.	11	94	9	2	.818	78	56	64	1.72
1947	Boston	A. L.	4	9	0	1	.000	5	10	10	6.00

Year	Club	Lea	G	IP	W	L	Pct	SO	BB	H	ERA
1948	Boston	A. L.	6	7	0	0	.000	4	7	9	6.43
1949	Boston	A. L.	26	152	11	6	.647	70	75	145	4.03
1950	Boston	A. L.	32	169	12	7	.632	78	88	158	5.11
1951	Boston a	A. L.	34	170	10	9	.526	75	74	180	4.76
1952	Chicago b	A. L.	38	135	7	12	.368	73	72	118	3.13
1953	Washington	A. L.	27	153	11	8	.579	67	44	146	3.29

Major League Totals 7 Yrs 167 795 51 43 .543 372 370 766 4.17

a Traded with Mel Hoderlein to Chicago White Sox for Don Lenhardt and Randy Gumpert, November 13, 1951.

b Traded to Washington Senators for pitcher Miguel Fornieles, Dec. 3, 1952.

STUART, MARLIN HENRY

Born, Paragould, Arkansas, August 8, 1918.
Bats Left. Throws Right. Height, 6 feet, 2 inches. Weight, 180 pounds.

Year	Club	Lea	G	IP	W	L	Pct	SO	BB	H	ERA
1940	Mayfield	Kitty	40	216	13	14	.481	186	135	223	4.83
1941	St. Joseph	Mich. St.	15	82	6	3	.667	81	78	82	4.94
1941	Paragould	N. E. Ark.	8	38	1	4	.200	30	32	32	5.92
1942	Springfield	I. I. L.	29	186	15	9	.625	111	102	161	3.53
1943, 1944, 1945		(In United States Military Service)									
1946	Elmira	E. L.	30	129	8	6	.571	80	77	112	3.49
1947	San Antonio	T. L.	32	177	9	15	.375	88	79	168	3.92
1948	Toledo	A. A.	4	11	0	2	.000	10	12	15	11.45
1948	Little Rock	S. A.	29	198	15	10	.600	106	93	203	4.68
1949	Detroit	A. L.	14	30	0	2	.000	14	35	39	9.00
1949	Toledo	A. A.	7	53	4	2	.667	26	21	41	2.72
1950	Detroit	A. L.	19	44	3	1	.750	19	22	59	5.52
1950	Toledo	A. A.	13	97	9	3	.750	48	22	84	2.23
1951	Detroit	A. L.	29	124	4	6	.400	46	71	119	3.77
1952	Detr.-St. Louis a	A. L.	42	117	4	4	.500	45	57	117	4.77
1953	St. Louis	A. L.	60	114	8	2	.800	46	44	136	3.95

Major League Totals 5 Yrs 164 429 19 15 .559 170 229 470 4.64

a Traded with pitcher Dick Littlefield and outfielders Vic Wertz and Don Lenhardt by Detroit to St. Louis for pitchers Ned Garver, Dave Madison and Bud Black and outfielder Jim Delsing. Aug. 14, 1952.

SURKONT, MATTHEW CONSTANTINE (MAX)

Born, Central Falls, Rhode Island, June 16, 1922.
Bats Right. Throws Right. Height, 6 feet. Weight, 205 pounds.

Year	Club	Lea	G	IP	W	L	Pct	SO	BB	H	ERA
1938	Cambridge	E. S. L.	21	158	9	10	.474	137	73	131	3.13
1938	Portsmouth	M. A. L.	2	2	0	0	.000	2	4	4	13.50
1939	Portsmouth	M. A. L.	35	218	14	13	.519	*193	*163	175	3.63
1940	Decatur	I. I. I.	33	234	19	5	.792	*212	94	193	*2.50
1941	Rochester	I. L.	38	163	10	6	.625	84	88	139	3.20
1942	Rochester	I. L.	32	193	10	*18	.357	94	107	182	5.04
1943, 1944, 1945		(In United States Military Service)									
1946	Rochester	I. L.	28	176	9	*17	.346	81	109	183	5.47
1947	Rochester	I. L.	38	190	15	10	.600	102	109	163	3.55
1948	Rochester a	I. L.	38	240	15	11	.577	142	109	229	4.16
1949	Chicago	A. L.	44	96	3	5	.375	38	60	92	4.78
1950	Sacramento	P. C. L.	31	255	18	13	.581	159	86	229	2.96
1950	Boston	N. L.	9	56	5	2	.714	21	20	63	3.21
1951	Boston	N. L.	37	237	12	16	.429	110	89	230	3.99
1952	Boston	N. L.	31	215	12	13	.480	125	76	201	3.77
1953	Milwaukee b	N. L.	28	170	11	5	.688	83	64	168	4.18

Major League Totals 5 Yrs 149 774 43 41 .512 377 309 754 4.01

a Drafted by Chicago White Sox, November 10, 1948.

b Traded to Pittsburgh with Sid Gordon, Sam Jethroe, Larry Lassalle, Fred Waters, Curt Raydon and cash for Danny O'Connell, December 26, 1953.

THOMPSON, JOHN SAMUEL (JOCKO)

Born, Beverly, Massachusetts, January 17, 1920.
Bats Left. Throws Left. Height, 6 feet. Weight, 180 pounds.

Year	Club	Lea	G	IP	W	L	Pct	SO	BB	H	ERA
1940	Canton	M. A. L.	7	29	1	1	.500	8	9	27	3.41
1940	Centreville	E. S. L.	27	208	18	5	.783	*268	74	144	*1.56
1941	Greensboro	Pied.	28	162	8	13	.381	105	64	158	3.56
1942-43-44-45	Scranton	E. L.	(In Military Service)								
1946	Scranton	E. L.	26	180	13	7	.650	146	97	164	2.60
1947	Toronto	I. L.	32	135	6	12	.333	69	55	128	3.80
1948	Toronto	I. L.	32	161	12	8	.600	92	93	166	5.09

Year	Club	Lea	G	IP	W	L	Pct	SO	BB	H	ERA
1948	Philadelphia	N. L.	2	13	1	0	1.000	7	9	10	2.77
1949	Toronto	I. L.	32	145	14	5	.737	121	63	111	2.73
1949	Philadelphia	N. L.	8	31	1	3	.250	12	11	38	6.97
1950	Philadelphia	N. L.	2	4	0	0	.000	2	4	1	0.00
1950	Toronto	I. L.	35	201	10	14	.417	115	100	209	4.57
1951	Philadelphia	N. L.	29	119	4	8	.333	60	59	102	3.86
1952	Baltimore	I. L.	39	231	13	14	.481	119	80	179	2.49
1953	Baltimore a	I. L.	25	154	10	4	.714	68	50	142	3.79
Major League Totals		4 Yrs	41	167	6	11	.353	81	83	151	4.28

a Drafted by Chicago White Sox, November 30, 1953.

TRICE, ROBERT LEE
Born, Newton, Georgia, August 28, 1928.
Bats Right. Throws Right. Height, 6 feet, 2½ inches. Weight, 190 pounds.

Year	Club	Lea	G	IP	W	L	Pct	SO	BB	H	ERA
1950	Farnham	Provinc.			5	3	.625	..	..	..	..
1951	Farnham a	Provinc.	23	152	7	12	.368	61	67	172	5.14
1952	St. Hyacinthe b	Provinc.	24	152	*16	3	*.842	68	29	162	3.49
1953	Ottawa	I. L.	38	229	*21	10	.677	57	84	207	3.10
1953	Philadelphia	A. L.	3	23	2	1	.667	4	6	25	5.48

a Played 27 games in outfield, 10 games at third-base.
b Played 62 games in outfield.

TRUCKS, VIRGIL OLIVER (FIRE)
Born, Birmingham, Alabama, April 26, 1919.
Bats Right. Throws Right. Height, 6 feet. Weight, 195 pounds.

Year	Club	Lea	G	IP	W	L	Pct	SO	BB	H	ERA
1938	Andalusia	Ala.-Fla.	38	273	*25	6	*.806	*418	125	143	*1.25
1939	Beaumont	T. L.	11	63	3	5	.375	38	41	57	3.43
1939	Alexandria	Evang.	24	173	13	5	.722	129	73	137	2.60
1940	Beaumont	T. L.	33	203	12	11	.522	142	92	170	3.50
1941	Buffalo	I. L.	33	204	12	12	.500	*204	76	164	3.22
1941	Detroit	A. L.	1	2	0	0	.000	3	0	4	9.00
1942	Detroit	A. L.	28	168	14	8	.636	91	74	147	2.73
1943	Detroit	A. L.	33	203	16	10	.615	118	52	170	2.84
1944, 1945		(In United States Navy)									
1945	Detroit	A. L.	1	5	0	0	.000	3	2	3	1.80
1946	Detroit	A. L.	32	237	14	9	.609	161	75	217	3.23
1947	Detroit	A. L.	36	181	10	12	.455	108	79	186	4.52
1948	Detroit	A. L.	43	212	14	13	.519	123	85	190	3.78
1949	Detroit	A. L.	41	275	19	11	.633	*153	124	209	2.81
1950	Detroit	A. L.	7	48	3	1	.750	25	21	45	3.56
1951	Detroit	A. L.	37	154	13	8	.619	89	75	153	4.32
1952	Detroit a-b	A. L.	35	197	5	19	.208	129	82	190	3.97
1953	St. L.-Chicago c	A. L.	40	264	20	10	.667	149	99	234	2.93
Major League Totals		12 Yrs	334	1946	128	101	.559	1152	768	1748	3.40
World's Series Record											
1945	Detroit	A. L.	2	13⅓	1	0	1.000	7	5	14	3.38

a Pitched no-hit games against Washington, May 15, and New York, Aug. 25.
b Traded with outfielder Johnny Groth and pitcher Hal White by Detroit to St. Louis Browns in exchange for outfielder Bob Nieman, catcher-outfielder J. W. Porter and infielder Owen Friend. Dec. 4, 1952.
c Traded to Chicago White Sox with Bob Elliott for Darrell Johnson, Lou Kretlow, and cash, June 13, 1953.

TURLEY, ROBERT LEE
Born, Troy, Illinois, September 19, 1930.
Bats Right. Throws Right. Height, 6 feet, 3 inches. Weight, 215 pounds.

Year	Club	Lea	G	IP	W	L	Pct	SO	BB	H	ERA
1948	Belleville	Ill. St.	16	97	9	3	.750	53	71	99	4.45
1949	Aberdeen	North.	33	230	*23	5	.821	*205	131	175	2.31
1950	San Antonio	T. L.	4	14	0	2	.000	10	19	15	9.00
1950	Wichita	Western	40	208	11	14	.440	153	118	213	4.28
1951	San Antonio	T. L.	34	268	20	8	.714	200	142	236	2.95
1951	St. Louis	A. L.	1	7	0	1	.000	5	3	11	7.71
1952-53	St. Louis	A. L.	(In Military Service)								
1953	St. Louis	A. L.	10	60	2	6	.250	61	44	39	3.30
Major League Totals		2 Yrs	11	67	2	7	.222	66	47	50	3.76

WADE, BENJAMIN STYROM
Born, Moorehead City, N. C., Nov. 26, 1922.
Bats Right. Throws Right. Height, 6 feet, 3 inches. Weight, 200 pounds.

Year	Club	Lea	G	IP	W	L	Pct	SO	BB	H	ERA
1940	New Bern	Coast. Pl.	4	23	2	1	.667	25	6	20	2.25

Year	Club	Lea	G	IP	W	L	Pct	SO	BB	H	ERA
1940	Durham	Pied.	1	1	0	0	.000	1	0	0	0.00
1941	Indianapolis	A. A.	32	127	4	5	.444	40	84	104	2.83
1942	Syracuse	I. L.	25	86	2	11	.154	53	67	82	5.86
1943, 1944, 1945				(In U. S. Military Service)							
1946	Birmingham	S. A.	11	47	1	7	.125	25	33	51	6.32
1946	Anniston	So'east.	21	160	15	4	.789	151	49	116	2.48
1947	Nashville	S. A.	36	239	17	11	.607	*145	73	*306	4.33
1948	Nashville	S. A.	30	194	14	10	.583	108	75	238	4.92
1948	Chicago	N. L.	2	5	0	1	.000	1	4	4	7.20
1949	Nashville	S. A.	38	217	18	8	.692	114	59	253	3.86
1949	Los Angeles	P. C. L.	3	5	0	0	.000	5	6	8	16.20
1950	Hollywood	P. C. L.	40	248	14	13	.519	156	83	222	3.67
1951	Hollywood	P. C. L.	30	200	16	6	*.727	134	76	186	2.61
1952	Brooklyn	N. L.	37	180	11	9	.550	118	94	166	3.60
1953	Brooklyn	N. L.	32	90	7	5	.583	65	33	79	3.80
Major League Totals		3 Yrs	71	275	18	15	.545	184	131	249	3.73
World's Series Record											
1953	Brooklyn	N. L.	2	2⅓	0	0	.000	2	1	4	15.43

WAUGH, JAMES ELDEN

Born, Lancaster, Ohio, November 25, 1933.
Bats Right. Throws Right. Height, 6 feet, 3 inches. Weight, 170 pounds.

Year	Club	Lea	G	IP	W	L	Pct	SO	BB	H	ERA
1951	Brunswick	Ga.-Fla.	18	119	10	8	.556	88	60	106	3.40
1951	New Orleans	S. A.	2	18	2	0	1.000	10	9	12	1.00
1952	Charleston	Sally	18	116	4	9	.308	63	63	112	3.18
1952	Pittsburgh	N. L.	17	52	1	6	.143	18	32	61	6.40
1953	Burlington	Carol.	9	87	6	3	.667	50	28	67	1.34
1953	Pittsburgh	N. L.	29	90	4	5	.444	23	56	108	6.50
Major League Totals		2 Yrs	46	142	5	11	.313	41	88	169	6.46

WEHMEIER, HERMAN RALPH

Born, Cincinnati, Ohio. Februray 18, 1927.
Bats Right. Throws Right. Height, 6 feet, 3 inches. Weight, 200 pounds.

Year	Club	Lea	G	IP	W	L	Pct	SO	BB	H	ERA
1945	Syracuse	I L.	16	102	4	8	.333	30	80	95	4.63
1945	Cincinnati	N. l	2	5	0	1	.000	0	4	10	12.60
1946	Columbia	S. A. L.	30	232	17	6	*.739	177	100	225	3.53
1947	Cincinnati	N. L	1	1	0	0	.000	0	0	0	0.00
1947	Syracuse	I L.	28	177	15	8	.652	81	98	150	4.12
1948	Cincinnati	N. L.	23	147	11	8	.579	56	75	179	5.88
1949	Cincinnati	N. L.	36	213	11	12	.478	80	*117	202	4.69
1950	Cincinnati	N. L.	41	230	10	18	.357	121	*135	255	5.67
1951	Cincinnati	N. L.	39	185	7	10	.412	93	89	167	3.70
1952	Cincinnati	N. L.	33	190	9	11	.450	83	*103	197	5.16
1953	Cincinnati	N. L.	28	82	1	6	.143	32	47	100	7.13
Major League Totals		8 Yrs	210	1053	49	66	.426	465	570	1110	5.21

WHITE, HAROLD GEORGE

Born, Utica, New York, March 18, 1919.
Bats Right. Throws Right. Height, 5 feet, 10 inches. Weight, 170 pounds.

Year	Club	Lea	G	IP	W	L	Pct	SO	BB	H	ERA
1937	Rome	Can. Am.	3	13	1	0	1.000	11	12	11	3.46
1938	Rome	Can. Am.	29	209	14	11	.560	168	98	217	4.09
1939	Buffalo	I. L.	4	8	0	1	.000	4	5	8	6.75
1939	Wilkes-Barre	E. L.	29	187	10	11	.476	89	56	198	3.27
1940	Buffalo	I. L.	34	196	16	4	*.800	92	40	165	*2.43
1941	Buffalo	I. L.	36	230	16	12	.571	109	65	229	2.74
1941	Detroit	A. L.	4	9	0	0	.000	2	6	11	6.00
1942	Detroit	A. L.	34	217	12	12	.500	93	82	212	2.90
1943	Detroit	A. L.	32	178	7	12	.368	58	71	150	3.39
1944, 1945				(In United States Military Service)							
1946	Detroit	A. L.	11	27	1	1	.500	12	15	34	5.67
1947	Detroit	A. L.	35	85	4	5	.444	33	47	91	3.60
1948	Detroit	A. L.	27	43	2	1	.667	17	26	46	6.07
1949	Toledo	A. A.	22	139	10	8	.556	59	52	130	3.24
1949	Detroit	A. L.	9	12	1	0	1.000	4	4	5	0 00
1950	Detroit	A. L.	42	111	9	6	.600	53	65	96	4 54
1951	Detroit	A. L.	38	76	3	4	.429	23	49	74	4.74
1952	Detroit a	A. L.	41	63	1	8	.111	18	39	53	3.71
1953	St. Louis b	A. L.	10	10	0	0	.000	2	3	8	2.70
1953	St. Louis	N. L.	49	85	6	5	.545	32	39	84	2.96
Major League Totals		11 Yrs	332	916	46	54	.460	347	446	864	3.69

WIGHT, WILLIAM ROBERT
Born, Rio Vista, California, April 12, 1922.
Bats Left. Throws Left. Height, 6 feet, 1¼ inches. Weight, 190 pounds.

Year	Club	Lea	G	IP	W	L	Pct	SO	BB	H	ERA
1041	Idaho Falls	Pio.	30	160	8	12	.400	109	124	157	3 83
1942	Binghamton	E. L.	3	15	1	2	.333	4	7	17	3.60
1942	Norfolk	P. L	14	100	7	5	.583	55	52	80	2.43
1943, 1944, 1945			(In United States Military Service)								
1946	New York	A. L.	14	40	2	2	.500	11	30	44	4.50
1947	Kansas City	A. A.	29	199	16	9	.640	75	71	202	2.85
1947	New York	A. L.	1	9	1	0	1.000	3	2	8	1.00
1948	Chicago a	A. L.	34	223	9	20	.310	68	*135	238	4.80
1949	Chicago	A. L.	35	245	15	13	.536	78	96	254	3.31
1950	Chicago b	A. L.	30	206	10	16	.385	62	79	213	3 58
1951	Boston	A. L.	34	118	7	7	.500	38	63	128	5.11
1952	Bos.-Detroit c	A. L.	33	168	7	10	.412	70	69	181	3.75
1953	Det.-Cleveland d	A. L.	33	52	2	4	.333	24	30	64	6.23
Major League Totals		8 Yrs	214	1061	53	72	.424	354	504	1130	4.11

a Traded to Chicago with Aaron Robinson and Fred Bradley for Ed Lopat, February 24, 1948.
b Traded with Ray Scarborough to Boston Red Sox for Joe Dobson, Al Zarilla and Dick Littlefield, December 10, 1950.
c Traded to Detroit with Walt Dropo, Fred Hatfield, Don Lenhardt and Johnny Pesky for Hoot Evers, George Kell, Johnny Lipon and Dizzy Trout, June 3, 1952.
d Traded to Cleveland with Owen Friend, Joe Ginsberg and Art Houtteman for Al Aber, Ray Boone, Steve Gromek and Dick Weik, June 15, 1953.

WILHELM, JAMES HOYT
Born, Huntersville, N. C., July 26, 1923.
Bats Right. Throws Right. Height, 6 feet. Weight, 190 pounds.

Year	Club	Lea	G	IP	W	L	Pct	SO	BB	H	ERA
1942	Mooresville	N. C. St.	23	108	10	3	.769	56	28	105	4.25
1943-44-45	Mooresville	N. C. St.	(In Military Service)								
1946	Mooresville	N. C. St.	*34	233	21	8	.724	185	50	*221	2.47
1947	Mooresville	N. C. St.	31	*250	*20	7	.741	198	92	*243	3.38
1948	Jacksonville	So. Atl.	6	11	0	0	.000	5	9	18	8.18
1948	Knoxville	Tri-Sta.	24	189	13	9	.591	104	62	194	3.62
1949	Jacksonville	So. Atl.	33	223	17	12	.586	126	92	198	2.66
1950	Minneapolis	A. A.	35	180	15	11	.577	99	64	190	4.95
1951	Minneapolis	A. A.	40	*210	11	14	.440	148	82	219	3.94
1952	New York	N. L.	*71	159	15	3	*.833	108	57	*2.43	2.43
1953	New York	N. L.	*68	145	7	8	.467	71	77	127	3.04
Major League Totals		2 Yrs	139	304	22	11	.667	179	134	254	2.72

WILLIS, JAMES G.
Born, Doyline, Louisiana, March 20, 1927.
Bats Left. Throws Right. Height, 6 feet, 3 inches. Weight, 175 pounds.

Year	Club	Lea	G	IP	W	L	Pct	SO	BB	H	ERA
1949	Alexandria	Evang.	22	165	14	5	.737	97	94	133	3.16
1950	Shreveport	T. L.	5	7	0	0	.000	2	3	11	7.71
1950	Greenville	Big State	13	46	2	4	.333	25	29	43	4.70
1950	Monroe	Cott. St.	15	60	3	5	.375	39	36	60	4.50
1951	Shreveport	T. L.	53	212	15	10	.600	79	123	208	3.65
1952	Shreveport a	T. L.	33	261	16	11	.593	106	113	222	2.73
1953	Springfield	I. L.	9	51	2	3	.400	24	25	62	3.71
1953	Chicago	N. L.	13	43	2	1	.667	15	17	37	3.14

a Drafted by Chicago Cubs, December 1, 1952.

WILSON, JAMES ALGER
Born, San Diego, California, February 20, 1922.
Bats Right. Throws Right. Height, 6 feet, 1 inch. Weight, 195 pounds.

Year	Club	Lea	G	IP	W	L	Pct	SO	BB	H	ERA
1943	Louisville	A. A.	28	57	0	5	.000	31	43	49	5.68
1944	Louisville	A. A.	38	237	*19	8	.704	*147	98	189	2.77
1945	Boston	A. L.	23	144	6	8	.429	50	88	121	3.31
1946	Boston	A. L.	1	1	0	0	.000	0	0	2	18.00
1946	Louisville	A. A.	22	158	10	6	.625	126	72	142	3.02
1947	Louisville a	A. A.	12	68	4	4	.500	47	38	45	2.65
1948	St. Louis	A. L.	4	3	0	0	.000	1	5	5	12.00
1948	Toledo b	A. A.	26	175	7	13	.350	108	75	177	4.01
1949	Philadelphia	A. L.	2	5	0	0	.000	2	5	7	14.40

Year	Club	Lea	G	IP	W	L	Pct	SO	BB	H	ERA
1949	Balt.-Buf.	I. L.	26	153	7	11	.389	100	63	187	3.94
1950	Seattle	P. C. L.	41	293	*24	11	.686	*223	76	254	2.95
1951	Boston	N. L.	20	110	7	7	.500	83	40	181	5.40
1952	Boston	N. L.	33	234	12	14	.462	104	90	234	4.23
1953	Milwaukee	N. L.	20	114	4	9	.308	71	43	107	4.34
Major League Totals		7 Yrs	103	611	29	38	.433	261	271	607	4.39

a Traded by Boston Red Sox with Pete Layden, Joe Ostrowski, Don Palmer, Roy Partee, Eddie Pellagrini, Al Widmar and estimated $300,000 for Jack Kramer and Vern Stephens, Nov. 17, 1947.
b Drafted by Philadelphia Athletics, Nov. 10, 1948.

WORTHINGTON, ALLAN

Born, Birmingham, Alabama, February 5, 1930.
Bats Right. Throws Right. Height, 6 feet, 2 inches. Weight, 200 pounds.

Year	Club	Lea	G	IP	W	L	Pct	SO	BB	H	ERA
1951	Nashville	S. A.	23	124	7	10	.412	77	83	79	4.57
1952	Nashville	S. A.	41	221	13	13	.500	*152	*140	194	3.54
1953	Minneapolis	A. A.	17	118	9	5	.643	74	50	114	2.90
1953	New York	N. L.	20	102	4	8	.333	52	54	103	3.44

WYNN, EARLY

Born, Hartford, Alabama, January 6, 1920.
Bats Both. Throws Right. Height, 6 feet. Weight, 200 pounds.

Year	Club	Lea	G	IP	W	L	Pct	SO	BB	H	ERA
1937	Sanford	Fla. St.	35	235	16	11	.593	106	81	224	3.31
1938	Charlotte	Pied.	29	179	10	11	.476	94	73	195	5.28
1939	Charlotte	Pied.	34	243	15	14	.517	150	98	254	....
1939	Washington	A. L.	3	20	0	2	.000	1	10	26	5.85
1940	Charlotte	Pied.	31	144	9	7	.563	76	57	154	4.25
1941	Springfield	E. L.	34	257	16	12	.571	126	84	*239	2.56
1941	Washington	A. L.	5	40	3	1	.750	15	10	35	1.58
1942	Washington	A. L.	30	190	10	16	.385	58	73	246	5.12
1943	Washington	A. L.	37	257	18	12	.600	89	83	232	2.91
1944	Washington	A. L.	33	208	8	*17	.320	65	67	221	3.38
1945					(In United States Army)						
1946	Washington	A. L.	17	107	8	5	.615	36	83	112	3.11
1947	Washington	A. L.	33	247	17	15	.531	73	90	251	3.64
1948	Washington a	A. L.	33	198	8	19	.296	49	94	236	5.82
1949	Cleveland	A. L.	26	165	11	7	.611	62	57	186	4.15
1950	Cleveland	A. L.	32	214	18	8	.692	143	101	166	*3.20
1951	Cleveland	A. L.	37	*274	20	13	.606	133	107	227	3.02
1952	Cleveland	A. L.	42	286	23	12	.657	153	*132	239	2.90
1953	Cleveland	A. L.	36	252	17	12	.586	138	107	234	3.93
Major League Totals		13 Yrs	364	2458	161	139	.537	1015	964	2411	3.66

a Traded to Cleveland with Mickey Vernon, December 14, for Ed Robinson, Ed Klieman and Joe Haynes.

YUHAS, JOHN EDWARD

Born, Youngstown, Ohio, April 5, 1924.
Bats Right. Throws Right. Height, 6 feet, 1 inch. Weight, 168 pounds.

Year	Club	Lea	G	IP	W	L	Pct	SO	BB	H	ERA
1942	Fond Du Lac ...	Wisc. St.	19	134	5	12	.294	116	123	104	4.30
1943-44-45-46	Fond Du Lac			(In Military Service)							
1947	Winston-Salem ..	Carolina	36	176	10	12	.455	154	77	187	3.89
1948	Rochester	I. L.	4	4	0	0	.000	1	5	6	15.75
1948	Omaha	West. L.	25	152	8	8	.500	132	72	165	4.09
1949	Rochester	I. L.	35	174	8	9	.471	84	69	191	4.45
1950	Rochester	I. L.	32	204	15	6	.714	95	108	214	4.54
1951	Rochester	I. L.	34	169	13	11	.542	87	81	163	3.04
1952	St. Louis	N. L.	54	99	12	2	.857	39	35	90	2.73
1953	St. Louis a	N. L.	2	1	0	0	.000	0	0	8	18.00
Major League Totals		2 Yrs	56	100	12	2	.857	39	35	93	2.88

a On disabled list from May 11.

BIBLIOGRAPHY

American League Green Book, Earl Hilligan. American League Service. Bureau, Chicago. Annual. Facts on the A.L.

Baseball Blue Book, L. Heilbroner and others. Heilbroner Baseball Bureau. Fort Wayne, Ind. Annual. Official rules, directories.

Baseball Cyclopedia, E. J. Lanigan. Baseball Magazine Co., N.Y. 1922–34. History, facts, rare box scores.

Baseball Is Their Business. Harold Rosenthal. Random House, N.Y., 1952. Leading figures from front office to field write of their specialties.

Baseball's Greatest Hitters, Tom Meany. A. S. Barnes, N.Y., 1950.

Baseball's Greatest Pitchers, Tom Meany. A. S. Barnes, N.Y., 1951.

Baseball's Greatest Teams, Tom Meany. A. S. Barnes, N.Y., 1949.

Best Sports Stories, I. T. Marsh and E. Ehre. E. P. Dutton, N.Y. annual.

Campanella, Roy, Dick Young. A. S. Barnes, N.Y., 1952.

Championship Baseball From Big To Little League, W. T. Lai. Prentice Hall, N.Y., 1954. By a college coach and major league scout.

Major League Baseball, Ethan Allen. MacMillan, N.Y., 1938. By a former major leaguer.

My Greatest Day in Baseball, J. P. Carmichael. A. S. Barnes, N.Y., 1945. Stars write about big moments.

National League Green Book, Dave Grote. National League Service Bureau, Cincinnati, Ohio. Annual. Facts on N.L.

Official Encyclopedia of Baseball, H. Turkin and S. C. Thompson. A. S. Barnes, 1951. Complete record book.

Official Baseball Guide, J. G. T. Spink. C. C. Spink and Son, St. Louis. Annual. Complete records of all organized ball.

One For The Book, Leonard Gettelson. C. C. Spink and Son, St. Louis. Annual. A record book.

Rizzuto, Phil, Joe Trimble. A. S. Barnes, N.Y., 1950.

Sports Golden Age, A. Danzig and P. Brandwein. Harper and Bros., N.Y., 1948.

The Little Red Book of Baseball, Seymour Siwoff. Al Munro Elias Baseball Bureau, N.Y. Annual. Official record book.

Most major league ball clubs publish annual yearbooks, available to the public. Publicity directors of each club have information on the purchase of these year books.

Lew Fonseca annually produces a motion picture of highlights of the World Series, and many other baseball films have been prepared by major-league clubs. Most are available to schools, clubs, and similar organizations. Information on the World Series motion picture is obtainable from A. G. Spalding and Company, New York City.